LJ

MAR 12 1992   LA JOLLA

BEACHAM'S POPULAR FICTION 1991 UPDATE

Volume 2
L-Z
Appendices I, II, III
Index of Titles
Cumulative Index

SAN DIEGO PUBLIC LIBRARY
LA JOLLA BRANCH

BEACHAM PUBLISHING, INC.
1991

3 1336 02800 7418

LA JOLLA

BEACHAM'S POPULAR FICTION 1991 UPDATE

Editors
Walton Beacham
David W. Lowe
Katharine McLucas
Charles W. Moseley

Editorial Assistant
Stephanie A. Fox

Library of Congress
  Cataloging-in-Publication Data

Beacham's Popular Fiction 1991 Update / edited by Walton Beacham, David W.
  Lowe, Katharine McLucas, Charles W. Moseley—Washington, D.C.:
  Beacham Publishing, Inc.

  Bibliography
  Cumulative index

  Recent publishing and critical history of best-selling American and
  world fiction writers included in *Beacham's Popular Fiction* and
  Popular World Fiction.

  1. Fiction—20th century— History and criticism. 2. Popular literature—History and criticism. 3. Best sellers—United States. I. Beacham, Walton, 1943

PS374.P63B43   1991   813'.5'09   86-25857

Copyright, ©, 1991, by Walton Beacham

All rights to this book are reserved. No part of this work may be used or reproduced in any manner whatsoever or transmitted in any form or by any means, electronic or mechanical, including photocopy, recording, or in any information storage and retrieval system, without written permission from the copyright owner, except in the case of brief quotations embodied in critical articles and reviews. For information, write the publisher: Beacham Publishing, Inc., 2100 "S" Street, NW, Washington, D.C. 20008.

Library of Congress Card Number: 86-25857
ISBN: 0-933833-26-1
Printed in the United States of America
First printing, April 1991

BEACHAM'S POPULAR FICTION 1991 UPDATE

RING LARDNER
1885-1933

Publishing History

Ringgold Wilmer Lardner was born in Niles, Michigan, on March 6, 1885; he graduated from Niles High School in 1901. Although his career as a writer took shape in the nation's two largest cities, Chicago and New York, Lardner remained in important ways defined by his small-town, midwestern upbringing. His enthusiasm for sports, his sense of decorum (and of its abuses), his satire of small-town midwesterners as "wise rubes" (and his satire of big-town easterners as exploitative anti-rubes) all derive from his experience as the son of a privileged family in Niles.

After several false starts as an office boy, "a third assistant freight hustler," and a bookkeeper, Lardner discovered his true vocation when, in 1905, he was hired as "society reporter, court-house man, drama critic, and sporting editor for the South Bend, Indiana, *Times*." Between 1907 and 1913 he served as a sports reporter for various Chicago newspapers; in 1913 he took over "In the Wake of the News" column in the *Chicago Tribune* and developed it into the versatile vehicle for the sports stories, poems, epigrams, and autobiographical anecdotes that made him one of America's top sports journalists. In 1914 he published in the *Saturday Evening Post* the first of his famous "busher" stories which would later be collected in *You Know Me Al* (1916) and two other volumes.

In 1919 he resigned from the *Tribune* and moved east, eventually settling on Long Island, where he became a neighbor and friend of F. Scott Fitzgerald. He began a widely syndicated "Weekly Letter," writing on all topics, and composed the continuity for a highly remunerative comic strip based on *You Know Me Al*. He continued to publish short stories, including several cycles of related stories that were subsequently collected in volumes such as *You Know Me Al, Gullible's Travels, Etc.* (1917), *Own Your Own Home* (1919), and *The Big Town* (1921). He pursued, less successfully, an ambition to write Broadway musicals and plays, and he undertook a campaign against what he took to be indecent lyrics in popular songs. He never wrote the novel which friends urged him to do. After several years of deteriorating health, he died of a heart attack on September 25, 1933.

Critical Reception, Honors, and Popularity

As a journalist and as a short story writer, Lardner was one of the best known writers of the post-World War I American scene. His "Weekly Letter" appeared in 150 newspapers with a total readership of eight million. Lardner's annual income from this column, from the "You Know Me Al" comic strip, and from the sale of his short stories to magazines reached nearly $100,000 in the 1920s. Although several of his story series were enormously popular when they were published in periodicals, they were only moderately successful when later issued as collections. *Round Up,* the 1929 collection of his best non-series stories, was Lardner's hardcover triumph, selling over 100,000 copies. He was much admired and imitated by contemporary journalists and short story writers (including the young Ernest Hemingway, who would later deride Lardner's prim aversion to "dirty words").

Lardner could claim the good opinion of Fitzgerald and H. L. Mencken, but the reviewers did not begin to take him seriously until the publication of *How to Write Short Stories* (1924), and he never achieved critical recognition as a major writer. Two factors depressed his reputation: his origin as a sports writer and his failure to compose a novel. Although he virtually ceased to write about sports after moving to New York, even the sympathetic Fitzgerald disparaged Lardner's affinity for "a boy's game." And Fitzgerald, who had been among those importuning Lardner to attempt something more ambitious than short stories, discounted his artistic achievement because he "never knew anything about composition, except as it concerned the shorter forms."

The principal critical debate involving Lardner has centered on the issue, implied in an early review by H. L. Mencken (1926) and developed by Clifton Fadiman (1929, 1933), of Lardner's misanthropy. Mencken, writing of the stories in *The Love Nest*, including the often anthologized "Haircut," described Lardner's satire as being "of the most acid and appalling sort—satire wholly removed, like Swift's before it, from the least weakness of amiability, or even pity." Fadiman expanded the charge, stating that Lardner wrote in "a cold frenzy," with "icy satiric power" and was left "without faith, hope, or charity." Other critics have emphasized the humorist over the satirist and argue that while his fiction did grow darker in later years, he never became an embittered hater of mankind. Lardner's fiction continues to be reprinted, and his stories (especially "Haircut," "Some Like Them Cold," and "The Love Nest") regularly reappear in anthologies. Four different collections of Lardner's work remain in print, and these have been supplemented by reprints of *You Know Me Al* and *The Story of a Wonder Man,* and by an edition of his letters. He has been the object of recent scholarly attention (a major critical biography, a new collection of late stories and sketches, and a number of scholarly articles). Because of all this recent attention, Lardner's ultimate place in American literature remains to be fixed.

Analysis of Selected Titles

YOU KNOW ME AL

You Know Me Al, 1916, short stories.

Social Concerns/Themes

You Know Me Al, Lardner's second book (the first had been a collection of occasional verse, *Bib Ballads*) is the best of the three volumes of *Saturday Evening Post* stories about the "busher" Jack Keefe, the self-involved, semi-literate, but not untalented pitcher for the Chicago White Sox. Each of the six stories in *You Know Me Al,* from "A Busher's Letters Home" to "The Busher Beats it Hence," consists entirely of Keefe's unintentionally revealing letters to his forbearing friend, Al Blanchard. They chronicle Jack's first two seasons in the major leagues (and, off season, his marriage and the birth of a son). Lardner achieves comic effects by exploiting Keefe's verbal incompetence, but he also uses the letters to develop a satiric commentary on the crudest type of know-nothing manhood, on baseball, and on marriage and parenthood in America.

Jack Keefe possesses the physical skills as a pitcher to get the great Ty Cobb to line out to the first baseman; his intellectual and verbal skills are less impressive. He responds to Cobb's challenge, "Pretty lucky Boy but I will get you next time" with the lame riposte, "I come right back at him. I says Yes you will." Jack represents the young, confident, technically competent American who lacks any sense of cultural or social tradition. He knows baseball and desires to know nothing else. Some of the humor of the book depends upon a knowledge of the rules and lore of baseball, but even readers unfamiliar with the game will easily grasp the self-serving tenor of Keefe's accounts of his performance; and the broader points of, for example, his negotiations with his owner, Charles Comisky, can be read as a commentary on workers and capitalists (a commentary which sanctifies neither). Because baseball rewards boyish behavior, Lardner can use the sport to satirize the prolonged adolescence which American culture seems to promote in young men. Jack's blundering relationships with women, especially his wife Florrie, further illustrate his immaturity. Both sexes exhibit shallow vanities and pursue self-gratifying designs.

Characters

Jack Keefe knows he is the hero of his own life. He is, in his own eyes, the most valuable member of the Chicago White Sox; his wins result from his excellence, his losses from the errors of his teammates. His egotism is so thorough and so naive that he never really comprehends that owners, managers, teammates, opponents, spouses, or even readers like the long-suffering Al might place a lower value upon his merits. He thoroughly monopolizes the narrative. His is the only voice, and his imperfect syntax and diction render a Keefeian version of the actions, speech, and thoughts of everyone else. In his narrative everyone takes a back seat to his version of himself. As a result, few other characters are individualized. Al may know Jack, but there is no way for the reader to know Al; Lardner does not present his responses to Jack's self-involved letters. Allen, a left-hander who joins the pitching staff at the same time as Keefe is a reappearing character; Jack and Allen are married to a pair of sisters, and the relations between the two couples provide some comic moments. Lardner employs actual baseball players in minor roles: Ty Cobb, Babe Ruth, and Christy Mathewson. Keefe's first manager, Jim Callahan, was, in fact, the White Sox manager from 1912 to 1914; his coach, Kid Gleason, was manager from 1919 to 1923.

Techniques/Literary Precedents

Jack Keefe's first letter begins: "Friend Al: Well Al old pal I suppose you seen in the paper where I been sold to the White Sox." The last letter, fourteen months later, ends, "You know me Al." The earliest English novels began with epistolary works like Samuel Richardson's *Pamela* (1740) and *Clarissa* (1747); Henry Fielding and Tobias Smollett were quick to exploit the form's comic possibilities. Lardner revives the device with an infusion of American vernacular humor. Jack Keefe writes the way he speaks, and Lardner has a fine ear for the way men like Jack speak. As a sportswriter, Lardner had travelled with the players; he wrote letters for some of them, and in one instance read menus aloud to an illiterate White Sox player. Jack Keefe gets his verbs and pronouns wrong ("the papers says," "you shouldn't ought to eats so much," "she has went to Detroit") and he often misspells words ("recruts," "appresiated"). Mark Twain is Lardner's great predecessor in the use of the vernacular and ungrammatical language in the service of humor. George Ade and Peter Finley Dunne were more immediate models; Ade's satiric portraits of Hoosiers in the big city and Dunne's use of dialect in his Mr. Dooley sketches clearly influenced Lardner.

Relation to Previous Works

Jack Keefe's further adventures were collected in two volumes, *Treat 'Em Rough* (1918) and *The Real Dope* (1919), dealing primarily with Keefe's enlistment in the army and military service in France. Two uncollected stories are reprinted in *Some Champions*. In the final busher story, Keefe manages to get himself sold to the "Philadelphia Athaletics" just before the White Sox entered the infamous 1919 World Series and earned the name "Black Sox." In 1930, in ill-health and needing money, Lardner returned to the device of the epistolary ballplayer, composing a six-part series for the *Saturday Evening Post* about Danny Warner, an outfielder for the Brooklyn Dodgers. Lardner also created some memorable baseball-playing protagonists who did not write letters and did not reappear in a series of stories. Three of the best are the title characters of "Alibi Ike" and "Hurry Kane" and Buster Elliott of "My Roomy" (all of which are included in *The Best Short Stories of Ring Lardner*). Finally, it should be noted that baseball was not the only sport to inspire Lardner's fiction: "Champion" is a relentless exposé of the vicious boxer, Midge Kelley; "Mr. Frisbie" and "A Caddy's Diary" dissect the more refined immoralities of golfers; "Contract" and "Who Dealt?" use the game of bridge to dramatize social interactions.

Lardner provides both sides of a correspondence in one of his best short stories, "Some Like Them Cold." Mabelle Gillespie, working girl, and Chas. F. Lewis, would-be songwriter, reveal their unappealing, shallow natures—she is crudely designing; he is thoughtlessly egocentric—as they engage in a comically unconsummated epistolary romance. "Haircut," probably Lardner's best known story, replaces letters with a special form of monologue, delivered by a barber to his captive audience (just as friend Al was the captive of Jack Keefe's correspondence). The busher and barber both belong to a morally obtuse class of self-satisfied Americans, but what was comically crude egoism in a baseball player acquires a darker tone in the barber's mindless approval of Jim Kendall's vicious practical jokes.

Adaptations

Between 1922 and 1925, Lardner wrote 3,744 panels for a syndicated comic strip based on the characters of *You Know Me Al* (collected in 1979). Several of his other sports stories were made into films: *The New Klondike* (1926), a silent film with a baseball theme by Lardner, directed by Lewis Milestone; *Fast Company* (1929), based on "Elmer the Great" by Lardner and George S. Kaufman (which, in turn, was based on Lardner's baseball story, "Hurry Kane"), directed by A. Edward Sutherland; *Elmer the Great* (1933), a remake of *Fast Company*, directed by Mervyn LeRoy and featuring Joe E. Brown; *Alibi Ike* (1935), based on Lardner's baseball story of the same title, and directed by Roy Enright, also featuring Joe E. Brown; *Cowboy Quarterback* (1939), another remake of *Fast Company*, shifting the sport to football, and directed by Noel Smith and featuring Harry Lynn; *Champion* (1949), based on Lardner's story of the same title, directed by Mark Robson and starring Kirk Douglas. John Sayles's 1988 film about the Black Sox scandal, *Eight Men Out,* based on the novel by Eliot Asinof, contains a Lardner character, played by Sayles himself.

THE BIG TOWN
The Big Town, 1921, short stories.

Social Concerns/Themes

The subtitle of this collection of related stories defines Lardner's theme and plot: "How I and the Mrs. go to see New York to see life and get Katie a husband." Getting his sister-in-law a husband leads Tom Finch, the "wise boob" narrator of the five stories, to contrast life in South Bend, Indiana, with that of booming postwar New York City. The autobiographical element in the stories—the Lardners made the same migration and even stayed at the Long Island hotel featured in two of the stories—led Lardner to include a humorous disclaimer in the 1925 edition. But clearly Tom Finch's midwestern reservations about the spendthrift habits and dubious manners and morals of the big town reflect an aspect of Lardner's own response to New York City at the beginning of the Roaring Twenties. "I just want to be where they's Life and fun": Kate's equating "Life" and "fun" with New York City underlies the satire of *The Big Town.*

Before the move, Tom had worked as a cigar salesman; but an inheritance from his war-profiteering father-in-law liberates the family, and they join the euphoria that characterized America between World War I and the Depression. In pursuit of a husband for Kate the Finches encounter three classes of New Yorkers. First, there are the established rich who are either accessible, but dull (Trumbull), disingenuous (Herbert Daly), or snobs (Lady Perkins). Second, there are the would-be rich—the ambitious young Wall Street broker who unfortunately prefers Ella to Kate, the ambitious young aviator whose airplane proves fatally imperfect, and the Ziegfield Follies comedian who has the ambition but not the talent to be a dramatic actor. Finally, there are the working men, Trumbull's chauffeur and Daly's jockey, who are more attractive than their employers, but who are handicapped by past marriages or past crimes. Having invested $25,000 in the Follies comedian, Kate finally makes her none-too-promising match.

On the final page Tom summarizes the action: "Do you remember what we moved to the Big Town for? We done it to see Life and get Katie a husband.

Well, we got her a kind of a husband and I'll tell the world we seen Life." They have, at least, seen enough of the "Big Town," and Ella readily agrees to his proposal that they "mosey" back to South Bend. *The Big Town* serves as Lardner's anatomy of American social life as he saw it in 1920. The satire is never bitter; the least wise of the boobs—Kate—may be infatuated with the idea of a Lady Perkins, but she is at least not taken in by the condescending Herbert Daley. The worst that can be said of the sophisticates is that they are drones who take the game of bridge too seriously or that they make improper advances to the wrong women.

Characters

Tom Finch is the epitome of the "wise boob" character which Lardner frequently employed in his social satires. Unlike the cruder, more self-absorbed "busher," Finch is a midwesterner with an awareness of his limitations, and he remains unimpressed by the socially ambitious, self-promoting people who surround him. Chief among these are his wife Ella and her sister Kate, who desire to escape what they perceive as the stifling confines of South Bend society and make their marks in the big city. Although Kate's role as the husband-hunting girl is stereotypical, Lardner employs the convention to develop a variety of humorous situations. Kate never seems to realize the folly of her pursuit, and Ella's realization that Life and New York City are not identical comes only at the end. Throughout, the plain-talking Tom Finch scores against the illusions of the fashionable and would-be fashionable that he encounters in his passage through the Big Town. Tom's own defects—his inattention to grammatical niceties and his affinities for drinking and gambling—are venial; his imperfect, honest voice embodies the standard against which the vanities of New York are measured.

Relation to Previous Works

Lardner had been mining this vein of social satire as early as *Gullible's Travels, Etc.* (1917). In the title story of that collection, the Gullibles, disdaining the "riff and raff" of their Chicago neighborhood, embark on an expedition to join the "Elight" in Palm Beach, Florida. Like the Finches, the Gullibles find high society impenetrable and hurry back to Chicago: "Ain't it grand to be home." In the final story, the Gullibles attempt to climb the social ladder at home with equally unhappy results; they slip on the exotic game of bridge. As in *The Big Town*, the husband is the narrator; he is cruder, however, than Tom Finch and more his wife's accomplice.

Adaptations

The Big Town was released as the movie *So This is New York* in 1948. It was directed by Richard O. Fleischer and featured Henry Morgan, Rudy Vallee, and Virginia Grey.

Other Titles

Bib Ballads, 1915 (verse); *Gullible's Travels, Etc.*, 1917 (short stories); *My Four Weeks in France*, 1918 (war correspondence); *Treat 'Em Rough*, 1918 (short stories); *The Real Dope*, 1918 (short stories); *Own Your Own Home*, 1919 (short stories); *Regular Fellows I Have Met*, 1919 (verse); *The Young Immigrunts*, 1920 (humorous essay); *Symptoms of Being 35*, 1921 (humorous essay); *Say it With Oil*, 1923 (humorous essay); *How To Write Short Stories*, 1924 (short stories); *What of It?*, 1925 (nonsense plays and nonfiction); *The Love Nest and Other Stories*, 1926 (short stories); *The Story of a Wonder Man*, 1927 (mock autobiography); *Elmer the Great*, 1928 (play with George S. Kaufman), *Round Up*, 1929 (collected short stories); *June Moon* (play with George S. Kaufman), 1930; *Lose With a Smile*, 1933 (short stories); *First and Last*, 1934 (nonfiction; edited by Seldes); *Shut Up, He Explained*, 1962 (nonsense and parody; edited by Rosamond and Morgan); *Some Champions*, 1976 (sketches and stories; edited by Bruccoli and Layman); *Ring Lardner's You Know Me Al. The Comic Strip Adventures of Jack Keefe*, 1979 (comics; edited by Bruccoli).

Additional Sources

Blythe, Hal, and Charlie Sweet. "The Barber of Civility: The Chief Conspirator of 'Haircut.'" *Studies in Short Fiction* 23 (1986): 450-453. A recent contribution to the debate concerning the crucial character of the barber-narrator in "Haircut." Blythe and Sweet argue that he has, in fact, planned the death of Jim Kendall.

Bruccoli, Matthew J., and Richard Laymon. *Ring Lardner: A Descriptive Bibliography*. Pittsburgh: University of Pittsburgh Press, 1976. Comprehensive; the standard resource.

Elder, Donald. *Ring Lardner, A Biography*. Garden City, NY: Doubleday, 1956. The first full biography of Lardner; an indispensable source of information.

Evans, Elizabeth. *Ring Lardner*. New York: Ungar, 1979. A sensible survey of Lardner's work.

Fadiman, Clifton. "Pitiless Satire." *Nation* 128 (May 1, 1929): 537. A review of *Round Up*.

———. "Ring Lardner and the Triangle of Hate." *Nation* (March 22, 1933): 315-317. Raises the question of Lardner's misanthropy. Fadiman accuses Lardner of hating his characters, of hating himself, and of creating characters who hate each other.

Friedrich, Otto. *Ring Lardner*. Minneapolis: University of Minnesota Press, 1965. A short survey of Lardner's life and work.

Geismar, Maxwell. "Ring Lardner: Like Something Going to Happen." In *Writers in Crisis*. Boston: Houghton Mifflin, 1975. Finds a "ceaseless masochism" in Lardner's fiction: "Lardner creates indestructible characters whom he vainly attempts to destroy."

Gilead, Sarah. "Lardner's Discourses of Power." *Studies in Short Fiction* 22 (1985): 331-337. Analyzes three stories—"Haircut," "Zone of Quiet," and "The Maysville Minstrel"—and finds the narrator, the authorial presence, and the reader trapped within the narratives.

Ingram, Forrest L. "Fun at the Incinerating Plant: Lardner's Wry Waste Land." In *The Twenties*, edited by W. French. Deland, FL: Everett/Edwards, 1975. Focuses upon *The Big Town* and *Round Up*.

Lardner, Ring, Jr. *The Lardners: My Family Remembered*. New York: Harper, 1976. Lardner's third son narrates the family's history from his parent's courtship in 1907 to the death of his mother and last brother in 1960.

Menken, H. L. "A Humorist Shows His Teeth." *American Mercury* 8 (June 1926): 255. The first exploration of Lardner's "misanthropy."

Patrick, Walton F. *Ring Lardner*. New York: Twayne, 1963. An excellent critical survey, emphasizing Lardner's style, structure, and narrative technique.

Smith, Leverett T., Jr. " 'The Diameter of Frank Chance's Diamond': Ring Lardner and Professional Sports." *Journal of Popular Culture* 6 (1972-1973): 133-156. An important article that explains Lardner's shift away from sports fiction as a response to what Lardner perceived as baseball's sacrifice of intelligent teamwork to crowd-pleasing action.

Spatz, Jonas. "Ring Lardner: Not an Escape, but a Reflection." In *The Twenties,* edited by W. French. Deland, FL: Everett/Edwards, 1975. Sees Lardner's career as a movement from gentle humor to pessimistic satire.

Yardley, Jonathan. *Ring, A Biography of Ring Lardner.* New York: Random House, 1977. An informed, well-written critical biography; Lardner's reputation will not suffer for want of this fine account of his life.

J. K. Van Dover
Lincoln University

EMMA LATHEN
Mary Lane Latsis
1927
Martha Henissart
1929

Update

In recent years, the output of "Emma Lathen" has slowed—from ten John Putnam Thatcher novels in the 1960s to seven in the 1970s and only three in the 1980s. Mary Jane Latsis and Martha Henissart, who have collaborated to produce twenty Thatcher mysteries as well as another series under the name R. B. Dominic, are now based in New Hampshire after many years in Cambridge, Massachusetts. Their only Thatcher novel since 1985, *Something in the Air,* was favorably reviewed and was a selection of the Mystery Guild, as well as an alternate selection of both the Literary Guild and the Doubleday Book Club.

Critical attention to mysteries in general has increased, and analytical articles on Lathen have appeared in several scholarly journals and in a book about major women mystery writers.

Analysis of Selected Titles

SOMETHING IN THE AIR
Something in the Air, 1985, novel.

Social Concerns

Like previous Thatcher stories, *Something in the Air* deals with a single financial enterprise—in this case, a no-frills commuter airline. While clearly accepting the capitalist system with all its implications, the novel raises questions about the relationship of labor and management that go beyond the treatment of this topic in Lathen's earlier books. Sparrow Flyways has an innovative profit sharing system and horizontal management, both of which become inconvenient for its founder during a period of proposed expansion. He then seeks to replace the system with a more conventional top-down management scheme. In the ensuing power struggle no faction is free of self-interest. The potential role of women also comes in for a greater share of attention than before, since one of the founding partners of Sparrow and the fiery leader of the workers' group are both female. By the end of the novel, Thatcher is wondering what will happen if and when his grown daughter—or his invaluable secretary, Miss Corsa—awakens to the kind of power which he sees wielded so ably by Eleanor Gough. Strong women have appeared in earlier Thatcher novels, but it is rare for Thatcher himself to think about what their strength may imply. The reviewer for the *New York Times Book Review*, not a habitual reader of mysteries, focused on this aspect throughout much of her review and concluded, "This no-frills mystery is quite a feminist tale."

Themes
As always, John Putnam Thatcher lives, works, and detects in a world motivated primarily by greed. Though the characters of *Something in the Air* pursue money just as eagerly as their counterparts in the earlier books, Lathen makes an explicit connection here between money and power that in the past was more often implicit, or sometimes not mentioned at all. Thus the murderer acts out of fear that something he did many years ago will be revealed, and in the belief that by removing his blackmailer he can continue to suppress the past. The fact that his old crime was itself based on greed is entirely secondary, and no financial benefit can come from the murder.

In addition to the murderer, other characters in *Something in the Air* seek out and use power as an end in itself. Phoebe Fournier, the outspoken representative of the Sparrow workers, uses her ten thousand shares of Sparrow stock as political leverage and urges the Sloan Guaranty Trust as trustee to do the same; money is useful in buying power, whereas in many earlier Thatcher books the power was the means and the money the end.

Critics have mentioned Thatcher's (and evidently Lathen's) admiration for work, implying a value system in which hard work is a virtue in itself. *Something in the Air* continues this idea, often playing off superficial, image-conscious characters against solid workers. Intelligence, charm, and even success are lower in Lathen's world of values than work.

Characters
As always, John Putnam Thatcher, vice president of Sloan Guaranty Trust, is wise, urbane, and tolerant. Over the years he has become somewhat more removed from the concerns and ways of the young; a visit with his daughter and her extended family leaves him happy to return to his quiet widower's life, and he clearly appreciates the mature personality of Eleanor Gough more than the dynam-

ic youth of Phoebe Fournier. For the first time in the series, an important part of the detective work is actually done by one of the other characters.

Of the Sloan staff, only Everett Gabler plays as large a role as usual, traveling to Boston to use his formidable accounting skills to ferret out secrets in the victim's financial records. The other Sloan characters put in only cameo appearances when Thatcher checks in at his home office, and they play no part in the action, probably because so much of the action takes place in Boston or at various airports.

Within Sparrow Flyways itself, flamboyant characters abound. Mitch Scovil, founder of Sparrow, is a typical boy wonder with little patience for the day-to-day operations which he leaves to his less colorful partners, Clay Batchelder and Eleanor Gough. The victim, Alan Whetmore, embodies the image of the egotistical, high-living commercial pilot, while Phoebe Fournier represents a combination of an idealistic approach with sound common sense and (perhaps most important) fiscal conservatism.

Techniques

Once again, Lathen cleverly uses a single financial body, this time a small commuter airline, to make the "closed society" of the classic detective story plausible. The death of the victim, a rather unpopular bachelor pilot, has no possible benefit for anyone outside of Sparrow Airways—but could be enormously useful to many within the company. Unlike most earlier novels in the series, however, *Something in the Air* has a variety of settings. Locale is not restricted to company headquarters and the Sloane, but includes two stunning airport scenes and a memorable boat excursion. This opening-up gives the action of the book a less contrived, more varied effect. Lathen had experimented with varying the scene with *When in Greece* (1969), much of which takes place on the road, but *Something in the Air* is a more successful effort. A comparison with Agatha Christie's classic *Death in the Air,* in which all the important action takes place inside a plane in flight, shows how far Lathen has departed from the usual limitations of a closed-world setting.

Even though she varies the usual cast of characters by removing most of the Sloan staff, and departs from the closed aspect by focusing on travel, Lathen nevertheless retains most of the essentials of the classic mystery. As in all the previous Thatcher books, Lathen draws attention to the formal structure of the work, and to the ironic, game-like quality of the classic puzzle-mystery, by a series of humorous chapter titles. This time, they are drawn from the language of bird watchers: "Labored Flapping" for negotiations gone wrong, "Helpless on Land" for airport closures after a walkout, "Sighted in Louisiana" for a misleading journey by one suspect, and so on. The minor false suspect (introduced early) and then the major false suspect (near the end), the exciting climax in the next to last chapter, and the concluding explanation by Thatcher, all satisfy the reader's expectations for the classic genre.

Relation to Previous Works

A popular author with a winning formula tends to repeat it, and Emma Lathen is no exception. Every Thatcher novel starts at the Sloan and ends with Thatcher's exposition of the crime in the last or next to last chapter; every Thatcher novel has comic relief by the supporting cast at the Sloan; and every Thatcher novel has as its unsung heroine Rose Theresa Corsa, secretary *par excellence*.

For the most part, the novels concern themselves with management and owners more than with workers (except in very special kinds of businesses, for example, the hockey players in *Murder Without Icing*). Only one previous novel has explored the nature of management-employee relations in any detail: *The Longer the Thread* (1972). In this book, set in Puerto Rico in politically troubled times, it is clear that the reader, and Thatcher, should support management and oppose a radical powerbase at the factory; indeed, a funny but wholly admirable ILGWU negotiator, Annie Galiano, is brought in: she is one of Lathen's ultra-competent, middle-aged female characters. In *Something in the Air,* however, the wants and needs of management and workers are more evenly balanced and the reader's sympathies are divided with excellent effect.

Another previous book with close ties to *Something in the Air* is its immediate predecessor, *Green Grow the Dollars* (1982). Here too, money is more than an end in itself; the murderer is motivated as much by his need for fame and continuing reputation as he is by simple greed. As a research scientist who has not had a breakthrough in ten years, he must produce or retire—a prospect which he clearly cannot face. His brilliant past controls his mediocre present just as much as the criminal past of the murderer of *Something in the Air* controls his.

In the only previous Lathen title involving the murder of a blackmailer, *By Hook or By Crook,* the motive differs greatly. The murderer's initial "crime" falls under the heading of illegality but not, in any ordinary sense, of wrongdoing; he is forced to kill only because, with his grasp on his company and on his fortune threatened already by family feuding, his position both in his company and in his family depends on maintaining his false identity.

Finally, Thatcher's admiration for the formidable Eleanor Gough resembles Congressman Benton Safford's longstanding alliance with Congresswoman Elsie

Hollenback, "the scourge of the Department of Defense," in the R. B. Dominic series by the same authors. For the first time in the Thatcher series, another character—and a female character, at that—appears who, though less central in the novel, is fully Thatcher's equal.

Additional Sources

Bedell, Jeanne. "Emma Lathen." In *10 Women of Mystery*, edited by Earl F. Bargainnier. Bowling Green, OH: Bowling Green State University Popular Press, 1981. An interpretative essay covering the novels through 1978, this remains the fullest interpretation available, with particularly good coverage of Lathen's comedy.

Christopher, J. R. "Can We Reach Agreement?" *Mystery Fancier* 8, 1 (1984): 14-15. A short article examining a sentence (in *Green Grow the Dollars*) in which a plural pronoun refers to a singular antecedent.

Lawrence, Barbara. "Emma Lathen: The Art of Escapist Crime Fiction." *Clues: A Journal of Detection* 3, 2 (1982): 76-82. An analysis of Lathen's output up to 1982 (sixteen Thatcher books) as a special type of "procedural novel."

Sarjeant, William A. S. "Crime on Wall Street." *The Armchair Detective* 21, 2 (Spring 1988): 128-145. A comprehensive overview of the first nineteen John Putnam Thatcher mysteries.

Steinberg, Sybil. "Something in the Air." *Publishers Weekly* 234 (September 9, 1988): 123. A favorable review.

Wasserstein, Wendy. "Something in the Air." *New York Times Book Review* (October 9, 1988): 23. A favorable review, commenting on Thatcher's new view of women.

Caroline Hunt
College of Charleston

JOHN LE CARRÉ
David John Moore Cornwell
1931

Update

In recent years there have been two dominant trends in criticism of John le Carré. The first is a group of critics who regard le Carré as the best writer of spy fiction in the world, and they treat him as an important author. The second, more recent group believes that le Carré's formula for spy fiction is outdated; the seeming end of the cold war has, according to this view, robbed le Carré of his subject matter: the contest between East and West which he superbly inaugurated in *The Spy Who Came in from the Cold*. The fall of the Berlin Wall, which some commentators have asserted is an essential image in le Carré's tales of espionage, heralds the fall of his fiction.

Le Carré has published two novels in recent years; in both *The Russia House* (1989) and *The Secret Pilgrim* (1991) le Carré provides responses to those critics who regard the spy novel as something that could only be credible while the cold war existed. *The Russia House* includes references to the changes in relations between the Soviet Union and the West. It asserts that some of the changes in the Soviet Union are superficial, while noting that many political undesirables still die anonymous deaths in Soviet forced labor camps, Soviet master torturers still ply their trade, and Soviet spy agencies still permeate the Western world. Ned says, "Listen to the insiders and you realize the picture hasn't altered by a brushstroke."

In *The Secret Pilgrim*, the question of the end of the cold war is presented in more ambivalent terms: master-spy George Smiley asserts that the need for vigilance is ever present if Western freedom is to be preserved, despite an admission that the deception essential to successful spying can be destructive to people's liberties. The book sounds a melancholy note, suggesting that even if the cold war has truly ended, the Soviet Union still represents a dire military threat that must be watched carefully by the spies of other governments.

Analysis of Selected Titles

THE RUSSIA HOUSE

The Russia House, 1989, novel.

Social Concerns

One of the aspects of le Carré's fiction that critics most admire is its careful examination of the social implications of spying. In *The Russia House,* the Soviet Union is in the midst of *glasnost,* through which the government is trying to adopt a more reasonable attitude toward the Western world. The novel is full of examples of the changes, such as when KGB guards exchange a wink with a British book agent over their admiration of a beautiful Russian woman. The previously hostile attitude toward foreigners has seemingly relaxed. On the other hand, *The Russia House* portrays a dark world in which superficial friendliness can disguise vicious rivalries. The Soviets still torture people into confessions; Western spies believe that no one, however well trained, can avoid betraying all they know to Soviet interrogators. Western spy agencies, too, have their dark sides, although they do not practice torture. Interrogations by British and American spy agencies are cruel and humiliating, treating even innocent civilians as if they were traitors.

As is usually the case in le Carré's fiction, right and wrong are ambiguous concepts. Neither East nor West can honestly claim the moral high ground in the world of espionage; indeed, there is neither a traditional heroic figure nor a traditional villainous figure in this novel. Instead, *The Russia House* explores the grey areas that lie between good and evil, focusing on how realistic human beings cope with fear and a desire for better lives. This explains the novel's ambiguous ending: Is Barley a hero for saving the life of the woman he loves and her family, or is he a villain for selling out the CIA and British intelligence? In reality neither East nor West has a true claim to his allegiance. In a world of calculated cruelty and sometimes foolish spy games, Barley finds the one true claim on his fidelity: individual human beings whose private fears and joys are the only fully meaningful aspects of life. In the end, Barley is true to his best nature; he saves innocent lives at a great risk to his own. Compared to the simple reality of individual human needs, the desperate secret espionage war seems insignificant.

Themes

Part of what makes le Carré's fiction appealing to critics is its emphasis on human nature. Le Carré's novels are not about great armies of spies that clash in the night, deciding the fate of all humanity. Instead, they are stories of individual people, whose personalities shape what they do. Central in *The Russia House,* is Barley's personality, not the characteristics of his government, or his spy agency, or the Western world. Ned recognizes this, which is why he knows well ahead of time what Barley really intends to do. Ned's colleagues do not realize Barley's intentions; they naively think their training has somehow fashioned Barley into the faithful drudge that he could never truly be. Thus, they are surprised by his betrayal.

Characters

Le Carré's characterization is an outstanding feature of almost all of his fiction. His studies of the effect of a world predicated on mistrust, lying, and betrayal on individuals add depth to his fiction, making the stories meaningful in simple human terms. The impact of espionage on the world is almost always destructive. Lying becomes habitual, even preferable to straightforward truth. Betrayal turns into a complex game in which the loss of human lives is merely a way of keeping score. The reaction of many of le Carré's characters to deceit and death is to deny the reality of the darkness inherent in spying. British spy masters refuse to believe that there is a traitor in their midst, even when that traitor sells out the lives of countless agents. They delude themselves into thinking that their "friends" would never betray them. When George Smiley reveals that there is an enemy agent working in the highest offices of the British espionage establishment, they punish him for revealing how they had been deceived themselves, as if Smiley were guilty of betraying them. Other of le Carré's characters become hardened to their trade; they trust no one and ruthlessly use other people. Some, like Smiley, retain a beleaguered sense of humanity; they weary of the cruelty of their work, yet see it as a necessary defense of their nation.

Into this lopsided world in which evil often looks like good and good often looks like evil comes Scott Blair, known as "Barley." He is an unlikely secret agent—he drinks far too much, is filled with self-hate, and regards himself as a loser. His fragile personality is thrown into a world that would be confusing to even the most stable of people. Through him, readers can see how an ordinary man achieves extraordinary things and responds to the bizarre world of professional spying. For a time Barley forgets himself, losing track of who he is. For instance, he is at one point surprised at his own physical strength; he had known that he was a strong man, but had forgotten it in the strain of trying to remember the multitude of deceptions required of him.

Barley's story is told in the first person by Horatio Benedict dePalfrey, also known as "Old Palfrey," "Palfrey," or most often "Harry." Harry is the resident lawyer for British intelligence. Timid and officious, he seems unlikely to sympathize with the melancholy and undisciplined Barley. But like many others in *The Russia House,* Harry hides another personality beneath his stern veneer. Sympathetic toward those who are drawn into his world, he speaks with satisfaction about how Niki Landau turns out to be a straightforward patriot who keeps his word exactly as he has given it. He expresses discomfort over how Barley continually looks at him, as if asking for moral support or comfort. Barley recognizes in Harry what Harry himself does not see—a kindred spirit.

Harry's concern for people and their needs makes him a good narrator; he takes time to expose individual's motivations and personalities. His reliance on law requires him to be very careful about presenting details. An honest man—even though he characterizes himself as deceitful—Harry makes it clear whenever he is speculating and not speaking from fact. His world is ambiguous and he is not sure of what is going on. The events, although fictional, appear credible, as if le Carré is presenting a true story.

Yekaterina "Katya" Borisovna Orlova is in some ways a typical heroine of spy thrillers. Katya is beautiful, goodhearted, and warm—a seemingly unrealistic portrayal given the ruthless realism of everyone else in the novel. One justification for her stereotypical portrayal is that the novel's narrator, Harry, is smitten by her and does not want to admit any frailties. She must also serve as a powerful motivation for Barley to risk everything to save her life. Barley loves her; he sees in her all the good that is missing in his life. It is little wonder that through the eyes of Barley and Harry, she seems the embodiment of great human virtues.

Ultimately, the success of *The Russia House* rests on the characterization of Barley. If the reader does not believe in Barley, it would be difficult to accept the premise of the novel. Big, strong, hard drinking, a lovable lost soul, he could easily become the stock character of a multitude of adventure novels. It is a sign of le Carré's mastery of characterization that Barley does not simply become a shallow gathering of eccentricities. Instead, he comes alive as a worldly man in search of an identity; he does not realize it, but his life has been a search for himself, for the man underneath the eccentricities, that hide his unhappy personality. At first it seems that his British and American spy masters have given him his identity. His insecurities are replaced with crafts of the trade. He assumes the identity of the confident spy who can betray others easily because he has no firm notion of right and wrong. The man who routinely uses and betrays women in the early part of the novel seems to ideally fit the role of a secret agent—someone who must ruthlessly use people. Yet, Barley finds another answer, one only Ned recognizes at first, and Harry comes to understand only after the novel's main events are over. Barley discovers individual lives are not worth the secrets he is supposed to protect. Thus, when he betrays his country to the Soviets, he paradoxically remains true to his best self.

Techniques

The Russia House is told in the first person by Harry. This colors the events of the novel, and Harry frequently reminds readers that they are seeing events through the eyes of a biased witness. Like George Smiley and other significant figures in le Carré's fiction, he yearns for a clean, honest, successful spying operation. The ambiguities of his life in the secret service gnaw at him, costing him sleep and troubling his conscience. He confesses that his image as an unemotional and fastidious lawyer is part of an act. He often mentions his love affair with a woman married to one of his colleagues. She wishes to marry him, and in his heart, he wishes to marry her. Even so, he is afraid of her and of the powerful emotions she represents. Thus he uses his secret work as an excuse not to commit himself to her; in essence his work becomes a way of escaping from himself. It is no wonder that he delights in the simple courage and faith of Niki Landau, and that he finds the case of Barley intensely meaningful. Barley has the courage to act on his best principles once he finds them; Harry admits that he cannot do the same.

Le Carré makes Harry more of an observer than a full participant in the action. In addition, he takes advantage of the opportunities Harry's first-person narrative provides. Harry contrasts well with his subject, Barley. Superficially, they seem to be men who have no sympathy for one another. Harry is prim and punctilious; he behaves as if his job were all-important to him. On the other hand, Barley is a dissipated alcoholic whose self-pity seems always ready to burst to the surface of his personality. Yet, the men recognize their kindred natures. Barley often turns to Harry for support. His pleading gaze causes Harry discomfort because Barley's fears and self-hatred reflect his own fears and disgust with himself. Harry's dry, matter-of-fact prose understates his agony over the conflict between individual decency and the indecencies life imposes on people.

Literary Precedents

In the early 1960s, le Carré and another important British novelist, Len Deighton, set new standards for the spy thriller. The early years of the cold war had seen a multitude of fictional spies who, like James Bond, tended to be larger than life and have amazing adventures in a secret world of technological marvels. In *The Spy Who Came in from the Cold* and Deighton's *The Ipcress File*, a more realistic kind of spy novel found a large and responsive audience. Le Carré was then still working in the British secret service; he used a pen name instead of his own because his government required him to do so. The unexpected success of his hard-nosed, no-nonsense account of intrigue, betrayal, and fear earned him enough money to quit his government job and devote himself to his writing. Over the years, he has created a fictional world that seems starkly real. However, he has deepened and enriched his stories by showing in them how the realistically portrayed world of spying displays in high relief the universal human needs for love, hope, and faith.

Related Titles

Most of le Carré's novels are tied together by common characters, such as Harry and Ned. *The Russia House* is not really a sequel to any of the earlier novels, although Harry mentions a few events from them. This particular novel exists on its own, depending not so much on continuing characters or past intrigues as on unique figures such as Barley and Katya and on the effort of a Soviet scientist to tell the world the truth about the Soviet Union's nuclear weapons. As with le Carré's other novels, *The Russia House* presents a realistic, dark world in which the human mind becomes confused, losing the distinction between right and wrong, and between "our side" and "their side."

Adaptations

The motion-picture version of *The Russia House,* starring Sean Connery as Barley Blair, and Michelle Pfeiffer as Katya, was released in December 1990. Connery seems the embodiment of Barley, creating a character for the screen that shares all of the humanity of the character in the novel. In an interview, le Carré said that he was delighted with Connery's portrayal, although he himself had pictured Peter O'Toole in the role. The screenplay was written by playwright Tom Stoppard, and it emphasizes the interior lives of the characters and de-emphasizes action. Some parts of the movie are slow; the filmmakers dwell on sights and scenery, perhaps because of their eagerness to take advantage of being allowed to film freely on location in Moscow. The motion picture opened to positive reviews, with some reviewers noting that it is satisfying adult fare and it examines mature emotions intelligently.

THE SECRET PILGRIM

The Secret Pilgrim, 1991, novel.

Social Concerns

Although *The Secret Pilgrim* focuses on the conflict between the free Communist worlds, it does not present many comparisons between Western and Eastern societies. The novel acknowledges Communist governments' torture and abuses of human rights, but it is more concerned with how deception affects individuals. The practice of spying is shown to be necessary for Western democracies; they need to know how to fend off threats to their sovereignty and liberties. On the other hand, characters such as Ned and Smiley note that some aspects of spying are antithetical to the ideals of freedom which form the moral foundation of their democratic government. They want to see themselves as secret protectors of the public good, but they wonder whether such aspects of domestic spying as wiretaps, investigations into people's private lives, and the Official Secrets Act actually help or harm the people they are supposed to serve. Overall, the novel suggests that even though spying can be destructive to the personality of individual spies, it is necessary in a world in which many powerful countries have no respect for the rights of others.

Themes

In a series of loosely connected episodes in the career of ace field spy Ned, *The Secret Pilgrim* examines how people behave under extreme stress. The most dramatic of these episodes is the one in which Ned is tortured by Polish agents. With all his courage he resists giving them what they want. He is beaten and loses teeth; he is tied to a rack and worked over. Typical of the melancholy tone of the novel, Ned's determination and endurance turn out to have no real meaning. He thinks that the colonel in charge of torturing him is after important secrets that could cost the lives of agents working for the British; instead, the colonel is only testing him to see how tough he is. It turns out that the colonel wishes to betray the Communist government, and in a bizarre twisting of motivations, he has tortured Ned in order to work for him; the colonel wants a tough man to be in charge of his own spying for the British.

The colonel is in search of a kind of perverse truth: he wants to find an honest man who would be true to his commitment to him. Throughout the novel, people seek truth, knowledge, and reassurance. A curious contrast to Ned's episode with the Polish colonel occurs when an old British war hero visits Smiley, who works in an office where citizens can report what seem to be suspicious activities that may involve spying against their country. The old war hero has come to find out whether his son worked for British intelligence. When he visited his son in prison, his son had claimed that being in prison was only a cover for his being out of the country, spying on Russia. After his son is stabbed to death, he comes to Smiley in hopes of finding the truth. After investigating the case, Smiley learns that the son was a nasty, vicious criminal who had led a life of crime, and who had died as he lived, in a vicious stabbing. Yet, when the old war hero returns with his wife, Smiley lets him believe that his son was involved in ultra-secret work, and gives the couple cufflinks that are supposed to symbolize their son's rank in British intelligence; the cufflinks are actually a pair given to Smiley by his wife before she had an affair with a vile double-agent, precipitating the break up of their marriage. Ned speculates on why the hard-nosed Smiley would allow the old couple to believe a falsehood—that their degenerate son was actually a heroic secret agent. In the convoluted world of secret intelligence, the falsehood actually gave Smiley a kind of truth. In the world of espionage, agents seldom know how their work will turn out; the case of the bereaved parents of a criminal son gave Smiley a moment of certainty in an otherwise uncertain career.

Characters

Ned's memoirs provide the foundation of the novel. He reminisces about aspects of his career as he listens to Smiley give a talk to a class of future spies whom Ned teaches. Ned believes that the world is changing as nations form new relationships made possible by the Soviet Union's collapsing empire. It is his hope—and Smiley's belief—that old brutal practices of the cold war have become obsolete, that future British secret agents will lead lives that will be less hypocritical and dehumanizing than were the lives of the agents of his own generation. From episode to episode, Ned traces his own growth into a top secret agent. He begins as an idealistic young man. In training he is paired off with Ben, one of British intelligence's leading lights. He feels himself inferior to his partner, and his superiors also seem to think that Ben is much better. Once in the field, Ben transgresses and betrays his government; from this, Ned learns a hard lesson about what spying can do to people. He also learns not to trust people the way he had trusted Ben.

Ned decides that his life is "to be a search." He dedicates himself to ferreting out information and looking for truth. In one episode after another, he learns that absolute truth is hard to find. Almost nothing is ever what it seems to be in spying. Why does Jerzy, the Polish colonel, torture him? Obviously, it must be to force Ned to give him secret information; yet, in truth, the obvious is wrong. Jerzy tortures Ned not to receive information but rather so he can give it. Ned comes to suspect betrayal from any source. After all, Smiley had revealed that one of Britain's most trusted secret agents was actually working for the Soviet Union. The response of Smiley's superiors was to punish him by relegating him to insignificant work. By the 1980s, Ned has become tired and unsure of what he has accomplished in life. He dislikes spying, being uncertain of its value. He hopes the kind of life he led will no longer be necessary in the future because of new arrangements with the Soviet Union. Even so, when he follows the news about how the Baltic republics are trying to break away from the Soviet Union, he wonders whether his government is now "diligently breaking" a cold war promise to help the Baltic peoples.

Ned's memories and questions are triggered by George Smiley, a master spy of the generation before Ned's own. In some ways, Ned sees a parallel between their two careers, each having shared similar rewards and punishments. As Smiley chats with Ned's students, he seems to be a repository of wisdom. He scoffs "at the idea that spying was a dying profession now that the cold war had ended." On the other hand, at the novel's end Smiley declares that his way of doing things is outdated and that therefore he will no longer come to the school for spies; the world will require new approaches to espionage. Still, when Ned studies his students, he sees in them what he and Smiley once were. Smiley represents what happens to a good man who must almost daily take charge of other people's lives and how having to lie to them, use them, and discard them—often without ever allowing them to know exactly what they are risking their lives for—can generate self-doubt and self-reproach inside the best of men. Among his students, Ned sees idealists like himself and the young Smiley; he sees the iconoclasts and the emotionally unstable who are nonetheless necessary to British intelligence because of their special talents; and he sees women, who now attend previously all-male classes, as a sign of changing times. The careers of Ned and Smiley represent a past that they hope the new secret agents will not have to follow. Ned's own weary, melancholy attitude suggests that this hope may be as elusive as finding truth or happiness in the necessarily deceitful world of spying.

Techniques

The Secret Pilgrim is one of le Carré's most brilliantly written novels. It is a "framed" story, an outer story that surrounds the main story; the frame is Smiley's talk with Ned's students. This frame allows for three different generations of spies to interact. Smiley represents the World War II generation, which joined British intelligence when anything seemed possible, when the world seemed ready to be made good, peaceful, and safe, with the British Empire still intact. For Smiley's generation, the 1950s and 1960s were profoundly disillusioning. Ned represents the generation that joined British intelligence during the height of the cold war, when spying was a murderously desperate contest between nations. His students represent the future; they are the hope for better days, when it may be possible that spying will become less of a deadly war for national self-preservation. The interactions among these characters provide perspective on the main narrative. Ned is able to refer back to comments made by Smiley and his students in order to provide insights into the tales of human suffering that make up the bulk of the novel.

The novel is episodic, with the character of Ned providing most of the links from one event to another. Like Smiley, Ned has become sensitive to humanity. He feels the losses of those he has known deeply and remembers their hopes having been dashed just as his own were. He calls his life a search, but as he tells it, it is more of an education in human strengths and weaknesses. The episodic organization of the novel allows him to examine several different kinds of people, such as Jerzy, who believes that his own cruelty has cost him his emotional life. Jerzy concludes that "by ceasing to feel he was ceasing to exist," so he spies for the British in part just to generate feelings and thus feel alive. Bella, the beautiful and sexually dynamic Soviet expatriate who is suspected of being a double-agent, turns out to be exactly what she seems, a strong, honest woman; Hansen, the brilliantly talented agent who survived the horrors of the genocidal war waged by Pol Pot in Cambodia, sees his daughter's personality destroyed by Marxist ideology, and now lives with her while she follows the only life that gives her a feeling of belonging, that of a brothel prostitute. These are colorful people whose portrayal makes them also realistic.

The episodic novel has at least three potentially significant weaknesses: the characters may not be well developed and may be merely one-dimensional stereotypes; the characters may become confused with one another and be easily forgotten; and the narrative may not flow, encouraging readers to close the novel after an episode and not reopen it. In *The Secret Pilgrim,* the characters are brilliantly realized. Ned's narrative has a stark, documentary feel to it, making the novel's events seem as though they may have actually happened. This carefully controlled realistic tone, enhanced by well observed details of locale and local customs, provides a fine background for the characters who are made more real by the world they inhabit.

Ned's primary interest is in what happens to people who risk their lives to serve others and he studies them in depth. For instance, Hansen emerges as a compelling figure. His life is a great modern tragedy played out against the most horrifying events of his time. His treatment at the hands of the Communists points out that there are vital reasons why he and Ned must ply their trade. Hansen himself is a complex man, talented yet whimsical. Something of a lost soul, he finds an anchor for himself in a bizarre and out-of-control environment, and it is this humane anchor that the novel implies is essential for survival. He loves his daughter and gives himself to her. Ultimately, the essential aspect of working for the public good demands that one focus on individuals and their welfare.

Literary Precedents

The Secret Pilgrim is in the tradition of le Carré's *The Spy Who Came in from the Cold*. It is a typically gritty account of the work of spies, with an emphasis on the human cost of the cold war. Le Carré has recently expressed weariness with this type of spy novel, so he may be moving on to other literary traditions.

Related Titles

The Secret Pilgrim takes place in the British intelligence community that le Carré has included in most of his earlier work. It is more clearly linked to his earlier work than *The Russia House* because of the inclusion of George Smiley, who appears prominently in earlier novels, most notably the "Smiley trilogy" of *Tinker, Tailor, Soldier, Spy* (1974), in which Smiley unmasks a Soviet agent working in a high position for British intelligence, an event that is discussed in *The Secret Pilgrim; The Honourable Schoolboy* (1977), in which Smiley helps the British intelligence community recover from the chaos created by the enemy agent; and *Smiley's People* (1980), in which Smiley pursues his archenemy, the Soviet master spy Karla.

Additional Sources

Bloom, Harold, ed. *John le Carré*. New York: Chelsea House, 1987. Part of the Modern Critical Views series, this volume gathers together eleven previously published reviews and essays on le Carré's work. Not as good as Bold's *The Quest for le Carré*, but scholars and students will find it useful.

Bold, Alan, ed. *The Quest for le Carré*. London: Vision Press, 1988. New York: St. Martin's Press, 1988. Part of the Critical Studies Series, this is a gathering of nine essays, plus a good introduction, focusing on aspects of le Carré's fiction. An ideal resource for students.

Brissenden, R. F. "A Perfect Spy: 'Like Huckleberry Finn.' " *Quadrant* 30 (December 1986): 45-49. Compares le Carré's *A Perfect Spy* to Twain's *The Adventures of Huckleberry Finn*.

Cohn, Jack R. "The Watch on John le Carré." *Studies in the Novel* 20 (Fall 1988): 323-337. Surveys several studies of le Carré's fiction.

Geoghegan, Jack. "The Spy Who Saved Me—A Thriller Starring John le Carré." *New York Times Book Review* (December 4, 1988): 16. Geoghegan tells of how the novel *The Spy Who Came in from the Cold*, by a then little-known novelist, le Carré, came to be published by his firm, Coward-McCann.

Silver, Brenda R. "Woman as Agent: The Case of le Carré's *Little Drummer Girl*." *Contemporary Literature* 28 (Spring 1987): 14-40. Discusses "a recurring theme in his novels: a distinction between wife and agent that brings into play concepts such as love and desire, lawlessness and law, subject and object" as it applies to *Little Drummer Girl*.

Wolfe, Peter. *Corridors of Deceit: The World of John le Carré*. Bowling Green, OH: Bowling Green State University Popular Press, 1987. A comprehensive critical study of the major themes and characters of le Carré's books.

Kirk H. Beetz
National University, Sacramento

URSULA K. LE GUIN
1927

Update

Ursula K. Le Guin's literary activity since 1985 has been impressive in its quantity, quality, and variety. Always a lively writer of children's books, she has published four new works for younger readers. *A Visit from Dr. Katz* (1988) is intended for kindergarten through third grade readers, and *Fire and Stone* (1988) for the first through third grades. Two works for slightly older children are *Catwings* (1988) and *Catwings Return* (1989). With their beautifully detailed drawings, they are appealing books with a captivating storyline about four flying cats who leave their alley home in the city to seek a better life. In the second book, they return home just in time to help their mother and a younger sister. Le Guin effectively endows each of the cats with a distinct personality. When these remarkable flying felines are assisted by some gentle children, young readers are quick to imagine themselves in this helpful role.

Le Guin's flair for innovation was revealed in the publication of her first play, *King Dog* (1985). A genre rarely used in science fiction, it deals effectively with a king's quest for freedom, and his encounter with a traveler from the stars, whom he calls the Lord of Death.

In 1989 Le Guin won the annual Pilgrim Award of the Science Fiction Research Association, designed to honor a lifetime of achievement in science fiction. In her acceptance speech, she argued fervently for incorporating science fiction and fantasy into the standard literature courses in college, rather than ghettoizing them into separate categories. Her argument was that literary quality, not genre, should be the standard of acceptance.

Her own continuing work in fiction, although innovative in many ways, is still in the large realm of the fantastic rather than the realistic. The title story of her collection *Buffalo Gals and Other Animal Presences* (1987) is indicative of both a new focus and an old interest: traditional native American myth. In this story a child drops from the sky, sole survivor of a plane crash, and enters a primitive Dream Time, a place inhabited by talking animals. The most important is Coyote, a wise and maternal figure, based on American Indian myths of that clever creature. When the child finally must return to reality, she is reluctant to leave the natural world of animal presences. Le Guin places new emphasis on the feminist perspective, which is also a factor in her recent critical writings.

Her recent anthology, *Dancing at the Edge of the World,* is a critical miscellany of talks, essays, and reviews. Some of the items are reprints of earlier publications, but many are new or hitherto unpublished. Le Guin also offers the reader a set of symbols as keys to the content of each piece: Feminism, Social Responsibility, Literature, and Travel, with the symbol for Feminism occurring most frequently. The volume chronicles her growing interest in the feminist approach, which has become central to her work. Along with her concern with problems such as world hunger and environmental pollution, she expresses her anger over the persistent inequality of women. She also discusses her changing views on narrative, rejecting the Aristotelian theory of linear narrative. She points out that such directionality does not exist even in the structure of matter, for neither the atom nor the gene is directional.

A feisty and provocative book, *Dancing at the Edge of the World* is lively reading and a good introduction to the concerns of Le Guin's recent fiction. The title, derived from North American Indian lore, is also indicative of an interest which dominates her latest novel and recent short stories.

Analysis of Selected Titles

ALWAYS COMING HOME

Always Coming Home, 1985, novel.

Social Concerns/Themes

Always Coming Home is a remarkable novel, totally unconventional in its narrative presentation, in which Le Guin deals with several social concerns. Set in northern California, the novel deals with people who "might be going to have lived a long, long time from now." In this imaginative "archeology of the future" Le Guin envisions two rival societies, the Kesh, who are the peaceful inhabitants of an idyllic Valley, and the Condor, a warlike society to their north. The Kesh are matriarchal, the Condor patriarchal.

Ecological consciousness is also a major theme of the novel. The Kesh, who live in a rural and tribal society, are ecology-minded. They live in harmony with nature, in contrast to the Condor, who are urban and national, and who routinely exploit nature. The ambiguously futuristic setting is a California five hundred years from now, which has largely been depopulated by catastrophe and contamination. The Kesh practice rituals based on nature, and respect the birds and beasts with whom they live. Although they have advanced technology, they do not use it aggressively or industrially. There is no pollution in the Valley. Their household animals are not known as "pets," a condescending word, but as "commensal," which means people living together.

The novel is also concerned with the nature of economic justice. The Kesh communities are socialistic rather than capitalistic, a fact reflected in their language and rhetoric. There is, for example, no word for "famine" because in their economy of sharing and their healthy environment such a phenomenon is simply non-existent. Their proverbs also reflect their attitudes toward wealth, such as "Owning is owing, having is hoarding." In their use of language words function as rhetorical tools of their ideology. The same word means "to give" and "to be rich."

Feminism is a central theme, in part focused on the figure of Stone Telling, a woman whose life story offers the single narrative line within this complexly organized, non-linear book. Stone Telling, who in her youth is known as North Owl, represents the cultural dialectic in the novel: her mother is of the Kesh and her father of the Condor. She feels an outsider among the Condor, not merely because they are patriarchal but because they scorn and abuse women. Among them she feels humiliated for they believe that women do not even have souls. It therefore becomes her goal to return to the place of her birth and eventually become Woman Coming Home. The feminist theme is also carried by the choral figure of Pandora, who speaks five interpolated sequences in the book. Her ironic asides offer commentary on women's roles.

Always Coming Home is also an anti-war book. Not only are the Condor negatively represented as a society that is aggressive toward other groups, but the absurdity of the act of war is stressed throughout. The concepts of heroism in battle and of glory in conquest are repeatedly devalued, both through the action and by the comments of outsiders like Pandora.

Characters

In a real sense the main character of the book is not an individual but a society, for Le Guin gives considerably more attention to her account of the Kesh culture than to any one character. There are, however, some major characters.

Stone Telling's account of her own life occupies about one-fifth of this long book. As a child, she lives among the Kesh, her mother's people; but she becomes restless and decides to join the Condor, among whom her father dwells. Her movement through life is reflected in her name changes. Stone Telling is her name as retrospective narrator. She marries (her husband is named Stone Listening) and has a daughter before finally returning home, when she becomes Woman Coming Home. Her account of her experiences is sensitive and moving.

As Stone Telling occupies the center in the book, the ambiguous character of Pandora occupies the circumference, for her interspersed remarks comment on all aspects of the narrative. The figure of Pandora is based on the mythic figure who was both the giver of all gifts and the mother of human woes. Pandora opened the box given to her by Prometheus, which released evils into the world but also held Hope at the bottom. Her role in *Always Coming Home* is not easy to specify. She may be seen as the alter ego of the author, a choral commentator, or a representative of the reader. She functions in all of these roles, and her incisive language makes her lively and appealing. Structurally and thematically she provides much needed irony. Frequently acerbic, she dismisses "smartass utopians" and scorns those who think they know the answers as "boring, boring." She also adds a welcome touch of humor to the novel.

Most of the other characters offer vignettes of their personalities and their roles in the contrasting societies of the book. Both of Stone Telling's parents appear, as does her husband, Stone Listening, but all are described by her and not fully developed as individuals.

Techniques

Always Coming Home is a highly experimental novel. Le Guin's guiding intention was to invite collaboration between the writer and the reader, so that reading would not be a merely passive exercise. Here the reader must in effect create the novel through the materials the author has provided. Le Guin's techniques are boldly unconventional, and the responsive reader can collaborate in a rich creative experience. One can begin reading *Always Coming Home* at any point, not just at the beginning, since the reading experience is not one of following a suspenseful plot to a climactic resolution but rather of moving in a multiplicity of directions around a visionary center.

The book is constructed of a variety of materials. About one-fifth is the autobiographical account of Stone Telling, spaced out in three separate sections. There are also poems, plays, short stories, information, commentary, and music. Of the various literary forms, poetry is predominant, with over seventy pages of poems, many ceremonial or improvisational. Some are children's songs. The highlight of the dramatic works is the play called "Chandi," a Kesh version of the Job legend, which employs pantomime, costume, and gesture as well as language to communicate its meaning. In addition to the plays and poems, the book contains short stories, prose essays, and a chapter of a novel in progress.

Along with these interpolated literary items, the novel also contains a long section called "The Back of the Book," which contains a variety of informational items about the Kesh culture. There are short articles about food, clothing, music, medicine, games, animals, even recipes. Also included are theoretical essays about language, literature, and narrative mode. All of these informational items are presented in the first person by the "archeologist of the future," the one who has supposedly discovered the evidence of the Kesh people who "might be going to have lived a long, long time ago."

Finally, the author has also provided audio and visual evidence of the Kesh. The novel is illustrated by Margaret Chodos, whose many line drawings represent flora and fauna, animals and artifacts, buildings and scenes. Furthermore, the novel is packaged with a cassette of Kesh music, by composer Todd Barton, including a variety of love songs and other lyrics. When one reads the poem about the dance of the heron, one can also see the line drawing and listen to the actual music of the dance. The novel concludes with a fourteen page glossary of Kesh words.

Literary Precedents

Le Guin's presentation of a total culture inevitably invites comparison with what J. R. R. Tolkien called his "secondary world" of Middle Earth. Whereas the Kesh will have lived far in the future, Middle Earth existed in the distant past. The prelapsarian innocence of the hobbits contrasts with the post-catastrophic isolation of the Kesh. In terms of narrative, the essential difference between the two is that Tolkien's miscellaneous information about the customs and history of Middle Earth exists largely outside of his novels whereas Le Guin's is included as an integral part of the novel. Tolkien added appendices and gathered background materials in other fictional collections, for it was not his purpose to seek creative collaboration with the reader. Their similarity is in the scope of the complete worlds they created, but not in the narrative form in which they are presented.

Relation to Previous Works

Although *Always Coming Home* is innovative, there are connections between it and Le Guin's earlier work. She had begun to interpolate mythic and historical material into her narratives in both *The Left Hand of Darkness* and the *Earthsea* trilogy. She has also interwoven material from her knowledge of North American Indians in earlier works. Her idealized cultures, including the dream world in *The Word For World Is Forest* as well as the *Earthsea* trilogy, are pastoral, non-technological societies. The Indian way of life is also depicted in the post-catastrophic image of the western United States in *City of Illusions*.

Le Guin has created imaginary worlds in many of her fantasy and science fiction works, but in *Always Coming Home* the reader is asked to participate in the act of creation by assembling the scattered materials. Furthermore, in this work Le Guin is attempting to forge links between fiction and other art forms, including art, music, and dance. Not only is the novel itself illustrated and accompanied by a cassette of music, but dance pieces inspired by the Kesh culture have been choreographed and performed by the Portland Dance Company. A highly innovative novel, *Always Coming Home* posits a revolutionary challenge not only to future novel writers but also to future novel readers, who are asked to become active collaborators in the act of creation.

TEHANU: THE LAST BOOK OF EARTHSEA
Tehanu: The Last Book of Earthsea, 1990, novel.

Social Concerns/Themes

For a novel announced as a sequel to a fantasy trilogy, *Tehanu* is surprisingly concentrated on contemporary social issues. The major themes of this "last book of Earthsea" are gender roles, child abuse, social justice, and aging. All of these concerns are depicted in the actual events of the novel and also discussed as explicit subjects by the characters.

The issue of gender roles is central. The protagonist, Tenar, youthful heroine of the second Earthsea volume, has recently been widowed. Her husband was a farmer, and she has an adult son and daughter. What must have been her late husband's stereotypical sense of women's duties is reflected in their son, Spark, a sailor who visits home and scornfully refuses to help in the kitchen with what he considers "women's work."

Tenar exemplifies conflicting views. After leaving her enforced role as priestess in the earlier work, she studied with the mage Ogion. As his student, she learned some of the language dragons speak, but never became a wizard. Instead she left her studies to marry a farmer. Now middle-aged, she raises the question whether women can ever become wizards and has a long but inconclusive conversation with Ged, hero of the trilogy, about this. Ged feels that a woman can never become a mage because magery is a distinctive male power. As he explains it, "If women had power, what would men be but women who can't bear children? And what would women be but men who can?" Tenar challenges his view, but is not able to define the distinctive nature of female power.

The subject of child abuse is treated in the story of Therru, whom Tenar and her friends rescue from her father who beat her and threw her into a fire. The child is severely scarred on one side of her face, blinded in one eye, and bears an even deeper psychological scar. For a long time she is passive, silent, and docile in her response to people, but eventually Tenar's love and care restore her.

The issue of social justice figures into the treatment of Therru's brutal father and his associates. Ged almost kills him when he attempts to break into Tenar's farmhouse in order to "punish" both Therru and Tenar. As he lies dying, Tenar and Ged decide to save his life even though they know him to be a murderer as well as a child abuser; they want to see him brought to justice. After he is tried and sentenced to death, they believe justice has been achieved.

Tehanu also deals with the theme of aging. Both Ged and Tenar, whom the reader first met as vigorous young people, are now experiencing the problems of age. Ged has not only lost all of his powers of magery but also is keenly aware of the loss of his physical strength. Tenar, an aging widow, finds herself having to deal with the problems of taking care of the house and the farm by herself. Tenar's friend, Moss, an aging local witch, also has problems of disability caused by age.

Characters

The protagonist of *Tehanu*, Tenar, is not at all the same young innocent whom readers met in the *Earthsea* trilogy. Now a widow, she lives alone on her farm, which she tends with the help of an elderly couple. Her maternal care for the injured child Therru shows her strength as well as her gentleness. She is courageous, as dramatically illustrated in the episode where a gang of vicious men try to break into her house, and she has only a butcher knife to defend herself. For the most part, however, hers is the quiet heroism of a woman leading a mundane but intense domestic life.

Her children are totally different from each other. Her son, Spark, is a "macho" personality, who regards his mother primarily as cook and housekeeper but who is happy to inherit the farm. Her daughter, Apple, is much kinder to her mother. The local witches, Ivy and Moss, are aged but expert in their knowledge of herbal healing.

Three male characters from the trilogy reappear in *Tehanu*. Ogion, the venerable mage, dies very early in the book. Ged, the former archmage, is a completely changed character. Having lost his powers of magery, he is reduced to humble circumstances, working as a goatherd, and his timid, defeatist language sounds humiliating for a man whose heroic deeds were sung throughout Earthsea. Lebannen, the young man who was about to become king at the end of the trilogy, is now king. In contrast to Ged, he is an idealized figure: handsome, wise, with a firm but gentle air of authority.

The child, Therru, develops during the course of the novel. Her early trauma leaves her unnaturally reticent, but her quiet life on the farm and the tutelage of Tenar and Moss help her to recover. The reader learns late in the novel that she can speak the language of dragons and that she clearly has magical powers. There is even a hint that she may one day become the next archmage, in spite of Ged's conviction that magery is limited to men.

A dragon is a significant character in all the Earthsea novels. Here it is Kalessin, who appeared near the end of *The Farthest Shore* to bring Ged and Lebannen back from the land of the dead. His purpose here is also rescue, and he comes in response to Therru's call for help. He offers to take the gifted child with him, but she refuses, preferring to stay with Ged and Tenar. His reaction to her decision is tantalizingly ambivalent: "an immense furnace-blast of laughter or contempt of delight or anger—Hah!"

Techniques

Le Guin's most important technique in *Tehanu* is an artful blending of realism and fantasy. In spite of its Earthsea setting, the narrative is essentially realistic. The major themes—gender roles, child abuse, social justice, and aging—are those one would expect in realistic fiction. The descriptions of setting are also realistic. Much of the action takes place on Tenar's farm where we learn about the goats, the fences, the cooking pots, the mending, and all of the homely details of rural life. The events are for the most part real, not fantastic. The brutal attack on the child, the frightening episode where Tenar finds that the invading gang can enter the house through a door with a broken lock, the scenes involving cooking, mending, and farm work are all quite realistic. The elements of fantasy are limited to the appearance of the dragon Kalessin and to references to witches and mages. The dragon scenes are effective, carrying the resonance of the trilogy.

The use of symbols is an important part of Le Guin's fictional technique. The most important is the scarred face of the child Therru, which is strongly reminiscent of Ged's scar, acquired in his encounter with the Shadow in *A Wizard of Earthsea*. Therru's scar is worse, in that it covers fully half of her face, discoloring as well as disfiguring it. But the scar is still the visible symbol of the Shadow, here of the whole Earthsea society, not just of an individual. It is a sign of something wrong in Earthsea, and also a sign that the guilty must be punished for such a brutal deed.

Le Guin's consistently understated style is also an effective technique, and her handling of dialogue is naturalistic. Much of the narrative is told in short paragraphs, and descriptions are brief and concrete. The style relies on the single, striking, sensuous detail. The overall point of view is third person, but some passages also communicate an individual character's private thoughts.

Relation to Previous Works

The full title, *Tehanu: The Last Book of Earthsea,* indicates that this Earthsea book will not have a sequel. For readers who enjoy the mythic fantasy of the original Earthsea trilogy, this novel may not seem like a sequel, even though the characters of Ged, Tenar, Lebannen, and Kalessin are present. Unlike the psychological emphasis of the Earthsea trilogy, the focus in *Tehanu* is decidedly social. Furthermore, the ideal of Taoist balance which seemed to be achieved after Ged's heroic adventures here seems to have been lost. A follower of the sorcerer Cob who destroyed the balance between life and death in *The Farthest Shore* is a new threat. Unlike the positive ending of the trilogy, with Lebannen about to assume the role of king and restore peace and order, the ending here is at the same time vague and negative. Tenar and Ged and the child who speaks the tongue of dragons decide to live in Ogion's house. They know that the male-dominated society of Earthsea is a failure, but they turn their attention to the garden and the goats. The conclusion of the sequel thus repudiates the mythic vision of the trilogy. On the other hand, the domestic vision which replaces it has a sad beauty of its own.

Other Sources

Collins, Robert A. "A Jarring Postscript." *Science Fiction Research Association Newsletter* 174 (January/February 1990): 45-47. The reviewer finds the emphasis on social criticism at odds with the mythic world of the trilogy. He admires the writing and the structure of the novel but sees it as an anticlimactic sequel.

Cummings, Elizabeth. *Understanding Ursula K. Le Guin.* Columbia: University of South Carolina Press, 1990. This book is divided into five chapters. The first provides biographical information; the other four analyze Le Guin's major worlds, Earthsea, Orsinia, Hainish, and the futuristic American West Coast. Cummings' clear analyses combined with footnotes and a complete bibliography make this an exceptionally useful work.

Delaney, Samuel R. "The Kesh in Song and Story." *New York Times Book Review* (September 29, 1985): 31. Delaney has high praise for what he considers Le Guin's most satisfying novel. He cites the Kesh cultural concept of the hinge, a connecting principle that both holds things together and permits them to move separately, as the key to their attractiveness as a people. He finds the pseudoanthropological materials an enhancement of the fictional narrative.

Gray, Paul. "History of an Imagined World." *Time* (October 19, 1985): 98. The reviewer suggests that Le Guin's book is a blueprint for an allegedly better world, with the Kesh representing her idealized vision and the Condor her attack on contemporary power politics.

Jahner, Elaine. Review of *Always Coming Home*. *Parabola* 11 (February, 1986): 100-104. The reviewer sees the book as a presentation which goes beyond the boundaries of the novel as a form.

McKinley, Robin. "The Woman Wizard's Triumph." *New York Times Book Review* (May 20, 1990): 38. This reviewer stresses the feminist focus in this work, seeing it as a sad but moving novel about feminine magic disguised as domesticity, as opposed to the more traditional magic of male wizards.

Charlotte Spivack
University of Massachusetts at Amherst

ELMORE LEONARD
1925

Update

Since early in the 1980s, Elmore Leonard has been one of the major figures in American crime fiction. His books, all popular and critical successes, have been regularly reviewed by major newspapers; he has made promotional appearances on the national broadcast media; he has been the subject of magazine articles; and film versions of *Stick* and *Fifty-Two Pickup* were released in 1985 and 1986. In 1989 the first book-length study of him—David Geherin's *Elmore Leonard*—was published, and in 1986 a personal account of his long bout with alcoholism (he quit drinking in 1977) appeared in Dennis Wholey's *The Courage to Change*.

Another effect of the belated recognition of his work is that he has become a leading moneymaker among his contemporaries in the genre. After *La Brava* won the Mystery Writers of America Edgar Allan Poe Award in 1984, Leonard received $360,000 for its paperback rights. The rights to his next novel, *Glitz* (1985), brought $500,000 after it made national best seller lists, and he was paid $1 million in a deal with Warner Books that included the paperback rights to *Bandits* (1987). As the decade ended, Arbor House offered $3 million for *Freaky Deaky* (1988) and his next novel, *Killshot* (1989).

He published two best sellers in 1987, *Bandits* and *Touch*, the latter written in 1977. An unusual novel (as the author himself puts it), *Touch* is about "mystical things happening to ordinary people," and its central character is a man who apparently is afflicted with stigmata. Bantam, an occasional Leonard publisher, bought the manuscript in 1977 for $60,000 in a deal that included *Gold Coast*, after a dozen other firms had turned it down. Even after typesetting the book, Bantam delayed its publication for eight years, uncertain about critical and public response to the atypical work and unwilling to take a risk. When *Glitz* soared to the top of the lists in 1985, confirming Leonard's position as a leading crime fiction writer, Bantam decided to publish the 1977 manuscript (originally entitled *The Juvenal Touch*, after its main character). Leonard, however, discovered that the rights to the book had reverted to him, and his agent, H. N. Swanson, then sold it for $300,000 to Arbor House, which published it as *Touch*. Since then, film rights also have been sold, making it one of over twenty Leonard novels bought by filmmakers. He began the new decade with *Get Shorty* (1990).

Popular and critical success has not inhibited Leonard's adventurous, even experimental, creative tendencies. His locales and characters differ considerably from book to book, and he still eschews continuing characters, although Ernest

Stickley, Jr. ("Stick") and Jack Ryan are notable exceptions, each appearing in two novels. By avoiding adherence to formula writing, Leonard differs significantly from most of his contemporaries in crime fiction, and indeed may have outgrown the genre writer label. Some hallmarks of his earliest novels do remain, however, including the realistic, usually urban settings; his keen ear for dialogue; a rapid succession of tense, action packed scenes; and a memorable gallery of singular characters. Increasingly, a strong social conscience has come to pervade the novels, with Leonard taking his cues from recent events and problems.

Perhaps the most important reasons for Leonard's continuing success after thirty-three years and twenty-eight novels are the naturalness of his style and his focus upon the essentials of storytelling. According to mystery author Donald Westlake, "He's so good, you don't notice what he's up to." There is an authenticity, an honesty, to the characters, the milieus, and the situations.

Analysis of Selected Titles

FREAKY DEAKY

Freaky Deaky, 1988, novel.

Social Concerns

Social activists of the 1960s who are aiming to settle old scores in the 1980s are the focus of both the narrative and the social aspects of *Freaky Deaky*. Now in their late thirties, the former revolutionaries are no less angry than they were two decades ago. Skip Gibbs and Robin Abbott remain unreconstructed outsiders. However much their disruptions helped to advance social change, they still live in the past, haunted by old hurts and bent on revenge. At the other end of the social spectrum are the rich boys, Mark and Woodrow Ricks. Encouraged by a superficially liberal mother, they flirted with the fashionable left-wing politics of the 1960s, but then evidently betrayed their radical friends. In the 1980s, Mark and Woody are also maladjusted, although cushioned by vast wealth. Amidst this quartet of aging former rebels, Leonard has placed Donnell Lewis, a former Black Panther who emerged from the radical movement as an unscrupulous golddigger and the amoral lacky of oafish Woodrow Ricks. Ironically, the moral paragon of the cast of characters is a bomb-squad detective, Chris Mankowski. Also a college student in the 1960s, Mankowski protested in Washington and participated in Woodstock; he then shipped off to Vietnam, where he was wounded. Although

Leonard portrays him sympathetically, Mankowski—like his adversaries—is a psychological and social misfit who flirts with criminality.

In *Freaky Deaky*, Leonard explores the seamy underside of the legacy of the 1960s and dramatizes a series of human problems, even tragedies, that had their origin in that hectic and heady period.

Themes

The search for identity and one's proper place in society is the primary thematic focus of *Freaky Deaky,* and is developed in different ways through the varied group of characters. Skip Gibbs, "a thirty-eight-year-old-kid," is a pony-tailed, bearded demolition expert whose twenty-year odyssey (with time out for a prison term) has taken him from coast to coast and to Europe. But at the end of the novel he is still searching, and his final thought is that he is "too old for this." Robin Abbott, his compatriot and former lover, also remains torn at age thirty-seven between the stable and affluent world of her parents and the revolutionary society of her college days. Symbolic of her continuing identity crisis is the escapist romantic fiction she writes under a pseudonym. Mark Ricks cannot fully establish his own identity because he is financially dependent on his brother and must do his bidding, despite his own desires. His brother, Woodrow, their mother's heir, is an obese lout, usually in an alcoholic fog and scarcely knowing who he is. Donnell Lewis, a black man out of place in an alien milieu, is technically Woodrow's servant but actually runs his life. He attempts to gain total control over Woodrow, although he lacks a clear sense of what or even who he wants to be. Chris Mankowski is drifting and rootless in another way. His relationships with women and his father are in flux, as is his career. Symbolic of his lack of stability is the fact that he does not have a home of his own, which leads the Detroit police department to suspend him. A minor character, though important to the identity crisis theme, is Ginger Jones, an aspiring actress whose real name is Greta Wyatt; her indecisiveness about which name to use reflects a debilitating ambivalence about who or what she is.

Characters

The novel begins and ends with Mankowski. More than just a police detective attempting to solve a series of crimes, he is the moral center of *Freaky Deaky*. A pleasant guy, committed to his career but struggling to keep a job on the force, Mankowski is portrayed in a thoroughly believable manner. In 1985, Leonard said in an interview: "My cops, I feel, are real cops . . . . I try to make them as real as possible. My cops cut corners a little bit, just as the real ones do." This is not to say, however, that Mankowski is in any way tainted by corruption. He is an ordinary person in a scrape, but by the end of the novel, the reader is certain that Mankowski will prevail. He is the hero, and in Leonard's books the protagonists always succeed. Career success, however, may not necessarily extend to Mankowski's personal life. He has difficulty establishing enduring relationships with women, which is in ironic contrast to his father's success in this regard; but Greta, equally at loose ends, may turn out to be the one that Chris has been seeking. Chris, then, is a lost soul groping his way through the city's "mean streets."

Also groping are the criminals Skip Gibbs and Robin Abbott. Having served time for blowing up an army recruiting office in Detroit in 1971, they have since been involved in murder, extortion, drug dealing, and theft. This pair of disreputable thrill seekers may be amoral, but they are not entirely despicable. Like many villain heroes, they are intriguing, compelling, and complex; and while Leonard provides little room for sympathizing with their actions, readers may admire the social conscience that initially motivated their unremitting struggle against social authority. But there is reason to question their motives, for Skip says to Robin: "You gonna tell me we were trying to change the world? We were kicking ass and having fun." And political philosophy does not motivate Robin's plot against the Ricks brothers. She aims to settle an old score and maybe make some big money at the same time. She and Donnell Lewis, at one time sexual as well as political partners, have a common goal, though his is as much racially as financially motivated. Donnell differs from the other characters because of his sense of humor, and since Leonard presents the life and times of Woody Ricks from Donnell's perspective, his wryness imbues the situation with a comic absurdity.

With many of the characters in *Freaky Deaky*, as in most of its predecessors, Leonard has blurred the distinction between the good and the bad. The result is that the characters are less stereotypical and more realistic than is usually the case in crime fiction.

KILLSHOT

Killshot, 1989, novel.

Social Concerns

In *Killshot*, his twenty-seventh novel, Leonard dramatizes the traumatic effect that ineffective law enforcement has on innocent people. Though much of the novel probes the depths of the criminal psyche in a manner that recalls Truman Capote's *In Cold Blood* (1965), Leonard is as interested in the husband and wife victimized by Armand Degas and Richie Nix. City police, sheriffs' deputies, and FBI men invariably are indifferent and insensitive; frequently they also are inefficient and bumbling. The only completely sympathetic characters in the novel are Carmen and Wayne Colson, the couple whose lives are changed when they happen to be in the wrong place at the wrong time. That they manage to survive and prevail despite the authorities' incompetence is testimony to their own persistence, courage, and ingenuity.

Leonard aims critical barbs not only at police, but also at the criminal justice system. Both of the novel's psychopathic villains have been in and out of prisons, and no matter how serious and how frequent their crimes, they make it back into society. Degas and Nix are not run-of-the-mill thugs, but cold-blooded murderers who cannot even remember how often they have killed. Armand, familiarly called Blackbird, is half Ojibway and half French-Canadian and does not recall his father; Richie, as he describes himself, has "lived with women in foster homes and women since then." Implicit in the novel is Leonard's concern that in very diverse places (the book is set in locales in the United States and Canada), the system fails so utterly that such asocial men emerge. His disappointment in the system is heightened by the portrayal of Armand as a man with a keen sense of his Ojibway roots and devotion to the grandmother who personifies them. Richie may be a drifter, but Armand is not, which makes the tragedy of his life even more troublesome.

Themes

Interwoven with tense confrontations and murder episodes are realistically developed scenes involving ironworkers (of which Wayne Colson is one) and their families. In *Killshot* Leonard transcends mere crime fiction with these domestic and on-the-job interludes. What emerges is the belief that these men and their families have a stability deriving from their membership in a group, and that vital to the social units of work and home are trust and interdependence. By contrast, Armand and Richie are loners who have never had any lasting relationships, personal or otherwise. Though they become partners early in the book, live together for a while, and even share the same woman, theirs is a relationship of convenience; they do not trust, like, or respect one another. The partnership ends as it began, with one man pointing a gun at the other.

To an extent, then, the novel celebrates the family and the traditional work ethic, as well as man as a social being. An aging Mafia don is the first person Armand murders in *Killshot*, slain at the behest of his son-in-law. Right after the killing, Armand crosses the border into Canada to visit—for the first time in nine years—his Indian grandmother, but she had died the previous winter. In the next episode, Leonard introduces the Colsons, in love with each other and with their son, who is in the navy. This juxtaposition of contrasting portraits—the Mafia's perversion of family, Armand's loss of the last link with his roots, and the Colsons' embodiment of an ideal family—sets up a fundamental contrast that provides the thematic foundation for the novel.

Characters

The characters in *Killshot* are credible largely because there is a minimum of authorial intrusion, and Leonard regularly shifts his narrative point of view to accommodate each of his major figures. A result of this method is that *Killshot* lacks some of the suspense that typifies the genre, but nevertheless there is a succession of gripping episodes; the lengthy introspective passages provide insight into characters' thoughts and plans and heighten the tension. Being informed of Armand and Richie's intentions does not guarantee foreknowledge of how they will act.

Armand (Blackbird) is the most compelling figure in *Killshot*, and Leonard avoids making him a stereotypical villain by focusing upon his Ojibway background and his spiritual link to his grandmother, an Indian mystic. A gun-for-hire and a determined loner, he establishes temporary ties with others only to serve his immediate purposes. But he is complex. Near the end of the novel, disgusted with Richie, Armand dismisses him as "something stuck to the bottom of your shoe you couldn't get rid of, like . . . chewing gum." At the same time Armand thinks about taking Donna (with whom he and Richie are living) to Memphis to see Elvis Presley's Graceland: "Why not? She was a stupid woman, but that was okay, he was tired of being alone in hotel rooms, bars, motels—take her on a trip, play some Yahtzee . . . . One moment he felt relieved, a weight lifted off him . . . the next moment he didn't feel so good." Having lived a joyless life, Armand does not even gain satisfaction from his professional successes, perhaps because he is too introspective, too bright, and too disciplined. A master of his craft, he is impatient with partners—including his brother—who act impetuously and risk their own well-being and that of others.

Richie Nix is a different type of criminal from Armand. He wants to rob a bank in every state and gain mention in *The Guinness Book of World Records;* he has only thirteen states to go. Along the way, however, he has spent time in prison and boasts that "he had an NCIC sheet that printed out of that national crime computer as tall as he was: six feet in his curl-toed cowboy boots with three inner soles inside." Neither a true six-footer nor the big time operator he thinks he is, this man-child conceives of a scam that he believes is "higher class" than bank robbery and "took more thought." However, the extortion scheme he attempts with his new acquaintance, Armand, is a disaster, partly because Richie is no more than a small-time bank robber with a murderous bent. Instead of Armand rescuing him and salvaging the scheme, Richie draws both of them into a fatal abyss. Immature and not very bright, he is a born loser who craves the love and attention that he was denied even as a child.

Leonard's narrative technique, including interior monologues, enables the reader to see things from Armand and Richie's perspectives and to gain an understanding of them. It is difficult to sympathize with them, however, because they always act wholly antithetically to accepted social norms.

By contrast, Carmen and Wayne Colson are Leonard's middle American ideals: happily married for twenty years, they have a son who was a varsity athlete in high school and then joined the navy. Wayne is a union member who wears a jacket with the legend "IRONWORKERS BUILD AMERICA" and goes deer hunting. Carmen dabbles at handwriting analysis and works for a realtor, nursing the dream that Wayne will someday work with her. Accidentally caught in a trap intended for someone else, the Colsons are strong, resilient, and resourceful. They even endure a period in the Witness Security Protection program that is notable mainly for the boorish behavior of Ferris Britton, a macho deputy on the make.

For much of the book, whether set in their hometown, Algonac, Michigan, or Cape Girardeaux, Missouri, where the federal government sets them up, Carmen lives in a state of siege. With Wayne usually at work or on the road, she bears most of the burden of confronting their adversaries. When the climactic moment finally arrives, she hesitates: "It was loaded . . . Now, go do it. And thought, I can't. And told herself, Don't think. But at the bedroom door, her hand on the old-fashioned key sticking out of the lock, she started thinking again, she couldn't help it." But later: "That fast, Christ, she had it aimed at him, holding it in both hands with her eyes wide open—not scared-to-death open, just open, staring at him . . . . And she shot him. Fired his own gun at him . . . and she shot him again, socked him in the chest with it so hard he went back against the chair and sat down. She was still pointing the gun at him." By the time Wayne returns from Missouri, Carmen has rid their house of all traces of the siege, and the novel ends with Wayne the same bad listener he always has been, but encouraging Carmen to try deer hunting with him this year: "Hey, it's something we could do together." Evil overcome, normality returns; and, after all, nothing much has changed in the lives of these ordinary people.

Literary Precedents

Leonard's first venture into crime was his reading of such writers as Frederic Brown and Erle Stanley Gardner, from whom he learned plotting and the usefulness of humor to leaven tension. His close reading of Ernest Hemingway (particularly *For Whom the Bell Tolls*) focused Leonard's attention on dialogue and narrative point of view, but he claims to differ significantly from Hemingway: "I see more absurdity. I like people more. I'm more tolerant." In terms of attitude, he is similar to Mark Harris and Kurt Vonnegut, Jr., contemporaries whom he favors. Another acknowledged influence is the novel *The Friends of Eddie Coyle* (1972) by George V. Higgins, which utilizes dialogue and monologues as means of increasing realism. Finally, Leonard's use of urban settings and focus on ordinary people (including policemen) in trouble are in the tradition of Raymond Chandler and Dashiell Hammett.

Relation to Previous Works

In most of his crime fiction over the years, Leonard has stayed close to home; from *Fifty-Two Pickup* in 1974 to *Split Images* in 1981, he produced seven novels in which the Detroit area was his primary milieu. (The others are: *Swag, Unknown Man No. 89, The Switch, Touch,* and *City Primeval.*) After using the South and Atlantic City for several books in the early 1980s, he returned to his old haunts in 1988 with *Freaky Deaky*. In it, Raymond Cruz, hero of *City Primeval*, briefly reappears, as do some other Detroit policemen.

Leonard also has a habit of reworking old characters. Donnell Lewis, Woody's houseman in *Freaky Deaky*, recalls Cornell Lewis, also a black servant, in *Stick*. In addition to similarities of name, race, and occupation, both are handsome and witty fellows who function as social commentators. Armand Degas of *Killshot* also has forebears, primarily Bobby Leary of *Unknown Man No. 89* and Roland Crowe of *Gold Coast*. The latter, like Degas, is an enforcer for the mob, a former inmate, and a frequent murderer. Crowe's last name and Degas' nickname, Blackbird, also suggest a kinship.

More significantly, the later novels share with their predecessors Leonard's grim realism and keen ear for spoken language that are hallmarks of his fiction. He also continues to avoid a commonplace of the genre: a recurring hero who copes with crime in a predictable manner.

Additional Sources

Geherin, David. *Elmore Leonard*. New York: Continuum, 1989.

Lupica, Mike. "St. Elmore's Fire." *Esquire* (April 1987): 169-172.

Most, Glenn. "Elmore Leonard: Splitting Images." *Western Humanities Review*, 41, 1 (Spring 1987): 78-86.

Skinner, Robert E. "To Write Realistically: An Interview with Elmore Leonard." *Xavier Review* 7, 2 (1987): 37-46.

Sutter, Greg. "Getting It Right: Researching Elmore Leonard's Novels, Part 1." *The Armchair Detective* 19, 1 (Winter 1986): 4-19.

―――――. "Advance Man: Researching Elmore Leonard's Novels, Part 2." *The Armchair Detective* 19, 2 (Spring 1986): 160-172.

Gerald H. Strauss
Bloomsburg University

ROBERT LUDLUM
1927

Update

Ludlum's 1980 novel *The Bourne Identity* was made into a four-hour, two-part television movie, which aired in May 1988. Directed by Roger Young, the film starred Richard Chamberlain as Jason Bourne and Jaclyn Smith as his love interest, Marie St. Jacques. The first two hours of the movie are suspenseful, as the action follows amnesiac Jason Bourne, who desperately seeks to learn his identity while a variety of people try to kill him. The film bogs down somewhat at the beginning of the second part, but the climax is swiftly paced and exciting. All told, the movie is above-average fare for television.

Ludlum has recently published two new novels: *The Icarus Agenda* (1988) and *The Bourne Ultimatum* (1990). His novels continue to be best sellers, and total sales of his books now approach one hundred million copies.

Analysis of Selected Titles

THE ICARUS AGENDA

The Icarus Agenda, 1988, novel.

Social Concerns

Ludlum carefully researches the backgrounds of his novels, a practice evident in *The Icarus Agenda* by the use of Arabic words and phrases and the geographical details of the coast of Oman. Such background detail gives his adventure story a tone of authenticity. Ludlum further enhances the credibility by taking one of the novel's important themes—terrorism—from the headlines of the 1980s.

The terrorists are mostly Palestinians who consider themselves heroic warriors fighting the enemies of their people. For Ludlum, however, they abuse and murder civilians; he portrays them as thoroughly vile, hypocritical, and stupid. As the novel begins, the terrorists have seized the American embassy in Oman; they have periodically dumped corpses from the embassy windows while the crowds outside cheer. Although the terrorists are mostly religious fanatics, they are funded by a businessman whose interest is in gaining a monopoly on the construction business in the Arab world. Although the businessman calls himself "the Mahdi," which is the title of a religious figure, he has little interest in religious faith. Thus, for all their proclamations about their willingness to die for God and claims that their fight is against Israeli oppression, the terrorists actually serve the ends of a greedy businessman. They not only kill children as well as adults, but they also justify their murder of innocent people as revenge for their own suffering. Ludlum carefully develops the theme of terrorism; the terrorists have their say in the novel, but their claims pale compared with the horrors they perpetrate on others. Their actions do not bring about a Palestinian nation or the promotion of their religion, but rather an increase in enemies of their cause and their own futile deaths.

Even though the terrorists are frightening and have a perversely plausible logic for their deeds, they do not dominate Ludlum's depiction of the Arab world. Instead, Ludlum takes care to show that they are a tiny minority. He humanizes the Arabs, showing both their strengths and weaknesses. They are generally intelligent people, capable of heroic sacrifice to protect their nations and culture. They also have their poor and venal, as illustrated by the "red-light" section of the city of Masqat. Such characters as the Sultan of Oman complain of how the Western world seems to view the Arab world as peopled by bloodthirsty savages. Ludlum clarifies some of the divisions in Arab society, giving a balanced view of the conflict between good and evil in a part of the world that few Americans understand.

Themes

The principal theme of the novel is the danger posed to democracy by the ambitions of the few to rule the many. Ludlum illustrates this theme by showing the people who are the American vice president's closest advisors. Like the Mahdi, they are motivated by greed, and just as the Mahdi hopes to gain control of the construction business in the Middle East, the vice president's advisors try to use him to gain control of America's weapons business. One of the vice president's advisors actually employs the same terrorists who held the American embassy in Oman; he wants them to murder Evan Kendrick, the novel's main character and a potential rival for the vice presidency in the upcoming presidential election. Their effort to make themselves the hidden rulers of America causes the deaths of many innocent people. Plainly, if these advisors/businessmen were to actually gain control of the presidency then the American people as a whole would suffer.

The theme of the dangers posed by the efforts of the few to rule the many is more subtly embodied in the organization that calls itself the Inver Brass, which was formed by wealthy men during the Great Depression. They used their wealth to help prevent riots and other violence and to encourage the passage of legislation in Congress that would ease the national suffering. They also developed ways of adding new members to Inver Brass as old ones passed away. By the time of the events in *The Icarus Agenda*, they have a sophisticated intelligence network run by people strongly committed to the well-being of America. Yet, in spite of their good intentions, the members of Inver Brass are little better than the despicable Mahdi and the vile advisors of the vice president. Coldly calculating, members of the Inver Brass find the deaths of a few innocent people acceptable as long as their aims are served. They use their immense wealth and power to propel Evan Kendrick into the vice presidency, even though he wants nothing to do with the office. The results of their attempt to secretly manage the country are disastrous for nearly everybody, including one of their members, Dr. Winters, who commits suicide when the CIA finds out what he has been up to. Dozens of CIA agents, terrorists, and innocents are doomed by the conniving of Inver Brass. In their efforts to save America, they forget about the importance of America's individual citizens, and their work stirs up some very nasty people, leaving corpses scattered across America and the Arab world.

Characters

The main character of the novel is Evan Kendrick, a stereotypical American hero. George Washington declared that all he really wanted to do was farm his land; he was a general and politician out of necessity. Kendrick similarly declares that all he desires is to run a construction business; his involvement in politics is necessary to clean up the political life of his congressional district. He is handsome, tall, bold, courageous, intelligent, and rigidly ethical. These traits make him the ideal political candidate for the secret society, Inver Brass, which seeks to keep the United States on a sound moral course. Kendrick is a reluctant politician, but Inver Brass intends to force him to become vice president by maneuvering him into a public position from which he cannot escape. The American public will see him as such a great hero that it will demand that he accept the vice presidency. Eventually, President Jennings himself makes such a demand.

The love interest of *The Icarus Agenda* is Khalehla, an exotically beautiful woman of keen intelligence and selfless courage. One of the subplots involves her and Kendrick pretending not to love each other; they deny that a brief sexual interlude early in the novel had any special emotional meaning. Eventually, they drop this pretense and become lovers. In addition to having courage and love in common, she and Kendrick also have the ability to shoot and not miss, even in the dark, and they are passionately committed to the United States.

Among the supporting characters is Manny Weingrass, an elderly but tough Jew who is a father-figure for Kendrick. He has connections to the Mossad, Israel's intelligence agency, and is very wise in the ways of espionage. Part of Weingrass' function in the novel is to illustrate Kendrick's goodness; when Weingrass is sick, Kendrick takes him home and cares for him, paying three nurses to attend him. Another of his functions is to help build suspense. He is lovably irascible, and readers are likely to care about what happens to him. He seems forever in harm's way, and his survival is often in doubt. Ludlum is merciless with the supporting characters, letting the forces of evil kill them throughout the novel. Weingrass is granted only a short reprieve from this, and at the novel's end, he is slowly dying from a horrible disease that a corrupt physician has injected into him.

Of the many supporting characters, perhaps the most interesting is the computer expert Gerald Bryce. He is seldom at the center of the action in *The Icarus Agenda*, yet his unseen hand is everywhere. Early in the novel, Ludlum teases the reader with the inclusion of remarks that an unknown figure is entering into a computer log. This figure notes how his "appliances" are providing him with good information that allows him to manipulate Kendrick into risking life and limb to save the American hostages in Oman. Is this enigmatic figure Dr. Winters, the brilliant historian and master political manipulator? More likely it is Milos Varak, the Czech masterspy who is dedicated to the well-being of the United States and who serves as the chief intelligence agent of Inver Brass. It is he, after all, who first presents the name of Evan Kendrick to the board of directors of Inver Brass; he persuades them that Kendrick is the ideal candidate for the vice presidency. Throughout the novel, he maneuvers and schemes, uncovering the traitor among the directors and making Kendrick into a national hero. Yet, when he dies, the scheming continues; the mysterious schemer is neither Varak nor Winters. A minor computer expert in the State Department, regarded by his colleagues as incapable of the sort of treachery required for the manipulation of Kendrick's career, continues to write entries into the log. Bryce, the true mastermind of the events of the novel, has taken over Varak's job, and he is well pleased with the success of his work. This lends an ominous tone to the end of the novel.

Early in the novel, the leaders of Inver Brass agree that after becoming vice president, Kendrick is to become president eleven months later; this is all part of their Icarus project. The creator of the plan, Bryce, is still at work. President Jennings may have made himself a candidate for premature death by persuading the reluctant Kendrick to become his running mate.

Techniques

The Icarus Agenda has a fine, classic structure. It is written in three clear movements, with each one developing a different aspect of the Icarus scheme. The novel begins with the Mahdi movement. It is a complete novel by itself; even without the rest of the book it could stand alone with an exciting plot, interesting characters, and a satisfying climax. In the Mahdi movement, the archvillain is the evil businessman who calls himself the Mahdi. He was responsible for the murder of all of the employees of Kendrick and Weingrass' Middle Eastern construction firm. When Kendrick learns of the strange hostage taking in Oman, he realizes that the secret financial backer of the terrorists must be the Mahdi, who uses terrorist groups to drive competing businesses out of the Middle East. Ludlum drops hints that the Mahdi story has wider implications, usually by showing the computer log entries of an unnamed mastermind, but otherwise the Mahdi movement's plot develops toward its own conclusion, the death of the Mahdi. All of this movement is found in Book One of the novel.

Book Two represents the main movement of *The Icarus Agenda*. It turns out the Mahdi story was told in order for the second movement to make sense. This main movement is the working out of the Icarus agenda: using Kendrick's supposedly secret heroism to propel him into the presidency. The main actors in the Mahdi movement were Kendrick and the Mahdi; in this section they are Inver Brass and the advisors to the vice president. When the traitor from Inver Brass alerts the vice president's inner circle to the scheme to make Kendrick the new vice president, the two groups fight a secret war. In panic, one of the vice president's advisors hires the terrorists Kendrick had outwitted in Oman to kill him. Much of the action now becomes bloody thrust and counter-thrust as the two contending forces vie for control of not just the vice presidency but of the presidency itself. Inver Brass see themselves as visionaries who know that America should spend less on its military and more on easing its economic troubles, whereas their rivals want the big profits that their stealing from the military spending brings them. The Inver Brass traitor sees military spending as the best way to promote scientific research, because the military spends huge sums on research that may lead to new weapons. Neither side is an attractive group, although Inver Brass is more genteel than its rivals and is able to couch its killings and betrayals in high-sounding language. Thus, it falls to Kendrick to form the moral center of the plot. He acts altruistically, but almost inevitably his selfless acts themselves make him a pawn of the Icarus agenda. The climax of the second section leaves Kendrick right where Inver Brass wants him.

The third section is brief. Like a short story, it has only a few main characters and a single, clear plot line. Kendrick must come to terms with his knowledge that his status as a public hero was created by Inver Brass, but he finds himself needed as vice president. He is reluctant to assume that position not only because he views his public stature as a sham, but because he does not want to make politics a career. He ran for Congress to unseat a corrupt representative, and he intended to see to it that a new, clean politician replaced him after he had served a term. Instead, the president of the United States persuades him to take on new political responsibilities. Unlike the first two sections, which had clear and satisfying climaxes, the third section leaves many things unresolved. It does have its own climax, with Kendrick agreeing to do as President Jennings asks, but the novel neither reveals whether Inver Brass will indeed remove Jennings from office eleven months after the election nor whether the CIA will be successful in tracking down the rest of the Inver Brass leaders, after having uncovered Dr. Winters's treachery. And it does not say whether terrorists will try to slay the archenemy Kendrick, rather than see him become the vice president of one of their most feared enemies, the United States.

Literary Precedents

The Icarus Agenda is a novel of political intrigue that is commonly found on best seller lists. Its antecedents include such diverse novels as Fletcher Knebel and Charles W. Bailey's *Seven Days in May* and John le Carré's *Smiley's People,* which have in common the creation of realistic backgrounds and tough, direct prose, which enhances their matter-of-fact tone. They differ from such tales of international espionage as the James Bond books in that they avoid high flights of technological fantasy and prodigious sexual performances of their heroes. Still, they are fantasies to some degree; for instance, Kendrick is almost without character flaws, and his wild adventures are implausible at best, with his escape from a Mexican island requiring several unbelievable acts, from disarming a trained and murderous FBI agent to shooting down his enemies in darkness.

To some degree, Ludlum is his own literary precedent. His novels have been immensely popular since the early 1970s and have helped to create the audience that voraciously reads the novels of many of his colleagues, as well as his own recent efforts. One of the standards he has helped set is clear structure; like *The Icarus Agenda*, his other novels tend to have straightforward dramatic movements, allowing the reader to follow the action even when the intrigue becomes complex.

THE BOURNE ULTIMATUM

The Bourne Ultimatum, 1990, novel.

Social Concerns

During a conversation with Marie Webb, Alex Conklin says, "God bless, favorite lady." She responds, "*He* abandoned us, Alex. God doesn't exist." This idea is repeated throughout *The Bourne Ultimatum*. The main character, David Webb/Jason Bourne, declares himself an agnostic. The KGB agent Dimitri Krupkin notes that he is officially atheistic, even though he sometimes calls on God. Although other characters also call on God, as Alex does when talking to Marie, the novel repeatedly emphasizes that calling on God is futile. If He exists, one character suggests, then the horrors visited on innocent lives mean that He is a "sadist." In the worlds of espionage, terrorism, and organized crime, people operate in an absence of divine justice; the people are amoral or, like Webb/Bourne, they are lost souls searching for meaning in the unrelenting cruelty of their lives.

Themes

Ultimately, *The Bourne Ultimatum* is about a search for self-knowledge. Although he focuses on killing Carlos the Jackal, Webb/Bourne searches for his own identity as he races around half the world in pursuit of his obsession. He is certain that for his family to be safe, he must kill Carlos, who is determined to avenge himself by destroying everything Webb/Bourne holds dear. A megalomaniac, Carlos is angry not only because Webb/Bourne has outwitted him in the past, but because Jason Bourne's reputation as an assassin almost eclipses his own. Bourne was created by the CIA to rival Carlos—to build such a reputation that Carlos would expose himself to his enemies in a desperate effort to eliminate his greatest rival. This CIA plot failed, but it left Webb/Bourne with a permanent identity crisis. Is he the kindly, professorial David Webb, or is he the cold-blooded killer, Jason Bourne? When he pursues Carlos, Webb/Bourne actually pursues a part of himself: his Bourne personality and that of the Jackal are virtually identical. Webb/Bourne needs to kill Carlos in order to free himself from the bitter, cruel identity of Bourne the assassin.

Characters

The character David Webb/Jason Bourne is one of Ludlum's best creations. Webb/Bourne is a complex man, with great depth to his personality. At the beginning of *The Bourne Ultimatum*, he is college professor David Webb, married with two small children. He wants to stay as far away from the violent life of international intrigue as he can. The CIA helps him in this by hiding his identity from all but a few high-level agents and by pretending that the mythical figure of Jason Bourne had died in Hong Kong eight years before. In spite of the efforts to protect him, Webb's identity is leaked to Carlos the Jackal. Once he knows that the Jackal is out to murder his family, Webb/Bourne decides that he must kill Carlos, and the novel becomes an account of how the two men try to trap each other, with traps containing yet more traps and reversals.

In the first novel in the series, *The Bourne Identity*, Webb/Bourne received a terrible blow to his head, leaving him with a fragmented memory of who he once was. Throughout *The Bourne Ultimatum*, bits and pieces of his previous life come back to him. He knows that during the war in Vietnam he had joined a secret military organization called Medusa, which operated behind enemy lines. This vicious group of criminals and misfits wreaked terror on the Viet Cong, and the original Jason Bourne was one of its vilest members. He not only was a cutthroat, he also was a traitor who sold out his comrades. The original David Webb had joined Medusa in order to have his revenge on the North Vietnamese fighter pilot who had murdered Webb's Cambodian wife and their two children. This hope for revenge proved futile, but it later motivates Webb/Bourne to hunt down Carlos in order to save his new wife and children.

Known in Medusa only as Delta One, Webb kills the original Jason Bourne when he discovers Bourne selling out to the North Vietnamese. He is persuaded to assume Bourne's identity in order to pretend that he is the murderous rival of the international terrorist, Carlos the Jackal. In *The Bourne Ultimatum*, Webb/Bourne finds himself having to kill Bourne all over again. The injury to his head has left him a fragmentary personality, with its Webb and Bourne parts competing for supremacy. This means that throughout the novel, he is on the edge of insanity. At times he breaks down, becoming a crying madman who is overwhelmed by the conflicts within himself. These conflicts and their complex development in the violent world of the novel make *The Bourne Ultimatum* a fine work of literature. Through the competition between the gentle David Webb and the savage Jason Bourne, Ludlum peers into the human soul of Webb/Bourne, who must continuously choose between fragmented aspects of himself.

Carlos the Jackal is offstage for much of the novel, yet his presence is felt throughout. His real name is Ilich Ramirez Sanchez, and he is originally from Latin America. He was once a trainee at the Soviet Union's elite spy school, Novgorod. There, his Soviet teachers decided that he was insane and had to be killed, but a Russian colonel warned him and he escaped, taking with him two years of training in espionage and murder, as well as an abiding hatred for Novgorod, which he believed had betrayed him. Carlos set himself up as a freelance assassin, and he eventually became known as the world's most effective terrorist. He killed anyone if the price was right and if it served to destabilize the enemies of Communism, a cause to which he remained fiercely loyal. Jason Bourne's presence in the world of international terrorism angered him. Whenever Carlos killed someone, Bourne claimed credit. This was the CIA scheme: to kill no one themselves, but to claim for the mythical Bourne the crimes of Carlos. Supposedly Carlos would eventually seek out Webb/Bourne, who had been superbly trained to fight Carlos. In *The Bourne Identity*, this scheme almost worked.

In *The Bourne Ultimatum*, Carlos is sixty years old and sick; he is nagged by a cough. Over the years, he has become even more unstable than he was back in Novgorod. He is obsessed with killing Jason Bourne and everyone Bourne loves. A clever man with a gift for survival, he is a worthy adversary of the brilliant Bourne. The two men do a dance of death from the Caribbean to Paris to Moscow to Novgorod, with Carlos always just a step ahead of Bourne.

The Bourne Ultimatum is rich with supporting characters. Marie, David Webb's wife, is a stunningly beautiful professional economist; her tendency to look at every situation in economic terms irritates some of those around her, but her courage and keen intellect make her an attractive figure. Alex Conklin is an ex-CIA agent who has lost a foot. He is Webb/Bourne's closest friend; troubled by guilt over his role in turning Webb into Bourne, he fights to give Webb/Bourne what he needs to survive. Morris Panov is a lovable psychiatrist who strives to keep David Webb from completely becoming Jason Bourne.

Techniques

The Bourne Ultimatum is one of Ludlum's most skillfully plotted novels. The traps and counter-traps flow one into another seamlessly, without impeding the main plot line. Ludlum's principal narrative problem is keeping the conflicts within Webb/Bourne clear. Ludlum does this by switching from one name to another depending on what aspect of Webb/Bourne's personality is dominant: David Webb, Jason Bourne, the Chameleon, and Delta One. The Chameleon is a sub-personality of Bourne; when the need for disguises arises, Webb/Bourne shifts to the Chameleon, changing himself into a new person. Delta One is part Webb and part Bourne; when the international crime syndicate Medusa holds Webb/Bourne's attention, he shifts to Delta One to recall what he knew about the original Vietnam organization. These shifts from one name to another may sound confusing, but in the novel they serve to quickly and easily clue the reader in to what is going on in Webb/Bourne's mind.

Literary Precedents

Like *The Icarus Agenda*, this novel is in the genre of the espionage thriller. Its clearest precedent is John le Carré's *The Spy Who Came in from the Cold*. Webb/Bourne wants to come in out of the cold world of international spying; he yearns to live a peaceful life. As in le Carré's novel, *The Bourne Ultimatum* presents a world of moral ambiguity, in which right and wrong are easily confused.

Relation to Previous Works

The Bourne Identity tells of amnesiac Jason Bourne's quest for his own true identity. In this novel, Bourne is primarily a cold blooded killer whose skills suggest that he really is an international terrorist. He meets Marie St. Jacques, famous economist, who becomes his wife after he recovers some of his lost personality. Like its sequels, *The Bourne Identity* has almost nonstop action, and the mystery of Bourne's true identity adds to its suspense. *The Bourne Supremacy* (1986), the second novel in the series, takes place in the Far East. In an interview, Ludlum explains that he originally conceived the novel without Webb/Bourne in it. After establishing what the novel was to be about, he needed a strong central character who would make sense of events for his readers. Unable to create the needed character without taking up hundreds of pages of exposition explaining who the character was and why he was in the Far East, he realized that he already had a fully drawn character in Webb/Bourne, so he placed Webb/Bourne in the middle of the exciting events of the novel.

Additional Sources

Sherwin, Lanny. "The Ludlum Techniques." *Writer's Digest* 67 (July 1987): 18-24. Ludlum explains how he writes a novel.

Kirk H. Beetz
National University, Sacramento

ALISON LURIE
1926

Update

In 1988 Alison Lurie published her eighth novel, *The Truth about Lorin Jones*. Previous novels include *Love and Friendship* (1962), *The Nowhere City* (1965), *Imaginary Friends* (1967), *Real People* (1969), *The War between the Tates* (1974), *Only Children* (1979), and *Foreign Affairs* (1984). *The Truth about Lorin Jones* has proved less popular with the critics than *The War between the Tates* and *Foreign Affairs*, her two most highly acclaimed novels. Although Lurie's latest novel maintains the author's usual acerbic edge, the characterization of Lorin Jones is fragmented and the ending facile.

Analysis of Selected Titles

THE TRUTH ABOUT LORIN JONES

The Truth about Lorin Jones, 1988, novel.

Social Concerns/Themes

Lurie uses the plot of *The Truth about Lorin Jones* to explore the implications of the feminist movement that began in the 1960s and to criticize women who use the movement to denigrate men. Polly Alter, the major protagonist, is one of these misguided women. She begins researching the life of the dead painter Lorin Jones in order to prove an anti-male thesis: the men in Lorin's life, from her half brother to her husband to her lover, prevented her from realizing her full potential as an artist. What Polly discovers from her research is that Lorin was responsible for her own failing as an artist. She used mind-altering drugs and took unnecessary risks that led to an early death. Polly's recognition of Lorin's own culpability leads her, by the end of the novel, to a pro-male thesis: the men in Lorin's life, rather than oppressing her, were themselves oppressed by the artist's selfishness.

By embracing a new view of Lorin's career, Polly also reassesses her own lifestyle, specifically her relationship with a separatist feminist, Jeanne. Jeanne distrusts all males, including Stevie, Polly's ingenuous teenaged son, and Mac, Lorin's former and Polly's current lover. Jeanne nearly convinces Polly of the inherent evil of males, but Polly's love for these two men and her new opinion of the men in Lorin's life lead her to reject Jeanne's viewpoint.

Thus, by the end of the novel, Polly has fully altered (a pun on her last name "Alter") her assessment of separatist feminism and has embraced a supposedly better understanding of Lorin Jones and her own desires. Unfortunately, the quality of this new understanding is suspect. Not only does the reader wonder if Polly is deluding herself about finding happiness with Mac in Florida, but the reader also suspects that Polly's new understanding of Lorin is faulty. At the end of the novel, Polly exonerates all the men in the artist's life, even Lorin's husband who clearly frustrated the artist's creative impulses when he tried to impose his own artistic theories on her work. A more convincing and accurate conclusion would be for Polly to believe that Lorin's failure as an artist is attributable to her own destructive lifestyle as well as interference from some men in her life.

Characters

Lorin Jones has been dead for years when the novel opens, so the reader must learn about her from the people Polly Alter interviews. A consequence of this technique is that the reader has only fragmented glimpses into Lorin's life. The "truth" of Lorin Jones, thus, is never satisfactorily realized. For example, Polly discovers that Lorin briefly disappeared as a child. When she was found, her panties were missing although she did not appear molested. People who knew Lorin felt that this incident affected her personality, but it is not clear to what degree and in what way. The people that Polly interviews also agree that Lorin maintained a distance in her relationships with others, but they provide different explanations for that distance. Some refer to her single-minded obsession with her art; others refer to her shyness; still others refer to her arrogance. The reader learns interesting facts about Lorin—she once turned all the furnishings in her room backward or upside down; she maliciously gave her stepmother an abstract painting of her deceased mother; she kindly saved photography books for her niece—but the sum of these facts does not create an understanding of the motivation and values of Lorin Jones. The only characteristic of Lorin that is clearly portrayed is her obsession with art and her subsequent expectation that others in her life—particularly her lover Mac—share in that obsession.

Techniques/Literary Precedents

The Truth about Lorin Jones is a retelling of Henry James' nineteenth-century novel of social criticism, *The Bostonians*. In *The Bostonians*, Verena Tarrant, a lecturer, is caught between two forceful personalities: Olive Chancellor, a feminist who hates all males and is perhaps a lesbian, and Basil Ransom, a Southerner who wants Verena to live a conventional life as his wife. At the end of the novel, Verena chooses Ransom. In Lurie's novel, Polly Alter, a biographer, is also caught between two forceful personalities: Jeanne, a feminist lesbian who hates males, and Mac Cameron, the former lover of Lorin Jones. At the end of the novel, Polly, like Verena, chooses a relationship with a man when she decides to move to Florida to live with Mac.

Criticisms leveled at *The Bostonians* also apply to *The Truth about Lorin Jones*. Henry James meant *The Bostonians* to express misgivings about American society in general; feminism was to be merely an example. Since the ideology of feminism is the forefront of this novel, it is difficult for readers not to see the book as an indictment of women's rights. Similarly, Lurie intended to criticize the separatist leanings of some feminists rather than feminism itself; however, the vitriolic spirit of the anti-male feminists in the novel and Polly's ultimate rejection of her own feminist lifestyle suggest that the book is indeed an indictment of feminism. Both *The Bostonians* and *The Truth about Lorin Jones* have additionally been criticized for the vapid characterization of the central protagonist. Verena and Polly are such malleable persons—shaped and reshaped by the people they meet—that it is difficult to see why strong-willed people would find them fascinating.

One criticism that James escapes and Lurie does not is the credibility of the ending. James ends *The Bostonians* by acknowledging that marriage to Basil will bring Verena sorrow. Lurie's ending, however, is complacently happy. Although Polly knows that living with Mac will be not be a perfect life, the emphasis is on the happiness it will bring: he will write a good biography of Lorin Jones; she might return to her own career of painting; and she might even have another child. There is no recognition that Polly, who only months ago abandoned her marriage to live a self-sufficient life in New York, will have any regrets living a marginal life with Mac in Florida.

Relation to Previous Works

With *The Truth about Lorin Jones,* Lurie continues her acerbic exploration of American society, specifically the relationship between men and women as it has been defined since the sexual revolution of the 1960s. In *The War between the Tates,* Lurie explores the changing relationship between husband and wife; in *Foreign Affairs,* she juxtaposes the romantic longings of a middle-aged woman with those of a young man; and in *The Truth about Lorin Jones,* she describes the trials of a newly divorced woman. Although these novels emphasize the flawed nature of society and romantic love, each novel ends with re-establishment of the status quo. After rejecting marital commitment, Erica and Brian at the end of *The*

War between the Tates plan to reconcile, as do Fred and Ruth at the end of *Foreign Affairs*. Similarly, at the end of *The Truth about Lorin Jones*, Polly, who had planned to reject heterosexual commitment, decides to live with Mac.

Underscoring the thematic connection among *The War between the Tates, Foreign Affairs*, and *The Truth about Lorin Jones*, the Zimmern family appears in all three novels. In *The War between the Tates*, Leonard and Danielle Zimmern are friends of the Tates. In *Foreign Affairs*, Leonard is the critic who scorns Vinnie's work; his daughter Ruth March is married to Fred. In *The Truth about Lorin Jones*, Lorin is Leonard's half-sister. During her search to recover Lorin's life, Polly interviews Leonard, Danielle, and Ruth.

In *The Truth about Lorin Jones*, Lurie continues to explore techniques used in *Foreign Affairs*. In both novels Lurie uses an alternating sequence for point of view. In *Foreign Affairs*, the chapters alternate between Vinnie's point of view and Fred's, while in *The Truth about Lorin Jones*, a section on Polly's life is followed by the voice of one of the people Polly interviews. Both of these works by Lurie are also an imitation of Henry James' novels. For *Foreign Affairs*, Lurie borrowed the international setting that James used in his early novels to explore the clash between American and British society. In *The Truth about Lorin Jones*, Lurie turns to *The Bostonians*, a novel James wrote during his middle period, to explore the consequences of imposing change on traditional values.

Additional Sources

Ferrell, Sarah. "Research for a Love Affair." *New York Times Book Review* (September 4, 1988): 3. Interview with Lurie on her latest novel.

Prescott, Peter S. "A Mannerly Comedy of Morals." *Newsweek* (October 10, 1988): 74. Finds Polly Alter too willing to absorb the opinions of others.

Taylor, Paul. "Hunt the Victim." *Punch* (July 22, 1988): 52-53. Finds Jeanne a fascinating character but objects to her being portrayed as representative of the entire feminist/lesbian movement.

White, Edmund. "A Victim for the Male Establishment?" *New York Times Book Review* (September 4, 1988): 3. Briefly compares *The Truth about Lorin Jones* to two James' novels, *The Bostonians* and *The Turn of the Screw*.

Margaret Ann Baker
Iowa State University

NORMAN MAILER
1923

Update

Since the publication of *Tough Guys Don't Dance* (1984), Norman Mailer has written and directed the screen version of the novel. His new work of fiction, *Harlot's Ghost*, which has been variously termed a CIA or spy novel, is scheduled for publication in August 1991. While Mailer has granted interviews, appeared on television, and written a few magazine articles, he has concentrated his efforts on the new novel and generally avoided involvement in public affairs. He has set aside the idea of the trilogy he announced in interviews given at the time of the publication of *Ancient Evenings* (1983).

Analysis of Selected Titles

TOUGH GUYS DON'T DANCE
Tough Guys Don't Dance, 1984, novel.

Social Concerns/Themes

In most of Mailer's writings, both fiction and nonfiction, he has been concerned with the role of violence in American life. In his seminal essay, "The White Negro" (1957), he contrasted individual violence to the collective violence of the state. To Mailer, the state was capable of inflicting much more damage on individuals than individuals could inflict on themselves. In fact, for Mailer, an individual act of violence might even be a defensible rebellion against the repressive nature of society. Consequently, he has tended to create fictional heroes—such as Stephen Rojack in *An American Dream* (1965)—who renew themselves through violence. In *Tough Guys Don't Dance*, Mailer reverses the usual order of things in his fiction. The novel begins with its hero, Tim Madden, wondering whether the severed head he discovers in his marijuana hideaway is the gory result of a drunken evening's debauchery which turned violent. Waking up with no memory of the night before, Madden fears he has given way to the wild impulses stimulated by his estranged wife, Patty Lareine. The violent side of himself sickens Madden. In order to make himself whole again, he sets out to discover what part he played not only in his wife's death but in the decapitation of another woman who resembled her and whom Madden met on the night that has been expunged from his memory.

Characters

Tough Guys Don't Dance is narrated in the first person by Tim Madden. The use of this voice is an effective way for Mailer to pursue the theme of identity and for Madden to discover what actually happened and what he is capable of as a man. It is Madden's quest to act honorably and courageously that is most important. His role model is his father, a stoical Irishman who fought hard for what he believed. His nemesis is his wife, a hard but beautiful blonde, who has tried to use him in pursuit of wealth and power.

The characters relate to each other as in a medieval romance, and Madden even refers to his wife as "my long lost medieval lady." Lareine, after all, means "the queen," and as in the Arthurian legend, Madden discovers she has had another lover, Deputy Police Chief Alvin Luther Regency, a powerfully-built, maniacal rival. Complicating matters further for Madden is the lurking presence of his former schoolmate, Meeks Wardly Hilby III, who was also once married to Patty Lareine.

Clearly the underdog, and the one character who doubts both his probity and his sanity, Madden is meant to engage the reader's sympathies. He comes from immigrant stock, is a writer, and naturally the one to solve the mystery that threatens to engulf him. If Madden can make sense of the two murders, he can also begin to put his life back together—including his failed relationship with Madeleine Falco, his witty, tough counterpart who left him when he took up with Patty Lareine and who now finds herself mired in a bad marriage to the dangerous Regency.

Techniques/Literary Precedents

Mailer has clearly taken the mystery story as the model for his novel. It is his only work of fiction in which suspense plays a key part and the perpetrator of a crime must be discovered through detective work. As in a traditional mystery, each chapter thickens the atmosphere of ambiguity and at the same time provides several clues that hint at a solution to the crimes. The reader is faced with several questions: Did the same person kill both women? What was Madden's role in these murders? What exactly is Regency's interest in the case? Several vital facts are withheld from both Madden and the reader until late in the novel—such as Regency's affair with Patty Lareine and his marriage to Madden's former flame, Madeleine Falco.

Mailer departs from the traditional constraints of the murder mystery in his narrator's digressions into character analysis and metaphysical speculation. Madden believes, for example, that people live with two opposing souls, which make them capable of great good and great evil. The universe itself, in his opinion, is defined by a struggle between God and the Devil, and each human being, therefore, is a part of that conflict. This is why he can be his own suspect. Unlike the traditional mystery story, the detective in this case contemplates the possibility that he himself has committed the crime.

Relation to Previous Works

Tough Guys Don't Dance is a provocative variation of Mailer's earlier novels. Like Mikey Lovett in *Barbary Shore* (1951), Madden is an amnesiac trying to reconstruct his life and to remember an important event. Like Stephen Rojack in *An American Dream*, Madden is beset by an ambivalent relationship with his wife. Both are wealthy women who dominate their men; both are women who express Mailer's concern with the fragility of the masculine ego. The women seem secure in their identities whereas the men struggle to find and maintain an identity, lacking the biological tie to life that makes women superior to men in this respect. Mailer has made this point in many interviews and in *The Prisoner of Sex* (1971), suggesting there is a willed, almost contrived quality to the male identity.

Adaptations

In the novel, Patty Lareine never actually appears; instead, she comes alive in Madden's sorrow over her departure and death. Since Mailer could not rely on a narrative voice in his screen adaptation (1987), he introduced Lareine as a character. Initially, Mailer's plan was to rely only on dramatized action in the film, but in the end he was forced to use some voice-over narration to clarify Madden's point of view and certain plot elements. Most reviews of the film were negative, citing an uneven tone and unduly complicated plot. Reviewers wondered whether Mailer was intentionally parodying himself or taking himself too seriously. They also panned his direction of the film, pointing to a lack of cinematic rhythm, and faulted his writing, finding some of his more foreboding lines ludicrous.

Additional Sources

Jaehne, Karen. "Mailer's Minuet." *Film Comment* (July-August 1987). Informative account of the movie production with comments by Mailer.

Lennon, J. Michael, ed. *Conversations with Norman Mailer*. Jackson: University Press of Mississippi, 1988. A superb collection of interviews with Mailer covering his life and work, including *Tough Guys Don't Dance*. Also contains a bibliography of Mailer's published books, an introduction, chronology, and index.

Lennon, J. Michael, ed. *Critical Essays on Norman Mailer*. Boston: G. K. Hall, 1986. The most recent collection of reviews and essays on Mailer's work, enhanced by a valuable overview of the critical literature on Mailer.

Merkin, Daphne. "His Brilliant (New) Career?" *American Film* (October 1987). Informative account of the movie production.

Wenke, Joseph. *Mailer's America*. Hanover, NH: University Press of New England, 1987. One of the most recent critical studies of Mailer, which is fair, accurate, and comprehensive.

Carl Rollyson
Baruch College
The City University of New York

BERNARD MALAMUD
1914-1986

Update

Since his death in 1986, Malamud's unfinished novel and a number of his uncollected stories have been published. Edited by his friend and publisher, Robert Giroux, *The People and Uncollected Stories* (1989) contains a useful biographical memoir by Giroux. It begins with an account of Malamud's first published story, written in Washington, D.C., in 1940, and ends with Saul Bellow's moving tribute to him as "a myth maker, a fabulist, a writer of exquisite parable," whose work invariably carries "the accent of hard-won and individual emotional truth."

At the time of his death, Malamud had completed sixteen of twenty projected chapters for his novel, and only the first few chapters had undergone the kind of rewriting to which the writer typically subjected his work. Nevertheless, the novel seemed worth publishing along with the fugitive pieces. *The People and Uncollected Stories* is vintage Malamud, about a Jewish peddler who becomes the adopted chief of a tribe of American Indians in the Pacific Northwest during the last century. As the dust jacket describes it, "Chief Jozip takes on his shoulders all the suffering the tribe is subjected to by the U.S. government, including their brutal mistreatment and their tragic, genocidal fate." The novel thus contains elements of the wit and fantasy that characterize Malamud's earlier fiction, as well as *God's Grace*. The stories, eleven in all, span the writer's career, from "Armistice" (1940) to "Alma Redeemed" (1984).

Analysis of Selected Titles

GOD'S GRACE

God's Grace, 1982, novel.

Social Concerns

In his last published novel before his death, Malamud has written a dark fable of the end of the world. It is set sometime in the future, after the thermonuclear war in which the Djanks and the Drushkies have destroyed not only themselves but all human life, or almost all of it. A single human being survives along with some chimpanzees, a shy gorilla, and a band of baboons. Trying to rebuild a civilization based upon mutual respect and love for all creatures, Calvin Cohn, the son of a rabbi and the sole survivor of the ultimate holocaust, educates the chimpanzees. He teaches them to talk and tries to instill in them a moral code drawn from the Judeo-Christian tradition. In the latter attempt, he fails utterly. Malamud seems to be saying that the instinct to aggression is supreme and for that reason all civilizations are doomed to failure.

Themes

Education, love for living creatures of all kinds, respect, and tolerance are among Malamud's principal themes, or moral imperatives, in this novel. Their counterparts—murderous aggression, jealousy, pride, and vengeance—are also prominent, and as Malamud shows, they are finally no match for the gentle virtues that Calvin Cohn practices and tries to teach.

Characters

The chief character in the novel is the sole human survivor of a nuclear war, Calvin Cohn. The other important character is Gottlob, a chimpanzee who also survives aboard the research vessel that carried Cohn to the depths of the ocean while the war briefly raged. Cohn nicknames the chimp Buz, and together they form a close, loving relationship, during which Cohn discovers that Buz can talk. When they land on an island, they set up housekeeping in a cave and later find other survivors, a gorilla whom Cohn names George, and a band of chimpanzees, whom Buz names Esau, Mary Madelyn, Melchior (an elderly chimp), and the twins, Saul of Tarsus and Luke. God also plays a role, especially at the beginning, when he talks with Cohn and warns him that his survival is the result of a minuscule error.

Techniques

Malamud's basic technique in *God's Grace* is reproducing the fable, complete with talking animals, Edenic landscapes, and overt moral exhortations. Cohn's conversations with God also reflect the narrative techniques of the Old Testament. Throughout the novel, Malamud mingles realism and fantasy, interspersing both with humor, especially Jewish humor, well-laden with irony. The humor lightens the fable's darkness, until the final catastrophe, where it is no longer appropriate.

Literary Precedents

Malamud borrows from the stories in the Old and New Testaments, particularly accounts of the Garden of Eden and Noah and the flood. He also draws heavily upon Defoe's *Robinson Crusoe*, but in a prefatory note he specifically acknowledges Shalom Spiegel's *The Last Trial* and Jane Goodall's *In the Shadow of Man*. Neville Shute's *On the Beach* is another novel that treats the aftermath of nuclear war, though in a different way, and Angus Wilson's *The Old Men at the Zoo* deals with the theme of man's relationship with animals, particularly as war affects that relationship.

Related Titles

In "The Jew Bird," an early story, Malamud introduces a talking animal and treats the theme of loving kindness between human beings and other creatures. Overcoming suffering and isolation is handled in *The Assistant* as well as *The Fixer*, where the outlook is more optimistic, even though the situations are in some respects more brutal and are treated with less humor. In his first novel, *The Natural*, Malamud utilizes an archetypal structure as he does in *God's Grace*, but the sources of his archetypes derive from other myths and legends.

Additional Sources

Bloom, Harold, ed. *Bernard Malamud*. New York: Chelsea House, 1986. Harold Bloom's introductory essay places Malamud in critical context and gives an overview of the twenty essays in this anthology. These essays, which discuss themes and issues in Malamud's work, represent a wide range of theories and perspectives. Useful as an introduction to Malamud's critical reputation.

Helterman, Jeffrey. *Understanding Bernard Malamud*. Columbia: University of South Carolina Press, 1985. This concise study of Malamud is designed to provide guidance for students and general readers. Themes, imagery, and characterization are discussed for the major works. Although some will find the interpretations overly simplistic, most newcomers to Malamud should find much of the information helpful.

Solotaroff, Robert. *Bernard Malamud: A Study of the Short Fiction*. Boston: Twayne, 1989. Solotaroff combines biography with an explication of forty-five stories to demonstrate Malamud's craft and themes, the most important of which is the meaning of being human in an inhumane universe. This book also contains interviews with Malamud, excerpts from critical reviews, a chronology of Malamud's life, a bibliography, and an index. This is a good, basic resource for studying Malamud at any level.

Salzberg, Joel, ed. *Critical Essays on Bernard Malamud.* Boston: G. K. Hall, 1987. Similar to other volumes in this series, this anthology offers reprints of important critical essays, original essays, and an introduction that provides an overview of the writer's reputation and place in literary history. Contributors include Harvey Swados writing on *The Natural*, Alfred Kazin on *The Assistant*, and James Mellard on *Dubin's Lives*. Salzberg's introduction points out the tasks confronting Malamud scholars and suggests directions for further research. Helpful notes and an index are included.

Studies in American Jewish Literature (Fall 1988). Contains essays by Ellen Pifer, Daniel Walden, Leslie Field, Daniel Fuchs, Harold Fisch, and others, besides a bibliographical essay by R. R. O'Keefe and a memoir by Joel Salzburg.

Jay L. Halio
University of Delaware

KATHERINE MANSFIELD
1888-1923

Publishing History

Katherine Mansfield's life was short. Born in New Zealand in 1888 and educated at Queen's College in London (1903-1905), she moved permanently to Europe in 1908. Between August 1908 and January 1923, when she died in France, Mansfield resided at over forty different addresses in England and on the Continent. She married twice, had a number of intense relationships with both men and women, and suffered several debilitating diseases. In the process, she managed to write sixty-two short stories, a number of which are considered masterpieces of the genre.

Most of these stories were written in two periods of her life, 1910-1913 and 1917-1922. Stories from the early period first appeared separately in *New Age, Rhythm,* and *Blue Review,* and were later collected as *In a German Pension* (1911) and *Something Childish and Other Stories* (1924). Mansfield's major stories derive from the second period. These stories were published separately in *New Age, English Review, Arts and Letters, Athenaeum, London Mercury, Nation, Sphere, Weekly Westminster Gazette, Sketch, Story-Teller, Collier's,* and *Adelphi,* and were then collected in *Bliss and Other Stories* (1920), *The Garden-Party and Other Stories* (1922), *The Dove's Nest and Other Stories* (1923), and *Something Childish and Other Stories.*

Critical Reception, Honors, Popularity

Mansfield remained an obscure writer during most of her lifetime, until the publication of *Bliss and Other Stories* in 1920. That collection was a critical and popular success, and the succeeding collections that were published during her lifetime and posthumously were equally well-received.

In the decade after her death, she became almost a cult figure, remembered as a writer of great promise whose life was cut tragically short. Today critics consider her one of the primary influences in the development of the modern English short story. As critic T. O. Beachcroft notes, "she is the only author who has placed herself in English literature, and indeed in Western literature, by a few short stories alone."

Analysis of Selected Titles

THE LITTLE GOVERNESS

"The Little Governess," 1915, short story.

Social Concerns

"The Little Governess" concerns the fall of a young innocent when she finds herself in new and unfamiliar surroundings. The governess of the title is travelling through continental Europe for the first time on her way to a new employer in Germany. She has been given strict instructions by the lady at the Governess Bureau to avoid contact with strangers, but she responds to the attentions of a seemingly kind old man whom she meets on an overnight train, only to discover too late that his intentions are not honorable.

Mansfield gives the reader little background about the title character, but the fact that the young woman is a governess tells the reader a great deal about her. In pre-World War I society, a governess was the career alternative for genteel women of scant means who needed to support themselves. These women were cast offs, victims of a male-dominated society that gave them few options for happiness and fulfillment outside the bonds of matrimony.

Themes

In this story, the young woman awakens briefly to the world of the senses and desire, but then withdraws in fear and panic when she discovers that she has deceived herself about the intentions of the old German gentleman she meets on the train. He offers her a day in Munich to do whatever she wants—she calls it "her last day to really enjoy herself in"—and tempts her with such exotic culinary delights as strawberries, white sausages, and chocolate ice cream, all of which she devours eagerly and unquestioningly. With each morsel, her ability to resist his next invitation weakens until she finds herself alone with him in his quarters. When he reveals his lustful intentions, she flees to the hotel where she was to meet her new employer, only to discover that she has missed her appointment.

Characters

None of the characters in the story is named. They are stock figures playing out their appointed roles in a little drama that is governed by the dictates of custom and manners. Yet "The Little Governess" is more than a comedy of manners, for Mansfield enters fully into the thoughts and feelings of the governess.

In addition to the young woman and the old man, there are a number of minor characters: an aggressive railroad porter who grabs the governess' bags at the station in Munich; a group of rowdy young men in the next train compartment who invite her to join them; a surly hotel waiter in Munich who resents the governess' stiff English manners; and several German women in the tram that the governess takes when she flees from the old man. Mansfield uses these characters in two ways—to create the governess' sense of an indifferent, vaguely hostile world through which she passes, and, in their fleeting observations, to offer ironic commentary on the events that are of such dramatic moment to the title character.

Techniques

In "The Little Governess," Mansfield uses a limited point of view. The story moves back and forth between the governess' interior monologue and dramatic action, offering the reader a double perspective. One not only sees events from the governess' point of view but also observes her fall into the fairly obvious trap of the lascivious old man, whom she mistakenly regards as her "fairy godfather." The narrator of the tale remains in the background but occasionally intrudes as when she makes the following speculations about the old man's motives: "Perhaps the flush that licked his cheeks and lips was a flush of rage that anyone so young and tender would have to travel alone and unprotected through the night. Who knows he was not murmuring in his sentimental German fashion: 'Ja, es ist eine Tragodie! Would to God I were the child's grandpapa!' " Even if a cynical reader is fairly certain that the old man's color comes from lust, rather than grandfatherly concern, the narrator invites the reader to consider an alternative interpretation. The narrator also invites the reader to see the governess as a victim of circumstance and upbringing rather than a foolish young woman who willingly falls into an old man's obvious trap.

Relation to Previous Works

"The Little Governess" was written in 1915, right before Mansfield began work on "The Aloe," in which she experimented with narrative patterns. It confirms her mastery of short story techniques revealed in the collection of stories *In a German Pension* published in 1911. In that collection, a number of stories were closer to sketches or vignettes than full-fledged stories. While "The Little Governess" retains the immediacy and fine attention to detail of the earlier work, it also possesses a stronger underlying plot than many of those stories.

Thematically, Mansfield works with material that she developed in many other stories. Just as a journey is a favorite situation in a Mansfield story, so is the misreading of someone else's thoughts and actions a common plot device. The climax of many of her stories involves the main character's sudden (often traumatic) realization that her reading of an event was in some way dangerously inappropriate.

Literary Precedents

When Mansfield wrote "The Little Governess," James Joyce, A. E. Coppard, and D. H. Lawrence were developing their own techniques in short fiction. Although their stories were quite different, together their efforts transformed the English short story, creating what T. O. Beachcroft called "the Chekhov kind of short story." Chekhov is an important antecedent for Mansfield. One of the best stories from her early period, "The Child-Who-Was-Tired," is a reworking of a Chekhov story, and in her journals she wrote admiringly of the Russian author. Although "The Little Governess" is a relatively early attempt, it bears the marks of this new style: the title character is presented seriously; her thoughts are permitted to speak for themselves; the reader is not directed to see them ironically or satirically; and the events of her journey are revealed dramatically, with relatively little commentary from the narrator.

PRELUDE and AT THE BAY
"Prelude," 1918, and "At the Bay," 1922, short stories.

Social Concerns

Both of these stories present events in the daily life of the Burnells, a New Zealand family that resembles the household in which Mansfield was raised. "Prelude" concerns the family's move from town to country. "At the Bay," which takes place some time after "Prelude," concerns the passing of one day spent at the family's vacation bungalow by the sea. In both stories, the reader observes the complexity of the interrelationships which keep the family together yet apart. While the members of the family are closely joined by emotional bonds, each character remains a separate individual, never fully relating to anyone else, and isolated in the privacy of his or her own thoughts and responses.

Themes

Women dominate the Burnell household. Even though Stanley Burnell rules when he is at home, there is always the sense that he is an intrusive presence in his own house. When Stanley leaves for work in "At the Bay," all the women heave a collective sigh of relief—"There was no man to disturb them." In "Prelude," the women are responsible for the smooth handling of the move as they try to accommodate Stanley's needs and wishes. While Stanley may appear domineering and managerial, the reader is always aware that he remains subservient to the will of his wife. As one critic notes, in this story Mansfield portrays "four stages of womanhood" in the principal female characters in the household: Linda Burnell, the mistress of the household; Beryl Fairfield, her beautiful unmarried sister, who is in search of an identity; Kezia, one of Linda's children, who is still young enough to experience life naturally and unselfconsciously; and Mrs. Fairfield, Linda and Beryl's mother, who runs the household for her married daughter. In terms of plot, little occurs, but each of these characters is caught in revelatory moments which reflect her sense of identity and her period of life.

An important theme in "At the Bay" is the passage of time. The story opens with "very early morning." Only after the natural setting is discovered in the dawn does the first human being appear. At the end of the story, darkness has fallen, the last person has disappeared from view, and all is still. Death and the meaning of existence are repeatedly alluded to in the conversations of different characters. In a central episode, Kezia learns about death from her grandmother who is thinking about the early, untimely death of one of her sons. Kezia refuses to accept the inevitability of Mrs. Fairfield's death when her grandmother tells her everyone must die.

Male characters are more important in "At the Bay" than in "Prelude," even though women continue to dominate the life of the household. Ambitious Stanley Burnell is here balanced by his brother-in-law Jonathan Trout who pities Stanley because of "his determination to make a job of everything," but who later reveals himself to be equally pitiable since he can never escape the demands of a job which requires him to sit "on a stool from nine to five, scratching in somebody's ledger." He likens his job to a prison and sees himself as an insect which has "flown into a room of its own accord" but then discovers it cannot get out and spends the rest of its existence ceaselessly "banging and flopping and crawling up the pane." Significantly, Jonathan shares an emotional sympathy with his sister-in-law, Linda, who feels trapped in her role as wife and mother.

Characters

In "Prelude" and "At the Bay," unlike other Mansfield stories, there is no single controlling point of view. Both stories are episodic, and the center of consciousness shifts from character to character. While nearly every character has his or her moment of illumination, the three characters who are developed most fully are Stanley, Linda Burnell, and Beryl Fairfield.

Linda Burnell should be the dominant woman in the household. She is the wife of an important businessman and the mother of his children, but she has left the running of the household and the raising of her children to her mother. Her relationship to Stanley is characterized by remoteness. At times her sister appears to be more Stanley's wife than Linda. Beryl plays cribbage at night with Stanley, and Beryl flirts with him as Linda remains lost in her dreams. Linda is analytical about her emotions and her lack of feelings for her children. Childbearing (both the actual experience and the dread of the next pregnancy) has left her drained, incapable of giving her children any love. When thinking of Stanley, she sees "all her feelings for him sharp and defined, one as true as the other. And there was this other, this hatred, just as real as the rest."

Beryl Fairfield is in a different position. Unlike her sister Linda, Beryl is not married and has no prospects of marriage. Whereas Linda is frustrated by the limitations imposed on her by her role as Stanley's wife, Beryl is frustrated by the uncertainty and ambiguity of her situation as an unmarried woman. Both stories end with episodes in which Beryl is alone in her room, contemplating who she is and who she might become. In "Prelude" she tries to catch a glimpse of her real self in a mirror but always sees Beryl playing a role. In "At the Bay," it is late at night and Beryl imagines herself in the arms of a lover, when Harry Kember (a local seaside Don Juan) calls to her from the garden. She goes out to him only to run away, horrified at the shoddy reality of what she has been imagining.

Stanley Burnell, the main male figure in this female household, is far more limited than the women. His happiness appears to depend on their moods, and his ability to imagine beyond immediate, practical concerns is limited. In "Prelude," when he thinks of joining a church, he hears "himself intoning extremely well: 'When thou didst overcome the *Sharp*ness of Death Thou didst open the *King*dom of Heaven to *all* Believers.' And he saw the near brass-edged card on the corner of the pew—Mr. Stanley Burnell and family." Obviously the words from the service have made no impression on Stanley's mind or heart.

Techniques

Mansfield's aim in "Prelude" and "At the Bay" was to recreate the life she knew as a child in New Zealand. Each story consists of a series of episodes presented sequentially. Characters are not so much introduced or described as discovered within scenes; the reader learns about them and their lives from direct observation. T. O. Beachcroft points out that in this method there is no narrator. Mansfield allows "no comment from any implied narrator"; she makes "the scene and the events of the story reveal themselves." Another critic calls the form "dramatic in character, revealed rather than told." The cumulative effect of these short episodes is greater than the sum, for at the end of each story, the reader feels that he knows these people and their lives intimately, even though he is ignorant of most details of time, place, and class which would conventionally be used to define character in longer works of fiction.

Literary Precedents

Two possible antecedents for these stories come from different periods of literature: Theocritus and T. S. Eliot. Mansfield used the XVth idyll of Theocritus as a model for a piece on the Coronation of George V that appeared in *New Age* in 1911. As T. O. Beachcroft notes in *The Modest Art,* this idyll "comes as near to a modern short story as anything in the world . . . the mime form gets rid of the need to prove the authority of the narrator." Characters are revealed through dialogue with no "comment, explanation, and moralizing" from an intrusive narrator. This form was well-suited to "scenes from everyday life." In both subject and method, "Prelude" and "At the Bay" can be compared with the XVth idyll of Theocritus.

According to Anthony Alpers, when T. S. Eliot's "Love Song of J. Alfred Prufrock" first appeared in 1917, Mansfield read it out loud to the guests at Lady Ottoline Morrell's estate in Garsington. Later Mansfield would tell Virginia Woolf that she didn't think of Eliot as a poet, because "Prufrock, is after all a short story." Just as Eliot experimented in poetic form to jettison expository or narrative encumbrances, so Mansfield attempted to achieve the immediacy of a dramatic scene or poem in the form of a short story.

Relation to Previous Works

In 1915 Mansfield began "The Aloe," which was to be a novel about New Zealand. On several occasions, Mansfield planned or began work on novels, always to abandon them. She got much further with "The Aloe" than with any other, but eventually she stopped writing it. The work she did on "The Aloe" was later cut and revised, becoming "Prelude," a departure from anything Mansfield had written before. The narrator has been virtually eliminated and the story divided into independent episodes. Mansfield used this episodic technique in only one other completed work, "At the Bay."

BLISS

"Bliss," 1918, short story.

Social Concerns

"Bliss" introduces Bertha Young, a thirty-year-old, well-to-do woman who apparently has everything she could possibly want, but who lives a shallow existence in a world of showy pretense. Although Mansfield's main aim is to reveal Bertha's delusions, she also satirizes Bertha's arty upper-middle-class set.

Themes

Bertha is eager to discover the source of her bliss, a deep burning sensation inside her body that she can just barely suppress. This bliss appears to be an essentially adolescent feeling, a desire "to run instead of walk, to take dancing steps on and off the pavement, to bowl a hoop, to throw something up in the air and catch it again, or to stand still and laugh at—nothing—at nothing, simply." Throughout the story, it keeps welling up in little bursts of laughter as if it would escape. But there is a discrepancy between Bertha's emotion and its apparent causes. In many Mansfield stories, the reader observes characters either misjudging external stimuli ("The Young Governess") or interpreting the stimuli in highly idiosyncratic ways ("Prelude"). This story is different; here the main character appears to be suppressing her true feelings.

According to Saralyn R. Daly, "what Bertha tells herself and the responses she makes to stimuli within the story are in conflict." Thus, Bertha feels maternal delight in claiming her rights as a mother from the nurse and feeding her baby herself, but the scene that Mansfield describes is at odds with what the character asserts about it. Similarly, Bertha later claims to have shared a moment of emotional communion with one of her dinner guests, Pearl Fulton, when there is no evidence that anything has occurred on Miss Fulton's part. At the very end of the story, she observes her husband arranging a rendezvous with Pearl Fulton, and her bliss evaporates instantly. When she finally asks, "Oh, what is going to happen now?" a reader may see that as a question she has been avoiding throughout the story.

What Bertha is suppressing is open to various interpretations. On the surface, it would appear to be a knowledge of her husband's affair with her friend, but there are other levels of meaning. In particular, her rambling thoughts reveal aspects of her own sexuality that she has not fully recognized. When Pearl Fulton is introduced, the reader learns that when she and Bertha first met, "Bertha had fallen in love with her, as she always did fall in love with beautiful women who had something strange about them." Later, after her supposed moment of communion with Pearl, Bertha feels desire for her husband for the first time in her life when "something strange and almost terrifying" darts into her mind: she thinks of their being "alone together in the dark room—the warm bed," and she recalls how cold she has been in the past. In this reading of the story, what has so long been suppressed is not knowledge of her husband's affair but knowledge of what Kate Fullbrook calls her "sexual need." At this moment of discovery, the ill-defined feeling of bliss turns into an "ardent" longing for her husband, only to be replaced almost instantly by despair as she discovers that Harry Young has found consolation elsewhere.

Characters

Mansfield makes Bertha and her responses the focus of her story; the two important people in Bertha's life, Pearl Fulton and Harry, are scarcely characterized. Pearl is not much more than a presence: "she seldom did look at people directly," and a "strange half smile came and went upon her lips as though she lived by listening rather than seeing." Harry is a go-getter, full of energy and life. Bertha thinks of him as her pal through most of the story; only at the very end is she aware of a different side to his nature after she observes him turn Pearl "violently to him" and then hears, moments later, the sound of his voice speaking to herself "extravagantly cool and collected."

In addition to the members of this triangle, there are other guests at Bertha's dinner party, people from the arts who are superficially lively and witty but shallow. It is no accident that Eddie Warren's departing words to Bertha are about the "*dreadfully* eternal" qualities of tomato soup as a poetic image. These characters help define the values of Bertha and Harry's world where style and appearance have become ends in themselves. Earlier in the story, Bertha had carefully arranged a bowl of fruit to bring out the color in her carpet, and she rearranged the pillows in the drawing room which made the room "come alive" even without the presence of people.

Techniques

This story reveals Mansfield's mastery of several techniques. There is no conventional narrator. The story moves freely back and forth between interior monologue and dramatic scene. By the final page, Mansfield can create a dramatic scene and depend upon the reader to imagine its impact on Bertha without the use of interior monologue. Thus, as if in the same instant at which it occurs, the reader hears the trivial conversation Bertha is having with Eddie Warren, catches the brief exchange between Pearl and Harry that Bertha sees, and witnesses the change in Bertha's state of mind. The scene has the impact of a moment of theater conveyed in the form of the short story.

Relation to Previous Works

This story, written in 1918, represents the flowering of Mansfield's mature style. If one compares it with "The Little Governess," written in 1915, one notes the absence of exposition and the elimination of a narrative voice. Whatever the reader needs to know is discovered by observing the main character in action and in thought.

JE NE PARLE PAS FRANÇAIS

"Je ne parle pas français," 1920, short story.

Social Concerns

The setting for "Je ne parle pas français" is Paris—a world of small cafés, crowded hotels, and gloomy rooming houses, populated by artists, writers, pimps, prostitutes, and gigolos. In this post-World War I story, society has lost its moral center. Raoul Duquette, the main character, sees feeling as the only sign of human worth. The exploitation of others for his own personal amusement and gain has become such a habit that Raoul is unaware of any standard of judgment besides self gratification.

Themes

Two important themes in the story are sexual ambiguity and victimization, what critic Kate Fullbrook calls the "inescapable victimization and universal warping of desire." The sexual orientation of each of the three main characters is in some way twisted or ambiguous. Raoul Duquette, the narrator of the story, had been repeatedly molested by an African laundress when he was a child, starting at the age of ten. His loss of innocence brought an early end to his childhood so that he "seemed to understand everybody and be able to do . . . what he liked with everybody." His English friend Dick Harmon has never been able to break the bonds of a domineering mother and is apparently unable to maintain relationships with either women or men. The young woman in the story, Mouse, may be fragile and delicately attractive, but she has masculine characteristics and several times is likened to a boy by Duquette. The story concerns the victimization of Mouse when she is abandoned in a strange city by both men. They, of course, have both been victimized early in their lives by women.

The mask is a more general theme in this story. All the characters in some way mask their true feelings and identities from others and from themselves. Raoul Duquette in particular practices a kind of conscious self-deceit. At one point, he describes himself practicing his pose as a man of letters in front of a mirror; he decides that if one looks the part, one must be the part.

Characters

"Je ne parle pas français" is first and foremost a revelation of the character of Raoul Duquette, the narrator. In the first half we encounter him sitting in a cafe, musing about himself, his world, and other people. Raoul is a fraud; he calls himself a writer, but as readers learn more about him, they become aware of his real business in that cafe. He is waiting; the others, whether they be women or men, always make "the first advances."

Midway through the story, Raoul recalls Dick Harmon. When they first met, Raoul was obviously attracted to Dick. They became fast friends and went everywhere together, but Dick had the disturbing habit of backing off. As Raoul notes, when they were out together with "a little woman," Dick would depart "just when she would not expect him to get up and leave her, but quite the contrary." Eventually, just as if Raoul were that little woman (or as he calls himself, a "fox terrier"), Dick got up and left him, returning to England with no prior warning.

But Dick comes back to Paris, bringing with him Mouse. Apparently they had run away together to share the Bohemian life, but he abandons her on their first night in Paris, leaving her a note, saying that it would kill his mother were he to carry out their plan. Raoul, who had arranged for their lodging and accompanied them to the rooms, witnesses this abandonment and is touched when Mouse reveals that she cannot return to England because she told everyone she was getting married. The reader knows the least about Mouse, perhaps because Raoul knows less about women than men. Earlier he lumped all women together: "But from little prostitutes and kept women and elderly widows and shop girls and wives of respectable men, and even advanced modern literary ladies at the most select dinners and soirées (I've been there), I've met invariably with not only the same readiness, but with the same positive invitation."

Raoul breaks his rule about making "first advances" by offering to come the next day to help Mouse, and she responded to his invitation by coming "out of her hole . . . timid . . . but she came out." Raoul Duquette, the cynic, never goes back to see her, but he is astounded by his responses to this woman whose suffering was real and spontaneous.

Techniques

In "Je ne parle pas français," Mansfield comes closest to writing the kind of stream of consciousness fiction pioneered by Joyce's *Ulysses* (1922) and Faulkner's *The Sound and the Fury* (1929). However, the story is not one long monologue without punctuation and paragraphing. It is broken up into short units, reflecting the narrator's shifting focus of attention which moves freely back and forth between the present setting, past events, and philosophical statements.

Literary Precedents

The most obvious literary precedent for "Je ne parle pas français" is Dostoyevsky's *Letters from the Underworld* (1864). In both works a self-absorbed man reveals his own nature, and both works end with stories from the narrator's past. When Mansfield's husband, John Middleton Murry, read the manuscript of the first part of the story, he wrote her, "It's utterly unlike any sensation I have ever yet had from any writing of yours, or any writing at all except Dostoyevsky's."

Another possible influence on this story might have been impressionist painters like Toulouse-Lautrec, Monet, Cézanne, Manet, and Matisse. Critic Rhoda B. Nathan has pointed out that the Paris Raoul Duquette inhabits is the Paris of Toulouse-Lautrec and that the technique of the story represents Mansfield's "attempt to do with language what the impressionists and post-impressionists were doing with brush and palette."

Relation to Previous Works

"Je ne parle pas français" is unlike most of Mansfield's earlier stories, not only in its use of a first-person narrator as the central character of the story but also in its development of a masculine point of view. The story is also more open about sexual matters than most of Mansfield's earlier work, particularly in the unexpurgated version that Mansfield wanted published. Unfortunately, the censored version is usually published, and Mansfield's portrait of Duquette loses much of its edge.

THE GARDEN-PARTY
"The Garden-Party," 1922, short story.

Social Concerns
"The Garden-Party" is built on the contrast between families from two social strata: the wealthy, upper-class Sheridans, who live in a spacious house with a large, well-tended garden; and the Scotts, their working-class neighbors in the next lane, who live in a "little mean" dwelling with an ugly garden patch filled with "nothing but cabbage stalks, sick hens and tomato cans." Both families have been caught in characteristic moments: the Sheridans are giving a large afternoon party requiring careful attention to superficial details of arrangement and decoration; the working-class family has been struck by the sudden, accidental death of the father, the breadwinner for a family of seven.

Themes
The main theme of the story grows out of this contrast. Laura, one of the Sheridan daughters, has been given the job of supervising the last-minute arrangements for the garden party. When she accidentally learns from a workman of the tragedy in the next lane, she thinks the party should be cancelled, but no one else in the family agrees. After the party, Mrs. Sheridan has "one of her brilliant ideas," that they give the party leftovers to the Scotts, who will find them useful in their hour of need. Laura is assigned to deliver the food, and the story ends with Laura's encounter with grief and death. As Laura enters the crowded lane where the Scotts live, she feels that she is the object of attention of all the neighbors. The only clear images Laura sees are the swollen face of the grieving widow and the face of the departed Mr. Scott, who appears to be "sleeping so soundly, so deeply . . . so remote, so peaceful."

Characters
Laura like Kezia in "Prelude" and "At the Bay" is another version of the young Mansfield. More sensitive and artistic than the rest of her family, she

identifies with the workmen who are helping get the house and the garden ready for the party. But hers is clearly a childish identification borne out of rebellion against the artificial atmosphere in which she has been raised. The rest of the family is indifferent to the plight of the Scotts, seeing them as part of a community that is an eyesore and has "no right to be in that neighbourhood at all." When Laura suggests cancelling the party, Mrs. Sheridan stands on class prejudice: "People like that don't expect sacrifices from us. And it's not very sympathetic to spoil everybody's enjoyment as you're doing now."

Techniques

"The Garden-Party" belongs to Mansfield's last group of stories. A number of these stories are held together by plot, what critic Joanne Trautmann Banks calls "a line that moves softly to an end"—a story element that almost disappeared from stories in Mansfield's middle period. This story line controls the direction of the work rather than the particular point of view of any individual character. Laura does not dominate in the way that Bertha Young dominates "Bliss" or Raoul Duquette dominates "Je ne parle pas français." Rather, early in the story we encounter a multitude of attitudes toward the afternoon festivities, one of which is Laura's. Even at the end of the story where Laura's point of view is dominant, the total picture of Laura's visit to the grieving family is as memorable as Laura's individual responses to the face of death.

Literary Precedents

Theocritus's XVth idyll serves as a literary precedent for the shape of "The Garden-Party." In that dramatic poem, two young women visit the festival of Adonis. Most of the dialogue concerns their sophisticated, superficial comments about their lives and about what they see in the crowded streets as they make their way to the festival. As T. O. Beachcroft notes, they are "foolish, yet endearing . . . put before us in all their human frailty with loving care." When the two Greek women arrive at the festival, they witness a performance of a mystical poem about Adonis which deeply moves them. After the performance, they are unable to articulate the experience they have had.

In "The Garden-Party," the presentation of the Sheridan family is at first characterized by bright, airy conversation as the various members of the household prepare for the party. The Sheridans appear both foolish and endearing as they go about their business. In the second part of the story, Laura is transported to a different order of experience when she enters the neighbors' lane and encounters the unveiled faces of grief and death. Taken by themselves, Laura's remarks to her brother when she returns from the dead worker's cottage appear completely inadequate to what she has witnessed. Nevertheless, because of their essentially dramatic form, both works leave the reader with the impression that something important, perhaps transcendent, has occurred.

Relation to Previous Works

Like "Prelude" and "At the Bay," "The Garden-Party" is based on events that occurred in New Zealand during Mansfield's youth. In 1907, the year before she left New Zealand for good, Mansfield's mother gave a garden party that was marred by a fatal accident in the working-class neighborhood on the next street. The Sheridans are essentially the same family as the Burnells in the other stories, only at a later point in their history.

Other Titles

Poems, 1923; *The Journal of Katherine Mansfield*, 1927; *The Letters of Katherine Mansfield*, 1928; *Novels and Novelists*, 1930 (criticism); *The Scrapbook of Katherine Mansfield*, 1939 (journal); *Katherine Mansfield's Letters to John Middleton Murry, 1913-1922*, 1951; *The Journal of Katherine Mansfield*, 1954 (a new edition combining materials from the 1927 journal and the 1939 scrapbook); *Katherine Mansfield: Publications in Australia, 1907-1909*, 1977 (fiction); *The Urewera Notebook*, 1980 (notes from a 1907 camping trip); *The Collected Letters of Katherine Mansfield*, 1984-1987 (two volumes of a projected five volumes).

Additional Sources

Alpers, Anthony. *The Life of Katherine Mansfield.* New York: Viking, 1980. The standard biography of Mansfield.

Banks, Joanne Trautmann. "Virginia Woolf and Katherine Mansfield." In *The English Short Story, 1880-1945: A Critical History*, edited by Joseph N. Flora. Boston: Twayne, 1985. Banks discusses Woolf and Mansfield separately, concluding with a discussion of the "link" between the two writers.

Beachcroft, T. O. *The Modest Art: A Survey of the Short Story in English.* London: Oxford University Press, 1968. Beachcroft discusses Mansfield's position in the development of the English short story.

Berkman, Sylvia. *Katherine Mansfield: A Critical Study.* New Haven: Yale University Press, 1951. An early discussion of Mansfield's oeuvre. Berkman traces the "interacting relationship" between Mansfield's life and work.

Bowen, Elizabeth. "Introduction." *Stories by Katherine Mansfield.* New York: Vintage, 1956. Bowen's introduction offers an overview of Mansfield's contribution to the English short story.

Daly, Saralyn R. *Katherine Mansfield.* Boston: Twayne, 1965. Daly offers careful, analytical discussions of the stories.

Fullbrook, Kate. *Katherine Mansfield.* Bloomington: Indiana University Press, 1986. Critical analyses of the major stories, including excellent discussions of "Je ne parle pas français" and "Bliss."

Magalaner, Marvin. *The Fiction of Katherine Mansfield.* Carbondale: Southern Illinois University Press, 1971. Critical analyses of the major stories, including excellent discussions of "Prelude" and "At the Bay."

Modern Fiction Studies (Autumn 1979). This issue was devoted to Mansfield and includes essays by leading scholars.

Nathan, Rhoda B. *Katherine Mansfield.* New York: Continuum, 1988. A critical introduction to Mansfield's works.

Tomalin, Claire. *Katherine Mansfield: A Secret Life.* New York: Knopf, 1988. A recent biography that offers a reinterpretation of Mansfield's life based on medical evidence.

Edward V. Geist
University of Bridgeport

PAULE MARSHALL
1929

Publishing History

Paule Marshall was born April 9, 1929, in Brooklyn to Barbadian parents who immigrated to New York after World War I. She graduated Phi Beta Kappa from Brooklyn College in 1953 and attended Hunter College in 1955. Marshall worked as a librarian and then as a staff writer for *Our World* magazine. Her work for *Our World* allowed her to travel throughout the Caribbean and Brazil, during which time she became reacquainted with her Barbadian and West Indian roots. In 1957 she married and moved to Barbados, and in 1959 she published her first novel, *Brown Girl, Brownstones*.

Since then she has lived for extended periods in the Caribbean, and her "Bajun" (Barbadian) heritage figures largely in her writings. *Soul Clap Hands and Sing*, a collection of four novellas, appeared in 1961. She published a second novel, *The Chosen Place, the Timeless People*, in 1969, and in 1983 published a third novel, *Praisesong for the Widow*, and a collection of short stories, *Reena and Other Stories*. Marshall has contributed essays and short stories to a number of journals and anthologies. Currently, she lectures and is a professor of African-American literature and creative writing at universities in the United States and abroad.

Critical Reception, Honors, and Popularity

Marshall's first two books garnered critical acclaim, earning her several honors during the 1960s, including a Guggenheim fellowship, the Rosenthal Award, grants from the Ford Foundation and the National Endowment for the Arts, and an award from the Yaddo Corporation. In 1984 she won the Before Columbus American Book Award for *Praisesong for the Widow*. In spite of critical acclaim, her works have not been commercially successful.

Brown Girl, Brownstones; Soul Clap Hands and Sing; and *The Chosen Place, the Timeless People* were out of print for several years; but because of renewed interest in her work, Marshall's books are again available. *Brown Girl, Brownstones* and *Reena and Other Stories* are published by Feminist Press, and *Soul Clap Hands and Sing* is available from Howard University Press. Recently, her works, as well as those of other African American women writers, are being read by a larger, more diverse audience.

Analysis of Selected Titles

BROWN GIRL, BROWNSTONES

Brown Girl, Brownstones, 1959, novel.

Social Concerns/Themes

Brown Girl, Brownstones has been described as a *bildungsroman* of a black female, and it is often compared to Zora Neale Hurston's *Their Eyes Were Watching God.* It is a novel of initiation that follows the life of Selina Boyce, as she grows up a first generation American, the daughter of Barbadian immigrants. As she matures, she struggles to resolve the conflict between succumbing to materialism and retaining the customs, rituals, and folkways of her parents' native land, Barbados. In developing this theme, Marshall contrasts "Bajun" with American culture, and immigrant with American culture, and seems less concerned with Selina Boyce's race than with her status as a first generation American. *Brown Girl, Brownstones* examines the corruption and loss of identity that accompanies the obsessive pursuit of property, in this case, an obsession to purchase brownstones. Cultural assimilation and financial security replace warmth and love, and real poverty is exchanged for spiritual poverty.

A second theme in the novel involves Selina's search for her identity as a woman and as a daughter of Barbadian immigrants. She must learn to transcend the stereotypes and repressive definitions of "woman" established by a patriarchal Caribbean community, as well as to carve out a meaningful place for herself in America.

Characters

The development of identity is at the core of *Brown Girl, Brownstones.* Through the eyes of Selina Boyce, the reader sees the struggles of her mother Silla and the women of her Barbadian Brooklyn neighborhood, which is the major setting of the novel. Deighton Boyce, Selina's father, represents a back-home-in-Barbados mentality, a kind of fantasy of spirit, gentleness, love, passion, and warmth. Silla comes to reflect a cold, unfeeling, competitive materialism, which is the face that America presents to the Bajan immigrant. Silla and Deighton's relationship embodies the extremes of the Barbadian immigrant experience in America. The old culture—and the old gender definitions—must be refashioned to suit a new life. Silla and her friends must find ways of coping with being disparaged as black, female, and foreign. Selina is pushed out into a large, hostile world and must find out who she is in order to make her way.

Techniques/Literary Precedents

Marshall pays homage to an oral storytelling tradition. In "Shaping the World of My Art," Marshall describes listening as a child to her mother and her mother's friends telling stories in the kitchen of their brownstone. Marshall calls these women the "kitchen poets" for their skillful use of language. Marshall learned early that the key to good storytelling is characterization, and in this novel, the simple linear plot turns on character portrayal. The drama and suspense in the narrative is married to the characters—especially Selina—and their search for identity. The language of Marshall's immigrants is indeed poetic, dramatic, and alive, and often leavened with irony and humor.

Defining oneself and establishing self autonomy is not new to literature nor to African-American letters, but Marshall's first novel is in a sense atypical in its portrayal of strong female protagonists. *Brown Girl, Brownstones* has been favorably compared with Zora Neale Hurston's *Their Eyes Were Watching God*, Dorothy West's *The Living Is Easy*, Nella Larsen's *Quicksand*, Ann Petry's *The Street*, as well as some of her drugstore fiction found in the *Miss Muriel and Other Stories* collection, and Gwendolyn Brooks' *Maud Martha*.

THE CHOSEN PLACE, THE TIMELESS PEOPLE

The Chosen Place, the Timeless People, 1969, novel.

Social Concerns/Themes

Identity, culture, and history are three elements which shape Marshall's second novel. It is set in the Bournehills area of Bourne Island, an imaginary island in the Caribbean that serves as a metaphor for the Third World. The inhabitants of Bournehills are largely uneducated, poor, and the descendants of slaves. But they are proud of their past and their independence, which was secured by an uprising led by Cuffee Ned. Bournehills remains poor, undeveloped, and seemingly frozen in time.

Various economic development projects have experimented with ways to "bring the people into the twentieth century," but these efforts invariably fail. These efforts to transform Bournehills symbolize the intrusion of the Western world, namely the U.S., which seeks to impose its own standards, ideals, and will on the inhabitants. They operate by throwing money at the "problem" with little regard for the people involved. The people of Bournehills endure by clinging to their heritage. They refuse to be influenced or reshaped by dollars and technology at the cost of giving up their identity, customs, and beliefs.

Marshall's main premise is that the history and heritage of a people must be accepted on its own terms, rather than dismantled to fuel "progress." A culture must be free to shape its own destiny. Otherwise, revolution like that led by Cuffee Ned may be the only resolution.

Characters

The major characters represent two conflicting forces in a struggle to control the world of the novel. On one side are the outsiders (or the people from "away" as referred to by the Bournehills residents), who include Saul Amron, the leader of a research team doing the advance work for a development project; Harriet, his wife; and Allan Fusso, statistician of the team. Harriet dispenses favors, does good deeds, and saves people—all with good intentions. But she fails to understand her underlying need to manipulate and control. She sees herself as improving the lot of the people, but mistakenly assumes that her value system is the only correct one. In this sense, she embodies an extreme presentation of the attitudes of industrialized countries toward the Third World.

The time-locked inhabitants of Bournehills are represented by Delbert, a rumshop owner and leader in Spiretown village; by Stinger, a cane cutter; by Leesy Walkes, an elderly widow; and by Vere Walkes, nephew of Leesy. All hold fast to the spirit of Cuffee Ned, which places independence and community above individual gain and materialism.

Perhaps the most interesting character of the novel is Merle Kinbona, who has lived in and been part of the Western world, but who is spiritually tied to Bournehills. Merle moves among the outsiders and among Bournehills blacks. Her private troubles reflect those of the Bournehills area, but she represents the possibility for change. As the story progresses, it becomes evident that Merle must heal the rift of worlds within herself. Only by confronting her own past and accepting it, can she hope to control her life and define her future.

Techniques/Literary Precedents

Characterization is the cohesive force of this novel. The development of the major characters, especially Merle Kinbona, moves the plot. The landscape and events blend with the characters to emphasize the interdependence of humans and their reliance on nature. Marshall employs extensive metaphors and draws analogies between the Bournehills landscape and the people. For example, Merle describes a cassia tree in her yard that appears dead. But when it seems time to cut it down, leaves appear and it flourishes anew. Roads always disappear; the waves are described as mourning for those of the diaspora drowned in the ocean or who died as slaves. The abuse of the environment parallels the abuse and oppression of the Bournehills residents.

Linking nature and characters in fiction or utilizing the landscape to reflect cultural or political themes is not new. But Marshall's mastery of the technique, coupled with her portrayal of black women as beings of integrity, is a credit to the tradition of African-American women writers, particularly Zora Neale Hurston. Hurston's famous pear tree scene in *Their Eyes Were Watching God* is perhaps the best example of blending nature, character, and theme.

PRAISESONG FOR THE WIDOW
Praisesong for the Widow, 1983, novel.

Social Concerns/Themes
Praisesong for the Widow addresses the African diaspora and the plight of the African American in the struggle with what W. E. B. DuBois called "double consciousness"—an attempt to merge the dominant Eurocentric culture with an awareness of African origins and culture. Avey Johnson, the protagonist in this novel, experiences the pain of an empty life complicated by the notion that she must cut all ties to an African heritage or black American culture to be happy. She aches and doesn't know why. She suffers in part from double consciousness.

Avey Johnson embraces an American materialism but begins to lose her passion for life. Avey and her husband, Jerome, believe that they must discard every vestige of their past life of poverty in Harlem—listening to gospels, dancing to jazz and blues, going on picnics and boat rides on the Hudson with the other black folks—to prove themselves worthy of living in middle-class North White Plains. They are painfully trying to expunge the essence of their African heritage in order to "fit in."

As a child, Avey spent each summer in the South with an aunt who took her ritually to a place called Ibo Landing. There the aunt told her the story of slaves who walked across the Atlantic back to Africa. Avey's Aunt Cuney also taught her other pieces of an African connection, such as the Ring Shout. She insists that "Avey" use her real name—Avatara—because a nickname hearkens back to the attitudes of slavery when humans were property. A nickname was a way of dehumanizing Africans, as when Kunta Kinte became "Toby," and was treated like a cow or a dog.

Avey, who is recently widowed, embarks on a summer trip to the Caribbean island, Carriacou, where she begins to find the strength to heal, to unite her past and present, and to find her roots in the African diaspora. Here, Avey recalls Ibo Landing and the myth attached, and makes her connection to Africa—a connection that resolves the major conflict of the novel. Avey finds her true identity and cures the disease of double consciousness, by renewing her connection to the larger black world and her African roots.

Characters

Praisesong for the Widow is Avey's story. In her mid-sixties, Avey has spent a lifetime trying to come to terms with the world and her place in it. The struggle to affluence which killed her husband, Jerome, also alienated them from the African-American community. Two of Avey's three daughters, Sis and Anawilda, are so materialistic and divorced from their roots that they are not aware of the missing piece of their identity.

During Avey's childhood, Aunt Cuney was the keeper of traditions and culture, like the musicians and storytellers of her African ancestors. But only when Avey makes the pilgrimage to Carriacou does she find the kind of guide and teacher she had in Aunt Cuney in the person of Lebert Joseph. Both Aunt Cuney and Lebert Joseph point Avey in the right direction, alternately through relating myths, by example, and by antagonism. Both characters are sometimes mystical and always symbolic of the life force that becomes central to Avey's being: Africa.

Techniques/Literary Precedents

Character development is the most outstanding feature of the novel. Flashbacks are used to show Avey's connection to the past and her heritage, and they also move the narrative. Flashbacks reveal the pieces of time and experience Avey needs to draw on and use to heal herself and to use in the future when she follows in the footsteps of Aunt Cuney and passes on the lessons of identity to her grandchildren.

Relation to Previous Works

During a conference of the Zora Neale Hurston Society, Marshall said that she writes in an effort to answer questions such as, how does a black woman writer survive in this republic? The answer is in part that Marshall, like the female characters she creates from Selina to Avey, must understand and define herself through the larger black world of the West Indies, Africa, and the Diaspora. Women are at the heart of Marshall's fiction. They emerge as healers of the spirit and as cultural guardians. In this sense, *Praisesong for the Widow* is the culmination of the themes of Marshall's previous novels. Selina in *Brown Girl, Brownstones* seeks a new identity that Merle finds in *The Chosen Place, the Timeless People*. In this third novel, Marshall reveals through Avey the inner strength of how she has become firmly grounded in her African heritage.

Other Titles
Soul Clap Hands and Sing, 1961 (novellas); "The Negro Woman in American Literature," *Freedomways*, 1966 (essay); "Shaping the World of My Art" in *New Letters*, 1973 (essay); "Some Get Wasted" in *Harlem, USA*, 1974 (short story); *Reena and Other Stories*, 1983 (short stories).

Additional Sources
Braithwaite, Edward. "West Indian History and Society in the Art of Paule Marshall's Fiction." *Journal of Black Studies* 1 (December 1970): 225-238. An approach to *The Chosen Place, the Timeless People* in which the resolution of the problems raised by the novel will be found only through self discovery as revealed by ethnic history.

Brown, Lloyd W. "The Rhythms of Power in Paule Marshall's Fiction." *Novel* 7 (Winter 1974): 159-167. Discusses themes of Pan Africanism and sexual politics in Marshall's short stories and novels.

Callaloo 18, 6 (Spring-Summer 1983). Contains a special section on Marshall which begins with an excerpt from her "From the Poets of the Kitchen," and continues with essays on the early short fiction, and concludes with an analysis of *Brown Girl, Brownstones, The Chosen Place, the Timeless People*, and *Praisesong for the Widow*.

Christian, Barbara. "Sculpture and Space: The Interdependence of Character and Culture in the Novels of Paule Marshall." In *Black Women Novelists—The Development of a Tradition, 1892-1976*. Westport, CT: Greenwood Press, 1980. Excellent treatment of culture, gender, and sexual politics in *Brown Girl, Brownstones*.

———. "Paule Marshall." In *Dictionary of Literary Biography, Afro-American Fiction Writers After 1955*, edited by Thadious M. Davis and Trudier Harris. Detroit: Gale Research, 1984. Best short reference on Marshall.

Cook, John. "Whose Child? the Fiction of Paule Marshall." *CLA Journal* 24 (September 1980): 1-15. Marshall's work is characterized by a "search for a political perspective," discussions of politics of culture, and the use of myth.

Kapai, Leela. "Dominant Themes and Techniques in Paule Marshall's Fiction." *CLA Journal* 16 (September 1972): 49-59. Discusses the themes of race, gender, and African-American heritage in *Brown Girl, Brownstones,* and *The Chosen Place, the Timeless People*, based in part on notes supplied by Marshall.

McCluskey, John, Jr. "And Called Every Generation Blessed: Theme, Setting, and Ritual in the Works of Paule Marshall." In *Black Women Writers, 1950-1980*, edited by Mari Evans. New York: Doubleday, 1984. Discusses the sociopolitical and sociocultural issues, the use of setting, the "interplay of individual and collective history" in Marshall's fiction.

Washington, Mary Helen. "Black Women Image Makers." *Black World* 23 (August 1974): 10-18. Discusses Marshall's "Reena" and the title character as representative of a black middle-class woman.

———, ed. *Black-Eyed Susans/Midnight Birds*. New York: Anchor/Doubleday, 1990. Introduction to Marshall's short story, "Reena," which is included in this collection of stories by and about black women. Contains useful comments referring to the theme of cultural identity and the role of the African-American female.

Muriel W. Brailey
Wilberforce University

BOBBIE ANN MASON
1940

Publishing History

Bobbie Ann Mason's imaginative vision is firmly rooted in working-class America, particularly the experience of provincial American life as it is increasingly shaped by shopping malls, television, fast food, and popular music. In her own adolescence, Mason was a devoted fan of the Hilltoppers, a Kentucky pop quartet, and as the president and chief publicist for the Hilltoppers' Fan Club, she first became acquainted with the allure of popular culture and its impact.

It was, however, at the University of Kentucky that Mason developed an interest in literature, particularly Ernest Hemingway, F. Scott Fitzgerald, J. D. Salinger, and Thomas Wolfe. After receiving her degree in 1962, Mason moved to New York, where she worked for a year as a staff writer for various movie and television fan magazines. Mason gave up popular journalism to return to the State University of New York at Binghamton, where she received her master's degree in 1966. Mason began studies toward her doctorate at the University of Connecticut in the following year, and in 1969 she married fellow graduate student, Roger B. Rawlings.

Mason received a doctorate in 1972 for a dissertation on Vladimir Nabokov's *Ada*. Her thesis was subsequently turned into her first book, entitled *Nabokov's Garden: A Nature Guide to "Ada"* published by Ardis in 1974. She then turned her critical attention to the popular narratives of her youth, and one year later published a study of books for young girls, entitled *The Girl Sleuth: Feminist Guide to the Bobbsey Twins, Nancy Drew, and Their Sisters*. Although this critical study foreshadows her later fictional explorations of the impact of popular culture on American life, Mason did not begin to write fiction until the late 1970s. By her own count, her twentieth short story, "Offerings," was accepted for publication by *The New Yorker*, and it appeared in the magazine in February of 1980. Despite her relatively late arrival on the literary scene, Mason soon experienced a flood of critical success. Her 1982 collection of short stories, *Shiloh and Other Stories*, received considerable critical acclaim, and her first novel, *In Country* (1985) was both a commercial as well as a critical success. Her most recent novel, *Spence + Lila*, was published in 1988; that has been followed by a second collection of short stories, *Love Life*, published in 1989.

Critical Reception, Honors, and Popularity

Although many of its stories had been published previously in magazines, *Shiloh and Other Stories* established Mason's reputation as a writer of national prominence. Nominated for the National Book Critics Circle Award and the American Book Award, it won the Ernest Hemingway Foundation Award in 1983. The same year, Mason received a National Endowment for the Arts fellowship and a Pennsylvania Arts Council grant, and in 1984 she was the recipient of a Guggenheim fellowship. The enthusiastic response to her regional realism encouraged a sizable investment by her publisher in her 1985 first novel, *In Country*. The first printing ran to over forty thousand copies, and was matched by a $40,000 advertising campaign, a movie option, offers to acquire foreign rights, and selection by the Book-of-the-Month Club. While many critics have drawn attention to the limited range and development in Mason's novel, her work has been celebrated as an example of the revival of realistic writing in America and of the infusion of contemporary popular culture and its characteristic preoccupations into serious American literature.

Analysis of Selected Titles

SHILOH AND OTHER STORIES

Shiloh and Other Stories, 1982, short stories.

Social Concerns/Themes

Typical of realistic writing generally, Mason's first collection of short stories is strongly oriented toward documenting the social lives of her characters. In Mason's version of life in western Kentucky, these concerns are predominantly economic and familial. On the one hand, Mason demonstrates at great length the disjunction between the limited horizons of predominantly rural Kentucky life and the world of television and consumer culture with which it collides. This generates one of Mason's often repeated themes, that of the person who desires to flee a constraining environment. On the other hand, she also asserts the powerful pull of familial connections upon these often frustrated individuals.

The emotional world of Mason's fiction is one that is governed frequently by disappointment, compromise, divorce, and diminished expectations. This, however, is principally true of those figures who grew up under the shadow of the end of provincial life and the arrival of mainstream America in western Kentucky. Typically, they have factory jobs in an increasingly threatened industrial base, or they pursue a living on the low-paying fringes of commercial life. The older generation, frequently rural and seemingly innocent of or indifferent to the contemporary world, is the source of familial affiliations, and many of Mason's female characters find themselves torn between the roles of daughter and independent woman in a transformed social world.

The female characters are also usually the focus of the narration, and her work is in this respect characteristic of recent women's fiction in America. But what is perhaps distinctive about Mason's fiction is her singular preoccupation with popular culture. Her frequent references to television programs, popular music, brand names, and fads is used to suggest the limitations of the characters she explores, but it is also a means of demonstrating the emotional sophistication of the responses and the wit of her characters, who exploit this range of references often as an ironic counterpoint to and commentary upon their lives.

Characters

The title story of the collection is typical of the development of Mason's characters throughout the volume. In "Shiloh," LeRoy Moffit has suffered a leg injury which has curtailed his career as a truck driver. He and his wife, Norma Jean, live in a small, nondescript house in Kentucky, while he pursues dreams of building a log cabin for himself and his wife. Norma Jean embarks on a course of self-improvement, pursuing programs in everything from physical fitness to English composition. Like many of Mason's characters, Norma Jean's aspirations for individual development appear somewhat naive and limited; however, they do have real consequences.

Norma Jean's mother has constantly urged Norma Jean and Leroy to visit the Civil War battlefield at Shiloh, the site of her own honeymoon, and when they do visit the site, partly to escape from their own disintegrating relationship, Norma Jean announces that she is leaving Leroy. Typical of Mason's characters, this breakdown seems both inevitable and pathetic. Neither is able to grow in the present circumstances, yet Leroy is unable to formulate the means to make their relationship a ground for real individual development.

Much the same dilemma is faced by the older couple Mary Lou and Mack Skaggs in "Rookers." While Mary Lou plays cards with older women friends and socializes in town, Mack stays home with the woodworking projects that are both his livelihood and his refuge from the world. He tries to read to keep up with their daughter who is away at college, but when she comes home before her exams, Mack is largely unable to communicate with her. This attitude is best captured at the end of the story by his telephone calls to the weather recording, which allows him to feign communication without speaking.

This sense of estrangement also characterizes Mason's women. The young girl, Peggy Jo, in "Detroit Skyline," visits her aunt and uncle in Detroit with her mother shortly after the introduction of television in America. During this visit her mother suffers a miscarriage, while Peggy Jo learns of the nascent world of television and about the "red scare" that is worrying her uncle and jeopardizing his job. For Peggy Jo, the promise of Detroit's skyline seems both alluring and threatening, and her experiences are very distant from her home in Kentucky.

Much the same distance is described in "Drawing Names," when Carolyn Sisson attends a Christmas dinner with her family. She and her sisters try to maintain a sense of familial harmony, but this often means placating their husbands or boyfriends, and Carolyn's own lover, Kent, fails to show up for the occasion. Most difficult of all are Carolyn's father and Pappy, her mother's father. Carolyn ultimately elicits a compassionate response from Jim, the man living with her sister, Laura Jean, whose presence at this family dinner is not entirely well received, particularly by the other men. Jim's outsider status as a northerner and as someone who is morally suspect in this conservative family gives him insight into Carolyn's feelings of alienation. And although Carolyn feels closer to Jim at the end of the story and somewhat free of her family's often oppressive judgments, her estrangement from this supposed harmony is not diminished.

In the story "Nancy Culpepper," the title character searches for a photo of her namesake great-great-aunt, and this search becomes emblematic of a larger attempt to connect herself to her ancestors. She, like other female figures in Mason's work, feels distanced from her family, but Nancy's distance has been caused by her move to the North and her advanced education.

On the whole, Mason's stories depict characters who are experiencing both a transformation of the family and a dissolution of the ways of economic life that had traditionally defined their families. Within this context, they are forced to establish a separate identity to achieve reconciliations, however temporary, with their lovers, parents, and siblings.

Techniques

Mason's fiction has been described by one reviewer as "shopping mall realism," and one of its most conspicuous achievements is its overall appearance of artlessness. This avoidance of obvious stylization is consistent with the aspiration of a realistic writer to present fiction as an accurate and faithful transcription of the real world, not as an elaborate and contrived story. To substantiate this claim to authenticity, Mason dwells upon the circumstantial details of the experience she describes, and this is particularly true of her use of popular culture. In contrast to those writers who depend upon references to other literary works to give their texts resonance, Mason relies upon popular culture as source of many of her allusions. For example, Norma Jean of "Shiloh," as the narrator notes, bears the real first names of Marilyn Monroe.

Shiloh and Other Stories belongs to the literary tradition of the related short story series. James Joyce's *Dubliners* is a good example of such a text, but much closer to Mason is Ernest Hemingway's first book of short stories, *In Our Time*. With respect to her contemporaries, Mason is squarely within the tradition of recent American minimalist writing, and one might compare *Shiloh and Other Stories* with the similar collection by Raymond Carver, *Cathedral*.

Related Titles

While *Shiloh and Other Stories* might be said to anticipate much of Mason's subsequent fiction in its thematic concerns and technical strategies, at least one story foreshadows a subsequent work. The Culpepper family is the subject of Mason's second novel *Spence + Lila*, which is in many a ways a metaphoric extension of the events outlined in Mason's story, "Nancy Culpepper."

IN COUNTRY

In Country, 1985, novel.

Social Concerns/Themes

Mason's first novel, *In Country*, belongs to the growing body of recent American fiction dealing with the events and aftermath of the Vietnam War. Unlike many of those novels and memoirs, Mason's fiction is told not from the perspective of a direct participant or even an eye witness to the period, but from the perspective of the daughter of a soldier killed during the height of the war in 1967. Samantha Hughes, better known as "Sam," devotes herself to the attempt to discover something of her father's experience, but she finally uncovers in large part only the distance that separates her from the motives and experiences of the Vietnam era. In this novel, Mason confronts Vietnam largely as an incomprehensible experience for the people of Kentucky generally, who found the political turmoil at home and the repudiation of traditional values beyond assimilation. Throughout the novel Sam is told again and again of the bewilderment both of the people who went to Vietnam and of those who stayed at home.

In addition to exploring the impact of the Vietnam War upon provincial America, *In Country* examines the themes of initiation and Sam's psychosexual fascination with her absent father. Like many of Mason's characters, Sam resides in a fragmented familial situation and is struggling to overcome emotional estrangement. At the same time, the process of emotional identification is filtered through popular culture, in particular America's fascination with Vietnam in its various guises, whether it be the television displacement of Vietnam into Korea in M*A*S*H or the critical nostalgia of Bruce Springsteen's song "Born in the U.S.A."

In its preoccupation with history and its impact upon western Kentucky, *In Country* might be Mason's most socially concerned fiction, and, in its documentation of Sam's initiation, perhaps the most representative Mason narrative.

Characters

Mason's novel focuses on Samantha and her quest to discover herself and her relation to her deceased father. Sam graduates from high school in 1984 and spends the summer considering her possibilities—going off to college or marrying her boyfriend. Unable to fix positively on the course for her own future, she lives with her uncle, Emmett, who has suffered physically and mentally as a consequence of his combat experiences in Vietnam. Emmett has a continuing problem with acne and experiences headaches and stomach pains, all signs, Sam believes, of Agent Orange poisoning, and he refuses to participate fully in mainstream economic life.

Sam's mother has moved to Lexington with her new husband and her infant child, and Sam's own decision to remain in Hopewell is a sign of her attachment to her father and to a familial possibility erased by his death. Sam's mother is realistic about the past and discourages her from probing into the culture of the Vietnam era, which she remembers as being a painful and disturbing time. Sam, however, persists through her relationship with another veteran in Hopewell. At a crucial point she retreats to Cawood's Pond where she attempts to recreate the experience of being out in a remote jungle position in Vietnam, but this effort largely fails. It is only when Sam and Emmett travel with her father's mother to Washington to the Vietnam Memorial that she experiences a moment of reconciliation. Here she finds her father's name and, curiously enough, also the name of a "Sam Hughes," and here Emmett begins to come to terms with the experiences that he has evaded for so long. While in many respects, Mason's novel emphasizes the ways in which historical experience escapes us, it also suggests the possibility of overcoming our emotional distance from the past.

Techniques/Literary Precedents

Mason draws upon the literature that has emerged from the Vietnam War to provide the circumstantial detail in her novel. For example, Mark Baker's 1981 collection of interviews with Vietnam veterans, entitled *NAM*, provides the source for at least one military anecdote in *In Country*. Mason's use of Dwayne's journal, her imitation of a soldier's combat journal, is similarly designed to render an authentic image of the Vietnam War. But Mason is not so much concerned with presenting the actual war experience, as with the perception and impact of that experience in provincial America. In this respect *In Country* is very different from most fiction that discusses the war, such as Robert Stone's *Dog Soldiers* or Norman Mailer's *Why Are We in Vietnam?*; Mason's novel is primarily concerned with America and American attitudes.

In terms of its narrative structure, *In Country* might best be described as a novel of initiation. Sam's quest to understand her father is also an attempt to understand her own identity, and the relation between daughter and absent father here is one which invites a feminist reading of the psychosexual aspects of Sam's development.

Related Titles

In Country is very much part of the same imaginative landscape that Mason first explored in *Shiloh and Other Stories*. The concern here with female initiation and history is most closely connected to the title story from the earlier collection and tales such as "Detroit Skyline, 1949" and "Nancy Culpepper."

Adaptations

In Country was made into a very successful 1989 film for Warner Brothers. It was directed by Norman Jewison and starred Emily Lloyd and Bruce Willis, as Emmett.

SPENCE + LILA

Spence + Lila, 1989, novel.

Social Concerns/Themes

In her second novel, Mason returns again to western Kentucky and to the Culpepper family, the subject of her earlier story, "Nancy Culpepper." In this narrative, however, the focus is not on Nancy, but upon the family dynamic and particularly the role and character of her mother Lila. Unlike *In Country, Spence + Lila* is not explicitly concerned with the wider social world, except as it intrudes upon life in Kentucky. Here Mason demonstrates the ground for a continuing familial sense of optimism, despite the threats of mortality and generational distances.

Characters

Spence + Lila is the most sentimental of Mason's works, and it might appear to confirm the suggestion that Mason often portrays her Kentucky figures so sympathetically that they become somewhat naive and insubstantial. However, what saves this novel from empty sentimentality is the figure of Lila, who must endure a mastectomy and at the same time continue, even from her hospital bed, the nurturing role that brings together her three children and her husband, Spence. Lila is by turns bawdy and reserved, but perhaps her greatest virtue is her tolerance for life in all its myriad forms. It is no accident, for example, that after her return from the hospital, her first act is to tend her garden.

Spence, her husband, is a taciturn farmer, who is at the same time largely a vegetarian and a fan of rock and roll music. Spence's affection for his wife is shown through his teasing and often clumsy gestures, which act both as a screen and a release for his emotions. Like his wife, Spence is tolerant of the very different lives of his children, but like Lila, he frequently worries over their precarious emotional and economic circumstances.

Each of the three Culpepper children is deeply concerned with their parents and the health of Lila, but each responds in a characteristic way. Nancy, the most audacious of the three, is critical both of the treatment that her mother receives from her doctors and the hospital staff and of what she considers to be the unhealthy lifestyle of her parents, particularly their diet and her mother's smoking habit. Cat, on the other hand, is much more sympathetic to her parents, in part because she herself has remained in Kentucky. Estranged from her husband, she nonetheless shares her mother's intuitive understanding of human nature, and her first response to any situation is generally one of tolerance and compassion.

Though their dispositions are very different, the Culpepper daughters are in turn very different from their brother, Lee. The Culpepper son resembles his father in his emotional reticence, but unlike his father he is fully immersed in the need to survive economically. He frequently works overtime in order to pay his mortgage and to support his family in town, and while his concern is real, he is perhaps most distant from the other family members.

Techniques/Literary Precedents
Spence + Lila continues in the realistic tradition of Mason's earlier fiction, but in its efforts to chronicle the triumph of Lila's compassion over threats to her own health and to the emotional stability of her family, this novel might well be compared with the recent tradition of familial fiction, perhaps best exemplified in the work of Anne Tyler.

Related Titles
By returning to the Culpepper family in this novel, Mason invites comparison with her earlier portrait of this family in *Shiloh and Other Stories*. But this novel also recalls Mason's other explorations of the dynamics of marriage and familial affection in "The Rookers" and "Drawing Names." More than *In Country*, *Spence + Lila* is a direct extension of the fictional world first represented in *Shiloh and Other Stories*.

Other Titles
Nabokov's Garden: A Guide to "Ada," 1974 (literary criticism); *The Girl Sleuth: A Feminist Guide*, 1975 (literary criticism); *Love Life*, 1989 (short stories).

Additional Sources
Brinkmeyer, Robert H. Jr. "Finding One's History: Bobbie Ann Mason and Contemporary Southern Literature." *Southern Literary Journal* 19 (Spring 1987): 22-33. Considers *In Country* in the context of southern history and the Vietnam War.

White, Leslie. "The Function of Popular Culture in Bobbie Ann Mason's *Shiloh and Other Stories* and *In Country*." *The Southern Quarterly* 26 (Summer 1988): 69-79. Good discussion of popular culture, particularly in *Shiloh and Other Stories*.

Wilhelm, Albert E. "Making Over or Making Off: The Problem of Identity in Bobbie Ann Mason's Short Fiction." *Southern Literary Journal* 18 (Spring 1986):

76-82. Considers the difficulties of individual identity and the problem of self in early stories.

―――――. "Private Rituals: Coping With Change in the Fiction of Bobbie Ann Mason." *Midwest Quarterly* 28 (Winter 1987): 271-282. Studies the role of initiation in Mason's fiction.

Thomas Carmichael
University of Western Ontario

PETER MATTHIESSEN
1927

Update

In 1989 Random House published Peter Matthiessen's collection *On the River Styx and Other Stories*. Although most of the fictions in this volume appeared in the chapbook *Midnight Turning Gray* (1986) and are, for the most part, reprints of work originally published in the 1950s and 1960s, Matthiessen's virtuosity as a prose stylist is apparent in the two newer stories included. They demonstrate, as well, his continuing thematic focus on the intersections of competing cultures. Random House has also reissued all of Matthiessen's early novels in a uniform series of Vintage paperbacks—perhaps as a prelude to the 1990 publication of *Killing Mister Watson*, Matthiessen's first novel in fifteen years, and his most ambitious. A film version of *At Play in the Fields of the Lord*, for which Matthiessen collaborated in writing the screenplay with director Hector Babenco, began filming in the fall of 1990, with an anticipated release date of 1991.

Analysis of Selected Titles

KILLING MISTER WATSON
Killing Mister Watson, 1990, novel.

Social Concerns/Themes

Matthiessen's persistent concern with a primitive landscape bearing the incursion of white "civilization" is re-presented in *Killing Mister Watson*. However, instead of displacing this fundamental conflict to South America or the Caribbean, Matthiessen sets it in America, on the west coast of the Florida Everglades. It is here, among the "dark mangrove walls closing out the world, with the empty Everglades to eastward where the sun rose, and that empty Gulf out to the west where the sun set, the silence and miskeeters and the loneliness," that Matthiessen locates his chronicle of the life and death of Edgar J. Watson—farmer, businessman, and outlaw gunman.

Matthiessen has at times been criticized for his tendency to posit the superiority of the primitive over the civilized, but in *Killing Mister Watson* there is no "primitive" who receives unalloyed praise. These "frontiersmen" of the Everglades are themselves hanging on tenuously to the American continent, and are thus already infused with the values of American civilization, for better or worse. Indeed, a recurrent subject of meditation for the narrators is the question of how much white blood someone has, and in what mixture with what other strains. Even though Sarah Hamilton, one of the narrators, remarks that "this whole darn foolishness of blood will be the ruin of this country," she too proceeds to catalogue her forebears and their nationality. It is as though Matthiessen acknowledges here America's inability to escape this essential concern with racial purity, regardless of its impertinence. The enemy, finally, is shown to be as much within us as without: the Everglades and its wildlife are threatened both by the plume hunting of the settlers, which destroys vast heron rookeries, and by half-baked ideas to dredge the swamps or build a road across the Florida peninsula.

Matthiessen has remarked in a television interview that Watson, the shifting center of this novel, can be seen as "a metaphor for the violence of the frontier." If so, that "frontier" is simultaneously the geographical edge of the continent, the intersection of civilization and its opposite, and a frontier of morality in both the individual and community. With the same clarity that the reader sees Watson recede, attention is drawn to Matthiessen's chief focus, highlighted in the novel's title. The book is an exploration not so much of Watson or his actions, but of the act of killing him—a communal act defying any clear ascription of agency, an act even the description of which is multiple and various.

Certainly, the novel draws attention to that particularly American tendency to celebrate its desperadoes even as it despises and fears them, but it also compels one to consider an even more desperate position, where individual responsibility for a collective act of violence is evaded by recourse to recapitulation and myth. As Matthiessen himself notes, his story is drawn from "a mix of rumor, gossip, tale, and legend that has evolved over eight decades into myth." It is this human propensity for myth-making, for the remaking of "history" as fiction, that takes center stage in the novel and reveals a murkiness of motive and morality at the center of things that rivals Watson's persona in desperation and menace. When one man's final verdict on the reasons for killing Mr. Watson comes down to "folks just got tired of him, I guess," something has gone very wrong.

Characters

Killing Mister Watson is narrated by a potpourri of characters—ten in all, plus a fictionalized "historian"—who act in the "story" they relate but also stand outside as commentators and reflectors. They include Henry Thompson, Watson's foreman and devoted surrogate son; Richard Hamilton, a Calusa Indian midwife and patriarch of one of the county's most prolific families; Bill House, one of

Watson's executioners; and Carrie Watson, his daughter, who exhibits changing perceptions and loyalties, and is an exemplar of an ineffective and well-dressed feminine morality. In these narrators, Matthiessen has assembled a cast who, through a series of narrative "interviews," provide access points into the multiplicities of the Watson legend. Along with those who speak directly, the reader is also introduced to a community of coastal farmers, hunters, and fishermen, and a ragbag of oddball types who give depth to the fictional construct. These range from Jean Chevalier the eccentric French ornithologist, treasure hunter, and cynic, to Hannah Smith, a "wild woman" who hacks her way clear across the Everglades only to be murdered on Watson's plantation.

To an extent, this varied cast provides a typology of character that exemplifies strains of the novel's thematics—Hamilton the Indian sage, Jim Cole the small town politico, Frank B. Tippins the resolute lawman, Mamie Smallwood the storekeeper's durable wife—yet the trajectory of the narrations moves the reader farther away from any sense of certainty as to what events actually took place amid the "thousand islands" of the Everglades. Instead, these voices reveal only the intricacies of self-interest and self-justification. Although many of the characters are striking in their evocation, any attempt to privilege one of their voices over another ends in futility; each is subsumed by the ensemble. They are in a sense less characters than eyes, variously trained on the variability that is E. J. Watson.

Techniques/Literary Precedents

By cancelling as much as possible the authorial presence and giving over the act of narrating entirely to objectified others, Matthiessen's novel gives the lie to conventional notions of univocal historical truth, substituting a choir of competing voices in its stead. The collection of interview transcripts, diaries, news clippings and historical records that constitutes the novel gives Matthiessen an opportunity to display his formidable powers as a stylist and his unerring ear for the nuances of voice—talents always in evidence in his work, but never more superbly executed. But Matthiessen does not employ stylistic brilliance for its own sake; indeed, coming to grips with the formal innovations of *Killing Mister Watson* is crucial for an understanding of the novel's themes.

Comparisons of this novel to the work of earlier writers—the social criticism of Sinclair Lewis, for example, or the evocation of the humid moral wasteland of Joseph Conrad—were made in the earliest reviews of the book, and will no doubt continue. In addition to these, *Killing Mister Watson* shows striking similarities to William Faulkner's *Absalom, Absalom!* (1936). Like Faulkner's Thomas Sutpen, E. J. Watson comes from nowhere to raise a plantation from the swamps; both are of dubious character but express undeniable physical and psychological force. Even the absenting of Henry Sutpen and the debacle of Judith's wedding in *Absalom, Absalom!* find parallels in Matthiessen's novel. But, while *Absalom, Absalom!* also explores the multiple points of view that make up history and the power of that history's hold upon its survivors and interpreters, Faulkner retains through his novel's diffusion of voices the characteristic and immediately recognizable Faulknerian style. Matthiessen, conversely, goes one step further, thoroughly fragmenting his voice into a multiplicity of styles that dissolve a fixed center of reference altogether.

Relation to Previous Works

Besides the connections to the other Matthiessen works that have already been noted, the novel's investigation of "evil" and focus on the individual and community response to that evil echoes themes explored in *At Play in the Fields of the Lord*. In technique, Matthiessen continues the fragmentation of voices and points of view found in *Far Tortuga*. In spite of these similarities, *Killing Mister Watson* is a major advance for Matthiessen; in complexity and maturity, both thematic and formal, the novel goes far beyond his previous work and is an achievement of great originality. Perhaps the most pertinent connection to his previous work lies simply in the recurrence of Matthiessen's boldness of vision.

Additional Sources

Bawer, Bruce. "Nature Boy: The Novels of Peter Matthiessen." *The New Criterion* 6, 10 (June 1988): 32-40. Simplistic and ultimately reductive reading of Matthiessen's fiction.

Bonetti, Kay. "An Interview with Peter Matthiessen." *The Missouri Review* 12, 2 (1989): 109-124. Interesting interview wherein Matthiessen surveys his major works and themes, and comments on his compositional processes. Also available as part of the American Audio Prose Library Series.

George Bishop
D'Youville College

ANNE MCCAFFREY
1926

Update

During 1985 and 1986 Anne McCaffrey was quietly adding more novels to her Pern series and creating other works of science fiction—her strongest medium. Also during this time many of her romances and non-science fiction novels were reissued, including *The Kilternan Legacy*, *The Mark of Merlin*, and *The Ring of Fear*. She also produced new romances, including *Stitch in the Snow* (1984), *The Year of the Lucy* (1986), and *The Lady* (1987). Generally, these novels are based in Ireland and have gothic or mystery elements.

In 1987 an illustrated edition of McCaffrey's science-fiction novella, *The Coelura*, was issued. That same year *Killashandra* won the Science Fiction Book Club's first annual award, based on club selections. As a testament to McCaffrey's established niche as a creator of a believable science-fiction world, in 1987 Jody Lynn Nye, author of *The Dragonlover's Guide to Pern*, published *Dragonharper*, the first non-McCaffrey novel based on the Dragonriders of Pern.

In 1988 McCaffrey's two Pern novels which focused on women, *Moreta: Dragonlady of Pern* (1983) and *Nerilka's Story* (1986), were released as audio recordings. McCaffrey herself reads *Nerilka's Story* and is credited with animating the personality of Nerilka. Also, Robin Wood, in collaboration with McCaffrey, published *The People of Pern* (1988), a rendering of over sixty portraits of characters from the Pern series.

In 1989 McCaffrey's newest addition to the Pern collection, *Dragonsdawn*, spent three months on the *New York Times* bestseller list. She followed this in 1989, with *The Renegades of Pern*. McCaffrey also collaborated with Elizabeth Moon to produce the first volume of the Planet Pirate series, *Sassinak* (1990), which was quickly followed by a second volume, *The Death of Sleep* (1990). McCaffrey has continued to produce novels centering on psionics and parapsychic research occuring in the future, including *Pegasus in Flight* (1990) and *The Rowen* (1990).

McCaffrey has continually offered to her readers a practical author's note: "I have green eyes, silver hair, and freckles—the rest changes without notice." Probably the best news, then, for McCaffrey readers is the publication of her three-volume autobiography (1991). McCaffrey attributes her success in writing science fiction to high expectations set for her by her mother, who also serves as the model for McCaffrey's strong female characters.

Analysis of Selected Titles

DRAGONSDAWN

Dragonsdawn, 1988, novel.

Social Concerns/Themes

Dragonsdawn shows McCaffrey's timely awareness of social issues. The colonists of Pern are doing what some of McCaffrey's readers would like to do: get away from Earth, forget the past, and start over. While the Earth and its colonies have advanced to become the Federated Sentient Planets (FSP), Earth's principal problems are old and familiar: a pollution-plagued environment, and rule by a technocratic bureaucracy. Since Pern is too far from Earth to be commercially exploited, the colonists establish an agriculturally-based economy, with a minimal, localized political structure.

Concern for the planet's ecology plays a large part in all decisions affecting the survival of the colony. The colonists bring many animals, plants and microorganisms from Earth, and biologists and genetic engineers help with integration and adaptation to Pern's ecology. Grazing animals are genetically altered to digest Pern's grasses. Metasynth dolphins, altered to communicate mentally with fishermen, are introduced. Scientists carry out genetic alterations on indigenous life forms to combat Thread. A geneticist creates the flaming dragons from the fire lizards, and a biologist shapes the grubs which eat ground-burrowing Thread.

The colonists acknowledge that they will be exchanging their technological lifestyle for a basic, if not feudal, existence. Most of them willingly make that trade—preserving the environment while maximizing their intelligence, integrity, and resourcefulness. This reliance on human resources also encourages greater racial and cultural integration, and colonists of all ethnic and minority groups are valued equally as they shape Pern's culture and environment.

Characters

In accordance with McCaffrey's environmental theme, the principal "character" is Pern itself. The novel opens with the sending of mobile probes down to the planet's surface to study its complex ecosystems to plan for the impact of Earth biology on Pern.

McCaffrey pairs the main human characters in the novel, either linking them as companions or using them as foils in illustrating aspects of Pern society. The first dyad is Admiral Paul Benden and Governor Emily Boll. Strong leaders in the FSP and the only characters that retain their former titles, they are united in their desire to forget their past sacrifices to a dying system, in their mutual respect for each other's strength, and in their hope to see the Pern colony prosper. While Benden and Boll are not official leaders in Landing (the first settlement), in emergencies the colonists look to them for guidance.

The second pair is Sorka Hanrahan and Sean Connell. These two are Irish children; Sean is from a tinker family and Sorka is from a middle-class family (her father is a veterinarian, her mother is a child-care professional). Both children exhibit the sharp-wittedness and sense of unity that will promote the survival of Pern. Sean and Sorka grow up together, marry, and share a love for animals, particularly horses. McCaffrey grooms them to be Pern's first dragonriders and future leaders.

In the third dyad, McCaffrey contrasts Sallah Telgar and Avril Bitra, doubling the impact of an almost archetypal theme from pioneering life and tales: the expulsion from Eden. While both women are strong-bodied and good strategists, their motivations and ambitions are violently opposed. The colonists have discovered the serpent in the garden—Thread—and lose their Edenic illusions of Pern; Bitra becomes the second serpent. She brings to Pern her Earthly sense of greed and seduces men to get power and gemstones. She kills Kenjo and injures Ongola to steal a shuttle to get back to Earth's colonies and a life of luxury. Telgar heroically stops Bitra from returning to Earth, but is unable to return to Pern, and becomes the second murder victim in Eden. In contrast to Bitra, however, she programs probes to study a potential Thread source, then dies as her husband finally declares his love for her. In spite of the high melodrama of her death, Telgar's story touches the Pernese colonists and readers. As the first hero and martyr of Pern, she exemplifies the kind of sacrifices and commitment that is needed to ensure the integrity of Pern.

The remaining characters, while being depicted in almost stereotypical ways (the Chinese as mysterious, the tinkers as unfriendly), illustrate a utopian ideal: diverse characters united for the benefit of all. McCaffrey realizes that utopias are not created without some conflict, and she uses a humane and creative punishment for one family: shunning by the rest of the colony. *Dragonsdawn* has a very large cast; many characters are sketches rather than full portraits, and readers do not get a clear shape of this young utopia.

Techniques

Dragonsdawn is divided into three parts. "Landing" encompasses the establishment of Landing, the central staging area and focus of the expanding community as claims are staked and land explored. The second section, "Thread," begins eight years later with the first Threadfall experienced on the planet and the tragic consequences. "Crossing," the final section, adds to these tragic events with the unexpected eruption of a volcano near Landing and the emergency evacuation of the settlement to the North Continent. These catastrophes emphasize the hardship, loneliness, and commitment of the colonists. Scenes of hard work and disaster are punctuated by delightful glimpses of the growing dragons. Readers again feel the wonder of dragon-love and dragon-flight, while the colonists hope the dragons can preserve their planet.

Setting moves the novel's pace and plot; Pern has benign and maleficent aspects, and the colonists must make some quick and far-reaching decisions. While Thread threatens the colony, the discovery of caves gives the settlers protection from Thread. The volcano also threatens Landing, but moving to the North Continent offers safety. While the North is rockier, providing better Thread protection, the arable land is less fertile than the South, thus limiting agricultural production, and making crop protection from Thread imperative. The colonists decide to move to the North Continent, creating Fort Hold, the oldest Hold in the modern dragonrider's time.

Literary Precedents

Dragonsdawn's most striking literary antecedent is Johann Rudolph Wyss' *Swiss Family Robinson* (1812). Like the famous family, the colonists are equipped to establish themselves in their new home, and they are quite ingenious in adapting to their new environment. Like another famous castaway, Robinson Crusoe, they are fiercely self-sufficient and renounce their dependence on Earth when Thread devastates their homes and families.

The theme of the survival of a colony is reminiscent of tales of the American pilgrims and Puritans and pioneer tales of the westward expansion, particularly narratives told mostly by women—a newly-rediscovered genre of American literature. McCaffrey does not depict the colony as a western-style boomtown, with bars and brothels as the first establishments, but as a homesteading community, where the first priorities are farms and schools. She even follows the old homesteading guideline: you own as much land as you can work, but no more.

Relation to Previous Works

Science fiction and fantasy writers frequently expand their short stories and other short works into novels. From the beginning of the Dragonriders of Pern series,

McCaffrey has included an introduction, which has been revised since its inception, giving the origins of the Pernese and their ongoing struggles against Thread. Avid fans who have been watching the changes in these essays now have a full novel on the founding of Pern. *Dragonsdawn* may also signal a new Pern cycle, answering questions and developing interesting new characters. Because *Dragonsdawn* is a prequel to the other Pern novels, McCaffrey creates a new cast of characters. However, these new characters are not totally unfamiliar; they have left their namesakes in Pern's weyrs and holds. Ironically, these heros and antiheros have been forgotten by their descendants, who, in *Renegades of Pern*, begin to seek for their lost history.

RENEGADES OF PERN
Renegades of Pern, 1989, novel.

Social Concerns

Renegades of Pern, unlike most of McCaffrey's novels, shows little of the popular dragonriders and leaders, Lessa and F'lar. Instead, the novel answers the question, what about the common people of Pern? The underclasses of Pern consist of the holders who are dependent on the Lord Holders; the traders who migrate between holds; the holdless, anyone who does not have a permanent home, safe from Thread; and the renegades, criminals who raid others. All these underpriviledged classes want a piece of the action—land in the Southern Continent.

McCaffrey continues themes concerning the changing government of Pern begun in *Dragonsdawn*. First, F'lar claims some of the Southern Continent for dragonriders to eliminate their dependency on Hold tithes during the Intervals (Pernese measurement of time) when there is no Thread to fight. The second change comes from Robinton's search for the past, and the Crafthall's increasing attraction to the colony's lost technology. All of these ambitions will make dramatic changes in the political and social organization of Pern.

Themes

Resilience and cleverness are recurring elements of McCaffrey's writing, and form an integral part of *Renegades of Pern*. At first, the reader believes that the term "renegade" refers to Thella, a Telgar noblewoman, and her gang of holdless raiders. While she is a clever and pernicious raider, she is not the only renegade on Pern. As the novel progresses, "renegade" is applied to most of the major characters, including Lessa, Robinton, and Piemur, who are developing as leaders. Thus McCaffrey explores the positive and negative sides of cleverness, leadership, and ambition.

Characters

The book begins with an introduction to the new cast of characters—the holdless. Unfortunately, many characters, holdless and otherwise, are not developed as fully as possible. However, using the holdless as a guideline, finding the central characters becomes easier. Three major characters emerge: Thella, Toric, and Jayge.

Thella is aggressive, high-handed, and athletic—a warrior woman, with all the positive and negative connotations of that title. She refuses to be married off by her brother, the Telgar Lord Holder, to a lesser holder. Thella is masculine by Pern's standards because she wants to establish herself as Lord Holder over her own hold. To do so she needs to attract the holdless to work for her. Because of setbacks, she decides that raiding other holds and holdless traders is easier. She becomes malicious and violent, one of McCaffrey's most lethal characters.

Toric, who resides in the Southern Continent, also plans to establish himself as a Lord Holder. Being ambitious, he wants to hold all of Southern Continent and import holdless from the North. His ambition is checked by his inability to be compassionate to the emigrant holdless (except when it serves his needs), and by the political influence of F'lar, Lessa, and Robinton.

Jayge, in contrast to both Thella and Toric, falls into holding by accident. He and his wife, Aramina, escape Thella's vengeance by running away to the Southern Continent. After surviving shipwreck and illness, they establish a hold in the ruins of a colonist's home. Piemur and Robinton encourage Jayge to declare their hold and invite others to join them. Jayge becomes a renegade, establishing a new hold by very old homesteading rules.

While Jayge represents holding in the future, Aramina's gift for hearing dragons ties together all threads of Pernese social fabric: her parents are disinherited holdless, she is protected by the weyrs, kidnapped by renegades, married to a trader, and honored by the harpers.

Techniques

With *Renegades of Pern*, McCaffrey enlarges the canvas of Pern. She intertwines characters' lives in a complex plot, which requires a great many narrative breaks. Thella's sneak attack on Aramina and Jayge is not only violent but also abrupt.

In the prologue, McCaffrey introduces the renegades: ten characters who for various reasons have become holdless. Some will defy expectations; others will become outlaws. While this initial listing can confuse even a careful reader, McCaffrey does integrate the stories of all ten major characters. Because *Renegades of Pern* overlaps with the ends of the previous trilogies, readers familiar with *The White Dragon* and *Dragondrums* will find pivotal conversations repeated exactly, but from the point of view of the other character.

Literary Precedents
Thella and her collection of holdless outcasts are reminiscent of other renegade groups: pirates tales like *Treasure Island*, or for a more domestic flavor, western outlaw gangs or Robin Hood gone awry. Thella, like the typical head honcho, has a favorite weapon—throwing daggers—and a brawny, loyal sidekick, Dushik, who takes care of "problems" for her. No one challenges her leadership decisions; she is obeyed.

The story of Jayge and Aramina, as well as the settlement of the Southern Continent, harks back to *Dragonsdawn* and the old colonizing imperatives: holding and working land, fighting disease, and raising children. Piemur continues his intrepid exploration and map-making that make him a Natty Bumpo, Kit Carson, or Robert Peary among the Pernese.

Relation to Previous Works
This novel takes on the remarkable task of tying together seven novels: The Dragonriders of Pern trilogy, The Harper Hall of Pern trilogy and *Dragonsdawn*. It covers the same time span as all three Dragonrider novels, explicitly repeats or refers to events in the Southern Continent from the last book of both trilogies, and implicitly includes details from *Dragonsdawn* which explain the current archeological discoveries. Each chapter of *Renegades of Pern* begins with a chronological and geographical note that is consistent with the previous Pern novels.

KILLASHANDRA
Killashandra, 1986, novel and short stories.

Social Concerns
When critics discuss McCaffrey's startling female characters, Killashandra Ree is a prime example. McCaffrey created Killashandra of the Heptite Guild of Ballybran in reaction to macho space-operas. McCaffrey's female character has it

all—a fulfilling career with extravagant perks and privileges, good looks, male attention, long life, and respect for her intelligence and power. But McCaffrey is also a foresighted reactionary. This maverick author (who admits to many similarities to Killashandra) honestly illustrates the drawbacks of this "success": the paradox of working hard to get away from crystal but being inextricably drawn back; and suffering infertility, debilitating memory loss, and alienation from other humans.

The Heptite Guild requires that applicants have "perfect and absolute pitch." With this strange and stringent requirement, it is no surprise that Killashandra and other guild members have extensive musical training. Here, McCaffrey explores the physical and psychological power of music. First, music serves a very practical purpose, as perfect pitch is needed to be able to identify the dominant notes of the crystal being cut and to tune the cutter to that note or harmonic variants. A strong sense of pitch and harmony is needed to identify and repair malfunctions of engines with crystal drives. Also, musical talent is used as a means of manipulating others. First, Killashandra uses her knowledge of opera characters like Lucia, Lady Macbeth, or Isolde to cope with her own problems and to perform her own scenes of bluff and dazzle for officious agents and audiences. At a more extreme level, music on Optheria's organs illegally controls the emotions of the populace through subliminal undertones and neural stimulation.

Themes

McCaffrey focuses on Killashandra's drive to excel as a performer and a crystal singer. Killashandra herself notes that her desires to be a Stellar-class opera diva and a crystal singer are actually the same: to be first-class. Both professions also emphasize solo performance—to be the only center of attention, in operatic productions or in dramatic crystal-mounting or repair. While Killashandra seems rather blind to her obsession, the reader soon sees the dark side to her virtuoso drive. This professional compulsion is much like crystal-thrall, which blocks out memories of the past and thoughts of personal safety, and which inhibits compassion for others and encourages selfish elitism. *Killashandra* explores the vices and virtues of excellence.

Characters

Killashandra is one of McCaffrey's most complex characters. She is a self-possessed, gutsy, intelligent woman with a light sense of humor. She is also capable of tremendous antagonism in order to get what she wants, is sometimes compassionate, and is rather obsessive in all her relationships—whether crystalline or masculine. While McCaffrey has been praised for her "subconscious" feminist agenda (she does not admit to being a feminist), some critical studies of Killashandra note an interesting paradox. While she is admittedly strong and self-willed, her greatest pleasures are found through submission: first, to the Ballybran symbiote, then to the seductive danger of singing crystal and crystal-thrall, and finally to the men in her life.

While Killashandra is demanding and manipulative, she is also unable to see how easily she is manipulated by men. Lanzecki, Guild Master in *The Crystal Singer*, places the Guild first in his life. He pushes Killashandra into finding black crystal soon after her startling Milekey transition, which puts her in great danger. As Lanzecki describes it, her finding crystal is demanded by the Guild and by himself; anything else she gives him (stimulating conversation, food, or sexual pleasure) is a gift, to be enjoyed only for the moment, which he decides.

Lars Dahl is equally manipulative. He kidnaps Killashandra to try to gain her sympathy with his group, which seeks to overthrow the government of Optheria. Fortunately for her, she was assigned to repair the Optherian organ and investigate complaints made by this very group. Their ensuing intimate relationship has powerful effects on Killashandra; but after many love scenes between Lars Dahl and Killashandra, a reader must wonder how much of the relationship is political and sexual, and how much is honest love and commitment—by both parties.

Perhaps Killashandra's greatest appeal is that, in her complexity, readers can find their own strengths, weaknesses, and concerns reflected in her.

Techniques/Literary Precedents

Killashandra's plot puts McCaffrey's hero through a series of adventures in order to discover the secrets hidden by the placid Optherian rulers. Frequently, McCaffrey breaks off the chapter at a cliff-hanging moment, which helps the novel maintain a rapid pace. Killashandra also assumes a series of disguises: a guileless music student for Corish (another spy for the FSP), a lusty island wench for Lars Dahl before she reveals her identity to him, and a demanding, masterful Heptite Guild member for the Optherian Council. Frequently, Lars Dahl wonders which woman he loves? This woman of many disguises and roles performs, as her training would imply, like a fine opera diva.

In spite of the warmth generated by Killashandra's relationships with her beloved Lars Dahl and the annoying Optheria Council, Killashandra herself comes from a rather cold and distant world. Her home world of Fuerte lives by the FSP right of Privacy—no intrusion is allowed in one's private life, nor is one even required to share space with anyone else. Ballybran is a harsh world, beaten by violent and deadly storms, and socially isolated by a Code 4 listing—a dangerous and restricted planet. With this background in *Crystal Singer*, putting Killashandra on a balmy, happy-go-lucky island world gives a new view to her character.

In contrast to the Pern series, which is science-fiction but seems like fantasy, the Crystal Singer series is conventional science fiction, sporting the hardware of sleds, identification bracelets, crystal cutters, and intergalactic travel. The potential cosmology is as extensive as Isaac Asimov's Foundation series, while her adventure intrigue and romantic explorations are much like Robert Heinlein's later novels of Lazarus Long and the Howard families.

Relation to Previous Works

While *Crystal Singer* is the first novel about Killashandra Ree, she originally appeared in short stories, which were rewritten into the novels. One short story, "Killashandra—Coda and Finale," tells of Killashandra's eventual mental deterioration, betrayal, and murder. While her future does not seem very bright, her story may be rewritten in a later novel.

McCaffrey takes pains to tie her fictions together in a single universe through various hints and allusions. In *Dragonsdawn*, McCaffrey identifies the Pern colonists as members of the Federated Sentient Planets (FSP), the result of Earth's extraterrestrial growth. In *Killashandra*, the galactic ruling body is also the FSP. *The Ship Who Sang* introduces us to Helva, the brain of a FSP ship, with various brawns/humans as companions. In her novel, Killashandra leaves Optheria with Samel and Chadria as the brains and brawn combination of her Scout ship.

Additional Sources

Arbur, Rosemarie. *Leigh Brackett, Marion Zimmer Bradley, Anne McCaffrey: A Primary and Secondary Bibliography*. Boston: G. K. Hall, 1982. An outstanding collection of sources of McCaffrey's fiction, nonfiction, and critical studies of her works through 1981.

Barr, Marleen. "Science Fiction and the Fact of Women's Repressed Creativity: Anne McCaffrey Portrays a Female Artist." *Extrapolation* 23 (1982): 70-76. Examines Menolly's strategies to remain a musician by assuming a male persona who flourishes in exile while developing her talents and earning the respect of others.

Brizzi, Mary T. *Anne McCaffrey* (Starmont Reader's Guide 30). Mercer Island, WA: Starmont House, 1986. A valuable collection of insightful essays on McCaffrey's works that also contains a good bibliography of primary and secondary sources.

Heldreth, Lillian M. "Speculations on Heterosexual Equality: Morris, McCaffrey, Le Guin." *Erotic Universe: Sexuality and Fantastic Literature*, edited by Donald Palumbo. New York: Greenwood Press, 1986. An insightful discussion of *Crystal Singer*'s proposed equality but actual undercutting of that theme.

McCaffrey, Anne. "Retrospection." *Women of Vision*, edited by Denise Dupont. New York: St. Martin's, 1988. This collection contains autobiographical insights shared by well-known women science fiction and fantasy writers.

Wood, Robin. *The People of Pern*. Norfolk, VA: Dorning, 1988. Contains over sixty portraits and scenery of characters from the Pern collection. Text and introduction by McCaffrey.

Lynne Facer
Brigham Young University

MARY MCCARTHY
1912-1989

Update

Mary Therese McCarthy, called by Norman Mailer the "first lady" of American letters and holder of the Charles Stevenson chair of literature at Bard College, was a leading artist, intellectual, and social critic for most of this century. She has also enjoyed considerable popular success. Her celebrated novel, *The Group* (1963), was made into a successful movie; and *Memories of a Catholic Girlhood* (1957), regarded as her most important work, continues to be reprinted, anthologized, and discussed in classrooms. Her most recent novel, *Cannibals and Missionaries* (1979), in which terrorists highjack a plane filled with art collectors and liberal members of a human rights group, explores the conflict between personalities and perspectives, art and life, form and feeling. A collection of her essays from the 1970s and 1980s was published as *Occasional Prose* in 1985. Many of these essays are memorials to well-known friends, such as James Baldwin, or to those with whom she shared personal history, such as Philip Rahv, the *Partisan Review* editor and leftist critic with whom she lived during the 1930s. Others reflect her interest in international affairs, history, and historiography, such as articles on the Italian philosopher, Nicola Chiaromonte, or on nineteenth-century and contemporary Russian literature, especially her "favorite," Tolstoy's *Anna Karenina*.

In 1987 the first volume of an intended multi-volume autobiography appeared in book form (parts had been published earlier in *The New Yorker* in 1986, embellished with family photos. Entitled *How I Grew*, the memoir recounts her adventures between her birth "as a mind" in 1925 (when she was thirteen), and her graduation from Vassar and marriage to actor Harold Johnsrud. These frank and entertaining memoirs shed light on her fiction (the autobiographical setting for *The Group*) and her enduring themes—initiation and the development of new awareness, hatred of cant and self-deception, the importance of discipline, and the education of the self.

McCarthy, drama critic, essayist, and novelist, died in New York of cancer in October, 1989. She had lived the last decades in Paris with James West, a diplomat, her husband since 1961. Reuel K. Wilson, her son from her second marriage to Edmund Wilson, is her only child; Kevin McCarthy, the actor, is her brother. In remarks at her memorial service held at Pierpont Morgan Library on November 8, 1989, and in the press, Elizabeth Hardwick, Arthur Schlesinger, Jr., and others detailed the central themes of her life: the history of political activism, dating from her early involvement with the *Partisan Review* and continuing through her later books on Vietnam and Watergate; the childhood marked so decisively by her parents' death of flu in 1918; and the biting and sometimes controversial social commentary in novels such as *The Group* (1963), a fictionalized account of life at Vassar, and short stories such as "The Man in the Brooks Brothers Suit," with its famous Pullman car seduction scene. Tales were recounted of the causes she had championed, from Trotskyism to the hand-milled coffee grinder, and to her celebrated friendships and enmities. At her memorial service Arthur Schlesinger, Jr., spoke of the generosity and fidelity to standards which marked both McCarthy's art and life.

Analysis of Selected Titles

HOW I GREW

How I Grew, 1987, memoir.

Social Concerns/Themes/Techniques

Set almost entirely in Seattle, where she lived with her grandparents, Harold and Augusta Preston, after her parent's death, *How I Grew* is an emotional and intellectual autobiography that details McCarthy's growing sense of self—her emerging identity as an intellectual, her interest in defining a moral life, and her deft analysis and debunking of cant and pretense.

Couched in an eighteenth-century "Dear reader" epistolary style and a firmly implanted authorial presence, *How I Grew* uses the motifs of childhood—the child's verse, the tale of the orphan (*Jane Eyre*)—to document a young girl's growing sense of self and personal destiny amid an atmosphere at once isolated and invigorating. In these pages her grandmother, grandfather, and uncle come to life, as do the upper-middle-class Seattle suburbs and summer places. McCarthy excels in the depiction of contemporary manners and culture which played so large a role in her fiction. She details her sentimental education through girlhood crushes and competitions and the more enduring friendships of young adulthood. The young McCarthy lives a secret life hidden from her family (she speaks of being an accomplished liar), and among the most memorable episodes is the account of her sexual initiation at the age of fourteen in the back seat of a local boy's Marmon.

Here, too, is the story of McCarthy's more formal education, undertaken in the family's library as well as in public and private schools, most notably the Annie Wright Seminary in Tacoma. Ever conscious of her emerging identity as an intellectual, McCarthy speaks the value of a classical and liberal education and the admirable but underappreciated female teachers who oversaw her intellectual growth. Her political education, heretofore virtually ignored, begins in earnest when she became radicalized when reading John Dos Passos' account of the Sacco and Vanzetti trials in *The 42nd Parallel* (1930). Throughout, McCarthy refers to her encounters with her Jewish heritage and the Catholicism that, although formally abandoned at an early age, was so much a part of her imagination.

How I Grew also provides a glimpse into the aging process through its depiction of a consciousness grappling with the haze of memory, the spontaneous flashbacks to incidents previously forgotten, and the tempering of emotional intensity by time and circumstance. The emerging butterfly of McCarthy's mature personality is often overshadowed by the awkward, self-conscious adolescent, harshly critical of her own "total absence of early talent." McCarthy's self-portrait is self-critical and self-revealing—a girlhood plagiarism, awkwardly short dresses, a hangover at graduation, and adolescent cruelties—forming the outline of a sometimes overly-critical, painfully absolutist character who shows a strong sympathy for the underdog and the orphan. Pain and loss are present as well, as McCarthy remembers herself at twenty-seven with a new baby, new husband, and "my first husband. . .dead as well as the young man I had left him for."

Additional Sources

Kakutani, Michiko. "Our Woman of Letters." *New York Times Magazine.* (March 29, 1987): 60-61.

"Memorial Service at Pierpont Morgan Library." *New York Times* 4, 27 (November 9, 1989): 1.

Stevens, Elizabeth. "The Way She Was." Review of *How I Grew*. *Women's Review of Books* 4, 10-11 (July-August 1987): 29-30.

Schlesinger, Arthur, Jr., "Mary McCarthy: 1912-1989." Memorial remarks in *The Partisan Review* 62, 1 (1990): 14-15.

Janet Polansky
University of Wisconsin-Stout

COLLEEN MCCULLOUGH
1937

Update

The 1977 publication of *The Thorn Birds*, a loosely autobiographical family saga set in the Australian outback, catapulted Colleen McCullough from obscurity as a research associate in neurophysiology at Yale University into overnight celebrity. The record-setting auction for paperback rights to *The Thorn Birds* garnered a great deal of media attention and forced the author to make significant changes in her life plans.

McCullough was born in Australia in 1937, the daughter of a meanspirited father who worked the sugar cane plantations and a mother who was determined to see that her children received a solid education. McCullough and her brother were both gifted and shared a very close sibling relationship. His death twenty-five years ago was a deep personal loss for her. McCullough focused her academic attention on science, and although she loved her work, she began writing on the side to supplement her income. The result was *Tim*, her first novel which was so quietly received in 1974 that many readers mistakenly assumed *The Thorn Birds* was her first novel instead of her second.

McCullough was preparing to embark for England to start nurse's training and gather background for a hospital novel she planned to write when she delivered the manuscript for *The Thorn Birds* to her publisher. When it sold for a record-setting paperback advance and made headlines, the loss of anonymity forced McCullough to abandon her nursing plans.

The fame and fortune which the phenomenal success of *The Thorn Birds* brought McCullough—to date it has sold eight million copies in paperback—made it difficult for her to continue living in mainstream society. When she learned of Norfolk Island with its controlled population, she applied to live there. Located in the South Pacific, a thousand miles from Australia, Norfolk Island is small (fifteen square miles) with a population of about two thousand people. At age forty-six McCullough met and married a man thirteen years her junior, Ric Robinson, a descendant of one of the *Bounty* mutineers. Today they live on Out Yenna, a fifteen-acre compound complete with two guest houses, which are in constant use. Her husband raises kentia palms and she writes her novels on the twelve typewriters she keeps on hand. Frequent power outages on the island make a word processor unreliable. Two facsimilie machines are their lifeline to the outside world. Robinson is active in the local government and McCullough is involved in charity work on the island.

Since *The Thorn Birds*, McCullough has published four more novels: *An Indecent Obsession* (1981); *A Creed for the Third Millennium* (1983); *The Ladies of Missalonghi* (1987); and *The First Man in Rome* (1990). *The Ladies of Missalonghi*, which McCullough calls her "fairy tale," is an illustrated novella. In 1988 accusations of plagiarism were levelled against McCullough by the family of Canada's most prominent author, L. M. Montgomery, best known for *Anne of Green Gables*. They charged that McCullough had taken her plot directly from the pages of *The Blue Castle*. Although there were parallels between the two stories, McCullough denied the charges. Instead, in a November 23, 1990, interview with *The Washington Post*, McCullough said the life she gave Missy was based on the hardships her mother faced and her own personal experiences that had given her a "particular fascination with the old maid." Montgomery's family never brought legal action against McCullough and the episode died quietly.

McCullough's recently published historical novel, *The First Man in Rome*, is the culmination of thirteen years of painstaking research. Her fascination with the period of Republican Rome began thirty years ago when McCullough first read the Penguin translations of Greek and Roman classics in college. She reread them after *The Thorn Birds* and was so impressed by the first-hand accounts of that period, written by the men who had made the history, that she decided she wanted to explore that world as a novelist.

To research the period, McCullough amassed a collection of two thousand volumes which she claims is the largest private library on Republican Rome anywhere in the world. She also hired a full time researcher, fluent in four languages, to travel and interview experts in many countries. The researcher also located portrait busts of prominent Romans which McCullough sketched herself for illustrations in *The First Man in Rome*. To accurately depict the settings in the book, McCullough traveled to various historic sites to get a feel for the topography. Over two million words of research were committed to paper before she tackled the novel itself.

Critical Reception, Honors and Popularity

The First Man in Rome is the first of a five-book series which her former hardcover publisher was reluctant to undertake. The publisher wanted her to drop the first two planned volumes and begin with the third in the series. McCullough changed her publishers rather than compromise her ambitious project. *The First Man in Rome* received favorable advance reviews in *Kirkus* and *Publishers Weekly*. Post-publication reviews were generally favorable although several British reviewers were decidedly negative. The novel was a Book-of-the-Month Club selection and had a 300,000 pre-publication advance printing. It spent weeks on the *New York Times* bestseller list. In the fall of 1990 McCullough spent two and a half months touring the U.S., Australia, and Europe to publicize the book. McCullough has completed the manuscript for the second volume, tentatively titled *The Grass Crown.*

Analysis of Selected Titles

THE FIRST MAN IN ROME
The First Man in Rome, 1990, novel.

Social Concerns

In *The First Man in Rome,* McCullough tells her story against the backdrop of the competitiveness, quarreling, and infighting between the classes of Roman society. This society was stratified into very distinct, well-defined classes. All citizens were either patricians or plebeians. The patrician class represented the original Roman aristocracy, and its members traced their lineage to ancient families. Not all were wealthy, yet they were distinguished by a prestige of birth that no plebeian could ever attain. The plebeian class consisted of all Roman citizens who were not patricians and was further segmented into economic subclasses. While membership in the patrician class guaranteed honor, it did not guarantee a more honorable, intelligent breed of men. Some of the most venal men in the novel are patricians.

The political system of Rome was closely linked to and organized around its class system. In following the maze of political debates, intrigues, and alliances, McCullough makes it clear that political corruption is a universal, age-old phenomenon. Ironically, many politicians who claimed to be acting for the "good of Rome," were, in actuality, more interested in advancing their own personal gain. Government could be bought for a price.

Roman government was so mired in tradition and preoccupied with maintaining the status quo, that it inadvertently sowed the seeds of the decline of the Roman republic. The government refused to adapt to changing times and circumstances. This is one reason Marius was so unpopular with many conservatives in the Senate. He was forward-thinking; they were always looking to the past. The old guard felt threatened as their power base was slowly being eroded by the growing strength of the plebeians. They felt the best way to look after the interests of Rome was to retain the government of the many by the few.

In *The First Man in Rome* McCullough deftly explores the interconnectedness of the Roman social and political systems, and the integral role it played in shaping Roman life.

Themes

In *The First Man in Rome*, as in her previous writings, McCullough displays an exceptional understanding of human emotion and motivation—the undercurrents of personality which compel men and women to love, hate, succeed, and kill. In *The First Man in Rome*, the politicos and military men are driven by greed, pride, and ambition. Relationships are often held together or torn apart by love.

Foremost among these human motivations is ambition, exemplified in the characters of Gaius Marius and Lucius Cornelius Sulla. Both men aspire to become consul of Rome and eventually to rise to the pinnacle of political greatness and become the "First Man in Rome." This title, which was held by only a handful of Romans, indicated that a man was the first among his equals in rank and opportunity. The pre-eminence and honor of such a title were not bestowed upon a man but had to be earned by him through his climb up the military and political ladders.

Both Marius and Sulla strongly believe they are destined for greatness and have been favored by the goddess Fortuna. Both, as Gaius Marius puts it, have "the luck." Events in each man's life serve to reinforce this belief. While serving in a military campaign in Africa, Gaius Marius meets Martha, a Syrian prophetess, who proclaims he will be consul seven times, save Rome from a great peril, and be regarded as the Third Founder of Rome. In Sulla's first encounter with the beautiful Julilla, she fashions a crown of grass and presents it to him, unaware of its significance. The *Corona Graminea*, or Grass Crown, was awarded to a man who saved a whole legion or, on rare occasions, a whole army. Sulla regards this episode as an omen of things to come and, from that point on, sees his luck and future inextricably linked to Julilla. These encounters fuel each man's ambition and spur them on to realize their destinies, whatever the cost. Later in the story, while spying among the Germans, Sulla fathers twins (a good omen) with his German wife Hermana, which further reinforces his belief that he has "the luck."

Both Marius and Sulla marry for political gain. Each marries a daughter of Gaius Julius Caesar Nepos for the social rank and *dignitas* that marrying into one of the oldest, most respected aristocratic bloodlines affords them. To be aligned with the

Caesars guarantees political and social esteem. For Marius, it is also, happily, a union of love. For Sulla, who feels himself incapable of love, it is a union fraught with disappointment, pain, and unhappiness. Yet for both men, marriage is a means to furthering their political ambitions.

Ascending the political ladder requires not only the proper class and social standing but also money. Buying the necessary votes and supporters to gain office was an expensive business. Marius is a very wealthy man, but Sulla, although born into one of the oldest, most venerable patrician families of Rome, is penniless thanks to an alcoholic father who drank up the family's fortune. To get the money necessary to fulfill his political birthright, Sulla murders his mistress, his stepmother, and the stepmother's cousin.

Both Sulla and Marius are single-minded and determined to achieve greatness. Yet to be great and to excel beyond other men does not mean to be without flaw. Sulla is shrewd enough to recognize this in himself and Marius. When Catalus Caesar is on the verge of sacrificing his Roman army to the Germans because of his pride, military ignorance, and poor leadership, Sulla, ordered by Marius to save Caesar's army at all costs, leads the soldiers in a mutiny. In the confrontation that follows, Sulla says to Catalus Caesar, "One day, you know, I'll be the First Man in Rome. The tallest tree in the world, just like Gaius Marius. And the thing about trees so tall is that no one can chop them down. When they fall, they fall because they rot from within."

Pride and greed are also powerful motivations and McCullough examines these traits through some of the novel's secondary characters. The Roman Senate and political system are rife with politicians willing to sell themselves, their favors, and their votes to the highest bidder. These same politicians are willing to bestow largesse on their clients in exchange for political support and loyalty. The verdicts of juries are often paid for in advance. Some men, like Quintus Servilius Caepio, are willing to sacrifice the lives of innocent men to enhance their own personal wealth. While serving as consul, Caepio commands Roman legions against the Germans near Tolosa. Three years earlier, while serving as the governor of Further Spain, Caepio had heard the tale of the lost gold of Tolosa. After the city surrenders, Caepio becomes obsessed with finding the gold. When he succeeds, he transports the gold to Narbo for shipment to Rome, presumably for the Roman treasury. However, the wagon train is ambushed en route to Narbo, six hundred Roman soldiers are killed, and the gold disappears. Everyone assumes the bandits made off with the gold, but the ambush was actually arranged by Caepio himself so the gold would be his.

In class conscious Rome, many patricians harbor a snobbish sense of superiority over those who are in the plebeian class or are considered as "New Men."

Sometimes this stubborn pride produces catastrophic results. As a consul, Gnaeus Mallius Maximus, a New Man, is in command of Roman forces along the Rhodanus near Aurasio. Quintus Servilius Caepio, a patrician, is ordered by the Senate to join his forces with those of Gnaeus Mallius Maximus and subordinate to the junior counsel. Caepio repeatedly refuses to obey because he, a patrician, will not stoop to take orders from a New Man. The two commanders squabble and fail to join legions to combat the Germans. As a result, the Germans brutally defeat the Romans at a cost of eighty thousand Roman soldiers and twenty-four thousand non-combatants—all because Caepio's pride and patrician status made him unwilling to serve under a New Man. As a Marsi soldier who survived the battle so aptly summarizes the situation, so many lives were lost "because some overbred Roman idiot bore a grudge against some underbred Roman idiot."

Julilla, still a young girl, develops a crush on Sulla when she first meets him. Sulla knows her father would not approve of her relationship with someone of his reputation, so he ridicules her in an attempt to discourage her affections. Julilla becomes so obsessed with Sulla that she plots to manipulate him and her family through self-imposed starvation. Julilla thinks if she can make Sulla believe she is ill, he will feel sorry for her and give in to her appeals. All the while she secretly sends him love letters, begging him to admit his love for her. Although Sulla does eventually marry Julilla, he does so for political advancement. Julilla marries Sulla, though, because she desperately loves him. While awaiting his return from the military campaign in Africa, Julilla surmises about her love for her husband: "any evidence whatsoever of discipline or self-control was proof positive of an inferior brand of love; love of the highest order should overwhelm, invade, shake down the spiritual walls, drive out all vestige of rational thought, roar tempestuously, trample down everything in its path as if some vast elephant."

Sulla, on the other hand, feels that he is incapable of love. Yet, he does have tender feelings for his German wife, Hermana, who is the polar opposite of his Roman wife Julilla. He does love his children, "and loved them deeply too, a very different kind of feeling from any he had ever experienced for either man or woman. Selfless and pure, untainted and rounded." Sulla also feels a deep affection for Netrobius, the handsome young actor, with whom he has occasional homosexual trysts. Sulla's unfortunate childhood circumstances have yielded a self-centered, aloof, calculating man. Burdened by a father whose love for the bottle exceeded his love for his son, Sulla learns emotional detachment and parsimony early on.

Julilla and Sulla are temperamentally ill-suited, yet their lives are inextricably entwined by their need for each other. Sulla needs Julilla for the social prestige she offers, and she needs him because she loves him. Because of the grass crown,

Sulla feels his destiny, his "luck," is eternally bound to Julilla. He supposes he loves her as much as he is capable of loving any woman.

While Sulla may unknowingly love Julilla, her love for him is so intense he feels suffocated and devoured by its demands. To Sulla, love is an incidental emotion; for Julilla her spirit and reason for being are enveloped in her love for Sulla. When Julilla learns of Sulla's German wife, she questions him about his feelings for Hermana and why he liked her so. Sulla replies, "she never expected me to be what I'm not . . . . She belonged to herself, and she didn't burden me with herself. You're a lead weight chained about my neck. Hermana was a pair of wings strapped to my feet."

Characters

The central characters in *The First Man In Rome* are Gaius Marius, a country squire from Arpinum, and Lucius Cornelius Sulla, an impoverished blue-blooded Roman aristocrat. Both men are ambitious, determined, shrewd, and intelligent, and both aspire to rise through the Roman political ranks to become the First Man in Rome.

Marius is a New Man, not born into the patrician class. As his nemesis Quintus Caecilius Metelus so derisively refers to him, he is "an Italian hayseed with no Greek." Marius is a natural born leader and military genius; soldiering and embracing the military life are his love. He commands the affection and respect of his soldiers because he, in turn, is genuinely concerned for their welfare. Marius is an unorthodox thinker and he is not adverse to going against tradition if it will accomplish his purpose. This tendency, though, earns him many political enemies. Marius is also a military reformer who shocks the Roman aristocrats when he wants to recruit soldiers from among the Head Count. He infuriates many conservative senators by breaking the rules and serving as consul six times. He is a natural competitor, a man driven to excel, a man who welcomes a challenge. When Sulla remarks to Marius about the difficulty of handling the intricacies of politics, Marius replies, "No, Lucius Cornelius, it isn't ever easy, is it? But that's what makes it worth doing! What man of true excellence and worth honestly wants a smooth path? The rougher the path, the more obstacles in the way, the more satisfaction there is."

Sulla is a handsome young aristocrat with impeccable family lineage but no money to facilitate the political career which is his birthright. Because of his father's drinking, he grows up in poverty and shame. To obtain the education his patrician status dictates, he prostitutes himself to raise the money. As a young man, Sulla earns the reputation as a carouser, a womanizer, and an indulger in sexual excesses. He is a ruthless, cold-blooded, calculating, self-centered man who will let nothing or no one stand in his way. When he becomes convinced of his political destiny, he needs money to enter the senate and murders three people to obtain it. When he and Marius become aligned through their marriages to the daughters of Gaius Julius Caesar Nepos, Marius takes on the role of mentor. Sulla seizes the opportunity to learn everything he can about soldiering and politics under Marius's tutelage. He is determined not to let his past low-living sully his future aspirations, so he exerts great patience and self-discipline to become a model soldier and right-hand to Marius.

While *The First Man in Rome* is dominated by male figures, there are several well-developed female characters. Julilla, the flighty, spirited wife of Sulla, is perhaps most memorable because of her tragic end. She, too, is self-centered and demanding and consumed by a possessive love for her husband which he cannot reciprocate. She is manipulative and shrewd when it comes to getting her way. As Julilla's marriage to Sulla becomes increasingly troubled, her elder sister Julia observes, "Julilla was ageing at the gallop—not physically, not even mentally—a process of the spirit, rather, intensely self-destructive."

Julia is wise, intelligent, educated, and level-headed. Although her father arranges to marry one of his daughters to Gaius Marius to ensure the financial and political security of his sons, Julia is delighted when Marius chooses her. They marry for love, as well as expediency. Raised in the house of the Caesars, she is well versed in politics and is treated with respect by the men around her.

The third female character of note is Aurelia Cotta who weds the youngest Caesar son, Gaius Julius Caesar Junior and gives birth to Julius Caesar. She is a patrician by birth and is greatly admired for her beauty. She and her family are besieged by hundreds of suitors. She is educated, intelligent, and of sound judgment. Because her family finds it impossible to pick a husband for her, she is permitted to make the choice herself. Although women's roles were quite restricted by Roman society and custom, Aurelia displays a refreshing independence. She and Gaius Julius invest in an *insula* in the Subura where they live in one apartment and rent out the rest. While Gaius Julius is away on military duty, Aurelia decides to run the *insula* herself. She is fascinated by the fact that she is not living among the patricians, and she is able to liberate herself, to some extent, from the constraints imposed by her aristocratic birth.

Techniques

McCullough's sixth book, *The First Man in Rome,* is the author's first foray into historical fiction, and her extensive historical research is very much in evidence throughout the text. In some passages, this information is seamlessly and unobtrusively woven into the narrative. At other times, however, the historical facts are disembodied from the fictional flow. The vast amount of Roman history and culture which permeates the novel is regarded by some reviewers as a strength, by others as a liability.

As in her previous works, McCullough employs a straightforward narrative structure and prose style. Her gift for description and detail create finely drawn portraits of Roman life, politics, landscape, and military operations. Whether maneuvering the reader through the labyrinthine streets of the Subura or sweeping overland with the Roman legions on the march, McCullough's descriptive and narrative power draw the reader into the scene.

McCullough's skillful use of descriptive language and metaphor create many beautiful and arresting images. For example, after becoming betrothed to Julia Caesar, Gaius Marius visits the pearl vendor to buy an engagement gift: "she was his pearl beyond price, so to her must come pearls, the tears of a distant tropical moon that fell into the deepest ocean and, in sinking to its bottom, froze solid."

In *The First Man in Rome* McCullough employs a device heretofore unused in her works. She uses numerous lengthy letters, exchanged between Gaius Marius and his dear friend Publius Rutilius Rufus, as a way of giving additional background information, much of it dealing with extraneous events that have little direct bearing on the events of this novel. In fact, the letters often interrupt the plot and impede the action or they divert attention from character development. The author defends their use as necessary to provide a background for events to come in later books in the series. (*The First Man in Rome* is the first of five planned volumes.) Despite these drawbacks, some of the letters of Publius Rutilius Rufus are gossipy and witty reports of the double dealing, intrigue, and crafty political machinations that riddle the Roman senate. His philosophical observations of his fellow Romans offer insight into the attitudes, values and morals of his day. In his letter to Marius following the defeat of the Germans, for instance, Publius wrote,

> There is something terribly reassuring about being in politics to enrich oneself. It's normal. It's human. It's forgivable. It's understandable. The ones to watch are the ones who are in politics to change the world. They do the real damage, the power-men and the altruists. It isn't healthy to think about other people ahead of oneself.

McCullough has provided a key to the cast of characters and also compiled an extensive glossary of terms and names which gives the reader additional explanation of the Roman era and its culture. She has devised a pronunciation guide to the many Latin names and terms which abound in the text. She also drew the maps, charts, and sketches of portrait busts which illustrate the novel.

Literary Precedents

The First Man in Rome is a historical novel, a genre that has been tackled by various writers with varying degrees of success. Robert James of the *Orange County Register* wrote, "at a time when the historical novel is languishing for the lack of a truly worthwhile writer, McCullough steps in. Michener has lost his mastery of the form long ago, and Jakes never had it in the first place. But McCullough has crafted an education in the Roman Republic, circa 100 B.C., and it reads as good, if not better, than any historical novel written since Michener's heyday in the '50s and '60s." Set in closer proximity of time frame and civilization, *The First Man in Rome* invites comparison to Taylor Caldwell's *A Pillar of Ironies*, whose central character is Cicero, stated Rita Mae Brown for her *Washington Post* review. She regards Caldwell's writing as "effortless" and preferable to McCullough's historical writing.

Relation to Previous Works

In *The Thorn Birds* McCullough examined the love relationship between Meggie and Father Ralph de Bricassart, the ambitious priest. Theirs was an unequal relationship. While Meggie loved Ralph totally and unconditionally, Ralph loved Meggie, but because of his ambitions in the church, he would never fully commit himself to her. In *The First Man in Rome,* McCullough explores the love relationship between Julilla and Sulla which, like Meggie and Ralph's, is a source of much pain and unhappiness.

McCullough also explored ambition as a motivating force in *The Thorn Birds*. Father Ralph de Bricassart was an ambitious priest who aspired to rise to the top in the church's hierarchy. While his methods were not as ruthless as Sulla's, his success was realized at the expense of his and especially Meggie's personal happiness.

Linda G. Faison

THOMAS MCGUANE
1939

Update

A few new critical works on Thomas McGuane's fiction have appeared in the past five years and are noted below. Of special importance are the interviews, since in some ways the best critical works to be found on McGuane are his own remarks. McGuane has continued his turn to less overtly comic novels in a chain from *Nobody's Angel* through *Something to be Desired* to *Keep the Change*. McGuane's personal life has apparently changed little: the champion cutting horses he raises continue to improve in quality, as do his novels.

Analysis of Selected Titles

KEEP THE CHANGE

Keep the Change, 1989, novel.

Social Concerns/Themes

Those familiar with McGuane's work will recognize in *Keep the Change* his continuing indictment of the unreflective acquisitiveness of American society. That the father of protagonist Joe Starling keeps a brace of dogs named Neuritis and Neuralgia and horses called Hart, Schaffner, and Marx is one more instance of McGuane's ironic notation of the infection of all facets of American life by the corporate ethic. Yet McGuane's treatment of this theme is less explosive here than in his earlier novels; rather, it is taken as a given, the necessary condition of contemporary life against which the individual struggles to establish a sense of more permanent value.

Emerging from the contrast between various kinds of lives enacted in suburban Minnesota, the Florida keys, the Montana prairie, and elsewhere, is Starling's sense that what he is looking for, finally, is "home." Much of the novel therefore engages in an exploratory definition of what that space consists of, the possibilities inherent in the end of restlessness. The resolution of this question is at best provisional and temporary, yet it is more clearly and hopefully realized here than elsewhere in McGuane's work. Starling's trek from Florida to Montana (again, favored McGuane locales) provides an opportunity to show the essential disconnectedness of American life, where the American plains appear to be one enormous mobile garage sale—all taken in randomly, while in flight. Still, while *The Bushwhacked Piano* ended with the inscription of Nicholas Payne's estrangement—"I am at large"—*Keep the Change* offers an abandonment of the desperado stance in Starling and his lover Astrid's shared acknowledgement that they "would pretty much have to see."

In large measure, this resolution works itself out through Starling's relinquishment of his inheritance—both the profits of his labor on the ranch, and ultimately the very deed itself. In doing so, he is ostensibly giving up his own dream of home, but the relinquishment is itself a kind of repossession of his soul, of another kind of home. His gift of the ranch to Billy Kelton signals not so much the reunion of their friendship as it does their shared opposition to those who would own the land merely for the sake of doing so, rather than those who work it and belong to it. In Starling's exchange of his own labor for the complex of frauds that his uncle devises, McGuane presents a complicated interweaving of fraud and honesty that ultimately displaces and transcends those categories. The novel begins and ends with a contemplation of the ruins of past effort and the possibilities inherent in ownership in the house of the Silver King, where Starling goes with his father to see a painting of a snowy landscape that is later revealed to be only an empty frame on a plaster wall. In this densely layered metaphor, McGuane speaks to the aesthetics of modern art, the persistence of illusion, and the infinite adaptability of interpretation. The novel concludes with the sense that long-standing debts—to the past, to the land, to family, to love, to the illusions of youth—are finally discharged.

Characters

The novel's protagonist, Joe Starling, is a failed painter coming to terms with that failure, with his father's legacy, and with his own inadequacies and obsessions. Largely an observer of other people's lives, and not always a perceptive one at that, Starling's detachment from other people and things settles around him like snow. Yet he acknowledges his detachment wistfully and with a full measure of self-criticism, as when he notes that his character is "composed almost strictly of things I hate in other people."

On the other hand, Starling is presented with few examples of a commitment to values more compelling than his own. His father is ruthless; Mr. Overstreet is obsessed with completing his land's symmetry; and his friend Ivan Slater, another of the "new industrialists" in the C. J. Clovis mode, is devoted to a pet scheme of marketing a home lie detector. The odd, parodic marriage of his Aunt Lureen and Uncle Smitty provides some possibilities in their mutual devotion, but also stands as a criticism leveled at Starling's own parents and at marriage in general. In his dissociation from those around him, Starling resembles earlier McGuane protagonists, yet he goes beyond them in his attempt to bridge that dissociation.

Much of the impetus for his quest comes from women. McGuane's depiction of Starling's fumbling first love with Ellen Overstreet is startlingly realistic. In her apparent domesticity and suburban security she harbors a capacity to manipulate and use Starling for her own designs. Contrasted with Ellen is the Cuban sensuality and wildness of Starling's lover Astrid. The character of Astrid shows that criticism formerly leveled at McGuane's treatment of women is less cogent regarding *Keep the Change*. Certainly, she remains secondary to a protagonist who in his isolation is recognizably male and thus set apart from the feminine as opposite, and crude sexist jokes persist in this text despite their immediate labeling by both Starling and McGuane as "infantilism." But Astrid finally, for all her unlikelihood, or perhaps because of it, stands formidably and fiercely there in Starling's vision.

It is also noteworthy that Starling's lifelong enmity with Billy Kelton is dissipated at the novel's end. Kelton appears at first to represent the same kind of half-mad, half-dumb male adversary as Nichol Dance or Wayne Codd did in earlier McGuane novels. Yet his role in *Keep the Change* is an expanded one, even from the boyhood fight that teaches Starling the lesson that "life had as one of its constant characteristics a strain of unbearable loneliness." Upon seeing Billy's retarded daughter, the daughter that could have been his, Starling goes beyond compassion and identifies with Billy "in all his isolated, violent ignorance."

Techniques/Literary Precedents

The comparison of McGuane to Hemingway is still appropriate, perhaps now even more so. McGuane himself has noted that while Hemingway-bashing is a kind of approved stance in American letters, he remains in McGuane's words "a figure that casts a tremendous shadow for better or for worse." Here, with McGuane's focus on an isolated man fighting the forces of engulfment and in his lean and highly polished prose style, the comparison to Hemingway is accurate. The most important precedent, however, is to be found in McGuane's earlier work, to which *Keep the Change* serves as a kind of culmination.

An essentially realistic manner comes to the fore in *Keep the Change* as well. The novel elicits a sense of American life as filled with "things," and with the struggle of honest efforts on all fronts. McGuane devotes much space to the business of ranching and raising cattle, and ultimately realizes a combination of cold-eyed labor and dreamy desirousness that inhabits all the characters in one form or another. Even Ivan Slater, Billy Kelton, and Joe's father, "types" that would have been villainized in earlier McGuane novels, are here invested with the desire for something genuinely better than that which characterizes Starling himself. Much of Starling's revelation, then, is a gradual awareness of the connectedness of the people around him through this quality—an awareness that itself gradually yields into a sense of forgiveness.

Relation to Previous Works

Keep the Change follows a continuum of McGuane heroes from *Nobody's Angel* through *Something to be Desired*, moving closer to a solution of the dilemma best characterized by McGuane's own remark about *Something to be Desired:* "it really is a case of a man discovering that a narcissistic crisis is going to bear penalties which are permanent." These novels, taken together, constitute a progressive working out of the problem of living as a man in contemporary America. *Keep the Change* is less stylistically clever than McGuane's early novels, and less labored in its humor, which gives greater cleanness and clarity to the prose.

To some extent the McGuane landscape has altered. His rhapsodic view of Montana serves as an antidote to the plasticity of American urban life so roundly vilified in his earlier novels. This, like other sources of comfort, is only provisionally held, yet it is nevertheless there and real in its beauty, like the empty frame surrounding an absent and imagined canvas. In a very real sense, all of the resolution and forgiveness of *Keep the Change* is contained in the anecdote of the empty frame that itself frames the book, and in Starling's final realization that "it wasn't an empty frame; it was his father telling him that somewhere in the abyss something shone."

Additional Sources

Bonetti, Kay. "An Interview with Thomas McGuane." *The Missouri Review* 9, 1 (1985-86): 75-99. A wide-ranging and revealing conversation, including discussions of the writing life, the academy, comic and satiric fiction, Hemingway, Twain, and McGuane's own early work; this is the best interview. Also available as part of the American Audio Prose Library Series.

Goldsworthy, Joan. "Thomas McGuane." In *Contemporary Authors*. New Revision Series. Vol. 24. Edited by Deborah Straub. Detroit: Gale Research, 1988. Contains a brief 1987 interview with McGuane.

Klinkowitz, Jerome. *The New American Novel of Manners: The Fiction of Richard Yates, Dan Wakefield, and Thomas McGuane*. Athens: University of Georgia Press, 1986. Sees McGuane sharing formal and thematic characteristics with Yates and Wakefield, and provides brief, lucid readings of all McGuane's novels through *Something to be Desired*.

Wallace, Jon. "The Language Plot in Thomas McGuane's *Ninety-Two in the Shade*." *Critique* 29, 2 (Winter 1988): 111-120.

———. "Speaking Against the Dark: Style as Theme in Thomas McGuane's *Nobody's Angel*." *Modern Fiction Studies* 33, 2 (Summer 1987): 289-298. Taken together, Wallace's two essays provide a closely reasoned analysis of some of McGuane's stylistic idiosyncrasies.

George Bishop
D'Youville College

JAY MCINERNEY
1955

Update

In the years since the publication of *Ransom*, his second novel, Jay McInerney's popularity and critical reputation have continued to rise. The film version of his debut novel, *Bright Lights, Big City*, was released in the spring of 1988, and his novel, *Story of My Life*, followed that summer. In addition to these major events, McInerney published short fiction in *Esquire* and the *Atlantic*, and penned articles for the *New York Times, Esquire,* and the *New York Times Book Review.*

The movie *Bright Lights, Big City* was released through United Artists, and its cast included Michael J. Fox as McInerney's unnamed narrator (called "Jamie" in the film version), Kiefer Sutherland, John Houseman, Jason Robards, and Dianne Wiest. Critical opinion varied, but much of it pointed out the strengths of the novel and the failure of the film to capture them adequately. The loss of both the novel's unique second person narration and the narrator's flippant wit were mentioned by reviewers as problems in converting the novel into a film. The movie did, however, publicize both McInerney and his most popular novel to date.

Story of My Life, McInerney's third book, was well-received, with reviews in the *New Republic, National Review,* and the *New York Times Book Review,* as well as in popular magazines such as *Time, Newsweek,* and *People.* By creating a female counterpart to his narrator in *Bright Lights, Big City,* McInerney tapped many of the strengths of the earlier novel and was once again praised for his ability to capture the conflicts and catastrophes of modern life.

With only three novels in print, Jay McInerney has nonetheless entered the rarefied air formerly inhabited by Truman Capote, Ernest Hemingway, and others, the realm of the author as celebrity. Young, talented, witty, and handsome, McInerney himself has been the subject of many articles and interviews, and the first serious critical articles on his work have now begun to appear in print. By virtue of his talent and his visibility, McInerney must be regarded as one of America's most important young writers.

Analysis of Selected Titles

STORY OF MY LIFE

Story of My Life, 1988, novel.

Social Concerns

Like *Bright Lights, Big City*, *Story of My Life* is narrated by an observant, witty, and jaded member of Manhattan's party elite. Alison Poole's descriptions of drug use and casual sex reflect a slice of life in the present, which the novel's epigraph describes as an age of anarchy.

Drug use constitutes one of the major pastimes of Alison's crowd, and although she knows rationally that it is dangerous, she generally gets swept along with the crowd, willing to temporarily lose herself and her problems in a line of cocaine. A recurring plot element is a card with the emergency number of a drug treatment center which is transferred from character to character. At the end of the novel when Alison comes to her senses, she finally uses the card to call for help.

According to the characters in *Story of My Life*, love and sex in the modern world are hardly distinguishable; the continuous use of the phrase "in lust" blurs the distinction by blending the two. Sex serves many purposes in the novel: like drugs, it helps people to forget; it can create a momentary illusion of love and security; and it can be used to hurt. But the modern dangers of casual sex are also expressed through references to AIDS, as well as Alison's accidental pregnancy. None of the characters in the novel seems capable of a long-term relationship, and new liaisons are created almost from page to page. For Alison, much of her confusion about love and sex stems from her father's incestuous advances, which she says, almost soured her on sex forever.

Themes

Despite her other faults, Alison claims to believe in honesty, sometimes even taking it to an extreme. Although her behavior is not always consistent with her belief, the conflict between acting and being is a central one in the novel, expressed through the continual games of "Truth or Dare" and, paradoxically, through Alison's acting lessons. Although she is learning to act out roles, Alison's acting teacher encourages his students to draw from themselves to fill out the part. His highest praise, that someone is "inhabiting the role," comes only when he feels that the performance, and the emotions, are honest ones. Ironically, the money for Alison's acting lessons often comes through dishonesty, as when she tricks Skip into giving her money for an abortion she does not need, or when her father, who seems to be involved in some unsavory business dealings, sends money for her school.

Like McInerney's other novels, *Story of My Life* may be read as a *bildungsroman*, a novel that chronicles a character's coming-of-age and awareness of who he or she is. Alison faces many challenges, some sexual, some financial, all of which must be conquered if she is to become a complete person. At the end of the novel, Alison reaches some understanding about herself and who she is; even though she has not solved all her problems, her growing self-awareness and newfound acceptance of her own life must be read as a positive step.

Characters

Alison Poole is the novel's narrator and most-important character. Twenty "going on 40,000," she feels she has seen everything and done everything, and her jaded response to most of what she sees points out the emptiness of a life lived only from one thrill to the next. Her acting is the only thing that seems to give her life focus, and praise from her teacher seems to mean more to her than anything else. Her family and friends, for the most part, are hindrances; her sister Rebecca is an exaggerated version of what Alison might become, manipulating men for financial security, while their father is too busy pursuing girls Alison's age to make sure her financial arrangements are in order. Alison truly loves only her grandparents and her youngest sister, none of whom appears in the novel.

Dean Chasen, a thirty-two-year-old stockbroker who wants to be a writer, captures Alison's eye, and they circle warily into a short-lived relationship. Dean has just broken up with his girlfriend, and Alison later concludes that he only wanted someone to spend time with, but the desolation she feels after she betrays him with his friend Skip Pendleton suggests that their relationship had possibilities.

Didi is the ultimate party girl, attractive, sexy, and always carrying cocaine. Alison's feelings about her are mixed; on the one hand she recognizes Didi's sex appeal and feels inferior to her in some ways, yet she knows that Didi is often overbearing and manipulative, and that her drug use has gotten out of control. While Alison helps Didi get treatment, she does not entirely approve of the results, since Didi then criticizes her drug-using friends with the same vigor she once used to get them to snort cocaine with her.

None of the members of Alison's circle are satisfied with what they have, and all of them seek more—more money, more sex, more thrills. Only Alison's relationship with Alex, her first love, demonstrates the potential happiness that people can have together. Alison and Alex no longer have sex, but their friendship is one of the few stable areas in Alison's life, and consequently, in the novel.

Techniques

The first-person narration of *Story of My Life* allows interior views of the main character and captures the intelligence of a likeable character living on the edge. Alison's narration is more casual than the unnamed narrator's in *Bright Lights, Big*

City, with many digressions and casual interpolations, and the erratic nature of her storytelling reveals her manic energy and the lack of coherence in her life.

Literary Precedents

The narrative technique evokes works like *The Adventures of Huckleberry Finn* and *The Great Gatsby*, but a more important link to these works is McInerney's realistic approach to fiction. Like these two earlier novels, *Story of My Life* is a novel of manners, presenting the reader with an accurate picture of a certain time and place. The reader knows what the characters drink, where they eat, what drugs they take, what Broadway shows they see. This realism also has an artistic value: the shows Alison mentions, for example, are *Fences*, about the difficult relationship between a father and child, and *Les Liaisons Dangereuses*, a story of sexual misadventures and deceptions similar to Alison's own story. McInerney manipulates the concrete details so that they also illuminate character, plot, and theme.

Relation to Previous Works

With *Story of My Life*, Jay McInerney continues to chronicle a frenetic world of alienation and frustration, but this work is the farthest outside himself. Using Alison Poole as a narrator, McInerney gives the reader a feminine outlook on society that did not exist in *Bright Lights, Big City*, or *Ransom*. Although Alison is a typical McInerney character in search of meaning for her life, her outlook on men, sex, music, and fashions differs radically from the masculine viewpoint expressed in the author's earlier work.

Additional Sources

Kael, Pauline. Review of *Bright Lights, Big City*. *The New Yorker* (April 18, 1988): 120-121. Champions the novel at the expense of the film adaptation.

Pinsker, Sanford. "Soft Lights, Academic Talk: A Conversation with Jay McInerney." *The Literary Review* (Fall 1986): 107-114. Interview discussing *The Great Gatsby,* the novel of manners, and learning to write.

Steinberg, Sybil. Review of *Story of My Life*. *Publishers Weekly* 219 (July 29, 1988). Primarily positive review comparing the novel with *Bright Lights, Big City*.

Greg Garrett
Baylor University

PATRICIA A. MCKILLIP
1948

Update
Patricia McKillip continues to write fantasy fiction, but in her novels since the impressive *Riddlemaster* trilogy, she has turned more to science fiction. Without entirely abandoning the theme of magic, which she handled so well in the trilogy, she has incorporated conventional science fiction motifs, such as space flight and interplanetary exploration. She has also written fiction for young adults, such as *The Changeling Sea* (1988). This book, concerning a lonely girl orphaned by the sea and a prince who turns into a sea dragon, has the charm and simplicity of a fairy tale and is a genuinely moving story. Her latest novel, *The Sorceress and the Cygnet* (1991), returns to fantasy, playing out through archetypal characters and symbolic events the conflict between love and power.

Analysis of Selected Titles

THE MOON AND THE FACE
The Moon and the Face, 1985, novel. Prequel: *Moon Flash,* 1984, novel.

Social Concerns
A sequel to *Moon Flash* (1984), *The Moon and the Face* also contrasts a primitive, traditional culture and a technologically advanced one. Communication has been established between the unspoiled, Edenic Riverworld and other planets. McKillip expands this contrast to include completely different societies in unfamiliar worlds. A mysteriously abandoned all-white city, a ruin of a long dead civilization, raises the question of how such total destruction could have occurred. And the figure of the Alien, a radically different, non-human being, teaches the protagonist to respect "otherness," however strange it may appear.

Themes
McKillip's social themes focus on the relationship of cultures. She effectively integrates this idea with the psychological themes of growing up, the ties of family, the nature and demands of love, and the problems of communication. Kyriel, child of the Riverworld, must learn to accept and master the scientific knowledge available to her in the Dome, the way station of an interstellar civiliza-

tion, without sacrificing her deep emotional ties with home. Her maturation includes an evolving sensitivity to a variety of creatures and their lifestyles. She also comes to know the meaning of love, which, besides offering fulfillment, demands sacrifices. McKillip treats the theme of communication on many levels, ranging from interstellar technology to telepathic dreams.

Characters

As in *Moon Flash*, the protagonist of *The Moon and the Face* is Kyriel, a delightful "child-woman" brimming with curiosity and "swarming like a bee-hive with questions." When we first see her she is wearing a silver flight suit and flying an interplanetary pickup craft. Her adventures subject her both to outer danger and to inner conflict. The crash of her spaceship on a deserted moon leaves her desolate except for the presence of an Alien. More seriously, it leaves her with premonitory dreams of trouble at home. Her deep love for her father, the Healer, and for her betrothed, Terje, contends with her need to fulfill her mission. Terje is also subjected to the strains of growing up, for he learns that he is to become the new Healer of Riverworld. Although he does not feel equal to the awesome role, he must accept it.

The Alien, encountered by Kyriel on the moon, is an exceptional achievement in characterization. It is terrifying only in its extraordinary height; its general appearance is more bizarre than frightening. It has three eyes; its head is a mound of white fur; and its mouth a shiny white beak. The row of tiny, quivering, brightly-colored fur balls encircling its beak turn out to be babies. Above all, this strange creature is both benign and brilliant. Without its gentleness, good will, and technical assistance, Kyriel would not survive.

Techniques

Alternate chapters of *The Moon and the Face* deal with Kyriel's experiences in space and events in Riverworld. McKillip also uses Kyriel's dreams to reveal what is happening in her home land. While the novel is told in the third person, McKillip manages to communicate the point of view of the separate characters. Terje's anxiety, for example, is handled in language distinctively different from Kyriel's, a style that blends simplicity and poetic evocation.

Literary Precedents

Although the idea of contrasting societies is a venerable one, McKillips's specific vision of two worlds is highly original. Analogous to the unspoiled paradise are

Edgar Rice Burroughs's Tarzan books, and Jean Auel's novels of prehistoric humankind. The importance of dreaming in Riverworld also recalls the use of that motif in Ursula Le Guin's *The Word for World Is Forest* (1972).

FOOL'S RUN

Fool's Run, 1987, novel.

Social Concerns/Themes

Social concerns and themes are interwoven in this complex work of science fiction. Against a background of futuristic space travel, the action takes place within a variety of interplanetary settings. The major themes include justice and revenge, sanity and madness, verbal and nonverbal communication, music, and the nature of symbolism.

The nature of justice comes into play in the central plot line. At the beginning of the novel the reader learns that seven years earlier a young woman named Terra, in response to a vision, killed fifteen hundred people with a laser assault rifle. One of those killed was the wife of Aaron Fisher, who spends the intervening years dreaming of revenge and simply trying to understand the motive of the killer. Terra has been imprisoned in the Underworld, an orbital prison which is extremely difficult to enter and from which escape is impossible.

Opposed to this sympathetic individual desire for revenge or explanation is the overarching issue of justice, for Terra seems to be insane. Balanced delicately between the rival claims of justice and revenge is the elusive definition of sanity. McKillip artfully presents an equivocal view of the strange vision which prompted the multiple murders.

An important strand in this thematic web is the problem of communication, which is introduced early in the novel. As the protagonist plays music in a trance-like state, unaware of the chaos around him, the difficulty of communicating is explored on many levels. The scenes involving the spacecraft deal with the technical means of communication between ships and between the ships and the land base. The protagonist, called the Magician, communicates on a non-verbal level and also responds to psychic messages from another consciousness. While unaware of the chaos at hand, he is able to envision what is happening in the Underworld. Mental telepathy as a form of interpersonal language parallels the interplanetary technology in that both are able to transmit language mysteriously through space.

Closely tied to the theme of communication is an exploration of the nature of symbolism, for the Magician can respond to and use non-verbal language. At one point he discusses the role of symbolism as a component of human nature. His examples of culturally recognizable symbols include the wedding ring and the cross, but he goes on to cite symbols he has shared with Terra, including a bent oval on purple sand. He perceives this symbol as part of her vision and interprets its meaning as a call for transformation. He recognizes that all such symbols have a compelling necessity for those who envision them. Music also functions as theme and symbol in the novel.

Characters

The central character in *Fool's Run* is called the Magician or Magic-man, and his given name (Roger Restak) is referred to only fleetingly. In the dramatic opening scene he plays Bach on the piano non-stop for several hours, oblivious to the mayhem around him. Although he works as a bar band performer he is clearly much more, as evidenced by his psychic abilities. When he takes his band, Nova, for an experimental concert tour that includes the Underworld, his multi-faceted talents come into play, climaxing with an ingenious coding of Bach by number into the Underworld computer. His skills are mystical as well as musical, as evidenced by the fact that he alone can enter the mysterious visionary world in the mind of Terra.

Two other important male characters are Aaron Fisher, the widower seeking revenge, and Jason Klyos, the supervisor of the notorious Underworld. Aaron is a gentle soul, who is drawn to one of the women in the band who always wears a mask. Jason is cool, tough, and rational, as his job demands, but he is also sensitive to innuendo in dealing with people and is highly responsive to music. Both men are convincingly well-rounded characters.

In contrast, most of the female characters are more allegorical than realistic. Quasar, a member of Nova, is of French origin, and her speech is punctuated by French phrases. She is repeatedly depicted polishing her nails in brightly colored lacquer. As an essentially comic figure, she is almost a caricature.

The two most important women are Terra, the killer, and her twin sister, Michelle, whom we first meet in disguise. Terra's character is developed largely through her dreams, and eventually through her vision. Her mind inhabits a different order of consciousness from the other characters, with whom she is unable to communicate directly. Only the Magician can even begin to understand her. Michelle is introduced as the Queen of Hearts, a figure with an expressionless mask of gold painted on her face. Later in the novel she is individualized, and her account of her childhood with her twin reveals much about them. Aaron's attraction to this woman whose hidden face duplicates that of his wife's killer, is an appealing and tantalizing irony.

With the novel's emphasis on symbolism, it is not surprising that the principal characters are developed through their unconscious perceptions as well as their conscious actions. Their outward appearances reflect their inner being, which is more important than their social selves.

Techniques/Literary Precedents

McKillip uses a number of sophisticated literary techniques. Some are part of the conventions of science fiction, but many transcend the usual formulas of the genre. She emphasizes theme, character, language, and narrative structure rather than plot or setting, and downplays references to space technology. The novel is structured contrapuntally, with chapters alternating between the orbital prison called the Dark Ring of the Underworld and the locale of the Magician—at first the Constellation Club where his band plays, then his spaceship, the *Flying Wail*.

Counterpoint as a structural device is especially appropriate in a novel where music functions on many levels. The Magician's absorption in music is established by his playing of Bach at the opening of the novel. The musical motif reenters later at several points. A musical phrase becomes an essential factor in the intergalactic communication, and a search for a phrase from a Bach suite becomes a matter of cosmic urgency. The Magician also uses Bach's music as a device to stall the Underworld pursuit of his ship. By coding Bach into the Underworld computer, he achieves a forty-eight hour override. He explains the technique simply as "playing by number." The actual relationship of music and number is thus gracefully made part of the action without unnecessary technical explanation. Another musical motif is that of the cube. The Queen of Hearts is hired as a cuber for Nova. References to "cubing," or amplifying, abound. Cubing makes the air "pulse like a war zone."

McKillip's imagery employs the visual arts as well as music. There is much color in the novel: the gold-painted face of the mysterious Queen of Hearts; the bright-colored finger nails of Quasar; and the purple sand of the vision shared by Terra and the Magician. In conjunction with the prevalence of color imagery is the startling contrast of dark and light. The prison is termed the Dark Ring, and its most notorious prisoner is Terra, who massacred a crowd with a laser rifle in order to transform everything else into pure light. Repeated phrases, musical sounds and repeated shafts of color heighten the sensory impact of McKillip's narrative. Since the band can amplify visual as well as auditory effects, the intermingling of musical and color imagery is integrated into plot and theme.

Throughout the novel McKillip maintains a double level of symbolism and realism. Along with allegorical references to red suns and purple sand, the dialogue is effectively realistic and frequently comic. The Magician, for example, complains that "thinking about people scrambles my circuitry," and his friend Sidney laments that the art of conversation "went out with the bassoon." In general the crisp dialogue is male, and the imagistic, visionary language is female. The concreteness and the sensory effect of McKillip's prose make an unforgettable impression on the reader.

Relation to Previous Works
In *Fool's Run* McKillip charts new fictional territory and refines old techniques. Her earlier work focused on fantasy rather than science fiction, and in her adult and children's books she dealt at least in part with simple, pre-technological societies in which magic, dreams, and riddling play major roles. In her last two novels she employed classical science fiction motifs. But even in her adoption of these genre conventions, McKillip is innovative; the concept of an orbital prison and the bizarrely appealing Alien are both highly original. McKillip also brings to her new work the imagistic language that worked so well in the *Riddlemaster* trilogy. Episodes involving mystical experience, such as Terra's vision and the Magician's psychic awareness, use language similar to that in the climactic Wind Tower ascent in *Harpist in the Wind*. The Magician, although a distinctive individual, has a mythic dimension that recalls Morgon the Riddlemaster.

Additional Sources
Frey, Yvonne A. Review of *Fool's Run*. School Library Journal 32 (October, 1985): 184. Stresses the use of dichotomies in the novel, and cites its imagery and symbolism.

Miles, Margaret. Review of *Fool's Run*. Voice of Youth Advocates 10 (August 15, 1987): 132. The reviewer notes the intricate plot and explores the images of sound and color in the novel.

Smith, Rosemary. Review of *Fool's Run*. School Library Journal 33 (June/July, 1987): 117. The reviewer stresses McKillip's imaginative use of musical themes.

Charlotte Spivack
University of Massachusetts at Amherst

LARRY MCMURTRY
1936

Update

Larry McMurtry has published several novels since 1987. These novels fall into two broad categories: sequels to earlier works—*Texasville* (1987) and *Some Can Whistle* (1989)—and recreations of the historical west in the tradition of *Lonesome Dove* (1985)—*Anything for Billy* (1988) and *Buffalo Girls* (1990). All four novels were admired by critics and sold well, though they achieved neither the critical nor popular success of *Lonesome Dove*. That novel was made into a well-received television mini-series in 1989. It starred Robert Duvall and Tommy Lee Jones as Gus and Call and won numerous awards, including one from the Screen Writers Guild of America. *Texasville,* the sequel to *The Last Picture Show* (1966), was made into a film with the same director (Peter Bogdanovich), screenwriter (McMurtry), and actors who distinguished the earlier adaption. However, the film was considered a disappointment by reviewers.

Epic in its scope and ambition, *Lonesome Dove* (1985) remains McMurtry's best work. The American West, as imagined in the novel, has the texture of reality and the artfulness of myth. It is not the *real* West; better than reality, it encapsulates the heroic and brutal *idea* of the West—the large and spacious stage for epic drama; love and friendship, loyalty and honor, betrayal and death. The television version honored its original; the mini-series was a fortunate choice because it allowed time for the story to be told without the drastic concision dictated by the constraints of a theatrical release. The January 1991 re-run of the mini-series revived interest in the novel, and it reappeared again for several weeks on the *New York Times* paperback best-seller list.

The historical novels, both appearing briefly on many best seller lists, are interesting as examples of revisionist re-mythologizing of the legendary West. McMurtry combines old forms—the dime novel and the epistolary novel—with a retelling of old stories about historical characters—Billy the Kid and Calamity Jane. His purpose is not to set the record straight, de-mythologize these people, or to tell what really happened. Instead, McMurtry re-invents the characters of our western legends, whom he depicts as confused, aware that their time has almost passed, and agents of their own obsolescence. The result is a new myth that is equally exhilarating and melancholy.

McMurtry has published a collection of his critical essays, *Film Flam, Essays on Hollywood* (1989). He also continues to write screenplays, one of which is *Souvenirs,* based on a story by John Cougar Mellencamp, who also stars in the film.

Analysis of Selected Titles

SOME CAN WHISTLE
Some Can Whistle, 1989, novel.

Social Concerns/Themes
Set in the present, *Some Can Whistle* deals with a number of themes, the most important of which is the relationship between parent and child. This is a familiar theme in McMurtry's work, and he is both eloquent and convincing in his analysis of the dynamics of the relationship between an absentee father and his neglected and abused daughter, grown to adulthood surrounded by violence, fanaticism, and unnecessary sorrow. McMurtry examines this issue with delicacy and restraint. The novel also deals with the issue of aging—the tendency to withdraw from active participation in the business of living; the pain of learning to live a life that encompasses violence, murder, loss, and great love.

Characters
The novel's central character and narrator is Danny Deck, the hero of an earlier novel, *All My Friends Are Going to Be Strangers* (1972). That novel ended with Danny, his marriage over and his parental rights denied, destroying his novel and walking into the Rio Grande. His spirit haunts two other novels by McMurtry: *Moving On* (1970) and *Terms of Endearment* (1975). In both of these novels, Danny's friends assume that he is dead. *Some Can Whistle* depends upon McMurtry's little joke: rather than being literally dead in the waters of a river, Danny, a successful Hollywood writer, is figuratively dead as he uses his Hollywood wealth to isolate himself from friends, love and living. Into this living death bursts T. R., the grown-up child that Danny has never seen. Danny is a wonderful McMurtry character—eccentric, bewildered by almost everything, living alone with a housekeeper and keeping in contact with the outside world by telephone. But McMurtry's great triumph is T. R., who locates and invades Danny's protected half-life, demanding that he love her, save her and her two children, help her break her boyfriend out of jail, give her lots of money to spend on junk, protect her, and now, when it is too late, be her father. Poor Danny, bewildered but full of good will, tries to oblige, and the collision between the aging, reclusive, sophisticated father and the disaster-prone, redneck young daughter provides the novel with its plot and its central theme. That the two learn to love each other is amazing; that they lose each other violently is heartbreaking. Surrounding the central characters

of Danny and T. R. are a host of marvelous McMurtry creations: T. R.'s lover, Muddy, a failed burglar; her children, Bo and Jesse; and the man who kills her, Earl Dee.

Techniques/Literary Precedents

Some Can Whistle is a traditional realistic novel. It is a richly detailed account of modern life; set in Texas, it is less grounded in regional concerns than McMurtry's earlier works. It is also traditional in its use of the first person narrator. Danny Deck's voice is richly individual—elegiac, regretful, gentle, and detached, even in loss and sorrow. One is made aware of his loss of power through aging, his regret at that loss of power, and his mild gladness that the storms of youth are forever behind him. The first person narrative allows McMurtry to approximate the process of letting go that is a part of growing old. It is delicately and poignantly achieved.

Relation to Previous Works

The novel returns to both characters and themes of McMurtry's earlier works. The most marked change is the pervasiveness of a sense of the inexorability of time. Although this, too, has always been present in McMurtry's fiction, it assumes a new centrality in this novel. *Some Can Whistle* also provides a sense of closure to many of the unresolved questions of the earlier novels; it removes the mystery about Danny's fate and allows him to grow old and approach death in a realistic way rather than in the romantic and mysterious darkness of the swirling waters of the Rio Grande. This revisionist ending is more fitting and more disturbing than its rehearsal.

Additional Sources

Butler, Jack. Review of *Anything for Billy*. *New York Times Book Review* (October 16, 1988): 3. Representative of the criticism of the historical novels since *Lonesome Dove,* it recognizes the greatness of the idea, but dismisses the novel as "minor."

Peavy, Charles D. *Larry McMurtry*. Boston: G. K. Hall, 1977. Although dated, still the best full-length, scholarly study of the novels.

Schaeffer, Susan Fromberg. "Lonesome Jane." Review of *Buffalo Girls*. *New York Times Book Review* (October 7, 1990): 3. Insightful review that also considers McMurtry's larger purpose in rewriting the legends of the Wild West.

Schmidt, Dorey, ed. *Larry McMurtry: Unredeemed Dreams*. Living Authors Series 1. Edinburg, TX: Pan American University Press, 1978. Dated, but still valuable as a source.

Elizabeth Buckmaster
Pennsylvania State University

JAMES MICHENER
1907

Publishing History

James Michener proved himself to be a man of diverse interests long before he published his first major work at the age of forty. At fourteen he hitchhiked through forty-five states, and at fifteen he wrote a sports column for his local Pennsylvania newspaper. A graduate of Swarthmore in 1929 with a bachelor's degree in English, Michener taught at the Hill School in Pottstown, Pennsylvania, until he received the Lippincott Award that allowed him to study at St. Andrew's University in Scotland. After working his way home on a Mediterranean collier, Michener taught at the George School in Pennsylvania and the Colorado State College of Education until 1941, when he became an associate editor for Macmillan Company. In 1942, despite the pacifism of his Quaker religion, Michener volunteered for service in the United States Navy and was assigned to the Pacific in a capacity described by his biographer A. Grove Day as "troubleshooter and atoll-hopper." Michener's first major work, *Tales of the South Pacific,* was begun when he was "stranded on an island with nothing to do."

Since the publication of *Tales of the South Pacific* (1947), Michener has produced more than forty fiction and nonfiction works, most of which have been published by Random House. Some of his earlier works include *The Fires of Spring* (1949), a somewhat autobiographical novel; *Return to Paradise* (1951), a collection of short stories and travel sketches; *The Bridges at Toko-Ri* (1953), a novel of the Korean War; and *Sayonara* (1954), a novel depicting the love between an American soldier and a Japanese girl.

Not until Michener began writing novels of almost epic proportions, beginning with the 1959 publication of *Hawaii,* did he become a best-selling author. Some of these massive works, described by Caryn James of the *New York Times Magazine* as "monolithic tales of places," include *The Source* (1965), a novel describing the archaeological excavation of Tell Makor in Israel; *Centennial* (1974), a fictionalized history of Colorado from its early geological development until the present; *Chesapeake* (1978), a "history" of the Chesapeake Bay area from the sixteenth century to the present day; *The Covenant* (1980), an exploration of fifteen thousand years of South African history; *Poland* (1983), a fictionalized account of seven hundred years of Polish history; and *Texas* (1985), a "history" of Texas from the sixteenth century to the present.

Although Michener has always been a prolific writer, since 1986 he has been especially busy. Continuing his long association with Random House, he has produced four more novels: *Legacy* (1987), *Alaska* (1988), *Journey* (1989), and *Caribbean* (1989). *Alaska* and *Caribbean* are typical of Michener's popular historical epics, but *Alaska* is more varied than *Caribbean*. Although Michener is often didactic and violent, *Caribbean* contains too much of both qualities. Michener's focus in *Caribbean* is male-oriented (Spanish, French, and English explorers and Buccaneers), and interesting female characters are in short supply. When asked why he chose the Caribbean as the subject of his epic novel, Michener responded that the area was "going to be a part of the American problem . . . . We're going to have to assume the role that Britain had for many years, and that Spain had."

In one of his two shorter novels, *Legacy*, Michener describes the members of the Starr family, who have defended American rights for over two hundred years. While the Starrs are ostensibly the focus of the episodes in *Legacy*, the real protagonist of the novel is the Constitution of the United States. Michener's latest short novel, *Journey*, originally a section in *Alaska*, "depicts the courage that men and women can exhibit when dealing with adversity." Michener's publisher, who believed the Canadian episode in *Alaska* was intrusive, suggested that Michener cut the section. Because *Journey* was published as a short novel rather than as an episode in *Alaska*, Michener was able to lengthen the story of four noble Englishmen and an Irish peasant who forge their way through Canada to the gold rush.

During the last two years, Michener has produced four works in addition to those published by Random House. His nonfiction *Six Days in Havana* was published by the University of Texas Press in 1989. The text is illustrated with photographs taken by Michener's editorial assistant John Kings, who accompanied him to Cuba in 1988. Material gathered by Michener during this fruitful visit also appears in his novel *Caribbean*. The second work, *Pilgrimage*, published in 1990 by Rodale Press, describes his visit to Poland after an invitation from the same government which censored his novel *Poland* (1983). *The Eagle and the Raven*, a short biographical account of the lives of the adversary generals Sam Houston and Antonio Lopez de Santa-Anna, was published in 1990 by State House Press at the instigation of one of Michener's former aides, Debbie Brooks. Illustrated with the drawings of Charles Shaw, *The Eagle and the Raven* was originally written as part of *Texas* but was eliminated because it was more historical than narrative. His latest work is *The Novel* (1991), a treatise on his views of writing fiction.

Critical Reception, Honors and Popularity

Although Michener has won numerous awards in both America and abroad (the National Association of Independent Schools Award in 1954 and 1958; the Bestsellers Paperback of the Year Award in 1968; the Hungarian Studies Foundation

Award in 1970; the U. S. Medal of Freedom in 1977), he has received no literary honors since his 1948 Pulitzer Prize for *Tales of the South Pacific*. Yet Michener's popularity has never depended on the evaluation of critics. While many critics fault Michener for combining fiction with nonfiction, for attributing the exploits of historical figures to his own fictional characters, Michener has, in the words of Jim Shahin, a "seemingly permanent reservation at the top of the bestseller lists." Michener gives his own conception of his role as a writer in the prologue to *The Eagle and the Raven*:

> I was born with a passionate desire to communicate, to organize experience, to tell tales that dramatize the adventures which listeners might have had. I have been that ancient man who sat by the campfire at night and regaled the hunters with imaginative accounts of their prowess that morning in tracking down their prey . . . . The job of a story teller is to tell stories, and I have concentrated on that obligation.

Most of Michener's faithful readers would agree that he has successfully met that obligation.

Analysis of Selected Titles

TALES OF THE SOUTH PACIFIC

Tales of the South Pacific, 1947, related short stories.

Social Concerns/Themes

In *Tales of the South Pacific*, Michener explores themes common to most of his works: racism and bigotry; the brotherhood of humankind; the effects of war, violence, exploitation, and authoritarianism on the human psyche; and man's destruction of his environment. Michener has stated that the book was written "under extremely difficult circumstances. I was in the Navy on Espiritu Santo in the South Seas . . . . I was sure the people who were bitching so much about the Islands would not remember them that way. I try to anticipate history."

Characters

Lieutenant Tony Fry, who appears in nine of the nineteen tales, is one of the most anti-authoritarian of the American characters in *Tales of the South Pacific*.

Readers meet Fry in the first tale, "The South Pacific," when Admiral Millard Kester orders Fry to remove from the side of his old TBF the twelve painted beer bottles illustrating Fry's twelve "heroic" beer-ferrying missions. In the tale "Mutiny," which takes place on Norfolk Island, Fry becomes involved with a descendent of one of history's best known mutineers, Fletcher Christian. The old woman Teta Christian and her family object to the navy's building an airstrip on their island because the most strategic place for the airstrip is in the middle of a stand of pine trees planted by their ancestors. Siding with the mutineers, Fry dynamites a bulldozer in protest against the desecration of that "living cathedral." In "The Cave," Fry lives comfortably in a cave on Tulagi while he receives transmissions from the "Remittance Man," a British trader who risks death by sending reports of weather and troop movements to the U.S. Navy. Although Fry continues to laugh at military protocol, he succeeds in confessing his own fear of death and learns to respect the Remittance Man's courage. The Remittance Man's death leads Fry to question the nature of a courage that enables human beings to risk their own lives for a cause. In the story "The Landing on Kuralei," Fry gives his own life when he chooses to move inland with the Marines, thus becoming one of the legendary heroes whom the narrator describes as always being "somewhere further up the line." Through the evolution of Fry's character, Michener's readers learn the realities of war—and death.

In the third story, "An Officer and a Gentleman," Michener introduces Ensign Bill Harbison, Tony Fry's foil. Although Harbison is a man who begins his navy career with both intellectual and athletic promise, he should have enlisted in the army, where his abilities would have earned him quick promotions. Unfortunately, the snobbish Harbison believes that officers in the army are little better than enlisted men. Slowly rotting on Efate Island in his less-than-demanding role as recreation officer, Harbison exercises his body playing various sports and his mind playing with the emotions of navy nurses. However, none of the plebeian nurses are serious competition for Harbison's Vassar-educated wife, to whom he writes creatively passionate and melodramatic letters describing his "heroic" four-day adventure on a raft. Harbison, who spends much of his time trying to persuade his commanding officer to transfer him to active duty, finally receives his much desired transfer to combat before the climactic battle in "The Landing on Kuralei." When Tony Fry dies on Kuralei beach, Harbison, who has used his father-in-law's influence to obtain a rest and rehabilitation leave, is alive and well in New Mexico.

One of the navy nurses whom "gentleman" Bill Harbison sets out to seduce is Nellie Forbush, a romantic young woman from Arkansas who wants to experience life. Because navy nurses are officers, Forbush is forbidden to fraternize with the enlisted men of her own class, who might love her for herself. On Efate, Nellie Forbush is an officer's prize catch, a pretty white "rarity" among all the brown faces. A naive target for Harbison's wiles, Forbush is rejected when her marriage proposal shocks Harbison into seeing her as a woman he "wouldn't look twice at in the States."

To add to her disillusionment with love, Ensign Nellie Forbush is exposed to the unromantic reality of duty in the South Pacific. Having left Arkansas with a hunger for "new thoughts and deeper perceptions," Forbush recognizes the irony in the clipping from a Little Rock newspaper which declares her "Our Heroine." Nevertheless, Forbush's heart and her romantic idealism are soon captured by Emile De Becque, a wealthy and courageous plantation owner who fled his native France after knifing a bully. Although Forbush loves De Becque, who proposes honorable marriage, she refuses to marry him. As Harbison rejected Nellie Forbush because of class snobbery, so Forbush rejects De Becque because of racial bigotry. De Becque, who has lived in the South Pacific for twenty-six years, has fathered eight illegitimate daughters, two of whom are half Polynesian. Although rejecting a lifetime of bigotry takes a quieter kind of courage than storming a beach, it is courage which finally enables Nellie Forbush to be a "heroine" who can accept De Becque as a "man" and his dark skinned daughters as human beings.

The most memorable character in *Tales of the South Pacific* is the old Tonkinese woman, Bloody Mary, whom Michener introduces in the story "Fo' Dolla'." A source of entertainment for the bored marines, who amuse themselves by teaching her obscenities and buying her souvenirs, Bloody Mary is named for her betel stained mouth, which looks as if it has been "gashed by a rusty razor." Although Mary is one of many women from Tonkin China (Vietnam) who have indentured themselves to wealthy French planters like Emile De Becque and Jacques Benoit, she clearly subverts their exploitation of her talents. In one month, Mary earns more money selling grass skirts to Americans than she can earn in a year under the colonial system of indenture; thus, Benoit forces through laws which prohibit Mary and her cronies from selling the skirts. While officers are forced to uphold local laws, the enlisted marines see Mary as a rebel, a "symbol of age-old defiance of unjust laws."

Bloody Mary is the mother of lovely Liat, who lives on Michener's mythical Bali-ha'i, where wise Frenchmen have sequestered all their virgin daughters, no matter what race they are. Through Bloody Mary and Liat, Michener introduces a male/female relationship which is doomed because of racial bigotry. "Very fine" is the way Bloody Mary describes Marine Lieutenant Joe Cable, who is the scion of an old Philadelphia family and a Princeton graduate, and very fine is the life which Bloody Mary dreams of for her daughter. Although Cable feels that no self-respecting officer would make love to a "native" girl, he is obsessed by the delicate Tonkenese girl from the moment her mother introduces them. Yet, when Bloody Mary insists that Cable marry his young lover, he refuses, for no matter how much he loves Liat, he cannot introduce a Tonkenese wife to his Philadelphia parents. Lacking the courage that Nellie Forbush shows in a similar situation, Cable watches as Bloody Mary gives Liat to Jacques Benoit, a lascivious exploiter of young girls, and ironically, the same planter who is responsible for the laws which forbade Mary to better her economic standard. Disgusted by his own behavior, angry at his peers who plague him about his relationship with Liat, Joe Cable proves his bravery in the battle at Kuralei and dies, a "man" at last.

Another unusual figure in *Tales of the South Pacific* is Luther Billis, whom Michener describes as a "big dealer." A modern Long John Silver with his sagging belly, bare chest, numerous tatoos, long hair, and gold earring, Billis manipulates officers and enlisted men alike to get what he wants. When he wants to visit Vanicoro Island, Billis interests Lieutenant Tony Fry in the religion of that island, the worship of pigs. Vanicoro's sacred boars are staked out for seven years so that their tusks grow back into their jawbone, making a complete circle through the roots. These boars and the agony they endure are used as a metaphor to explain the pain, suffering, and death experienced by the men and women serving in the South Pacific.

In the last of the tales, "A Cemetery at Hoga Point," the first-person narrator of the story visits the grave of the dead hero, Lieutenant Joe Cable. Lying close to Cable's grave is the grave of Commander Hoag of the SeaBees, who miraculously constructed a landing strip in fifteen days and died in performance of his duty. Not far from both these men is the grave of a man whose death was the result of his own negligence: he drunkenly drove his jeep off a cliff. Heroes or cowards, rich or poor, black or white, officer or enlisted men—in a cemetery, there are no classes: "There are only men."

Techniques

Always extremely meticulous in his research, Michener wrote *Tales of the South Pacific* from his personal experience during World War II. A. Grove Days states that Michener thought of his South Pacific stories as a novel unified by "strong" themes, by a "changing but limited setting around the Pacific islands," and by a number of "recurring figures." The nineteen stories, which climax in the tale "The Landing on Kuralei," have three narrators: a first-person officer-narrator who tells thirteen of the stories; Lieutenant Bus Adams, who narrates two stories; and an omniscient narrator, who relates four tales.

Literary Precedents

Novels describing the adventures of white men in the tropics have fascinated western readers since the publication of Daniel Defoe's *Robinson Crusoe* in 1719. Herman Melville romanticizes his account of the Marquesans in *Typee* (1846). Robert Louis Stevenson's *Treasure Island* (1883) describes the adventures of the boy Jim and the pirate Long John Silver. Joseph Conrad, who explores the concept of courage in *Lord Jim* (1900), treats both racial and economic exploitation in *Heart of Darkness* (1902). Nordoff and Hall's *Mutiny on the Bounty* (1932) describes the life of sailors in the South Pacific as well as the famous eighteenth-century mutiny led by Fletcher Christian.

Novels stressing the futility of war also abound in western literature. These include Leo Tolstoy's *War and Peace* (1865-1869), which discusses Napoleon's invasion of Russia; Stephen Crane's *The Red Badge of Courage* (1895), which describes a young Union soldier's first battle experience in the American Civil War; and Erich Marie Remarque's *All Quiet on the Western Front* (1929), which explores World War I through the eyes of a German soldier.

Adaptations

In 1949, Rogers and Hammerstein were inspired by the tales "Our Heroine" and "Fo' Dolla' " to write one of Broadway's most successful musicals, *South Pacific,* starring Mary Martin as Nellie Forbush and Ezio Pinza as Emile De Becque. Michener himself fought to keep "You Have to be Taught," a song about racial bigotry, in the show. A film of *South Pacific* starring Mitzi Gaynor and Rosanno Brazzi was produced in 1958.

HAWAII

Hawaii, 1959, novel.

Social Concerns/Themes

Michener's publication of *Hawaii* was timely, occurring only three months after Hawaii was granted statehood. Yet A. Grove Day states that Michener's interest in writing a book about the islands originated over a decade earlier, in 1944, while he was escorting John Dos Passos around Manoa Valley. Five years later, during a longshoreman's strike, which caused an economic crisis in Hawaii, Michener decided to write a novel that explored the "social relations in this melting pot of the Pacific."

Like *Tales of the South Pacific*, *Hawaii* integrates themes of racism, bigotry, exploitation, and prejudice, especially religious prejudice. However, the novel's major theme is symbolized in the archetypal title of its last section, "The Golden Men." The "melting pot" of the Pacific has produced a new type of man whom Michener's narrator describes as "neither all white nor all brown nor all yellow, but somewhere in between"—a blend of Polynesian, Caucasian, Chinese, and Japanese, who is "wholly modern and American yet in tune with the ancient and the Oriental."

Characters

Each of the major characters in *Hawaii* represents one of the races making up the genetic pool of Hawaii's melting pot. Tamatoa, Teroro, and Marama, Polynesians who emigrate to Hawaii in 817 A.D., are the predominant characters in "From the Sun-swept Lagoon," the second section of Michener's novel. Like all of the emigrants who follow them, Teroro and King Tamatoa are unhappy with their fates, for as Michener's narrator states, "No man leaves where he is and seeks a distant place unless he is in some respects a failure." Disgusted by the bloodthirsty rites of the new god Oro, King Tamatoa and his priest-brother Teroro plan a five-thousand-mile odyssey to a fabled land guarded by stars known as Seven Little Eyes. Because she is infertile, the "moonfaced" Marama must remain in Bora Bora, and Teroro takes with him his second wife, Tehani. Although they are guided only by the words of an ancient chant, Tamatoa, Teroro, thirty-seven men, fifteen women, and six slaves courageously sail their provision-loaded canoe *Wait-for-the-West-Wind* to the island they name Havaiki-of-the-North. Teroro's name means "the intelligent one," but it is his wife Marama who has been the wise half of their union, and Teroro soon finds Tehani's sexuality an inadequate replacement for Marama's counsel. Returning to Bora Bora for Marama, who has, ironically, borne him a son during his two-year absence, Teroro also claims the stone which represents Pere, the volcano goddess, since a volcanic eruption makes it quickly evident his people will need Pere's protection in their new home.

Over a thousand years later, in the section Michener calls "From the Farm of Bitterness," American missionaries arrive at the Hawaiian Islands aboard the bark *Thetis*. The protagonists in this section are the Reverend Abner Hale, a Yale University graduate who offers the light of his Calvinist God to Hawaii, and his bride Jerusha Bromley Hale, the character to whom Michener gives his greatest tribute. Although it is his intention to ordain Hawaiian ministers as soon as possible, the bigoted Hale comes to believe that only white men are capable of administering God's word in Hawaii. Frustrated by pagan backsliding, Hale "love[s] the

Hawaiians as potential Christians . . . but despise[s] them as people." Jerusha Hale, who teaches of God's love rather than of his wrath, is the real Christian influence on Maui:

> From her body came a line of men and women who would civilize the islands and organize them in to meaningful patterns. Her name would be on libraries, on museums, on chairs of medicine, on church scholarships. From a mean grass house, in which she worked herself to death, she brought humanity and love to an often brutal seaport, and with her needle and reading primer she taught the women of Maui more about decency and civilization than all the words of her husband accomplished. She asked for nothing, gave her love without stint, and grew to cherish the land she served: "Of her bones was Hawaii built."

This section introduces several other relevant characters of Caucasian and Polynesian origins. The Americans include Dr. John Whipple and his wife Amanda, who come to Hawaii as missionaries but leave the mission because of its hypocrisy; the slave trader Captain Rafer Hoxworth, Jerusha's first love, who kicks Abner Hale in the head when he hears of Jerusha's death; and Captain Retire Janders of the *Thetis,* who exploits Hawaii's first great commercial enterprises, whaling and sandlewood. Interesting Polynesian characters are Malama, the enormous, mana-filled Alli Nui, whose incestuous royal marriage to her brother Kelolo gives Abner Hale much scope for Calvinist moralizing; Keoki, their son, whose desire to be a minister of God is thwarted by Hale; and their daughter, Noelani, whose disillusionment with Calvinism leads her to consummate the last sacred marriage of the Alli Nui and to marry Rafer Hoxworth.

The most memorable character in *Hawaii,* Char Nyuk Tsin, is introduced in the fourth section, "From the Starving Village." Abducted from her Hakka village, the Chinese peasant girl is placed in the custody of Kee Mun Ki, a Punti gambler who leaves his "civilized" but impoverished life in China to seek his fortune in Fragrant Tree Country [Hawaii] as an indentured plantation laborer. Nyuk Tsin, who is destined for a Honolulu brothel, is grateful that Mun Ki names her his second wife when they board Rafer Hoxworth's ship, the *Carthaginian,* yet she is aware that Mun Ki feels disdain for his skinny Hakka wife with her unbound feet. In Honolulu, both become the servants of John Whipple, whose gift of land begins Char Nyuk Tsin's rise in life. When Nyuk Tsin bears her husband the first of their five sons, a Chinese scholar names the boy Kee Ah Chow [the Kee who Controls the Continent of Asia] and renames her Wu Chow's Auntie [the Aunt of the Continents]. According to Chinese custom, her son's "real" mother is Kee Mun Ki's first wife, who lives in China. Grateful to Mun Ki for her rescue from prostitution and stoically accepting her husband's right to take their sons when he returns to China, Nyuk Tsin envisions her own future in Hawaii. During Nyuk Tsin's fifth pregnancy, Mun Ki contracts leprosy, an event which allows Michener to explore the horrors of the leper colony on Molokai. When Nyuk Tsin accompanies her husband to Molokai as an uninfected "kokua" [a helper], the dying Mun Ki no longer sees her large feet, forgets that she is a Hakka, and loves her as his real wife.

Because of her compassion on Molokai, Nyuk Tsin earns another name, the Pake Kokua, a name which gives her influence with whites, Polynesians, and Chinese. Thus, the Auntie of Five Continents becomes the matriarch of the powerful, respected, and wealthy Kee "hui" (syndicate) of Honolulu, led by her third son, Africa Kee, who studies to be a lawyer in America, and his son Hong Kong Kee, one of the first Chinese asked to join the "Fort," a consortium of the ruling first families of Honolulu. The indomitable ancestor of seven hundred American citizens, Char Nyuk Tsin dies at the age of 106 on the day she finally earns her own American citizenship.

Other relevant characters in "From the Starving Village" are those who manipulate systems of government, economy, agriculture, or education during the nineteenth century: Micah Hale, son of Abner and Jerusha Hale; Hale's nephew, "Wild" Whipple Hoxworth, grandson of Rafer and Noelani Hoxworth; and the British schoolteacher Uliassurai Karakoram Blake. A. Grove Day describes Wild Whip as a composite of all the nineteenth-century American enterprisers in the islands since he "single-handledly develops irrigation, sugar planting, the pineapple industry, and even the importation of the succulent mango." With his dignified, white-bearded Uncle Micah, Whipple Hoxworth also initiates the United States's annexation of Hawaii in 1898. But it is Ulliassurai Karakoram Blake, a character based on the historical figure Alatau Tamchiboulac Atkinson, who dooms the Caucasian power monopoly when he teaches the first Chinese boy the alphabet.

"From the Island Sea," as well as much of the final section of *Hawaii*, "The Golden Men," is devoted to the activities of the Japanese. The Sakagawa family, led by Sakagawa Kamejiro who emigrates to Hawaii from Hiroshima to work in the sugar fields in 1902, illustrates the drive of the Japanese to succeed. During his early years, Kamajiro not only works as a gardener and a dynamiter for Whipple Hoxworth, but during his "free" time he operates a hot bath for his own people. In 1915 Kamajiro marries Mori Yoriko when he and the labor organizer, Mr. Ishii, exchange proxy brides on their arrival at Honolulu. Blacklisted for his own work with the labor movement, Kamajiro moves his wife and their five children to Honolulu where he cleans privies and instructs his children in the values of education.

Although Kamajiro believes in the superiority of the Japanese way of life and dreams of returning to Japan, his children think of themselves as Americans. His oldest son Goro, a football hero, becomes a labor leader after the war, and his youngest son, Shigeo, educated at Hawaii's finest prep school, is elected a senator in the 1950s. All four sons prove their patriotism during World War II by serving in the U.S. Army in Europe; two of them, Tadao and Minoru, give the ultimate proof of their loyalty. Working in her father's barber shop, Kamajiro's daughter Reiko also rejects Japanese tradition by falling in love with a Caucasian soldier. Because of this dishonorable relationship, Reiko is forced to marry Mr. Ishii, whose pride in Japan's honor deludes him into believing that Japan won the war. After World War II, when Ishii's mother-in-law Yoriko writes to him of the devastation at Hiroshima, he is finally forced to accept Japan's loss of face, and the dishonored old man commits suicide on the steps of Hawaii's Japanese Consulate. Although they never become American citizens, the elder Sakagawas, who are disillusioned by post-war Japan, return to their true home where they see their descendants become Hawaii's Golden Men.

Techniques

Like all of Michener's works, *Hawaii* is based on extensive historical research. For this particular work, Michener and his Hawaiian expert, Mrs. Clarence V. Taylor, read or reviewed over five hundred books on Hawaii, New England, China, Japan, and the South Pacific.

In *Hawaii*, Michener originates the novelistic structure which insures his place as a major American popular author. In the first section, "From the Boundless Deep," Michener makes the land of Hawaii itself one of the most fascinating characters in the work. He describes the islands' formation from their geological birth in volcanic fire to the arrival of the birds and life on the islands before the voyages of the first human inhabitants. So impressive is this particular section that *Life* magazine printed it before *Hawaii* was published.

Each of the following sections describes the groups which come to inhabit the islands. Unifying the structure of each section is the depiction of the hardships of the voyage to Hawaii and the belief of each group that its racial purity should remain uncontaminated by intermarriage with other races. *Hawaii*'s narrator,

Hoxworth Hale, one of the Golden Men of Hawaii, is Michener's refutation of that belief.

Literary Precedents

The structure of *Hawaii* has many literary precedents, including Leo Tolstoy's *War and Peace* (1865-1869), Booth Tarkington's *The Magnificent Ambersons* (1918), and John Galsworthy's *The Forsythe Saga* (1922). All are old-fashioned narratives which weave generations of fictional families through documented factual events. According to A. Grove Day, Michener believes his function as a writer is to "report the world, factually or imaginatively, but also emotionally and even poetically." A writer who never forgets his origins as a history teacher, Michener's "classroom is the world."

Adaptations

Because of its length and numerous characters, *Hawaii* has not adapted well to film. Two adaptations of the book have been produced by United Artists: *Hawaii* in 1966 and *The Hawaiians* in 1970. The better of the two versions, *Hawaii*, which deals with the material in the section "From the Farm of Bitterness," stars Julie Andrews, Max von Sydow, and Richard Harris. *The Hawaiians*, which depicts events in "From the Starving Village," stars Charleton Heston and Geraldine Chaplin.

ALASKA

Alaska, 1988, novel.

Social Concerns/Themes

In *Alaska* Michener focuses on the major themes of his previous works. He is most concerned with man's intolerance and inhumanity toward his fellow man. Also typical of past works is his depiction of the white man's destruction of the environment and his exploitation of darker-skinned races. In "Reflection" at the end of *Journey*, Michener states: "I wanted to help the American public to think intelligently about the Arctic where large portions of future international history might well focus; I wanted to remind my readers that Russia had held Alaska for a longer period, 127 years . . . than the U.S. had held it." One of the best illustrations of Michener's themes is found at the end of the section "The Duel." When Russians arrived on the Aleutian Islands in 1741, the islands were the home of

18,500 Aleuts; when the Russians left, "ninety-four percent had been starved, drowned, forced into slavery, murdered, or otherwise disposed of in the Bering Sea."

Characters

Although the characters of *Alaska* live in periods of time as vast and as varied as the Alaskan terrain (some are not even human), most share one common trait: they have journeyed to and been captured by the Alaskan "Ice Castle." In many cases, this captivity is literal as well as metaphorical, for Michener's first wanderers are those who cross the Bering Strait from Asia to Alaska during the Earth's several ice ages, and they (or their descendants) are trapped when rising waters cover the land bridge during an interglacial period.

Animal characters, like human ones, encompass both prehistoric and historic times. These include Mastodon, who 385,000 years ago led his cows into Alaska, searching for a more plentiful food source; and valiant Matriarch, whose wiles protect her woolly mammoth herd from fire, but not from the danger of Alaska's first human inhabitants. Perhaps the most interesting of these animal characters is Nerka, the sockeye salmon, whose entire lifespan, as well as twentieth-century man's systematic decimation of his species, is graphically described.

Michener quickly establishes his major themes through the characters in "The People of the North." The exodus from Asia begins almost 29,000 years ago, when Varnak and his people walk across the Bering Strait. Like many nomads who precede and follow them, Varnak and his people have no knowledge that they have journeyed from one continent to another; they know only that they must follow the mammoth or die. Varnak kills the daughter of the mammoth Matriarch so that his people will survive, but this death allows Michener to establish a pattern which can be seen throughout the novel: Alaskans (both men and animals) who are weak, innocent, and peaceful are soon displaced by those who are strong, hungry, and violent.

In 14,000 B.P.E. during an interglacial period, Varnak and his people are joined by another group of Asian hunters who will someday be known as Eskimos. Although these Siberian seafarers are basically a peaceful people, their livelihood depends upon the courage and skill required to hunt whales in the Arctic Ocean. Therefore, the cross-eyed, awkward hunter Oogruk seems unheroic in the eyes of his people. Yet, Oogruk's wife Nukleet, daughter of the chief of the village, appreciates him for his integrity and compassion, traits which many better hunters do not have. The shaman of Oogruk's village, who uses his position to force himself on pretty Nukleet and overthrow her father's rule, is the catalyst which forces Oogruk to leave Asia. Incapable of fighting the shaman's power, Oogruk, Nukleet, her father, and her young daughter brave the icy Bering Sea in a small kayak to begin a new life in Alaska.

Two thousand years later, the people whom later cultures will name the Aleuts begin a trek of their own. Pushed out of Asia and mainland Alaska by more warlike tribes, the gentle people of the shaman Azazruk journey to the Aleutian Islands. As a benevolent shaman who serves his people instead of using them, Azazruk is directly contrasted to Oogruk's power-hungry shaman. With Azazruk, Michener illustrates the influence which a positive spiritual leader can have on his people. In their new home, Azazruk and his people are enchanted by a mother sea otter which, with an almost human face, floats on her back, resting her baby on her stomach. For Azazruk, the sea otter becomes a symbol of peace and maternal love, but for most of his people, hunting the silky-furred otters becomes impossible to resist.

As a part of his effort to expand Russia's sphere of influence, Tsar Peter the Great orders the Dane, Vitus Bering, to explore Alaska. In "The Explorers," the historical Vitus Bering and his fictional companion, the Cossack, Troflin Zhdanko, set out on a true odyssey, one which takes them eight years from St. Petersburg, across eighteenth-century Russia, to Siberia and Alaska. Russian imperialism and Russian explorers have a disastrous effect on Alaskan natives (both human and animal), for most of the Russian explorers lack Zhdanko's moral strength. One of the worst offenders is his step-son, ironically named Innokenti (Innocent), who exploits the Aleuts and their environment. Innokenti, like most of the Russians, feels no more remorse when he kills an Aleut than when he clubs the beautiful sea otter for its pelt; after all, an Aleut is "not human."

One Aleut who survives the extermination of her people is fourteen-year-old Cidaq. To further the decimation of the Aleuts, the Russians strip Cidaq's island of all its male inhabitants. Although there is food in the Arctic waters, Cidaq's people believe that hunting and kayaks are forbidden to women. Cidaq's courage is reinforced by that of her grandmother, Old One, who convinces her not only to touch the forbidden kayaks, but to embark on a whale hunt. Old One's courage and her determination to survive force her to "sell" Cidaq to Rudenko, a Russian criminal. Old One understands that the people of the island are doomed, and even a bad life for Cidaq is better than no life at all.

Two important aspects of civilization are brought to Alaska at almost the same time—the Russian church and the Russian state. Father Vasili Voronov, an idealistic young Russian Orthodox priest, whom Michener based on a historical figure, is sent to Alaska to bring enlightenment to the Aleuts. The title of this section, "The Duel," reflects the battle between Father Vasili and the last Aleut shaman for the minds and the souls of all the Aleuts, and for one Aleut in particular—Cidaq. Raped and tortured by her Russian "rescuer," Cidaq represents all the Aleuts who have been brutalized by Russian exploitation. Although she is Father Vasili's first convert, his rigid Christian philosophy decrees that she must become God's instrument to save Rudenko. Sincere in his good works, Father Vasili sees Aleuts and Creoles (the children of an Aleut and a Russian) as human, yet he renounces his marriage to Cidaq (now christened Sofia), and this "saint" leaves Alaska to become Metropolitan of All the Russians.

Aleksander Baranov, a major historical figure, bears the standard of law and order for Russian merchants when he is sent to Alaska to govern the territory and to insure their profits. Like Father Vasili, Baranov sees Aleuts and Creoles as the future of Russian America. Although Baranov is an able governor in both the Aleutians and in Sitka, he meets with adversities: rebellious Tlingit Indians and arrogant Russian aristocrats, who believe that only the upper class should rule. The Tlingits, who are led by the historical Kot-le-an and the fictional Raven-heart, prove to be worthy opponents as they repeatedly try to recover their stolen land. Honored for his courage and compassion by his enemy Raven-heart, Baranov is defeated by his countrymen. He leaves Sitka in 1819, a prisoner aboard a Russian warship and dies in chains before he reaches Russia.

When Russia sells Alaska to the U.S. in 1867, Alaska gains a new master, but not a better one. Since no one in Washington knows what legal status to give this new possession, Alaska has no law, Alaskans have no protection, and both become the prey of Captain Emil Schransky and his dark ship, *Erebus*. Looking like a Calvinist image of God the Father, with Nordic white hair and long full beard, Schransky slaughters gravid female seals and rips unborn cubs from their mothers' wombs. Worse is Schransky's exploitation of the Eskimos. Because he illegally sells them rum, entire villages of men, women, and children are wiped out. The Reverend Sheldon Jackson and Captain Michael Healy are an unlikely pair who unite to defeat Schransky. A "born missionary," Jackson hates Catholics, Mormons, Democrats, and alcohol. Healy is the "profane and hard-drinking" son of an Irish-Catholic father. That he is also the child of a black Georgia slave woman makes him a perfect foil for the white-bearded Schransky and his dark ship.

Other Americans who damage Alaska ecologically, politically, and economically include Portland merchant Malcolm Ross, who controls the goods which are shipped to Alaska and the ships which carry the goods; and Tom Venn, Ross's son-in-law, who builds one of the first salmon factories and is largely responsible for endangering the sockeye salmon. Although Ross and Venn convince themselves that their Alaskan "icebox will never have enough people to become a state," they are shrewd enough to hire Marvin Hoxey to prevent national legislation that would give Alaska home rule.

The years between 1897 and 1898 bring hordes of people stampeding through Alaska when an enterprising Portland reporter writes that a "ton of gold" has been discovered in the Klondike in Canada. In "Gold," Michener again focuses on the incredibly complicated and dangerous process of the journey itself by detailing the journeys of two of the major characters in the novel: John Klope and Missy Peckham. Klope, a poverty-stricken farmer from Moose Hide, Idaho, reaches the Klondike in four months. Succeeding only because of his stubbornness and his physical strength, he takes the route of the Yukon River, which freezes before he can reach his goal. In sub-zero weather, he walks fifty miles to Fort Yukon, then dog sleds the final stage to Dawson City to stake his claim.

Social worker Missy Peckham, her lover Buck Venn, who is on the run from the Chicago police, and his young son Tom take the route through Chilkoot Pass, which separates the American and Canadian borders. Canadian law requires Missy and each member of her party to carry two thousand pounds of supplies (food for the entire year) up the snow-covered Chilkoot so they will be self-sufficient in Canada. During her travels Missy is victimized by Alaska's lack of government. She meets Soapy Smith, who robs and kills gold miners; the Belgian Mare, a madame who imports her girls from Europe; and Will Kirby, a congenial Mountie who becomes her lover after Buck Venn is killed. John Klope finds gold, but it "slowly slips through his fingers"; Missy finds, not gold, but the Irishman, Matt Murphy (his fatal MacKenzie River route across Canada is the section which becomes *Journey*); and Tom Venn opens a store and becomes one of the wealthiest men in Alaska.

"The Railbelt," which follows the relationships of families already introduced (or their descendants), also adds several new characters. Looking for a place to build Malcolm Ross's salmon cannery, Tom Venn meets two descendants of the Tlingit Raven-heart, Tom Bigears and Tom's daughter Nancy. Although the Bigears family has owned their land for generations, Ross has no trouble dispossessing them of their rights. After removing thirty-two thousand crates of salmon from the Bigears' river, Ross "graciously" gives Tom Bigears permission to take one or two salmon a year. During the Great Depression, when Minnesota farmers Elmer and Hilda Flatch are given an all-expenses-paid ticket to Alaska by the U.S. government, Missy Peckham, now an outspoken advocate of Alaskan statehood, is on hand to greet the new arrivals. Later, young LeRoy Flatch helps to provide a much-needed means of transportation when he becomes a bush-pilot, while Flossie Flatch, over the objections of her parents, marries Nate Coop, an illiterate half-breed. The three male members of the Flatch family all contribute to the war effort during the 1940s: LeRoy, who joins the Air Corps, flies cargo planes to Moscow across the Arctic Circle; Elmer helps build the first Alaskan highway, the fourteen-thousand mile Alcan; Nate Coop, who joins the Alaska Scouts, takes part in a bloody defense of the Aleutians when the Japanese invade in 1943.

"The Rim of Fire" is an appropriate title for the last section. Alaska not only rests on an area of geological upheaval, it is in the throes of economic, ecological, and political upheaval. The greatest victims are its native peoples, as Kendra Scott begins to realize when she teaches Eskimo children at Desolation Point. In spite of government legislation to return native land, and in spite of education, the Eskimos of Alaska are an endangered species. Alcoholism and suicide run rampant in their culture. When the Native Claims Settlement Act is passed in 1971, two kinds of lawyers move to Alaska. They are represented by Jed Keeler, pragmatic but honorable, and Poley Markham, whose motto is "No matter what you do, leave a trail of paper proving that you didn't do it." At the end of the novel, Jed Keeler dies, swept out to the ocean with the tsunami, leaving Poley Markham and the Poleys of the world in possession of Alaska.

Techniques/Literary Precedents

Because Michener's novels include such a variety of information, he has been accused of using an army of researchers to help him. But Michener, with degrees in English, philosophy, and history, is his own best research assistant. Since 1972, his editorial assistant, John Kings, has read and commented on Michener's works before they are sent to the publisher. In *Alaska*, Michener uses techniques he has perfected in his previous novels. After a geological description of the Alaskan terrain, Michener depicts the arrival of its prehistoric animal and human occupants. He develops more completely events and people in historic eras, and in the last two sections, explores modern political, social, and economic repercussions for Alaska and its inhabitants. One especially striking technique in *Alaska* is Michener's use of the epic journey. The odysseys of many of the human characters are among the most descriptive, as well as the most enjoyable passages in the novel.

Relation to Previous Works

In structure, content, and theme, *Alaska* is most similar to Michener's novels *Hawaii* and *Centennial*; they too emphasize racial prejudice, religious bigotry, and ecological exploitation. Characters in *Alaska* have their counterparts in *Hawaii*. The Eskimo woman, Nukleet, who encourages her husband to sail his kayak to

Alaska, is similar to the Polynesian woman Marama, who inspires her husband to sail from Bora Bora to Hawaii. Father Vasili Voronov, whose missionary zeal sends him to save the souls of Alaska's Aleuts, and Reverend Sheldon Jackson, who believes Aleuts and Eskimos should be Christians but not citizens, have predecessors in Reverend Abner Hale, who preaches Christian love to his Hawaiian converts but refuses to allow a Hawaiian to be ordained. Even though Michener's novels are similar in form and content, he remains one of America's most popular novelists. Perhaps part of his appeal is based on the very predictability of his works. Readers know what to expect, and when they open a Michener novel, their expectations are met.

Additional Sources

Day, A. Grove. *James A. Michener.* 2d ed. Boston: Twayne, 1977. Contains a brief biography of Michener, examines many of his nonfiction works, his Pulitzer Prize novel, *Tales of the South Pacific,* and many of his best novels.

―――――. *Dictionary of Literary Biography: American Novelists Since World War II,* 2d series. Detroit: Gale Research, 1980. Reflections on Michener's works not given in the 1977 edition of Day's *James A. Michener.*

James, Caryn. "James A. Michener." *New York Times Magazine* (September 8, 1985). Discusses Michener's major works and the reasons for his popularity.

Michener, James A. "Reflections." In *Journey.* Toronto: McClelland and Stewart, 1989. Relates his publication problems with *Alaska.* Discusses themes of both *Alaska* and *Journey* and the inspiration for *Journey.*

―――――. "An Old Apple Tree." In *The Eagle and the Raven.* Austin: State House Press, 1990. Discusses Michener's reasons for writing ten works during the years 1986-1990.

Shahin, Jim. "The Continuing Sagas of James A. Michener." *The Saturday Evening Post* (March 1990). Discusses Michener's works during the years 1988-1990.

Diana Wells Barrow
University of Tennessee at Chattanooga

N. SCOTT MOMADAY
1934

Publishing History

N. Scott Momaday, a member of the Kiowa tribe of North American Indians, begins the story of his life with his great-grandparents. All of Momaday's writing stems directly from his life and his ancestors' lives. His father, Albert Morris Mammedaty (the family changed the spelling of their name after 1932), was raised in a small community near Rainy Mountain, Oklahoma, with Kiowa traditions. His mother, Mayme Natachee Scott, on the other hand, was raised in Kentucky and only later rediscovered her native-American heritage. Born February 27, 1934, he says that the first notable event in his life was at the age of six months, when his parents took him to Devil's Tower in Wyoming, where Pohd-lohk gave him his Kiowa name, Tsoai-talee: Rock-Tree Boy. While his parents struggled to retrieve and reform their identity, Momaday was well on the way in his search for his cultural identity.

He also learned about native-American culture in other ways. His earliest friends in Gallup and Shiprock, New Mexico were Navajo, and he learned their language and stories. In Hobbs, New Mexico, in 1943, Momaday began to see native Americana through the eyes of other Americans: as blankets, bows and arrows, and broken English. His best friend was Billy Don and his hero was Billy the Kid, a recurring character in Momaday's poetry and painting. At this time, he began keeping journals in which he recorded long stream-of-consciousness impressions of his responses to his friends, World War II, other native Americans, school, and sports. In 1946 his parents took teaching positions in New Mexico canyon country among the Jemez Pueblo, where Momaday was influenced by the Navajo, Tanoan, Jicarilla, and Mexican cultures. All of these cultures, which can be found in Momaday's *House Made of Dawn* (1968), exerted a powerful influence on his perceptions about language and the creation of stories.

Momaday's first book *The Journey of Tai-me* was printed in a limited edition of only one hundred copies. But that book, which Momaday describes as archetypal, steered him toward success as a writer. His first novel, *House Made of Dawn*, put him in the literary limelight. Shortly after *House Made of Dawn* was released, Momaday revised *The Journey of Tai-me* (1967), releasing it as *The Way to Rainy Mountain* (1976), with illustrations by his father, Al Momaday.

Momaday then produced four books of poetry, based on his graduate training under Yvor Winters at Stanford University and his experiences as a young man in New Mexico. Momaday turned to biography, and told his story, as well as that of his ancestors, in *The Names* (1976), which combines folk tales, pictures, memories, and created history. Most recently, Momaday has returned to the novel. A part of his work-in-progress, known as "Set," has been released under the title, *The Ancient Child*. While the novel has received mixed reviews, it exhibits the interwoven plots, the sense of the historical and the mythic, and the search for identity that Momaday began in *House Made of Dawn*.

Critical Reception, Honors, and Popularity

Critical recognition of Momaday's works has been quiet but persistent. He received a great deal of attention for being the first native American to win a national literary prize, when he received the Pulitzer Prize in 1969 for *House Made of Dawn*. His works are heavily anthologized in collections of native-American literature, and his novel is often taught in American literature courses. Other native-American authors, particularly Paula Gunn Allen, cite Momaday's literary work as an encouragement to continue writing in a native-American tradition.

Since *House Made of Dawn*, Momaday has turned to essays, poetry, and painting. In 1959 he received the Academy of American Poets prize from Stanford for his poem "The Bear," which, he explains, was based on William Faulkner's story. He won a Guggenheim Fellowship in 1966, and was inducted into the Kiowa Gourd Clan in 1969. In 1974, Momaday and David Muench received the Geographic Society of Chicago Publication Award and the Western Heritage Award for *Colorado*, for its outstanding poetry and nature photography. The Oklahoma Heritage Association inducted Momaday into the Oklahoma Hall of Fame in 1987. He is currently a professor of English at the University of Arizona in Tucson.

Analysis of Selected Titles

HOUSE MADE OF DAWN

House Made of Dawn, 1966, novel.

Social Concerns

Despite the novel's initial popular appeal as a "protest novel" against the discrimination and degradation of native Americans, and the psychological ravages of war, the strength of the novel lies in its depiction of Abel, a native American, who is being healed by cultural and spiritual means from the pain of these events. Within this framework, Momaday depicts the power of language upon Abel—the white culture's silencing and the Indian culture's healing. Momaday, like Alex Haley in *Roots*, depicts the ability of a strong cultural heritage to unite and connect an individual and a people.

His work also is specific to Southwestern Indian cultures. Momaday captures a patchwork of the dying traditions of the Navajo, Jemez Pueblo, and Kiowa. He records Abel's experiences with these fading cultures, not with a sense of loss, but with a sense of discovery. An important part of these cultures is their attitude toward the land. Building an affinity with these scattered roots of the self and the past involves developing a sense of belonging to the land. This is stressed by Momaday's impressive descriptive passages of mesas, canyons, and villages as well as depictions of battlefields and cities.

Themes

Momaday's special concern with language stems from his background as a member of a culture with a strong oral tradition, in which language has the power to create and destroy. Abel's destruction comes about through language: from Tosamah's daunting preaching to the "legalese" at his trial, which silences him. Abel is unable to communicate his need to be healed, and his silence pervades the novel. Abel's recreation also comes through language and ritual. His friend, Benally, teaches him to recreate himself as a native American; "House made of dawn" is the beginning of a Navajo ritual of healing, which encompasses and orders the world. These reminders of his cultural heritage restore Abel, and give him courage to go back to the reservation and become a "longhair"—a participating member of his tribe.

This ordering power of language also embraces Abel's search for the sacred, which Momaday locates in ancient ritual and a bonding to the land. Abel has many guides who lead him through the landscape of the spirit: the paganism and witchery of the albino, the catholicism of Father Olguin, Tosamah's peyote road, Benally's Navajo chants, and Francisco's death. Although these guides can show Abel the spiritual paths that he can follow, he must create his own language and his "center"—he alone is ultimately responsible for his healing.

Characters

While Momaday has denied a conscious awareness of his choice, many readers first connect Abel to the biblical Abel, the first victim. The novel explores whether Abel will become a victim and surrender his identity or whether he will become a longhair in a white world. Along the way, Momaday associates Abel with animals: a caged and helpless eagle, hundreds of fish struggling on the shore at night, and the bear (Momaday's favorite animal) with its dark strength and its mythical and spiritual power. Momaday does not offer simple solutions for Abel; even in the dawnrunner ceremony at the end of the novel, Abel finds his voice and sings, but he also stumbles and falls.

To get to this point, Abel has had the benefit of guides who embody a certain use of language and a certain stance toward their culture. The Reverend John Big Bluff Tosamah is, as his name implies, "conviction, caricature, callousness." As the Priest of the Sun, he preaches and conducts peyote prayer meetings with his congregation. As a preacher, he creates a humorous caricature of Christianity, undercutting words of love and peace with encouragements to get ahead in the world. As an American Indian priest, he denies the power of his heritage, except when a cheap imitation will profit him. Tosamah's second address, which tells how he gained strength from finding his Kiowa heritage at Rainy Mountain, is an ironic restatement of one of Momaday's better-known essays. Tosamah rejects and harasses Abel, because Abel is silent, "primitive," and "ungrateful"—a longhair.

Benally, the night chanter, is a less-developed but essential character. He lives in Los Angeles and is content; he has created a balance between living, working, and drinking in the city and remembering the language of his youth on the reservation. Benally's memories are basic and elemental; they center on horse chants and his own horse—small, fast, and a little wild. As Abel's friend, Benally shares with him the Navajo healing chants. From Benally, Abel learns what is essential to be a human and a native American.

Techniques

The novel begins and ends with the traditional Jemez Pueblo words that begin and end a ritual chant or a story. This mythic, timeless quality is not dispelled by Momaday's use of dates and places to mark Abel's linear, seven-year journey. The prologue is actually the end of the story (1952); the narrative then begins in 1945. This disjointed structure circles back on itself, framing the novel which seems to come from Abel's memories.

The novel itself divides into four parts, four being a sacred cultural number. Each part is dominated by a particular character and represents a segment of Abel's journey.

The first section "The Longhair" (1945) establishes Abel's context and his conflicts. Through interspersed memories readers learn of Abel's childhood alienation from his tribe because of his illegitimacy. The letters which the Catholic priest, Father Olguin, reads and admires illustrate how detached the white world is from native-American cultural values. The conflict is intensified after Abel loses a ritual game, is humiliated by the winner—a "white man," or albino—and later kills him. Only his grandfather, the longhair, misses him.

The second section, "The Priest of the Sun" (1952), offers Abel alternatives to the reservation. Tosamah's ironic sermons and his numbered list of materials for the peyote ritual parody spiritual leaders but reject the power of land and language. Framing the two sermons, Momaday relates the story of Milly, who has attempted to integrate herself into white society by becoming a state social worker. She is lonely among her white friends and shares painful memories from her reservation life with Abel. Both characters seem to wear masks which hide their true expressions from those around them.

The third section, "The Night Chanter," consists mostly of Benally's stories and memories, interspersed with Abel's pain and his memories after being beaten and left for dead. These scenes show his final conflict with Tosamah, his being beaten by a malicious policeman, and his resolution to return home.

The final section, "The Dawn Runner," connects the two ends of the story to create a circular structure. Francisco, Abel's dying grandfather, tells stories about his life as a spiritual man and as a Dawn Runner. Both Francisco and Abel are longhairs and Dawn Runners, and Abel understands the strength of being spiritually connected to a place and a way of life.

The narrative's limited omniscient voice moves through current happenings to remembrances, often when Abel is drunk or in pain; the text depicts Abel's consciousness, the perspective of others who tell their experiences and memories in letters (offset from the text), and stories told to Abel (in italics). Yet these voices and memories conceal the lack of actual dialogue, reflecting Abel's painful silence. This blending of voices, which includes vivid descriptions of the land and oblique character development, requires careful and sensitive reading.

Literary Precedents

Readers familiar with Ira Hayes, the Indian hero of Iwo Jima, will notice an immediate similarity to Abel. Both Abel and Ira were war heroes who came back home and became victims of white prejudice and the lack of opportunities for American Indians. While the plot is cast in familiar Anglo-American terms, much of the power of the images and concepts stems from early native-American writers, such as Black Elk, Lame Deer, and others who recorded visions and preserved sacred traditions of the culture. Contemporary literature, like *Cogewea, the Half Blood* by Mourning Dove (1927), or *The Man Who Killed the Deer* by Frank

Waters (1942/1970) recorded the struggle of halfbloods, illegitimate children, and other misplaced American Indians who must discover where they belong.

While much of the cultural material is clearly based in native-American texts, Momaday also owes much to traditional American writers, particularly William Faulkner. From Faulkner, Momaday learned to create a rich style, and to mold the passage of time by tale-telling and memory-sharing. Also, like Faulkner, Momaday insists that all his works are part of a larger story. Repeating stories throughout his works establishes a sense of continuity and reveals their autobiographical source.

Momaday has also established a strong example for many other native-American writers, identifying many themes accepted as common to native-American experience, and exhibiting the variety of genres and styles (from Ernest Hemingway to James Joyce) that can portray those experiences.

Relation to Previous Works

Momaday sees his works as parts of one overall story, similar to Faulkner's portrayal of Yoknapatawpha County. In *The Way to Rainy Mountain*, he tells of a pilgrimage to his grandmother's grave and of his connection to the Kiowas and the myth of the bear-boy. In *House Made of Dawn*, Tosamah repeats this, with significant differences, as his second sermon which ends "The Priest of the Sun" chapter. The mixture of Tosamah's words with Momaday's make John Big Bluff seem ironic, in light of his attitude toward the traditional. Yet the end of the chapter points out to the reader where Abel will go—to his own Rainy Mountain.

Adaptations

Kay Bonetti taped an interview with Momaday in 1983, recorded in his home in Tucson ("N. Scott Momaday"). A second recording ("N. Scott Momaday Reads") captures him reading excerpts from *House Made of Dawn*, *The Names*, and his poems "The Gourd Dancer" and "Tsoai," revealing his deep and lyrical voice. Both recordings are available through American Audio Prose Library. Also, *House Made of Dawn* was made into a movie which used an American Indian film crew and cast.

THE WAY TO RAINY MOUNTAIN

The Way to Rainy Mountain, 1969, personal narrative.

Social Concerns/Themes

Unlike *House Made of Dawn*, with its obvious involvement with social concerns, *The Way to Rainy Mountain*'s greatest appeal is its treatment of the personal and spiritual aspects of human life.

The narrative began as *The Journey of Tai-me*, a collection of Kiowa oral myths and legends, woven into a relatively complex and thematically diverse work. Reworked and published as *The Way to Rainy Mountain*, the text retains the journey motif. This journey realistically depicts the landscape and landmarks, such as the Big Dipper, meadows, and pronghorn antelope encountered on the way to Devil's Mountain in Wyoming. The journey also reveals Momaday's growing awareness of relationships and connections to the world. Spiders, his grandfather Mammedaty, visions, and bay horses all become emblematic as he draws connections between the past and the present.

The narrative progresses toward a place that is both geographically and spiritually central, encompassing "a landscape that is incomparable, a time that is gone forever, and the human spirit, which endures."

Characters

The book differs from a novel in that the narrator is the only character. This narrator, ostensibly Momaday himself, acts as a companion to the reader, who functions as a silent partner on the journey. The narrator expects some sort of response or reply to his creation, which requires the reader to interact with the text as she or he would in an oral tradition. As the text and the reader interact, Momaday occasionally peoples the story with his ancestors, such as Mammedaty his grandfather, and Ko-sahn his grandmother, as well as divine beings from his mythical history, such as Tai-me, grandmother spider, and the Kiowas' migrations. Momaday characterizes himself in *Ancestral Voice* as a "wordwalker," making his way with words—and taking his reader with him.

Techniques

The text itself is framed at the beginning and end with poems about coming and going, movement and stillness. The prologue introduces Tai-me, the object of the Kiowa's migration, Momaday's journey, and our own "imaginative experience." The introduction gives the geographic landscape of the journey, and the spiritual significance of Tai-me to the Kiowa. Three distinct parts correspond to parts of the journey: The Setting Out, The Going On, and The Closing In.

Each section consists of a number of loosely connected stories, told by three distinct voices: the mythic voice, telling the cultural legends and lore that shape the "imaginative experience"; the logical, almost anthropological voice, interpreting the myth and giving the "historical" experience; and, finally, the personal voice of Momaday which joins the other two and tells its own story. Each voice has its own position on the open pages—the mythic on the left, the historical and personal on the right—and its own typeface. The interplay of these voices gives the text an almost spiral movement, tying together the spiritual reality with the objective and subjective reality.

The book is illustrated with line drawings by Momaday's father, Al Momaday, whose simple but forceful style adds a visual "voice" to the narration. The epilogue records Ko-sahn's witness of the fall of Tai-me and the Kiowa's loss of their religion. Yet at the end of the journey is also the sense of beauty, joy, and play.

Literary Precedents

Because of its origins in tribal history and oral traditions, *The Way to Rainy Mountain* is more similar to the sacred writings of Black Elk and Lame Deer than to a modern novel. As a narrative, it owes much of its presentation to other early American types, especially captivity, slave, and travel narratives. Its journey motif goes back to the dawn of almost all western literary traditions, including the Sioux tradition of the vision quest. While the text is rooted in ancient predecessors, the innovative use of various narrative voices and the dynamic between a narrator/storyteller and reader/audience give it a distinctly contemporary cast.

Relation to Previous Works

The book began as a collection of Kiowa tribal history and literature which was gathered into *The Journey of Tai-me*, only a hundred copies of which were printed. Sections of the text appeared in *House Made of Dawn*, and a year later, *The Way to Rainy Mountain* assumed its final shape.

THE MAN MADE OF WORDS

"The Man Made of Words," 1970, essay.

Social Concerns/Themes

Princeton University was the site of the First Convocation of American Indian Scholars in 1970. The convocation was planned, organized and presented by native

Americans as an opportunity for American Indian scholars "to come together and take the lead in formulating clear-cut stands and goals on the [political] issues" that affect all tribes. The participants' goal was "to form a solid basis for education accomplishment, and to unite our scholarly forces on behalf of our people."

Momaday begins his assembly presentation, "The Man Made of Words," with the question, "What is an American Indian?" He first defines Indian as "an idea which a given man has of himself," then pinpoints the ramifications of this definition: the idea must be articulated in language to become reality, therefore, imagination and storytelling are integral parts of being an American Indian.

Momaday illustrates his discussion of imagination with a story about a vision he had of Ko-sahn, the old woman at the end of *The Way to Rainy Mountain*. After writing the book, Ko-sahn was as real as he was—a combination of "living memory" and "verbal tradition." This power of imagination is the first step toward preserving the environment, as it fosters a new regard for the land.

A corresponding aspect of being an American Indian is storytelling, which Momaday describes as an exertion of the force of language upon the unknown, ourselves included. He then goes on to answer some questions about oral tradition and its relationship to art and reality, language and words, and to the connection between what people are and what they say: "The state of a human being is an idea, an idea which man has of himself. Only when he is embodied in an idea, and the idea is realized in language, can man take possession of himself."

These two elements, imagination and storytelling, are essential for the American Indian and the larger human family.

Characters

In this essay, Momaday tells two stories that have been the most significant to him throughout his life. The first is the vision of Ko-sahn at the completion of *The Way to Rainy Mountain*. Momaday dreams about how old she might have been, and if she could remember the meteor shower that foretold the end of the Kiowa people. Ko-sahn arrives with the sense of play that Momaday attributed to her, laughs at him for thinking she was only a dream, and explains that she exists just as surely as he. She also explains to Momaday that a racial or cultural memory allows her to be there, and allows both Ko-sahn and Momaday to remember the genesis of the Kiowa and their fateful meteor shower. Through this charming and wise woman, Momaday teaches the power of imagination to create.

The imagination expresses itself through words, which Momaday illustrates with the story of the Kiowa arrowmaker who faces an unknown enemy. While the arrowmaker draws the bow, his real weapons are his words, the request that the enemy identify himself or be killed. Ultimately the risk and responsibility of language is the weapon: to request a response, and the lack of a response identifies the unknown figure as an enemy. The arrowmaker is the man made of words, and he is us: "He has consummate being in language; it is the world of his origin and of his posterity, and there is no other. But it is a world of definite reality and of infinite possibility."

Techniques

"The Man Made of Words" was presented as an assembly address. In it Momaday uses a technique that he frequently uses in his interviews. He answers a question with a story, then discusses the story to explain and illustrate his answer. This approach in an address makes an engaging combination of the metaphorical and the analytical. The essay consists of narrative, dialogue, poetry, a rhetorical question-and-answer session, and a folktale, all which define and illustrate Momaday's purpose of helping the participants recognize the power of language to make and preserve contemporary native-American culture.

Literary Precedents

Public forums such as addresses at convocations and conferences have often been a pulpit for political and professional preaching. Abraham Lincoln, Elizabeth Cady Stanton, Martin Luther King, Jr., and Jesse Jackson have all promoted their causes and established their personal reputation through public addresses. As a literary scholar, Momaday studies the function of narrative and rhetoric in native-American texts. He also serves as a critic of common cultural misconceptions and a voice calling on other native Americans to realize the strength of their own traditions.

Relation to Previous Works

Both the story of Ko-sahn's life and the tale of the arrowmaker appeared in *The Way to Rainy Mountain*, as well as the themes of imagination, language, and storytelling. The phrase, "The Man Made of Words" also describes Momaday and his sense that all he is doing is retelling aspects of the human story. With this articulated view of himself as a writer of American Indian culture, Momaday has had a powerful effect on other native-American writers, such as Paula Gunn Allen and Leslie Marmom Silko; many native-American writers have come to view themselves as primarily storytellers, and secondarily as political activists.

Adaptations

While copies of "Man Made of Words" are difficult to obtain, important sections of this essay are available on a cassette tape entitled *Land as Symbol: The American Indian*, recorded by National Public Radio.

Other Titles

The Complete Poems of Frederick Goddard Tuckerman, 1965 (edited by Momaday); *The Journey of Tai-me*, 1967 (narrative); *Colorado: Summer, Fall, Winter, Spring*, 1973 (poetry, photography by David Muench); *Angle of Geese and Other Poems*, 1974 (poetry); *The Colors of Night*, 1976 (poetry); *The Gourd Dancer*, 1976 (poetry); *The Names: A Memoir*, 1976 (autobiography); *The Ancient Child*, 1989 (novel).

Additional Sources

Aithal, S. K. "The Redemptive Return: Momaday's *House Made of Dawn*." *North Dakota Quarterly* 53 (Spring 1985): 160-172. Studies how Momaday uses myth, legend, and history to create the unique identity of native Americans and how he envisions their redemption from spiritual and cultural disintegration.

Antell, Judith A. "Momaday, Welch and Silko: Expressing the Feminine Principle through Male Alienation." *American Indian Quarterly* 12 (Summer 1988): 213-220. Examines the connections between male alienation from traditional culture and the feminine principle as represented by Indian women and tribal affiliations in *House Made of Dawn*, *The Death of Jim Loney*, and *Ceremony*.

Bartlett, Mary Dougherty, ed. *The New Native American Novel: Works in Progress*. Albuquerque: University of New Mexico Press, 1986. Contains Momaday's "Set," an early excerpt of *The Ancient Child*.

Blaeser, Kimberly. "*The Way to Rainy Mountain*: Momaday's Work in Motion." In *Narrative Chance: Postmodern Discourse on Native American Indian Literatures*, edited by Gerald Vizenor. Albuquerque: University of New Mexico Press, 1989. Blaeser uses reader-response theories as a context for discussing how Momaday first creates the text by his reading of history, and then how he involves his readers in their own creation of Rainy Mountain.

Bruchac, Joseph. *Survival This Way: Interviews with American Indian Poets*. Tucson: University of Arizona Press, 1987. This interview, also published in *The American Poetry Review*, reveals Momaday's love for poetry, as he discusses his own poetry and how it reflects an oral culture.

Hirsch, Bernard A. "Self-Hatred and Spiritual Corruption in *House Made of Dawn*." *Western American Literature* 17 (Winter 1983): 307-320. Examines how Abel threatens Martinez, Tosamah, and Benally by exposing their rejection of native culture.

Indian Voices: The First Convocation of American Indian Scholars. San Francisco: Indian Historian Press, 1970. Published source of many outstanding addresses and assembly presentations at the convocation, including Momaday's "The Man Made of Words."

Lincoln, Kenneth. "Tai-me to Rainy Mountain: The Makings of American Indian Literature." *American Indian Quarterly* 10 (Spring 1986): 101-117. Documents some of the difficulties in getting *Way to Rainy Mountain* published, including communication between the author and editor, mixed reviews of the manuscript, and a discussion of native-American aesthetics.

Raymond, Michael W. "Tai-me, Christ and the Machine: Affirmation through Mythic Pluralism in *House Made of Dawn*." *Studies in American Fiction* 11 (Spring 1983): 61-71. Rejects a narrow, traditional interpretation of *House Made of Dawn* as American Indians overcoming alienation or avoiding integration with white society. Rather, the novel focuses on accepting cultural diversity and finding one's place in it.

Roemer, Kenneth M., ed. *Approaches to Teaching Momaday's* The Way to Rainy Mountain. New York: Modern Language Association, 1988. Roemer begins by contextualizing *The Way to Rainy Mountain*; various contributors then discuss critical and pedagogical approaches.

Scarberry-García, Susan. *Landmarks of Healing: A Study of* House Made of Dawn. Albuquerque: University of New Mexico Press, 1990. Analyzes *House Made of Dawn* in terms of its themes of healing (central to native-American writing), the ritual's connection to the landscape, and mythic references that underlie the novel.

Schubnell, Matthias. *N. Scott Momaday: The Cultural and Literary Background.* Norman: University of Oklahoma Press, 1985. Contains a chapter of biography and other chapters about Momaday's theories concerning language, imagination, and the land, as well as chapters on his books. Includes extensive bibliography of primary and secondary writings on Momaday. A major work.

Velie, Alan R. *Four American Indian Literary Masters.* Norman: University of Oklahoma Press, 1982. Velie shows connections between Momaday's life and his works, and also between Momaday's "post-symbolist" poetic style and his mentor, Yvor Winters.

Weiler, Dugmar. "N. Scott Momaday: Story Teller." *The Journal of Ethnic Studies* 16 (Spring 1988): 118-126. This interview focuses on the characters of *House Made of Dawn* and on Monaday's poetry and painting.

Woodward, Charles L. *Ancestral Voice: Conversations with N. Scott Momaday.* Lincoln: University of Nebraska Press, 1989. A product of years of interviews and friendly conversation, delving into how Momaday views self-knowledge, places, journeys, story-telling, aesthetics, and appropriateness. Also contains artwork by Momaday.

Lynne Facer
Brigham Young University

TONI MORRISON
1931

Update

Even before Toni Morrison received the 1988 Pulitzer prize for fiction, an increasing number of public admirers were complaining that the high quality of her previously published four novels had for too long gone unrecognized. *Beloved* was awarded the Pulitzer Prize, however, not because of public pressure, but because of unanimous praise by critics and general readers alike for the novel's distinctive achievement. Besides being included in books on African-American women writers, Morrison has been awarded prestigious honorary degrees, including one from Harvard University in 1989.

Analysis of Selected Titles

BELOVED

Beloved, 1987, novel.

Social Concerns/Themes

Before *Beloved*, Morrison wrote only of the painful rise, and occasional overreach, of African Americans of her own lifetime. In a 1989 *Time* magazine interview, she explained why she had "this terrible reluctance" about revisiting the period of slavery in America. In part, she was overwhelmed by its duration (three hundred years) and its enormous human costs (60-200 million individuals), and felt inadequate to the task. In approaching the subject, she felt compelled to research it thoroughly, if only to overcome her own participation in what she called a case of "national amnesia." What moved her especially were the "torturous restraining devices" that were inflicted on slaves even while they worked, to complete their humiliating subjugation.

Even as she elaborated the historical aspects of her novel for the sake of authenticating the past, Morrison was intent on revealing, by implication, the remnants of racism in modern America. *Beloved*'s central theme—the coexistence of past and present—functions as the invisible underpinning for what otherwise might be mistaken for a ghost story, too incredible to be taken seriously, involving the return of a murdered child. But because Morrison examines more subtle forms of enslavement, the theme of the ever-present past involves each generation's obligation to its predecessor, especially within the framework of the family. Morrison has always revealed a special concern for depicting what defines and sustains family life. Part of her investigation in *Beloved,* therefore, includes such potential forms of "enslavement" as a mother's right to dominate and even take her daughter's life.

Characters

The most spectacular event in *Beloved* is Sethe's murder of her two-year-old daughter. The young mother, a fugitive slave, is prepared to kill her children and herself rather than surrender any of them to the Kentucky slaveowner who has pursued them to Ohio with the intention of returning them to captivity. Instead, Sethe is imprisoned for cutting her child's throat. Besides such mitigating circumstances as Sethe's preference for death over the loss of freedom, she is without her husband, Halle, also a slave, who has not succeeded in escaping. Nor has she had time to seek the advice and assistance of his old mother, Baby Suggs, with whom she lives. Nevertheless, her personal sense of guilt and of frustrated maternal love allows her conscience no peace. She is disturbed but also relieved, therefore, when the restless spirit of Beloved returns, years later, first as a ghostly presence, then in the flesh. Beloved, now an eighteen-year-old, has mixed feelings herself—of revenge, of reconciliation, of needing to know if her death was in fact an act of love. But even the terrible agony of her confusion is better than the limbo afterlife she has endured.

Paul D, another fugitive slave who once worked alongside Halle, eventually arrives, offers Sethe physical comfort, but soon suffers from seeming to be Beloved's rival. Denver, her younger sister, is also the victim of Beloved's derangement. Sometimes they are hostile competitors, sometimes co-conspirators, in their relationship with Sethe. When Sethe defends Beloved with an ice pick against a crowd of townspeople intent on exorcising the girl as an evil spirit, Beloved does disappear, perhaps because she is convinced by Sethe's behavior that she is in fact loved. Certainly she is missed by Sethe, who needs to be reassured in turn, by Paul D and by Denver, that she is "the best thing" because she considered her children "the best thing."

Techniques

The problem which Morrison sets herself in *Beloved* is how to combine raw authenticity—the demeaning, daily, historic, horror of slavery—with extrasensory experiences of the troubled spirit, without letting the latter seem merely symptomatic of insanity or superstition. Sethe might easily be interpreted as a young, uneducated woman prone to hysterical fantasies, were the sections that explore her inner consciousness not filled with examples of genuine sensitivity to her womanly role as a life-provider. That her "ghostly" experiences must be taken seriously and are not hallucinations is reinforced by the maturity which Paul D brings to the same "apparitions" and by the natural innocence of Denver. In the final chapter Morrison daringly provides the stream of Beloved's consciousness as she lives/relives her time among the dead. All these techniques have a single purpose: to persuade persons of all cultures, not just African Americans, to consider these events, both natural and supernatural, as real possibilities.

Literary Precedents

With equal seriousness Henry James' *The Turn of the Screw* dwells on a similar series of ghostly events. James, however, leaves ambiguous the question of whether the governess is lying, hallucinating, or projecting sexual desires when she declares that she is defending her young wards against evil-spirited former servants. *Beloved* is far more elaborate and certainly far more profound in its social implications than is James's story.

As for the right of a mother to take back the life of her child, precedent was set in *Sula* when the grandmother Eva burned to death her alcoholic, mindless son rather than have him continue to waste away. However, Eva shows little sign of suffering terrible pangs of conscience, as Sethe does.

Relation to Previous Works

In *Beloved* Morrison continues her poetic expression of the rich culture inherited by African Americans. Within those considerable dimensions, there is an evolving sense of worth assigned to male characters. In her first two novels they were virtually invisible and generally undependable; in *Song of Solomon* Milkman was allowed to reach a maturity beyond his earlier manipulation of females, only in what may have been his last minutes alive; in *Tar Baby* Son's ultimate acceptance of his cultural heritage is left unresolved. Paul D, however, is a person of strength and resilience, devoted to Sethe's needs, patient, caring, and thoughtful. The principal innovation in the novel, beyond this growth in male worth, is Morrison's decision to explore the nightmare that haunts descendants of slavery: whether they have proven their humanity to themselves, if not to others; or, whether like those who once declared themselves masters of the Africans, African Americans have themselves become authoritarian, abusive, possessive, self-justifying victims of the same urge to be superior, rather than equal. As usual, Morrison writes from a moral viewpoint, urging hope and reconciliation, not rejection.

Additional Sources

Angelo, Bonnie. "The Pain of Being Black." *Time* (May 22, 1989): 120-122. Interview with Toni Morrison.

Christian, Barbara. *Black Feminist Criticism*. New York: Pergamon, 1985. Three chapters feature Morrison's novels: one examines the use of community and nature; one considers the concept of class; and one is a review of *Tar Baby*.

McKay, Nellie Y. *Critical Essays on Toni Morrison*. Boston: G. K. Hall, 1988. National and international writers, with varied perspectives, contributed to this work, which focuses on Morrison's standing as a member of the African-American and American literary traditions.

Naylor, Gloria, and Toni Morrison. "A Conversation." *The Southern Review* 21, 3 (July 1985): 567-593. This twenty-seven page conversation is unique because of its length and the wealth of information presented. Morrison and Naylor share their philosophies about writing fiction as seen in Morrison's first four novels.

Otten, Terry. *The Crime and Innocence in the Fiction of Toni Morrison*. Columbia: University of Missouri Press, 1989. Otten purports that Morrison views the fall from grace as a vital sign of freedom for the characters who choose to live genuine lives. He explores the idea of the sin of innocence in a fictional world where good and evil constantly change.

Leonard Casper
Boston College

ALICE MUNRO
1931

Update

Since the publication of *The Progress of Love* (1986) Alice Munro has continued her established publishing pattern. She first publishes stories in magazines like *The New Yorker*, then publishes them as collections. Her most recent volume of stories is *Friend of My Youth* (1990). Additionally, she has reviewed books and expressed her ideas in interviews and miscellaneous essays. Her critical reputation and popular sales both continue to grow. Academic attention to her work is mainly limited to Canadian scholars. The first book-length study of her work, other than collections of essays, is W. R. Martin's *Alice Munro: Paradox and Parallel*. Published in Canada in 1987, it is distributed in the United States by the University of Nebraska Press.

Analysis of Selected Titles

FRIEND OF MY YOUTH

Friend of My Youth, 1990, short stories.

Social Concerns/Themes

The ten stories collected in this volume share recurrent themes; there is a unity in Munro's work that is more easily recognized than defined. One of the facets of Munro's subtle craft is her ability to surprise. Not only is the reader often surprised by a twist of plot and or by quirks of character, but also when the point of a story begins to seem apparent, it too may slither off in an unexpected direction. While varying thematic points are made, all tend to arise from a treatment of, as one reviewer put it, "the restlessness of intelligent women forced to live in constricted surroundings." The surroundings constrain in various ways: the social mores of a small town provide little flexibility; stern religious beliefs breed intolerance for the unusual; a husband, trapped in his gender-defined role, may be insensitive to his wife's feelings. This restlessness often manifests itself sexually; adulteries are frequent in these stories.

Munro's female protagonists are generally trying to comprehend the past. In their mature years, they attempt to understand how they got to be where and who they are. Thus, while it is accurate to say that these stories are relevant to contemporary women's issues, Munro avoids the merely topical by placing these issues in a larger historical and cultural context. She seems to suggest that to understand not only contemporary feminism but the complexities of human relationships, it is necessary to recognize the often quirky ways in which class, religion, social environment, and family and friends act on imagination to shape character, ideas, and action. Each case is unique; no easy generalizations are available and thematic truth must constantly be redefined.

Characters

The short story form is too short for extended character development; in short fiction a character's nature is often a given, directly stated by the author. In Munro's work, however, a sense of a character's complexity is nearly always revealed through the development of relationships with others. Munro reveals her narrator's character primarily through her judgments and responses to those whom she describes. Through the focus on relationships, character is effectively integrated with plot and theme.

The relationships Munro describes are mainly those between men and women, or between women and other women. A number of stories focus on the connections between a contemporary woman and one from an earlier generation. In terms of men, Munro turns several sexual positions on their heads. Freud's famous question, "What does a woman want?," is melded with Zorba's description in *Zorba the Greek* of women as "the female species" when, at least implicitly, Munro's narrators ponder the question "what does a member of the male species want?" The story "Hold Me Fast, Don't Let Me Pass," for example, ends: "Meanwhile, what makes a man happy? It must be something quite different."

Although some men in the stories, such as Robert Deal in the title story, are presented unfavorably, there is no general hostility to men. Rather, the attitude of the female narrators towards men seems to comprise a mixture of attraction, pity, and bemused puzzlement. While there is little respect for males, there is a certain tolerance of the male as "the weaker sex." Reversing another cliché, Munro's characters often seem to say of men, "you can't live with them, and you can't live without them." The forms taken by this paradox are worked out differently in the relationships in each story, ranging from Averill's romanticized fantasy of the ship's captain in "Goodness and Mercy" to Maya's describing, in "Differently," her extended adulterous affair with Harvey as "exercise."

If the contemporary, mature women, who are central in all of Munro's stories, define themselves in part through their relationships with men, they are also revealed, perhaps more significantly, in their interactions with other women:

childhood friends, rivals, mothers, or women from the past. Summoned by the narrator's imagination working on bits of memory, these women of an earlier generation are probably the most vivid characters in the book. Almeda Roth, the poet in "Meneseteung," and Mora Grieves in "Friend of My Youth" are especially memorable for the apparent pathos of their lives, ennobled by their inner strengths. Women, then, may be separated by generations, by rivalry over men, or by class differences, but they are united by a common bond of sisterhood.

Techniques/Literary Precedents

Central to the construction of each story is the concept of "epiphany." The term, in its literary sense, was developed by James Joyce and exemplified in his collection of stories *Dubliners* (1914). An epiphany involves a sudden, significant revelation arising from a series of seemingly trivial and disconnected incidents. Munro expresses the idea in the story "Differently" when she speaks of "accidental clarity"; it is this type of insight that Hazel gains in "Hold Me Fast, Don't Let Me Pass."

As in Joyce's *Dubliners*, such insights often emerge from mundane frustrations. Munro writes (as did Anton Chekhov to whom she has been compared) generally of the frustrations of provincial life. Her stories, with their Canadian settings, also share the quality of using a regional identity to generate a sense of universal truth, similar to Eudora Welty's stories of the American South. Both Chekhov and Welty use imagery and symbolism to suggest their points, as does Munro. For example, in *Friend of My Youth*, hair takes on a symbolic significance as an indication of the moral condition of a character—a streak of white hair suggests integrity, hair "the color of brass candlesticks" the opposite.

Although irony and humor are present in Chekhov, Welty, and Joyce, in Munro's stories the humorously ironic is more pronounced. In "Wigtime," for example, a character grotesquely disguises herself to comically spy upon her husband's adulteries.

What most distinguishes Munro's style is her manipulation of point-of-view and time structure. The title story provides a striking example; in it, a contemporary woman narrates a story, the germ of which she learned from her mother, of a woman who was that mother's "friend of my youth." Thus, the tale simultaneously presents the actors in the drama from the past, the mother's view of the story, and the primary narrator's view of the past and her mother's attitude towards it. It sounds like, and indeed it is, a complex presentation, but with Munro's skilled technique it all works; the reader gains insights that a more straightforward narration would not provide. Similarly, in the other tales, shifting points-of-view add greatly to the reader's insight and pleasure. Although influenced, as is any writer, by various literary precedents, Alice Munro has created her own unique way of telling a story.

Relation to Previous Works

When compared to Munro's earlier books, *Friend of My Youth* provides no major surprises. Beginning as a skilled realistic writer of stories about ordinary people mainly in small-town Ontario, by her fifth book, *The Moons of Jupiter* (1982), Munro had expanded her range of settings and honed her craft. While maintaining a mastery of the carefully chosen detail, she has become more experimental in technique, especially in manipulating point-of-view and time structure. She continued and expanded this experimentation in *The Progress of Love* (1986). *Friend of My Youth* demonstrates a mature mastery of the techniques found in *The Moons of Jupiter* and *The Progress of Love*. While in these previous books the reader is sometimes conscious of the technical experimentation, in *Friend of My Youth* Munro makes her craft seem entirely natural. Even the complex weaving together of the past and present (also seen in *The Progress of Love*), seems lacking in artifice. Munro, having challenged herself to avoid easy writing, has mastered the art of making the difficult appear simple.

Additional Sources

Martin, W. R. *Alice Munro: Paradox and Parallel.* Edmonton: University of Alberta Press, 1987. The first full-length study of Munro's fiction, Martin's work subjects individual stories to close reading, and attempts unifying generalizations. A number of interesting insights are generated, but as a whole the study lacks the coherence that could have been provided by a more penetrating overview of Munro's works.

William B. Stone
Indiana University Northwest

V. S. NAIPAUL
1932

Publishing History

Born in Chaguanas, Trinidad, on August 17, 1932, Vidiadhar Suraiprasad Naipaul did so well when he entered school that he was awarded a scholarship to Queens Royal College. Following six years of study, largely in French and Spanish, Naipaul briefly taught at the college, leaving in 1950 to study at University College, Oxford, where he earned a degree in English. While studying literature Naipaul developed his writing, completing the manuscript of *Miguel Street,* a collection of linked stories, in 1955, the same year he married Patricia Ann Hale.

In "Prologue to an Autobiography," from *Finding the Centre* (1984), Naipaul recalls his own beginnings, and indicates that the most significant influence on his choice of a literary career was his father's frustrated career as a writer. Naipaul's success is, in many ways, a tribute to his father. *A Turn in the South* (1989), Naipaul's investigation of the contemporary American South and the religion that appears to organize it, is dedicated to the memory of his father.

While Naipaul experienced early success with *The Mystic Masseur* (1957), *The Suffrage of Elvira* (1958), and *Miguel Street* (1959), *A House for Mr Biswas* (1961), which dramatizes the conflicts between a character similar to his father and his wife's powerful Brahmin family, was his first major critical success. In the early works the characters comically exploit the contradictions of Trinidad's culture. In *A House for Mr Biswas* these contradictions are painfully felt, giving the author's own feeling of homelessness a larger dimension.

To counteract this feeling of belonging nowhere, Naipaul took to travel, journeying to the West Indies, India, and East Africa. London, which had become almost an organizing principle in Naipaul's life, ceased to be so, as he accepted a condition of permanent exile.

Signs that this condition would be modified began to appear in the 1970s. Dropping his apolitical stance, Naipaul became more politically active, spurred by the disaster of Bangladesh. By the mid-1970s, Naipaul began to see the possibilities of becoming a world citizen, proposing standards of conduct throughout the world. As a world citizen, Naipaul could be engaged by a wide range of cultural problems: Africa in *A Bend in the River* (1979), liberation politics in *Guerrillas* (1975), India in the nonfiction *India: A Wounded Civilization* (1977), Argentina in the nonfiction *The Return of Eva Peron* (1980), and the modern American South in the nonfiction *A Turn in the South* (1989).

Naipaul's most recent book, *India: A Million Mutinies Now* (1990), surprised critics because of its favorable view of modern India. Naipaul has long been regarded as an expatriate who has been particularly critical of his ancestral land. But years after his highly critical works, *An Area of Darkness* (1962) and *A Wounded Civilization* (1977), Naipaul has retraced his old journey to produce a sympathetic book about the tragedies of a nation caught between modernity and tradition. His sanguine insights and his ability to revive Indian voices speaking of their history and heritage make this one of the most important books for understanding India at the end of this century. Naipaul likely will never lose his feeling of homelessness, perhaps the central principle of his fictional world.

Critical Reception, Honors, Popularity

Naipaul has received a number of awards for his fiction: the John Llewellen Rhys Memorial Prize in 1958 for *The Mystic Masseur*, the Somerset Maugham Award in 1961 for *Miguel Street*, the Hawthornden Prize in 1964 for *Mr. Stone and the Knights Companion* (1963), the W. H. Smith Award in 1968 for *The Mimic Men*, and the Booker Prize in 1971 for *In a Free State* (1971). In addition Naipaul is a member of the Society of Authors and a fellow in the Royal Society of Literature.

Interestingly, the awards are nearly always for Naipaul's fiction. His travel narratives, histories, and journalism have not been as well received. Among the novels, almost all critics consider *A House for Mr Biswas* and *The Mimic Men* major works. Opinion on *Guerrillas* is more divided, with some critics resisting the novel's political theme. When Naipaul becomes politically involved and the idea of homelessness is muzzled, his works tend to be judged for their politics as much as their art. The portrait of the revolutionaries in *Guerrillas* is not flattering, and it produced condemnation in some political and literary circles.

The political responses of critics increase when one moves from Naipaul's fiction to his nonfiction. Of his histories and travel books, *Among the Believers: An Islamic Journey* (1982) has sustained the heaviest attacks. After touring Iran, Pakistan, Malaysia, and Indonesia for seven months, Naipaul attributed the civil and social disorder he witnessed to the rise of Islamic fundamentalism. This, predictably, alienated a number of Arab critics who accused Naipaul of viewing Islam from a biased Western viewpoint. Many American southerners did not like Naipaul's treatment of the South in his more recent *A Turn in the South*. It is not surprising that Naipaul's literary reputation was freer from controversy when he was portraying alienated victims in his fiction than when he asserted a role as cultural critic.

Analysis of Selected Titles

THE MYSTIC MASSEUR

The Mystic Masseur, 1957, novel.

Social Concerns/Themes

If one could wash away the comic satire from Naipaul's first novel, it would be seen as a story of the rise of Ganesh Ramsumair from humble beginnings to Member of the British Empire. Such a story, as long as the hero and the society are viewed as admirable, serves as a model for readers to emulate (much like the American Dream). However, in *The Mystic Masseur* neither the hero, Ganesh, nor the culture, Indian settlements in Trinidad around the time of World War II, are admirable.

The years depicted in the novel were critical for Ganesh and for Trinidad. They mark a transition from a traditional, almost feudal, colonial culture of large sugar plantations to a more capitalist, Western oriented culture. Ganesh is a product of both the Indian Hindu tradition in which he was raised and the Western values he learns at Queens Royal College. When Ganesh finally begins to act as a healer, a mystic masseur, he learns to cynically use the values of both cultures in pursuit of success. Over and over Ganesh markets his Eastern culture in the service of commercial and political success.

While there are disturbing faults in Ganesh, such as vanity and laziness, the culture is lacking as well. The chief cultural void is the absence of standards. Success is applauded, and even plausible failure is rewarded. Trinidad seems a hopelessly mixed cultural stew of British, Muslim, Hindu, and African elements from which no rational standards can arise. To use one of Naipaul's favorite words, all is "absurd" in this comic novel.

Characters

Characters in *The Mystic Masseur* are either Ganesh's helpers or else adversaries over whom he can triumph. Beharry, a shopkeeper in Fuente Grove, is a helper, one of the few people in town who can read and a person who believes Ganesh is of a higher caste and therefore worthy of cultivation. Leela, Ganesh's wife, is his helper (unless she is irritated with his laziness), as is the Great Belcher, an aunt who gives Ganesh old Hindu books which he uses in his cures.

Ramlogan, Leela's father and a wily shopkeeper, who never fails to pursue his self-interest under the hypocritical guises of friend and father-in-law, is one of

Ganesh's chief adversaries. Although Ramlogan makes arrangements for the funeral of Ganesh's father, it is with the goal of capturing Ganesh, a person of higher caste, as a son-in-law. Under the guise of friend, Ramlogan, who pretends to be "modern" like Ganesh, seeks to dispense with a dowry. Ganesh, while something of a fool throughout the novel, nonetheless sees through Ramlogan's plan and forces money out of him through the manipulation of Eastern and Western traditions. During a ceremony in which the bridegroom is ceremonially bribed to eat kedgeree, Ganesh forces Ramlogan's generosity. Later, Ganesh writes a newspaper article about Ramlogan's great gift in establishing a cultural center in the nearly treeless Fuente Grove which again squeezes Ramlogan's purse.

Indarsingh, a Trinidadian educated at Oxford, and Narayan, a critic of Ganesh's later success, are Ganesh's adversaries in the political arena. Indarsingh loses an election to Ganesh because his acquired British identity causes him to totally misread Trinidad's Indian population. To defeat his former Queens College friend, Ganesh exploits his Indian heritage. Narayan, who hoped to manage a large grant from an Indian industrialist, loses his political hold when Ganesh fills Narayan's organization with his own cronies.

The narrator, who appears in the story significantly at the beginning and the end, is neither a helper nor an adversary. At the beginning, he is a young black boy whose mother brings him to Ganesh for medical help. Although Ganesh's treatment is unsuccessful, the boy is impressed by Ganesh's books and finds him amusing. At the end of the novel, as a student at an English university in 1954, the narrator is to be host to one of his countrymen, G. R. Muir, Esq., M.B.E. The narrator's guest turns out to be a haughty Ganesh. The narrator, subject to the same vices of vanity and hypocrisy one sees in the other characters, has a double reaction to Ganesh—he likes him, even as an adult student in England, but he knows Ganesh's weaknesses, the lies in Ganesh's autobiography, *The Years of Guilt,* and his many foolish whims and petty vanities.

Ganesh is a delightful comic character. Lazy and dull, he nevertheless manages to forge a respectable and successful career. At times, when he is working as a strike negotiator or healing, he almost seems admirable. The enjoyment of seeing Ganesh get the better of his adversaries is that of seeing one confidence man outwit another.

The cure of a black boy pursued by the hostile black cloud shows Ganesh at his best. This cloud is a projection of the boy's guilt over the death of his brother. The guilt resulted from the boy's sending his brother on an errand in which he was run over by a truck. Ganesh tries to rid his "patient" of guilt and pretends to see the boy's cloud. Ganesh, after establishing the mood with religious paraphernalia and

Hindu chants, creates a visible black cloud that quickly dissipates. Although Ganesh fools the boy and his family, he does cure the child. Greedy but caring, a trickster who also privately prays for the success of his trick, Ganesh advises the family, "If you want to send me anything, send it. But don't go around telling all sorts of people about me." Ganesh knows that the family will tell everyone about him and send him more money than they can afford in gratitude. But Naipaul does not linger on Ganesh's successes; he rushes through Ganesh's political career, collapsing ten years of Ganesh's life in fifty pages, so that readers see more of Ganesh's struggle than his success.

Techniques/Literary Precedents

The Mystic Masseur is a straightforward comic novel. Except for the handling of narrative point of view, there is nothing technically innovative in the book. Using traditional novelistic techniques, Naipaul has created a character, Ganesh, that is a target of comedy and the recipient of affection.

The narration is chronological, except for the narrator's introduction of himself and Ganesh at the novel's beginning, and shows a skillful use of the participant narrator. This young black man feels Ganesh to be a person much like himself, and yet, since the narrator is more clever than Ganesh, he can see his shams, lies, weaknesses, and petty vanities. The narrator's judgments, however, never drain sympathy from Ganesh, but allow the comic foibles of this pundit and politician to be delightfully exposed. Ganesh's own writing, such as his autobiography, *The Years of Guilt*, which the narrator quotes, cunningly points to a seemingly great man while also exposing the pretension of such a vanity publication.

Some have criticized Naipaul's handling of narrative pacing and the magnitude of successive episodes in *The Mystic Masseur*. They feel that the ending is rushed and that Ganesh's later political success is not as detailed as the early years of failure. Other critics claim that there is too much summary, at too great a distance from Ganesh, softening the comic potential of the book and blurring the satirical focus.

Relation to Previous Works

Three of Naipaul's stories written before *The Mystic Masseur* feature Ganesh Pundit to varying degrees. He appears in "Man-Man" of *Miguel Street* as a person who has a relation to God that the title character imitates, but it is merely a passing reference of less than a paragraph. In "How I Left Miguel Street," the last story in the collection, the narrator's mother bribes Ganesh, now a popular politician, to give her son a scholarship to study in London. The story depicts Ganesh in a comic crying contest between the narrator's mother and Ganesh over the size of the bribe. "My Aunt's Gold Teeth," published in *A Flag on the Island,* shows an ineffective younger Ganesh who hastens the death of one of his patients, but who also consoles the patient's widow, who feels guilty for offering Christian prayers. Interestingly, each of these views of Ganesh comes from a different period of his life: before his success as healer, in the middle of that success, and after he moves on to a political career.

The narrative perspective of *Miguel Street* is a more significant bridge to *The Mystic Masseur.* Both books have character-narrators, but the narrator in *Miguel Street* is too close to Ganesh to provide an objective view of him. *The Mystic Masseur* employs a retrospective participating narrator who can reconstruct events and motivations from a mature perspective. This participating narrator exhibits a greater control of tone than the narrator in *Miguel Street.*

A HOUSE FOR MR BISWAS

A House for Mr Biswas, 1961, novel.

Social Concern/Themes

While there is much humor in *A House for Mr Biswas,* the dominant tone of the novel is melodramatic, even tragic. The novel presents the struggle for identity for an Indian in Trinidad whose agrarian values are challenged by Western cultural influences when he moves to the city. Mohun Biswas must reconcile the apparently contradictory values and traditions of East and West, and forge an authentic self in relation to both family and society. This quest is not simply a recognition of some inner traits, but rather the gradual unfolding of choices made within the context of new situations, restraints, and sources of fulfillment. Mohun's journey is from an agrarian village ruled by the whimsies of a Hindu pundit to the towns of Trinidad and finally to Port of Spain. During the course of this journey he becomes a herder, acolyte to a pundit, sign painter, store owner, overseer, welfare worker, and journalist.

However, Mohun's career changes are not the primary focus of *A House for Mr Biswas;* the most important changes in the novel involve the changing nature of family relationships. Thinking that his son's body is submerged in a stream, Raghu, Mohun's father, dives for it, and, in his rescue attempt, drowns. His death breaks up the family; Mohun's older brothers and mother go to work as farm help, while Mohun finishes his education and serves Pundit Jairam before rebelling and becoming a sign painter. Work, though, is of lesser importance to Mohun than learning to live as a poor relation to his Aunt Tara and later as a son-in-law of the powerful Tulsi family. Defining his place among these families is especially important to Mohun.

The house in Naipaul's title thus becomes significant; it is the site and symbol of Mohun's independence and familial responsibility. Creating a home is an essential part of Mohun's development; but it must also satisfy the needs of his wife Shama, his son Anand, and his daughter Savi. In each house where Mohun lives as a dependent, the families with whom he lives have different responses to traditional culture and religion and the accommodation to Western values, religion, and standards of personal success. Just as these houses pose cultural dilemmas for Mohun, so too do the houses he builds, buy, or rents.

Characters

Characters in *A House for Mr Biswas* can be viewed in relation to the clash between traditional Indian culture and Western values. Mohun responds to them in terms of his need for survival and independence, and the claims and counter-claims they make for traditional Indian culture.

As a child among his relatives, Mohun Biswas responds with love and guilt to his mother, Bipti, who can provide warmth but no protection, comfort but no answers to his questions. Tara, his maternal aunt, can provide protection and physical comfort, but only at the cost of his obedience to traditional culture.

The education that should lead Mohun to the traditional life approved by his aunt, instead provides him with skills for life in the city. To him Hindu ceremonies appear empty; he is drawn to a Western view of work, painting, calculating, and the Christian weighing of choice and motive.

The most difficult people for Mohun to deal with are the Tulsis, who are alternately Christian or Hindu, depending upon the situation. Allowing himself to be trapped into a dowry-less marriage to Shama is Biswas's greatest error. He allows himself to be manipulated by the Tulsi family overseer, Seth, and by his mother-in-law, Mrs. Tulsi, a strong woman who seeks domination in terms of traditional culture and success in Western terms. While Mrs. Tulsi uses her faith to rule the family, she sends her sons to Christian schools for their education. Although the Tulsi homes provide a kind of sustenance and security for Mohun, he continually revolts, either by clowning and caricaturing the homes' power structure, or by his plan to create his own home. Once Mohun's children are born, however, he must achieve freedom not only for himself but for his family. The Tulsis, even more than his Aunt Tara, succeed in Western ways. The old religion and caste structure are irrelevant to success in the towns and cities. There, education and the acquisition of property are the roads to freedom.

Even on these terms Mohun knows that his possibilities are limited. Work as a newspaperman or as welfare worker is as high as he can practically aspire, and he sees the family's only hope as residing in his children. While Mohun attempts to fashion a life between East and West, his children will succeed in Western terms. Europe, not Trinidad, is the only secure measuring rod.

If, as some critics have speculated, Mohun's son, Anand, is the implied narrator, *A House for Mr Biswas* can be seen as a means for Naipaul to come to terms with a part of his past. Mohun provides the cultural mediation necessary for his son's development in another culture much as Naipaul's own father did for him.

The house, then, frail and a swindle, is only a temporary claim to a life of achievement, a house of cards ready to topple at the universe's slightest quiver. Anand will not live in his father's house; he will not return from England but will live abroad in a still more foreign land.

Techniques/Literary Precedents

Two radically different novelistic traditions have influenced *A House for Mr Biswas*: the nineteenth-century English social novel, with its focus on an individual life story amid a large cast of characters, and the existential novels of Camus, particularly *The Stranger* (1942). Camus, an Algerian in France and a Frenchman in Algeria, poignantly describes the lack of connection between cultural traditions, beliefs, and life. Naipaul, a dispossessed Indian in Trinidad, and a dispossessed colonial in England, experienced a similar difficulty charting a life among traditions that seem alien to him. Just as the existentialists tried to force an answer to the absurdity of life through personal choice and willed behavior, Mohun tries to build a home that challenges his life's absurdity. The house is less important as a structure than as an idea and symbol of emotional commitment. For Naipaul a colonized culture with a diverse immigrant ethnic population is a natural absurdity. In such a situation individual lives are deformed by a combination of bankrupt immigrant traditions and colonized social expectations.

Relation to Previous Works

A House for Mr Biswas is a more mature and assured work than Naipaul's earlier novels, which are lighter in tone and more comic. Part of the reason for the complexity of *A House for Mr Biswas* is its narrative point of view. Although the narration is in the third person, the "Prologue" and "Epilogue" have a more personal quality, almost as if Anand were telling the story. Unlike Naipaul's earlier novels where the comedy is external, the comic element in *A House for Mr Biswas* is more internal and connected to the title character. The comic humiliations of Mohun are both funny and sad. As Mohun moves from an extended to a nuclear family, from country to city, from a traditional culture to Western values, one is not certain whether to applaud his individuality or to laugh at him and censure his selfishness. He is comic butt, comic clown, melodramatic victim, and, at times, a tragic hero.

GUERRILLAS

Guerrillas, 1975, novel.

Social Concerns/Themes

The status of *Guerrillas* as a major novel rests on its classification as a political novel. Unlike *A House for Mr Biswas*, *Guerrillas* has a small cast of characters. Only three are of major importance: Peter Roche, a dispossessed white victim of South African oppression, who has emigrated to the nameless Caribbean island that is the novel's setting; Jimmy Ahmed, a half-Chinese, half-black "revolutionary" leader; and Jane, a Canadian who seems to be hoping for a personal definition through these two men.

For such a situation to express political concerns, the individual relations of the characters must be symbolic of a larger social relationship. In short, the personal relations should give an outline of a culture, as each character represents a part of the social world. Such an action tends toward allegory, and an initial interpretation of *Guerrillas* might be that of a story in which a white radical befriends a black revolutionary, and their friendship becomes the emblem of a new, just society. This view, however, does not account for the character of Jane, who, except for the excitement involved, is basically indifferent to the political dimension.

But this view of *Guerrillas* as a simple political allegory is inadequate. No one in the novel truly represents any social group. Consequently, the novel presents a web of tortured personal relations, much self-ignorance on the part of Jane and Jimmy, and the rape and murder of Jane as well as of the land itself.

Characters

Except for Peter Roche, who represses his own self-knowledge, the major characters in *Guerrillas* are self-deceived and ignorant of their own natures. Jane is not even in harmony with her body, mistaking, as she does, rape for love; she is careless of the feelings of others and ignorant of her own. Her awkwardness is a sign of her splintered self, which has lost contact with its extremities. For her, pain and rape are welcome because at least they allow feeling to exist.

Jimmy Ahmed, the supposed revolutionary, is actually a creation of his own lies and the propaganda of others. His radical commune raises nothing and houses a group with no relation to him or to each other. Politics, posters, and slogans are part of Jimmy's fantasies of power. While these fantasies are sometimes political, more often they are thinly disguised sexual fantasies of raping grateful white women. Women are basically threatening to Jimmy; he is much more comfortable with his homosexual lover, Bryant, whose jealousy he appeases by offering him Jane's life. Like the stories and novels Jimmy is forever trying to write, he can only begin actions, not complete them.

Peter Roche, supposedly tortured for his political views in South Africa, cannot make sense or create value from his past suffering. The only thing he has learned is to flee pain. For him there is no tragic recognition, no solace for suffering. Just as he flies from England when threatened with death, he flees back to England from the island. Rather than attempt to understand and shape experience, Peter only desires to escape Jimmy and erase his memory of Jane.

Techniques/Literary Precedents

The most important literary influence on *Guerrillas* is Joseph Conrad, whose *Nostromo,* (1904), *The Secret Agent* (1907), and *Under Western Eyes* (1911) are portraits of revolutionary lands and cultures. Conrad, like Naipaul, was moved by social injustice, and yet he never described political actions, particularly radical ones, with any favor. To him all such actions were undermined by selfishness and weakness. Like Conrad, Naipaul condemns exploitation, such as the rape of the island by an American corporation, but he portrays Jimmy as even more despicable than the corporation. Although he is unsparing in his criticism of social injustices, Naipaul does not believe that revolutionary movements are the answer.

Relation to Previous Works

Like all of Naipaul's fiction, *Guerrillas* deals with unsettled individuals in an unsettled society. His literary advances in *Guerrillas* are in two broad areas: the portrayal of lives shaped by external political and economic forces and the use of a narrative strategy of symbolic compression. Naipaul's social grasp is larger in *Guerrillas* than in earlier novels, and the compression results from a conscious change in narrative form. Gone is the model of the nineteenth-century social novel, filled with a multitude of characters and mimetic detail; here it is replaced by a story line as compressed as that of a Hawthorne romance. It is as if Naipaul had discovered deeper reasons for the unsettled lives and societies of his earlier works.

Other Titles
The Suffrage of Elvira, 1958 (novel); *The Middle Passage*, 1962 (travel); *Mr. Stone and the Knights Companion*, 1963 (novel); *An Area of Darkness*, 1964 (travel); *The Mimic Men*, 1967 (novel); *A Flag on the Island*, 1967 (short stories); *The Loss of El Dorado*, 1969 (history); *In a Free State*, 1971 (short stories); *The Overcrowded Barracoon*, 1972 (articles and interviews); *India: A Wounded Civilization*, 1977 (travel); *A Bend in the River*, 1979 (short stories); *The Return of Eva Peron*, 1980 (journalism); *Among the Believers: An Islamic Journey*, 1982 (travel); *Finding the Centre: Two Narratives*, 1984 (autobiography); *The Enigma of Arrival*, 1987 (fiction); *A Turn in the South*, 1989 (travel journalism); *India: A Million Mutinies Now*, 1990 (social analysis).

Additional Sources
Hamner, Robert D. *V. S. Naipaul*. New York: Twayne, 1973. Hamner includes an analysis of Trinidadian culture before turning to the short stories and novels.

———, ed. *Critical Perspectives on V. S. Naipaul*. Washington, DC: Three Continents Press, 1977. Published after *Guerrillas*, a seminal novel in Naipaul's career, the critical views in this collection are less aesthetic and more political.

Hemenway, Robert. "Sex and Politics in V. S. Naipaul." *Studies in the Novel* 14, 2 (Summer 1982): 189-202. Hemenway does a good job in focusing on the absence of positive heterosexual relations and mothering in the works.

Morris, Robert K. *Paradoxes of Order: Some Perspectives on the Fiction of V. S. Naipaul*. Columbia: University of Missouri Press, 1975. An attempt to show how Naipaul's characters try to order the world in their own images, only to discover how their order breaks down and reveals their falsified selves.

Theroux, Paul. *V. S. Naipaul: An Introduction to His Work*. New York: African Publishing, 1972. One acclaimed novelist looks at another.

Thorpe, Michael. *V. S. Naipaul*. Harlow, Essex: Longman, 1976. A bit scandalized by the graphic portrayal of murder and rape in *Guerrillas*, Thorpe nevertheless makes useful points.

White, Landeg. *V. S. Naipaul: A Critical Introduction*. London: Macmillan, 1975. Written before *Guerrillas*, White's book focuses largely on the existential dilemmas of the characters in the early stories and novels.

Woodcock, George. "V. S. Naipaul and the Politics of Fiction." *Queen's Quarterly* 87: 679-692. Interesting criticism by one of the best authorities on anarchism.

Craig Barrow
University of Tennessee at Chattanooga

R. K. NARAYAN
1906

Publishing History

R. K. Narayan published his first novel, *Swami and Friends, A Novel of Malgudi*, in 1935; his latest work of fiction, *The World of Nataraj* came out in 1990. In the intervening years he has published at least twelve novels, seven collections of short stories, three travel narratives, English adaptations of the two great Indian epics, *The Ramayana* (1972) and *The Mahabharata* (1978), and a memoir. Such a long and steady history of publication gives a measure of Narayan's success as the leading Indo-English writer of his generation. But the bare facts also conceal the immense difficulties he faced initially in getting his works into print. For although a few of his novels are now always stocked by leading book-sellers in India, Britain, and the United States, he had a difficult time securing publication of the books he wrote in the 1930s and the 1940s.

When Narayan, a South Indian from the city of Mysore, finished his first novel, he had no hopes of having it published in India. It was simply too much to expect that his countrymen would read a novel written in English by another Indian, even though the tradition of Indo-English literature dates back to the nineteenth century and in spite of the fact that the novel in question dealt with recognizable Indian landscapes, situations, and character types. Narayan therefore sought an English publisher. To do so, he enlisted the services of an Indian friend at Oxford, who eventually got the English novelist Graham Greene to look at *Swami and Friends*. Greene persuaded Hamish Hamilton to publish the book. But although this first novel got good reviews, sales were so low that Hamish Hamilton refused to invest in the second, *The Bachelor of Arts* (1937). Narayan again approached Greene, by then a good friend and destined to be a lifelong advocate. Greene recommended the book to the publishing house of Nelson. The book met with enthusiastic reviews but poor sales, and Nelson balked at publishing Narayan's third novel, *The Dark Room*. Greene brought the novel to the attention of Macmillan, which published it in 1938. But his third change of publishers made no difference in sales: as usual, reviewers had good things to say about his writing, but the public was unimpressed.

Narayan's fourth novel, *The English Teacher*, was published by Eyre & Spottiswoode in 1945. This time, however, Narayan's tragi-comic novel, based on the death of his wife and the events that led him to accept her death, attracted enough attention for him to continue with Eyre & Spottiswoode for his fifth novel, *Mr. Sampath* (1949). By then, Narayan could count on a small but devoted international readership, and even though he changed publishers for his next book, *The Financial Expert* (1952), he could look forward to a period of economic stability.

The 1950s, in fact, were a turning point in Narayan's career as a professional writer. The books he wrote in this decade consolidated his reputation as a major novelist, and for the first time his books began to appear outside England. In the United States, for instance, Pocket Books published *The Bachelor of Arts* in 1951, while Michigan State University Press brought out six of his novels in quick succession between 1953 and 1955. Narayan's novels even found publishing outlets in India.

Narayan's reputation as a writer of captivating novels about Indian life probably peaked with the publication of his eighth novel, *The Guide*, in 1958. This story of an ex-convict who puts on the mask of a holy man and ends up being one has come to be recognized as a minor masterpiece. Indeed, *The Guide*, along with *The Financial Expert* and *The Man-Eater of Malgudi* (1961), represents the high-water mark of his art. These novels established Narayan's Malgudi as a fictional region almost as compelling as Faulkner's Yoknapatawpha County.

At present a number of Narayan's books are in print. In recent years, soft cover editions of his novels and short stories have been published by the University of Chicago Press and Viking/Penguin. In Britain, Heinemann and Penguin continue to print his novels. A number of works have been translated and published in Russia, Poland, France, Israel, Germany, Sweden, Norway, Finland, Holland, and Yugoslavia.

Critical Reception, Honors, and Popularity

Although fame came to Narayan rather late in his life, Narayan was compensated for the relative neglect he suffered in the first two decades of his writing career when *The Guide* was awarded India's highest literary award, the National Prize of the Indian Literary Academy, in 1958. In 1964 he became the recipient of the Padma Bhushan, another honor conferred by the Indian government for his contribution to Indian letters. The University of Leeds offered him an honorary doctorate in 1967; in 1980 he was given the A. C. Benson Medal by the Royal Society of Literature; and in 1982 he was made an Honorary Member of the American Academy and Institute of Arts and Letters. His autobiographical work, *My Days; A Memoir*, received the English Speaking Union Book Award in 1975.

Narayan has been commended by some of the leading writers of this century. Graham Greene, who played such a crucial part in his career, has compared him to Tolstoy, Henry James, Turgenev, and Chekov. Another major contemporary novelist who became an early admirer is V. S. Naipaul. He has his reservations about Narayan's fiction but has written eloquently about Narayan's religious dimension, finding the novels at their best to be classic expositions of Indian life. In the United States, one of Narayan's most vocal admirers has been John Updike, who invoked Charles Dickens in trying to describe "the effect of colorful teeming" that Narayan's fictional city of Malgudi conveys.

Updike's appreciative comments on Narayan, published in *The New Yorker*, also compare him to Faulkner, since the Indian novelist, like the great chronicler of the American South, is a writer "immersed" in his material, and able to weave tales from "a community of neighbors." But while Malgudi is only a region in India, alert critics have noted that it is meant to be a metaphor for the human condition. Additionally, critics have praised Narayan for his sense of place, his simple, straightforward style and unaffected use of Indo-English speech rhythms, his gift for comedy and eye for human idiosyncracies, and his sensitivity to the pathos of life and India's spiritual heritage.

Narayan, indeed, has something of a cult following in many countries. But while Narayan devotees have welcomed almost every new edition to the Malgudi tales, there have been those who have expressed their dissatisfaction with his later work. A major complaint, especially among the new generation of Indo-English writers, is that he has not been receptive to change and that he writes about an India which seems more or less untouched by the contemporary world. Anita Desai, one of the leading novelists of this generation, expresses this point of view when she writes in a review of a recent Narayan novel that "There are many of Narayan's readers who feel that his fiction does not reflect the chaos, the drift, the angst that characterizes a society in transition and that his 'rootedness' is a relic of another pastoral era even now shaken and threatened beyond recovery."

Desai, however, is willing to affirm that Narayan is a very assured and accomplished writer. After all, he has successfully written about Malgudi life without making it seem narrowly provincial, and he has managed to sustain a high level of excellence over a career which now enters its sixth decade. Even though his preeminence in Indo-English writing has been challenged, there is universal recognition of his importance in recording the tales of twentieth-century Indian life.

Analysis of Selected Titles

THE FINANCIAL EXPERT

The Financial Expert, 1952, novel.

Themes and Social Concerns

In outline, *The Financial Expert* sounds much like a fable. It is the story of Margayya, a man first seen under a banyan tree with a tin box, eking out an existence by advising peasants in obtaining loans from a co-operative institution. He is then seen acquiring considerable wealth through questionable means, only to lose everything and return to the banyan tree with his tin box and a condition close to penury. Narayan's point seems to be a simple but profound one: the wealth Margayya acquired was illusory; true riches can never accrue when one makes money into a god.

The Financial Expert probes dubious paths to wealth: Margayya's work as a "financial expert"; his successful stint as a publisher of a semi-pornographic book by a Dr. Lal that masquerades as a work on domestic harmony; and his phase as a money-lender who bases his business on the strategy of withholding the interest from the first installment on the loan. The desire to amass money, Narayan seems to suggest, leads to moral blindness. Certainly, in its exposure of the folly and delusion of Margayya and its focus on the transience of human action, *The Financial Expert* is typical of Narayan's best work.

The story of the modern-day "financial expert" comes to us, in a manner which is uniquely Narayan's, with the trappings of Indian religious myths. Margayya's fate, Narayan suggests obliquely, has been decided as much by his own dealings as by the ongoing quarrel between Lakshmi, the Hindu goddess of wealth, and Saraswati, the goddess of knowledge and enlightenment. In other words, when Margayya has wealth, he cannot have enlightenment; at the end of the novel, and at a point when he has lost all that he acquired, he is closer perhaps to self-knowledge than he had ever been. Nevertheless, he goes back to his old profession of adviser to peasants seeking money, showing thereby a spirit that is indestructible, and untouched by the war between deities.

Characters

Margayya, the central character of *The Financial Expert*, is a good example of Narayan's skill in drawing complex characters. Shrewd and mean but also susceptible to a kind of mysticism in his feelings about money, comic and energetic but also tragically drawn to the ruin of what he had accomplished, capable of contemptible behavior but also incredibly naive, he is a convincing study in obsession and moral confusion. What is especially remarkable about his portrait is the way Narayan presents his ugly, predatory side without withdrawing his sympathies from this driven but vulnerable man.

Margayya's portrait also draws strength from his links with other, equally fascinating characters. Thus Dr. Lal, the aggressive, confidence man author of the book Margayya publishes, is another remarkable study. An outsider in Malgudi who does not care for traditional values and dabbles in sociology to make money, he is not unlike Dr. Tamkin, the memorable character created by Saul Bellow in *Seize the Day*. Margayya is also shown with his spoiled and inconsiderate son Balu, who does everything he can to ruin his indulgent father. Also impressive are the scenes between Margayya and his brother, between whom there is no love lost, and the encounter between Margayya and the enigmatic priest who tells him about the unending war of the gods and conveys a sense of holiness. Strangely enough, the priest manages to sound somewhat skeptical and irritable when he prescribes the rituals Margayya must follow in his quest for wealth. The holy man, like Margayya, illustrates Narayan's feelings about the ambiguity of human actions and the inexplicable mysteries of our behavior.

Techniques

The Financial Expert is an excellent example of Narayan's deft and economic mode of storytelling. The prose is unforced and clear, and Narayan's use of Indian locutions and concrete details from everyday life flavor the narrative and make Margayya's story very much an Indian one. Narayan's tone, typically, is light but cool, firm but humorous. A dramatic novelist, he manages to stay out of his fictions, preferring scene to summary or editorial comments. Instead, he puts every detail to work until ordinary events come to have a representative significance.

THE GUIDE

The Guide, 1958, novel.

Themes and Social Concerns

Widely considered to be Narayan's best book, *The Guide* is the story of Raju, a scamp who ends up becoming a saint. For most of his life Raju had managed to manipulate other people's emotional needs for his own advantage, but the novel shows him going beyond himself to do a genuinely disinterested act at the cost of his life. Raju, in other words, dies so that others may live.

Raju begins his professional life as the owner of a sweetmeat stall at the railway station in a region that has become a popular tourist attraction. He soon discovers that he has a knack for telling people what they would like to hear and becomes a full-time guide. This profession leads him into an affair with one of his clients, Rosie. She is the wife of Marco, a man who does not really care about her aspirations to become an exponent of Indian classical dance. Raju encourages Rosie to make her dreams come true and in the process he becomes a successful impresario and the manager of a very popular dancer. But greed overwhelms him and he begins to exploit Rosie for money while scanting her artistic inclinations. Indeed, his lust for riches makes him forge her signature in a bid to acquire her family jewels. This leads to Raju's incarceration. After he has served his term, though, he finds himself in a village where an innocent villager, Velan, mistakes him for a *sadhu* or holy man. Velan's admiration and Raju's old instinct for utterances that satisfy the longings of his auditors make him revered throughout the village. However, drought soon threatens the region and one of his gnomic pronouncements is taken by the villagers to mean that he will fast till the rains come. This is a moment of truth for Raju: will he escape from the consequences of his decision to be satisfied with the role of a *sadhu,* or will he live up to the expectations he has aroused in the villagers and act like a holy man who will give up life for others? Raju chooses in the end to fast, and the last scene of the novel suggests that Raju has achieved transcendence from his body. Raju exclaims that he can feel the rains coming but does not indicate clearly whether the end of the drought is a fact or the delusion of a man who has been without food for a long time. One thing is clear: Raju had ended his life as a true guru, or spiritual guide, in demonstrating that life should be lived by more than self-interest.

Characteristically, Narayan gives a greater significance to his major theme by interlacing the narrative with references to Hindu theology. Raju's progress from excessive worldliness, his craving for wealth, and inordinate desires are precisely what the Hindu metaphysical tradition cautions against as obstacles in the path of true self-realization. Raju, according to this philosophy, must come to see the world as *lila,* a stage, or as *maya,* an illusion. He must stop playing roles and embrace his *dharma,* or the part assigned him by his fate, and demonstrate *bhakti,* or true devotion.

Characters

Raju is a splendidly realized character. Not given to thought, drifting in and out of situations, and until the last stage of his life ruled by an individualistic spirit which carries him away from family, friends, and morality, he will ultimately learn what it is to act responsibly. But even when he is selfish and full of guile, he is immensely likable, especially because he wants to please other people as much as he can. Except for forging Rosie's signature on a truly reprehensible impulse, he never strikes readers as a wicked character. And although he deludes others as well as himself from time to time, he likes to see things grow and tries to help people achieve their ambitions.

Because Raju narrates most of the novel, readers tend to see the other characters through him. Still, Rosie is another finely wrought portrait of a complex personality. When Raju first meets her she is leading an unfulfilled life because her archaeologist husband, Marco, has no time for her, preferring cave paintings to the real, vital woman. With Raju's help, she becomes a successful dancer, one who comes to see classical Indian dance as a vocation and not a trade. She seems to represent the repressed, creative side of her culture reasserting itself, for her dances are rituals which enact a vital and ultimately uncontrollable force. For this reason Raju loses his hold on her; although he has helped make her famous, he becomes more interested in her value as a marketable commodity and ceases seeing her as an artist in touch with primeval spirits.

Techniques

Narayan is not usually given to elaborate technical experiments or overt display of his artistic skills, but *The Guide* is one of his few works that draws attention to itself because of its somewhat unusual narrative method. In telling Raju's story, Narayan alternates third-person and first-person narration and uses such cinematic techniques as flashbacks and jumpcuts. When we first encounter Raju, he is about to meet Velan, and he is seen at this point from the perspective of an omniscient narrator. Then Raju takes over the narrative chores and relates his progress from sweetmeat seller to jailbird to Velan. In between, the omniscient narrator punctuates Raju's narrative by showing him dealing with the villagers as a holy man. At the end, Raju ceases to be a narrator as he loses his hold on his consciousness. The omniscient narrator concludes the story, showing us a Raju who is about to achieve transcendence. While not as technically sophisticated as classic modernist works, *The Guide*'s flexible narrative mode is a notable achievement and is well suited to the tale of a man who is seen to rise above himself and his unsatisfactory past.

Narayan's technique here, as in his other novels, involves the use of images and symbols rooted in Indian life, but having universal appeal. To take one example, at the end, as Raju is drowning himself, he has his eyes turned towards the mountains. As the villagers look on, the morning sun suddenly illuminates everything. The whole scene is a simple but effective way of utilizing an Indian village setting to symbolize the death by drowning that will give rise to the birth of hope. Raju seems to derive inspiration from the heavens by submersing his worldly self and becoming a true guide who will show his charges the path from this world to the next.

Adaptations
There have been two unsuccessful attempts to represent *The Guide* in other mediums: a film version produced in India, which Narayan has decried for taking all sorts of liberties with the text; and on off-Broadway adaptation by Harvey Breitt and Patricia Rhineheart that folded after three performances in 1968.

THE MAN-EATER OF MALGUDI
The Man-Eater of Malgudi, 1961, novel.

Themes and Social Concerns
This novel has been interpreted in two different ways: as an allegory of good and evil and as a study in identification and displacement. Readings of the work as an allegory focus on the relationship between the narrator Nataraj, the passive and well-meaning printer of the town of Malgudi, and Vasu, the eccentric taxidermist and out-of-towner who forces his way into Nataraj's attic and uses it to house himself and practice his seemingly grisly profession. In the allegorical view, Narayan represents Indian passivity while Vasu embodies the aggressive forces of modernism poised to threaten and destabilize Indian society. Certainly, Vasu unsettles the whole community and seems to overwhelm everyone with his brusque personality and anti-social tendencies. This version of the plot of *The Man-Eater of Malgudi* derives credibility from the mythological underpinnings of the narrative: Vasu is cast in the novel as a *rakshasha,* one of the demons who challenge the gods and introduce chaos into existence. Specifically, Nataraj's assistant Sastri characterizes Vasu as Bhasmasura, a demon in Hindu myths who blights everything he touches, defies the heavens, and makes ordinary human beings suffer. In the end, however, Bhasmasura overreaches himself and self-destructs—an example of pride that inevitably leads to a fall. In the novel itself Vasu frightens everyone in Malgudi, disrupts the lives of its citizens, and attempts to obstruct its rituals. Ultimately, however, he kills himself while trying to squash a mosquito which lands on his forehead.

The other, radically different reading of *The Man-Eater of Malgudi* treats it as a narrative of identification; a work where the narrator-protagonist Nataraj is aroused from his inconsequential mode of existence by the energetic Vasu. According to this version, Nataraj increasingly acts and thinks like Vasu until he reaches a point when he has to get rid of the man who embodies the more primitive and instinctive self that has been bottled up in him for such a long time. Nataraj, in other words, emerges as a much stronger figure at the end of the novel and is even able to displace Vasu by forcing him into a corner from which he has no way out except through self-destruction.

Characters

Vasu is a fascinating creature, not only brutal, self-centered, unpredictable, and indifferent to tradition, religion, or the claims of everyday morality, but also spontaneous, good-humored, and endearingly no-nonsensical in his way of looking at others. If one side of him suggests the demonic, another represents the doer, the man of action who hates small talk and petty-mindedness. Significantly, he is a patriot; he joined the civil disobedience movement aimed at ending British rule in India and was jailed for his nationalistic activities. Clearly, he is a man to be admired as well as hated.

The narrator, Nataraj, may appear to be easygoing, friendly, and meek, and in most ways a model citizen, but he too can be aggressive, cunning, and motivated by self-interest. Outwardly inoffensive and altruistic, he can be inwardly skeptical, resentful, or impatient with his fellow citizens. And as the narrative progresses and he is provoked by Vasu to take a stand, he becomes increasingly petulant, irrational, and obsessive. A measure of his complexity is the way he responds to Vasu: he alternates between admiration and indignation in viewing the taxidermist's actions.

Narayan concentrates in this novel on tracing the involutions of the Vasu-Nataraj relationship, but he also peoples his narrative with a captivating cast of minor characters. Nataraj's friends and neighbors, Vasu's mistress Rangi, and a host of other citizens of Malgudi make the novel memorable through their beliefs, eccentricities, and reactions to Vasu's impact on their settled mode of life. Taken together, they testify to Naipaul's joy in the variety of creation and the comedy of life. Fantastic and yet very human, these minor characters constitute solid evidence of Narayan's skills as a chronicler of a corner of India that has become representative of the whole world.

Techniques

Like most of Narayan's novels, *The Man-Eater of Malgudi* is written in clear, straightforward prose. Narayan's dominant tone is of gentle irony; Narayan seems to be incapable of heavy-handed satire or cynicism. He shows a marked ability to control the narrative pace, shifting adroitly from the slow-moving opening scenes to the fast-paced end where Natavaj and the townspeople maneuver to thwart Vasu. Since *The Man-Eater of Malgudi* is a first-person narrative, we are made to share Nataraj's growing tension and anxiety at Vasu's actions; and yet the novel never ceases to be funny. And although the book has mythical overtones and some very fantastic happenings—for instance, the manner of Vasu's death—it is almost always realistic in its depiction of Indian settings and culture.

Other Titles

Swami and Friends, 1935 (novel); *The Bachelor of Arts*, 1937 (novel); *The Dark Room*, 1938 (novel); *The English Teacher*, 1938 (novel; published in the United States as *Grateful to Life and Death* in 1953); *Mysore*, 1939 (travel); *An Astrologer's Days and Other Stories*, 1947 (short stories); *Mr. Sampath*, 1949 (novel; published in the United States as *The Printer of Malgudi* in 1955); *Waiting for the Mahatama*, 1955 (novel); *Lawley Road*, 1956 (short stories); *My Dateless Diary*, 1960 (travel); *Gods, Demons, and Others*, 1965 (short stories); *The Vendor of Sweets*, 1967 (novel); *A Horse and Two Goats*, 1970 (short stories); *The Ramayana: A Shortened Version of the Indian Epic*, 1972 (translation); *My Days: A Memoir*, 1975 (autobiography); *The Painter of Signs*, 1976 (novel); *The Emerald Route*, 1977 (travel); *The Mahabharata: A Shortened Prose Version of the Indian Epic*, 1978 (translation); *Malgudi Days*, 1982 (short stories); *A Tiger for Malgudi*, 1983 (novel); *Under the Banyan Trees*, 1985 (short stories); *Talkative Man*, 1986 (novel); *The World of Nataraj*, 1990 (novel).

Additional Sources

Alam, F. "Plot and Character in R. K. Narayan's *The Man-Eater of Malgudi*: A Reassessment." *Ariel* 19, 3 (1988): 77-92. Sees in the story a plot line based on identification and displacement.

Chew, Shirley. "A Proper Detachment: The Novels of R. K. Narayan." In *Readings in Commonwealth Literature*, edited by William Walsh. Oxford: Clarendon Press, 1973. A sensible introduction to the novels, though somewhat dated.

Cronin, Richard. "Quiet, Quiet India: The Despair of R. K. Narayan." *Encounter* 64, 3 (1985): 52-59. Evaluates some novels by Narayan not discussed in this entry.

Desai, Anita. "R. K. Narayan and the Grand Malgudi Circus." *Washington Post Book World* (September 4, 1983): 3, 9. Review of *A Tiger for Malgudi*, but also a brief overview from the perspective of the next generation of Indo-English novelists.

Garebian, Keith. "Strategy and Theme in the Art of R. K. Narayan." *Ariel* 5, 4 (1979): 70-81. Helpful comments on the way in which Narayan's technique helps reinforce his thematic concerns.

Greene, Graham. "Introduction." In *The Bachelor of Arts*. London: Heinemann, 1978. Comments on Narayan's achievement by a leading English novelist who helped launch Narayan's career.

Mahood, M. "The Marriage of Krishna: *The Man Eater of Malgudi*." In *The Colonial Encounter: A Reading of Six Novels*. Totowa, NJ: Rowan & Littlefield, 1977. A reading of the novel as an allegory of good and evil.

Mukherjee, Meenakshi. *The Twice-Born Fiction: Themes and Techniques of the Indian Novel in English*. New Delhi: Arnold-Heinemann, 1974. Places the fiction in the overall context of the Indo-English novel.

Naipaul, V. S. *An Area of Darkness*. London: A. Deutsch, 1964.

──────. *India: A Wounded Civilization*. New York: Alfred A. Knopf, 1977. Two evaluations by a major novelist and student of post-independence India; provocative but useful.

Ruthfork, John. "Hindu Mysticism in the Twentieth Century: R. K. Narayan's *The Guide*." *Philological Quarterly* 62, 1 (1983): 31-41. Thoughtful attempt to explain the religious dimension of the novel.

Updike, John. "Alive and Free from Employment." *The New Yorker* 50, 28 (September 2, 1974): 80-82. Review of Narayan's memoir, *My Days*, and a judicious assessment of the work.

Walsh, William. *R. K. Narayan: A Critical Appreciation*. Chicago: University of Chicago Press, 1972. The only widely available book-length study of the writer—sympathetic and suggestive.

Westbrook, Percy D. "The Short Stories of R. K. Narayan." *Journal of Commonwealth Literature* 5 (1968): 41-51. Overview of Narayan as a writer of short fiction.

Woodcock, George. "Two Great Commonwealth Novelists: R. K. Narayan and V. S. Naipaul." *Seewanee Review* 86, 1 (1979): 80-82. Contrasts the two writers and defends Narayan against Naipaul's description of him as "an instinctive, unstudied writer."

Fakrul Alam
Clemson University

LARRY NIVEN
1938

Update

Niven's work in recent years (aside from his new Smoke Ring series) has consisted of extensive collaboration with other writers in the hard science fiction tradition. He collaborated with Jerry Pournelle on the best-selling *Footfall* (1985) and with Steven Barnes on *The Barsoom Project* (1989), a sequel to *Dream Park* (1981). Niven, Pournelle, and Barnes have also produced *The Legacy of Heorot* (1987). Niven was one of eleven writers to contribute to Harlan Ellison's anthology, *Medea: Harlan's World* (1985). His most recent anthology, *Limits* (1985), contains collaborations with three other authors, as well as individual works. Niven has allowed writers like Poul Anderson and Dean Ing to create stories using the background of his Known Space series in *The Man-Kzin Wars* (1988). Niven's most important individual work is *The Integral Trees* (1984), a story that takes place within his Leshy Circuit series, and its sequel *The Smoke Ring* (1987). Niven also published a book of essays entitled *Niven's Laws* (1984).

Niven remains a popular science fiction writer, well regarded for his inventiveness, humor, and rigorous logic; but he has received relatively little critical attention. In recent years he has been content to cover well-worn territory, rather than develop in new directions. *The Integral Trees* was nominated for the Nebula and Hugo awards and remains, along with *Footfall*, his most highly regarded work in recent years.

Analysis of Selected Titles

THE INTEGRAL TREES

The Integral Trees, 1984, novel; Sequel: *The Smoke Ring,* 1987, novel.

Social Concerns/Themes

This work combines two of Niven's favorite themes: the need for freedom, and the necessity for exploration and discovery. The heroes, outcasts of the Quinn tribe, are descendants of space travellers who mutinied against the totalitarian authority of Earth and settled on Smoke Ring, an asteroid belt with its own atmosphere that circles a neutron star. The people of the Smoke Ring live in varying degrees of savagery, inhabiting floating jungles or gigantic flying trees shaped like integral signs. The novel is structured as a series of escapes, revolts, or exiles which are also voyages of discovery. Through this plot structure, Niven suggests that although freedom brings danger, it also brings an excitement that makes life worth living.

The novel presents a frequent theme in Niven's fiction, the double-edged nature of science and technology. The people of London Tree use the superior technology they have preserved from their ancestors to enslave their neighbors. Sharls Davis Kendy, a former Checker for the State, now a human machine, plans to reestablish his control over the Smoke Ring dwellers by means of the almost magical powers that he can offer to any would-be dictators. Niven neither shrinks from the dangers inherent in scientific progress nor retreats into technophobia. His characters manage to snatch the Promethean flame without burning their fingers, in keeping with his basically optimistic philosophy.

Characters

In keeping with science fiction traditions, Niven devotes little space to in-depth characterization. He is concerned with man's interactions with his environment rather than with his fellow man. The main characters follow familiar lines: Clave, the leader, man of action, and lover; Jeffer, the scientist; Gavving, the young hunter who comes to maturity during his adventures. The female characters, Minya, Lawri, Merril, and others, are depicted as equal to the men as warriors and scientists. Interestingly, though the Smoke Ring dwellers are technologically backward and organized along tribal lines, Niven does not depict them as savages enslaved by superstitions. Though only the tribal scientists and their apprentices understand science, most of the characters accept scientific explanations for unfamiliar phenomena. This skepticism helps them to deal with Kendy and reveals Niven's confidence in the power of reason.

The Checker, Sharls Davis Kendy, is perhaps the most interesting character in the novel. A fanatic, whose only purpose is to serve the state, his form follows his function. His personality is recorded in the computer of the ramship *Discipline*, turning him into an un-aging sentient machine, a fusion of technology and totalitarianism. Niven effectively begins and ends *The Integral Trees* with Kendy, establishing him as a continuing threat to the mutineers' descendants. Though a sinister figure, Kendy is also an impressive one.

The Smoke Ring itself, with its bizarre flora and fauna, might be viewed as the central "character" in the book. Niven dazzles his readers with integral trees, floating cotton-candy jungles, mobies, dumbos, elongated human giants, and other wonders. His carefully worked out speculations are more fantastic than many worlds presented in fantasy novels, yet they are always logical.

Techniques/Literary Precedents

The Integral Trees is an exercise in constructing an alien environment, a standard form of science fiction. While some writers like Ursula K. Le Guin, Frank Herbert, or C. S. Lewis make exploring a new world a spiritual journey with the alien world symbolic of the human consciousness or soul, Niven, like other science fiction world builders, makes the Smoke Ring a new part of the physical universe. Niven challenges himself to design a free-fall environment scientifically consistent and filled with details ranging from astronomy to anthropology. *The Integral Trees* may be best compared to such works as Poul Anderson's *Fire Time* (1974), Robert L. Forward's *Dragons Egg* (1980), and Niven's own *Ringworld* (1970). Niven, in fact, dedicated *Integral Trees* to Forward for his help in designing the Smoke Ring. Niven exercises care in presenting his Smoke Ring without slowing down the plot with exposition. He buttresses his text with maps, diagrams, and a glossary. The story itself begins with no formal exposition and provides background information with flashbacks, reminiscences by Kendy, and computer research consulted by the tribesmen. In this way, the reader gradually gets accustomed to the Smoke Ring and experiences a sense of awe-struck wonder at this creation.

Niven also follows in the libertarian tradition of Robert Heinlein, Anderson, and Pournelle. Coercive statism, represented in the novel by Kendy, the London Tree's copsik-runner (slavers), and the chairman of Quinn tribe, are all threats to the heroes' freedom. Niven does not specify what kind of state Kendy serves because its structure, fascistic or communistic, is not as important as the fact that it holds absolute power. The novel's sequel, *The Smoke Ring*, closes with the hint that Kendy will play a larger and more direct role. Niven seems to feel that statists like Kendy cannot be finally defeated.

Related Titles

The Integral Trees forms part of Niven's Leshy Circuit series which also includes *A World Out of Time* (1976). The link in these stories is the totalitarian state of Earth which colonizes other planets with ramships. *The Integral Trees* and its sequel can stand on their own since their main interest is the unique environment of the Smoke Ring. Though critics have found Niven's attempt to create a free-fall environment fascinating, the series does not have the scope or inventiveness of Niven's Known Space series. The Smoke Ring continues the adventures of the remnant of the Quinn tribe in exploring the Smoke Ring. The ending of this sequel implies that a third novel will be written. *The Smoke Ring* remains an enjoyable adventure story.

Additional Sources

Barron, Neil, ed. *Anatomy of Wonder*. 3d ed. New York: R. R. Bowker, 1987. Provides a brief commentary on some of Niven's recent fiction and helpful connections to other works.

Lawler, Donald L. "Larry Niven." In *Twentieth Century Science Fiction Writers*. 2d ed. Edited by Curtis C. Smith. Chicago: St. James Press, 1988. A brief article with a useful bibliography.

Anthony Bernardo
Rutgers University

JOHN NORMAN
John Frederick Lange, Jr.
1931

Update

In recent years John Norman has published three additional books in his series of novels about Gor, a planet which orbits the sun exactly opposite and on the far side from Earth, thus escaping Earth's notice. *Renegades of Gor* (1986), *Vagabonds of Gor* (1987), and *Magicians of Gor* (1988) bring the series to twenty-five novels. As with previous books in the series, feminists have much cause to detest these novels, and critics, in general, have ignored them.

Analysis of Selected Titles

MAGICIANS OF GOR

Magicians of Gor, 1988, novel.

Social Concerns

Although Norman's alter ego is a professor of philosophy, the philosophical aspects of the Gor novels have not often been examined. The novels' emphasis on sadomasochistic sexual practices has obscured some of the lessons Norman puts into Tarl Cabot's first-person narration. Sometimes Cabot launches into extended philosophical disquisitions. Some of what Cabot says, when stripped of its social science jargon, is common sense: weakness attracts bullies and weak nations are frequent victims of ruthless enemies; people need a sense of direction in their lives. When society breaks down, as Ar does after it surrenders to the forces of Cos, young people form gangs and carve out their own small territories; defending them against others becomes their purpose. At least on the surface, this parallels what has happened in some large American cities. Another, perhaps more disturbing, series of observations that appears in *Magicians of Gor* focuses on the abuse by their own people of brave soldiers who were defeated while defending Ar. Instead of honoring or helping these veterans, the citizens of Ar revile them, blaming them not only for the loss of the war, but for having any war at all. This seems Norman's comment on the experiences of many of America's Vietnam War veterans. Through propaganda and the citizenry's fear, Cos shifts from being seen as a remorseless enemy to the wronged friend of Ar which has liberated the city from tyranny. Norman seems to have a low view of people's ability to think for themselves; the citizens of Ar believe almost anything if it sounds close to what they want to believe.

Most of the Gor novels are concerned with the idea of biological determinism. A popular scientific and philosophical view in the twentieth century, biological determinism maintains that most of what people become is determined by their genes, hormones, and other legacies of millions of years of evolution. These determine what each individual person will be like, with environment having only minimal influence. This concept has appealed to some futurist thinkers who have suggested that techniques such as genetic testing could rid society of incorrigible undesirables or create utopian societies in which people were good because they were forced to be through advanced technology. Norman takes the notion of biological determinism and, within the context of a "primitive" warrior society, applies it to the relationships between men and women.

It is possible that Norman intends to ridicule notions of biology as destiny—that people are born to be what they become as adults. Some critics suggested in the early 1970s that in the Gor books Norman was merely working out his own sexual fantasies on paper and was sharing those fantasies with his readers. This may be so, but the intellectualism interjected frequently in *Magicians of Gor* suggests that the sadomasochistic society of Gor is more than just wish fulfillment for a sexually frustrated male. Repeatedly, Tarl Cabot, the narrator, declares that women are biologically meant to be slaves and men are meant to be masters. On earth, he notes, men and women are usually unhappy with one another. This is because earthly society (probably meaning American society) has forced ordinary people into unnatural social roles to suit small social elites that seek power for themselves at the expense of the welfare of others. For Cabot, when women act like men, they are defying their true selves, dooming themselves to miserable lives. To be happy they should be slaves to men. Thus when a Gor slaving raider brings earth women to Gor, the women soon find themselves happier than they ever were before. As slaves, they serve men totally, which is what evolution meant them to do. Cabot constantly refers to slave women as being truly feminine, while free women are lost in unhappiness because they lack true femininity. On the other hand, men are unhappy when they must try to deal with women as if men and women were equals; this unnatural relationship can only be rectified by the man becoming a master. He must learn that women are biologically meant to serve his every whim, with total obedience; he must learn that no woman is truly happy unless she is a man's slave.

Most psychiatrists would probably cringe at Cabot's radical view of the proper relationship between the sexes. Human relationships seem too complex for Cabot's reasoning to hold true, yet it is Cabot's point that earthly relationships have been made artificially complex. On Gor, the complexities are stripped away to reveal the truly simple relationships nature intended. The whole idea that women want to be degraded, to literally lick men's feet, to be whipped to remind them that they are entirely in a man's power, and to be chained and regarded as no more than a domesticated animal seems perverse. Simplistic answers may satisfy some adolescent minds, but the real-life experiences of adults suggest that most women hate to be abused.

Could the Gor series be a savage satire on the whole notion of biological determinism? After all, Norman is the pen name of a real-life philosopher whose academic work suggests that he is well acquainted with the confusions of modern philosophical views. Much of twentieth-century philosophy depends on the notion that only what is physical exists, that there is no supernatural aspect to the universe. Biological determinism is the logical result of the belief that people have only physical brains—no minds, no spirits, no God. On Gor, biological determinism runs rampant. The gods of Gor are not really like the Christian God; they are somewhat cowardly insect-like creatures, making the spiritual lives of Goreans seem ridiculous and suggesting that biological determinism does not properly deal with people's spiritual needs.

Even the most mystical events on Gor, such as when Boots Tarsk-Bit seems to make a woman disappear, can be explained in purely physical terms by hard-headed Tarl Cabot. Yet, under all the cynicism, all the brutality and acting out of biological drives, is a contradiction. Cabot and his companion Marcus act altruistically—not in the self-interest that their biology would dictate, but in the interest of others. The sadomasochistic world of Gor seems insane, and perhaps it is meant to be.

This does not absolve Norman from responsibility for the views of men and women he presents in his fiction. If the Gor series is a satire, it is a joke almost no one understands. Further, his book *Imaginative Sex* (1974) indicates that he may be serious about sadomasochism and the idea that women must submit to their masters in order to be happy. How many of the many millions of readers of the Gor books take the biological theories seriously is open to conjecture. After all, the books are presented as fantasies, and the sex as no more than fantasy; for their readers they may be no more than light entertainments. Further, those who charge the Gor books with being pornographic are exaggerating. They may be deeply offensive, but being offensive does not make them pornographic.

In fact, the sex in *Magicians of Gor* is not described in detail. It occurs but is obliquely presented; a careless reader might miss it entirely. Still, the novel opens with a free woman being seized and enslaved for trying to sleep with a handsome male slave. The scene is horrifying, with the woman bound in a net, her life thrown to the wind. Soon thereafter, Marcus abuses his own slave, Phoebe, who delightedly licks his feet clean of the dirt and dust they had gathered from walking in Ar's streets. Phoebe is presented as overjoyed to serve her master in such a humiliating way, but for those readers who are unprepared for it, the scene is a shocker. Elsewhere, women are "cuffed"—struck with back or palm of the hand—for minor transgressions against the code of conduct all slaves must follow. These cuffings may easily call to mind those women who are beaten by their husbands or boyfriends in real life. Their battered faces are not romantic, and in those cases in which the battered woman insists she loves the man who beats her, the woman appears pathetic and foolish, not as though she were a beautiful love slave whose beatings made her a sex goddess. Critics of the abuse of women have every reason to be appalled by *Magicians of Gor*.

Another disturbing aspect of *Magicians of Gor* is the subject of slavery. The plot of the novel is slight; about three-fourths of the book is devoted to depictions and justifications of slavery. The practice is commonplace on Gor, and characters find slavery mildly troubling only when they contemplate male slaves having to be subservient to women. Such qualms are rare. In general, the practice is treated as being a natural consequence of biology; some people are born stronger than others. The strong rule the weak. All women are weaker than men and thus all women should be slaves of men. For those men who are weak—especially those who treat women as equals or at least as people whose feelings matter—slavery is seen as suitable for them because in slavery they would at least be serving real men, natural men who dominate as biology intends.

The Greek and Roman names of the native Goreans suggest a parallel with the classical world. In these and many other ancient and primitive societies, slavery was a common practice, but America's own experiences with slavery suggest that the practice was not only despicable but destructive of the personalities of both slave and owner. This is not apparent in *Magicians of Gor*. Further, the constant insistence on the glories of female slavery on Gor and of how that slavery is honest, whereas earthly practices are hypocritical, implies that female slavery is superior to earthly ways.

On Gor, slavery is a legal institution and is governed and protected by law. Women are slaves because they must be; they are branded because they are like animals and have no choice; they may be bought, sold, traded, tortured, put to any kind of labor whatsoever, and may be killed entirely at the will of their owners. Tarl Cabot once, in the earliest Gor novels, was troubled by Gor's slavery; he is no long bothered by it.

Themes

The main theme of *Magicians of Gor* is a complex speculation about reality, about what really exists and what does not. At the end of the novel this theme is explained in relation to the Home Stones, over which wars are fought and for which people will give their lives. Cabot explains that the Home Stone "exists, which goes beyond, which surpasses, meaning. In this primitive sense the Home Stone is simply that, and irreducibly, the Home Stone. It is too important, too precious, to mean. And in not meaning, it becomes, of course, the most meaningful of all." This idea that what is not may be more than that which is, is not only complex, it seems contradictory to the idea that being exactly what one is and nothing else is what is most important to people. Women are inherently slaves, the reasoning goes, thus they must be slaves to be really themselves. Yet, the novel's principal theme suggests that in not being what one is, in denying the fact that one exists, one can become more than what one was before. On the one hand, people find fulfillment in reducing their relationships to their own fundamental natures, those of slave and master, and on the other hand the philosophical underpinning of the novel is that in denying what one is, one can become greater than oneself. By being without meaning, the Home Stone has intense meaning because it is so obviously just a rock, yet inspires intense emotions in people.

Elsewhere in the novel, the theme turns up in other forms. For instance, self-denial shows up several times, often in relationship to sexual desire. By denying that there is desire, a master inflames himself and his slave; the greater the denial, the more powerful the desire. The slave Milo exerts an attraction for free women as if he were not a slave; no free man is more idolized. Seremides, a military lord in Ar, has become the power-behind-the-throne of the city by surrendering to the forces of Cos; as a defeated warrior he has won Ar. Adding to the confusion is the frequent assertion that the women in the novel are only truly liberated when they are total slaves. The liberation comes from their becoming their true selves, which means that they are meaningless property. Eventually, the theme finds its fulfillment not in the disquisition on the meaning of Home Stones, but in Talena, Ubara (Ruler) of Ar. She has been made legally a slave, owned by Tarl Cabot, but she is to live as if still a free woman; she legally has nothing, but she is to seem as if she has everything.

Characters

The characters in *Magicians of Gor* are not well developed. A reader new to the Gor series might have difficulty figuring out who the narrator is, although people familiar with the series would realize that the narrator is Tarl Cabot, once of Earth but now a skilled warrior on Gor. When he allows himself some reflection about himself, Cabot notes that he is in most ways just an ordinary man, but nature has given him the extraordinary physical gifts that make him a natural swordsman. He is embarrassed to be so immodest as to admit that he is among the best fighters on Gor. His modesty, however, does not extend to his looks; he thinks he is a handsome man and does not like to hear that any man may be better looking. As the novel unfolds, he is also revealed to be a clever man with the ability to outthink clever enemies. His schemes lead to the recovery of the Home Stone of Ar's Station, a city to the north of Ar, and to the enslavement of his enemy Talena.

Cabot's companion is another skilled warrior, Marcus, of Ar's Station. Marcus, courageous but a bit dense, learns that his sex slave, Phoebe, came from Cos. Cos has crushed Ar's Station in war, so Marcus takes his anger out on Phoebe, using her as a representative of Cos. Phoebe is meek, utterly servile, and loves her master. When he returns her love, she is happy and contented.

Other characters are not presented at length. Boots Tarsk-Bit makes an appearance as a traveling magician and uses sleight of hand to retrieve the Home Stone of Ar's Station from its display area in Ar. Disowned by her father, the true Ubar of Ar who disappeared in a punitive raid in the mountains, Talena is an evil character who seems willing to do anything for power. She shamefully sends free women off to be slaves in Cos under the pretense of doing a moral and righteous act; she says they are to serve as reparations for Ar's supposed crimes against her conqueror, Cos. When she discovers her fate at the end of the novel, she curses mightily and expresses contempt for all men.

Techniques

When the Gor series began in the 1960s, reviewers compared it to the fiction of Edgar Rice Burroughs. Some reviewers hoped that Norman might exceed Burroughs as a creator of vivid fantasies of adventure. This did not happen. Even in the early novels signs of weaknesses are evident. For instance, *Outlaw of Gor* (1967) takes forever to get its action underway and seems a mere prologue to the real story which comes in *Priest Kings of Gor* (1968). *Magicians of Gor* seems to wander endlessly. The plot of the novel does not become evident until after more than sixty pages. About three-fourths of the novel is devoted to descriptions of the pleasures of slavery. Purely as a matter of technique, the repetitive descriptions are without the variation or originality which might liven them up as sex fantasies. The sadomasochistic aspect of the novel is its primary interest, with the plot decidedly secondary. The early novels are marked by well-told high adventure. For instance, in *Priest-Kings of Gor*, the reader seems in the presence of a master storyteller. The secret of the Priest-Kings is sought and eventually revealed, and the primitive practices of Gorean society form an exotic backdrop for the earthman who is discovering the wonders of a strange new world. But after uncovering the truth about the nature of the Priest-Kings, Cabot seems to have little left to discover. The subsequent novels slowly drift into the pattern of *Magicians of Gor*, a clever plot buried under layers of sexual titillation. To Norman's credit, he still practices the essentials of the novelist's craft. He ties the seemingly pointless events of the first chapter to Cabot's scheme to enslave Talena, and builds suspense for the next novel in the series. Further, he has a gift for evocative description, making strange buildings in Ar and camps outside it come alive. The flair for creating an exotic environment in which anything might occur is still present in Norman's fiction, but not much actually happens.

Literary Precedents

The Gor novels were once seriously compared with the novels of Edgar Rice Burroughs. Both Norman and Burroughs present wish-fulfillment stories; they write daydreams. Like *Magicians of Gor* such Burroughs novels as *At the Earth's Core* present semi-naked beautiful women, robust heroes, and bizarre situations. However, Burroughs presents the more complete daydream, with exciting and courageous heroines to complement the heroes and with many diversions besides sex. Burroughs' heroes, with their many self-doubts and misunderstandings clouding their motivations, tend to be more complex and interesting than those of the Gor books.

Kirk H. Beetz
National University, Sacramento

JOYCE CAROL OATES
1938

Update

Since 1985, Joyce Carol Oates has continued to teach at Princeton and to publish at the rate of several books a year. Five novels have appeared—*Marya* (1986), *You Must Remember This* (1987), *American Appetites* (1989), *Because It Is Bitter, and Because It Is My Heart* (1990), and *I Lock My Door Upon Myself* (1990); two volumes of short stories—*Raven's Wing* (1987), and *The Assignation* (1988); a reprinted collection of poems—*The Time Traveller* (1989); a collection of essays—*Woman Writer: Occasions and Opportunities* (1988); and a book-length essay—*On Boxing* (1987). In addition, Oates caused a stir when to the astonishment of her publisher, E. P. Dutton, she submitted a novel under the pseudonym of Rosamond Smith to Simon and Schuster. Oates said that she was not trying to deceive, but that she wanted to find a new identity as a writer to see if this might generate a new voice. In *Lives of the Twins* (1987), she addresses the theme of double identity, a theme underscored by the fact that she played on her husband Raymond Smith's name when she chose her pseudonym. Oates maintained the pseudonym for two other novels, published by Dutton, *Soul/Mate* (1989) and *Nemesis* (1990), and seems to be reserving it for novels that fall into the popular thriller genre. She continues to show interest in being both a popular and a serious writer: she regularly discusses her craft and describes her sense of obligation to reflect the world as she sees it, and she has recently discussed her personal life more freely in interviews and in print.

On numerous occasions, Oates has answered charges that she is too prolific or too violent. By talking about her habits of revision, she has also attempted to dispel the myth that she indulges in a kind of automatic writing. Although there is still an "anti-Oates" faction of critics, reviewers have treated her work more seriously, and scholars have contributed an increasing number of book-length studies.

Since 1985, Oates has also continued to have plays produced, and indeed, much of her fiction seems adaptable to dramatic forms. Martin Scorsese holds the film rights for *You Must Remember This*, but to date only one film adaptation—*Smooth Talk* (1985)—has appeared, which is Joyce Chopra's version of Oates' short story "Where Are You Going, Where Have You Been?" In it, Chopra captures the frenetic quality of shopping mall America and, by adding a number of adolescent friends for Connie, emphasizes that adolescents make choices that are both dangerous and exciting. The film's grounding in realism overwhelms much of the metaphoric quality of Oates's story. Chopra may have chosen to have Connie return to her family after she is "raped" by Arnold Friend to emphasize the initiation archetype over the adolescent warning many see as the focus of the film.

Analysis of Selected Titles

MARYA: A LIFE

Marya: A Life, 1986, novel.

Social Concerns/Themes

One of Oates's most autobiographical novels, *Marya* traces the journey of the child Marya from her origins in the poor communities of Innisfail and Shaheen Falls in upstate New York to a successful academic career, a career as translator at the international level, and finally, back home as she decides to search for the alcoholic mother who abandoned her to a paternal aunt and uncle after her father was murdered. The structure enables Oates to address issues that have concerned her in much of her fiction: the defenselessness of a child, particularly a female child; the conformity and rebellion of the adolescent and the violence of adolescent behavior; the place of the brilliant, sensitive person in an ordinary world; the struggle with religious faith; and the politics of the academic world. While *Marya* pulls together many of Oates's themes, it also reflects a new attention to issues of feminism that she began to address in *Solstice*. Oates uses that novel's vision of women locked in a relationship based on a power struggle in her portrait of Marya and her college friend Imogene. But where *Solstice* ended on the cyclical nature of the power struggle, *Marya* ends on the need for women to accept their origins by coming to terms with their relationship—or lack of relationship—with their mothers.

Oates's refusal to ignore the violent nature of society continues in *Marya*. The novel opens with the violent murder of Marya's father and places Marya in a number of personally violent encounters, most notably a near-rape where her hair, the symbol of her womanhood, is cut off by a group of drunken peers. The motif of violence culminates in an international conference on torture that Marya attends, the emphasis here suggesting not just the global nature of violence but also how much it is linked to sexual abuse of women.

Despite the emphasis on violence, *Marya*, like most of Oates's novels, is not nihilistic. Its belief in the value of life connects to Oates's feminist perspective, which does not harbor illusions that women's relationships are always supportive but does see the possibility of women finding value in themselves by acknowledging their origins. Neither a male nor a female relationship brings Marya out of her coldness, but her sense of her living, though not pregnant womb, connects her to the universal quality of birth and particularly to her mother. Marya's womb-life echoes the French feminist criticism of Hélène Cixious, Luce Irigaray, and Julia Kristeva that focuses on the internal and biological, on a state of being that is preconscious and, therefore, uncontaminated by patriarchal language. Oates is too much of a realist merely to endorse abstract French feminism, so she has Maya abandon feminist theory and polemics in favor of her need to confront her relationship to her roots. By so doing, she suggests that while there may be value in trying to find a woman-identity apart from social and language definitions, there is also the need to acknowledge one's individual social definitions.

Characters

The book is clearly Marya Knauer's, and Oates creates a convincing view of the protective coldness that children of alcoholics or the victims of child abuse often adopt. The novel's structure allows Oates to emphasize significant people who have shaped Marya's life: Lee, a cousin who bullies and abuses her; Mr. Schwilk, the junior high school teacher whom students harass out of the classroom; Father Shearing, the priest who helps Marya understand faith; Emmett, Marya's first boyfriend who will never rise out of Shaheen Falls and would like to keep Marya there with him; Imogene, her college friend and rival; Maximilian Fein, the brilliant, married professor who becomes her lover; Gregory, her colleague with whom she must compete for a tenured position; Eric, her lover who in death teaches her to relinquish her protective shell; Vera, the aunt who has raised her and who directs her at the end of the novel toward her mother. While the fictional characters are individualized in the context of Marya's life, they also represent significant teachers or clergy or lovers or friends in the reader's own life.

Techniques/Literary Precedents

Marya's eleven chapter episodic structure creates a female heroic journey involving departure, initiation, and return. Where the male heroic structure tends to propel the hero on a solitary journey with encounters that involve conquering obstacles, Marya's journey propels her into encounters that involve negotiating relationships. Her return home does not complete the journey as much as it begins the most significant part where she will negotiate her sense of self by coming to terms with her mother. Marya is a twentieth-century Jane Eyre who survives an abusive childhood, but where *Jane Eyre* (1847) comes to a neat closure involving the heroine's marriage, *Marya* ends without any outcome predicted in the search for the mother.

Many of the chapters of *Marya* were published as separate short stories, and they stand up well as complete stories. This does not, however, detract from the sense of the wholeness of the novel. Oates achieves this wholeness by repeating image patterns—stones or barriers that block relationships; cars, bicycles, roads, canals that define the territory of the journey; voice and dream patterns that keep recalling Marya's past; images of blighted nature, such as the image of Queen Anne's lace marred at its center by a black dot. These images keep the novel recursive and memory driven. Its first chapter is modern with its fragmented, disconnected voices, but the novel is also realistic and traditionally plotted in its episodic structure.

Relation to Previous Works

With the publication of *Marya*, Oates returned to the rural landscape of her early fiction set in western New York. Its beginning chapters connect to Oates's large output of stories about adolescents. Its chapter on Father Shearing connects to the theological issues Oates has addressed in many essays, particularly ones on Kafka and Flannery O'Connor in *New Heaven, New Earth* and on O'Connor and Simone Weil in *The Profane Art*, in numerous short stories, and in *Son of the Morning*. Its later chapters about Marya's academic life address issues Oates has looked at in her short stories about academics and her academic novel *Unholy Loves*, and its chapter about Marya's college friends echoes the adult version of female friendships in *Solstice*.

YOU MUST REMEMBER THIS

You Must Remember This, 1987, novel.

Social Concerns/Themes

Set in Oates's fictional Port Oriskany, New York, the university town setting of the college student section of *Marya*, *You Must Remember This* captures the atmosphere of the 1950s where the middle classes could live well and where they could blind themselves to the violence lying just beneath the surface of their society. The novel draws on Oates's interest in boxing as a metaphor for this controlled violence as she traces the relationship between the adolescent Enid Maria Stevick and her father's illegitimate half-brother Felix, a boxer. It asks the reader to remember that beneath the tranquil American 1950s there was sexual turmoil, embodied in Enid's adolescent affair with Felix and her parents' asexual marriage; the fanaticism of McCarthyism and its role in the Rosenbergs execution; and the bomb, the ultimate weapon that can annihilate humanity, despite the naive act of building bomb shelters. The link between the physicality of adolescence and of boxing enables Oates to make her point that physical experiences are the most profound experiences of our lives, even as we try to transcend them in our attempt to be spiritual beings. As she links the male experience of boxing with the female experience of abortion, she dramatizes her vision of the transcendent power of violence.

The rebellion of Enid and Felix against the complacency of the 1950s is risky. They try to control life's experiences as the boxer tries to control violence in the ring or the artist tries to give shape to experience in the art object. But life finally controls Enid and Felix, and they are both deeply scarred by Enid's eventual abortion. For Oates, though, such experiences need not destroy; rather, they represent the life-force that allows people to enter, survive, and bring order to the uncontrollable physical bouts of life. That Oates believes it is possible to transcend the physical through the physical is evident in the last scene where Enid's parents, Lyle and Hannah Stevick, make love after eighteen years of abstinence, self-imposed because of the Catholic church's stand on birth control. Copulating in their backyard bomb shelter, Hannah does not respond physically, yet still she declares her love, and Lyle, sexually fulfilled, remembers young love. Through this groping act Oates suggests that we can continue to live if we remember and continue to seek moments that sustain at the same time that they do not mask the violent nature of life.

Characters

Enid and Felix represent two of Oates's major interests: the adolescent who rebels and will survive and profit from her rebellion only if she remembers it and acknowledges why it was necessary; and the boxer who survives life by trying to control it in a metaphoric boxing ring. While Felix emerges as Oates's central character, Enid and her family, more than Felix's boxing world, emerge as the central character group. Lyle Stevick, Enid's father, is a second-hand furniture store owner who reads intellectual literature and is accused of being a communist. Spending his spare time building a bomb shelter, Lyle leads a life of quiet desperation. Lyle's wife, Hannah, represses all the unpleasantness of life so fully that she seems unaware of her own desperation. Rather than confronting Enid about a coded notebook Enid has been keeping, she burns it, as if burning will erase its contents and Enid's hidden sexual life. Other members of the Stevick family include Enid's sisters, Geraldine who is married and pregnant and Lizzie who is probably the mistress of her voice teacher; her brother Warren, a wounded Korean War veteran who protests the bomb; and Lyle's brother, Dominic, a priest who represents the belief that everything will be fine as long as one follows Catholic teachings.

Techniques/Literary Precedents

With its omniscient point of view and chronological plot, *You Must Remember This* has as its precedent the traditionalist view that the novel should tell an interesting story. Its unflinching look at society recalls naturalistic fiction, but it is more hopeful than novels in that tradition because it suggests that people can rise above the forces that act to control them. As the novel probes the American nightmare, it also shows a belief that the American dream can co-exist with the nightmare.

The novel's most distinguishing feature is the way it integrates details from the 1950s, from the first Philco televisions and Arthur Godfrey to the Eisenhower-Stevenson campaign and bomb shelters stocked with Campbell's soup. It recreates that era much as Dos Passos recreated the 1930s, but instead of using Dos Passos's fragmented clips, Oates weaves the era into an integrated story line.

Relation to Previous Works

As in *Marya*, Oates has returned in *You Must Remember This* to the locale of her early novels. With the emphasis on the adolescent, one also thinks of her many short stories and of *Childwold*, her version of Nabokov's *Lolita*. It is interesting to note that this novel about boxing was published the same year as Oates's book-length essay *On Boxing*.

BECAUSE IT IS BITTER, AND BECAUSE IT IS MY HEART
Because It Is Bitter, and Because It Is My Heart, 1990, novel.

Social Concerns/Themes

The central event of *Because It Is Bitter, and Because It Is My Heart* is Jinx Fairchild's murder of Little Red Garlock while Iris Courtney, the girl Garlock has been chasing, watches. Like *Marya* and *You Must Remember This, Because It Is Bitter, and Because It Is My Heart* examines the connection between adolescence and violence, and, like them, it is more controlled and purposeful in its intent than Oates's early fiction. Iris Courtney's journey from her adolescence in the small upstate New York city of Hammond to Syracuse University replicates Marya's journey. Like Marya, Iris protects herself from the scars of her father's drinking and gambling, of her mother's alcoholism and promiscuity, and of her parents' eventual divorce by adopting a cold, shell-like exterior. Despite its bleak view of the quality of life in mid-twentieth-century America, Oates finds a way of endorsing the fact that this kind of life is better than no life at all.

Where *You Must Remember This* found something sustaining in the metaphor of the controlled violence of boxing, *Because It Is Bitter, and Because It Is My Heart* finds beauty in the metaphor of art and photography. Iris becomes an art major at Syracuse and her uncle is a photographer who regularly photographs her and her mother. The photograph is a pose, just as Iris's parents' early life together was a pose and Iris's marriage to the son of one of her art professors will be a pose. She marries without ever telling her fiancé or his family about her past, and the novel closes with Iris being fitted into an heirloom wedding gown in which she can adopt the perfect pose. Some editorial intrusions indicate that Iris's marriage will last and that, even though she will be an emotionless wife, she will survive her life experiences, which include not only witnessing a murder but also being attacked by a gang of young males.

The position of the adolescent within the family or within society, the pervasiveness of violence, and the nature of art have all been concerns that Oates has explored throughout her career. Although she has always implied an interest in how social and class structures shape lives, *Because It Is Bitter, and Because It Is My Heart* is her most sustained look at these structures. Oates achieves her purpose by juxtaposing the Courtneys' varying social class against the hillbilly Garlock family and against the African-American Fairchild family. But Oates does more than create stereotypes of social class. When she has Jinx Fairchild murdered and has Iris attacked by a car full of black toughs, one has to ask why she chooses to equate violence with the black community. Because she has chosen also to show Jinx saving Iris from white violence, she not only stereotypes the black community as violent but highlights as well how much class and race struggles have defined the modern world. Filled with references to Kennedy, to the civil rights movement, and to Vietnam, the novel forces us to ask how we can cope in such a bitter world. As Stephen Crane suggested in the poem from which Oates takes her title, we can cope only if we force ourselves to acknowledge that life is bitter and only if we eat of it anyway. Like Crane's beast that "Held his heart in his hands, / And ate of it," and liked it "Because it is bitter, / and Because it is my heart," Oates's latest novel insists, as her work has always insisted, that confronting the real nature of the world we have created is a first step toward transcending that world.

Characters

Iris Courtney and Jinx Fairchild are mirror characters. They are both placed into social classes that have not been empowered by education or money, and both sense themselves as different from others in their social class. It is this sense of difference that draws them together. Iris's advantage is that she is white, while Jinx's is that he is male, but their respective disadvantages victimize them. Iris is a survivor, but at the expense of her capacity for emotion and honesty, while Jinx probably dies in the Vietnam War. One of Jinx's last acts is to send Iris a photograph of himself, taken by her uncle, an act that Oates uses to suggest that Iris should remember the violent and bitter event that connected her to a part of life she may be trying to ignore in her comfortable marriage.

Most of the other characters in *Because It Is Bitter, and Because It Is My Heart* are defined by the family to which they belong. Duke and Persia Courtney play Fred Astaire and Ginger Rogers roles until their lifestyle spirals downward from middle-class standards. Leslie Courtney, Duke's brother who loves Persia, succeeds with his photography and remains in the middle class, perhaps because he uses photography to shape his vision of what he wishes life to be rather than solely for commercial purposes. Jinx Fairchild's family reveals the same kind of pressures to succeed and the same kind of misguided notions about how to do it as Iris's family. His mother, Minnie, places all the family's hopes on Jinx's success; his father Woodrow places all his hope in God; his wife Sissy Weaver seems beyond the possibility of hope and follows the same pattern of alcoholism, promiscuity, and downward mobility that Persia Courtney follows. The Garlock family is overwhelmed by poverty, incest, abuse, while the wealthy, intellectual Savage family that Iris marries into, protect themselves from the bitterness of life by trying to live as if their lives were a photograph of a perfect dinner party.

Techniques/Literary Precedents

As in *You Must Remember This*, Oates creates the atmosphere of the 1950s and 1960s by numerous references to popular culture and political movements: Jack Palance and Ava Gardner; Hell's Angels and "Great Balls of Fire"; the Kennedy assassination that precipitates the opportunity for Iris being attacked and that, along with the Vietnam War, is the central metaphor for the character of the twentieth century.

Oates cuts back and forth between families. Iris is at the center of the Courtney family and connects it to the Garlock and Savage families; Jinx is at the center of the Fairchild family, which Oates examines less closely than the Courtneys. Perhaps this is because she feels better able to fictionalize a white, female experience than a black, male experience. She juxtaposes Iris's upward mobility against the downward mobility of most of the other characters. With its quick cuts between families, the novel is a bit like one of Leslie Courtney's photographs, a snapshot look at how social structures frame who we are and become. Its title places it in the tradition of Stephen Crane, a writer who also used a photographic technique but whose vision of life was more bitter than that of Oates.

Relation to Previous Works

Since 1985 Oates has returned to the unmitigated look at violence that drew negative criticism in her early work. In *Marya, You Must Remember This*, and *Because It Is Bitter, and Because It Is My Heart* she looks at violence in the lower and middle classes, while in *American Appetites* she shows that the American appetite for material and intellectual success can turn as nightmarish as the appetites of any of the social classes. With its theme of racism, *Because It Is Bitter, and Because It Is My Heart* most recalls *them*, though Oates in her later fiction is spending less time creating a consciousness of violence and more time using art to shape a way to respond to violence.

Additional Sources

Anthony, Carolyn. *Family Portraits: Remembrances by Twenty Distinguished Writers*. New York: Doubleday, 1989. In the section she wrote for Anthony, Oates provides much information about the violence within her ancestral family and about the support of her immediate family.

Bender, Eileen Teper. *Joyce Carol Oates: Artist in Residence*. Bloomington: Indiana University Press, 1987. Bender provides close discussions of Oates's work in the context of how the artist reflects the communal experience.

Bloom, Harold, ed. *Joyce Carol Oates*. New York: Chelsea, 1987. Part of the Modern Critical Views Series, this book collects previously published essays addressing a variety of aspects of Oates's works.

Grant, Mary Kathryn. *The Tragic Vision of Joyce Carol Oates*. Durham, NC: Duke University Press, 1978. This early study suggests that Oates may be so prolific because she believes the world has meaning but that it needs to be healed and reawakened.

Johnson, Greg. *Understanding Joyce Carol Oates*. Columbia: University of South Carolina Press, 1987. A general introduction to Oates that sees her in the context of the visionary experience.

Milazzo, Lee, ed. *Conversations with Joyce Carol Oates*. Jackson: University Press of Mississippi, 1989. Collects interviews Oates has given since the beginning of her career to the present.

Severin, Hermann. *The Image of the Intellectual in the Short Stories of Joyce Carol Oates*. New York: Peter Lang, 1986. This published dissertation defends the numerous short stories Oates has written about academics as being complex, well-crafted works, rather than repetitive satirical attacks.

Waller, G. F. *Dreaming America: Obsession and Transcendence in the Fiction of Joyce Carol Oates*. Baton Rouge: Louisiana State University Press, 1979. This book stops before Oates's *Son of the Morning* (1978) but accurately predicts that Oates will turn her attention to an eastern visionary experience. Waller believes that Oates uses violence and obsession as a way of achieving transcendence.

Sharon L. Dean
Rivier College

O. HENRY
William Sidney Porter
1862-1910

Publishing History

It is hard to imagine an American writer with a more frenzied career than O. Henry's. In less than a decade he flashed across the literary sky, produced a dazzling display of a couple of hundred stories, and then disappeared as quickly as he appeared. Although he had written humorous sketches while in Texas, William Sidney Porter developed his short story technique in earnest while in prison. He served a little over three years (from 1898 until 1901) in an Ohio penitentiary for a crime of which he maintained his innocence, long after it ceased to matter. While there, William Sidney Porter chose his pen name: O. Henry. The origins of his pseudonym remain to this day cloaked in obscurity. O. Henry would have preferred it that way: a symbol of the obscurity in which he wished to shroud his entire prison experience.

O. Henry was profoundly ashamed of his stint in prison, but in the longer view of his life it proved valuable. It gave him a first-hand view of a wretched stratum of society with which he had little contact. He came to know not only criminals, but also those from urban backgrounds and from poor ghettos. In the long evenings when he served as a nurse and pharmacist, he honed his writing skills. Furthermore, the inmates provided him with some good stories—not the least of which is "A Retrieved Reformation." More important than any particular story, though, his experience behind bars revealed to O. Henry a fertile area for material: the lower classes. Long after he had left prison he habitually observed strangers and the down-and-out, gathering material for his stories from people in the street.

While in prison, O. Henry sold his first stories to national magazines, and in some respects these are as technically well-written as anything he did. Obviously, he had the time to lavish attention on them—something that would not happen in later years when he was always hard-pressed for cash. "Whistling Dick's Christmas Stocking" was published in *McClure's* in 1899, and "Georgia's Ruling" appeared in *Outlook* in 1900. "Money Maze" and "Rouge et Noir" were both purchased by *Ainslee's*.

After his release from prison in 1901, he visited his daughter in Pittsburgh, a city he found dismal. The editors of *Ainslee* advanced him a hundred dollars to come to New York City, initiating a pattern that became habitual—of receiving advances from editors for unwritten stories and then struggling to deliver. O. Henry was nearly forty before he set foot in the metropolis that would become so closely linked with his own name. He viewed the city, therefore, with the eyes of a stranger, not someone who was familiar with its streets and alleys.

O. Henry entered the ranks of New York magazine writers at a propitious time. With national literacy rates on the rise, there was an increasing demand for reading material that appealed more to the common person, rather than the upper classes. As a result a new group of "democratic" newspapers and magazines appeared, containing fiction, articles, travelogues, exposés, recipes, and pictorial essays, with something of interest for everyone. The demand for sentimental fiction was enormous. Like many other story writers, O. Henry focused on how to generate and maximize income from the plethora of periodicals in the marketplace. Books were a mere afterthought. Never in his career would book publishing occupy a central point in O. Henry's literary life. As a result, stories in his books frequently exhibit little in common. The selections are rather haphazard, the quality uneven.

Some of the unevenness of his work has to do with O. Henry's writing itself. He did not develop or grow very much as a writer. He wrote superb stories early in his career and later in his career, right alongside forgettable ones. He wrote sixty-five stories in 1904 and fifty in 1905, states one source. Another source says that he wrote over a hundred stories in thirty months for the *New York World*. Whatever the precise count, he worked at a feverish pace. His *Complete Works* lists over 270 stories. Taken together, O. Henry's stories provide a vivid portrait of a city and an era. But his furious pace took its toll. In 1910 O. Henry collapsed and died, barely 48. His passing was mourned by critics and public alike who sensed America had lost a national treasure.

Critical Reception, Honors, and Popularity

In spite of his popularity, O. Henry continued to view himself as a hard-working hack, and his reward was the paychecks he squandered with good-natured abandon on the denizens who provided him with many of his ideas. Indeed, he was somewhat embarrassed when praised. But critical and public acclaim almost immediately followed his first publications. In recognition of his short story "While the Auto Waits," which appeared in the May 1903 issue of *Ainslee's*, the *New York Times* said, "We defy anybody to produce a short story writer capable of producing anything finer." The London *Spectator* said O. Henry had "a remarkable gift of literary expression."

Frequently, O. Henry wrote about New York, lightly and at times darkly, but always affectionately. The people of New York—the Four Million—responded with an outpouring of admiration. In O. Henry, they had found a champion. A few years after walking out of prison, O. Henry was famous, sought after eagerly by magazines willing to pay him huge sums for anything from his pen. In 1918 the O. Henry Memorial Award was established to honor O. Henry and the best American story of the year.

The years have not been especially kind to O. Henry's reputation as a writer. The short fiction of Hemingway, Fitzgerald, Sherwood Anderson, Faulkner, and Steinbeck has moved the short story a long way from the contrived sentimentality of O. Henry. Yet his short stories continue to be anthologized and reissued in various editions and collections. Some of his stories have become American folk tales; "The Gift of the Magi," "The Last Leaf," and "A Retrieved Reformation" are three examples, to which could perhaps be added "Two Thanksgiving Day Gentlemen," "The Ransom of Red Chief," and "The Trimmed Lamp." Whatever the critics might say, he is still read eighty years after his death, a claim that can be made by few other short story writers of that era.

Analysis of Selected Titles

THE FOUR MILLION

The Four Million, 1906, short stories.

Social Concerns/Themes

As was his wont, at times O. Henry would slip into a story something specific from his life. In the story that leads off *The Four Million*, "Tobin's Palm," O. Henry makes a literary declaration. One of the characters in the story is a writer who comments: "I wander abroad by night seeking idiosyncrasies in the masses and truth in the heavens above. The rapid transit is poetry and art: the moon but a tedious, dry body, moving by rote." This is just as O. Henry did. " 'Ye will put me in a book,' says Tobin, disgusted; 'will ye put me in a book?' 'I will not,' says the man, 'for the covers will not hold ye. Not yet'." O. Henry tried mightily to put the characters of New York into a book, and if he failed in his own eyes, he nonetheless succeeded better than any other short story writer of the day.

The Four Million, O. Henry's second collection of short stories, was the first to bear all the recognizable O. Henry traits. As he said in another of his books, he was the voice of the city, giving it expression and reality. New York was the gateway to America then, and immigrants were pouring in from all parts of the world. O. Henry celebrated that ethnic diversity.

O. Henry was the conscience of the city, too. He not only spoke eloquently of the plight of the poor in such stories as "The Skylight Room" and "An Unfinished Story," but he brought romance and adventure, excitement and glamour to those who had too little of it in their lives.

What made O. Henry a thoroughly American artist was his conviction of the essential benevolence of life. Put another way, he was the spokesman for the American Dream. He wrote for an audience that was not far removed from the immigrant experience; if they were not immigrants themselves, probably their parents were. America was a country of immigrants. Most came to America looking for a better life. True, they often found poverty, but there was also hope, and O. Henry gave expression to that ideal in his fiction. Despite the vastness of the city, lost lovers can be reunited as they are in "Tobin's Palm" and "Springtime à la Carte," a young woman can be rescued from suicide in "The Skylight Room," and true love can win out in "An Adjustment of Nature" and "Mammon and the Archer." In "The Green Door" adventure and romance beckon. Despite poverty, the lovers have each other in "The Gift of the Magi" and in "A Service of Love," and that is more than enough, O. Henry maintains. In "Lost on Dress Parade" and "The Coming-Out of Maggie" the characters filch a bit of glamour for their otherwise drab lives.

Still, tragedy is rarely far away. "Life is made up of sobs, sniffles, and smiles, with sniffles predominating," O. Henry wrote. That may sound coy, but suicide is the conclusion of "The Furnished Room," made more tragic by callous indifference, and in "An Unfinished Story" it is clear that degradation is not far ahead, the result of loneliness, despair, and poverty.

Characters

O. Henry was not just the poet of the poor. The twenty-five stories in this collection depict every stratum of society. "The Skylight Room" is about a poor working girl, but "Mammon and the Archer" is a story of self-made wealth. There are stories about the young and the old, the upper class and the lower, the bohemian artist, the young working man, the down-and-out bum and, of course, O. Henry's favorite character type, the shop girl.

There is an inherent nobility in an O. Henry character, whatever his or her social status. The couples of any of the various love stories will do for examples. Even Soapy, in "The Cop and the Anthem," a bum who "viewed with swift horror the pit into which he had tumbled, the degraded days, unworthy desires, dead hopes, wrecked faculties and base motives that made up his existence," attempts to regain his lost decency. Rarely is there ever a villain in an O. Henry story, unless it is poverty, dreariness, or loneliness. Defeat is often the result of weakness, not active evil. Perhaps, O. Henry suggests, evil that results from indifference is the greatest iniquity of all.

Techniques/Literary Precedents

O. Henry's writing is irrevocably linked with the surprise ending. Indeed, the term "O. Henry ending" has entered the literary vocabulary. However, the O. Henry ending was *not* merely something tacked onto the body of the story to astound the reader, it was a natural illumination of character. The surprise ending was an expression of his philosophy of life. Take, for instance, the well-known "The Gift of the Magi," the second story of *The Four Million*. The surprise ending not only epitomizes the character of these two self-sacrificing lovers, but it also epitomizes the character of love itself, the very theme of O. Henry's story. Theme and character are embodied in the surprise that really is not a surprise lurking at the end.

In the same way the climax of "The Love-Philtre of Ikey Schoenstein" drives home the point of the story. Ikey, using his wiles, tries to trick his rival and gain the heart of his beloved. But his rival, more honest than Ikey, adheres to the philosophy "if you get the girl get her on the square." At the surprising conclusion, Ikey discovers that he has failed precisely because he is not on the square. Ikey may not be any wiser, but the readers are.

O. Henry's works have been most closely identified with the short fiction of Guy de Maupassant and Anton Chekhov. All three were prolific in the shorter forms, writing stories frequently of the lower class, and often using the slice of life story for revelation. But there is an amorality about Maupassant and a fatalism about Chekhov that O. Henry would have been unable to accept. Many American writers have attempted to emulate the slangy story-telling of O. Henry, few as successfully as Ring Lardner.

Relation to Previous Works

For his first several months in New York, O. Henry wrote stories about many locales other than New York; the West, Central America, the South. So when his first book was issued, it focused on his Central American stories. By the time *The Four Million* was published, O. Henry was hitting his stride. He had found his peculiar place and voice in American literature.

THE TRIMMED LAMP

The Trimmed Lamp, 1907, short stories.

Social Concerns/Themes

O. Henry brought Romanticism squarely into the twentieth century. He showed that industrialism and Romanticism were not incompatible. The gritty aspects of modern city life—"the crash of the elevated trains, clanging cars," smoky factories, bums on park benches, and department stores—all formed the fabric of his fiction. He thrust this seemingly fragile and delicate art into the hustle and bustle of the streets, into the squalor of the tenements, the dingy apartments of shop girls, and the furnished rooms of transients. Romanticism not only survived, it flourished under his pen. O. Henry protested against the "club of realism." Alongside the negative aspects of the city, there was also much that was positive. There was glamour, excitement, and the endless variety of the urban experience.

Central to O. Henry's conception of life is the question, "What's around the corner?" For O. Henry, the future represented a challenge; it was magical, brimming with excitement, with the possibility of surprise. A policeman could be a millionaire tomorrow; a shop-girl could fall in love and marry a wealthy young gentleman. This was the Land of Opportunity, and Americans had great faith in the vision of social mobility; wealth and fame could be attained by anybody with the talent, ability, and perseverance.

Good or bad, happiness or sorrow, the moral fulcrum of an O. Henry story is often equally balanced. In "The Trimmed Lamp" the goodness of Nancy who refuses to be "a traitor to herself" is balanced against Lou who becomes a wealthy man's mistress. In "The Last Leaf," Johnsy's gallant struggle against death is weighted against Old Behrman, who dies helping her by painting the last leaf on the window.

A light-hearted writer, O. Henry was unafraid to address many of the pressing issues of the day: alcoholism, poverty, child neglect, poor housing, working single women. Yet as he chronicled these stories, he knew the problems might be insoluble. The conclusion of "The Trimmed Lamp" has a policeman walking his beat, ignoring a weeping woman: "He was wise enough to know that these matters are beyond help so far as the power he represents is concerned, though he rap the pavement with his nightstick till the sound goes up to the furthermost stars."

Characters

Once again O. Henry presents a kaleidoscope of characters; the millionaire, the bum, the shop-girl, the bohemian, the artist, the gang member, the tourist, all are here in abundance, all seeking elusive happiness. O. Henry's forte was not the closely and deeply drawn character. Within the confines of the short story, in a couple of thousand words, he painted his characters with swift and broad strokes. What O. Henry lacked in subtlety, he made up for in penetrating insight, honest emotion, and keen, good humor.

Techniques/Literary Precedents

One of the trademarks of O. Henry is the way in which pithy gems of observation and insight are scattered throughout a story—"the raisins in the dough of existence," he called it. For instance, in the title story from *The Trimmed Lamp*, O. Henry makes the following observation: "If you live in an atmosphere of luxury, luxury is yours whether your money pays for it, or another's." Or he describes the dull, but dependable Dan "in his neat but obviously ready-made suit, his ready-made tie and unfailing, genial, ready-made wit." Or a line or two later O. Henry says, "He was of that good kind that you are likely to forget while they are present, but remember distinctly after they are gone."

O. Henry loved to play with the English language. His stories are filled with malapropisms, outrageous puns, silly jokes, and light-hearted slang. Sometimes the stories are so slangy that the reader—not familiar with turn-of-century phrases—can miss the point.

Relation to Previous Works

Intentional or not, *The Trimmed Lamp* seems to sound a darker note than *The Four Million*. Alongside the light-hearted stories, there are many tales of despair. Often in these stories a sudden gush of pain will erupt. At times a story ends on a note of bleak tragedy and hopelessness. The word "lost" echoes time and again. "Brickdust Row" ends with: "But man, it's too late, I tell you. It's too late. It's too late. It's too late." The story of "Elsie in New York" tells of young girls who are "lost thus around us every day." "The Guilty Party" chronicles the neglect of a young child, who eventually kills her lover and commits suicide. The hero of "The Assessor of Success" concludes with a cry of despair, "God! I wish I could die."

Adaptations

The best-known adaptation of the stories of O. Henry is a 1952 film titled *O. Henry's Full House*, released by Twentieth Century Fox. Cast and production were first-rate. John Steinbeck introduced the five stories: "The Cop and the Anthem," screenplay by Lamar Trotti, directed by Henry Koster, starring Charles Laughton, David Wayne, and Marilyn Monroe; "The Clarion Call," screenplay by Richard Breen, directed by Henry Hathaway; starring Dale Robertson and Richard Widmark; "The Last Leaf," screenplay by Ivan Coff and Ben Roberts, directed by Jean Negulesco, starring Anne Baxter, Jean Peters, and Gregory Ratoff; "The Ransom of Red Chief," screenplay by Nunnally Johnson, directed by Howard Hawks, starring Fred Allen and Oscar Levant; and "The Gift of the Magi," screenplay by Walter Bullock, directed by Henry King, starring Jeanne Crain and Farley Granger.

Hollywood has also extensively used the O. Henry character The Cisco Kid in twenty-three films—sound and silents—with varying degrees of authenticity. Besides films, there was also a 1950s television series, *The Cisco Kid,* starring Duncan Renaldo.

A number of O. Henry stories have been filmed over the years. Most are just titles, now, but a few are still remembered: *The Green Door,* 1917; *An American Live Wire,* 1918; *Everybody's Girl,* 1918; *You're Fired,* 1919; *Alias Jimmy Valentine,* 1920; *The Texan,* 1930; *Doctor Rhythm,* 1938; *Llano Kid,* 1940; *Black Eagle,* 1948; and *The Big Chief,* April 1960.

In 1957 there was a television series based upon the short stories of O. Henry. It was titled *The O. Henry Playhouse.* The thirty-minute anthology, hosted by Thomas Mitchell, lasted for thirty-nine episodes. Among the stories adapted for the small screen were "Georgia's Ruling," "Between Rounds," and "Hearts and Hands."

Other Titles

Cabbages and Kings (1904); *Heart of the West* (1907); *The Voice of the City* (1908); *The Gentle Grafter* (1908); *Roads of Destiny* (1909); *Options* (1909); *Strictly Business* (1910); *Whirligigs* (1910); *Sixes and Sevens* (1911); *Rolling Stones* (1912); *Waifs and Strays* (1917); *O. Henryana* (1920); *Letters to Lithopolis* (1922); *Postscripts* (1923); *O. Henry Papers* (1924); *O. Henry Encore* (1939); *The Complete Works of O. Henry* (1953); *Collected Stories of O. Henry* (1979).

Additional Sources

Abrams, Fred. "The Pseudonym 'O. Henry': A New Perspective." *Studies in Short Fiction* 15 (Summer 1978): 327-329. Abrams examines the evidence for the origins of Porter's pen name and offers his own suggestion concerning the obscure pseudonym.

Arnett, Ethel Stephens. *O. Henry from Polecat Creek*. Greensboro, NC: Piedmont Press, 1962. This biography has a North Carolina slant to it and focuses on O. Henry's birthplace and childhood.

Clarkson, Paul S. "A Decomposition of *Cabbages and Kings*." *American Literature* 7 (May 1935): 195-202. A study of how the stories for O. Henry's first book were brought together from various sources.

———. *A Bibliography of William Sydney Porter (O. Henry)*. Caldwell, ID: Caxton, 1938. The most exhaustive listing of works by and about O. Henry covering works to 1938.

Current-Garcia, Eugene. *O. Henry (William Sydney Porter)*. New York: Twayne, 1965. A fair and scholarly examination of the American writer. An excellent volume for beginning a study of O. Henry because it provides biographical information, a literary assessment, and a selected bibliography.

Davis, Robert H., and Arthur B. Maurice. *The Caliph of Bagdad*. New York: D. Appleton, 1931. A charming, intimate look at O. Henry in New York City by a good friend.

Firkins, O. W. "O. Henry." In *Modern Essays*, edited by Christopher Morley. New York: Harcourt, Brace, 1921.

Gallegly, Joseph. *From Alamo Plaza to Jack Harris's Saloon: O. Henry and the Southwest He Knew*. The Hague: Mouton, 1970. Gallegly focuses on O. Henry's time in and stories about the Southwest, especially Texas.

Jennings, Al. *Through the Shadows with O. Henry*. New York: H. K. Fly, 1921. Jennings was a long-time pal of O. Henry's. The book is an affectionate, chatty, informal look at the writer from a non-literary point of view.

Kramer, Dale. *The Heart of O. Henry*. New York: Rinehart & Company, 1954. A fictionalized, but accurate, account of O. Henry's life. Kramer does a fine job of providing a vivid portrait of O. Henry's dynamic first wife, Athol.

Langford, Gerald. *Alias O. Henry*. New York: MacMillian, 1957. Perhaps the most thoroughly documented biography of O. Henry. It presents a fair, objective view of the writer.

Long, E. Hudson. *O. Henry: American Regionalist*. Austin, TX: Steck Vaughn, 1969. One of the foremost authorities on O. Henry, Long looks at the writer from the standpoint of the tradition of the regional writers at the turn of the century.

———. *O. Henry, The Man and His Work*. Philadelphia: University of Pennsylvania Press, 1949. A scholarly view of the relationship between the biography and the short stories.

McLean, Malcolm D. "O. Henry in Honduras." *American Literary Realism* 1 (Summer 1968): 39-46. O. Henry's short time in Central America, when he was fleeing criminal charges, is examined here.

O'Connor, Richard. *O. Henry The Legendary Life of William S. Porter*. Garden City, NY: Doubleday, 1970. An even-handed, swiftly moving eminently readable biography of the writer.

Peck, H. T. "The American Story Teller." *Bookman* 31 (April 1910): 131-137. One of the first articles on O. Henry to examine both his strengths and weaknesses as a writer.

Smith, C. Alphonso. *The O. Henry Biography*. Garden City, NY: Doubleday, Page, 1916. Smith was an "official" biographer. As was common in those days by biographers, he focused a great deal of attention on O. Henry's family background.

Stuart, David. *O. Henry: A Biography of William Sydney Porter*. Briarcliff Manor, NY: Stein & Day, 1986. The latest biography of O. Henry.

Van Doren, Carl. "O. Henry." *Texas Review* (later *Southwest Review*) 2 (January 1917): 248-259. Van Doren provides a balanced, early assessment of the writer's work.

Williams, William Wash. *The Quiet Lodger of Irving Place*. New York: E. P. Dutton, 1936. An informal, highly readable account of O. Henry in New York. The book is based on Williams' personal recollection of the writer.

Jesse F. Knight

WALKER PERCY
1916-1990

Publishing History

Walker Percy was trained as a doctor, not a writer. In 1942, while serving a residency at Bellevue Hospital in New York City, he was infected with tuberculosis. During a long recuperation, he read extensively, particularly the Christian existentialists Søren Kierkegaard and Gabriel Marcel, the existentialist novelists Jean Paul Sartre and Albert Camus, and the Russian novelists Fyodor Dostoevski and Leo Tolstoy. The experience lead to his conversion to Catholicism in 1947 and a conviction that he wanted to write.

He began his publishing career with an essay "Symbol as Need," which appeared in the journal *Thought* in 1954. The essay is a response to Suzanne Langer's *Feeling and Form*, and it argues for a theory of language as "a means of knowing in the Thomist and existential sense of identification of the knower with the object known." The essay announced many of the linguistic, existential, and religious themes that would concern Percy for the rest of his life. However, before he could explore those philosophical concerns in novels that would appeal to a popular audience, Percy had to struggle to find a colloquial—and often humorous—voice. The break-through came in 1961 with his first published novel, *The Moviegoer*, written after two failed attempts at novels. It received the National Book Award in 1962, and Percy continued to publish novels until his death in 1990: *The Last Gentleman* (1966), *Love in the Ruins* (1971), *Lancelot* (1977), *The Second Coming* (1980), and *The Thanatos Syndrome* (1987).

The six novels vary in emphasis. Three of the novels—*The Moviegoer*, *The Last Gentleman*, and *The Second Coming*—are primarily concerned with an individual's alienation. The other three—*Love in the Ruins*, *Lancelot*, and *Thanatos Syndrome*—are more concerned with society and attempts to reform society (which in Percy's view are doomed to failure, since the roots of social problems are not found in society but in mankind's existential situation). In novels such as *The Moviegoer*, Percy is not so much concerned with social problems as he is with the attempts of the alienated individual to come to terms with that society so that he, as Percy puts it, "can live through an ordinary fall afternoon."

He also continued to publish essays, articles, and reviews on language, literature, southern culture, science, psychiatry, existentialism, and religion in Catholic publications, including *Commonweal* and *America*; in scholarly journals, including *Georgia Review* and *Michigan Quarterly*; and in popular magazines, including *Harper's* and *Esquire*. Most of his important essays can be found in two collections: *The Message in the Bottle: How Queer Man Is, How Queer Language Is, and What One Has to Do with the Other* (1975) and *Lost in the Cosmos: The Last Self-Help Book* (1983).

Critical Reception, Honors, and Popularity

At the time of his death, Percy was considered one of the leading philosophical novelists in the country, one of the best southern novelists of the post-World War II period, and the most notable American Catholic writer since Flannery O'Connor. One of his major accomplishments was to attract a popular audience while pursuing serious philosophic and religious concerns. His first novel won a National Book Award; his second, *The Last Gentleman*, was nominated for another; and *The Second Coming* was nominated for the PEN/Faulkner prize. Percy has not been without his detractors, however. In particular, his conservative views on sex and women's issues have been attacked by more liberal critics. Other critics have tended to ignore or misunderstand some of the more orthodox aspects of his Catholic faith; others have complained that his writing sometimes becomes too didactic. Even then, however, critics have taken Percy seriously. Walter Clemons, writing a hostile review of *The Second Coming* in *Newsweek* wrote: "He is a beguiling, uniquely gifted novelist who deserves to be read in order and in full. His worst novel, this one, is still more interesting than most other writers' best shot."

Analysis of Selected Titles

THE MOVIEGOER

The Moviegoer, 1961, novel.

Social Concerns

Walker Percy has one concern and one theme in all of his novels: alienation—people's alienation from themselves, from others, from society, and, foremost, from God. Percy shares this general concern with the European existentialists, and his concern with mankind's alienation from God is shared by Christian existentialists such as Kierkegaard and Marcel. But Percy has made clear in interviews and essays that he believes mankind's alienation (or "exile," as the Catholic prayer *Salve Regina* expresses it) is the ancient, central Christian doctrine of the Fall. To put it colloquially, as Percy does in his novels, people are in pretty bad shape these days (and always have been), and they need to "get right" with themselves, one another, society, and God.

Since Percy believes all forms of alienation stem from a central Fall from grace, it is not always possible to separate an individual's attempt to overcome his alienation from himself with his attempts to overcome his alienation from others, from society, and from God. All of Percy's novels present a central character (always an affluent, white southern male) attempting to overcome these alienations. The novels also include attacks on society, usually for its racism, a sign of society's alienation from itself (Percy has argued that no southern writer can fail to address the racial problem), and for what he views as its sexual abuse (promiscuity and homosexuality), a sign of people's alienation from one another, as well as from their true selves. Percy also attacks "Christendom," as opposed to Christianity (following Kierkegaard's distinction), for allowing racism and sexual abuse to continue.

Themes

The Moviegoer is Percy's most conscious and consistent attempt to express Kierkegaard's existentialism in concrete form: to depict an alienated individual struggling to find his way out. The epigram of the novel is from Kierkegaard's *The Sickness Unto Death*: ". . . the specific character of despair is precisely this: it is unaware of being despair." Binx Bolling, however, knows that he is in despair; he knows that his life is no longer working for him. He is on a search that "anyone would undertake if he were not sunk in the everydayness of his own life." His search incorporates Kierkegaard's philosophical strategies to breakthrough everydayness—"rotation" and "repetition"—but, as a novelist, Percy gives the philosophical strategies concrete form. Put colloquially, Binx likes to have sex with his secretaries and go to the movies.

True to his Christian existentialism, Percy carries his reader to the end of his search. In an interview Percy commented that, at the end of the novel, "Binx jumps from [Kierkegaard's] aesthetic [stage] clear across the ethical [stage] to the religious [stage]." However, the Christian—and explicitly Catholic—theme is much more subtly handled than the Kierkegaardian theme. Some critics are not convinced, despite Percy's statement that Binx "returns to his mother's religion" at the end of the novel. *The Moviegoer* is perhaps the most accessible of Percy's novels for readers who share Percy's existentialism, but not his Catholicism.

Characters

Binx Bolling is the first in a line of Percy's typical central characters: affluent, white southern males, somewhat confused, but often with good instincts for finding their way through society. Binx has "a good nose for *merde*" and Will Barrett of *The Last Gentleman* has his "radar." Above all, Percy's heroes are alienated, and they know it. Binx believes everyone around him is "dead," and he makes no special case for himself, except that he, unlike most of his friends, admits that his life is no longer working for him. Despite the major hold his Aunt Emily has over his life, he knows that her southern stoicism no longer provides a sense of values for his life. (Critics have pointed out that Aunt Emily is modeled after Percy's uncle, Will Percy, who adopted and raised him and his two younger brothers after the suicide of their father and death of their mother in an automobile accident.) On the other hand, Binx does not accept his mother's Catholicism.

Binx becomes entwined with his cousin Kate, who is undergoing therapy. She is as alienated as Binx, and a good deal less able to find her way through an ordinary afternoon. In general, critics have complained that Percy does not create strong women characters—Aunt Emily, who is much older, and, with some reservations, Allison in *The Second Coming* are exceptions. According to these critics, Percy's women generally fall into the "lady or whore" syndrome, and the ladies, like Kate, are weak, confused characters who need to be told what to do.

Lonnie, Binx's younger, and dying, brother plays a slight role in the novel, although his death is very significant to the ending. He is first in a line of suffering younger people depicted in Percy's novels, the most memorable being Jamie in *The Last Gentleman*.

Techniques

The body of the novel is a monologue in which Binx narrates the events of the week of Ash Wednesday in New Orleans. Reviewers generally praised the novel's evocation of New Orleans, and in particular, Percy's descriptions of the white heron and the swimming snake that Binx sees while fishing with his mother. Although critics generally have been favorably impressed with Percy's ability to capture the physical sensations of a particular time and place, some have maintained that much of Binx's narration is intentionally flat, detached, and self-conscious. It is only in the epilogue, they point out, that Binx can speak directly and naturally. There he addresses Kate, to whom he is now married, and comforts his brothers and sisters before Lonnie's impending death.

By the epilogue, according to Percy, Binx has made his Kierkegaardian "leap of faith" and returned to the religion of his mother's family. The epilogue is focused around Lonnie's death, but, as are all of Percy's novel, it is also focused around one of the sacraments of the Catholic church. Lonnie's sister accepts that her brother is dying, but she wants to make sure he has been anointed (received extreme unction). Binx assures her that he has, and then professes an orthodox belief in the resurrection of the body on the last day. This explicitly Catholic element of the conclusion is much less dramatic than the baptism of the dying Jamie at the end of *The Last Gentleman*, and is much more easily passed over by critics; but, at least for a religious reader, it creates a ritual-like emotional power.

Literary Precedents

Although Percy's sensibility and much of his content are shaped by his southern heritage, the literary precedents for this novel are more clearly European. He commented that after the failure of two attempts to write novels, "It crossed my mind, what if I did something that American writers never do, which seems to be the custom in France: Namely, that when someone writes about ideas, they can translate the same ideas to fiction and plays . . . . So it just occurred to me, why not take these ideas I'd been trying to write about, in psychiatry and philosophy, and translate them into a fictional setting in New Orleans, where I was living." The French novelists and playwrights which Percy probably had most in mind are Camus and Sartre, although his philosophical ideas, expressed in the essay "The Man on the Train" (collected in *The Message in the Bottle*), are more in tune with Kierkegaard and Marcel. The novel's conclusion is clearly modeled on the conclusion of Dostoevski's *The Brothers Karamazov* (1879).

Relation to Previous Works

All six of Percy's novels (and most of his essays) are closely linked by similar concerns and themes. In each, a central character finds himself confused, alienated from himself and society, and unsure what to do with his life. In each novel, this character begins a search, usually misguided at first: Binx's seductions and moviegoing; Will Barrett's search for answers from Sutter in *The Last Gentleman*, and his attempt to force God to prove his existence in *The Second Coming*; Lancelot's disastrous search for the un-Holy Grail in *Lancelot*; and, Tom More's scientific lapsometer in *Love in the Ruins* and *The Thanatos Syndrome*. All these characters, however, are offered at least the opportunity for a more authentic search and the possibility of grace, symbolized by a religious sacrament at the end of each novel:

the anointing of the dying in *The Moviegoer*; baptism at the end of *The Last Gentleman*; eucharist at the end of *Love in the Ruins*; possible confession and absolution at the end of *Lancelot*; impending marriage at the end of *The Second Coming*; and eucharist, again, at the end of *The Thanatos Syndrome*. Along the way, each character pursues a romantic interest, and, in almost every case, the character is forced to choose between an "inauthentic" romantic interest and an "authentic" one. Binx must give up his secretaries for his cousin Kate, Tom More must choose between three women in *Love in the Ruins*, and Lancelot must move from the adulterous Margot to the possibility of a new life with Anna. Finally, in keeping with Percy's particular Christian linguistic concerns as expressed in the essay *The Message in the Bottle*, at the conclusion of almost every novel, the central character is poised to hear the "good news," the gospel, from someone who has the authority to proclaim it. In *Love in the Ruins*, Tom More goes to confession, is admonished by the priest, and returns to mass, as he does in *The Thanatos Syndrome*; in *Lancelot*, Lance is prepared to listen to his old friend Percival, who has become a priest; and at the end of *The Second Coming*, Will Barrett is prepared to receive religious instruction from Father Weatherbee. One exception to this pattern is Will Barrett at the end of *The Last Gentleman*. He is so intent on being told what to do by Sutter that he is not prepared to listen to the priest who baptizes the dying Lonnie. The other exception is Binx Bolling, at the conclusion of *The Moviegoer*. Of all of Percy's main characters, he is the only one to give the instruction himself—to his brothers and sisters.

THE SECOND COMING

The Second Coming, 1980, novel.

Social Concerns

In *The Second Coming*, as in many of his novels, Percy is more concerned with the attempts of two individuals to overcome their personal alienation from themselves, from others, and from God, than with their attempts to overcome their alienation from society. But these attempts are interrelated, and, in *The Second Coming*, Percy makes his clearest statement of the traditional belief that marriage is the basic social unit. At the end of the novel, Will and Allison have, to some extent, overcome their alienation, are preparing to marry, and, significantly, are planning to help others build a community.

The novel is also a satiric attack on Christendom. Percy comments that his central character "lives in the most Christian nation in the world, in the most

Christian part of that nation, the south, in the most Christian state in the south, North Carolina, in the most Christian town in North Carolina.'' Yet the people live in a "death-in-life" trance of greed, lust, and hate. Will's pentecostal daughter and Jack Curl, the Episcopal priest who wears jump suits and is uncomfortable with "religious talk," are particular targets of Percy's satire.

Themes

Love—both human and divine—is a constant theme in Percy's novels, but in *The Second Coming*, Percy provides his most thorough analysis of love and marriage as a way through the alienation of the fallen world. Will Barrett, the central character, consciously (and comically) searches for God, or at least a sign of God, in this novel, but, instead of finding Him, he literally "falls" into love with a woman named Allison. Will and Allison are both alienated, which is to say "fallen" human beings, but by coming together they find a way back to their true selves and each other: "She was moving against him, enclosing him, wrapping her arms and legs around him, as if her body had at last found the center of itself outside itself." Their love is described in allegorical language that recalls both the Christian doctrine of the Fall and the neo-Platonism of Dante: he is a "faller" and she is a "hoister," but Percy is also simple, direct, colloquial: "His need of her was as simple and urgent as drawing the next breath."

Their love is sexual, but it is also sacramental. At the conclusion of the novel, Will asks for a sacramental (in this case, interestingly enough, Episcopal) marriage. In the traditions of the Catholic church, the sacrament of marriage is not complete until it is consummated, and, in the allegorical tradition of the Church, the physical act of intercourse is taken as a symbol of the hypostatic union of the human and the divine. It is in that context that Percy can have Will say, at the conclusion of the novel, as he looks at the priest: "Is she a gift and therefore a sign of a giver? Could it be that the Lord is here, masquerading behind this simple holy face? Am I crazy to want both, her and Him? No, not want must have. And will have." This is the most profoundly optimistic conclusion that Percy ever wrote: Will Barrett has found both love and the sign he had searched for so desperately.

Characters

Will Barrett, the central character of *The Last Gentleman*, is also the central character of *The Second Coming* (Percy wryly observed "the title refers to that, among other things"). Will, although older than in the earlier novel, is still a typical Percy hero: able to manage, but confused about what to do about life. The surprise of the novel is Allison. She is not the typical weak woman that Percy usually creates; some critics have speculated that Percy created her as a conscious response to critical attacks on his female characters. Allison does have problems: she has escaped a mental ward where she has undergone shock therapy, which has, among other things, impaired her ability to speak. But for Percy her awareness of her alienation is a virtue, as it is for his male characters. As Allison phrases it in her delightful, zany way: "our lapses are not due to synapses" (with Percy's theological pun on "lapse" for "fallen"). Will responds: "No, they are as they should be."

Allison is not a totally independent person: she needs Will "to give her the words." Yet their need is mutual (he falls, she hoists him up). In having her need him to provide words for her, Percy is not only following his own interest in semiotics (his own younger daughter was born deaf), he is following the "intersubjectivity" concepts of the Christian existentialist Gabriel Marcel: consciousness must be shared, through language and symbol, before it can truly come into being. In sharing language, Will and Allison create a shared consciousness.

Techniques

The novel begins with a chapter on Will, then one on Allison. Chapters alternate, occasionally linked very directly: one chapter ends, "He remembered everything" and the next begins, "She remembered nothing." The novel seems to conspire to bring these two lovers together, using coincidences that strain credibility (for example, it turns out that Allison is the daughter of Kitty Vaught, Will's girlfriend in *The Last Gentleman*). Percy may have intended to make a point with this string of coincidences; in a similar way, *The Last Gentleman* seems to conspire to baptize Jamie, whether he likes it or not. However, critics have complained that this technique and the unabashedly optimistic ending makes the novel overly sentimental.

Literary Precedents

The Second Coming, in providing a concrete, physical situation for philosophical and theological concerns, follows Percy's general approach, borrowed from the French existentialists. Again, much of the philosophical framework is provided by Kierkegaard, although the theme of love as a redemptive power is certainly related to neo-Platonic thought, as seen in Dante's *Divine Comedy,* and the action of the novel is a re-working of the Christian myth of the Fall. A sub-plot—Will's attempt to come to terms with the suicide of his father, and his realization that his father had intended to kill him—is handled in a Faulknerian way, even though Percy is one of the few modern southern writers who was not strongly influenced by Faulkner.

Related Titles

The most obviously related novel is *The Last Gentleman*, in which a younger, more confused Will is the central character. This Will Barrett has made a fortune as a lawyer in New York, has married into an even larger fortune, and has retired early. Percy's point is that Will's metaphysical problems are certainly not related to an inability to deal successfully with the world.

Also, even though *The Second Coming* is a more thorough consideration of the redemptive power of love and marriage, the optimism of this conclusion recalls a similar joyous conclusion to *Love in the Ruins*: "To bed we go for a long winter's nap, twined about each other as the ivy twineth, not under a bush or in a car or on the floor or any such humbug as marked the past peculiar years of Christendom, but at home in bed where all good folk belong."

Other Titles

The Last Gentleman, 1966 (novel); *Love in the Ruins*, 1971 (novel); *The Message in the Bottle: How Queer Man Is, How Queer Language Is, and What One Has to Do with the Other*, 1975 (essays); *Lancelot*, 1977 (novel); *Lost in the Cosmos: The Last Self-Help Book*, 1983 (essays); and *The Thanatos Syndrome*, 1987 (novel).

Additional Sources

Broughton, Panthea Reid, ed. *The Art of Walker Percy: Stratagems for Being*. Baton Rouge: Louisiana State University Press, 1979. Critical essays on Percy's novels and essays.

Hardy, John Edward. *The Fiction of Walker Percy*. Chicago: University of Chicago Press, 1987. One of the most comprehensive and current book-length studies of Percy's work.

Hobson, Whitney. *Walker Percy: A Comprehensive Descriptive Bibliography*. New Orleans: Faust, 1988. The most current comprehensive bibliography on Percy

Lawson, Lewis A., and Victor A. Kramer, eds. *Conversations with Walker Percy*. Jackson: University Press of Mississippi, 1985. Collects twenty-seven interviews with Percy.

Luschei, Martin. *The Sovereign Wayfarer: Walker Percy's Diagnosis of the Malaise*. Baton Rouge: Louisiana State University Press, 1972. Argues that the major intellectual influence on Percy is European existentialism: Percy's "great achievement may prove to have been translating Kierkegaard into concrete American terms."

Percy, William Alexander. *Lanterns on the Levee: Recollection of a Planter's Son*. 1941. Reprint. New York: Alfred A. Knopf, 1966. Autobiographical essays by "Uncle Will," Walker Percy's uncle and adoptive father, whose "southern stoicism" was a major influence.

Tharpe, Jac. *Walker Percy*. Boston: Twayne, 1983. Concise, but fairly comprehensive overview of Percy's life, thought, theory of art, and artistic techniques.

James Reynolds Kinzey
Virginia Commonwealth University

S. J. PERELMAN
1904-1979

Publishing History

S. J. Perelman was one of the most popular, successful, and influential humorists in American literary history. During a remarkable professional writing career that spanned fifty years, he wrote over six hundred prose pieces for a variety of journals, including *Holiday, Travel and Leisure, Broun's Nutmeg, Brown Jug, College Humor, Contact, Diplomat, Escapade, Funny Bone, Judge, Life, McCalls', Redbook, Stage Magazine, The Country Book, The New Masses, The Saturday Evening Post, This Week Magazine, TV Guide, Venture,* and *What's New*. The most notable of the magazines to which Perelman contributed was *The New Yorker* (in which he published 278 "casuals"). Indeed, along with James Thurber, E. B. White, and Robert Benchley, Perelman was one of the forces that created the *"New Yorker* Style" and made the magazine one of the most popular and successful in literary history. Four-hundred-forty-one of his individual essays appeared in his twenty-three volumes of collected works. He was so popular that two of these volumes were published after his death, and several have since been reprinted. In addition, he published one novel, scripted eight dramas, and worked on the scripts of eleven films.

Critical Reception, Honors, Popularity

Given the size of Perelman's oeuvre, the quality of his work, and his influence on other humorists of his generation and later, it is surprising that relatively little scholarly attention was paid to him before his death. Still, there were some fine book sections and chapters (most notably Norris W. Yates's "The Sane Psychoses of S. J. Perelman" in his *The American Humorist: Conscience of the Twentieth Century* in 1964 and Walter Blair and Hamlin Hill's "Benchley and Perelman" in their *American Humor: From Poor Richard to Doonesbury* in 1978) and outstanding individual essays written about him before 1979 (these include John Wain's "A Jest in Season: Notes on S. J. Perelman, with a Digression on W. W. Jacobs" and J. A. Ward's "The Hollywood Metaphor: The Marx Brothers, S. J. Perelman, Nathanael West").

Much of the critical attention to Perelman's work came in the form of book, film, and play reviews, some written by important critics or major literary figures. In fact, Steven H. Gale's "Sidney Joseph Perelman: Twenty Years of American

Humor," published in the January-March 1972 issue of *Bulletin of Bibliography* was the first scholarly publication specifically about Perelman.

Douglas Fowler's *S. J. Perelman* (1983) was the first full-length study devoted to Perelman. Steven H. Gale's *S. J. Perelman: A Critical Study* (1987) followed soon afterward. These two volumes remain the only critical monographs on Perelman to date. Gale's *S. J. Perelman: An Annotated Bibliography* (1985) is considered the standard bibliography. The academic community has concentrated primarily on Perelman's prose pieces (his stylistics have attracted attention from the beginning of his career and lately this topic has been a popular focus).

As a youngster, Perelman won a prize for his essay, "Grit," in a 1917 contest sponsored by *American Boy*. Much later he received an Academy Award and a New York Film Critics Award for his screenplay for the cinematic adaptation of Jules Verne's *Around the World in Eighty Days* (1956). He was awarded an honorary doctorate by Brown University in 1965. He also received, posthumously, New York City's 1979 "Mayor's Award for Arts and Culture." He received the two most prestigious honors of his long career twenty years apart when he was elected to the National Academy of Letters in 1958 and when he received the first Special Achievement Award of the National Book Awards Committee in 1978.

One mark of Perelman's success is the fact that his short magazine pieces were popular enough to warrant reprinting in book form. His first collection, *Dawn Ginsbergh's Revenge*, attracted some attention, though it did not sell well. *Strictly from Hunger* met with the same reception, but this second anthology contained an introduction by Robert Benchley, one of the most important humorists of the time. Benchley's comments were prophetic. Perelman, he wrote, "took over the *dementia praecox* field and drove us all to writing articles on economics for the *Commentator*." Three years later *Look Who's Talking* sold two thousand copies in the first two months, and in 1948 *Westward Ha!*, his collection of travel tales, sold more than sixty thousand copies. According to the editors of *The New Yorker*, Perelman was one of their most popular authors, and his popularity led to film-script and playwrighting offers as well as assignments to write travel stories.

Among his contemporaries and successors, Perelman has been accorded great respect. Besides the Benchley assessment, Thurber and E. B. White praised him, and in an introduction to *The Best of S. J. Perelman*, published in 1958, Dorothy Parker called the humorist the best in his field. Numerous writers of "serious" literature have recognized his talent, too, and the list of those who admit to having been influenced by his writing is impressive (from Woody Allen and Peter Sellers to John Updike, Kurt Vonnegut, and Nathanael West).

Perelman's anthologies can be grouped according to content: collections of pieces related to life on his Pennsylvania farm; essays on his travel adventures; and miscellaneous topics. *Acres and Pains* was the first and the best of his farm-theme collections, *Westward Ha!* the first and best of his travel collections, and *The Most of S. J. Perelman* is his most representative anthology.

Analysis of Selected Titles

ACRES AND PAINS

Acres and Pains, 1947, essays.

Social Concerns

The first of the humorist's thematic collections, *Acres and Pains* is an anthology of pieces that, according to Perelman, were "the by-product of a dozen years of country living." Each of the twenty-one stories is set on Perelman's farm, which he called the Rising Gorge (in 1961 he published the volume entitled *The Rising Gorge* which was another collection of tales about life on his farm). All but one of the segments were initially printed in the *Saturday Evening Post* (the other appeared in *The Country Book*), and each details a particular aspect of country living. Perelman's topics range from interactions with his neighbors to experiences with architects and remodeling his farmhouse, from swimming pools to maids, from milk cows to country doctors, and from hoboes to dogs. His chapters on vegetable gardening and on the effect of solitude on the country dweller are the funniest and most representative.

Only in the largest sense is Perelman interested in social concerns in this volume. While there is certainly commentary on people's relationships and on individuals coming to terms with themselves and their world, his primary focus is on the everyday experiences faced by a city dweller who moves to the country to live on a farm. As is traditional with humor, however, one purpose of Perelman's satirical writing is to point out social and individual foibles. As much as anything else, Perelman's work is typified by his constant attempt to puncture pretension.

Themes

The basic theme in *Acres and Pains* is that civilized man and rural life are not compatible. In what starts out as a journey back to nature, the author discovers that there are no Rousseauistic noble savages among the locals—who constantly take advantage of his pocketbook, gullibility, and inexperience in a rural environment. The reality of chiggers, dry wells, cracked walls, dying trees, termites, and mosquitoes soon undermines his idealized vision of country life.

Characters

Although there are minor characters such as the attorney Newmown Hay, the real-estate agent Dewey Naivete, and an abundance of hired hands all named Lafe, together with the protagonist's wife and two children scattered throughout the tales, there is really only one predominant character, the protagonist. The Perelman persona is a version of the "Little Man" character which was to a large extent developed in tandem with Robert Benchley and James Thurber in the pages of *The New Yorker* during the 1930s and 1940s. The Little Man figure is average, usually a victim of an illogical outside world that he cannot control and which is epitomized by that frightful generic monster, Woman. Perelman's Little Man is at once jaundiced and hopeful, expecting the unexpected as well as the expected, and encyclopedic while self-centered.

Techniques

The use of the Little Man persona is a technique in itself. Perelman's writing also is characterized by an ironic tone, first-person narration and monologue, a sense of values, parody, dialect humor, incongruous juxtaposition, a mixture of literal and figurative usages, and a combining of two or more fragments by superimposing one upon the other.

In addition, there are four principal stylistic components that are evident throughout virtually all of Perelman's prose: his use of clichés, his allusions, his use of puns, and his Yiddish background. In the humorist's writing some clichés are utilized as though they are literally true, some are used figuratively, and some start in one mode and finish in the other. The wide range of allusions that abound in Perelman's writing reflects an arcane knowledge in his reference to cultural figures and styles of the past, obsolete words, and oddities of architecture.

Perelman's felicity with puns, which many consider his trademark, is enhanced by his immense vocabulary and extensive storehouse of cultural tidbits. In fact, many of his puns evolve out of clichés or allusions, a feature that is exemplified by his titles—another well-recognized trademark and a source of humor in themselves (*A Child's Garden of Curses* rather than verses, for instance). Finally,

Perelman's Yiddish background, the American-Jewish culture in which he matured and functioned as a professional writer, is apparent in the device of the *schlemiel* and the stratagem of the *shpritz*, a free-form eruption of fantasy, nonsense, and satire that feeds upon itself. Perelman has said that he likes Yiddish words "for their invective content."

Literary Precedents

There were several major influences on Perelman's themes and style. A voracious reader throughout his life, Perelman publically admitted to having been influenced by popular fiction (the Toby Tyler books, *Graustark, Girl of the Limberlost, Trail of the Lonesome Pine, The Woman Thou Gavest, The Mystery of Fu Manchu, The Winning of Barbara Worth, Three Weeks, Scaramouche, Polyanna*), the Horatio Alger success story, the novels of Charles Dickens, and the writings of H. L. Mencken, George Ade, Stephen Leacock, Max Beerbohm, Ring Lardner, Robert Benchley, Donald Ogden Stewart, Frank Sullivan, Flann O'Brien, W. Somerset Maugham, T. S. Eliot, Raymond Chandler, E. M. Forster, Henry David Thoreau, George Jean Nathan, and James Joyce. The humorist's early interest in cartooning also clearly affected his writing and scholarly analyses have demonstrated the impact of Yiddish and American humor traditions and Hollywood films as well. There is even some evidence of an association between Perelman's humor and the American frontier humor tradition in his utilization of those elements of straightfaced exaggeration and journalistic humor in the tradition of Mark Twain, Artemus Ward, Henry Wheeler Shaw, Finley Peter Dunne, Mencken, and Lardner.

Relation to Previous Works

In tone, technique, and the use of the Perelman persona, *Acres and Pains* is similar to the collections that preceded it. The primary difference between this volume and those collections of miscellaneous stories that the humorist had already published is that *Acres and Pains* is thematically oriented by virtue of the author's focus on his life at the Rising Gorge farm.

WESTWARD HA!
OR AROUND THE WORLD IN EIGHTY CLICHÉS

Westward Ha! Or Around the World in Eighty Clichés, 1948, essays.

Social Concerns/Themes

Perelman expresses the same kinds of concerns in *Westward Ha!* as in *Acres and Pains*. Again his paramount interest is to portray the adventures and reactions of his protagonist rather than reflect on social issues, although Perelman would undoubtedly consider the improvement of manners a significant social issue for he saw manners as emblematic of a society's level of maturity.

The twelve selections in this collection, all originally published in *Holiday*, are intended to provide insights into the writer himself, to explore the human condition through the metaphor of travel, and to comment on the locales visited. Together with *Eastward Ha!* and *The Swiss Family Perelman,* this volume forms a travel book sub-genre in his canon, yet *Westward Ha!* is more concerned with the world that surrounds the author than with the author himself, who takes centers stage in the other two books.

Characters

The Perelman persona, as usual, is the primary character in these essays. The tales are full of incidental characters that the writer meets along the way (Cass Register, the deposed Emperor of Annam, servants, the Prince Regent's Belgian shepherd dog), but the only other person of consequence in the volume is Perelman's travelling companion, Al Hirschfeld, the *New York Times* caricaturist. Hirschfeld, according to Perelman's account, is a fellow sufferer at the hands of foreigners whose cultures do not accommodate the visitors. Still, the narrator's unrealistic self-idolizing combined with self-deprecation and the other characteristics of the Perelman Little Man persona make him more vulnerable than his friend to discomfiture in foreign lands.

Techniques

The essays in *Westward Ha!* are longer than Perelman's typical pieces and contain more descriptive material than usual, for he is describing foreign scenes to a travel-oriented audience. Stylistically, the volume is superior to the majority of Perelman's later travel pieces. It is more compact, with less filler and very little wasted verbiage, and it is more cleverly structured; almost every line is funny or composed to set up a funny line.

Literary Precedents

Besides the general literary precedents discussed in connection with *Acres and Pains, Westward Ha!* draws on the conventions of travel writing. In England and

Europe this tradition was at its height in the eighteenth and nineteenth centuries, and is exemplified by Samuel Johnson's *Journey to the Western Isles of Scotland* (1775) and James Boswell's *Journal of a Tour to the Hebrides* (1785). In American literary history some of the most famous travel books are John Woolman's *The Journal of John Woolman* (1774), St. Jean de Crevecoeur's *Letters from an American Farmer* (1782), William Bartram's *Travels*, Sarah Kemble Knight's *The Private Journal of a Journey from Boston to New York* (1825), Herman Melville's *The Encantadas* (1854), and John Steinbeck's *Travels with Charlie* (1962).

Perelman's travel books differ from these in that he uses travel primarily as a pretext for making humorous commentary rather than purely to describe those surroundings and his comments are filtered through the perceptions of his specially designed persona.

Relation to Previous Works

In tone, technique, and the use of the Perelman persona, *Westward Ha!* is similar to the collections that preceded it. The principal difference between this and earlier collections is that *Westward Ha!* is thematically directed by events that took place during the humorist's travels around the world.

THE MOST OF S. J. PERELMAN

The Most of S. J. Perelman, 1962, essays.

Social Concerns

Perelman's satiric attack on pomposity and pretension, especially as exhibited by bureaucrats and salespeople is more prevalent in the pieces selected for this anthology than earlier collections. How one person treats another is a central concern in many of these essays. Thus, while Perelman is often considered a parodist, his satires demonstrate that he clearly is concerned with the nature and directions of social intercourse.

Themes

There are 120 pieces in *The Most of S. J. Perelman*, including *Acres and Pains* and *Westward Ha!* in their entirety, and selections from *Swiss Family Perelman*. Originally published between 1930 and 1958 in *The New Yorker*, *Holiday*, *The Saturday Evening Post*, *The Country Book*, *College Humor*, *Contact*, and *Life*, these pieces represent the widest range of Perelman's writing and serve as an excellent introduction to his prose. Basically a social writer, Perelman's topics are the annoyances of the kind that will always plague humankind (travel, appliances with minds of their own, movies, pompous clerks, and so forth). He celebrates a life that is full of surprises, pleasant and unpleasant, an adventure that leads to downfalls but not defeat. Along the way he takes time to point out those human haracteristics that keep the universe from running smoothly.

Characters

The Perelman Little Man character is present in a preponderance of the stories contained in *The Most of S. J. Perelman,* though not necessarily as Perelman's persona. The collection contains too many characters to try to describe them all even as character types. For instance, Santa Claus appears in "Waiting for Santy," Fleur Fenton Cowles, directress of *Look* and other magazines, is satirized in "The Hand that Cradles the Rock," "Somewhere a Roscoe" is narrated by a private detective in the vein of Dashiell Hammett, "A Farewell to Omsk" is a Dostoevskyian dialogue between Afya Afyakievitch and Pyotr Pyotrvitch, letters supposedly written by Paul Gauguin compose "Beat Me, Post Impressionist Daddy," and the protagonist of "Frou-Frou, or, the Future of Vertigo" is a woman.

Techniques

The techniques found in *Acres and Pains* and *Westward Ha!* resurface again in *The Most of S. J. Perelman,* though Perelman became more adept and more imaginative in his handling of language as he matured. Because he uses many different narrative structures in this volume, there are several additional techniques not seen in the earlier, more unified, volumes. Perelman frequently establishes his initiating premise by quoting a newspaper story, filler, or advertisement. On occasion he writes from a female point of view, or structures a number of his pieces as scenarios (in short play format). Several of his subjects are films or books that he was exposed to as a youth and which he reconsiders as an adult.

Literary Precedents

The same basic literary precedents that informed his other volumes are present here. Especially in his earlier period it is clear, too, that he was influenced by the American college and humor magazines that were popular in the 1920s and 1930s—*Judge, College Humor, Brown Jug,* and others. Perelman's topics and his approach to his material in the earliest pieces is typical of what appeared in those publications.

Other Titles
Dawn Ginsbergh's Revenge, 1929 (essays); *Parlor, Bedlam and Bath*, 1930 (novel, co-authored with Quentin Reynolds); *The Third Little Show*, 1931 (stage play); *Monkey Business*, 1931 (screenplay); *Horse Feathers*, 1932 (screenplay, written with Bert Kalmer and Harry Ruby); *All Good Americans*, 1933 (play, written with Laura Perelman); *Sitting Pretty*, 1933 (play); *Even Stephen*, 1934 (play, written with Nathanael West); *Florida Special*, 1936 (screenplay); *Strictly from Hunger*, 1937 (essays); *Sweethearts*, 1938 (screenplay); *Ambush*, 1939 (screenplay, scripted with Laura Perelman); *Boy Trouble*, 1939 (screenplay); *Look Who's Talking*, 1940 (essays); *The Golden Fleecing*, 1940 (screenplay); *The Night Before Christmas*, 1941 (play, written with Laura Perelman; movie version released in 1948); *Larceny, Inc.*, 1942 (screenplay); *The Dream Department*, 1943 (essays); *Crazy Like a Fox*, 1943 (essays); *One Touch of Venus*, 1943 (play, written with Ogden Nash and Kurt Weill); *Greenwich Village*, 1943 (screenplay); *Sweet Bye and Bye*, 1946 (musical play, written with Ogden Nash, Al Hirschfeld, and Vernon Duke); *Keep It Crisp*, 1946 (essays); *Listen to the Mocking Bird*, 1949 (essays); *The Swiss Family Perelman*, 1950 (essays); *A Child's Garden of Curses* 1951 (essays); *The Ill-Tempered Clavichord*, 1952 (essays); *Hold That Christmas Tiger!*, 1954 (essays); *Perelman's Home Companion*, 1955 (essays); *Around the World in 80 Days*, 1956 (screenplay, co-written with James Poe and John Farrow); *The Road to Miltown*, 1957 (essays); *The Beauty Part*, 1961 (play); *The Rising Gorge*, 1961 (essays); *Chicken Inspector No. 23*, 1966 (essays); *Baby, It's Cold Inside*, 1970 (essays); *Vinegar Puss*, 1975 (essays); *Eastward Ha!*, 1977 (essays); *The Last Laugh!*, 1981 (essays, edited by Paul Theroux); *That Old Gang O' Mine*, 1984 (essays, edited by Richard Marschall); *Don't Tread on Me: The Selected Letters of S. J. Perelman*, 1987 (edited by Prudence Crowther).

Additional Sources
Many of Perelman's writings contain autobiographical details, particularly collections such as *Acres and Pains*, *Westward Ha!*, *The Rising Gorge*, *Eastward Ha!*, and *Swiss Family Perelman*. Unfortunately, he frequently took liberty with the facts, so it is sometimes difficult to determine when he was writing fiction for the sake of the story and when he was reporting factual information. "How I Learned to Wink and Leer," Perelman's homage to satirical cartoonist Tad in *The*

York New Times (April 23, 1978) is one of the pieces that can be considered reliable. Four selections that were published in *The Last Laugh!* (New York: Simon and Schuster, 1981) under the heading *The Hindsight Saga*, "The Marx Brothers," "Nathanael West," "Dorothy Parker," and "Three Little Photoplays and How They Grew," appeared as "Fragments of an Autobiography," a project that Perelman never completed but which provides accurate biographical information. Finally, several interviews are important for the biographical information that they contain, along with details about his techniques, philosophies, and so forth. These include: William Cole and George Plimpton's "The Art of Fiction: S. J. Perelman," Roy Newquist's *Conversations*, Arthur Whitman's "A Perelman Sampler," and William Zinsser's "That Perelman of Great Price Is Sixty-Five."

Blair, Walter, and Hamlin Hill. *American's Humor: From Poor Richard to Doonesbury*. New York: Oxford University Press, 1978. The section on "Benchley and Perelman" is an admirable analysis of Perelman's use of fantasy. A first-rate study of the American comic tradition.

Cole, William, and George Plimpton. "The Art of Fiction: S. J. Perelman." In *Writers at Work: The Paris Review Interviews, Second Series*, edited by George Plimpton. New York: Viking, 1963. Less factual detail included than in the Zinsser interview, but includes Perelman's views on his own work and his theories regarding the nature of humor.

Cooke, Alistair. *The American in England: Emerson to S. J. Perelman*. Cambridge and New York: Cambridge University Press, 1975. Considers Perelman in the context of the history of American literature.

Fowler, Douglas. *S. J. Perelman*. Boston: Twayne, 1983. Part of the American Authors series, this first full-length study of Perelman is an interesting introductory overview of the author's life and work, with special attention to his place in both American and Jewish comic traditions and to elements of his style. Perelman is seen as primarily a caricaturist and parodist.

Gale, Steven H. "Around the World in Eighty Ways: S. J. Perlman on Scrumoritis." *Studies in American Humor* Vol. 4, No 3 (Fall 1985): 142-160. Examines Perlman's screenplays.

―――. *S. J. Perelman: A Critical Study*. Westport, CT: Greenwood Press, 1987. A thorough examination of Perelman's prose writing, stage plays, and film scripts. Attention is paid to the relationship between the writing and the humorist's life. An in-depth explication that analyzes themes and style and concludes that Perelman is concerned with the social impact of his satire.

———. *S. J. Perelman: An Annotated Bibliography*. New York: Garland, 1985. The standard bibliography. Includes over 650 listings of Perelman's individual publications and 380 entries of critical and scholarly reactions to Perelman's cannon. Gale's *S. J. Perelman: A Critical Study* contains a bibliographical essay updating this volume.

———. *S. J. Perelman: Critical Essays*. New York: Garland, 1991. Useful because it contains reprints of his most important and best interviews, reviews of his books, films, and plays, and scholarly treatments of the humorist's writing all in one volume.

———. "S. J. Perelman: The Kennest Hatred of Chickens." *Studies in American Humor* 3, 2-3 (Summer/Fall 1984): 228-236. Discusses the topics of money in Perlman's works, particularly in *The Beauty Part*.

Herrmann, Dorothy. *S. J. Perelman: A Life*. New York: Fireside/Simon and Schuster, 1986. The only book-length biography of Perelman, Herrmann's volume is obviously the most complete and comprehensive collection of information on the writer's life. Telling a captivating story and full of interesting information, Herrmann's biography is limited by a lack of fully developed connections between the humorist's life and his writings. In both content and style Herrmann is clearly writing for a popular audience without regard for scholarly studies of her subject's career.

Newquist, Roy. *Conversations*. New York: Rand, McNally, 1967. Includes an interview in which Perelman stresses his sense of tradition and notes his literary influences.

Wain, John. "A Jest in Season: Notes on S. J. Perelman, With a Digression on W. W. Jacobs." *The Twentieth Century* (June 1960): 530-544. One of the best overall analyses of Perelman's style, this fine, insightful article compares Perelman with the Edwardian humorist W. W. Jacobs in order to comment on the nature of humor and to analyze Perelman's satire.

Ward, J. A. "The Hollywood Metaphor: The Marx Brothers, S. J. Perelman, Nathanael West." *The Southern Review* 12 (July 1976): 659-672. An interesting comparison of the material used by Perelman, West, and the Marx Brothers as representatives of reactions to Hollywood.

Wilk, Max. *And Did You Once See Sidney Plain?: A Random Memoir of S. J. Perelman*. New York: W. W. Norton, 1986. Remembrances by an author and friend of Perelman's.

Yates, Norris W. *The American Humorist: Conscience of the Twentieth Century.* Ames: Iowa State University Press, 1964. Contains "The Sane Psychoses of S. J. Perelman," an attempt to place Perelman in an American literary tradition revolving around the character type of the Little Man, mixed with a psychoanalytical approach and a brief examination of Perelman's Jewish heritage as it is expressed in his writing.

Zinsser, William K. "That Perelman of Great Price is Sixty-Five." *New York Times Magazine* (January 26, 1969): 26+. Perhaps the best interview with Perelman in terms of providing information on his early activities and other biographical background. Also contains his comments on the literary figures whom he felt most influenced him.

Steven H. Gale
Kentucky State University

ANN PETRY
1908

Publishing History

Ann Lane Petry was born October 12, 1908, in Old Saybrook, Connecticut, to Peter and Bertha James Lane. Her family owned and operated drugstores in Old Saybrook and Old Lyme, Connecticut. A 1931 graduate of the University of Connecticut College of Pharmacy, Petry followed the traditional family profession as a pharmacist. After operating the drugstore in Old Lyme, Petry gave up pharmacy to pursue another family tradition—storytelling.

Petry's fiction pays homage to the storytelling tradition so prominent in the fabric of African-American life. In interviews and in her own essays Petry tells of the way in which her parents could shape and dramatize stories, and how these stories helped a young black child survive in a white society. Although Petry was encouraged to become a writer in high school, she did not pursue a career as a writer until after becoming a practicing pharmacist.

Ann Lane married George Petry in 1938 and moved to New York City, her husband's home. She wanted a job that would involve writing and went to work for a newspaper. Petry was an advertising salesperson and a writer for the *Amsterdam News* (1938-1941), and a reporter and women's page editor for *People's Voice* (1941-1944), both Harlem-based newspapers. She taught in a special language skills program for inner-city children and was a member of the American Negro Theatre, the spawning ground of Ruby Dee, Frederick O'Neal, Sidney Poitier, and Ossie Davis. She was the founder and secretary of Negro Women, Inc. and a member of the famed writing workshop of Mabel Louise Robinson at Columbia University.

Because black authors had difficulty getting their work published by mainstream publishers, Petry's first work appeared in 1939 in the *Afro-American,* a weekly Baltimore newspaper. She received five dollars for the short story "Marie of the Cabin Club." In 1941 she published "On Saturday the Siren Sounds at Noon," in *Crisis,* an NAACP magazine founded by W. E. B. DuBois. In 1946 she published *The Street.*

Petry's major works of adult fiction include *Country Place* (1947), *The Narrows* (1953), and *Miss Muriel and Other Stories* (1971). While Petry continued to write for adults, she also wrote books for children and juveniles. These works include *The Drugstore Cat* (1949), *Harriet Tubman: Conductor of the Underground Railroad* (1955), *The Girl Called Moses: The Story of Harriet Tubman* (1960), *Tituba of Salem Village* (1964), and *Legends of the Saints* (1970).

Critical Reception, Honors, and Popularity

Petry won the Houghton Mifflin Literary Fellowship in 1945 for her manuscript, *The Street*, the work for which she is still best known. When it was published, *The Street* sold over a million copies, making Petry the first African-American woman to author a best seller. Her story, "Like a Winding Sheet," was voted the Best American Short Story for 1946. Among her other awards, Petry was honored with a Lifetime Achievement Award during the fifth annual Celebration of Black Writing held in Philadelphia in 1989.

Accompanying a burst of interest in the works of African-American women writers, Petry has been rediscovered by general readers as well as by scholars. Her out-of-print books have been republished, and scholars have turned to analyzing her writing. Her work is widely represented in anthologies of African-American letters, and is becoming firmly established in the canon of African-American literature. Critic Calvin Hernton describes Petry as a pioneer in portraying black women as victims of the multiple oppressions of race, gender, and socioeconomic class; he writes that *The Street* "is a pioneer work in womanist/feminist prose and that most of all, she treats black women as both black and female, and, in addition to racism and capitalism, Petry incorporates the third dimension in black women's lives—sexism."

Petry has been a visiting professor at the University of Hawaii, and her work has been the subject of doctoral dissertations. The forerunner of Toni Morrison and Alice Walker, Petry continues to write in the tradition of the storytellers of her family.

Analysis of Selected Titles

THE STREET

The Street, 1946, novel.

Social Concerns/Themes

The Street, Petry's best-known work, is often compared to Richard Wright's *Native Son* (1940). While there are similarities between the two novels, particularly in the portrayal of the economic plight of African Americans in northern cities, *The Street* moves in different directions. Both in its thematic concerns and its depiction of a black female protagonist, the novel is unique and significant. Petry was ahead of her time in focusing on what are considered contemporary social concerns: latchkey children, single parenting, and the way the politics of sex establishes an unending maze of oppression. *The Street* examines the unique role of the African-American woman in maintaining sanity amid the triple threat of classism, sexism, and racism. The novel presents the black woman as the center of the family and the community, as the person who shoulders the moral and ethical responsibilities of a race, and discusses how her relations with whites shapes the nature of interracial dynamics.

Characters

The Street presents a relatively small number of characters. These include Lutie Johnson's deceased grandmother, Granny, who was a major influence on Lutie and a source of kindness and comfort, and her grandfather, Pop, a bootlegger and ne'er-do-well. Lutie, the main character of the novel, marries Jim Johnson right after high school. They live in a frame house in Jamaica, New York, and at first Jim is the model husband and father. But when Jim loses his job, he begins to bring other women home while his wife is at work. Eventually, Lutie leaves Jim and moves to Harlem. There Lutie and her eight-year-old son, Bub, move into an apartment building in which Mrs. Hedges, an important presence on the "street" of the novel's title, operates a whorehouse. William Jones is the perverted building superintendent who lusts after Lutie. When Lutie's rejects him, he tricks her son and gets him in trouble.

The remaining characters are Junto, a white man who owns Harlem real estate, whorehouses, and bars, and is a partner of Mrs. Hedges. He, too, tries to seduce Lutie. Boots Smith, who works as a musician in Junto's bars, traps Lutie in his apartment and is killed by her after an attempted rape.

The real protagonist of the novel is the street on which Lutie lives and, by extension, the seedy and downtrodden residents of Harlem. Lutie Johnson is at the heart of the novel and represents one of the "walking wounded" of the ghetto. She believes the American Dream of a comfortable life is attainable if she works hard enough. In the end Lutie sees she is not included in the American Dream, and when she realizes that no amount of sacrifice and work will save her or Bub, she deserts her son and runs away to Chicago. Lutie is a victim of economic racism and the bias of sexism, evils which prevent African-American men from earning a living and turn black women into virtual slaves and beggars.

Techniques/Literary Precedents

The Street is often described as a female version of Richard Wright's *Native Son*, and Lutie Johnson has been called a female Bigger Thomas. Petry's first novel is also seen as an example of the naturalism characteristic of twentieth-century African-American fiction. But to see Petry as a lesser Richard Wright is to slight her achievement.

The Street protests the racism and sexism in the urban North. Zora Neale Hurston's *Their Eyes Were Watching God* (1937) is another novel of womanist protest that has an African-American female protagonist. But Hurston's protagonist, Janie Crawford, is rural and southern and transcends her condition through self-discovery and self-definition. *The Street* presents a poor northern urban protagonist and does not go beyond protest. While Janie protests her condition as black and female and eventually transcends her status, Lutie's story is one of protest and defeat, and she eventually flees the life on 116th Street. Lutie is sexually pursued by both black and white men, and it is this lust based on the conception of African-American females as fair sexual game which ultimately destroys Lutie. Indeed *The Street* is the first novel written by an African-American woman that details the triple oppression of African-American women—race, gender, and class. The novel is a pioneering rather than a derivative work.

Relation to Previous Works

Often seen as a single-work author or a children's writer, Petry published six short stories prior to *The Street*. "Marie of the Cabin Club" appeared in the Baltimore *Afro-American* newspaper in 1939; in 1943 "On Saturday the Siren Sounds at Noon" appeared in *Crisis*. Other stories preceding *The Street* were published in so-called "Negro Journals." These were written during Petry's stint as journalist. In 1944 "Doby's Gone" was published in *Phylon*, the scholarly journal associated with W. E. B. DuBois and Atlanta University. In 1945 "Olaf and His Girlfriend" and "Like a Winding Sheet" appeared in *Crisis*. In each of these stories female characters figure prominently.

COUNTRY PLACE

Country Place, 1947, novel.

Social Concerns/Themes

Country Place is almost a direct opposite of *The Street*. The novel is set in Lennox, Connecticut, a place similar to the town in which Petry grew up. The narrator is a white male druggist and the major characters are all white; a housekeeper is the only character of color. Petry's major themes are the prevalence of provincialism and materialism and how these societal ills destroy the town's moral fiber. This seemingly idyllic village contains many of the same problems as urban areas. Human frailties in Lennox are fueled by the townspeople's search for happiness in materialism and their spiritual poverty. It is a time of the collapse of traditional values following World War II and of a stifling routine existence with little room for creativity. The inhabitants, especially those women and few men who remained during the war, are trapped in a tortuous and empty life.

Characters

The narrator is the town druggist who is privy to all the intimate details of the lives of the Lennox residents. The novel opens with the return of Johnny Roane, an army veteran, and ends with his departure to study art. Although the story traces Johnny's relationship with his wife Glory, Lil, Johnny's mother-in-law, and Glory, mother and daughter, are the central characters. Both women have affairs with Ed Barrell. Lil marries Mearns Gramby, the son of the wealthiest woman in Lennox, but does not find fulfillment with him or the things he can give her. Mearns controls and manipulates his wife, for he knows she does not love him and that she thinks she will be rich after his mother dies.

The single character of color is Neola, the housekeeper and maid, who is loyal to Mearns' mother. Neola is contrasted with Glory and Lil early in the novel. Lil, though from humble beginnings, scoffs at Neola and feels superior to her not because Neola is a maid, but because she is black. She makes derisive comments about Neola's getting a divorce, asking whoever heard of "a nigger divorce." The irony is that Lil remains trapped in a loveless marriage and Neola is freed from hers. In the contrasts between Neola and the white women, Petry shows that though women experience sexual oppression, gender discrimination is not necessarily a unifying factor for all women; race is a stronger source of conflict.

It is Neola and Portulacca, "Portugee," the Gramby gardener, who represent hope and moral justice in Lennox. The two plan to marry and are willed the Gramby mansion and a lifelong maintenance allowance.

Techniques/Literary Precedents

Described by some as a "race free" novel, plot as well as character are often secondary to descriptions of the "country place" of Lennox. The town is presented as a commonplace town with calm and commonplace citizens. Petry summons the violence of nature to reveal the reality of the town. The hurricane that whips the water, thrashes the vegetation, and damages the buildings, also rips the veneer from the violent, greedy, and immoral lives of the major characters. Petry focuses on the physical details of the damage done by the storm.

THE NARROWS

The Narrows, 1953, novel.

Social Concerns/Themes

Petry has stated, if you are African American and a writer, it is inevitable that the subject of race will appear in some form in your work. Her third novel explores the intersection of race and class, and its destructive effects on a New England community. A subplot concerns an affair between a black man and a white woman which bears some resemblance to the tragic story of Romeo and Juliet. The novel also develops themes of violence and materialism in American culture.

Characters

As in Petry's first novel, female characters are prominent. African-American women are both major and minor characters, and they move the plot and shape the themes.ABigail Crunch is very much a New Englander, and strives to uphold that image. The major difference between Abbie and other New Englanders is her race: she is an African American. However, Abigail is out of touch with the real world, and lives vicariously through the men in her life: her late husband, the Major, and her adopted son Link Williams.

Link, a focal character, is killed at the end of the novel because of his involvement with Camilla Treadway, the white heiress of a gun factory. A boarder in Abbie's house, Malcolm Powther, is a butler to the Treadways and is indirectly responsible for Link's murder. Powther is almost as stiff as Abigail Crunch, and they both feel distant from the blacks who live in "the Narrows" section of the town. Malcolm Powther is the opposite of saloon keeper, Bill Hod, who is having an affair with Powther's wife, Mamie.

Mamie Powther is a sensual being in love with life. She is almost a stereotype of the whorish black female. Nevertheless, she is arguably the most interesting character of the novel. When Mamie is compared to Camilla Treadway, who is also involved in an extramarital affair, one can see the role of history and racial politics in the shaping of images of the African-American female. Also evident is the significant element of race when gender oppression is at issue. A minor character, F. K. Jackson feels herself an anomaly for being female and black.

Other characters add humor and spice to the novel. Cesar the Writing Man chalks prophetic biblical verses on sidewalks. Cesar is not merely the voice of doom, he chastises the people of Monmouth for their intolerance, greed, and racism. Weak Knees, a kind but gruff cook who acts shell-shocked, is sometimes a foil for Bill Hod.

Relation to Previous Works

In addition to her novels, Petry published short stories and essays. Between 1947 and 1953, when *The Narrows* appeared, she published three short stories, "Solo on the Drums," "The Necessary Knocking on the Door," and "The Bones of Louella Brown." A novella, *In Darkness and Confusion*, based on Harlem riots appeared in 1947, as well as an essay for *Holiday* entitled, "Harlem." All of these works reflect the problem of race and the peculiar social and psychological place of the African-American woman.

Adaptations

According to a 1987 interview, the film rights to *The Narrows* was sold in 1955, but a completed film has never materialized.

Other Titles

"Tribute to Mr. Gentry," 1946 (essay); "My Most Humiliating Jim Crow Experience," 1946 (autobiographical essay); "What's Wrong with Negro Men?" 1947 (essay); "The Great Secret," 1948 (essay); "The Novel as Social Criticism," 1950 (essay); *Harriet Tubman*, 1955 (biography); "Has Anybody Seen Miss Dora Dean?" (short story); "Miss Muriel," 1963 (short story); *Tituba of Salem Village*, 1964 (young adult novel); "The New Mirror," 1965 (short story); "The Common Ground," 1965 (essay); "This Writing Business," 1965 (essay); "Migraine Workers," 1967 (short story); *Legends of the Saints*, 1970 (biography); *Miss Muriel and Other Stories*, 1971; "The Witness," 1971 (short story); "The Moses Project," 1986 (short story).

Additional Sources

Bell, Bernard. *The Afro-American Novel and Its Tradition*. Amherst: University of Massachusetts Press, 1987. Compares Petry's novels with those of Richard

Wright and Chester Himes. Bell concludes that Petry moves "beyond the naturalistic vision of Himes and Wright to a demythologizing of . . . Afro-American character."

Bell, Roseann P., Bettye Parker, and Beverly Guy-Sheftall, eds. *Sturdy Black Bridges: Visions of Black Women in Literature*. Garden City, NY: Doubleday, 1979. Basically a reprint of a 1973 interview.

Carby, Hazel. *Reconstructing Womanhood: The Emergence of the Afro-American Woman Novelist*. New York: Oxford University Press, 1987. Mentions *The Street* as representative of the intersection of race, class, and sexuality in the novels of African-American women.

Christian, Barbara. *Black Women Novelists: The Development of a Tradition, 1892-1976*. Westport, CT: Greenwood, 1980. Focuses on a discussion of *The Street* and tends to compare Petry with Richard Wright. Mentions Petry's other novels in passing.

Coffey, Michael. "Black Writers Debate 'Being Human in the 20th Century'." *Publishers Weekly* (February 17, 1989): 16-17. Mentions lifetime achievement award for Petry, and includes an overview of her career.

Davis, Arthur P. *From the Dark Tower*. Washington, DC: Howard University Press, 1974. Petry is one of the African-American writers included in this important reference work. Discussion of literary career and works and valuable biographical data.

Hernton, Calvin. *The Sexual Mountain and Black Women Writers: Adventures in Sex, Literature, and Real Life*. Garden City, NY: Doubleday, 1987. Devotes a chapter to Petry. Hernton sees Petry as forerunner of writers such as Alice Walker, and claims that Petry was first to write a novel of protest against racism and sexism.

Hull, Gloria T., Patricia Bell Scott, and Barbara Smith, eds. *All the Women are White, All the Blacks are Men, but Some of Us are Brave*. Old Westbury, CT: Feminist Press, 1982. This primary work in Black Women's Studies devotes a section to the work of Petry. Includes a partial listing of reviews and evaluates secondary sources.

Ivy, James W. "Ann Petry Talks About First Novel." *Crisis* 53 (January 1946): 48-49. Interview focusing on *The Street*.

Lattin, Vernon. "Ann Petry and the American Dream." *Black American Literature Forum* 123 (1978): 68-70. Lattin focuses on Lutie in *The Street* and discusses the manner in which capitalism and the quest for materialism (the American Dream) is a nightmare for blacks and especially black women.

McDowell, Margaret B. "*The Narrows*: A Fuller View of Ann Petry." *Black American Literature Forum* 14 (1980): 153-159. Stylistic and thematic discussion of the novel with a consideration of historiographic issues.

O'Brien, John, ed. *Interviews with Black Writers*. New York: Liveright, 1973. In this significant interview Petry gives the reasons for the topical nature of her fiction.

Pryse, Marjorie, and Hortense Spillers, eds. *Conjuring: Black Fiction and Literary Tradition*. Bloomington: Indiana University Press, 1985. Two chapters are devoted to Petry's work. One treats motherhood with the focus on Lutie in *The Street;* the second, written by Bernard Bell, reiterates much of what appears in his own book.

Shinn, Thelma J. "Women in the Novels of Ann Petry." *Critique: Studies in Modern Fiction* 16 (1974): 110-120. Analyzes Petry's novels as an examination of gender oppression.

Wade-Gayles, Gloria. *No Crystal Stair: Visions of Race and Sex in Black Women's Fiction*. New York: Pilgrim Press, 1984. Focuses on Petry's first novel; considers gender and racial oppression as core themes of Petry's "artistic vision."

Washington, Gladys J. "A World Made Cunningly: A Closer Look at Ann Petry's Short Fiction." *CLA Journal* 30 (September 1986): 14-29. Focuses on what Washington refers to as the drugstore stories. One of a few scholarly articles treating some of Petry's short fiction.

Washington, Mary Helen. *Invented Lives—Narratives of Black Women 1860-1960*. Garden City, NY: Anchor, 1987. Petry is included in a chapter with Dorothy West. Moves past the criticism which emphasizes *The Street* and suggests that the best way to approach Petry's work is to hold in the forefront the exploitation of black women instead of stressing the environment as the primary determining factor in the women characters' lives.

Weir, Sybil. " *The Narrows:* A Black New England Novel." *Studies in American Fiction.* 15 (Spring 1987): 180-193.

Wilson, Mark. "A *Melus* Interview: Ann Petry-The New England Connection." *Melus* 15 (Summer 1988): 71-84.

Muriel W. Brailey
Wilberforce University

JAYNE ANNE PHILLIPS
1952

Update

For *Machine Dreams* (1984), Jayne Anne Phillips received a National Book Critics Circle Award nomination, and the novel was cited among American Library Association Notable Books and *New York Times* Best Books of 1984. In 1987, with the support of her second fellowship from the National Endowment for the Arts (1978, 1985), Phillips published *Fast Lanes*, a volume of seven short stories, three of which deal with characters who also appear in *Machine Dreams*. Many of these stories had previously been published in magazines or in limited editions.

Throughout this period, Phillips has continued to teach creative writing at Boston University. In 1986-1987 she also held the Fanny Howe Chair of Letters at Brandeis University in Waltham, Massachusetts. In addition, she has published short stories in a number of magazines, among them *Granta*, *Grand Street*, *Esquire*, and *Rolling Stone*.

Analysis of Selected Titles

FAST LANES

Fast Lanes, 1987, short stories.

Social Concerns/Themes

In *Fast Lanes*, as in her earlier fiction, Phillips depicts the dislocations in contemporary American life. She examines in minute detail the impermanence of human relationships and the resulting destruction of individuals. Confronted with an impersonal society and disintegrating families which supply no enduring values, Phillips' characters can rely only on their own limited inner strength for support in their inevitable personal crises. Generally they have experienced—or are experiencing—either actual losses or omens of such losses. While the forms of their reactions vary, Phillips' people recognize the frailty of their psychological balance and use emotional detachment to shield themselves from further pain.

Thus handicapped, Phillips' characters sometimes try to establish bonds with others, but such attempts seem always doomed to failure. Rayme, the title character of her story, has moved back and forth among communal houses and the homes of relatives but she carries with her the isolation resulting from her parents' divorces and her mother's suicide. Thus, she remains the perennial outsider. Mickey, in "How Mickey Made It," describes the women he has lived with, most of whom are older than he; yet none of these women can compensate for his rejection by his adoptive mother. Five years after her divorce, Kay regards her marriage and her children as "Something That Happened"; just as her physical pain was eliminated when half her stomach was removed, so she has recovered her emotional equilibrium by withdrawing from the lives of her husband and children. At the same time, Angela, the youngest daughter, has adopted values more conventional than Kay's; she too is detached from other people, however, especially her parents and siblings.

Most of Phillips' families are dysfunctional, but inescapable. Unable to cope with the difficult twelve-year-old who had been abused, Mickey's adoptive parents made him a ward of the state and so, in his words, shipped him off to a correctional facility. Yet Mickey remains bound to them by an obsessive hatred, and he constantly disparages his entire family. In "Fast Lanes," both of the principal characters are alienated from their families. The narrator feels compelled to return home to visit her ailing father, but she dreads the moment of her arrival and knows she will soon leave again. Thurman, her companion, sporadically visits his mentally confused father and alcoholic mother in the decaying family home. Thurman is still trying—unsuccessfully—to find meaning in his family's losses; so, despite his assertion that he should stay away, he continues to hold his home together, physically and emotionally.

Likewise, while trying to understand her family's painful past, Danner Hampson of "Blue Moon" provides a psychological anchor, not only for her emotionally aloof parents, but also for her brother and his unstable girlfriend. "Bess" tells of a sister and brother, as they first understand the types of love, the meaning of death, and the extent of their mutual dependence. Born just thirteen months apart, the two youngest in a family of twelve children, Bess and her brother Warwick grow up as twins; the age gap sets them apart from their older siblings and their aging parents, and their primary loyalty is to each other. Except for Bess's brief marriage, which Warwick refuses to acknowledge, the two remain together until Warwick's death forces the sale of the farm and scatters the remaining family.

In "Bluegill," another account of obsessive love, a pregnant woman addresses her unborn child, whose father she does not name or acknowledge. Living among strangers, this narrator is cut off from her past, and her world consists of only herself and the fetus she thinks of as an almost mythical sea creature. Although she receives monthly checks from her baby's father, he is indistinguishable from the other men in her past and less real to her than some local fishermen who have been shipwrecked and presumed drowned.

Phillips' choice of "Fast Lanes" as the title story suggests that these stories, taken together, serve as a commentary on sanity as a precarious balance between reality and illusion. At one extreme, Rayme has chosen delusion, rejecting all forms of conventional reality. To a lesser degree, Mickey's prospective music career represents a triumph of self-delusion, as does the pregnant woman's belief that she and her child will be able to live in a dream world that unites them and excludes all others. Likewise, Angela and Kay in "Something That Happened" irrationally and whimsically pursue the interrelationship of the emotions and the body systems.

It is Danner Hampson, however, who consciously considers the question of reality and illusion, as a central character in "Blue Moon" and "Fast Lanes" and perhaps the anonymous narrator of "Rayme." Danner sees the destructive effects of illusion in the parallel cases of her mother's devotion to a long-dead fiancé and Kato's obsession with Billy. Equally damaging is the illusory wife/mother whom Warwick invents to perpetuate the fiction of his emotionally incestuous relationship with Bess. By allowing Warwick to claim Mitch Hampson as his son, Bess forces Mitch to deal with the double rejection of Warwick's coldness and abandonment by his supposed mother.

Danner's self-delusion involves her attempts to escape the reality of her family's failures and losses, to lose her past and herself through ceaseless wandering, moving in the fast lanes. She envies earlier generations, who seemed to see reality clearly and to accept their lot, but she wonders if her view of such people is only another illusion. Thurman, who claims to have left the fast lanes, reassures her that his grandfather possessed a sense of certainty and that acceptance is difficult but still possible; both Thurman's incessant travels and Bess's concluding story of Warwick, however, undercut this assertion, suggesting that life is, at best, an equilibrium of reality and necessary illusions.

Characters

Most of Phillips' major characters are psychologically scarred by the deterioration of their families and their subsequent uncertainties about their own identities. Their emotional stability varies from the madness of Rayme and the manic egocentricity of Mickey to the resignation of Thurman and the placid acceptance of Bess.

Rejected when her father chooses the children who will remain with him and abandoned when her mother starves herself to death, Rayme responds by deliberately choosing behavior which will further set her apart. She gloats in the link to her mother which her madness supplies, and she refuses to acknowledge conventional concepts such as ownership or the distinction between edible and inedible substances.

Kato Black, who was abandoned by her mother in "Blue Moon," depends for her sense of identity upon her role as Billy Hampson's girlfriend, and when Billy's mother pressures him to enroll in a boarding school, Kato finds the proposed separation unendurable. Her suicide attempt, a desperate attempt to keep Billy in Bellington, has precisely the opposite effect, ensuring that Billy will be sent to boarding school, and she will be sent to live with her aunt.

Mickey, the recently fired bartender and would-be musician talks non-stop to the customer who has picked him up. His stories of the many older women he has slept with, and of the brilliant music career awaiting him in London, do not conceal his insecurity and self-doubt. Although he brags about his power over women, he finally reveals his rejection by his adoptive mother, the only person he has ever really loved.

In "Blue Moon," Danner Hampson finds herself caught between a number of opposing forces: her father's failures and her mother's resentment; Kato's obsession with Billy and Mrs. Hampson's fierce desire to protect her son by controlling his life; her own immaturity and her need to understand the adults around her. Although Shinner Black tries to explain the past's hold on him and Jean Hampson, Danner does not realize that the death of Tom has caused her mother to feel completely isolated, deprived of her love and her dreams. Danner cannot comprehend such loneliness until, in "Fast Lanes," she has experienced equally devastating losses. Where Jean tried to escape through marriage to Mitch, Danner has tried sex, drugs, and rootlessness—living in the fast lanes, passing everything. Returning home forces her to acknowledge the futility of all these attempts and leads her to question the possibility of achieving the apparent certainty of people in earlier times.

Thurman offers Danner hope; he claims to have quit running from his family and his past, though he still cannot fully understand either. The youngest son of a famous high school football coach, he has always been a misfit, preferring woodworking to football. Because he could not measure up to his father's expectations as an athlete, Thurman tries to gain his father's attention by recklessly inviting serious injury in the final game of his senior season. When his father seems more interested in the championship trophy than in his concussion, Thurman's behavior becomes increasingly unconventional. For a while, he becomes a ski bum, then he runs dope, next he serves a stint in the Peace Corps in Ceylon, and finally he becomes a hippie carpenter. Accepting responsibility for his mentally incompetent parents, he returns two or three times a year to check on their welfare and to arrange for routine maintenance of the family home, but in their attempts to escape reality, his father refuses to admit that any repairs are needed, and his mother acquiesces in this delusion.

By taking Danner to his parents' home, Thurman shows her the destructive results of refusing to accept reality. His brother, like Danner's, chose to go to Viet Nam where he was killed. But Thurman's mother, like Danner, clings to the illusion that her son is alive; and her delusion leads to alcoholism and mental confusion.

The character most accepting of the past is Bess, Danner's grandmother. From the perspective of her eighty years, she recalls her dead siblings, especially her brother Warwick, whom she regarded as a virtual twin. When she was twelve, the traditional age of maturity, Warwick took her to a concealed spot where they could watch sexual intercourse between their brother and his wife. From Warwick, too, Bess learned about death as she helped to nurse him through a near-fatal allergic reaction. She believes her voice called him back from death then, but sixteen years later she could not save him from death in the coal mine. Though she eloped with a man, who later deserted her, and bore a child that Warwick would not allow him to acknowledge, she remains bound to him—vicariously experiencing his death but this time too far removed, physically and psychologically, to call him back again. Now an old woman, Bess sees how his illness and his later death not only changed the course of her life, but initiated her into the mystery of death.

Techniques/Literary Precedents

The themes of individual isolation and reality/illusion are ancient and almost universal. Modern precedents include the fiction of Joseph Conrad, Edith Wharton, Virginia Woolf, and James Joyce, whose technique of the interior monologue may have influenced the story "Bluegill." Similar emphasis upon the question of illusion is seen in the novels of John Barth and John Irving and in the plays of Edward Albee and Eugene Ionesco. Phillips' portraits of the disintegrating family find parallels in the work of Gail Godwin, Anne Tyler, and Bobbie Ann Mason.

In technique *Fast Lanes* is in the tradition of Thomas Wolfe, William Faulkner, and Sherwood Anderson. The lyrical quality of Phillips' prose is reminiscent of Wolfe's prose poems in *Look Homeward, Angel*, and the themes of family failure and individual alienation are equally typical of Wolfe. Like Faulkner and Anderson, Phillips has assembled a collection of stories linked by related or recurring characters, and by themes, upon which the stories provide multiple perspectives. *Fast Lanes* resembles Faulkner's *Go Down, Moses* in its portrayal of several generations of one family and in its multi-faceted development of the isolation theme. Phillips' emphasis upon the warping influence of obsessive self-delusion also recalls Sherwood Anderson's *Winesburg, Ohio*.

Relation to Previous Works

The stories of *Fast Lanes* continue to develop the themes introduced in *Black Tickets* and *Machine Dreams*—the disintegration of the family, the isolation of the individual, and the contemplative person's search for values and identity. Other similarities include Phillips' use of a variety of narrators and narrative techniques: the monologue in "Bluegill" and "How Mickey Made It"; the reminiscence in "Rayme," "Bess," and "Blue Moon"; and the retrospective narrative in "Fast Lanes" and "Something That Happened."

Additional Sources

Adams, Michael. "Jayne Anne Phillips." In *Dictionary of Literary Biography Yearbook*. Detroit: Gale, 1980. Brief biographical sketch with critical analysis of stories in *Black Tickets* and a limited bibliography.

"Jayne Anne Phillips" In *Contemporary Literary Criticism*. Vol. 33. Detroit: Gale, 1985. Succinct excerpts from reviews of *Machine Dreams*.

Shepherd, Kenneth R., and Jean W. Ross. "Jayne Anne Phillips." In *Contemporary Authors*. New Revision Series. Vol. 24. Detroit: Gale, 1988. Biographical sketch with critical analyses and extensive list of reviews. Also includes a transcript of a 1987 telephone interview.

Charmaine Allmon Mosby
Western Kentucky University

CHAIM POTOK
1929

Update

Potok has continued to receive both critical and popular attention. Many critics found *Davita's Harp*, which appeared in 1985, disappointing. His most recent novel, *The Gift of Asher Lev* (1990), has been given a mixed reception by reviewers.

Potok continues to be the subject of journal articles, and the first book-length study, *Chaim Potok* by Edward A. Abramson, appeared in 1986. In the most thorough treatment of Potok's work so far, Abramson is sympathetic and admiring, but candidly acknowledges Potok's flaws. He provides a useful chapter on Potok's life and a detailed, two-page biographical chronology. The remainder of the book includes chapters on all of the novels up to *Davita's Harp* and on Potok's nonfiction book *Wanderings: Chaim Potok's History of the Jews*.

Since 1985, Potok has continued to give lectures on college campuses and elsewhere throughout the United States. During 1985, he was a Visiting Lecturer at Bryn Mawr College in Pennsylvania. He is currently chairman of the Publications Committee of the Jewish Publication Society.

Besides *The Gift of Asher Lev*, Potok's publications since 1985 include *Theo Tobiasse: Artist in Exile* (1986), a nonfiction book on a Jewish artist, with numerous illustrations; "The Culture Highways We Travel," the printed version of a lecture, in *Religion and Literature* (19, 2 [1987]); "Neighbors," a reminiscence from his wife's childhood for *Seventeen* (December 1987); an introduction to *Last Traces: The Lost Art of Auschwitz* by Joseph P. Czarnecki (1989), which discusses art produced in Nazi concentration camps. Potok has also written two plays, *Out of the Depths* and *Sins of the Father*, both performed in Philadelphia in 1990.

Analysis of Selected Titles

THE GIFT OF ASHER LEV

The Gift of Asher Lev, 1990, novel. Prequel. *My Name is Asher Lev*, 1972, novel.

Social Concerns

Like several of Potok's other novels, *The Gift of Asher Lev* deals with a Jew's place in the world and with the artist's role in society and duty to his community and family. Again, Potok deals with "core conflicts" that go to the center of human self-definition. The demands of art are pitted against familial loyalties; the politics of modern secularism—the environment in which Asher creates much of his art—are pitted against the dedication and religious needs of the orthodox faithful.

Themes

The theme of friendship is again prominent: the friendship between Asher and his late mentor, Jacob Kahn; between Asher and his wife Devorah; between Devorah and her cousin, Max (with whom she hid during the Holocaust); between two sets of fathers and sons—Asher and his father, and Asher and his son.

Once more, Potok looks at his characters' responses to their pasts, but here he is more concerned with their futures. Though Asher must face up to the pain his artistic choices have caused those he loves most dearly, he ultimately focuses more on his own future and on the future his son may provide in his stead for the community Asher has left.

Characters

The novel portrays Asher Lev—whom we have come to know in an earlier novel, *My Name Is Asher Lev*—in the aftermath of his exile from the Ladover Hasidic community. Since then he has married Devorah and fathered two children: Rocheleh and Avrumel. Against a montage of significant minor characters, the book focuses on Asher, now a prominent and respected (though often hated) artist. At the novel's beginning, Asher acknowledges that his critics may be right in stating that his art tends to repeat itself. And even as these critiques are being published, Asher's life begins to imitate his art. He sees himself in his own cycle, retreading ground he thought he had left.

When he returns to Brooklyn from France for his uncle's funeral, he is persuaded to remain for two months, during which time he learns that his uncle has willed him a priceless art collection (which creates great family dissension) and that Asher's parents and the revered Rebbe want young Avrumel to prepare to succeed the Rebbe. These revelations force Asher Lev to examine his conflicting loyalties and to find some balance between his duties to art and to family. Through what he learns as the cycle of his life unfolds—a cycle that ultimately will replace him with his son—he returns to his art with renewed strength, renewed pain, and renewed anger—all of which revive and refocus his talent and give his work tremendous power.

Techniques

Throughout the novel, Potok moves back and forth between past and present and between America and Europe, often through Asher Lev's dreams (both waking and sleeping) and once through a miraculous vision of the Rebbe. There are fairly obvious symbols throughout. Images of light and darkness are prominent, as are the riddles of mysticism.

Literary Precedents

Like the earlier novel about Asher Lev, *The Gift of Asher Lev* concerns the role of the artist. It is thus influenced by the tradition of novels about an artist's development, especially James Joyce's *A Portrait of the Artist as a Young Man* (1916) and *Ulysses* (1922). Like Joyce, Potok deals with the artist's conflicts with his family, community, and religion. Though, like Joyce's Stephen Dedalus, Asher Lev has gone into exile, in this second novel he achieves a more satisfying reconciliation with his community than Joyce's hero does.

Relation to Previous Works

The Gift of Asher Lev is a sequel to *My Name Is Asher Lev* and deals with many of the same themes, especially the conflict between an artist and his family and community. Since almost twenty years elapsed between the publication of the two books, some readers and critics have tried to assess Potok's development as a writer during those years. Though some see improvement, culminating in *The Book of Lights,* others (including many who enjoy Potok's work) have seen a decline in the quality of the novels that followed *My Name Is Asher Lev*, especially *Davita's Harp*, and some claim Potok has been repeating himself. Critical response to *The Gift of Asher Lev* has been more positive, seeing it as less ponderous than *Davita's Harp* and, though flawed, as demonstrating Potok's continuing ability to depict cultural conflict.

Additional Sources

Cowan, Paul. "The Faiths of Her Childhood." *New York Times Book Review* (March 31, 1985): 12-13. This review of *Davita's Harp* praises the novel's "rich" prose style and calls it Potok's "bravest book, but not his best."

Dembo, L. S. "Asher Lev: The Mariolatry of a Hasid." In *The Monological Jew.* Madison: University of Wisconsin Press, 1988. Using ideas derived in part from Martin Buber, Dembo views the title character of *My Name Is Asher Lev* as drawn toward "mother worship," primitivism, paganism, and "aesthetic idolatry."

Kauvar, Elaine M. "An Interview with Chaim Potok." *Contemporary Literature* 27 (1986): 291-317. Potok reveals his views on various aesthetic and cultural questions and talks about his novels and his development as a writer.

Kremer, S. Lillian. "Eternal Light: The Holocaust and the Revival of Judaism and Jewish Civilization in the Fiction of Chaim Potok." In *Witness Through the Imagination*. Detroit: Wayne State University Press, 1989. This chapter on Potok considers his use of the Holocaust in *The Chosen, The Promise, In the Beginning,* and an early story and compares his treatment of the subject to that of other Jewish writers.

Ratner, Rochelle. "Variations on a Theme." *Midstream* (March 1986): 60-61. Review of *Davita's Harp* that emphasizes the book's flaws.

Review of *The Gift of Asher Lev. Publishers Weekly* (March 16, 1990): 61. Briefly discusses the book, praising its dramatic tension but finding the dialogue wooden and the prose burdened by excessive details of art techniques.

Soll, Will. "Chaim Potok's *Book of Lights*: Reappropriating Kabbalah in the Nuclear Age." *Religion and Literature* 21, 1 (1989): 111-135. Discusses Potok's use of Jewish mystical texts in a novel set in the twentieth century and dealing (among other things) with the devastation wrought by the atomic bomb.

Stiller, Nikki. Review of *The Gift of Asher Lev. New York Times Book Review* (May 13, 1990): 29. In this mostly negative review, Stiller claims that "the predictable prevails" and that the book "offers simplistic answers" to the question, "How can the artist and the community be reconciled?"

Zvirin, Stephanie. Review of *The Gift of Asher Lev. Booklist* (February 1, 1990): 1050. A positive review, calling the book "an extraordinary, compelling sequel to *My Name Is Asher Lev*" and praising Potok's "fine," "rich" prose.

Bruce W. Young
Margaret B. Young
Brigham Young University

MANUEL PUIG
1932-1990

Update

In 1988 Puig published his last novel, *The Tropical Night Falls* (*Cae la noche tropical*). He was preparing to review the English translation of the novel when he died in Cuernavaca, Mexico, on July 22, 1990. He was fifty-seven years old.

In the last years of his life, Puig renewed his interest in film and continued to write and adapt for the stage. One of his film scripts, an adaptation of a short story ("El impostor," "The Imposter") by Argentine writer Silvina Ocampo was produced in Mexico as *Place Without Limits* (*Lugar sin límites*) in 1984. Puig also published, in English translation, a two-character play, *Mystery of the Rose Bouquet* (*Misterio del ramo de rosas,* 1988) which was performed to critical acclaim in London and Los Angeles in 1987 and 1988 respectively.

Analysis of Selected Titles

PUBIS ANGELICAL

Pubis Angelical, 1986, novel. *Pubis angelical,* 1979.

Social Concerns

This novel tells the seemingly unconnected stories of two female characters: Ana, an Argentine woman confined to a hospital bed in Mexico in the 1970s and a nameless beautiful Viennese woman in the 1930s who becomes a Hollywood movie star. Their stories, though set in different locales and times, are parallel tales that reveal similar social concerns; these, reduced to their minimalist core, are in turn integrated into a set of futuristic, science fiction episodes introduced in the third part of the novel.

The paramount social concern of the novel is the problematic relationship between men and women. This is conveyed through the characters' fruitless yet relentless pursuit of the ideal male, the superior man who might satisfy a woman's complex set of needs. This position is slowly articulated by Ana from her hospital bed, as she reflects on her unsatisfying relationships with men and critiques her partners' imperfections. Although at times her criteria seem frivolous and her critical (and self-critical) resolve shaky, she cannot escape the inevitable conclusion that she has failed in her quest. Ana ultimately indicts all men in her life. Her father, husband, and lovers, to varying degrees, have all disappointed her.

Ana's reflections on her failure to find the superior man every woman wants and needs is mirrored in the lives of the European beauty and the young woman who appears in the futuristic passages. And while Puig creates a seemingly rich variety of male characters, from the Viennese woman's revered brilliant, scientist-father to the handsome female impersonator spy-cum-maid who orchestrates her escape from a husband who oppresses her, not one of these men is able to satisfy a woman's deep longings, fill her loneliness, or dispel her melancholy.

A second, important social concern of the novel is the way in which politics, repressive political systems in particular, affect the intellectual and moral lives of individuals. Puig pursues here the theme he first explored in *Kiss of the Spider Woman*. Using political developments in Argentina during the 1970s after the death of Juan Perón, Puig sees signs of danger as he watches his country evolve toward a modern version of Nazi Germany. Of particular interest to him is the Argentinean search for a national identity and the inherent threat that this quest might deteriorate, as in Nazi Germany, into fascism. Puig appeals to several historical and ideological parallels between Argentina of the 1970s and Germany of the 1930s: a heightened sense of nationalism; a high standard of living; a superior level of culture; a deep love of music; and Argentina's pioneering appreciation, years before most countries, of important new currents of thought and aesthetics. Pozzi, an idealistic lawyer and one of Ana's lovers, embodies the country's dilemma. He is altruistic and self-denying and defends political prisoners. He is also a partisan of Juan Perón, portrayed as Latin America's Hitler and Mussolini. Ana, whose self-described political innocence and ignorance are undermined by her questioning of Pozzi, asks how he can reconcile his humanitarian principles and a concern with human rights with his membership in the Peronist movement. Does he not realize that to be a leftist and a Peronist is a contradiction? The eventual fate of Pozzi suggests that this is not merely a rhetorical question.

Puig's political concerns are also evident in the utopia portrayed in the futuristic episodes of the book, where his detachment from specific political dogma gives way to pessimism. An all-knowing repressive government reigns supreme. As in George Orwell's *Nineteen Eighty-Four,* Puig constructs a world in which the state has attempted to obliterate the individual; names have been replaced with initials and numbers, and personal autonomy has all but disappeared. The young protagonist of these pages is W218. Her basic needs, as well as society's, are fulfilled in a manner that is fair, efficient, and methodical.

A third, and less prominent social concern of the novel is the class distinctions to which characters cling although they are acknowledged as shallow and meaningless. Ana is especially vulnerable to class snobbery. Much of the mutual attraction between her and Pozzi revolves around their perception that they belong to different classes: Ana to the upper class and Pozzi to the lower. She finds his poverty, his rumpled clothes, and the fact that he is working his way through school, exciting. She feels puzzled and betrayed when she discovers that his family is comfortably middle class. Likewise, Pozzi is suitably impressed by Ana's demeanor, clothes, speech, and especially her habit of using certain words and avoiding others, a self-described sign of high class. While she first tells Pozzi that she learned this at home, she later admits to having borrowed the affectations from classmates at school where she was the poorest pupil. Ana's pretentiousness allows her to sustain an interest in Alejandro, a wealthy landlord who becomes her second lover. She overlooks his reprehensible politics, both social and sexual, as well as his controlling personality, as long as he remains generous toward her and her family.

Themes/Characters

In *Pubis Angelical* Puig recreates one of his favorite themes, that of the interplay between reality and fiction, between fact and illusion, and the propensity of individuals to take refuge in a world created exclusively by the imagination. Ana, the main character, is also the master fictionalizer. She is first introduced in a hospital room, sick and in pain, suffering the post-operative effects of a seemingly unsuccessful surgery to remove a tumor. She is in pain and in need of frequent sedation throughout the novel. Her counterpart, the Viennese beauty, is also introduced as helpless and devoid of autonomy, sedated, and a prisoner not of her own body or of the hospital but of her powerful husband.

As Ana slowly reveals the details of her life through several interlocutors, the reader learns of the mysterious Viennese actress through descriptions by a third person narrator. All details concerning her are narrated with a distinct sense of unreality; her life is distilled into a hazy and narcotized rendition of a series of highly unrealistic events such as a seduction, a daring escape, a trans-Atlantic crossing, an accidental but necessary murder, a Hollywood movie contract, and so on. The logic of the parallel display of Ana's "realistic" dialogues and thoughts and the more chimeric passages—not unlike Puig's use of film descriptions in *The Kiss of the Spider Woman*—becomes clearer as the reader learns the details of Ana's life and the connection between the two women. We learn of Ana's early disenchantment with her husband; for her sake, he urges her to pretend to be someone else during lovemaking. We learn how Ana, unhappy as a housewife and mother, leaves home to work for Buenos Aires's principal opera house, to a life that is glamorous and exciting. Likewise, the Viennese beauty leaves her husband, kills her lover rather than be trapped by him, gives up their child in return for a movie contract, and proceeds to enjoy unprecedented critical success in Hollywood. Yet all is not well; she is unhappy, lonely, and melancholic, and more than anything fears turning thirty. Before the dreaded birthday, she is run over by a car while on location in Mexico to make a film.

The young woman of the utopian episode, W218, is also fated to die from an incurable disease contracted, perhaps voluntarily, in the course of her work. Ana, however, appears to be spared death before thirty. When at the end of the novel she gets the first optimistic prognosis from her doctor, she decides to ask her mother and daughter to join her from Argentina. As in the closing scene of the futuristic text, the centrality of the bond between mother and daughter is acknowledged for the first time. Ana has always dismissed the affectations of her mother and daughter in her futile quest for the superior man, and only at the end, in a redemptive tone that echoes the science fiction text, is she willing to recognize her emotional ties with them.

As for the men portrayed in the story, none proves worthy of the female characters' trust and affection. Pozzi, the altruistic lover who visits Ana in Mexico, wants to use her to entrap Alejandro, the rich conservative landlord, and swap him for political prisoners. He also compromises her by going back to her Buenos Aires apartment, without her consent, where he is eventually gunned down by agents of the government. The Viennese beauty, as W218, is seduced and betrayed.

Ana, following her husband's advice, masterfully designs imaginative strategies to help her survive the pain and pessimism of her medical ordeal. At the end, she appears poised for survival. Or perhaps, having exhausted the melodramatic possibilities of a Hollywood ending and the austerities of science fiction, could the middle class ideals of motherhood be a new, promising direction for her fictions? The reader never knows with certainty. In this, as in his other novels, Puig masterfully continues blurring the line between reality and illusion.

Techniques

In *Pubis Angelical,* as in other novels, Puig makes use of a variety of narrative techniques. The text alternates between the two main characters without regard for traditional boundaries of chapters and parts. And while the essential plot lines evolve in a mostly progressive manner (especially the actress and the science fiction storylines) the novel lacks a clear chronological focus because Ana's recollections are fragmented.

There is, however, a distinctive style and tone for each narrative segment. When Ana is the main character, for example, we learn about her through her friend Beatriz, who visits her often; through her lover Pozzi who is in Mexico for political reasons; and, finally, through her own diary entries. With both Beatriz and Pozzi, Ana holds curt discussions on the main social concerns of the novel: sex rules, the meaning of feminism, and politics. In her diary, on the other hand, Ana rearranges her past in a series of directed, expansive recollections that add texture and shape to the cerebral talks with her visitors.

When the Viennese actress is the focus, a third person narrator relates the highly improbable action sequences, selecting, as in a movie of the 1940s, rich, descriptive details of pose, texture, color, sight, and sound. These are all glazed by a sort of semi-transparent film or mist that keeps us from seeing and understanding things clearly. The narrator is superficial and withholding, offering only sufficient detail of the life of the "most beautiful woman in the world" to conform to the basic requirements of a movieland fiction. In *Pubis Angelical,* however, the fiction exists as a Hollywood reality, not as a movie, as a living version of an illusion rather than as its celluloid counterpart.

The futuristic narrative, likewise, is presented by a third person narrator who reports, faithfully and dispassionately, W218's frustrations and longings. The language here is cold and formal, and the reader is made aware of the incongruity between the icy, mechanical, impersonal environment and the emotions of the protagonist. The somewhat sentimental ending of this segment, perhaps meant as parody, surprises the reader both because of its tone and also because the rather simplistic lesson W218 learns will inform Ana, rather than the other way around.

In the final analysis, Puig's novel demands active involvement on the part of the reader, who is constantly challenged to conspire with the author in the futile attempt to distinguish between reality and fiction within his fictions.

BLOOD OF REQUITED LOVE

Blood of Requited Love, 1984, novel. *Sangre de amor correspondido,* 1982.

Social Concerns

Set in the small town of Cocotá, in the State of Rio, Brazil, this novel tells the story of the relationship between Josemar Ferreira and María da Gloria Rossi. Through dialogues and monologues the broad outline of their story is gleaned. The reader learns that Josemar lives in the country a few miles outside of town, and is the middle of eleven children of a poor farming family. He is despised and picked on by his father and protected and adored by his mother. While the reasons for the father's rejection are never explained, Josemar's appearance might hold the key. He resembles neither of his parents nor any of his brothers and sisters. He is handsome, white, and has curly, chestnut-colored hair. According to unconfirmed rumor, Josemar might be the son of the local landlord; the young man shares the landlord's good looks and a passion for soccer. It is in part Josemar's appearance, (supported by the rumors about his birth) that allows him to pursue his ambitious dreams and the love of María da Gloria, the blond, middle-class daughter of Italian immigrants who is the obsessive object of his thoughts and a principal interlocutor of the novel.

Josemar's preoccupation with making something out of himself, with fame and fortune, is one of the principal social concerns of the novel. In spite of his sense of entitlement, his hard work, and his willingness to try different occupations, Josemar fails. He never gets to buy a car, never gets to be the elegant, progressive person he wants to be, and never escapes the poverty into which he was born. Last, but not least, he never gets to live happily ever after with the woman of his dreams. This discourse of failure is as much an indictment of the closed social system of Brazil with its vast economic underclass as it is of the weaknesses and self-delusions of Josemar.

The second social concern of the novel is the preoccupation with seduction and sexual conquest, and the complacency with which both men and women, young and old accept the figure of the macho seducer. In fact, the dynamic of the novel is provided by different and conflicting versions of the core of Josemar's thoughts and actions: the seduction and "deflowering" of María da Gloria.

But this approach to women also informs all relations between the sexes, not just Josemar's; his black adopted brother, his father(s), and all significant males in the novel are driven by it. They consider a man's sexual possession of a woman a sort of territorial imperative. And while Josemar, as a child, feels sympathy for his mother when she waits at home for the return of a philandering husband, he fantasizes about seducing his own school teacher. As an adult Josemar consciously reflects on his father's behavior and absolves him, accepting male lust and infidelity as the way of the world; he goes on to emulate and surpass any of his childhood models.

A particular obsession for Josemar is the seduction of virgins and its attendant problems, such as the pain and difficulty both partners might endure and the amount of blood that the act might produce. He follows with great interest and anticipation several local girls' passages into puberty, especially María de Gloria's.

When he first notices her she is twelve years old; he awaits her development and "seduces" her only after she comes of sexual age. This patience reveals a certain code of conduct in sexual matters; it is a source of pride for Josemar, among his many regrets, and serves to distinguish his relations with women from relations with animals, especially the mean and cantankerous cow his father asks him to milk.

Themes/Characters

Unlike some in Puig's other works, none of the characters is especially mysterious or profound. In *Blood of Requited Love* the mystery for the reader lies in the question of if and when the protagonists, Josemar in particular, will ever tell the truth. And, although the contradictory details of the text contribute to the elusiveness of the story, the details of the lives of the principals are simple and routine, conforming, as they do, to the broad outlines of normalcy in a small provincial town. Lovers meet in the town square, go to dances together, see each other at soccer games, and after church. They take long walks in the country, listen to birds, and admire the stars. They go to school, make out behind shade trees, and fantasize about the future.

The town proves too small to contain Josemar's ambitions. He needs to leave to make something of himself; he works as a mason and then for the electric company. Neither job gives him the money and glory he so desperately wants, and his meager savings are spent to treat his mother's painful and debilitating arthritis. He fathers two children out of wedlock and is unable to support them. Their mother, a teacher, cares for them and helps nurse Josemar's ailing mother. To add to the complete deconstruction of the character's hopes, his mother anticipates having to sell the humble house in which they live in order to pay her medical expenses. In sum, years after leaving town in search of fame and fortune Josemar has nothing, not even a roof over his head. When he returns to Cocotá almost a decade later, he has little to show for his absence except rich fictions about the past, endless tales of sexual prowess, and equally fictive accounts of his soccer feats.

María da Gloria, though a main character and a frequent discursive partner in the novel, reveals little of herself. From the third person narrator we learn that she is an intelligent, resourceful, and independent girl. In collusion with her mother, she appears willing to defy her father's orders that she not see Josemar, a youth whose country roots and lower-class origins make him an unacceptable boyfriend. As for her role in the seduction, the reader never learns the extent of her complicity. After he leaves Cocotá, immediately after the alleged act, he never contacts her nor exhibits any overt curiosity about her fate. We do learn that during Josemar's long absence, she suffers from a nervous condition and is seldom seen in public. This conscious indifference on Josemar's part is hard to reconcile with his mental life, which remains dominated by thoughts about María, visions and revisions of the seduction, recollections about their past together, and illusions about what could have been.

María da Gloria eventually recovers, resumes her studies, becomes a teacher, and is poised to accept the romantic entreaties of a friend from her youth newly returned to Cocotá, professional degree in hand.

Unlike Josemar, the rest of the characters of the novel, including María, appear resigned to their plight, and life in Cocotá, with or without Josemar, continues at its predictable small-town pace.

Techniques

The novel consists of twelve chapters and an epilogue. Each unit shares a similar structure and is evenly balanced in the treatment of characters, actions, and themes. The montage techniques at which Puig has excelled in other novels is discarded here in favor of a more subtle, and confounding, structure. Without clear warning to the reader or markers of any sort, juxtapositions appear within each chapter, created by the three, not always distinct, principal voices of the story. Josemar is the main discursive subject of the novel and dominates the book; the second main voice belongs to an anonymous third person narrator, and the third belongs to Josemar's discursive partner.

The third person narrator fills in highly subjective and critical "factual" details about Josemar but does not display either omniscience or control. In fact, this voice sounds much like Josemar's; the narrator is full of doubt and often interrupts his own discourse seeking information and approval from an unidentified and invisible interlocutor through questions such as "right?" "is that clear?" "do you understand?"

Aside from Josemar and the narrator, there is a second voice, perhaps not always the same, but always in the dual role of witness and interrogator. At times, but not always, it is clear that the voice belongs to María da Gloria. Through her distant and reproachful (yet pointed) questions, she sometimes assists Josemar in the production of a version of the events surrounding the seduction; at other times, she contradicts him and deflates his tale by creating her own. In these passages, there is no mimetic dialogue. She delivers her question, more a dare than a doubt, and Josemar or the narrator scrambles to incorporate her query into a new (re)vision of the truth.

Puig is especially equivocal in his use of time and the progressive development of the characters and their story. While Josemar has been away from Cocotá for many years, and not in a position to know what happened during his absence, he is not deterred from refashioning information without regard for chronology or consistency. Details of the relationship between the protagonists are juxtaposed, and the present, past, and distant past are in collusion with the subjects in the creation of their conflicting versions of the truth. In theory, the characters may continue their dialogues and monologues endlessly since the fictive possibilities of their predicament are inexhaustible.

Aside from the fact that Josemar is a failure, little else about this book is really clear, since neither Josemar nor María ever authenticates any one version of what happened between them. Neither does the third person narrator. The end result then is that since the text provides no anchor, the reader is no better equipped than any of the participants in the fiction to relate the facts.

Additional Sources

Lavers, Norman. *Pop Culture into Art: The Novels of Manuel Puig.* Columbia: University of Missouri Press, 1988. A seventy-page analysis of Puig's success in integrating traditional views of "low" and "high" culture in his writing. Directed at the non-specialist, this short book relies heavily on interviews with Puig and provides brief summaries of his novels translated into English.

Kerr, Lucille. *Suspended Fictions: Reading Novels by Manuel Puig.* Urbana: University of Illinois Press, 1987. A carefully argued study of Puig's narrative techniques with particular emphasis on critical theory. Among contemporary Spanish American self-critical writers, Kerr considers Puig one of the most radical in his "desire to alter and disrupt the conventions of literature."

Clara Estow
University of Massachusetts at Boston

THOMAS PYNCHON
1937

Publishing History

Although Thomas Pynchon has published only four novels and a handful of short stories, he has earned a reputation as one of the most important writers of the twentieth century. The breadth and depth of his works would be sufficient to qualify him as a significant novelist, but Pynchon's unique contribution has been his use of scientific concepts in his fiction. Although many imaginative writers have addressed the impact of science and the scientific mentality on the modern world, few are as qualified to discuss this subject from both the artistic and the scientific perspective as Pynchon.

A student of English and engineering at Cornell, Pynchon reportedly still devours technical journals "as if they were comic books." An early short story, "Entropy" (1960), advanced one of his major themes based on scientific principle: the application to human society of the Second Law of Thermodynamics, that is, the tendency of all the energy in the universe to equalize so that there is no kinetic force left ("heat death"). Pynchon thinks that recent human history can be traced to our failure to understand the finality of this condition, to our prideful assumption that the earth's resources, even the universe, are here merely for us to use (which in practice often means "waste") and discard, producing what Pynchon calls an "addiction" to the use of energy that threatens the survival of the planet.

With his early short stories (most reprinted in the collection *Slow Learner*, 1984), Pynchon established his skill at describing a scene in detail, manipulating symbols, and constructing complex plots to support his philosophical ideas. His first novel, *V.* (1963), was a best seller and brought him instant acclaim. This *tour de force* novel blazes along from first page to last, replete with remarkable insights, stunning images, and powerful writing. With *V.* Pynchon also demonstrated a frequently overlooked talent: he is one of the funniest twentieth-century writers.

Pynchon called his second novel, *The Crying of Lot 49* (1966), a "story." This novel is generally considered his most accessible, partly because of its brevity.

In 1973, Pynchon published *Gravity's Rainbow*, an acknowledged masterpiece that advanced him to the rank of a "major twentieth-century writer." This huge book, bristling with detailed descriptive passages, ideas, allusions, symbols, jokes, and songs, follows over three hundred characters through the last days of World War II and the immediate post-war period in Europe. *Gravity's Rainbow* was highly praised by critics and became a best seller and book club selection. Few of the book's original purchasers were prepared for its complexity, however, and many complained that they could not finish it.

The critical and monetary success of *Gravity's Rainbow* ensured the financial security of the frugal Pynchon for some time. He published nothing for seventeen years except the collection of previously printed short stories, *Slow Learner*, which also contains rare personal comments on his ideas and techniques. In the early 1960s, Pynchon drew a veil of secrecy over his private life and became a mysterious figure. Finally in 1990, Pynchon published the novel *Vineland*, which became a book club selection and a best seller, perhaps mostly because of his reputation.

Critical Reception, Honors, and Popularity

Serious critical attention to Pynchon began with the appearance of his first novel, *V.*, after which his early short stories were reexamined for their thematic relationship to that work. Seldom does a first novel appear in which so many elements of the writer's craft are so fully developed; technically, it was difficult to fault. Critics, however, were disturbed by Pynchon's view of social entropy, his description of failed revolts and brutal repression, his vision of an increasingly grim future based on a past filled with disasters—all of which seemed to present an unnecessarily bleak philosophical view. Some critics attacked this as negativism; others countered that Pynchon was simply telling the truth as he saw it.

Perhaps a more telling criticism is that Pynchon does not create believable characters; everyone in the book is a grotesque. While it could be argued that such characters fit Pynchon's view that the world has gone mad, other writers who use unusual characters, such as Dickens and Faulkner, also give the reader normal characters as benchmarks or points of reference; Pynchon does not. The weirdness of Pynchon's characters in *V.* makes it difficult for the reader to penetrate the emotional world of *V.*

The suggestion that Pynchon could not create believable human characters was belied by his next novel, *The Crying of Lot 49*. The main character, Oedipa Maas, is considered his warmest creation and the character most likely to engage the reader's sympathy. *The Crying of Lot 49* may also be considered a concession to reader popularity, since it reprises Pynchon's major themes in a little over a hundred pages.

Gravity's Rainbow is such an overwhelming achievement that Pynchon's genius could no longer be denied. There was high praise for the novel, and—as an indication of its breadth—it was reviewed in *Scientific American*. The nominating committee unanimously voted to award Pynchon the Pulitzer Prize for fiction for *Gravity's Rainbow*, but the editorial board vetoed the recommendation, stating that the book was "unreadable and obscene." As a result, no Pulitzer Prize for fiction was awarded that year (1974).

Gravity's Rainbow was, however, granted the National Book Award, and the literary world was excited by the news that the reclusive Pynchon would appear at the banquet where the award would be given. "Pynchon" turned out to be comedian Professor Irwin Corey, hired by the novelist's publishers to impersonate him. The American Academy of Arts and Letters tried to award its Howells Medal to Pynchon, naming *Gravity's Rainbow* as the best novel of the decade, but Pynchon politely declined by letter.

Anything Pynchon produced after *Gravity's Rainbow* was fated to seem anticlimatic, and this has indeed been the reaction to *Vineland*, which some reviewers labelled a "potboiler." Despite these detractors, Pynchon's critical reputation continues to grow, as there are scores of books and hundreds of articles about his works and even a journal, *Pynchon Notes*, devoted exclusively to them.

Analysis of Selected Titles

V.

V., 1963, novel.

Social Concerns

Although the main action of *V.* is set in the mid-1950s, interpolated material extends the time frame back to the end of the nineteenth century, allowing Pynchon to view the entire twentieth century as a decline into decadence (the social and political equivalent of entropy). Another central feature of the novel is the opposition of the tendency toward dissolution embodied by various cabals and conspiracies—some noble, some sinister, some merely silly, but all failures. Pynchon implies that the decay has gone too far to be arrested.

Themes

The two major themes of *V.* are the tendency of twentieth-century society toward entropy (dissolution) on the one hand and conspiracy (control) on the other. Entropy, the running down of the universe through the depletion of energy, is sometimes assisted by the impact of conspiracy, as world powers maneuver to gain control of the world's resources and lines of communication.

The book begins in Norfolk, Virginia, on Christmas Eve, 1955, and initially concerns certain crew members of a U.S. Navy ship back from the Mediterranean. America's presence in the Mediterranean is dictated by its interest in the oil resources of the Middle East and the short cut to those riches, the Suez Canal. In the first of several lengthy flashbacks, the reader is returned to late nineteenth-century Egypt for a glimpse of the espionage activities of the agents of Britain and France, and others who are just available to the highest bidder. The same old imperial powers reappear for a last gasp on the world stage during the Suez crisis of 1956, also alluded to in *V*. Malta, the mid-Mediterranean transportation choke point, is the scene of much of the action, both in real time and flashback.

Another set of flashbacks to the genocidal campaign of the Germans against the native peoples of Southwest Africa in the early part of the century suggests that resources are not the issue in some cases, but that the exercise of power itself is the main feature of modern life. The oppressed fight back with conspiracies of their own, such as an effort by Venezuelan rebels to steal Botticelli's *Birth of Venus* from the Uffizi, seen in another flashback. This effort turns out to be as laughable as it sounds.

In this way Pynchon makes the reader aware that the history of the twentieth century has been, at bottom, a mad scramble for a dwindling supply of resources. Those caught up in the struggle are concerned with supply and power, not, as logic would suggest, with conservation and compassion. Those who seem oblivious to the struggle are still affected by it, as they drift along in its backwash without motivation or interest.

An important corollary theme is the replacement of human body parts by artificial devices, or, to look at it in a grimmer way, the invasion of the body by foreign objects, a change that leads to the replacement of human functions, including intelligence. This trend is amusingly and chillingly climaxed with a scene in which one of the main characters has a conversation with a robot and comes out decidedly second best. The V. of the title is a woman who gradually replaces her body parts with inanimate objects—a false leg, a jewel in the navel, and a glass eye with a watch in it. In a further branching of this theme, the body is seen as just another object which may be repaired or adjusted like a car, a tendency exemplified in a scene in which a female character gets her nose bobbed in an operation described in seat-squirming detail. In another macabre episode, a character shows a child an electrical switch implanted in his arm which, when thrown, changes his behavior, and explains that everything is an electro-magnetic phenomenon anyway. Pynchon implies through these and similar scenes that our concern with the physical universe and with science in the twentieth century has led us to think of ourselves as no more than objects, with the resultant loss of our humanity.

Another major theme, which appears in all of Pynchon's novels, is that of the questing hero. Just as the political and military powers are searching for more resources and more power, several characters are searching for evidence of conspiracies—not just conspiracies which they know to exist, but the principles behind the conspiracies. They believe that if those principles were found, they might at least bring meaning to a life which grows increasingly both more shallow and more bizarre. These personal quests turn out to be ironic, unsuccessful, and self-deceptive.

Characters

There are so many people in *V.* that it is difficult to designate a main character, but most of the action concerns three central figures: Herbert Stencil, Benny Profane, and V.

Herbert Stencil is the son of Sidney Stencil, a British agent during the turn of the century whose search for a mysterious woman named V., as described in his journals, motivates his son to continue the quest. The journal material also provides the source for the flashback sections.

The elder Stencil died at sea near Malta in 1919. Through the journals, Herbert Stencil learns that his father had tracked V. from her first appearance as a girl in Egypt not only through the previously mentioned adventures in Africa and Italy but also to Paris in 1913 where she was part of the *avant garde*. Further evidence suggests that she was present in Malta during the German bombing raids of World War II and died there, disguised as a false and seductive priest. V. may even have seduced the older Stencil, and therefore may be the younger Stencil's mother. The book ends in Malta with Stencil pursuing more leads in the search for V. Stencil seems less concerned with finding V. or the truth about her than engaging in the search.

One possibility for the conclusion of the search is that V. is not the key to understanding all the machinations of which she was a part; no meaning is revealed and the quest is pointless. Another possibility is that if Stencil were to find V. and determine what her life means, he would lose the meaning of his own life, which has been defined, as his father's was, by the quest itself. The idea that process is more important than goal is a dominant Victorian principle, and in linking the son to the father's quest, Pynchon may be suggesting, that, like the old imperial notion of glory for its own sake (i.e. rapine and slaughter without justification), the search for meaning in the twentieth century is both passé and fraudulent.

As bleak as that assessment of Stencil sounds, it is preferable to the condition of another main character, Benny Profane, a sailor from the Navy destroyer *Scaffold* who meets Stencil by chance through their mutual friendship with New Yorker Rachel Owlglass (who appears to be in love with her car). Benny accepts chaos and meaninglessness and as a result bounces through a series of relationships and jobs, including shooting alligators in the sewers of New York and tending the robots SHROUD and SHOCK. Profane describes his activities as "yo-yoing," a pointless moving from one location to another, such as riding the shuttle between Grand Central Station and Times Square for hours. One moves but really goes nowhere. In contrast to Stencil, who sees possibilities of meaning where there may be none, Profane is surrounded by associations, none of which he can pursue or even recognize—a true late twentieth-century man.

V. is seen so totally objectively, so completely from the outside, that it is difficult to think of her as a character. She appears to be more of a thing without a recognizable human personality, a condition which she tries to disguise, first by concealing her identity, then by replacing body parts with jewelry, prostheses, and mechanical devices. V. represents an alternative to Profane's reaction to twentieth-century life. Benny is buffeted by the natural objects of the world; V. retains a measure of power by attempting to become one with the natural universe.

There are a host of other characters in *V.*, each of which supplements or contrasts with the roles of the three main characters, among them Paola Maijstral (named after a Mediterranean wind which affects her birthplace, Malta), who provides a link with V.'s last known appearance; Pig Bodine, a slobbish Pan-like sailor who embraces animality with greater relish than Benny Profane; Hugh Godolphin, an associate of the elder Stencil who claims to have visited the magical land of Vheissu and thus adds another dimension to the Stencils' search for V.; Father Faring, a mad priest who ministers to the rats in the sewers of New York and whose favorite parishioner is a rodent named Veronica; and McClintic Sphere, a black jazzman suggested by the actual musicians Ornette Coleman and Eric Dolphy, who contributes one of Pynchon's few hopeful comments, "Keep cool, but care."

Techniques

Symbols abound in *V.*, starting with the title of the book, which is an abbreviation that stands for something else. It has been proposed that V stands not only for the character in the novel but for Venus (the shape of the alphabet letter suggesting erotic welcome), Vheissu, Venezuela, Veronica, or a number of other V's mentioned in the book.

The lengthy flashbacks are confusing to a reader who expects the novel to follow a more conventional form, as it is often difficult to determine who is the narrator of these sections. Usually the flashbacks are presumed to have been based on Sidney Stencil's journals, but events are described which he could not have known about and are sometimes presented from the viewpoint of another character. The first flashback, to Egypt, is written from the perspectives of eight characters. In such cases, the reader wonders whether the flashback narrator is supposed to be Sidney Stencil, a fantasizing Herbert Stencil, or Pynchon? Pynchon's pushing of the novel form past its natural narrative limits later becomes a major feature of *Gravity's Rainbow*.

Literary Precedents

With its intense attention to detail, breadth of erudition, and themes of conspiracy, paranoia, and the lone intellect questing for answers, *V.* has been compared to the novels of Vladimir Nabokov and Joseph Conrad. It can also be seen as a mutation of the spy novel genre as practiced by, for example, Eric Ambler, the exotic mystery story such as Sax Rohmer's Fu Manchu series (1913-1959), or the romantic adventure tale in the manner of Wilkie Collins's *The Moonstone* (1868), or H. Rider Haggard's *She* (1887).

THE CRYING OF LOT 49

The Crying of Lot 49, novella, 1966.

Social Concerns

In this short novel, Pynchon continues his concern with conspiracy and technological control of the society and adds a satiric dimension by setting the story in modern California. The main character yo-yos from the Bay Area to San Narciso, a stand-in for Los Angeles, where the street layout suggests to the main character the printed circuits of a transistor radio and the name suggests a city of the self-absorbed. The California backdrop gives Pynchon the opportunity to comment on substitutes for a spiritual center in modern life, from drugs to popular music.

Themes

In *The Crying of Lot 49*, Pynchon combines the themes of decay and conspiracy developed in *V.* with observations on communication theory. The main character,

Oedipa Maas, has been given the job of administering the estate of her deceased lover, Pierce Inverarity, who in addition to being a real estate tycoon, was also a stamp collector. In the course of investigating Inverarity's holdings, Oedipa uncovers a conspiracy against the postal system which dates back to the sixteenth century. The conspiracy, called Tristero, manifests itself in certain small ways such as counterfeit stamps in which the designs of official stamps are subtly changed. Members of the conspiracy deposit messages in trashcans marked "Waste," which, as Oedipa discovers, stands for "We Await Silent Tristero's Empire."

In a night journey through San Francisco, Oedipa discovers frightening signs of the existence of Tristero everywhere. She also watches a performance of an Elizabethan play, *The Courier's Tragedy* (Pynchon's hilarious parody of revenge tragedy), the director of which drowns under mysterious circumstances. This drowning suggests that Tristero, although invisible, is as alert and alive as that other invisible conspiracy which is reputed not to exist, the mafia.

There are other references to communication in the novel, such as Oedipa's husband's job as a radio disc jockey, which eventually drives him to drugs. In *V.*, the world is going to pieces, but the novel itself is intact. In *The Crying of Lot 49*, although the story is shorter and tighter than that of *V.*, the overall impression is much more unsettling; no communications can be trusted, and language itself offers not clarity but confusion. The title refers to the auction ("crying") of part of Inverarity's stamp collection ("lot 49") which Oedipa attends, fearful that Tristero agents are present but determined to find out if the conspiracy really exists. Significantly, from the standpoint of the theme of failure of communication, and ominously in terms of the plot, the novel ends just as the auctioneer is about to speak.

Characters

Oedipa Maas is generally agreed to be Pynchon's most appealing and human character. Like Herbert Stencil, Oedipa is on a quest, but Stencil's search seems rather crack-brained, and Oedipa's, although more frightening, is also more believable, because at first she thinks that she is merely doing a favor for a friend and gradually becomes drawn into Inverarity's secrets and the intrigues of Tristero. The reader identifies with Oedipa more than with the bizarre characters of *V.* because, just as Oedipa has to try to figure out the riddle of Tristero, the reader must try to piece together the meaning of *The Crying of Lot 49*. The *pieta*-like scene in which Oedipa tries to aid a derelict is one of the most powerful in Pynchon's work.

The rest of the characters are drawn from a gallery of grotesques, each of whom illuminates another facet of Pynchon's coruscating array of duplicitous and unsuccessful facades. Oedipa's husband, Mucho Maas, is a Bay Area disc jockey who thinks that his present occupation is as fraudulent as his previous job, that of used car salesman. Dr. Hilarius, Oedipa's psychiatrist, demonstrates his inability to help her by going mad himself. Randolph Driblette, the director of *The Courier's Tragedy* is reported to have committed suicide, but it is likely that he was dispatched by agents of Tristero who thought that his production of the play revealed too much. Stanley Koteks, an employee of the Yoyodyne Corporation, which Inverarity helped to organize, complains to Oedipa about the way this impersonal industrial giant cheats and uses its employees. Mike Fallopian is a member of the reactionary Peter Pinguid Society which opposes the greed and dehumanization of Yoyodyne and is a more ideological paradigm of Tristero. Metzger, the lawyer whom Oedipa meets in San Narciso, used to be a child actor named Baby Igor; Metzger's friend Manny di Presso (manic depressive—like Oedipa's own name, a joke on psychoanalysis) is an actor who used to be a lawyer.

In the light of all this confusion, mistrust, and shifting identity, it is not surprising that the rock group, which Oedipa meets is named The Paranoids. Dead when the novel begins but presiding over all of the novel, as does the absent Mrs. Newsome in James' *The Ambassadors*, is the mysterious figure of Pierce Inverarity, who, when alive, called Oedipa on the phone and used different voices; the last one was radio's Lamont Cranston, "The Shadow."

Techniques

Although *The Crying of Lot 49* is filled with Pynchon's usual mind-boggling accumulation of details, apparent digressions, and zany characters, it is also the most conventionally organized of his novels, since everything is seen from the third person limited viewpoint of Oedipa Maas. In Pynchon's other novels, it is often difficult to determine who is telling the story, and one often must assume that Pynchon himself is addressing the reader directly. Perhaps this traditional form is a result of Pynchon's originally having conceived of this book as a long story, since his short stories are tighter in form and easier to comprehend than his novels.

Literary Precedents

Besides the kinds of mystery and detective story parallels noted under *V.* above, *The Crying of Lot 49* also shares points of contact with the revenge tragedy form so beloved of Elizabethan dramatists, but with an interesting twist; in the novel, the machinations of the revengers are vaguely glimpsed by the victim, unlike the point of view of the original dramas, in which the audience was allowed to see the plotters plan their attacks. The two poles of the revenge tragedy come together when Oedipa views *The Courier's Tragedy*, Pynchon's parody on the revenge form, so that the effect on the reader of the novel is both laugh-provoking and chilling.

Two other parallels are not strictly literary: one is artistic and literary, the other scientific. Oedipa remembers seeing a painting (which actually exists) by the Spanish artist Remedios Varo of girls imprisoned in towers letting down their long golden hair like Rapunzel of the fairy tale. This image suggests the position of Oedipa herself, trapped and trying to understand the meaning of a creepy, märchen-like world. The other parallel is the scientific hypothesis of Maxwell's Demon, which Stanley Koteks explains to Oedipa. The "demon," as first posited by nineteenth-century British Scotch physicist James Clerk Maxwell, sits and sorts randomly moving molecules into slower and faster groups, thus defeating entropy without doing work. Critics with a scientific bent have pointed to the elaborate discussion of this idea and its application to communication theory in *Lot 49* as an indication that Pynchon may not be as pessimistic as is generally assumed.

GRAVITY'S RAINBOW

Gravity's Rainbow, novel, 1973.

Social Concerns

Pynchon sets *Gravity's Rainbow* in the midst of the most obviously mad scene of the twentieth century—World War II. But his intent is less obvious than that of most novelists who use this background. From the rationalist perspective, all war is a consequence of a breakdown in reason, and World War II—the greatest slaughter in history and the worst case yet of such a collapse—is a warning for future generations. From the moralist perspective, World War II may be considered a victory of the forces of light against the forces of darkness, the popular democracies which believe in the dignity and freedom of the individual (with the perplexing exception of the Soviet Union, of course) against a robotic, enslaving fascist nightmare of the soul.

To Pynchon, such views of the conflict are sophomoric. World War II is neither a collapse nor a triumph but just the bloodiest episode in the ongoing, centuries-old struggle for resources and power. To defuse the rationalist argument regarding the war, Pynchon gives the reader scientist villains on both sides of the conflict:

the Allies specialize in social scientist scoundrels, the Axis in natural scientist fiends—all of whom are concerned with mastery over the earth and its inhabitants, a mastery demonstrated by the power to destroy.

To disarm the moralists, Pynchon begins *Gravity's Rainbow* near the end of the war when its outcome was no longer in doubt and refers only briefly or not at all to the spectacular events that marked its close—the Normandy invasion, the Battle of the Bulge, the drive for Berlin, and the use of the atomic bomb. This focus deletes from the novel the high drama presaging glorious victory. Much of the novel takes place after the defeat of Hitler but before the fall of Japan in "the Zone" (occupied Germany, the capitulation of which is not even described). The machinations and intrigues which, in the first part of the book, seemed associated with the war effort, continue without stint, indicating that the war was only an eruption onto the world military stage of an ongoing contest, which had been going on before, and more ominously, continues.

Themes

The themes of Pynchon's stories and first two novels reappear more elaborately in *Gravity's Rainbow*. The rapid, mindless depletion of the earth's resources, hastening the process of entropy, is what the war was about, rather than ideology or morality. The war ended certain governments and eliminated certain leaders, but entropic decay goes on. Pynchon steps outside the framework of the war at one point to assert directly that living in the last half of the twentieth century (being a part of what Pynchon calls "The System") is like being a passenger on a bus (consuming petrochemicals, of course) driven by a madman bent on self annihilation and thereby, that of those who ride with him. The most frightening part of this simile is that one is only a passenger on the bus; the individual is powerless to stop the destruction even if he or she can understand its meaning.

Conspiracies and the fruit of conspiracies, the manipulation of other people, also abound on both sides of the fighting lines, and, for that matter, reach across them. The behavior of one of the main characters is finally discovered to have been shaped when he was a baby by social scientists on both sides of the Atlantic, partially as a result of the interests of I.G. Farben, a huge industrial cartel, which Pynchon regards as the real power in prewar and wartime Germany, even more powerful than the Nazis. The Herero tribesmen of Southwest Africa, victims of the German genocide described in *V.*, reappear as part of a cabal within the nation that attempted to exterminate them. Most of the characters on the Allied side are connected with the White Visitation office, home of PISCES (Psychological Intelligence Schemes for Expediting Surrender), a sort of psychic Office of Strategic Services at which the schemes often become ends in themselves and their aim, surrender, refers not to the Axis but to the mind and spirit of anyone who might fall into PISCES's web. The conspiracies and counter-conspiracies interpenetrate in dizzying fashion. Most of these schemes also involve Pynchon's familiar quest pattern as well.

Two more minor themes of Pynchon's first two novels become major themes in *Gravity's Rainbow*. Calvinist theology maintains that though all men are damned through the sin of Adam, some—the elect—are saved through the grace of God, and others—the preterite—are simply damned, and nothing can be done about this condition. Pynchon sees this view of God as horrifying and leading to the excesses of modern society, since a further corollary of this theology is that God rewards the elect during this life with the riches of this world. This rationale justifies greed and self-aggrandizement and makes it easier to exploit the poor and powerless through the assumption that, since they are not rewarded with worldly goods and status, they must be part of the preterite damned and therefore of no consequence. (Max Weber presents this analysis in his *The Protestant Ethic and the Spirit of Capitalism*, an important influence on Pynchon.)

Like Blake's Satan, Pynchon stands with and for the preterite in their hopeless struggle against a pompous, uncaring God. The political parallel to this conflict is the continual defeat of the underclass by the military-industrial-technological juggernaut, designed to fulfill the needs of the self-satisfied elect. The story of Rapunzel is an analogue for *The Crying of Lot 49*, and in *Gravity's Rainbow* some critics have found a parallel for the main storyline in the fairy tale Hansel and Gretel; but true to Pynchon's bleak view, in this version the witch wins.

Much of the book concerns the search for the location and purpose of the V-2 rocket 00000, which, near the book's conclusion, an evil scientist launches toward the north pole. Inside the rocket is his lover, a young boy, who becomes the Hansel inside the "oven" of this modern fairy tale. This episode also shows what happens when loving human emotions, as expressed in sexuality, become subsumed in the drive to power, and destruction is substituted for sexual climax.

The inverted fairy tale motif is itself part of a Pynchon's larger message that the familiar, comforting view of ordinary reality is no more than a facade, and that at any moment one may be plunged into a larger reality, that of horror and destruction.

Characters

There are hundreds of characters in *Gravity's Rainbow*, but most of the action of the novel revolves about the adventures of two main characters, American Lieutenant Tyrone Slothrop and German Major Weissmann, also known as Blicero, a German nickname for death. The paths of the two characters move towards each other as Weissmann builds rocket 00000, and Slothrop tries to find its meaning and location.

Tyrone Slothrop is a New Englander with Puritan forebears (characteristics he shares with Pynchon) who comes to the attention of workers at the White Visitation because the locations of his sexual conquests coincide with the later arrival of a V-2 rocket. His superiors, particularly Major Pointsman, want to discover if Slothrop has some psychic control over the rockets. Much later the reader learns that Slothrop, while an infant, was the subject of an experiment, based on the theories of the German social scientist Laszlo Jampf and using the synthetic plastic Imoplex-G, to produce in baby Slothrop an erection. Imoplex-G is also used to make V-2 rockets. Although the exact relationship is never completely explained (like most other elements in Pynchon's writings), it appears that Slothrop's organ is guiding the rockets to their targets.

Slothrop is a blend of *V.*'s Herbert Stencil and Benny Profane, since, like Stencil, he is on a quest but, like Profane, seems to drift into it. Near the end of the novel, Pynchon (or his narrative voice) states that Slothrop has faded out, disappeared and spread over the landscape. This fate is not as grim as it might sound; Slothrop's transformation resembles that of the Egyptian god Osiris, who was scattered into pieces but later reborn. (At one point in the novel Slothrop sails on the ship *Anubis*, named after another Egyptian god.)

Major Weissmann is a mad scientist out of the Doctor Frankenstein and Hollywood B movie tradition, a popular culture element which Pynchon specifically invokes. His principal aide is the Dutch spy Katje Borgesius, who penetrates the White Visitation itself. Much of the last half of the novel concerns the efforts of various characters to locate, assist, or thwart him, but rocket 00000 is launched with its human cargo, a representative of the preterite or the whole hapless human race. Like Slothrop, Weissmann also disappears at the end of the novel, but not entirely; Pynchon's narrative voice notes ominously that he is somewhere in the United States, suggesting that the American military-industrial complex has picked up the torch fallen from the hands of the Germans; although, as previously noted, no nation has a monopoly on madness, which is a basic human quality.

Here are a few of the characters who populate the novel's many sub-plots: Doctor Edward Pointsman manipulates Slothrop and tries to discover the secret of the American's connection with the rain of V-2 rockets; Roger Mexico, a worker at PISCES who is Pynchon's most sympathetic character after Oedipa Maas, falls in love with British girl Jessica Swanlake but loses her to a cloddish Briton when the war ends; Franz Pökler, a technician at the V-2 rocket works, loses his wife

Leni and their daughter Isle to a concentration camp, but the Nazis keep him at his task by allowing him to see his daughter (or a girl resembling her) once a year, a variation of the Persephone myth; Enzian, an African allied with Weissmann who tries to stop a group of Herero tribesman from launching a rocket of their own, is opposed by his half-brother, the Russian spy Tchitcherine. Although these last two are bent on destroying each other, in typically Pynchonian fashion, when they meet they pass without recognition.

Techniques

Symbolism is richer in *Gravity's Rainbow* than in Pynchon's other novels, all of it coming together around the image of the V-2 rocket, the German weapon against which there was no defense, and analogous to the American apocalyptic threat of the atomic bomb. All of the themes, characters, and episodes of the novel coalesce around the frightening missile, which is simultaneously a symbol of science and technology triumphant; reason has utterly fled, since the device has no purpose but mass destruction. At the end of the book, Pynchon tightens the screw by not merely giving the reader a questing main character to identify with, but by placing the reader in the novel as part of an audience in a theater waiting while the rocket descends on their helpless heads.

Aside from the central symbol of the V-2, the book is also organized around such symbolic systems as the zodiac, the Christian calendar of holy days and feasts, the Tarot, Talmudic and Kabbalistic tradition, and a panoply of mythologies, notably Egyptian, Greek, and Norse.

In his earlier novels Pynchon used techniques and described action which were both vulgar and obscene, and in *Gravity's Rainbow* this element is heightened. On the same page, one may encounter a reference to Teutonic legend, a bad Hollywood cowboy movie, a song sung by one of the characters (interpolated lyrics, familiar in Pynchon since *V.*, appear more frequently in *Gravity's Rainbow*) and a Leon Schlesinger cartoon, appearing in the midst of a chase scene resembling one from an Abbott and Costello film. Pynchon does not intend the low comic and popular culture features as relief from or even ironic comment on the more serious action. To Pynchon, all the action is both serious and comic, tragic and bathetic, high and low at once, just like human life itself. His mind is like an encyclopedia thrown in a Los Angeles trashcan which is then tumbled through a sewer and hurled around in a cyclotron. Sparing the reader nothing, Pynchon also includes a coprophagous scene and a clinical description of a castration (performed on the wrong person, of course) which echoes the nose job of *V.*. These episodes are presumably the sections of the novel which cost Pynchon the Pulitzer Prize.

The Pulitzer Prize was also denied on the basis of "unreadability." Aside from its sheer density of detail, *Gravity's Rainbow* is unreadable to some because of another of Pynchon's techniques which appears in *V.* and becomes a major organizing principle in *Gravity's Rainbow*. An episode begins with definite characters, setting, and point of view, but digressions lead to further digressions until the digressions have become another episode with different characters and settings and with an undetermined point of view. Often the reader must conclude that the point of view is that of Pynchon himself and that the reader is no longer "reading a novel" with the conventional expectations of what that experience involves, but directly engaged with the mind, ideas, and fantasies of Thomas Pynchon. Once the reader realizes that this is what is happening, the effect is frightening, unsettling, titillating, exciting, and funny—rather like watching a horror movie such as *King Kong*, one of Pynchon's favorites. Traditional imaginative literature often attempts to refine the reader's sense of reality by allowing him or her to observe a fantasy; Pynchon changes the reader's reality by overwhelming the reader and dragging him or her into a one-on-one confrontation with genius.

Literary Precedents

As noted, *Gravity's Rainbow*'s precedents include comic books, cartoons, and bad movies as well as literature, but it is a measure of the novel's greatness that it is most frequently compared with James Joyce's *Ulysses* (1922), another landmark of twentieth-century literature. Pynchon's novel shares with Joyce's the quantities of intricate detail, symbolic complexity, and philosophical profundity. The gloomy atmosphere and symbolic overlay of the novel have been compared to the works of T. S. Eliot. Critics also compare Pynchon's work to that of Herman Melville, particularly *Moby-Dick* (1851), since Slothrop's search for rocket 00000 resembles an ironic version of Ahab's quest for the white whale, and the many disguises Slothrop adopts are like those of the main character of Melville's *The Confidence Man: His Masquerade* (1857). Melville's sour philosophical position coupled with a volatile imagination also resemble that of Pynchon.

VINELAND

Vineland, novel, 1990.

Social Concerns

Vineland is set in California in 1984, and the setting is a clue to Pynchon's intentions. Although 1984 is in the past, for the post-World War II generation that year represented the future because of the political associations with George Orwell's novel. Most of the characters are survivors of the social changes and political upheavals of the 1960s, and the term "survivors" has a positive connotation in the novel. The characters have been strengthened by their experiences during this turbulent era, and *Vineland* is by far Pynchon's most hopeful work.

Themes

In *Vineland*, Pynchon again uses the themes of entropy, conspiracy, and the quest. The title of the book is a reminder that the new world, discovered by Leif Erickson long before Columbus, was Vinland—a green land, rich in natural resources. That land has now been replaced with freeways, industrial parks, and shopping malls. Where people used to look with wonder at a fecund natural world (still present in Northern California, where much of the action takes place in a town called Vineland), they now look at television. Not only do the characters in *Vineland* spend a lot more time looking at television than in Pynchon's other books, but often they seem to be acting out a life they have seen on television. Since they do have the option of turning the thing off, what happens to them as a result of watching television is as much their fault as that of those who would control them.

When Pynchon describes such programs as a made-for-TV movie about an actual playoff series between the Boston Celtics and the Los Angeles Lakers, one wonders not only where sports end and entertainment begins but where television ends and reality begins. Or does television ever end? For many people, life is a TV movie. *Vineland* features Pynchon's usual lineup of sinister conspiracies, such as the technological cartel Chipco (suggesting the importance of information) and the United States government. Pynchon suggests that television is another kind of conspiracy, not of the evil and power-hungry, but of the dumb and exploitative. Television is silly but fascinating, a combination that undermines perception and intellect.

Continued exposure to television is so debilitating that one of the characters has escaped from a tubal detoxification center where clinicians labored to free his mind from the grip of the electronic device. With details like this, Pynchon proposes an inversion of conventional wisdom of the type so beloved in the sixties; the drug which does the most damage to the individual mind and spirit is modern life itself and the agencies that keep it humming—television, advertising, the mercantile system, and the government. Illegal drugs are a refuge from this kind of life and offer fleeting solace. For this reason they really are a threat to the American lifestyle, but for social and economic reasons, not the health and psychological reasons officially stated. By "illegal drugs," however, Pynchon usually means only marijuana, the biggest cash crop in the region in which the story is set and a constant feature of the narrative (one of the characters is named Weed Atman).

Just as in *V.*, the quest in this novel is for a mysterious female figure, and, as in *The Crying of Lot 49*, the searcher is a woman. The unifying element of the plot is Prairie Wheeler's search for her mother, Frenesi Gates, who holds the key to Prairie's past and many of the mysteries of the story. As in *V.*, the quest involves a child trying to find its parent (V. may be Herbert Stencil's mother), but the darkness and sense of dread are missing from this attempt.

Critics have often noted that in his first three novels Pynchon's characters are extreme loners, unconnected to the world. In *Vineland*, people not only have families, but there is a definite sense of community, of resistance to the banality and madness of contemporary life. Even if the resistance does not succeed, things are brighter because those who protest, Pynchon suggests, at least have each other.

Characters
Most of the action of *Vineland* involves the family of Zoyd Wheeler, who lives near the town of Vineland and collects mental disability checks. He demonstrates his qualifications for the aid annually by jumping through the plate glass windows of a local bar. Zoyd has a daughter, Prairie, whose mother, Frenesi Gates, began life as the socially conscious daughter of an Old Left Wobbly family and during the sixties became a radical film maker. Frenesi's life was turned around by the novel's villain, Brock Vond, a federal prosecutor who forced Frenesi to become a sting operative for the Federal Bureau of Investigation. At the beginning of the novel, Frenesi's whereabouts are unknown, and her future is cloudy because the Reagan administration's budget cutbacks have caused her job to be eliminated.

Vond is trying to find Prairie so he can use her to influence his former lover, Frenesi. Prairie, while trying to stay away from Vond, searches for her mother and encounters such people as D. L. Chastain, a female friend of her mother from the past. The gangster Ralph Wayvone once hired D. L. to kill Brock Vond by means of an oriental technique, the "vibrating palm," which causes the victim to die one year after it has been applied. The wily Vond, however, causes D. L. to use this death grip on Japanese detective Takeshi Fumimota instead of himself.

Prairie eventually discovers the truth about her mother's past and the novel reaches a spectacular conclusion which also features a group of the undead called the Thanatoids. The plot is confusing and wacky and obviously more fun than Pynchon's other novels.

Techniques

Pynchon uses all of his familiar techniques in *Vineland*, including linked digressions, but the main line of the narrative is easier to follow than in any of Pynchon's novels except *The Crying of Lot 49*. Symbolism and elaborate plot structure are less prominent in this novel and the many references to contemporary life keep the focus satirical rather than archly literary.

Literary Precedents

For once Pynchon seems to have read and drawn from his literary contemporaries instead of basing his novel on classic works, mythologies, and popular culture sources. The first third of the novel, which establishes the setting and characters, is similar to the satiric novels of Tom Robbins, in presenting an array of strange, grotesque but emotionally warm characters. In suggesting the importance of a family-like group (such as the hippie communities of the sixties) as a refuge against the insanity of contemporary life, Pynchon shares the values of Kurt Vonnegut. It has often been suggested that Vonnegut is producing a popularized and more easily understandable version of Pynchon's worldview.

Additional Sources

Fowler, Douglas. *A Reader's Guide to Gravity's Rainbow*. Ann Arbor, MI: Ardis, 1980. Like Steven Weisenburger's book (see below), this volume takes the reader through *Gravity's Rainbow* page by page, explaining its references. It also contains lengthy critical essays on the meaning of the entire novel.

Levine, George, and David Leverenz, eds. *Mindful Pleasures: Essays on Thomas Pynchon*. Boston: Little, Brown, 1976. A collection of essays on all of Pynchon's novels except *Vineland*. Contains informative essays by Richard Poirier, Tony Tanner, W. T. Lhamon, Jr., and Matthew Winston, as well as a bibliography.

Mendelson, Edward. "Levity's Rainbow." *New Republic* 203 (July 9 & 16, 1990) 40-46. A lengthy review of *Vineland* which helps to place it in the context of Pynchon's earlier writings.

―――, ed. *Pynchon: A Collection of Critical Essays*. Englewood Cliffs, NJ: Prentice-Hall, 1978. A critical anthology with essays on all of Pynchon's novels except *Vineland*, including works by Tony Tanner, Edward Mendelson, and Robert Sklar.

Newman, Robert D. *Understanding Thomas Pynchon*. Columbia: University of South Carolina Press, 1986. An excellent short introduction to Pynchon's work with an annotated bibliography.

Pearce, Richard. *Critical Essays on Thomas Pynchon*. Boston, G. K. Hall, 1981. This collection is aimed at the literary scholar and contains an article assessing Pynchon criticism.

Pynchon Notes. A journal devoted to Pynchon's works published by the English Department of Wesleyan University, Middletown, Connecticut.

Slade, Joseph W. *Thomas Pynchon*. New York: Warner, 1974. This is the first full length study of Pynchon's works (except for *Vineland*) and is therefore designed as an introduction. A good place for the beginning researcher to start.

Tanner, Tony. *Thomas Pynchon*. London, Methuen, 1982. This survey of Pynchon's work to 1982 is by one of the most intelligent and readable critics of twentieth-century literature and is recommended for general audiences.

Weisenburger, Steven. *A Gravity's Rainbow Companion: Sources and Contexts for Pynchon's Novel*. Athens: University of Georgia Press, 1988. This book offers page-by-page explanations of Pynchon's references and allusions in *Gravity's Rainbow*. It also contains a bibliography of works useful in understanding the novel.

Jim Baird
University of North Texas

ISHMAEL REED
1938

Publishing History

"I don't mince words. Nor do I pull any punches, and though I've delivered some low blows over the years, I'm becoming more accurate, and my punches are regularly landing above the waistline. I'm not a body snatcher like Mike McCallum, and I usually aim for the head." For Ishmael Reed, "writing is fighting," and his publishing career consists of thirty-nine years of "boxing on paper." The boxing analogy works well for Reed's fiction. With quick, sharp satiric jabs, Reed circles and pokes at his opponents, often angering and enraging them in the process. And who are his opponents? Semiotician Robert Scholes claims, "whoever called him Ishmael picked the right name. His hand is against every man's and every woman's, too . . . . He is a black Juvenal."

Reed developed his pungent writing style early. He dates his first commissioned work to 1952, when his mother asked him to write a birthday poem for one of her fellow employees. A year later, at age 14, he was writing a jazz column for *The Empire Star Weekly*. After leaving the University of Buffalo because of a shortage of funds, Reed moved to New York City in 1962. Reed's New York period was crucial in his evolution as an artist. He co-founded *The East Village Other*, the first of the nonconventional newspapers to gain a national audience; he became a member of the Umbra Workshop, a black writers group that, Reed believes, "began the inflorescence of black poetry as well as many other recent Afro-American styles of writing." He separated from his wife; and, in 1965 and 1966, he wrote his first novel, *The Free-Lance Pallbearers*.

Reed left New York before the book came out because, he says, he wanted to make it on the merit of the book, "and not on the merit of playing tennis with George Plimpton or being at Town Hall with some liberal." Reed moved to Berkeley to avoid becoming literature's "token darkie." While the novel was fairly well received, its publication began what was to be a stormy relationship with literary critics.

Mumbo Jumbo (1972), Reed's third novel, was his most critically acclaimed and widely reviewed novel. Houston Baker, Jr., called *Mumbo Jumbo* "the first Black American novel of the last ten years that gives one a sense of the broader vision and the careful, painful, and laborious 'fundamental brainwork' that are needed if we are to define the eternal dilemma of the Black Arts and fruitfully work toward its melioration . . . . [The novel's] overall effect is that of amazing talent and flourishing genius." *Mumbo Jumbo* is generally acknowledged as Reed's supreme achievement to date.

Critical Reception, Honors, and Popularity

To say Reed's critical reception has been mixed would be a gross understatement. Reed maintains a sense of humor about the situation, however. *Mumbo Jumbo*'s dust jacket proclaims that the work of Ishmael Reed is a "laying on of hands" for American writing, "uniting divergent factions." There follows a list of negative comments about Reed's work, ranging from "propaganda" by the *New York Times* and "cute" by *The Writer* to "Unlike other young black novelists whose work I did praise, Mr. Reed has not yet written a book worth taking seriously," by Irving Howe in *Harper's* and, "This is diarrhea of the typewriter," by Kirkus Service. While Reed does have his supporters, most notably Henry Louis Gates, Jr., the ongoing battle between Reed and his critics has inspired an entire book, Reginald Martin's *Ishmael Reed and the New Black Aesthetic Critics*.

In spite of his mixed critical reception, Reed has been formally recognized by the literary establishment. In 1973 he became the only writer to be nominated for the National Book Award in both poetry and fiction. That same year he was also nominated for the Pulitzer Prize in poetry for *Conjure*. In 1974 he received a National Endowment fellowship for creative writing and a year later, a Guggenheim Memorial Foundation Award for fiction. Widespread popular acceptance, however, has not been forthcoming. As is often the case with satirists, Reed's readership must bring a certain knowledge to the work in order to understand what is being satirized. This has been a problem. Reed's lawyer-agent Ellis Freedman has been quoted as saying Reed does not sell large quantities of books because "he writes for a limited kind of audience." His one-time editor at Random House, Anne Freedgood, says, "It's not easy reading. You have to concentrate, pay attention."

Whatever the reason for his lack of popular success, Reed's books are all still in print, and he has remained a force in American literature. In the opening essay of his book *Writin' is Fightin': Thirty-seven Years of Boxing on Paper*, Reed writes, "The late Hoyt Fuller was right when he said that for one published Ishmael Reed, there are dozens of talented writers in the ghettos and elsewhere, who remain unpublished. And having lasted this long, I've been able to witness the sad demise of a lot of 'tokens' who believed what their literary managers told them, who believed that they were indeed unique and unusual."

Analysis of Selected Titles

THE FREE-LANCE PALLBEARERS

The Free-Lance Pallbearers, 1967, novel.

Social Concerns/Themes

Reed's first novel contains a myriad of stances and positions, all wrapped in a satiric, parodic narrative. Reed develops several themes in *The Free-Lance Pallbearers*, including an examination of what Reginald Martin calls the "oppressive, stress-filled, Western/European/Christian tradition." Other themes include a parody of the autobiographical style of earlier African-American narratives and an examination of the different strata in the black community, especially different kinds of black leaders. Random targets of Reed's satire are the academic community, the debate over the nature and purpose of art, and the American political system.

Nothing, it seems, and no one is safe from Reed's satirical barbs. The black community's various attempts to find a leader to rally behind, for example, are spoofed by the inclusion of a capricious black nationalist character who teaches purity but secretly eats pork, and black ministers who, beneath the piety, run numbers rackets and "sell reefer."

Linking the different parodies together is narrator Bukka Doopeyduk, an articulate, naive young black man who appears to favor assimilation and integration at the beginning of the book:

> "...it behooves me to start at the bottom and work my way up the ladder. Temperance, frugality, thrift—that kind of thing."

He later moves to more of an activist position:

> NOW I WAS DA ONE. NOW NOT ONLY WOULD I BE THE NAZARENE BISHOP WHICH WAS AFTER ALL PEANUTS, BUT I WAS GOING TO RUN THE WHOLE KIT AND KABOODLE. ME DICTATOR OF BUKKA DOOPEYDUK.

Ultimately, Doopeyduk is satirizing assimilated blacks and corrupt black militants.

Characters

Reed's characters in *The Free-Lance Pallbearers* are symbolic representations of the particular issue he is satirizing. At times, the issue/character is gently rendered,

Ishmael Reed

as with Doopeyduk. His naiveté and trusting nature make his early foibles easier to swallow, and the reader ends up feeling more sorry for Doopeyduk—and his real-life counterparts—than anything else. Much more often, however, Reed's characters are used to savagely attack what Reed sees as falsity and corruption. The "attack" characters' actions provide the novel with much of its vicious humor and relevancy.

Reed's critical views toward black leaders, for example, are portrayed by Elijah Raven, the muslim/black nationalist whose ideas of cultural and racial separation in the United States are contradicted by his actions again and again:

> "You'd better get on the right side, brother, because when the deal goes down, all backsliding uncle toms are going to . . . get it in the neck, Doopeyduk," Elijah scowled, moving his finger across his neck . . . revealing cufflinks . . . on which were engraved: "To Elijah from Sargent Shriver."

Other negative black characters are Eclair Porkchop, the minister and people's advocate who is later found having sexual relations with HARRY SAM, and the Free-Lance Pallbearers of the title, who allow their leaders to be killed and only arrive to bury and venerate the corpse. It is black leaders in general, though, who are the hardest hit by Reed's satirical punches:

> The leaders of the blacks . . . mounted the circuitous steps leading to SAM's assuring the boss dat: "Wasn't us, boss. 'Twas Stokely and Malcolm. Not us, boss. No indeed. We put dat ad in da *Times* repudiating dem, boss. 'Member, boss? You saw da ad, didn't you, boss? Look, boss. We can prove it to you, dat we loves you. Would you like for us to cook up some strange recipes for ya boss? Or tell some jokes? Did you hear the one about da nigger in da woodpile? Well, seems dere was this nigger, boss . . . ."

While Reed is highly critical of certain types of blacks, he certainly does not let the white power structure escape unharmed. Throughout the novel, most of the white characters are mired in a world of excrement: HARRY SAM, the chief power figure, has been in the "john" for thirty years, and he lives in a house surrounded by a moat filled with human waste; and Doopeyduk's mentor at Harry Sam College, U2 Polyglot, is first introduced as he is preparing a paper for an English literary quarterly entitled "The Egyptian Dung Beetle in Kafka's *Meta-*

morphosis." Doopeyduk finds Polyglot pushing a "light ball of excrement" around his office by the tip of his nose.

Bukka Doopeyduk is virtually the only character who is treated sympathetically by Reed. Doopeyduk suffers his lazy, hostile wife gladly, becomes humiliated as the star of a performance art exhibit, and pursues his spiritual Nazarene growth until he actually meets SAM and becomes disillusioned. Since his primary duty as an orderly is to empty bedpans filled with excrement, he is thereby initially aligned with the white characters. His slow transformation from obedient Nazarene apprentice to power-hungry black leader forms the narrative of the novel.

Techniques/Literary Precedents

"One of the problems with mono-ethnic critics approaching my work is that they don't know the full scope of the traditions I'm drawing upon," says Reed; "As I learn more and more about differing cultures in this country, the gap between my work and the viewpoint of some critics—especially those in the northeast—widens, and the critics become very frustrated. They call my style idiosyncratic; yet my style is older than the European tradition." While using that "old" style, Reed draws on sources ranging from Egyptian mythology to Caribbean voodoo to American black folklore to create his fiction.

Reed often uses phonetic spellings instead of standard spellings, capitalization for emphasis, and uses news flashes and radio voice-overs to comment on the book's action. The effect is a narrative that reads much like a motion picture or television show. The pacing and flow are very reminiscent of the way the media communicates its ideas.

MUMBO JUMBO

Mumbo Jumbo, 1972, novel.

Social Concerns/Themes

At its heart, *Mumbo Jumbo* is a struggle between the Judeo-Christian Ethic and what Reed calls the Neo-HooDoo Aesthetic. The catalyst for the struggle is a mysterious "anti-plague" called "Jes Grew," a "disease" that forces its "victims" to dance and let their inhibitions go. Since the Neo-HooDoo Faction feels "laughter washes the heart," they are excited and supportive of Jes Grew, whereas the secret society attempting to subdue the plague, the Knights Templar, is aligned with the Wallflower Order. They are intent on stopping Jes Grew before it gets to New York City.

Reed, as he has in other books, sprays his satirical buckshot far and wide, and there are many victims. Black nationalists again are perceived as being hypocritical and contradictory. In a 1974 interview Reed said,

> Some of the people who call themselves nationalists and revolutionaries are your worst enemies because, in many ways, they're sicker than the mainline critic who's a superficial expert on blackness. You get those blacks who feel that just because you're the same skin color . . . shit! Most of the time I'm cherry red. I'm beginning to see why black writers flee this country.

Reflecting this viewpoint, Reed created Abdul Hamid, the nationalist in *Mumbo Jumbo*. Hamid adjusts his wordplay depending on the audience he addresses, and is accused of "censorship to the very last. He took it upon himself to decide what writing should be viewed by black people."

The overriding theme of the novel is that prominent blacks are used by whites to achieve whites' hidden agenda. Many of the white characters attempt to manipulate black characters in order to stop Jes Grew. The white characters' primary aim is to get their dogma espoused by having black authority figures speak to other blacks. The "Talking Android" (a black figure used to "work within the Negro . . . to drive [Jes Grew] out, categorize it analyze it expel it slay it, blot Jes Grew.") is one way whites speak "through" blacks in *Mumbo Jumbo*. By using this theme, Reed not only exposes the white power structure, but condemns black leaders at the same time.

Mumbo Jumbo also seeks to show how history has been manipulated and revised by the white power structure. Reed spends a lot of time talking about the 1915 U.S. invasion of Haiti, and the efforts of the Atonists—Reed's term for defenders of the Judeo-Christian ethic—to suppress knowledge of the occupation. At the climax of the book is an extended retelling of the legend of ancient Egyptians Osiris and Set, a story that began "1000s of years ago in Egypt." The two brothers quarrelled over whether the Egyptians should dance and enjoy life, the Osiran view, or whether they should be modest and temperate as Set wished. Set won the battle, but Osiris was able to put his dances and rituals in a book, The Book of Thoth, that became the Text that the competing characters in *Mumbo Jumbo* seek to either reclaim or destroy.

The common historical omission of ancient Egyptian civilization as an important society is demonstrated by Reed when, as he finishes the Osiran section of the novel, he has a black character denounce it all. Reed makes it clear, as the character insists "serious works . . . began in Greece," that the effect of the historical omission is that blacks do not invest as much value in their own African-Egyptian history as they do in the "western" civilization popularly accredited to ancient Athens.

Characters

Mumbo Jumbo is a book with a great many characters. Some, like President Warren Harding and James Weldon Johnson, are actual historical figures. The overwhelming majority of characters are fictional, and two characters are at its center. The hero is PaPa LaBas, a HooDoo detective who, with his colleague Black Herman, tries to uncover the origins of Jes Grew and devise ways to keep the "anti-plague" alive. LaBas and Black Herman use conjuring, exorcising and healing in their work, and as a result, LaBas' critics call his headquarters Mumbo Jumbo Kathedral. Critic Henry Louis Gates, Jr. claims PaPa LaBas is "the chief detective in hard-and-fast pursuit of both Jes Grew and its Text. LaBas is the Afro-American trickster figure from black sacred tradition. His surname, of course, is French for 'over there,' and his presence unites 'over there' (Africa) with 'right here.' He is indeed the messenger of the gods, the divine Pan-African interpreter, pursuing, in the language of the text, 'The Work,' which is not only *Vaudou* but also the very work (and play) of art itself."

The other central character is Hincle Von Vampton. Von Vampton lives in a house called "Spiraling Agony," and is pursuing The Book of Thoth in order to destroy Jes Grew before it gets to New York. Von Vampton and his colleague, Herbert "Safecracker" Gould, manipulate naive, rural blacks, and those they cannot manipulate they steal from and misrepresent their writings. These two characters appear to represent the white power structure that carries out the practice of revising history and stealing from black culture. "Safecracker" Gould, throughout the novel, eavesdrops on black culture and records it, thereby becoming an "expert." This expertise, or lack thereof, is exposed when he fails to carry off his attempt to pose as the "Talking Android" in blackface.

Another character portrayed in blackface, even though he is black, is Woodrow Wilson Jefferson, a black farmhand from Re-mote, Mississippi. Jefferson, with his overly formal manner and his use of titles (he calls Von Vampton "Publisher Hincle Von Vampton" whenever he addresses him), embodies the image of the pretentious pseudo-middle-class black man who is actually quite naive and rural. Jefferson is hired at Von Vampton's publication, the *Benign Monster*, to write the Negro Viewpoint (a viewpoint Von Vampton will actually command, with Jefferson acting as figurehead). Seconds after being hired, Jefferson asks Von Vampton if he would introduce Jefferson to Karl Marx and Friedrich Engels. "[I'll] really have to mold this 1," Von Vampton thinks, "but it would give [me] good practice for when [I] discovered the Android." Eventually, Jefferson's Baptist minister father comes to New York to drag him back home.

The most complex character in *Mumbo Jumbo* is Abdul Hamid, the black nationalist. Hamid is shown to be brash and extroverted, yet confessional and intimate. He is always looking for a chance to get on a soapbox ("Abdul sees the doorway is empty. Deprived of an audience, he changes his demeanor. He suddenly becomes polite affable patient reasonable."), but also is one who sticks to his principles—indeed, dies for them. He obviously cares deeply for his people, but his attempt at "censorship," ostensibly to help blacks, actually accounts for the regression of Jes Grew. Hamid burns The Work—The Book of Thoth—that is the key to Jes Grew, and after the burning, Jes Grew "just withered up and died." In spite of the bad light Reed puts Hamid in, he also makes it clear that, however misguided, he does have blacks' best interests at heart.

Hamid is the character through which some of Reed's most prophetic statements are voiced. Early in the novel, for example, Hamid says, "People are beginning to trickle in here from down home and I'll bet sooner or later there will be an exodus rivaling the 1 of the Good Book . . . . Happy Dust is here now. What strange enslaving drugs will be here later?"

Relation to Previous Works

Reed's writing style matured greatly between *The Free-Lance Pallbearers* and *Mumbo Jumbo*. Critical response generally reflected this assertion, although a few critics felt that "the full-blown explication of Neo-HooDoo dulled the devilishly humorous cutting edge of the two previous novels." The characters are more complex in *Mumbo Jumbo* than in Reed's earlier works. In *The Free-Lance Pallbearers* the contradictions some characters displayed made them seem inconsistent. In *Mumbo Jumbo*, the characters all display contradictions but are drawn in such a way that the differences make them more human.

Techniques/Literary Precedents

Mumbo Jumbo is an experimental, postmodern novel that actually employs more textbook than novelistic conventions. It contains illustrations, footnotes, and a bibliography. Of particular critical interest is the "Partial Bibliography," an inclusion one critic calls Reed's "most brilliant stroke." Another critic finds that

Reed's bibliography "affirms his opinion of pedantry and outworn attitudes in literary circles."

Beyond the textbook-like feel of the novel, the text itself comprises a mish-mash of characters, conflict, and connections, all brought together in a style that shuns quotation marks, uses unusual spellings ("Kongress" instead of Congress; "Kathedral" instead of Cathedral), employs a selective use of commas, and substitutes numbers for numerical words. The technique makes for an interesting read. The novel is unconventional, but the differences add to the book's readability rather than detract.

One of the unusual aspects of *Mumbo Jumbo* is the usage of what critic Reginald Martin calls "HooDoo time," which he sees resurfacing through a "stylistic technique that produces a synchronic effect. Certain chapters which have detailed past events in the past tense are immediately followed by chapters that begin with present-tense verbs and present-day situations; this effect introduces simultaneity to the text, and elicits from the reader a response that mirrors the feeling of the HooDoo/oral culture. That is, the reader feels that all of the actions are thematically and rhetorically related, because they all seem to be happening in the same narrative time frame."

Reed talks about his usage of "necromancy" in his book of essays, *Shrovetide in Old New Orleans*: "I wanted to write about a time like the present or to use the past to prophesy about the future—a process called necromancy. I chose the twenties because they are very similar to what's happening now. This is a valid method and has been used by writers from time immemorial. Nobody ever accused James Joyce of making up things. Using a past event of one's country or culture to comment on the present."

In a 1974 interview, Reed, while commenting on the fact that a photograph of John Mitchell, Richard Kliendienst, and John Dean appeared in *Mumbo Jumbo* before the Watergate scandal broke, talked about some of his writing techniques—both conscious and unconscious:

> It's necromancy. You try to prophesy; you get strange feelings or impulses. I do believe that I get psychic information from sources I'm not aware of when I'm writing. That's prophecy. But that's only one element of the book. I took all these things, used the classic techniques of the detective novel, as well as Egyptology, Western history, black dance, American civilization, and the Harding administration—all myths to explain the present.

RECKLESS EYEBALLING

Reckless Eyeballing, 1986, novel.

Social Concerns

Although the dust jacket for *Reckless Eyeballing* says the novel is "men vs. women, blacks vs. Jews, North vs. South, and Ishmael Reed vs. everybody," certainly some of the alliances are more positive than they sound. The novel's central character, for example, playwright Ian Ball, has an excellent working relationship with his Jewish director, and while the battle lines between men and women are clearly drawn, there is an attempt at fusion by the book's end.

Reed's primary focus in *Reckless Eyeballing* is on the black women writers who routinely display black men in ways that mirror society's general misconception of black men. Reed came under heavy criticism for this novel, as many critics saw the book as a thinly veiled attack on Alice Walker and *The Color Purple*. The similarities between Walker and her novel and Reed's fictional character and her play are striking. Tremonisha Smarts, a black female playwright, has written a play called *Wrong-Headed Man*, where all the black men commit incest, and routinely rape and brutalize women. Her play is being adapted into film by a director who "did science fiction plots that were so embellished with special effects that you forgot the weak story lines and the bad acting." Also, direct references are made to "that lesbian business" and to a woman who puts "urine and spit into her guests' drinks," both, seemingly, direct allusions to *The Color Purple*. ("The book is a work of fiction," Reed maintains, dismissing the charges.)

It is clear, however, that Reed intends to expose the way some black writers could unwittingly be controlled by powerful whites. "I was writing about some brutal black guys," says Tremonisha Smarts, "who I knew in my life who beat women, abandoned their children, cynical, ignorant, and arrogant, you know these types, but my critics and the people who praised me took some of these characters and made them out to be *all* black men." This passage, late in the novel, demonstrates the way Reed's female characters come to understand Reed's position in a way Reed's real-life critics still have not come to understand. As a result, the criticism of *Reckless Eyeballing* was unusually harsh.

Several sub-themes run through the novel. The killing of a Jewish director at a racist southern religious rally, along with frequent ruminations about the difference between the North and South, simultaneously point to the North/South dichotomy while commenting on race relations.

The white feminist movement is also examined, and Reed offers an example of the way history is revised by those who have the power to do so. A white female producer is set to produce a play about the "exploitation" of Eva Braun and the rest of the women who were "forced" into cooperation with the Nazis. The producer has also bumped Ball's play to a smaller, less comfortable theatre so she can run the Eva Braun play at the larger, more prestigious theatre. By fusing the two themes—the discretionary power of those who produce and publish along with the way history revised—Reed shows not only that power exists, but how it is exercised and for what reasons.

Characters

As in his other novels, Reed's characters are symbols of the particular social ill on which he is commenting. There are a number of different story lines and characters to pursue those story lines. Ball, the central character of the novel, is a southerner—from the West Indies, not the southern United States—who is beholden to the materialism of the mid-1980s. The women, the gadgets, and the apartment are all a vital part of his life. So in order to become a successful, famous playwright, he is interested in getting his name off the feminists' "sex list." Ball writes *Reckless Eyeballing*, a play comprised mostly of women, as an attempt to placate the feminists. Ball is another in a long line of complicated Reed characters: he thinks one way and acts another and he struggles over whether to compromise his values for the money and prestige a hit play would bring. In the end, his duality takes control of him, the result of HooDoo practiced on him at birth by his mother's lover's wife. She "put a hex on the child . . . [saying] he would be born a two-head, of two minds, the one not knowing what the other was up to."

Although Ball travels from New York back to New Oya during the space of the novel, Tremonisha Smarts is the character who makes the longest philosophical journey. She begins the novel as a black man-bashing womanist, and ends the book acknowledging the way her views have been co-opted by whites for their own agenda. As a result, she leaves the New York theatre scene and accompanies her man to Yuba City, California, to begin a theatre group and have "lots of babies." Smarts is a broad character, who does not quite emerge as fully realized as she was probably intended. She finally becomes a character who acts the way Reed apparently wishes all black feminists would act. The area she must cover to come to an understanding of Reed's point of view is great, and, as a character, she doesn't emerge unscathed.

The chief power broker in *Reckless Eyeballing* is Becky French, the theatre producer. She is the person who insists on including a controversial scene in

Tremonisha Smarts' play, *Wrong-Headed Man*; she makes an important change in Ball's *Reckless Eyeballing*; and she is producing the Eva Braun play. This character is meant to symbolize the cannibalistic nature of the white power structure, and the way those wielding power can influence the artist. French doesn't change at all in the book. She's manipulative and mean throughout, and she drives the major characters away with her strong-arm tactics. By devising a powerful, immovable character, Reed illustrates the necessity of learning to get around the power structure with values intact.

Techniques

In writing *Reckless Eyeballing*, Reed does not employ as many of the unconventional experimental devices as in some of his earlier works. Still, Reed's basic underlying structure is that used in even the more experimental novels. A wide range of characters are introduced, some having very much to do with the direct plot, along with others that are loosely connected to the plot but carry on a separate subplot of their own. A good example is Lawrence O'Reedy, a white New York detective. O'Reedy serves a number of functions in the novel, from symbolizing the racist, murderous attitudes (and latent guilt) of some New York Police Department veterans, to exhibiting racist sexual attraction toward black women like Tremonisha Smarts (whose case he is investigating). O'Reedy, then, can provide an interesting subplot while commenting on the action of the main plot.

Neo-HooDooism is still at the core of the novel, as Reed uses HooDoo to explain the contrary actions of Ian Ball. His actions stem from a curse put on him at birth by a HooDoo practitioner. Reed also relates HooDoo to the novel in ways not immediately seen by the reader. Reginald Martin points out that Tremonisha Smarts' first name is drawn from a Scott Joplin opera of that title. "In Joplin's opera," says Martin, "the character Tremonisha represents the powers of assimilation into American culture in opposition to the 'powers of the HooDoo men.' Thus, not only does Reed's version of the Tremonisha character allude to the original Tremonisha's disagreement with early African-American currents, but she also becomes one of the critical forces that Reed has long opposed."

Some critics see the roots of *Reckless Eyeballing* as spreading further back than Joplin. Robert Elliot Fox, in *Conscientious Sorcerers: The Black Postmodernist Fiction of LeRoi Jones/Amiri Baraka, Ishmael Reed, and Samuel R. Delany*, equates Reed with the Trickster figure from African folklore; Reed "simultaneously indicts and 'validates' Jews, feminists, 'failed' artists, and so on, through a dialectical disputation between rival theories, fantasies, 'facts,' and emotions engaged in by various characters in the book," writes Fox. "This allows him to make his case, in a sense, against his enemies and his 'inconsistent' friends and allies, while at the same time appearing to present a variety of viewpoints, silly and serious, paranoid and playful. When Jake Brashford accuses Ball of being 'nothin' but a trickologist,' the reader is likely to turn this accusation against Reed himself, who has, in fact, consciously identified with the Trickster figures who function at the center of his fictions. Indeed, Reed's work is a vaudeville of the spirit, a militant minstrelsy, trickster tales to trouble the conscience of a contradictory society."

Relation to Previous Works

While Reed's use of a more conventional narrative form in *Reckless Eyeballing* makes him less "experimental," his subject matter keeps him mired in controversy. One source comments that Reed "seemed to relish the outrage his book evoked as 'publicity' and as a way of carrying on the project that seems to consume him." So the lack of postmodern markers in Reed's *Reckless Eyeballing* does not mean that his viewpoints themselves lack any of the same punch he carried in his earlier works of fiction. Reed's aim is to enlighten and educate, and his fiction does both, to those who'll listen. For Ishmael Reed, indeed, "writing is fighting."

Other Titles

Yellow Back Radio Broke-Down, 1969 (novel); *Catechism of D Neoamerican HooDoo Church: Poems*, 1970; *19 Necromancers from Now*, 1970 (edited by Reed); *Conjure: Selected Poems 1963-1970*, 1972; *Yardbird Reader, Volumes 1-5*, 1972-1976 (editor); *Chattanooga: Poems*, 1973 (editor); *The Last Days of Louisiana Red*, 1974 (novel); *Flight to Canada*, 1976 (novel); *A Secretary to the Spirits*, 1977 (poetry); *Shrovetide in Old New Orleans*, 1978 (essays); *Yardbird Lives!*, 1978 (edited with Al Young); *Calafia: The California Poetry*, 1979 (edited by Reed); *God Made Alaska for the Indians: Selected Essays*, 1982 (essays); *The Terrible Twos*, 1982 (novel); *New and Collected Poetry*, 1988; *Writin' is Fightin': Thirty-Seven Years of Boxing on Paper*, 1988 (essays); *The Terrible Threes*, 1989 (novel).

Additional Sources

Afro-American Encyclopedia. Vol. 8. North Miami, FL: Educational Book Publishers, 1974. This dictionary contains a biographical, anecdotal entry that concentrates on Reed's life to 1974.

Bellamy, Joe David, ed. *The New Fiction: Interviews with Innovative American Writers*. Chicago: University of Illinois Press, 1974. This interview was conducted in parts between 1971 and 1973, and primarily concerns *Mumbo Jumbo* and the heavy criticism Reed has received from both black and white literary critics.

Contemporary Literary Criticism. Vol. 2. Detroit: Gale Research, 1974; Vol. 3, 1975; Vol. 5, 1976; Vol. 13, 1980; Vol. 32, 1985. This journal reprints, in their entirety, book reviews and criticism of Reed's works.

Current Biography Yearbook 1986: New York: H. W. Wilson, 1986. This article, despite some incorrect dates, contains an excellent review of Reed's writings, and some interesting anecdotes on Reed's life and upbringing. Throughout the article, the author includes opinions taken from book reviews and criticism on Reed's works. As such, the entry provides not only a commentary on Reed's works, but the response his work generated in the literary community as well.

Fox, Robert Elliot. "Ishmael Reed: Gathering the Limbs of Osiris." In *Conscientious Sorcerers: The Black Postmodernist Fiction of LeRoi Jones/Amiri Baraka, Ishmael Reed, and Samuel R. Delany*. New York: Greenwood Press, 1987. Fox analyzes each of Reed's novels (with special emphasis on *Mumbo Jumbo*) through *Reckless Eyeballing*. He touches on the "Neo-HooDoo" aspect of Reed's works, and concretely explains the symbolism and imagery that make Reed's experimental novels "postmodern."

Gale, Steven, ed. *Encyclopedia of American Humorists*. New York: Garland, 1988. Reed's life and works are closely inspected within three sections (Biography, Literary Analysis, and Summary). He is called "the brightest contribution to American Satire since Mark Twain."

Gates, Henry Louis. "Ishmael Reed." In *Dictionary of Literary Biography*. Vol. 33. *Afro-American Fiction Writers After 1955*. Detroit: Gale Research, 1985. In this lengthy, comprehensive review of Reed's life and works, Gates calls Reed "one of the cardinal figures in the Afro-American literary tradition," and analyzes at length Reed's fiction and poetry up to 1984. There are also entries on Reed in *Dictionary of Literary Biography, Volume 2: American Novelists Since World War II*, 1978; and *Volume 5: American Poets Since World War II*, 1980.

Martin, Reginald. "An Interview with Ishmael Reed." *Review of Contemporary Fiction* 4, 2 (1984). Reginald Martin talks with Reed, for the most part, about the same subject matter that comprised Martin's subsequent book: *Ishmael Reed and the New Black Aesthetic Critics.*

―――――. *Ishmael Reed and the New Black Aesthetic Critics.* New York: St. Martin's, 1988. This four-chapter book begins with an extended, badly needed definition of the term "black aesthetic." In the middle chapters, Martin acts as literary referee, presenting the views of Reed's critics along with Reed's response to those critics. The last chapter, "Hoodoo as Literary Method: Ishmael Reed's 'True Afro-American Aesthetic,'" contains Martin's own comments on Reed's "Neo-Hoodoo Aesthetic."

―――――. "Ishmael Reed." In *Contemporary Authors.* Vol. 25. Detroit: Gale Research, 1989. This entry provides detailed listings of Reed's career moves, awards and honors, and writings. An analysis of Reed's works, particularly Reed's fiction, is included.

Bertram D. Ashe
Virginia Commonwealth University

RUTH RENDELL
1930

Update

In 1986 after writing thirty volumes of detective fiction, British novelist Ruth Rendell openly assumed the pseudonym Barbara Vine and began to create a concurrent literary reputation with psychological thrillers. She feels that the plot line determines whether a given work will be a Rendell or a Vine, because she believes that Barbara (her own second name which her friends and family use) is "a bit more feminine and perhaps less bossy" than Ruth. Even so, Vine criticizes her society more sharply than Rendell does, mainly through more controversial characterizations, like the "little lesbian theme" Rendell feels may have been responsible for Bantam's rejection of Vine's third novel, *The House of Stairs* (1989).

Since then Barbara Vine novels have been published in the United States by Harmony Crown, with the fourth, *Gallowglass*, released in 1990. Rendell's books have also changed hands, from Doubleday to Pantheon to The Mysterious Press, most recently with *Going Wrong* (1990), possibly indicating an attempt to put one of her works on the U.S. hardcover bestseller list, an achievement that so far has eluded her. Rendell is one of Britain's most popular authors, and she has received considerable recognition among her peers: a second Edgar Allan Poe Award from the Mystery Writers' Association, for the short story "The New Girl Friend," 1985; a Silver Dagger from the Crime Writers' Association for *The Tree of Hands*, 1984; and Golden Daggers for Rendell's *Live Flesh*, 1986, and Vine's *A Fatal Inversion*, 1987.

Rendell claims she writes too much. In her first twenty-five years as a novelist she averaged three books every two years, but between 1986 and mid-1990 she produced eight, a stepped-up pace she called in a 1989 interview "a pleasurable grind but . . . also hard work." In "How Do You Learn to Write?" Rendell indicated the keynote for her constant effort to improve her craft: "to make that which is very, very hard look easy." Reviewers seem to feel she is succeeding by increasing her psychological penetration and mastery of fictional technique.

The Rendell and Vine novels currently sell regularly in fourteen languages. Audio versions of *A Judgement in Stone* and *The Lake of Darkness* were enthusiastically received in 1987, a trend that continues, and in 1989 British television began filming Rendell's fourteen-novel series centered on Chief Inspector Wexford, her most likeable and popular creation.

Analysis of Selected Titles

THE VEILED ONE

The Veiled One, 1988, novel.

Social Concerns/Themes

The title of Rendell's fourteenth Wexford novel suggests its principal theme, carried out simultaneously in the crime that Wexford must solve and in his relations with his family and environment: the classical Greek philosophical fallacy that if she is veiled "you can recognize your own mother and not recognize her" —"something to do with all of us and our parents, and with knowing and not knowing." The veils modern society imposes on its members prevent individuals from distinguishing between the ideal and the real, with results that are all too often tragic.

Rendell explores several of these in her most richly textured Wexford novel to date. Her primary concern is to lay bare the twisted psychological motives behind the murder of a respectable middle-aged woman garrotted in a shopping center parking basement almost under Wexford's eyes. She also addresses sensitive current issues: a hypocritical media treatment of famine; the disregard of the old and infirm under the guise of a national socialized welfare system; well-intentioned but misguided police work that attempts to justify a brutal interrogation by achieving a suspect's confession and finishes in disaster; inter-family stresses brought on by a parent's helpless preference for one child over another; a wrongheaded refusal to compromise and adjust in marriage. Wexford sums it all up: "It's not so much a depraved society that we live in as an idealistic one"—and as Rendell reveals them here, the ideals that these individuals espouse, no less than the society which encourages them, often create darksome veils of deceit and self-delusion.

One of Rendell's favorite causes, anti-nuclear lobbying, enters *The Veiled One* through Wexford's favorite daughter, a prominent BBC actress whose public protests seem to bring on a car bombing that nearly kills Wexford. This "unveiling" turns out for the better; Sheila's father cringes at her well-publicized ban-the-bomb protests, but Sheila's openness about her activities and even her divorce and new lover at last teach Wexford a vital lesson: so what if the neighbors see?

Characters

A reviewer of *The Veiled One* has called Reg Wexford "the coziest, most approachable, least angst-ridden detective in today's major-league crime fiction," seeing Wexford's essentially well-adjusted composure as a necessary antidote to the baleful murk through which he plies his trade. Wexford's England has nothing to do with the tidy vicarages and romantic moors of other British crime writers. He must function amid pretentious phoniness, like the shopping center decked out in pseudo-medieval castle trappings, and a suspect's home hung with all-enveloping ivy.

Wexford is mature enough, secure enough, to be able to see beyond the facade of this crime, which appears to be the work of a random-striking homicidal maniac. But when he is temporarily incapacitated by the explosion of his daughter's car, the investigation passes to his right-hand man Mike Burden, himself an edgy new father groping into a second family as uncomfortable to him as the just-bought jeans that replace his former business suits. Burden's obsessive conviction that he has found the psychopath conceals both the identity of the real murderer and Burden's own capacity for error. Finally, Wexford humanely unravels the entanglement, smiling wryly to himself when he hears Burden admit for the first time, "We live and learn."

Rendell consistently succeeds with her dispassionate portraits of aberrant criminal behavior. *The Veiled One* overtly plays an unnatural mother-son combination against Wexford's healthy relationship with his daughter Sheila, making Clifford Sanders, the disturbed son of the woman who discovers the garrotted body at the beginning of the novel, eerily real. Rendell's psychological study of Sanders reveals both his fears and the twisted love that underlie the murders which open and close this case.

Techniques/Literary Precedents

Earlier in her career, Rendell subordinated character to plot, but her later books begin with her characters. She finds "abiding satisfaction" in contemplating perceptive portraits by Old Masters—"Slyness must lurk behind those eyes surely, cruelty in that thin-lipped mouth"—and she creates their counterparts for her books, a technique that seems to lend striking verisimilitude to her depictions of distorted personalities.

For some time, Rendell says, she has also been reading and rereading the great Victorian novels, to learn "how to evolve and develop a story and cliff-hang my protagonist at the end of a chapter." Each chapter ending of *The Veiled One* pulls inexorably into the opening of the next, an effect strengthened by Rendell's novelistic reticence, a technique she attributes to Ford Madox Ford's *The Good Soldier* (1915): the power to suggest and withhold information that she believes is essential to mystery fiction.

Relation to Previous Works

Chief Inspector Wexford made his debut in Rendell's *From Doom to Death* (1965), as a good-natured fifty-two-year-old professional given to appropriate quotations and gentle self-directed irony. He has aged gracefully into a tolerant grandfather figure who can look unscathed into the darkest depths of human nature and come away still believing in the goodness of mankind. In *The Veiled One* Rendell also uses to advantage her exceptional talent for depicting how well houses reveal their occupants' characters; the explosion that sent Wexford to the hospital turns the home he and his wife have lovingly built over the years into an obscene heap of rubble and packs them off to live in the very neighborhood where the murder took place. Out of it all, however, Wexford salvages his hope and his sense of humor. At the close of the novel, one of Rendell's darkest, he still can grin as he sees workers beginning to rebuild his house, which serves as a metaphor for his new insights into his own family relationships. Rendell believes that "one should write to please oneself," and the development of her Wexford series seems to illustrate her success in doing so, since her protagonist continues to grow and flourish into a consistently more fully realized human being.

THE BRIDESMAID

The Bridesmaid, 1989, novel.

Social Concerns/Themes

Inspector Wexford builds his outer and inner houses out of solid sanity and decorates them with a cheerful optimism, taking for granted that most of his fellow humans have a capacity for goodness; those who do not he must lock up. The bad characters do not so much construct their homes as to allow them to go to seed, producing the squalid decaying suburbs of Rendell's modern London that parallels her view of the contemporary British spirit. Rendell feels that if people have a choice of where they live, their houses reflect their characters, but if they are trapped by circumstance, "the effect on them must sometimes be very bad indeed."

In *The Bridesmaid* Rendell dissects one of the worst of those effects, the fatal combination of bad luck and bad choices. In a tale of two intertwining obsessions, she eerily demonstrates that whatever people turn their backs on gets them in the end. Young Philip Wardman at first appears the epitome of middle-class decency, caring about his widowed mother's happiness, looking as best he can after his sisters' welfare, and faithfully walking the family terrier. He has what he calls "a phobia" against violent death, but his irrational, passionate affair with Senta, an enigmatic woman he meets at his sister's wedding, leads him to just such an end.

Horrifyingly, as Wardman slips ever further into sexual bondage to Senta, who demands they each kill a person to prove their love for the other, he realizes the depth of his degradation. Blinded by lust he cannot see that the choices he makes for her are wrong, leading him to ignore his family and even his own moral sense for the sake of a tawdry affair with a woman at the edge of madness.

Characters

Rendell has said that "the time for a blackness and whiteness of characters . . . has long gone by." She maintains that characters can become "so unpleasant that we lose interest in their fate," and that even the most repugnant must exhibit love for someone or something to sustain a reader's attention. *The Bridesmaid* twists this concept unsettlingly back upon itself: only when Philip Wardman acknowledges that he has never really known how to love, that even as a boy he "fell out of love" with his adored cat once it grew old and decrepit, is he capable of knowing what crimes of the spirit he has committed. In Senta, a pathological liar and homicidal manic-depressive, Rendell has created a character so devoid of love for anyone or anything beyond herself, who is so filled with self-absorptive fantasy, that she no longer knows truth from reality. She is able to cloud the mind of common-sensical, decent Philip Wardman, who eventually learns to his own devastation what his love for her has cost him.

Techniques

At one time, Rendell declares, she found structure and the movement of characters to be her chief fictional problem. She lately has been following Graham Greene's advice to pare down sentences that involve violent action, stripping off adjectives and adverbs to leave bare simple sentences that shock the reader into sharing an awareness of the stark finality of incurable insanity, mutilation, or death, as at the climax of *The Bridesmaid*, when Wardman looked at Senta, whom he thought he loved, and suddenly "saw madness staring out of her eyes."

The Bridesmaid also exhibits a thin thread of comic relief new to Rendell's suspense novels. Wardman's work as a lowest-on-the-company-totem-pole interior designer takes him into the touchy area of remodelling bathrooms for shrewish women, a chance for Rendell to use authentic dialogue she picked up from builders working on a new kitchen for her home near Polstead, Suffolk, and to demonstrate that "in our hands houses suffer as well," with sometimes incongruous results.

Literary Precedents

In the area of horror fiction, Rendell has acknowledged that "Victorian ghost stories have a lot to teach us," especially Percival Landon, whose "Thurnley Abbey is the most frightening story I have ever read," with everything a writer needs to know about fear and how to create it. Suggestion is everything to this approach, making a reader's imagination create monstrous images out of the greenish-black gloom, the color of rotting corpses, that so often surrounds Rendell's unnatural characters and their deviant behavior.

Related Titles

In several previous novels, especially *Master of the Moor* (1982) and *The Killing Doll* (1984), Rendell used two psychopathic characters who, unknown to one another at the outset, meet with fatal impact at the conclusion of her story. Bringing such figures into intimate contact in *The Bridesmaid* multiplies the pathological symptoms in its atmosphere. Philip Wardman and Senta, with their respective obsessions, writhe indissolubly into one another from the start: during his first night in her foul-smelling basement lair, she tells him prophetically, "I don't just want to have you, Philip, I want to be you"—and by the end she has swallowed him up.

THE HOUSE OF STAIRS

The House of Stairs (written as Barbara Vine), 1989, novel.

Social Concerns/Themes

Like Barbara Vine's two preceding novels, *The House of Stairs* is a psychological novel more "literary" and "mainstream" than works published under Rendell's name. From the start, when the first-person narrator Elizabeth Vetch reveals that she has a fifty-fifty chance of developing genetically transmitted Huntington's chorea, Vine plays off the forces of heredity against people's "houses," again her metaphor for the restrictive environments they create for themselves. Now in middle age, Elizabeth is forced to relive events of fourteen years earlier when she glimpses Bell, a woman out of Elizabeth's past who has been released from prison, striding along a London street. Bell's crime and even its victim are not revealed until the final pages of *The House of Stairs*, but along the way Vine explores several contemporary themes, most related to perceptions of female sexuality. Vine declares here that society still condemns an older woman's need for a younger man and makes aging itself bitterly unfair: "Why," asks Elizabeth, "do we have to be old for so much longer [than men]?" The "little lesbian theme" between Bell and Elizabeth results from Elizabeth's fear of passing on the disease in a normal marriage, and the responsibility Elizabeth feels for Bell's crimes stems from Elizabeth's love of literature, by which she unknowingly supplied Bell both a motive and a means of murder.

Vine also included a secondary theme dealing with the process of writing itself, perhaps a comment on Ruth Rendell's career. Elizabeth turned her back on scholarly studies of Henry James and taught herself to produce salable fiction. Fourteen years later, she compares popular success with genuine achievement: "Writers perhaps don't achieve great success or fame unless they write from the heart," and looking back, she declares, "I might have at least tried to write something that was an examination of the human heart, but I didn't. I wanted money."

Characters

The women of *The House of Stairs*, as Vine's themes suggest, far overshadow their male companions. Each in fact builds herself a dwelling and in it, spider-like, destroys a physical or emotional mate. At the death of her prototypic English husband who believed that a man's home was a measure of his accomplishment, Cosette, the replacement mother Elizabeth chose for herself, flings herself into a 1960s bohemian lifestyle with drugged and alcoholic hangers-on she invites to her new house, the bizarre setting for most of the novel's action. Elizabeth Vetch's narrative passes one landing after another in Cosette's odd house until at the end she reaches the ominous room in the garret whose one window looks out into a void, a metaphor for the guilt-ridden life that her role in Bell's crimes has condemned her to live. Elizabeth's fear of the disease that has killed so many of her relatives may also echo circumstances in Rendell's own life; her mother died of multiple sclerosis, and Rendell admits that even though that disease is not supposed to be hereditary, "I used to be very twitchy about it."

Techniques/Literary Precedents

Clearly Henry James, that master of maddeningly subtle figures in early twentieth-century literarature dominates Vine's plot and characterizations in *The House of Stairs*. Vine, like Rendell in her psychological thrillers, rejects the format of traditional mystery fiction, which generally opens with the murder and proceeds to sort out clues to the killer's identity. With a Jamesian reliance on exploring the psychology of the criminal, Vine prefers to dissect motives, shadow by shadow, without making clear until the end exactly what the crime is and who has been victimized. In *The House of Stairs* she employs an ultimate cliffhanger worthy of James himself, closing on a ringing telephone that will determine Elizabeth's future.

Relation to Previous Works

One critic has observed that Ruth Rendell compares "her double authorial identity to a kind of controlled and benign schizophrenia." As her self-comparison with Henry James suggests, the development of her Vine novels seems to tend toward the kind of fiction James was beginning to create in his last years, especially his masterpiece *The Wings of the Dove* (1902), mentioned often in *The House of Stairs*. James' horrendously accurate portrayal of the spiritual corruption that the betrayal of innocence brings is the model for Vine's growing ability to suggest the enormous complexity of evil, far more powerful than attempting to delineate the unspeakable. More than any other literary characteristic, this seems to set her work apart from Rendell's, making Vine's the "examination of the human heart" that Rendell's books never quite achieve.

GALLOWGLASS

Gallowglass (written as Barbara Vine), 1990.

Social Concerns/Themes

The title of the fourth Barbara Vine novel comes out of a violent tradition in Celtic history: a "gallowglass" was a chieftain's bodyguard, sworn to stand constantly at his master's right hand, ready to taste food and drink and hurl himself in front of hostile spears or battle axes. Although Vine sets her story in contemporary England, society is scarcely less violent today than in the time of the druids, allowing her to focus on the modern phenomenon of kidnapping for ransom. Her dual protagonists, who alternately narrate the novel, are two "gallowglasses" whose fates converge on the figure of a "Princess," a lovely ex-model now married to a wealthy British businessman.

Joe, who speaks first, illustrates Vine's interest in the social misfits for whom Britain's National Health Service offers too little help too late. Raised by uncaring foster parents and ejected from a psychiatric ward by governmental cuts in welfare spending long before his depression is even alleviated, Joe comes close to throwing himself under an express train; rescued in the nick of time by Sandor, an enigmatic sadistic stranger with whom he falls into a selfless asexual love. Joe willingly becomes Sandor's gallowglass, at his side each step of the tortuous way that Sandor plots to kidnap Nina Apsoland.

Joe's opposite is Paul Garnet, hired by Apsoland to guard his wife. Garnet is as normal as Joe is skewed. After Garnet's wife left him, he accepted Apsoland's offer so that he could raise the daughter he loved. But falling in love with Nina Apsoland, Garnet opens a chink in the cordon of security he is supposed to be maintaining, endangering both Nina and his daughter Jessica.

The entangled lives Vine portrays as meeting in pursuit and defense of Nina Apsoland allow her to explore various faces of love. By Ruth Rendell's theory of creating sympathetic figures for her novels, Joe's dogged hopeless attachment to Sandor should make him acceptable to readers, if not wholly palatable. Garnet, on the other hand, falls in love with love, a physical passion for a beautiful woman blinding him to his duty and even to his concern for his child. Once Garnet's daughter becomes a lever in the kidnap scheme, he abruptly falls out of love with Nina: she had done "too much" for him, he told her, in offering to give herself up to the kidnappers in place of Jessica, and that meant death to their relationship.

Characters

Barbara Vine's absorption with unnatural psychological states dominates her portrayal of Sandor, more deadly by far in his separation from reality than Joe. Sandor's keen mind seems somewhere to have slipped over the thin line to outright obsession, at once his perverse strength and his fatal weakness. Sandor's pursuit of Nina had begun long before, when he and others had kidnapped her for ransom in Italy. The stories with which he hypnotizes Joe at last coalesce into the myth that has guided Sandor's actions ever since, the belief that he is a new Paris, abducting a Helen for whom he counts everything else in his warped world well lost. Sandor thinks nothing of slashing Joe gratuitously with a cutthroat razor when Joe, doglike, comes too close. But when Joe's adopted sister Tilly, one of Vine's most engaging grotesques, takes Sandor into her bed to seal their cooperation in the kidnap plan, Sandor's lackluster performance is perversely predicated on his brutal reminiscences. Out of the mouth of the rejected Joe come acute observations: Sandor, he, and Tilly are "three members of society who've been squeezed out of it," and Vine's devastating ending leaves no grounds to doubt that in her fictional universe a grisly justice must triumph when murderers have been loosed upon society too soon.

Techniques/Literary Precedents

In *Gallowglass* Vine departs from the Jamesian reticence she used in *The House of Stairs*, where she unveiled the crime at the novel's core with deliberate gravity, Here the kidnapping is plotted openly throughout the novel, but its real motivation lies hidden in the twisted mentalities she depicts. The surprises at the end of *Gallowglass* are produced not so much by revelations of guilt and innocence as by a strange denouement in which the old girl-meets-boy plot line is turned upside down. Normalcy, as Paul Garnet represents it, withdraws from commitment, while whatever psychological disturbances Joe and Tilly suffer only draw them closer together.

The device of dual narrators that Vine employs in *Gallowglass* allows a constant seesaw between the unholy trinity of Sandor, Joe, and Tilly and the conventional romantic triangle of Garnet, Nina, and Apsoland. Vine inverts the traditional happy ending of fiction, severing the largely physical bond between Nina and Garnet and allowing Tilly and Joe, raised as siblings though not related by blood, to find what happiness they can together, incestuous in spirit if not in fact. This taint in their relationship lends the closing of *Gallowglass* a note peculiar to Vine's absorption with abnormal psychology, both a condemnation of society's rejection of its misfits and a plea for compassion towards them: what no one seems to understand, Joe believes, "is that what's the wrong end of the stick for others may be the right end for you."

Relation to Previous Works

Rendell/Vine's technique of bringing two disturbed characters together at the climax of a suspense novel, seen most recently in *The Bridesmaid*, has modulated in *Gallowglass* into an overt comparison between the normal and the disturbed. The abnormal sexual patterns she has hinted at in several previous novels, like the experimental relationship between two women in *The House of Stairs* (though both characters claim it is not a lesbian affair), is limited in *Gallowglass* to the mildly incestuous overtones of Tilly's choice of Joe as lover. Joe seems incapable of any sort of physical passion: he asks plaintively,"However you look at sex, it's not attractive, is it?" Because of these shifts in emphasis, *Gallowglass* seems both more conventional and less powerful a novel than the earlier Vine books. This novel more closely resembles Rendell's Wexford novels, which conventionally pit normalcy against criminal aberration, occasionally to a degree that detracts from their author's attempts at advancements in fictional technique.

Other Titles
Writing as Ruth Rendell: *To Fear a Painted Devil*, 1987 (novel); *Heartstones*, 1987 (novel); *Live Flesh*, 1987 (novel); *Talking to Strange Men*, 1987 (novel); *Collected Short Stories*, 1987 (short stories); *Wexford: An Omnibus*, 1988 (collection); *Going Wrong*, 1990 (novel). Ruth Rendell as editor: *Warning to the Curious: The Ghost Stories of M. R. James*, 1987 (anthology); *Going Wrong*, 1990 (novel).

Additional Sources
Kimberly, Nick. Review of *The Veiled One*. *New Statesman* 116 (May 6, 1988): 26.

Klein, Andy. Review of the television movie made from *The Face of Trespass*. *Los Angeles Magazine* 33 (June 1988): 216.

Rubins, Josh. Review of *The Veiled One*. *New York Times Book Review* (October 9, 1988): 23.

Steinberg, Sybil. Review of *Collected Short Stories*. *Publishers Weekly* 233 (March 25, 1988): 53.

Turbile, Diane. Review of *The Bridesmaid*. *Maclean's* 102 (November 6, 1989): 94.

Winks, Robin. Review of *Going Wrong*. *New York Times Book Review* (October 14, 1990): 42.

Mitzi M. Brunsdale
Mayville State University

ANNE RICE
1941

Update

In 1985 Anne Rice moved back to New Orleans, her birthplace, after spending a large part of her adult life in California. She has continued writing the series of novels she terms the Vampire Chronicles and in 1988 published *The Queen of the Damned*. She plans a fourth book in the series, tentatively titled *The Body Thief*. In 1989 she published a horror thriller called *The Mummy, or Ramses the Damned* and in 1990 *The Witching Hour*, which received excellent reviews and immediately rose to the top of the best-seller lists. In it, the Mayfair family is cursed by an alliance with a demon named Lasher, who follows family members through several generations, moving from seventeenth-century Scotland to the world of New Orleans in the twentieth century. Rice has produced no new Anne Rampling books, but under the pseudonym A. N. Roquelaure, she published a trilogy of erotica: *The Claiming of Sleeping Beauty* (1983), *Beauty's Punishment* (1984), and *Beauty's Release* (1985). In a career spanning thirteen years, she has published eleven books.

In a 1988 interview Rice mentioned that she was working on a concept for a television series. Previous deals to adapt *Interview with the Vampire* and *The Vampire Lestat* for the screen have not as yet materialized.

Analysis of Selected Titles

THE QUEEN OF THE DAMNED

The Queen of the Damned, 1988, novel.

Social Concerns/Themes

Feminism, religion, equality among and between the sexes, the importance of family, conflicting concepts of good and evil, and the beneficent evolution of humankind are the major social issues Rice addresses in *Queen of the Damned*. Akasha, the queen of the damned, represents feminism carried to a radical extreme. She is committed to changing the role of all women. Believing that the world's troubles have been caused by men, Akasha decides that ninety percent of the world's male population must be destroyed so that war, rape, and other violence can be ended forever. She contends that with women in power all over the earth, there would at last be universal peace.

Rice has said in an interview, "We can found a code of morality on ethics rather than outmoded religious concepts. We can base our sexual mores on ethics rather than on religious beliefs. Most of the activities in this century to stop war, to feed the hungry, and to provide medicine for the ill have been accomplished by rebels against religion rather than by people associated with religions." She develops these ideas through the speeches of Lestat, Maharet (mother of the Great Family), Narius, Louis, and all the other vampires who, by their very nature are godless but who are nevertheless highly moral in their concern for humankind. Akasha, queen of the damned, intends to establish a new religion with herself as supreme goddess in the mold of the Virgin Mary and "the ancient Mother . . . the mother whose tiny naked statues were now and then found in the earth."

In *Queen of the Damned* allusions to Christianity abound, supporting the view that Rice's ideas about the power and expected obsolescence of religion are integral to the plot. Lestat, performing at his rock concert, is described as "Christ on the cathedral cross," recounting "his defeats, his resurrections." His concert in termed "this great Mass." The neophyte Daniel says, "Lestat was unkillable. He devoured the suffering forced upon him and emerged all the stronger. To join him was to live forever: This is my Body. This is my Blood." Lestat is in many ways a Christ-figure in his "mission" to show the way to others, to enlighten the world, to ruffle the feathers of those who would keep the masses ignorant and enslaved, and ultimately to risk all for the sake of humankind.

Sexual equality is so well handled that the reader is lulled into an unconscious acceptance of the tender, loving, and even erotic relationships that male and female vampires have with each other without regard to gender. In fact, the closest and truest relationships are those between vampires of the same sex: Louis and Daniel, Maharet and Jesse, Narius and Armand.

Family is shown as the foundation of eternal life. Maharet, who has kept track of her descendants through the female line for six thousand years, says, "I turned to the family as if it were the very spring of life itself . . . the family was my guide through time and space. My teacher, my book of life. The family was all things." Rice elaborates the traditional notion of family to include our own ancestors and all their descendants, with the implication that all are related to all. After six thousand years, Maharet's descendants are everywhere: "there is no nation on earth that does not contain some part of it [her family] . . . No people, no race, no country does not contain some of the Great Family. The Great Family is Arab, Jew, Anglo, African; it is Indian . . . Mongolian . . . Japanese . . . Chinese. In sum, the Great Family is the human family."

Characters

Many characters in *The Queen of the Damned* have appeared before in the Vampire Chronicles, including Lestat, Louis, Narius, Gabrielle, Armand, and Nael. Akasha and Enkil are introduced in *The Vampire Lestat,* and Akasha is a principal character in *The Queen of the Damned.* New characters are also introduced: Jesse (Jessica); Maharet and Mekare, the red-haired twins; Daniel; and Khayman, an Egyptian who like Maharet and Mekare was one of the first vampires. Daniel was the interviewer in *Interview with the Vampire.*

Akasha, revived from a centuries-long catatonic state by the music and antics of Lestat, the vampire rock star, sets about to remold the world. It should be peopled by newly liberated women and only a limited number of males, until such time as men are genetically or culturally freed of their aggressive tendencies. In pursuit of this goal, she begins annihilating whole villages of men as well as all the vampires who might oppose her. Lestat, along with his friends, are among the chosen few that she spares. When told by Lestat that her plan is horribly brutal, she says that limiting the number of males is no different from what has been happening to females over the centuries: "Don't you think the peoples of this earth have limited in the past their female children? Don't you think they have killed them by the millions because they wanted only male children so that those children could go to war?" She believes the eradication of males would produce a serenity the world has never before known: "we shall see for the first time since man lifted the club to strike down his brother, the world women could make and what women have to teach men. And only when men can be taught, will they be allowed to run free among women again."

Maharet, the keeper of the records of the Great Family, is one of the original vampires and has apparently evolved into such a benevolent creature that the reader tends to forget she is a vampire. Her main mission seems to be the preservation of the record of her family and finding her long-lost twin sister Mekare. She represents, intentionally or not, all that is admirable in those who would cherish family, who see family as a unifying concept, transcending ethnicity, nationality, and religion. Through Maharet, Rice contends that "we can search for love and maintain it and believe it . . . this age has demonstrated that the belief in the value of love will endure after religions have passed away."

Lestat is again a major character. He is the catalyst who creates the crises of the novel just as in *The Vampire Lestat.* With his capricious and lawless urge to reveal the existence of vampires, making them even more vulnerable than they already are, he not only plays into the hands of Akasha but also creates anger and fear in other vampires. He is sought by Akasha as an ally in her plan to exterminate most of the human male population and dissident vampires, and targeted for destruction by those vampires seeking to retain their anonymity. These create some of the major conflicts of the book. Rice has said in an interview that her vampire characters are the "perfect metaphor for people who drain us dry, for our fear of the dead coming back, for the outsider who is in the midst of everything and yet feels monstrous and completely cut off." She might have added that they also serve her well as spokespersons for her views on the state of the world, the increasing irrelevance of religions, the obsolescence of the notion that each sex has its own societal role, and other social ideas embodied in the novel.

Techniques/Literary Precedents

Queen of the Damned employs a great number of flashbacks, often so intricately that there is sometimes confusion as to what is happening at any given time. Lestat is ostensibly the teller of the tale and he begins with a first-person narration. However, he quickly shifts to the third person so that others' stories can be told. The connection of these stories is revealed only gradually. All the stories illuminate some relevant background either to the plot or to important characters, and all come together in a climactic scene where the still unpersuaded Lestat and Akasha confront the dissident vampires.

The flashback technique allows the plot to span the centuries as well as link the three main narrative threads to the previous Vampire Chronicle novels. The telling of a complex story over several related volumes is not unique with Rice. Writers such as William Faulkner and James T. Farrell have created a series of works around a set of characters. With six thousand years of history and immortal characters, some of whom have lived through all these millennia, Rice obviously has a wealth of material to keep the chronicles going for some time. Chelsea Yarbro, another contemporary writer, has used the vampire theme in a series of five books about the vampire St. Germaine. These are historical horror thrillers every bit as fascinating as the Rice series.

Relation to Previous Work

The Queen of the Damned begins where *The Vampire Lestat* ends. It carries that earlier plot to its resolution, resolving many of the unanswered questions. It develops the character of the interviewer, Daniel, from *Interview with the Vampire*, and gives a fascinating explanation of how the first vampires came to be. It is considered by critics to be gorier and less erotic than the previous Vampire Chronicle novels. The novel champions the modern world, even with its failings, seeing it as proof of human evolution to a higher ethical and spiritual plane.

Additional Sources

Holditch, W. Kenneth. "Interview with Anne Rice." *Lear's* (October 1989): 86-89, 155. Rice talks about the effect of New Orleans on her writing, what she tries to achieve in her Vampire Chronicles, and her views on religion and morality.

Bluestein, Ron. "Interview with the Pornographer." *Vogue* (April 1986): 212+. Rice's views on pornography and love, and a brief mention of the Vampire Chronicles.

Kraft, Eric. Review of *The Queen of the Damned*. *New York Times Book Review* (November 27, 1988): 12-13. Believes that Rice is wasting her "enormous ability" by continuing with her vampire series.

Ransland, K. M. "Interview with the Vampire Writer." *Psychology Today* (November 1989): 34+. Rice describes her fascination with vampires since childhood.

Wadler, J. "Anne Rice's Heart May Roam Among Vampires and Erotica, But Her Heart Is Right at Home." *People* (December 3, 1988): 131+

Jane L. Ball
Wilberforce University

MARY ROBERTS RINEHART
1876-1958

Publishing History

By her own account Mary Roberts Rinehart began her writing career when she was the mother of three young sons and the wife of a physician whose stock market speculations left the family finances in precarious shape. Her first published short story resulted from the suggestion of the nurse who cared for her during one of her many periods of ill-health. (In the first years of her marriage Rinehart suffered through three extremely difficult pregnancies, gynecological operations necessitated by them, as well as a number "childhood" illnesses, including diphtheria, contracted while caring for her young sons.) As sympathetic as readers might have been to her personal circumstances, the facts of her life do not explain the phenomenal popular and financial success Rinehart enjoyed from the moment she began writing for publication, and they tend to underplay her real literary talent. What her life did, however, was to provide Rinehart with a justification for becoming the principal breadwinner in her family at a time when married women were expected to devote themselves to domestic concerns and allow their spouses to support the family. Her independence and success, combined with the longevity of her own marriage and the contentment of her family life, contributed to the popularity and durability of her work among the readers of magazines such as *The Saturday Evening Post* in which much of her short fiction first appeared.

As a child, Mary "Mamie" Roberts had no literary pretensions, although she later admitted that she liked to sit down "with a clean sheet of paper and put words on it." She was also a voracious reader, especially of the "Deadwood Dick" adventure series, and in high school she undertook the less popular (and practical) English courses rather than the "general" or "commercial" courses available. Her real interest, however, lay in her desire to become a doctor, an unlikely career in the nineteenth century for a young woman of a genteel, although impoverished background. In 1892 when she was still a high school student, two of her short stories were published in the *Pittsburgh Press*. One of these stories featured the first Rinehart detective. Any further attempts at publishing were delayed for over a decade while she trained as a nurse and later married and gave birth to her three sons. The horrifying reality of her hospital experiences initially shocked Rinehart's sheltered, middle-class sensibilities, but later would provide her with material for her novels. *K*, one of her most popular books, is set in a hospital, and Nurse Hilda Adams, "Miss Pinkerton," is one of Rinehart's most enduring characters.

When Rinehart began her publishing career in 1903, her short stories appeared in popular magazines such as *All-Story* and *Munsey's*. According to her own handwritten account book, in her first year as a writer she sold over forty-five stories and earned $1,842.50. These first short stories had no common theme and consisted of almost every type of fiction from domestic drama to gothic romance. It was only in 1905 when the editor of *Munsey's* suggested a crime serial that Rinehart turned to detective fiction. She wrote *The Man in Lower Ten* in less than a month and followed it a year later with *The Circular Staircase*, destined to become a classic of the genre. Both appeared in serial form in *All-Story*. After Bobbs-Merrill brought out *The Circular Staircase* in book form in 1908, Rinehart's place atop the best-seller charts was assured. For almost thirty years Rinehart was one of the most successful writers in America. *The Man in the Lower Ten* was the first mystery novel ever to make the best-seller list; eventually, eleven of her novels would make the list in the year they were published. In 1910 the "Tish" stories, featuring the unflappable Miss Letitia Carberry, began appearing in *The Saturday Evening Post*. By the 1930s *The Post* would pay as much as $65,000 for the serialization rights to each of Rinehart's new novels. Her return to book-length detective fiction after a fifteen year absence with *The Door* in 1930 marked the debut of Farrar and Rinehart, her sons' publishing firm, which continued as her sole publisher until the end of her life. Beginning in 1915 with the first film version of *The Circular Staircase*, which also appeared in a stage version titled *The Bat* in 1920, Rinehart's work became the source for numerous commercially-successful films, plays, and later television productions.

Critical Reception, Honors, and Popularity

While Rinehart's popular and commercial success is unchallenged, the critical reception of her work has been mixed. She is often ridiculed as the founder of the "Had-I-But-Known" school of writing because of her ingenuous heroines who persist on walking into dangerous situations in spite of numerous warnings not to do just that. This style of writing has gained Rinehart countless, usually less talented, imitators and has also caused her to be viewed as a writer of the twentieth-century gothic or romance genre, both of which also rely heavily on this technique. Rinehart's own continued insistence that she began to write solely out of monetary motives and her early tendency to denigrate her own ability also contribute to the lack of critical appreciation for her writing.

Rinehart's place in the development of the detective novel is more assured. *The Circular Staircase* is a classic in that genre, and Rinehart was one of the first mystery writers to shift the emphasis away from the eccentric detective to the victim and the criminal. She is often faulted for the limitations of her plots: her mysteries always begin with an initial murder that leads to several other killings. She is noted, however, for introducing elements of romance and humor into the detective story as well as humanizing it, which may indeed account for the overwhelming popularity of her fiction among ordinary readers.

Although she is primarily remembered now for her mysteries, in her lifetime Rinehart's other novels were also popular. Indeed, none of her full-length works written from 1914 to 1930 were mysteries. In her autobiography *My Story*, published in 1931, Rinehart indicates that she saw herself as having moved from a young mother who dashed off as many short stories as possible in as short a period of time as possible in order to make money to a mature, serious writer. Critics seldom agreed with her assessment, and her novel *This Strange Adventure* (1929) received a lukewarm reception from both the critics and Rinehart's readers. *This Strange Adventure* represents an attempt to examine the lifestyle of a mature woman of Rinehart's own background and class. Ironically, the same subject matter presented two years later as the autobiography of Mary Roberts Rinehart, famous author, made the best-seller list. Critical recognition eluded Rinehart throughout her life, and she came to view this as a result of her conscious rejection of the use of suggestive or sexual themes in her writing. Conversely, her refusal to deal with contemporary social issues and problems in the last thirty years of her career make her attempts at more serious writing seem dated and add to the lack of critical appreciation of them. At the same time, her readers responded warmly to those themes and subjects which echoed their own more traditional beliefs and values.

Contemporary interest in women's studies has led to a reconsideration of Rinehart. The first full-length critical assessment of her as a popular novelist appeared in 1980. The importance of the female protagonists in her detective stories has undergone reexamination in many recent discussions of that genre. While she will probably never be viewed as a great writer, Rinehart will undoubtedly be seen as an enduring one.

Analysis of Selected Titles

THE CIRCULAR STAIRCASE
The Circular Staircase, 1908, novel.

Social Concerns

While Rinehart's comments on social issues would later be eagerly sought by the readers of mass market magazines such as *The Saturday Evening Post* and *Ladies' Home Journal*, in her early novels she concentrated almost entirely on plot and character. Yet *The Circular Staircase* is not devoid of an interest in the limitations of the author's own upper-middle-class environment. Its main character, Miss Rachel Innes, is a spinster, an anomalous figure in a society which saw wife and mother as the only acceptable roles for a woman. Most spinsters were financially dependent and condemned to stereotypically feminine (and low-paying) occupations such as teachers, nurses, shop clerks, and office workers. The fictional Miss Rachel Innes is released from those constraints in *The Circular Staircase* and is free to use her intelligence and insight to unravel the complexities of the situations in which she finds herself. The more traditional roles are represented in the novel both by Miss Rachel's timid maid Liddy and by her teenage niece Gertrude. Rinehart herself had longed to study medicine as a girl but was forced by family finances as well as social convention to train as a nurse. In her novels she liberates her female characters from the constraints placed upon them by their gender. There is also a great deal of witty commentary on that new social phenomenon—the automobile—one of which is owned by Miss Rachel's nephew Halsey.

Themes

As with all her detective novels, Rinehart's *The Circular Staircase* is concerned with the reaction of ordinary people who become innocently embroiled in situations beyond their control. Miss Rachel rents a summerhouse which turns out to have a secret room in which the proceeds from a bank robbery have been hidden. While her maid Liddy cowers in the background, Miss Rachel rises to the occasion in typical intrepid amateur sleuth fashion. While Rinehart's approach is comic, the examination of human reactions in the face of unexpected horror is serious.

Characters

The character of Miss Rachel Innes dominates the action of *The Circular Staircase*. Although she appears in only this one novel, she is the prototype for many of Rinehart's heroines, most notably "Tish," Miss Letitia Carberry, one of Rinehart's most popular creations. Not only does she face one terrifying event after the other with absolute equanimity, but she also takes great delight in her ability to do so. She is clear-sighted and practical, able to deal with murder and mayhem on the same terms as she does the more mundane distractions of the social lives of her young niece and nephew. She also exhibits genuine regret when the situation is resolved, and she must return to her ordinary existence.

Liddy, Miss Rachel's maid, is the flighty, easily-frightened female who embodies stereotypical views of women's behavior. Miss Rachel's niece and nephew, Gertrude and Halsey, not only provide her with a surrogate family but also allow for gentle satiric commentary on the amusements of young people in upper-middle-class society.

Techniques

All of Rinehart's detective novels were to follow the pattern set by *The Circular Staircase*. The initial crime is only the first in a series of violent events which strike the characters throughout the novel. Other elements introduced in this novel include the infamous "Had-I-But-Known" narrative technique, where the first person narrator laments that, based on hindsight, she would have acted very differently; the blending of romantic subplots with the main mystery storyline; the use of humor; and the shifting of attention from the detective to the victims and villains involved in the crime.

Rinehart also borrows a number of gothic elements for *The Circular Staircase*. It is set in Sunnyside, a rambling old mansion on Long Island, full of hidden rooms, secret passages, and things that "go bump in the night." The name of the house is, of course, ironic. While its surface appearance is benign, its interior hides great evil. The novel also features a middle-of-the-night disinterment in a cemetery, another direct borrowing from the gothic tradition.

Literary Precedents

The Circular Staircase is clearly a descendant of the fifty years of detective stories which preceded it. It is probably no coincidence that Bobbs-Merrill, the publishers of the novel, had also published Anna Katherine Greene's *The Leavenworth Case* exactly thirty years earlier. Greene also created a female detective, Violet Strange, now long forgotten. Although Rinehart writes firmly in the detective tradition of Edgar Allan Poe and Sir Arthur Conan Doyle, she shifts the focus from the eccentric detective with almost supernatural powers of detection to an ordinary individual caught up in a situation in which she must call on her powers of common sense to deal with the problem in front of her. While earlier practitioners of the genre had portrayed women in their more typical role as victim, Rinehart made her detective a woman. While it is true she is an unusual one, being free from the restrictions she would have faced had she been tied down with the responsibilities of caring for a husband and children, she is a woman nonetheless.

Related Titles

The spinster detective Rinehart creates in *The Circular Staircase* is clearly a forerunner of one of her most popular characters, the heroine of the long-lived "Tish" series. Miss Letitia Carberry first appeared in a short story written in 1910 and then in more short stories and a series of books: *The Amazing Adventures of Letitia Carberry* (1911); *Tish* (1916); *More Tish* (1921); *Tish Plays the Game* (1926); *The Book of Tish* (1931); *Tish Marches On* (1937); and *The Best of Tish* (1955). *The Saturday Evening Post* printed every new "Tish" story for over thirty years. While exceptionally popular, these stories usually have very little to do with the solution of a mystery. Their interest lies in the comic character of Tish, a spinster of indeterminate age who travels about the United States and Europe, encountering any number of off-beat and sometimes improbable situations which her own blend of morality and silliness always sees her through.

The Circular Staircase is also related to the "Miss Pinkerton" stories which feature Rinehart's other female detective, Nurse Hilda Adams. "Miss Pinkerton" is given her nickname by the police themselves because of her ability to solve crimes that elude them. Although "Miss Pinkerton" is cast in the same mold as Miss Rachel Innes and "Tish," she is a more realistic character. Rinehart obviously has drawn on her own youthful experiences as a nurse and her own advice to young writers: "If you are a housewife living in the South, why try to tell a story of French Colonials in North Africa?" The character first appeared in the short story "The Buckled Bag" in 1925 and then in the novel *Miss Pinkerton* (1932). Her adventures continue in a series of novels over the next fifteen years, ending with *Haunted Lady* (1942). The "Miss Pinkerton" stories present the curious proposition that because of the special role a nurse plays in her patients' lives, she has the right to take advantage of their weaknesses, both physical and moral, to expose their guilt. This, according to Rinehart, allows the nurse to be more highly effective at solving crimes than, for example, other professionals such as physicians and the police who are bound by legal and ethical codes. Since the character of Hilda Adams is clearly autobiographical, this view of the relative roles of nurse and physician undoubtedly reflects Rinehart's own experiences, as well as those of her readers, as repugnant as it may be to contemporary thinking.

The final Rinehart series which is related to *The Circular Staircase* features "Bab the Sub-Deb." Bab is an adolescent version of Letitia Carberry. Barbara Putnam Archibald narrates her wild adventures through the medium of the misspelled and ungrammatical essays written in response to her English assignments. In the "Sub-Deb" stories Rinehart is able to give full rein to her sense of the absurd. Although they are wonderfully comic, they also allow Rinehart to portray quite accurately the emotional life of an adolescent girl in all her wild enthusiasm and uncertainties.

Adaptations

The first film version of *The Circular Staircase* appeared in 1915. A television version appeared on CBS's *Climax!* series in 1954. More well-known, however, are the movies and television productions based on Rinehart's own adaptation of the novel for the stage as *The Bat*, one of the most commercially successful mystery dramas ever written. Rinehart and Avery Hopgood adapted *The Circular Staircase* for the stage under this title in 1920. Miss Rachel Innes became Miss Cornelia Van Horder; her maid Liddy was renamed Lizzie. The initial Broadway run of *The Bat* lasted for two years. (A 1953 revival with Zasu Pitts as Lizzie was nearly as successful, and after the play closed, Pitts starred in a television version.) To capitalize on the success of her play, Rinehart allowed Stephen Vincent Benét to fictionalize *The Bat*, and it was republished as a separate novel in 1926. The stage version of *The Bat* was used as the basis for a silent film in 1926, followed by a United Artists sound version with the title *The Bat Whispers* in 1930. The film was remade in 1959 by Allied Artists with Agnes Moorehead as Miss Van Horder and Vincent Price as "the Bat." The following year Helen Hayes and Jason Robards, Jr., were featured in a Dow Great Mystery Series television production of *The Bat*.

K.

K., 1915, novel.

Social Concerns/Themes

Rinehart's major themes in *K.*, the first of her novels to be based largely on autobiographical material and to depart from the mystery formula that had served her so well in earlier books, are those of individual freedom and identity. Its protagonist, Sidney Page, is a young woman bound by the social mores of "the Street," where she lives with her widowed mother who runs a boarding house. Sidney is about to enter training as a nurse, in keeping with the traditional expectations for a woman, but secretly she wants to escape; she longs for the freedom to do something, to do anything beyond what society expects of her. These desires to move beyond the expected social role are symbolized by her androgynous first name. She does not want her actions and achievements to be limited by her gender. Concurrent with Sidney's struggle against the limitations placed on her by her sex, Rinehart portrays the personal anguish of the great surgeon Edwardes whose faith in his own skill has been destroyed by the accidental deaths of three of his patients. Disguised as the mysterious new boarder, K. le Moyne, Edwardes enters Sidney's life just as she begins her training. Given Rinehart's own feelings and the sentiments of her audience, it is no surprise that Sidney's longing for freedom and K.'s self-doubts are all resolved by their growing mutual love.

Characters

Sidney Page is clearly modelled on the young Mary Roberts. Sidney's dead father, who bequeathed her "the dreamer's part" of her nature, certainly reflects Rinehart's own father, a failed inventor who committed suicide. Mrs. Page's insistence on maintaining respectability in spite of her lack of financial resources is based on the experiences of Rinehart's own widowed mother. The character of "Dr. Max," the egotistical and unscrupulous doctor with whom Sidney and every other student nurse fall in love, the horrifying scenes when Sidney confronts human suffering, many of the details of everyday life, are all drawn from Rinehart's experiences during her youth in Allegheny, Pennsylvania. Like young Mary Roberts, Sidney eventually sacrifices her own desires for freedom in the face of her love for a "good man," K.

Techniques

K. is one of the first books in which Rinehart attempted to write mainstream fiction. She does not rely on the comfortable formula of the detective novel, and the tone is completely serious. She also departs from her early tendency toward romanticism in favor of realistic depiction of everyday life, especially in the hospital scenes. Her handling of plot is not sure, however, and the conclusion seems banal, sentimental, and predictable.

Related Titles

K. is closely related to its immediate predecessor, *The Street of the Seven Stars* (1914), and looks forward to some of Rinehart's later attempts at serious novels, especially *This Strange Adventure* (1929). In *The Street of the Seven Stars* Harmony Wells, a gifted young violinist, must choose between her career and her love for the young physician Peter Byrne. In spite of the presence in the novel of Dr. Anna Gates, a proponent of women's rights, Harmony comes to the inevitable conclusion that if she is to have a career, it will be Peter's. Such an ending, of course, assured *The Street of the Seven Stars* a place on the best-seller lists.

In what was one of her last attempts to establish herself as a writer of serious fiction, Rinehart examines the life of Missie Colfax in *This Strange Adventure*. Again, largely autobiographical, the novel traces its protagonist's life from her childhood in a neighborhood very similar to that in which Rinehart grew up, to a loveless marriage to a wealthy philanderer, to a brief attempt at fulfillment through love (Missie, given her author's awareness of her audience, remains physically chaste), to a self-sacrificing return to care for her invalid husband, to the final stunning realization that her sacrifice for her son has been worthless. At the end of the novel, Missie returns to her childhood home intent on suicide, only to discover the gas has been shut off. She cannot even succeed at self-destruction. *This Strange Adventure* was an ambitious book for Rinehart, given the popular reputation she had built on happy endings. It was, not unexpectedly, largely unsuccessful and seems to have marked Rinehart's final attempt to move beyond the constraints of her own popularity.

Adaptations

A film version of *K.* appeared in 1918 under the title *The Doctor and the Woman*. Six years later Universal brought out *K.—the Unknown*.

Other Titles (selected)

The Man in Lower Ten, 1909 (novel); *When a Man Marries*, 1909 (novel); *The After House*, 1914 (novel); *The Amazing Interlude*, 1918 (novel); *Dangerous Days*, 1919 (novel); *Affinities*, 1920 (novel); *A Poor Wise Man*, 1920 (novel); *Spanish Love* (with Avery Hopgood), 1920 (play); *The Breaking Point*, 1921 (novel); *The Red Lamp*, 1925 (novel); *Two Flights Up*, 1926 (novel); *The Romantics*, 1929 (collected stories); *The Door*, 1930 (novel); *Mary Roberts Rinehart's Mystery Book*, 1930 (collected novels); *My Story*, 1931 (autobiography); *Mary Roberts Rinehart's Romance Book*, 1931 (collected novels); *The Crime Book*, 1933 (collected novels); *The State vs. Elinor Norton*, 1933 (novel); *Married People*, 1937 (short stories); *The Wall*, 1938 (novel); *Familiar Faces*, 1941 (short stories); *Episode of the Wandering Knife*, 1944 (short stories); *Alibi for Isabel and Other Stories*, 1944 (short stories); *The Swimming Pool*, 1952 (novel).

Additional Sources

Cohn, Jan. *Improbable Fiction: The Life of Mary Roberts Rinehart.* Pittsburgh: University of Pittsburgh Press, 1980. The only full-length critical biography available, invaluable for its assessment of the relationship between Rinehart's life and work. Contains a complete bibliography of all Rinehart's publications.

Craig, Patricia, and Mary Cadogan. *The Lady Investigates: Women Detectives and Spies in Fiction.* New York: St. Martin's, 1981. Contains a section on the "Miss Pinkerton" stories.

Davis, Robert H. *Mary Roberts Rinehart: A Sketch of the Woman and Her Work.* New York: Doran, 1925. Brief treatment which contains essays by Davis, Grant Overton, and Rinehart herself.

Hoffman, Arnold R. "Social History and the Crime Fiction of Mary Roberts Rinehart." In *New Dimensions of Popular Culture,* edited by Russel B. Nye. Bowling Green, OH: Bowling Green State University Popular Press, 1972. The most scholarly analysis of Rinehart's detective fiction and its relationship to popular culture.

Overton, Grant. *The Woman Behind the Door . . . Mary Roberts Rinehart.* New York: Farrar and Rinehart, 1930. Basically only a propaganda piece for the publishing company established by Rinehart's sons.

Rinehart, Mary Roberts. *My Story.* New York: Farrar and Rinehart, 1931; reissued as *My Story: A New Edition with Seventeen New Years,* 1948. Rinehart's autobiography with her recollections of the impetus for each of her major novels.

———. *Writing Is Work.* Boston: The Writer, 1939. Rinehart's description of her writing techniques.

Steinbrunner, Chris, and Otto Penzler, eds. *Encyclopedia of Mystery and Detection.* New York: McGraw-Hill, 1976. Brief overview of Rinehart's career with selected comments by Rinehart on *The After House, The Red Lamp, The Album, The Great Mistake,* and *The Yellow Room.*

Mary Anne Hutchinson
Utica College of Syracuse University

ALAIN ROBBE-GRILLET
1922

Update
Now in his late sixties, Alain Robbe-Grillet continues to write labyrinthine novels exemplifying the tenets of *nouveau roman* and, in the assessment of one reviewer, he "dislikes as comprehensively as ever the realism of most contemporary fiction . . . and movies." In 1985, he published *Le Miroir Qui Revient*. His latest work, *Angelique ou L'Enchantement* appeared in 1988. The two novels are said to be part of a series Robbe-Grillet is working on which the author himself calls "Romanesques." The third volume in the series is, according to a review of *Angelique* by John Sturrock in the *Times Literary Supplement* to be titled *La Mort de Corinthe*, but has not yet been published.

Analysis of Selected Titles

DJINN
Djinn, 1982, novel (Originally published 1981).

Social Concerns/Themes
In *Djinn*, readers familiar with Robbe-Grillet's work once again find themselves in a Kafkaesque world in which objects are so painstakingly described as to seem significant, although what they signify is never clarified, chronology is disordered, and events which seem to be taking place later appear not to have been "real" at all. Like *The Erasers* (1964; *Les Gommes*, 1953), *Djinn* is the story of a quest, although the object and purpose of the quest is far less certain here than in the earlier work. The narrator (he is called Simon LeCoeur, but his very identity is called into question throughout) enters a hangar at the appointed hour of six-thirty where he is to meet someone. Seeing a man dressed in hat and trenchcoat, like a detective from "some old . . . movie of the thirties," he presents himself and recites the coded message. When the "man" answers, Simon realizes that "he" is a she. Shortly afterwards, however, the narrator again makes a discovery: "she" is not even a person, but a mannequin. The voice he has heard is coming from a tape recorder placed somewhere out of sight. Ordered by this disembodied voice to proceed upstairs, Simon then meets the "real" woman, an American from Boston named Jean (Simon first pronounces it "Djinn" and is corrected), and her

double, Laura, who may or may not be a mannequin. As Simon is about to receive his first instructions, Jean/Djinn tells him, in what might just as well be a directive to the reader, that for reasons of "security" and "efficiency" she cannot reveal "the exact purpose of [the] mission nor the general goal of our undertaking."

The novel then proceeds to demonstrate—if it demonstrates anything at all—the veracity of that remark. The narrator follows his orders without knowing what is to be achieved; he often finds himself thwarted in his mission by seemingly random events (for example, missing the appointment at the Gare du Nord when a young boy crosses his path, trips, and falls unconscious, perhaps dead), but is unable to discern whether such events are, in fact, part of the plan. In the room where he takes the young boy, he encounters a mysterious girl-child, Marie, and is later told he is their "papa," but whether this is so is never clarified. Perhaps the strongest image of this narrative uncertainty is that of the blindfolded Simon, sitting in a room in an unknown place, listening to Djinn, who is once again only a disembodied voice, and peeking out of his blindfold only to find himself in a room full of blindfolded men. If readers look to authors to make sense of the fictional world for them, Robbe-Grillet seems here to be asserting that author and reader are equally blind; indeed, he seems to mock the very notion that there is a discernible truth to be found in the world. Perhaps he means to say of this fictional world what he once said of the real one: that it is "neither significant nor absurd—it is, quite simply."

Characters

The characters in *Djinn* are no more fully delineated than in Robbe-Grillet's previous novels, and may be even less coherent. Names are given, but the individuals to whom they belong seem to shift. The names Boris and Laura evoke the characters in *Un Regicide* (1978), but here, Boris might be Simon, and Laura might be a mannequin, or even Djinn/Jean, whom she resembles. Djinn/Jean is not only the name of the American female, but also the name of the young boy who is hurt, or dead (he "dies often" according to Marie), and a later version of Marie—now called Djinn—tells Simon "all little boys are called Jean." Simon himself may be Djinn; the name, like its equivalent, Jean, is masculine in French. Also, according to the anonymous narrator of the prologue, Simon/Boris/Robin was known by his students as Yann "which they spelled Jan . . . none of them could say why." Robbe-Grillet seems again to be mocking the very idea of character as a coherent entity who can be pinpointed in time and space. The fact that some of the "characters" in this story may be nothing more than lifeless mannequins echoes Henri Peyre's assertion, in *French Novelists of Today* that

Robbe-Grillet treated character as if it were a "mummy just good enough to be discarded." The mannequin Djinn/Jean is indeed discarded, "mortally wounded," although no wound is visible, oozing blood, even though mannequins do not bleed. Readers trying to get a clear sense of who is who in this novel may find themselves in the position of Simon's female alter ego near the end of the novel: "reason tumbling, into the void, in a vertiginous fall."

Techniques/Literary Precedents

The five chapters of the text, which are "found" by the anonymous narrator on Simon LeCoeur's desk, are narrated in the present indicative tense, as if what is being described were indeed happening at the moment of the reading. A similar narrative technique was employed in *Jealousy* (1959; *La Jalousie*, 1957), which begins with the word "now." Chapter six of *Djinn* is partially narrated in the past tense by a third person who seems to have limited omniscience, but shifts back to the first person, present tense towards the end, a mode which continues into chapter seven. About a third of the way through that chapter, the narration shifts inexplicably back to third person, past tense. Chapter eight is first person, past tense, but the narrator is no longer Simon; it is now a girl, presumably Djinn, telling her version of the events. After her "vertiginous fall" the narration shifts again to a first person narrator, past tense. He begins to tell the story of going to the hangar at six-thirty, as if the previous pages of the novel did not exist, but he gets no further than the point at which he steps forward to recite the coded message. Then the anonymous narrator steps forth, in the epilogue, to tell the reader that Simon LeCouer's story has ended. These shifts in person and tense keep the novel as fluid as time seems to be in Simon's story; past and present become meaningless terms. The young boy "dreams the future," but the events he dreams have already been described, which suggests that they are past; the same events that take place with Simon and the young Jean and Marie are repeated later with an older Jean and Djinn/Marie, as if past, present, and future are, in some sense, synchronous. This kind of disordering of time is common among writers of "the New Novel," such as Claude Simon, Michel Butor, Nathalie Sarraute, and, of course, Robbe-Grillet himself.

Relation to Previous Works

As previously stated, the names Laura, Boris, and Jean appear in an earlier novel. According to Ilona Leki in *Alain Robbe-Grillet* (1983), *Un Regicide* "contains so many seeds of the themes and novelistic concerns which were to develop later throughout Robbe-Grillet's work." It would seem then that, in addition to the literary influences of novelists like James Cain, Franz Kafka, William Faulkner, and Samuel Beckett, Robbe-Grillet is his own literary precedent. It is particularly intriguing to note the variations on the theme of the Oedipus myth throughout his work; it is suggested by the very title *Un Regicide,* built into the structure of *The Erasers,* where a man seeking a murderer finds it to be himself, alluded to in *Djinn,* in the image of the blind Simon being led by a child, and made explicit in Simon's musing that he "must have an Oedipus complex."

Additional Sources

Fraizer, Dale Watson. *Alain Robbe-Grillet.* Metuchen, NJ: The Scarecrow Press, 1973. This is an annotated bibliography of critical studies on Robbe-Grillet, covering the period 1953-1972. It includes a section on "general studies," chapters on seven of Robbe-Grillet's novels (both the original French and the English translations), bibliographies on the author himself, and one on studies in languages other than English.

Le Sage, Laurent. *The French New Novel.* University Park: Pennsylvania State University Press, 1962. Le Sage provides helpful information about the history and background of the New Novel, its philosophical basis, and what, exactly, characterizes the genre. He includes in separate chapters samples from the work of thirteen novelists from Beckett to Kateb Yacine (and including Robbe-Grillet).

Mercier, Vivian. *The New Novel: From Queneau to Pinget.* New York: Farrar, Straus and Giroux, 1971. Mercier takes issue with the premise that the New Novel is the embodiment of phenomenology, arguing that it is "the result of a literary rather than a philosophic movement." She discusses in some depth the work of seven novelists. Her discussion of Robbe-Grillet's work focuses on his adaptation and use of cinematic techniques in the novel.

Peyre, Henri. *French Novelists of Today.* Oxford: Oxford University Press, 1967. Peyre, who views modern criticism with some disdain, discusses Robbe-Grillet's work in the chapter on "Main Trends Since World War II." He is critical of Robbe-Grillet for being dogmatic and not altogether "coherent in his delineation of his own intentions."

Janis Karam
Palo Alto College

TOM ROBBINS
1936

Update

The witty social commentary that distinguished Robbins' earlier work and earned him his large readership reemerges in *Skinny Legs and All* (1990), his most recent novel. Accused of selling out to the commercial market in *Still Life with Woodpecker,* Robbins has chosen to return to his established, counterculture role as social physician, providing his readers with a diagnosis of society's ills as well as the prescription necessary to return it to good health. Promoted as one of his most serious and thought-provoking efforts, *Skinny Legs and All* has nevertheless attracted a large popular readership. In fact, shortly after its release, the novel appeared on the *New York Times* best-seller list, climbing to fourth in a three-and-a-half month run. Clearly, Robbins' renewed interest in and return to more substantial social themes as signaled in *Jitterbug Perfume* (1984) has been confirmed in *Skinny Legs and All.*

Analysis of Selected Titles

SKINNY LEGS AND ALL

Skinny Legs and All, 1990, novel.

Social Concerns/Themes

As he does in *Another Roadside Attraction* and *Even Cowgirls Get the Blues,* Robbins chronicles the failure of western society to live in harmony and peace with itself. He believes modern Western culture, particularly as it is represented in Christian fundamentalism, is responsible for much human unhappiness and social discord. According to Robbins, modern man has been deceived by a culture that has impaired his spiritual vision. To illustrate his position, Robbins uses the Middle Eastern Dance of the Seven Veils as a means to present seven illusions which keep the naked facts of life from our eyes. As the veils drop in the course of the dance, Robbins reveals his philosophical position: that through ignorance or dissembling our purpose in life is hidden; that we do not have dominion over plants, animals, and inanimate objects; that political expediency is often advertised as virtue; that organized religion diminishes rather than enhances our spiritual life; that valuing money clouds our minds as much as valuing organized religion; that living as if only the afterlife were important keeps us from fulfillment in the here and now; and that every individual is responsible for his or her spiritual growth.

Robbins believes that the cure for the diseased Western cultural system is a return to earlier and healthier feminine principles, like the veneration of Astarte, the pre-Christian goddess of fertility once worshipped across the Middle East. Additionally, he suggests that much of the political discord in the Middle East is a result of the various groups—whether Jews, Arabs, or Christians—losing touch with the older religious system they once shared. Cultural veils lead us to prefer dry spirit in place of fertile soul, the easy power of money in place of the mysterious creative power of magic which produces art.

Overlaying Robbins' social concerns is a tale of two artists who attempt to come to terms with art and each other. *Skinny Legs and All* develops the relationship between beautiful painter Ellen Cherry Charles and lame welder Boomer Petway, a twentieth-century romance between Venus and Vulcan. This love story connects the political, class, religious, and artistic themes of the novel.

Characters

As in his earlier works, Robbins employs an eccentric cast of characters. The protagonist in *Skinny Legs and All*, Ellen Cherry Charles, is tied to a double vocation as artist and waitress; her redneck husband, Boomer Petway, holds a similar twin calling as welder and artist. After the Airstream van that Boomer has welded into a giant roast turkey to win Ellen Cherry Charles as his wife becomes the latest sensation in the New York art world and Boomer gains overnight celebrity status, the marriage, which Ellen Cherry entered with some uncertainty, rapidly disintegrates. To support herself, Ellen Cherry Charles takes a job as a waitress at Isaac's and Ishmael's, a pacifist restaurant opened by an Arab and a Jew across from the United Nations. Joining Ellen Cherry Charles and Boomer Petway are additional outlandish characters, including Turn Around Norman, an artist whose creative expression leads him to rotate in front of St. Patrick's Cathedral so slowly his movements are imperceptible except to his devotees and inanimate objects; Buddy Winkler, a fundamentalist preacher intent on bringing about the second coming of Christ by fomenting war in the Middle East; and Salome, a virginal Lebanese nursing student by day, sexually charged belly dancer by night. Yet Robbins is not content with creating this odd assortment of human characters; his novel also includes a cast of inanimate characters: Conch Shell, Painted Stick, Sock, Spoon, and Can O'Beans. This unlikely group follows Ellen Cherry Charles and Boomer Petway across the United States to New York and, with the exception of Sock, makes its way across the Atlantic to Israel. The interaction between these unusual characters produces the fantastic situations which delight Robbins' fans.

Techniques

Skinny Legs and All is divided into seven major sections, each one corresponding to one of the seven veils dropped by Salome as she performs the Dance of the Seven Veils on Superbowl Sunday. As with each of Robbins' novels, this one manifests its author's delight with the written word, a delight reflected in his verbal humor, puns, stretched metaphors, and wordplay. Unlike his previous works, however, this novel is less experimental. The metafictional intrusion of the author into the work, which has been noted in *Another Roadside Attraction, Even Cowgirls Get the Blues,* and *Still Life with Woodpecker,* has given place to more traditional methods of exposition. Still, Robbins' latest fiction successfully merges fantasy with many of the elements of popular culture as a means of articulating his views on Western sexuality and spirituality.

Literary Precedents

Robbins has indicated that he appreciates works by E. L. Doctorow, Günter Grass, Thomas Pynchon, Ishmael Reed, and Alice Walker. *Skinny Legs and All,* though less innovative than his earlier work, still expresses the playful style and literary techniques reminiscent of Kurt Vonnegut.

Relation to Previous Works

Robbins' protagonist, Ellen Cherry Charles, plays a cameo role in his earlier novel *Jitterbug Perfume,* in which she first appears as one of the "Daughters of the Daily Special" who receives a grant from her sister-waitresses to pursue her interest in painting. More importantly, the author's treatment of issues concerning personal freedom, spirituality, organized religion, human sexuality, and art which appear in *Skinny Legs and All* have been previously introduced in earlier works. Robbins' experience as art critic for the *Seattle Times* and his research on Jackson Pollack appear to have provided him with much of the background for Ellen Cherry Charles' artistic philosophy, the character of Ultima Sommervell, the art dealer, and the New York setting. Once again, Robbins directs some biting satire toward his birthplace, the Richmond, Virginia, area. His fictional Colonial Pines, actually Colonial Heights, Virginia, is depicted as the constricting home of Ellen Cherry Charles and the home base for misguided fundamentalist preacher Buddy

Winkler. The area fosters an atmosphere that drives out art and encourages soul deadening religion.

Additional Sources

Donahue, Deirdre. "New Novel is Both Spiritual and Spirited." *USA Today* (April 18, 1990): D1-2. A cover story that provides a positive review of *Skinny Legs and All* and background information on Robbins' eccentric behavior and publishing success.

Queenan, Joe. "Then the Spoon Speaks Up." Review of *Skinny Legs and All*. *New York Times Book Review* (April 15, 1990): 12. A review appreciative of Robbins' stylistic achievements but critical of the themes and philosophical sophistication of the novel.

Kenneth B. Grant
University of Wisconsin Center-Baraboo

JUDITH (PERELMAN) ROSSNER
1935

Update

His Little Women, published in 1990, is Judith Rossner's first novel since *August* (1983). It was chosen as the main selection of the Literary Guild for April 1990. In the interim between novels, Rossner published a few short pieces in popular magazines.

Analysis of Selected Titles

HIS LITTLE WOMEN

His Little Women, 1990, novel.

Social Concerns/Themes

His Little Women, loosely based on Louisa May Alcott's classic, *Little Women* (1868-1869), is a contemporary treatment of the themes of sisterhood and daughterhood. Instead of being part of a stable family centered around a mother in the Alcott mold, Rossner's four sisters are set adrift by parents who are themselves coming apart. Sam Pearlstein, their charismatic father, has had three wives, each of whom he has left, abandoning his daughters at crucial moments in their young lives. *His Little Women* centers on the two older girls, Louisa and Nell, who meet for the first time at ages twenty-seven and seventeen at the funeral of Nell's second father, Tony. At that point Louisa has already abandoned her own young son to come to California in a bid for her father's love, and Nell soon embarks on a parallel quest. In their search for Sam's love and approval, they highlight a number of the social concerns of our decade: the role of women and their relationship to each other in the aftermath of women's liberation, the enduring worth of tradition and family in an unstable world, the destructive power of low self-esteem, and the lifelong need for parental love and support. Because both Louisa and Nell are writers, the story also explores the novelist's craft, most specifically the relationships between fact and fiction, between real people and fictional characters, and the dilemma that these tensions pose in today's litigious environment.

His Little Women suggests, at the least, an ambivalence toward the achievements of the women's movement in the United States. Some reviewers have termed the novel a "revisionist indictment" of the women's movement. In the novel Nell struggles between her admiration of a woman's independence and her personal need for comfort and support. As a young girl, mainly in reaction to Violet's inability to make a life for herself and her daughter, Nell develops contempt for women who are not self-reliant. Violet's insecurity is made tangible through her doll Mooty, which she has had since childhood and is "unwilling to let out of her sight." Nell thinks the attachment is silly and immature, yet years later, when she sees the doll in Violet's bag at the memorial service after Sam's death, she has a very different response; "I began crying," she writes, "and didn't stop for days. Or was it months."

The modern woman is expected to have it all and do it all: successful career, loving relationships, intellect, sensuality, and self-esteem. The promise of the women's movement seems to have gone slightly sour, however. Nell, while "liberated" by her career and the escape from her first marriage, hesitates to embrace a strong feminist position, especially "the humorlessness that went hand in hand with its militant posture, with its failure to acknowledge complexity, contradiction, and paradox." Eventually she puts aside her law career for a love relationship with Shimmy, a sixty-three-year-old friend of her father's who woos and wins her.

Louisa, too, while considered a spokesman for feminism in her writing, backs off from a strong feminist stance in her personal life as she comes to realize that the sisterhood espoused by the women's movement really goes against human nature, since, as she says, "if most girls purely and simply *love* their sisters, I don't know about it." In her opinion, women don't want to "overthrow men" but just to "make them behave."

As Rossner's heroines are backing off from feminism in this book, however, minor characters such as Violet (Sam's second wife), Lynn (Sam's third wife), and Dagmar (Sam's one-time mistress) are just discovering it. They join a women's support group and become the best of friends. Violet matures and admits that she "had never dreamed what a comfort women could be." Dagmar thrives in this new sisterhood also and seems more beautiful than ever. Lynn's transformation, however, is a disaster. Immersed in her new life, she rejects her former one entirely, turning to drugs and sex, and abandoning her daughters to a life of the same. Eventually she recovers somewhat, but her daughters are lost, one to suicide and the other to drugs.

Such abandonment of responsibility in favor of hedonistic pleasure is a repeated tragedy in the novel. Lack of self-esteem has been a problem for many of Rossner's characters, most notably for Theresa Dunn in *Looking for Mr. Goodbar*, and most try to escape reality through alcohol, drugs, sexual promiscuity, or other excesses. In *His Little Women*, the entire I-Land operation, the self-destructive lifestyles of Sonny and Liane, the seduction of all four daughters by the repulsive Hugo, the temptation and downfall of Jack Campbell, and even Louisa's and Nell's brief drunken indiscretions all highlight the emptiness and dangers of such behavior. Eventually, even Sam, who generally seems so in control of his life, destroys himself as the result of an eating and drinking binge he cannot control no matter how much those he loves try to stop him.

Finally, in *His Little Women*, only the traditional values of love and family can give people the strength they need to survive. The longing for parental love and approval is at the heart of *His Little Women*, as the title itself underscores. Despite Sam's absence from large parts of Nell's and Louisa's youth, he is the focus of all they do. Some critics have suggested that Rossner claims that women seek only their father's love and nothing else. Louisa and Nell compete for that love, and while at times it binds them together, it also sets them at odds. The drive for parental acceptance is so strong that Louisa abandons her own son to get it, seemingly oblivious to the irony. Most of the characters' problems as adults seem to stem from the absence or doubt of parental love. Violet, having lost her parents in the war, suffers through a lifetime of non-personhood; Sonny, alienated from her parents, commits suicide when she is rejected by Estella as well; Nell loses her father three times—first Sam, then Tony, then Sam again, and longs at the end to find a reasonable substitute in Shimmy.

All the characters seem to be searching for the elusive "real thing," and at the end it seems to be found in traditional morality and family ties, not careers or sensual pleasure or the women's movement. Eventually, even Sam finds that Hollywood success cannot satisfy him, and his final longings are for his humbler roots—his grandfather Moishe, the Jewish foods of his childhood, a concerned and loving wife (thus his proposal to the plain but caring nurse Clara). After Sam's death, the void inside Nell is unbearable. She feels, although she has "a perfectly good life," that she lacks the personhood to enjoy that life. Deep in despair, she rediscovers Shimmy and his daughter, whom she has known all her life, and recognizes that these people do, in fact, "have a life." As she comes to know Shimmy better, first as friend and then lover, she concludes that his strength comes from what she has been denied—years of "domestic bliss" and the stability, as he puts it, of "coming home at night to the familiar." The book ends with Nell abandoning her high-powered life as a lawyer to allow time for these simpler pursuits.

Important though all these relationships are in Rossner's book, they cannot eclipse an almost equally important issue for Rossner's characters and for Rossner herself—understanding the process by which fiction is created. Louisa and Nell discover that the writer's craft has far-reaching effects. Not only can a writer be sued for the stories she creates but, even more significantly, the writing becomes a major issue in family relationships. As Nell puts it, "fiction can be enjoyed in inverse relationship to one's proximity to the author." The sub-plot involving Jack Campbell's lawsuit against Louisa is not very important in itself—his is obviously a tenuous case at best—but for what it allows Rossner to reveal of her own doubts and concerns as a writer. Events "that might well have happened" seem as real as those that actually did. Rossner herself once admitted in an interview that "it's much more difficult for me to set down unaltered fact. I worry terribly that I'm not getting each detail exactly right. In fiction, I make the details." On another occasion she said, "I have the absolute urge to bend reality to my own needs." In *His Little Women*, Louisa seems to speak directly for Rossner regarding these issues. The characters, settings, and details in Louisa's book, *Joe Stalbin's Daughters,* are all amalgams of people and places she has known, and the uncanny parallels between her Jack and the real Jack Campbell are just coincidences that have arisen from totally unrelated details from Louisa's own life. Louisa is clearly innocent of libel, and her acquittal allows Rossner to express herself on an issue that is obviously important to her. Ronald Chow, Louisa's lawyer, states her message most eloquently in his summary statement: "We need to read wonderful stories as much as authors need to tell them. We need authors' flights of fancy because we want to soar with them out of everyday life and into realms the imagination makes interesting. We will not have places to go with our writers if their flights are grounded because the weather in the courts has grown dangerous."

As *His Little Women* ends, Louisa has written a new book, *False Light*, in which she means to tell only the truth. Nell observes that "for all *Joe Stalbin's Daughters* being labeled as fiction its characters are more recognizable to me than the ones in *False Light*." She then concludes, "I've come to think there is some complicity between reader and author in an account that makes no claim to the truth. My task in picking up *Joe Stalbin's Daughters* is to forget that it has anything to do with reality. While my task in reading *False Light* is to remember. It goes without saying that I would like the reader to regard my own account as an exception to this truth."

Characters

Just as in Alcott's *Little Women*, Rossner's book establishes the second daughter as the solid center of the action. Nell is presented as the most balanced character, avoiding the excesses of feminism, low self-esteem, or loss of self-control that plague the other characters. From the beginning she acknowledges her father as the "sole light of my life." Her attraction to Hugo, Saul, and Jack Campbell are only momentary diversions, and even Shimmy satisfies her mainly because through him she can preserve a bit of her father and rediscover herself. She loved Tony, her mother's second husband, who was a true father to her, who taught her a love of opera, and who even eclipsed her real father for a time. On the whole, so long as she has a secure base in a father's love, she is a happy, self-reliant woman.

Louisa, her older half-sister, is less secure, for she has been fatherless most of her life. At first she appears cynical and emotionally unattached to her father, but the truth soon becomes clear—she is in deadly competition with Nell to be his favorite daughter. Much later, when preparing for the Jack Campbell trial, she reveals her true feelings to Ronald Chow: "I was an only child. Then my father left us and had another daughter . . . . I knew who he was, and it turned out I could find him in the movie magazines. So now I had a father. And I had a baby sister. Half sister. The . . . little brat had *my father*, and I hated her!" As Nell and Louisa get to know each other, this childish hate is replaced by feelings more complex, and Louisa sometimes truly loves her sister, but the competition is never far beneath the surface. Louisa rejected her first child, a son, but welcomes her daughter, fathered by a sexy Australian bartender, and provides her with a loving home. The daughter, Penny, becomes Sam's fifth little woman and achieves for Louisa the closeness with her father she always craved. Penny eclipses them all as the new "girl" in Sam's life. Louisa's success as a novelist is important to her, but what she wants most is her father's praise of her work. After his death she is still seeking his approval, and so she writes *False Light* with a single purpose in mind: "The most important adult in my life has died and with his death I need to tell the truth about events seen in a false light in my fiction."

Sonny and Liane, the third and fourth daughters, seem to know they have lost the fight for their father's affections from the start. As children they have his love but when Louisa and Nell appear on the scene when the little girls are six and three, the younger pair is immediately supplanted. They develop into empty shells, Sonny at seventeen doing "a lot of dope" and "screwing around in such a way that the rest of the world had to be aware of what she was doing" and Liane, at fourteen, "ravishingly beautiful but also incredibly dumb and utterly self-absorbed." Sonny cares about no one but their housekeeper Estella, who disowns the family over Louisa's first book, *A Servant's Diary*, and refuses to return. A few years later, Sonny commits suicide in a final bid for Estella's attention, and her sister Liane drifts into a commune and is soon forgotten.

The sisterhood in this book is not limited to just Sam Pearlsteins's four daughters. A sisterhood of Sam's wives and lovers, consisting of Esther, Violet, Lynn,

Dagmar, and Clara also forms, and, once they begin to support one another, they become remarkably close. On the whole, except for Nell's mother, Violet, they are negligible women, eclipsed by their famous husband who, as Nell once put it, had a "way of moving through life as though each new group of people had been sent by Central Casting and could be replaced at will without anguish."

Sam Pearlstein himself is a remarkably attractive character. His women's love for him is believable, even though on an objective basis, he has been far from a model husband and father. An incident that occurred when Nell was five best illustrates his warmth and his capacity to love. Nell wanted desperately to see snow, so when a storm was predicted in New York, Sam had her nurse, Peg, fly her in from California for the occasion. When he met the plane before dawn, Peg told him he need not have got up so early to meet them and "he responded that he wouldn't for anything have missed watching me [Nell] see snow for the first time." That memory of being held by her father as "he stepped down from the curb, took several steps, gave [her] a kiss, and whispered 'Hey sunshine, look up at the sky' " sustains her through many lonely moments in the years ahead. Sam is similarly kind to both Nell and Violet when Tony dies, patient with Lynn during her difficulties, and an adoring grandfather to Penny. Sam Pearlstein is known in Hollywood as a powerful man, but as he reveals to Nell, he is a vulnerable and sensitive man, too. When she says his new face after cosmetic surgery "scares" her, he explains that "the rest of the world doesn't love me like you do, and the way I looked *then* was what was scaring everyone." As he approaches retirement, he becomes less and less sure of who he is and thinks back lovingly to his forgotten origins as a Jewish boy in New York. To his daughters, especially after his death, he has no flaws and grows larger than life, but the man himself has a touching humility that makes him human.

The other male characters in the book are of two types—the seducers, like Teddy and Hugo, who are quickly dismissed, and the father types, like Tony and Shimmy, who are capable of great warmth. Even Jack Campbell, for his spontaneous kindness to Nell on the day Tony's will was read, places himself among the fatherly group despite his later questionable activities. The men in *His Little Women* seem more capable of nurturing than the females. This is particularly true of Shimmy, who loves to take care of Nell. By finally accepting Shimmy's offer of a life together, Nell opens herself to the possibility of father and lover in a single person. As her father's closest associate, "whose force of personality is as great as my father's was," Shimmy allows Nell the freedom to love without being untrue to the man who will always be the "light of my life."

Techniques/Literary Precedents.

His Little Women is a frame narrative—a lawyer recounting the story of her father and sisters, one of whom, in turn, is also recounting the same story in a series of loosely autobiographical novels. Further complexity is introduced by the fact that there is a libel lawsuit arising from one of the sister's books and another libel lawsuit being defended by the narrator. As a final reminder of the frame within a frame, the narrator self-consciously addresses the reader at the close of the novel to plead for a favorable reading of her book.

In many ways such techniques are more reminiscent of the literary conventions of Louisa May Alcott's time than the present. The occasionally preachy moral tone and the doubling of narrator as self-conscious author are both typical of pre-modernist novels. The publishers correctly label the book "as romantic as a Victorian novel," with its surprisingly happy-ever-after ending, followed by a proper epilogue to let the reader know how all the characters fared in the "future."

The plot and characterization of *His Little Women* reflects Rossner's nineteenth-century models in numerous ways. Her opening quotation of a letter by Papa March from *Little Women* suggests the most significant one—that Sam's girls, like Mr. March's, must conduct themselves like "little women" while he is away so that he may return "fonder and prouder than ever of my little women." The circumstances are very different—Papa March is off in the Civil War, not moving from family to family, and Mrs. March is a strong, supportive mother, not a series of women of limited mothering skills—yet Alcott's and Rossner's girls share many of the same roles and personality traits. Like Nell, Alcott's Jo is the voice of the book, the writer, the "old maid" career woman, who does not marry until later and then to an intellectual almost fifteen years her senior. Alcott's Meg, the oldest, is like Louisa the "little mother" of the family, the first to provide her father with grandchildren, but she is far more taken with domestic life than Louisa will ever be. Beth, Alcott's third daughter, is frail and dependent; she dies young, the darling of the family, having never regained her strength after a childhood bout with scarlet fever. Rossner's Sonny, too, dies young, but this time for lack of love and at her own hand. Alcott's Amy, like Liane, is the youngest and prettiest, artistic and sociable. Liane resembles her with her striking blonde features and physical attractiveness, but in place of Amy's kind and charming personality, Liane's spirit is vapid and empty. The Pearlstein daughters, like the March girls, must be dutiful, brave, and strong during their father's many absences. Louisa and Nell must also be "little women" about his death, able to carry on and eventually, as grown girls, to "live a reasonable life unrelated to him."

The novel is not without its technical flaws, and critics have been quick to point them out. One reviewer characterized the novel as "laboriously contrived, rambling and lacking momentum." Another, while generally pleased with the book, is annoyed when Rossner "gets on her polemic high horse." Although the plot does get bogged down in the middle of the novel and Rossner's style is occasionally awkward and convoluted, the novel has definite strengths. Rossner makes skillful use of dramatic juxtaposition to foreshadow connections between seemingly unrelated details, particularly in her insertion of excerpts and synopses of Louisa's novels into the narrative. This has the effect of highlighting particular attitudes or observations about women or commenting on actions in the main plot line. She also does an admirable job of taking her readers inside Nell's mind through skillful management of the time line and frequent changes in style and voice to signal shifts in her mode of thinking.

Relation to Previous Works

Rossner's characters in *His Little Women* suffer from the same fears and insecurities that have troubled her previous characters—the longing for love, the fear of loss, and the need for self-reliance and a positive self-image. However, these characters choose different means of coping with these difficulties and have varying degrees of success in overcoming them.

Rossner's central characters always seem to lose their home support early in life: Theresa Dunn's favorite brother died at eighteen and devastated the family (*Looking for Mr. Goodbar*); Nadine's parents were killed in her youth in a freak swimming pool accident (*Attachments*); Dawn's mother committed suicide and her father drowned before her second birthday (*August*); and Nell's father left home and her mother never really took an interest in her (*His Little Women*). Dealing with these losses is a lifetime preoccupation for Rossner's characters.

His Little Women is different from Rossner's previous novels in a major way— the central character is able to cope while relying not on sex (Theresa) or marriage (Nadine) or a symbiotic relationship (Lulu and Dawn) but on herself. *Looking for Mr. Goodbar*'s Terry is a dual personality, insecure in her career independence, unable to accept the support of her fiancé or female friends, and apt to flee to bars in search of casual sexual partners to boost her self-image. This behavior eventually destroys her.

In *Attachments*, the duality between dependence and independence splits to two people—Nadine, who suffers from a fear of loneliness and a poor self-image, and her friend and sister-in-law Dianne, who is a successful lawyer and capable mother. The central character is Nadine, however, who, despite the constant presence of Siamese twins and Dianne in a double marriage, is still lonely. In *August*, Lulu (the psychiatrist) and Dawn (the patient) work out their loneliness and losses together and both are strengthened by the relationship. In *August*, Rossner's faith in the feminist conception of the sisterhood of women reaches its height, and men seem almost negligible.

His Little Women takes a step backward from this feminist position. Rossner's sisters here are only half-sisters, not only by blood but also in terms of their capacity for friendship. Rossner suggests that feminine instincts will let sisterhood go only so far before rivalries and frictions make women step back from each other. Lynn, Dagmar, and Violet's "sisterhood" produces a new self-assertiveness in Violet, but it too is suspect because of its failure to save Lynn. In *His Little Women*, finally, the strength has to come from the self. That self is bolstered by family and friends, but each person owes it to himself to "have a life." Nell achieves satisfaction neither through sex nor talking out her problems, but through the self-therapy offered by her writing. Louisa does the same. Although Nell needs the help and support of Shimmy to get her through a difficult time after her father's death, the implication is clear that self-reliance is an attainable goal. The quotation from *Little Women* with which Rossner introduces the epilogue leaves no doubt about where the strength must lie: "The love of power which sleeps in the bosoms of the best of little women woke up all of a sudden and took possession of her."

Additional Sources

Cloutier, Candace, and Jean W. Ross. "Judith (Perelman) Rossner." In *Contemporary Authors*, New Revision Series, Vol. 18, edited by Linda Metzger and Deborah A. Straub. Detroit: Gale Research, 1986. This article provides a detailed biography and a good overview of Rossner's writing through *August*. It also includes an interview with Rossner in which she discusses her writing habits and the themes of individual novels.

Cooper, Ilene. Review of *His Little Women*. *Booklist* 86 (January 15, 1990): 955. This review finds the book "entertaining and insightful."

Review of *His Little Women*. *Publishers Weekly* 237 (January 26, 1990). Finds the book disappointing.

Rossner, Judith. "The Unfaithful Father." *Mademoiselle* 92 (August 1986): 134+. This is a short story about the death of a mother, and her seven-year-old daughter's struggle to cope with her father's courtship and remarriage to her mother's sister.

See, Carolyn. "Daughters and Lovers." Review of *His Little Women*. *Book World* (April 22, 1990): 5. This mixed review discusses the themes of the novel in some detail.

Mary G. Bernath
Bloomsburg University

PHILIP ROTH
1933

Update

Several major events in Philip Roth's personal life have led to two important pieces of nonfiction along with another novel, *Deception* (1989). Minor surgery in the spring of 1987 turned into "a prolonged physical ordeal" followed by an extended depression. In "the period of post-crack-up meditation," as he calls it, Roth began to reconstruct his life, and the result was *The Facts: A Novelist's Autobiography* (1988). The book traces Roth's life from his boyhood in Newark, New Jersey, through his unhappy marriage, separation, and his first wife's eventual death in 1968. Framing the autobiography is an introductory letter to Nathan Zuckerman, explaining the reasons for writing and soliciting the surrogate author's opinion, and then Zuckerman's response in a long afterword that includes the advice: "Don't publish." The afterword is really a critique of autobiographical writing, specifically Roth's, whom Zuckerman sees rather as a "personificator" than an autobiographer. Nevertheless, the book contains a good bit of useful biographical information, however selectively arranged and ordered, including pseudonyms for Roth's first wife and others.

In 1988 Roth's father became afflicted with a massive brain tumor that would kill him within slightly longer than a year. That illness, his father's last months, and Roth's care and concern are beautifully and movingly portrayed in *Patrimony: A True Story* (1990). Included also are accounts of his mother's death in 1981 and its effects on the Roth family, as well as other events in Philip's personal life, most important of all the emergency quintuple by-pass surgery he underwent just weeks before the tumor finally took his father's life. Readers who misinterpret Roth's relationship with his family, particularly since Bessie Roth's death, became closer and more devoted, each to the other, than ever before. Unlike Zuckerman's father, Herman Roth adored both of his sons, Philip and Sandy, and never found anything in his writing to object to.

Roth's novel *Deception* (1989), published between these autobiographical works, is a departure from his earlier novels. For one thing, it is almost entirely in dialogue; for another, instead of using Zuckerman as his fictional surrogate, he uses his own name, even referring to the novels about Zuckerman in several dialogues. A major character from *The Counterlife*, Zuckerman's English wife, Maria, reappears here as "Philip's" mistress; and although Roth did not marry the actress Claire Bloom until April 1990, several references to "Mrs. Roth" and marital difficulties appear. In actual fact, Roth shared his life with Claire Bloom for years before they were married, spending part of his time in his home in Connecticut and part in London, where Claire lived and where he maintained a studio apartment in which to work. Much of the dialogue occurs in that studio, but the book is fiction, not autobiography, despite the evident pleasure Roth takes in playing with fiction and fact.

Analysis of Selected Titles

THE COUNTERLIFE

The Counterlife, 1986, novel.

Social Concerns

Roth resurrects the characters of his trilogy, *Zuckerman Bound*, to create his best novel since *Portnoy's Complaint* and his technically most complex. The novel contains a long section set in Israel in which Roth presents opposing views—right, left, and center—on Israel's mission, its occupation of the West Bank, and the infighting among Israelis. In a later chapter, he brings up the vexed question of anti-Semitism, particularly in England. Nathan Zuckerman woos and weds an English woman and, because of a child from her previous marriage, they move to London, where he encounters various incidents of more or less blatant bigotry. To his wife's surprise and his own, he becomes not only more fully conscious of his own Jewishness, but also very defensive about it—to the point where it threatens to destroy his marriage.

Themes

The main theme of *The Counterlife* is expressed by its title. As he did to a lesser extent in *My Life as a Man* (1974), where he first introduced the character of Nathan Zuckerman as the novelist Peter Tarnopol's alter ego, Roth here plays with alternative versions of a person's life, or fate. Thus, in the first section, Nathan's brother Henry undergoes surgery for a serious heart condition and dies, but in the next section he is alive and recovered from the surgery and living in Israel. In a still later section, not Henry, but Nathan, has the heart condition and dies, leaving his brother and his lover, Maria, to discover the drafts of the novel he is writing about them, most of which the reader has already read as the foregoing chapters. Henry's and Maria's comments, as well as the eulogy recited at Nathan's funeral, provide important insights into the nature of Zuckerman/Roth's fiction.

Characters

The novel's principal character is Nathan Zuckerman, an accomplished novelist, famous—or infamous—for his fourth novel, *Carnovsky* (which bears close comparison to Roth's *Portnoy's Complaint*). Nathan becomes his brother's confidant when, after a long estrangement as the result of *Carnovsky* and its treatment of their family, Henry feels he must talk with someone about his predicament. His heart ailment is being treated medically with a beta-blocker, which unfortunately also causes impotence and therefore seriously interferes with his sex life. Although he recognizes the dangers, Nathan does not talk him out of the surgery. When Henry is resurrected in the next section and abandons his family for life in Israel, Nathan hunts him down in Judea, where he has fallen under the sway of Mordecai Lippman, a militant Zionist. Nathan does not try to persuade his brother to return home, and during his visit he learns a lot about what made Henry decide to stay. Meanwhile, Nathan has successfully persuaded Maria Freshfield, the wife of his upstairs neighbor in New York, to divorce her husband and marry him. But in a later section of the novel, Nathan (like Henry in the first section) dies in surgery, leaving Maria to talk with his ghost. In the final section, Roth resurrects Nathan (as he did Henry), and shows him living in London with Maria and her daughter, trying to cope with his new surroundings, and attempting to establish a new life. Minor characters include Henry's wife, Carol, and their three children; Maria's mother and her sister, Sarah; and Nathan's Israeli journalist friend, Shuki Elchanan.

Techniques

In presenting his "counterlives," Roth uses a variety of traditional techniques, such as flashbacks, interior monologues, dramatic skits, and comic juxtapositions of events; but the novel's form as well as its theme is fresh and original. As the novel repeatedly doubles back on itself, the reader is compelled to reconsider characters and events in different contexts. This is the point of *The Counterlife*: to consider different ideas of a person's fate. In his alter ego, Nathan Zuckerman, Roth presents different or opposing ideas of his fate as a novelist. Despite these twists and counterturns, the novel is not difficult to follow once the reader grasps its basic technique.

Literary Precedents

The closest precedents in contemporary literature to *The Counterlife* are John Barth's use of himself as a character in some of his stories, or similar techniques used by the English novelist, B. S. Johnson. The French novelist Alain Robbe-Grillet and his follower in England, Gabriel Josopivici, have also written novels that double back on themselves, re-presenting characters and situation from altered perspectives.

Related Titles

The earlier life of Nathan Zuckerman appears in Peter Tarnopol's "Useful Fictions," the first two sections of *My Life as a Man* (1974). Roth presents Zuckerman's later career in the *Zuckerman Bound* trilogy, which consists of *The Ghost Writer* (1979), *Zuckerman Unbound* (1981), *The Anatomy Lesson* (1983), and an *Epilogue: The Prague Orgy* (1985). He also appears in *The Facts: A Novelist's Autobiography* (1988). There, Roth writes a letter to his alter ego and receives a critique of his book in a letter that concludes the volume. Some mention of married life between Zuckerman and Maria also appears in the letter, and in *Deception* (1989) Maria reappears as a major character.

Additional Sources

The Counterlife. Review by John Rubins II. *New York Review of Books* (March 26, 1987): 40. Rubins speaks of this novel as "frustrating and disappointing," that commenting that Roth pushes autobiographical fiction to its limits.

―――――. Review by Janet Fletcher. *Library Journal* (January 1988): 44. Calls this a "dazzling novel" that draws together many elements in his previous fiction.

―――――. Review by John Updike. *The New Yorker* (March 2, 1987): 107. Thinks the novel takes too many twists, which results in an unsatisfactory ending.

―――――. Review by Martha Amis. *Atlantic* 259 (February 1987): 89. Says Roth "is an electrifier . . . so formicably good...so perversely surprising."

Milbauer, Asher Z., and Donald G. Watson. eds. *Reading Philip Roth.* New York: St. Martin's Press, 1988. An important collection of thirteen essays, including an interview with Roth by the editors.

Schechner, Mark. "The Road of Excess: Philip Roth." In *After the Revolution Studies in the Contemporary Jewish Imagination.* Bloomington: Indiana University Press, 1987. Discusses all of Roth's major fiction up to but not including *The*

Counterlife; "In Roth's world, love is a front for aggression, sex is an occasion for failure, childhood is tragedy, adulthood farce."

Walden, Daniel. ed. *The Odyssey of a Writer: Rethinking Philip Roth.* A special issue of *Studies in American Jewish Literature* 8 (Fall 1989). Contains an introduction and ten useful essays, including a bibliographical essay by Ann Leavey and one by Melvin J. Friedman, "Texts and Countertexts: Philip Roth Unbound," that includes *The Counterlife* and *The Facts.*

Jay L. Halio
University of Delaware

SALMAN RUSHDIE
1947

Publishing History

Salman Rushdie, without a doubt the most controversial writer of recent years, was born in Bombay, India in 1947. He spent his early years in Pakistan where his family continues to live, and was educated in England (Rugby School and King's College, Cambridge). Rushdie came to fiction by way of the theater and advertising. He was an actor in fringe theater and authored the television films *The Riddle of Midnight* and *The Painter and the Pest*. His first novel, *Grimus* (1975), was written specifically with an eye to a science fiction prize offered by the publishing house of Gollancz. Despite good reviews, it was not reprinted until the success of *Midnight's Children* (1981), Rushdie's second novel.

When *Midnight's Children* was published in England, its critical and commercial popularity elicited an American edition. His third novel, *Shame* (1983), added to Rushdie's growing fame. These two complementary novels were soon translated into twenty languages. Although *Shame* was not as critically successful as *Midnight's Children*, it generated great expectations for Rushdie's literary career.

Rushdie's subsequent publication, however, *The Jaguar Smile; A Nicaraguan Journey* (1987), was a political travel narrative which received mixed reviews. Certainly this slight book, the outcome of a brief visit he made to Nicaragua in 1986, did little to further his literary reputation.

Still, Rushdie was considered an exciting new novelist, especially in Britain, where something of a publishing row broke out when he left his original publisher and signed with Viking/ Penguin for the sum of $850,000 for his next book, *The Satanic Verses*. This is the controversial book that has made Rushdie a political and cultural cause both in the West and in the Moslem world, and its publishing history is very much a part of the controversy. As soon as the book was made available to the public in Britain on September 26, 1988, it earned the opprobrium of Muslims all over the world. They found the book insulting and sacrilegious, and demanded that it be withdrawn. The book was immediately banned in India, and within the next few weeks Iran, Pakistan, Saudi Arabia, Egypt, Somalia, Bangladesh, Sudan, Malaysia, Indonesia, Qatar, and South Africa also prohibited the entry or circulation of the novel. Canada temporarily banned the import of the book on February 17, 1989, and some American bookstores removed it from display shelves soon after. As the storm broke out, and the book continued to be banned, proscribed, condemned, or censured in various parts of the world, the big question became whether Viking would publish it in the United States at all. It did so eventually on February 22, 1989. To date *The Satanic Verses* has been translated into fifteen languages, and five more translations are in preparation. As is often the case, the attempt to force a book out of print only made others more curious to read it. Within a year of its publication, over one million copies of a difficult literary work had been sold in English-speaking countries alone.

The publishing history of *The Satanic Verses* is also remarkable because of the furor over the question of paperback printing of the novel. A softcover edition is only available in America to members of the Quality Paperback Book Club since Viking Penguin has been reluctant to release the book in paperback. Paperback editions of the novel are available in France, Spain, Greece, and Holland.

And what about Rushdie's literary production as he was trying to ride out the storm in hiding? Much of his efforts since the publication of *The Satanic Verses* have gone into defending the book or ruminating on his situation as an apostate and a man with a price on his head. Thus *Newsweek* published in its February 12, 1990 issue his defense, "In Good Faith." The literary magazine *Granta* has printed in successive numbers a verse meditation, "6 March 1989," and the text of a lecture he had delivered at the Institute of Contemporary Poets in London on February 4, 1990 titled "Is Nothing Sacred?" The same issue of *Granta* included another Rushdie poem titled "Crusoe."

However, Rushdie's major work after *The Satanic Verses* is a children's book, *Haroun and the Sea of Stories* (1990). This is a story of a young boy whose mother has eloped with another man and whose father, a professional storyteller named Rashid, is unable to weave any more stories. Surprisingly light-hearted, comic, and readable, *Haroun and the Sea of Stories* is also an autobiographical work dealing with its author's current predicament: how to continue to write in the face of censorship and threats. In the fantastic world of the children's book (dedicated to Rushdie's son, Zafar), Haroun is able to restore the gift of storytelling to his father by defeating the tyrant Khuttam-Shud, and the book ends with the victory of speech over silence, storytelling over bans imposed on it, and light over dark.

Reviews of *Haroun and the Sea of Stories* have been mostly favorable, and most reviewers have commented on the ingenuity with which Rushdie has utilized the fairy-tale form to articulate his views about man's gift for storytelling and the importance of free thought. Evidently, Rushdie has won his own personal battle against Khuttam-Shud, for there is already talk of another novel and a collection of essays, titled *Imaginary Homelands,* from this fertile and continuously surprising writer.

Critical Reception, Honors, and Popularity

Although *Grimus* did not win the prize it was written for, and received only a scattering of critical applause, the lack of honors and the critical neglect were more than made up for after the publication of *Midnight's Children*. The novel won two of England's major literary prizes: the James Tait Black Memorial Prize and the prestigious Booker McConnel Prize. Reviewers, too, were enthusiastic, comparing the young author to Gabriel García Márquez, V. S. Naipaul, and Günter Grass. Almost no one in the West doubted that *Midnight's Children* was one of the major novels to have come out of the English-speaking world in recent years, while on the Indian subcontinent, where there is a long tradition of literature written in English, writers rejoiced at the recognition given a novelist who had forged an authentic and unique idiom based on the Indian political situation.

Although *Shame* did not receive the honors showered on *Midnight's Children*, it helped consolidate Rushdie's reputation as one of the finest novelists of his generation and the French version received the prize for the best translation of the year. If the reviewers were not quite as enthusiastic, they continued to invoke names such as Swift, Voltaire, Sterne, and Milan Kundera in their appraisals of Rushdie's achievement.

But while *Midnight's Children* and *Shame* were considered major works, they did not escape censure from some quarters. Indeed, in hindsight it is clear that Rushdie was always courting controversy by assuming the role of cultural gadfly. In fact, *Midnight's Children* infuriated the then Indian Prime minister, Indira Gandhi, for its explicit attack on her and her family. The novel even gave rise to a debate on censorship in India, and Rushdie had to apologize to the Gandhi family at one point. *Shame* managed to offend politicians in Pakistan and was promptly banned in that country; more ominously, it was attacked by fundamentalist Muslims, who saw the novel as ridiculing their faith.

Nevertheless, the furor caused by *Midnight's Children* and *Shame* was minor compared to the global hurricane that followed the publication of *The Satanic Verses*. A full record of the path of the storm is beyond the scope of this essay; interested readers, however, should consult *The Rushdie File* (Syracuse University Press, 1989), to get a sense of the intense emotions generated by the work. The book gave rise to demonstrations, riots, and diplomatic rows. Iran's Ayatollah Khomeni issued an edict against Rushdie and his publishers, pronouncing a death sentence on the writer for blaspheming Islam and its Prophet. Rushdie was forced into hiding and has been under continuous police protection since then. In Belgium, two moderate Muslim religious leaders who opposed censorship of the work were assassinated. At least a score of people were killed and hundreds of others were injured when Muslims around the world demonstrated to express their anguish and indignation at what they considered to be a defamatory, false, and repugnant book. A few Western writers and readers also condemned Rushdie for being irresponsible and for abusing his right to publish satirical fiction. Former President Jimmy Carter, for instance, felt that the novel "had opened the kind of intercultural wound that is difficult to heal."

On the other hand, *The Satanic Verses* was hailed as a great achievement by a number of Western critics. The novel was awarded one of England's premier literary awards, the Whitbread Literary prize for 1988, and was also shortlisted for the Booker Prize. In March 1989, the Nobel Prize Committee for literature reportedly split over considering the book and its author for their award. At the height of the controversy, Western intellectuals banded together to defend Rushdie's freedom to publish such a book. And although the hurricane created by *The Satanic Verses* has died down somewhat, criticisms of Rushdie and defenses of his work are still being published. In late 1990 Rushdie briefly emerged from hiding to autograph copies of his newest book and to offer apologies aimed at lifting the Islamic "death sentence."

Arguing that *The Satanic Verses* is a "moral fable" about a character who "has lost his mind because he has lost his faith," Rushdie has attempted recently to distance himself from the anti-Muslim sections of the book. He has also expressed repentance and a desire to be seen as a Muslim who never "attempted the book as an insult." However, most Islamic groups have rejected the apology and Iran has renewed its call for the execution of the author, who still remains in hiding and under continuous police protection.

Analysis of Selected Titles

MIDNIGHT'S CHILDREN
Midnight's Children, 1981, novel.

Social Issues/Themes

Midnight's Children is the story of Saleem Sinai, the thirty-year old narrator of the novel. Born at midnight on August 15, 1947, the moment of India's independence, Saleem's story has representative significance, for his birth and upbringing are meant to parallel that of India. The novel, however, encompasses over one hundred years of Indian history, since Saleem feels that his begetting is as much a part of his story as is his birth. The novel covers different periods of Indian history such as the era of British rule, the struggle for independence, partition, the progress of the two nations of India and Pakistan, Indo-Pakistani wars, the creation of Bangladesh, and Indian politics in the 1970s.

Saleem narrates his story to Padma, a girl who works in a pickle factory and is in love with him. Although autobiographical in mode, the novel partakes of the fantastic, for it is Rushdie's point that the history of India cannot be seen in realistic terms. Padma's simple but critical nature causes her to interrupt Saleem's narrative and ask him questions. These prevent Saleem's story from having any kind of consistent forward flow. Also, Saleem's mind tends to wander from time to time so that the novel moves back and forth in time and has more than its share of digressions.

Fantastic, disorderly, nonlinear, and digressive though it may appear to be, *Midnight's Children* yields up an elaborate plot to readers patient enough to follow the different patterns Rushdie weaves into a complex whole. One way of recreating the plot is to focus on the novel's division into three books. Book one evokes the past and takes us to the moment in Indian history when Western beliefs intermingled with Indian values in people like Saleem's grandfather. Book two deals with the India of Saleem's childhood, a land in which Saleem delights until he is thrust out into the adult world. Book three deals with Saleem's loss of innocence, with the proliferation of chaos, and with the entry into a darker world.

Another way of approaching the plot of *Midnight's Children* is to see it as the story of a changeling who must solve the mystery of his identity and come to terms with a fragmenting world. Saleem is the changeling for he is really the son of a common street singer made pregnant by a departing Englishman who is switched at birth in a nursing home by a politically radical nurse for the son of a rich Muslim couple. Saleem is thus brought up in affluence while the son of the rich Kashmiri family, given the name of Shiva, grows up as a street tough. Later, Saleem attempts to restore his lost identity by plunging into Shiva's world while Shiva tries to get to the top through force and cunning. Eventually, Saleem ends up in a slum where, though he is rendered impotent by overzealous family planning campaigners, he manages to regain access to his memory. At the conclusion of the novel, Parvati, Saleem's wife and another of midnight's children, gives birth to Shiva's child after being seduced and then abandoned by him. In this way a child is born who will have Sinai blood as well as the name—one wrong that has been righted, albeit in a strange manner. This is a cause for hope and the stage is thus set for a new generation that will replace the band of midnight's children and inherit the Indian earth without illusions.

A major theme of *Midnight's Children* is the predicament of the modern Indian, grappling with his unique history, split between the tendency to affiliate with Indian cultural traditions and his attraction to Western values. Rushdie is also intent on showing how the ideals of a secular, egalitarian India—expressed in the movement for independence—were shattered by subsequent political developments and how the dream had become a nightmare by the 1970s. *Midnight's Children,* in other words, is a satire on Indian politics and politicians, on the corruption, despotism, war-mongering, and zealotry that Rushdie sees everywhere in contemporary India.

Another theme that Rushdie pursues is the disintegration of traditional familial, cultural, and political structures in present-day India. In addition, Rushdie is bent on depicting India as a land where anything is possible, a land where the serious and the absurd, the fantastic and the earthy, the tragic and the comic complement each other. It is part of Rushdie's novelistic strategy to give his readers the feel of a mixed-up, fragmenting world.

For Rushdie India is a country where national history and individual progress are so intertwined that every national event is reflected in the lives of individuals.

Characters

Midnight's Children's narrator-protagonist Saleem Sinai leads a cast of characters who are among the most quirky and unforgettable created by a novelist in recent times. Saleem's most prominent physical characteristic is his ugly, oversized nose. He is gifted with telepathic powers but loses them when he undergoes a sinus operation. However, the operation results in heightening his olfactory abilities, which leads to his employment as a tracker. But somehow things are always happening to Saleem and his physical and social condition steadily deteriorates. In the course of the novel, he loses a tuft of hair, a part of his finger, and his sexual potency. His veracity as a narrator is suspect because his memory is fallible and his vision, especially towards the end, is apt to become fragmented. Moody, apologetic, and solemn at times, he can also be cynical and witty.

Saleem's family is also eccentric and memorable. His grandfather, Aadam Aziz, for instance, courts Saleem's future grandmother Naseem through a perforated sheet. Saleem's mother trains herself to love her husband part by part. His uncle, Hanif, devotes his life to making the perfect documentary film and is obsessed by the notion that he should play rummy until he completes a thirteen-card heart sequence. Saleem's sister, known as the Brass Monkey, is another fantastic creation whose favorite activity is to set fire to the family's shoes.

Saleem himself is only one of the supposedly one thousand and one children born at the first hour of August 15, 1947, all of whom are endowed with special gifts like Saleem's telepathic power. One of these children can travel through time; another can change sex at will. Still another, Parvati, who becomes Saleem's wife but mother of Shiva's son, is a sorceress. Shiva, of course, is another of midnight's children and Saleem's opposite in every way: cruel, unscrupulous, opportunistic, and destructive.

Still other characters exemplify Rushdie's desire to fill the novel with India's teeming, yet fascinating, humanity. Singh, a seven-foot Snake Charmer, also known as the Most Charming Man in the World, uses his snakes to promote Marxism. He is one of the many illusionists, contortionists, and exhibitionists who move through the pages of *Midnight's Children*. The variety of these supporting characters—the peepshow man, Methwold, Wee Willie Winkie, Nadir Khan, Commander Sabarmati—populate this novel with a representative mix of the melting-pot that is the Indian sub-continent.

Some of the characters that seem totally fantastic are based on real people. Among them is the Widow who decides to get rid of all of the midnight children and has them incarcerated in a hostel where she intends to have them sterilized. Rushdie uses this project to attack the excesses of Indira Gandhi's family planning campaign. Another character who seems tinged with unreality is the politician who drinks his own urine for health reasons; he too is based on a real-life Indian prime minister, Moraji Desai, who admitted to such a practice. Actuality, for Rushdie, can be every bit as bizarre as fiction.

Techniques

Reviewers hailed *Midnight's Children* as a stylistic tour de force and many studies have focused on Rushdie's technical virtuosity and originality. Rushdie is indeed not afraid to dazzle his readers with a rich excess. Some of the episodes of the novel are operatic in texture or have a dreamlike quality; still others use the form of the news-flash and newspaper report for startling effects. Rushdie is fond of juxtapositions, digressions, flashbacks, flash-forwards, and breathtaking changes of pace; but he can also offer pages of straightforward narrative and sections which are constructed with journalistic particularity or essayistic clarity. On occasion the narrator appears self-conscious, self-reflexive, and postmodern in his bid to convince readers of the fictionality of his work; at other times he sprinkles his narrative with Indian names and words and colloquialisms to give the feel of the Indian milieu in which his characters move. *Midnight's Children* can also be densely allusive, for Rushdie builds his contexts from Indian myths, history, popular culture, and magazine talk as well as from Western literary classics.

Literary Precedents

Even though *Midnight's Children* is an entirely original work, it is self-consciously in a distinct narrative tradition which can be traced as far back as Laurence Sterne's *Tristram Shandy* (1759). In fact, Rushdie echoes Sterne's masterpiece on several occasions and styles his narrative on the earlier novel's transgressive, teasing, digressive, and nonlinear style. Moreover, Saleem Sinai's birth, physical oddness, sensitivity, and playfulness owe a great deal to Sterne's conception of his hero.

Midnight's Children also echoes other celebrated works of world literature. Like Günter Grass's *Tin Drum* (1959) and Gabriel García Márquez's *One Hundred Years of Solitude* (1967), Rushdie's novel presents a national history through one family's extraordinary experience; and all three books employ the fantastic in the service of reality. Saleem's gift for telepathy parallels the talent of Oscar, Grass's hero, for seeing through the surface; both characters survive the cataclysms of recent history in unique ways. From Marquez, Rushdie seems to have learned the technique of "magical" realism that has become the hallmark of recent Latin American fiction. It is worth noting that *Midnight's Children* also recalls one of Rushdie's favorite literary works, the *Thousand and One Nights*. The number of children born on midnight on that fateful day is Rushdie's way of acknowledging his debt to the phantasmagoric mode of the oriental classic. In his literary affiliations, as in everything else, Rushdie displays his Eastern roots as well as his Western lineage.

SHAME

Shame, 1983, novel.

Social Concerns/Themes

Unlike the sprawling nature of *Midnight's Children*, *Shame* is a tightly controlled narrative. The novel begins with the strange birth of its "peripheral hero," Omar Khayyam Shakil, jointly born to three sisters named Chhunni, Munnee, and Bunny. Shakil is a peripheral hero because he is relegated to the margins of the action after the first three chapters. The focus then shifts abruptly to the linked destinies of two other families, the Harappas and the Hyders, and especially to the men who dominate these families, Iskander Harappa and Raza Hyder.

Iskander Harappa, a gambler and womanizer turned politician, is removed from power by General Hyder, the man he had promoted to a high public position when he became prime minister. On this level *Shame* is the story of the political rivalry between two men who were once in collusion but who inevitably become antagonists. However, Rushdie goes beyond this rivalry to highlight the tragic fortunes of Sufiya Zinobia, daughter of Hyder, and wife of Shakil. Although a brainsick girl since infancy, Sufiya is preternaturally aware of the shameful deeds being committed all around her by the men of her country. Ultimately metamorphosed into a beast of shame, a violent agent of retribution, not unlike Nemesis, she becomes a savage killer. As in an Elizabethan revenge play, the stage is littered with corpses in the final scenes as men who had pursued power in immoral ways face horrible deaths. Other women join Sufiya in becoming instruments of vengeance. Hyder, for instance, is killed by Shakil's three mothers sometime after he has had Harappa executed. Shakil, too, meets a violent death when Sufiya decapitates him. She then reverts to the retarded girl she was before the shamelessness around transformed her into a Beast of Shame.

If *Shame* resembles an Elizabethan revenge play or a Gothic novel, Rushdie, appearing throughout the novel as the author-narrator, tells his readers quite clearly that the events of his story are only "at a slight angle to reality." In fact, he leaves no doubt that *Shame* is an attempt to recreate the history of the state of Pakistan in the imaginative mode. Thus the novel must first of all be seen as a political allegory. Iskander Harappa is based on Zulfiqar Bhutto, prime minister of Pakistan in the 1970s, while Hyder is modelled on General Ziaul Huq, who usurped power from Bhutto in a military coup and had him hung. While there are no historical equivalents of Shakil and Sufiya, Harappa's daughter, Arjumand, an ambitious and sophisticated woman, clearly resembles Benazir Bhutto, who subsequently became Pakistan's prime minister. Rushdie's major premise is that the history of Pakistan is a shameful one, filled with coups, massacres, rigged elections, religious hypocrisy, and power-hungry, treacherous, mean-minded men who violated the ideals that led to the formation of a state meant to embody purity of faith. Rushdie attacks, among other things, "the mutually advantageous relationships between the country's establishment and it's armed forces" and emphasizes the psychic damage to that section of the population that must bear the brunt of the tyranny. Death and destruction, Rushdie appears to be saying in the apocalyptic conclusion, will spread throughout a land when a country's leadership is taken over by successive unscrupulous, repressive regimes. As far as Rushdie is concerned, Pakistan's history reads like a chapter from a book about the Middle Ages or any period when barbarians vied for power and left ruin in their wake. To make this point, Rushdie dates his story according to the hegerian calendar so that the novel's events literally take place in the fourteenth century.

Characters

As in *Midnight's Children*, *Shame* contains a gallery of fantastic, even bizarre characters, the most striking being Sufiya Zinobia. Made to blush at her birth by the disappointment of her father at the birth of a daughter, infected with brain fever at the age of two, married off to a man who does not care about her, confined to an attic to prevent her from walking the streets, and eventually transformed into the fiery, ravening beast of shame, Sufiya retains our sympathy throughout her strange, troubled story. Shakil, her husband, always at the edge of things, clearly embodies shamelessness. Obese, drunk, and an opportunist, he is also grotesque, but believably so.

Besides those characters modeled on historical figures, some are purely imaginary beings that advance Rushdie's allegorical points. Talver Ulhaq, Iskander Harappa's chief of secret police, for instance, is so clairvoyant that he can read people's thoughts before they can translate them into action. Still other characters stand out because they are given distinctive touches. Harappa's wife, Rani, embroiders a shawl to cope with the humiliation of being cast aside by her playboy-husband. The shawl is her way of getting revenge on him and it documents his political wrongdoings. Rushdie's characterization in *Shame* thus runs the gamut from the complex to the simple, from the psychologically realistic to the emblematically representative. All of the characters embody various forms of shame or shamelessness.

However, the most interesting of all the characters one encounters in *Shame* is the author-narrator. The novel contains not only the stories of the Shakils, the Harappas, and the Hyders, but also the ruminations, the likes and dislikes of a man driven to write about a country to which he is tied, as he puts it, with "elastic" bonds. As a matter of fact, there is a great deal about Rushdie's own life in the novel. The first five pages of the second chapter, for example, reads like an extract from Rushdie's own diary. There is nothing gratuitous about Rushdie's presence or his dark musings on Pakistan in the novel; his presence is needed to steer us through the bewildering series of events with our sense of reality intact.

Techniques

"I'm only telling a fairy story," says the author-narrator at one point. On another occasion he affirms that he is telling the truth, mainly, with only some "off-centering" of it. At still another point he confesses that he is forced to reflect Pakistani history in his narrative "in fragments of broken mirrors" since a straight realistic novel about his country would be too fantastic for most people. Such comments not only indicate Rushdie's self-consciousness about his narrative technique but also underlines the constant oscillation between fantasy and history that takes place in *Shame*. As in *Midnight's Children*, Rushdie has drawn from a variety of narrative forms: political allegory, revenge tragedy, the gothic-oriental tale, postmodernist metafiction, the fairy tale, the personal essay, and the moral fable. By turns serious and farcical, tragic and playful, surrealistic and realistic, eloquent and loquacious, Rushdie again displays in this novel his control over a wide range of fictional techniques. His prose shows his mastery of different levels of discourse: sophisticated English syntax, Indian English, bureaucratese, idioms based on Urdu, and words of Indian origin. Not surprisingly, Rushdie has been criticized for his stylistic excesses and self-indulgent prose, but that is the risk involved in his exuberant style and commitment to experimental fiction.

Literary Precedents

Many of the texts which were important in the literary genealogy of *Midnight's Children* remain primary for a work like *Shame*. The digressions, authorial interventions, and attempts to lay bare story-telling devices again bring to mind Sterne's *Tristram Shandy*. The technique of exaggeration, of fantasy put to use in the service of realism, the apocalyptic violence of the ending, the political consciousness, and the preoccupation with powerful families continues to echo Márquez's *One Hundred Years of Solitude* and other works of the "magical realism" tradition. The fabulous, phantasmagoric nature of most of the episodes continue to evoke the *Thousand and One Nights*; in fact, Rushdie alludes to that work quite clearly in his novel.

Shame also recalls two other writers as influences on Rushdie at this stage of his career. The savage irony of sections of the novel and satiric distinctions, such as that between the one-godly (Muslims) and the stone-godly (Hindus), show the impact of Jonathan Swift. (Swift made fun of Lilliputian factions by calling them Big Endians and Little Indians.) Rushdie's techniques and fictional concepts also show similarities to those of the Czech novelist, Milan Kundera, who alternates his "fairy tale" with an expatriate's comments on the politics of a country. Like Kundera, too, Rushdie is able to express his pain at what goes on in the name of ideology in his country without abandoning the comic mode.

THE SATANIC VERSES

The Satanic Verses, 1988, novel.

Social Concerns/Themes

The Satanic Verses has a convoluted plot, or perhaps it is better to describe the novel as having a complex main framing plot which allows Rushdie to include a number of subplots or embedded stories. The main plot concerns the coming together and falling apart of Gibreel Farishta and Saladin Chamcha. Both of them are Indian actors, but whereas Gibreel has become a superstar in his country by playing the role of gods in "theologicals," or films based on religious subjects, Saladin has had less spectacular success in England by lending his voice to television commercials and a situation comedy called *The Aliens Show*. The two men meet under extraordinary circumstances: they are on an Air-India jumbo jet which is taken over and then blown apart by Canadian Sikh terrorists. Their fates are conjoined as they miraculously survive the crash and fall down on an English beach. But if they manage to escape death, both Saladin and Gibreel undergo a weird transformation as they descend: Gibreel has a halo around his head and fancies himself an angel who will blow the trumpet of doom while Saladin is metamorphosed into a goat, complete with horns, legs, and hoofs. In his altered state, Gibreel spends most of his time having visions and exhibiting the symptoms of a paranoid schizophrenic. Saladin, however, is captured by police on the lookout for illegal immigrants, despite the years he has spent in England and his attempt to become an Englishman. Since at the moment of his arrest, Gibreel refuses to identify him, Saladin finds himself with twin goals: to regain his human identity and to take revenge on Gibreel for failing to stand by him. Soon Saladin finds himself in Brickhall, an Asian ghetto in London, where he becomes something of a cause celebre. Ultimately, Saladin does manage to destroy Gibreel through devilish cunning. Paradoxically, however, Saladin is not condemned for his part in the death of Gibreel. In fact, at the end of the novel Saladin positively grows in humanity as he rediscovers the power of love when he visits India to be at the bedside of his dying father.

The subplots of *The Satanic Verses* have to do with the visions Gibreel has after his fall. In a few of these dreams, cast in the "epic" style of Indian "theologicals," he revisions the founding days of a religion that is unmistakably Islam. Gibreel dreams thus of the episode of the satanic verses, a controversial event in the early history of Islam, when according to some disputed sources, the prophet Muhammad (here renamed Mahound), is misled for a while by the devil into compromising with the polytheists of Mecca (here Jahilia) but recovers in time to reassert the oneness of God and reject the temptations of Satan. In another of these episodes, the scribe Salman and the poet-satirist Baal reveal the disillusion of some after Mahound has set himself up as a lawgiver. Salman, for instance, retells the story about his attempt to corrupt the sacred words dictated to him by Mahound as the messenger of God. Two other of Gibreel's dreams that constitute the subplots of the novel are also "theological" in nature, but are taken from recent history. One of them is the portrait of an obsessive religious leader in exile, strikingly similar to the Ayatollah Khomeni in London awaiting the overthrow of the Shah of Iran. The other religious tale based on a recent event is the haunting story of a visionary butterfly-eating girl called Ayesha who, Pied-Piper like, leads almost everyone in an Indian village to the Arabian Sea, which she is convinced will part and take them to Mecca, the holiest city of Islam.

There are, in addition, many other stories that are linked in one way or another to the main plot. The best of them has to do with Rosa Diamond, the lonely old woman in whose house Gibreel and Saladin find themselves after their fall, and her dreams of the romantic moments of her life in the Argentine pampas. In the story of the Sufiyan family, typical Asians experience the stresses and transformations of immigrant life in England. Both Gibreel and Saladin have their love interests and these provide the occasions for more twists in the main plot. Gibreel, for example, has rejected his Indian mistress, Rekha Merchant, and pursues the beautiful mountain-climber, Alleluia Cone. Saladin is estranged from his wife, Pamela Lovelace, and goes back at the end of the novel to his Indian girl friend, Zeeny Vakil. All in all, *The Satanic Verses* is a potpourri of tales and episodes held together by the framing story of the emotional adventures of Gibreel Farishta and Saladin Chamcha.

Under extraordinary attack ever since the novel was published, Rushdie has been at some pains to clarify his thematic concerns. For instance, in an interview given in the *Observer* (September 25, 1988) Rushdie has called *The Satanic Verses* a novel "about transformations, about religious faith, from the point of view of someone who would no longer describe himself as religious," and about "imported cultures, that is to say, the immigrant experience." In another interview, broadcast on BBC television (February 14, 1989) Rushdie claimed that he intended to show in his novel the conflict "between the sacred text and the profane text, between revealed literature and imagined literature." In still another interview (*India Today*, September 15, 1988), Rushdie declared that one of his major themes is "religion and fanaticism" and that another was the "fact that an idea or a new thing in the world must decide whether to compromise or not."

After his book was banned in India, Rushdie committed himself to explaining his thematic intentions in a number of written statements. In one of them, an open letter to the prime minister of India, he affirms that "the book is not actually about Islam, but about migration, metamorphosis, divided selves, love, death, London, and Bombay" and "the phenomenon of revelation, and the birth of a great world religion." From hiding, and a year after the controversy had peaked, Rushdie published an extended essay in *Newsweek* (February 12, 1990), in which he reiterated his view that his novel is about the "immigrant condition" and called it a celebration of "the hybridity, impurity, intermingling, the transformations that come of a new and unexpected combinations of human beings, cultures, ideas, politics, movies, songs." At the same time, he admitted that his novel is "a secular man's reckoning with the religious spirit," written not to insult Islam, but to question it from the perspective of a radical dissenter.

If Rushdie's comments on his novel are accepted, *The Satanic Verses* deals seriously with two major themes: the phenomenon of immigration and the nature of religious faith. There can be little doubt that Rushdie is effective in his depiction of the situation of Indian immigrants in present-day England. Among the issues he explores with considerable sensitivity are the immigrant's encounter with racial prejudice and police brutality, the life of South Asians and West Indians in London ghettos, and the kind of subcultures sprouted by cultural migration. Rushdie also focuses on other aspects of the immigrant's experience: the tendency of first-generation Indians in England to hold on to their heritage; the defiant ways of second generation Anglo-Asians who must make a place for themselves in Britain despite their skin color and parental prohibitions; and the "Uncle Tomism" of an immigrant such as Saladin who at one point of his life is willing to do anything to be accepted by English society.

Rushdie also uses the novel form to comment on issues of faith and doubt and the question of religious truth. These issues, and topics such as the nature of prophecy and the origins and spread of Islam, are explored in the chapters devoted to Gibreel's dream visions. Rushdie is also interested in underscoring the thin line that divides good and evil, angel and devil, a theme embodied in the linked destinies of Gibreel and Saladin. In the episodes of the Imam in exile and the narrative of the butterfly-eating Ayesha, Rushdie's gaze is on people who become monomaniacs because of a sense of religious mission.

But Rushdie's tongue-in-cheek treatment of the Prophet Muhammad and the history of the birth of Islam undermine to some extent the claim that he has made that *The Satanic Verses* is a spiritual novel. He might have felt, as Melville did after completing *Moby-Dick*, that he was as innocent as a lamb; but he must have known that, from the point of view of many orthodox Moslems, he had written a wicked book. Episodes, such as the one in which a group of prostitutes adopt the name of the Prophet's wives to attract customers, irreverent references to people and practices sanctified in Islam, and Salman the scribe's cynical comments about Mahound, make Rushdie vulnerable to charges that he was being deliberately provocative and offensive.

Characters

In *The Satanic Verses* Rushdie provides a diverse and distinctive set of characters, some taken from contemporary life and some based on people mentioned in Muslim religious history. The most memorable is Saladin Chamcha, a character who is to some extent Rushdie's self-portrait. In his progress from Anglophilia to a renewed understanding of his Indian roots, in his journey from alienation to love, Saladin goes through the gamut of human emotions. Gibreel Farishta, a composite of two real-life Indian actors, is also a complex character, angelic on the outside, treacherous and hateful within. He is a remarkable study of a man in the process of disintegration, a star who has become so possessed by the semi-divine status attributed to him by his fans that he comes to believe he has angelic powers.

Among the minor characters, the most fascinating are the hate-filled Imam and the almost ethereal Ayesha. Rushdie is also convincing in his portrait of Indian women, such as Saladin's girl friend, Zeeny Vakil, who urges him to make a mature acquaintance with his country, or the tough-minded and uninhibited Sufiyan sisters. However, Rushdie's attempt at portraying English women such as Pamela Lovelace or Alleluia Cone seem contrived and uninspired.

Rushdie's historical characters are skillfully drawn. Salman the scribe's cynicism about the revealed world is like (Salman) Rushdie's own doubts about the authority of sacred texts. Abu Simbel, the leader of Mecca who has to come to terms with Mahound's growing influence; his heartless wife Hind; the poet Baal, whose profession falls into disrepute because of the teachings of the new religion and who numbers himself among the Prophet's enemies; and Mahound, the mystic and Law Giver are deftly drawn portraits of characters from an earlier period. But in choosing to present the Prophet in fiction and to rename him Mahound (a name which traditionally has had negative connotations for Muslims), and in showing him as a man who is fallible and opportunistic, Rushdie has managed to enrage Muslims all over the world.

Techniques

As in *Midnight's Children* and *Shame*, Rushdie resorts to a variety of narrative techniques to present his story. At times he parodies the excessive, artificial, melodramatic, and garish aspects of popular Indian films; on other occasions he adopts the self-reflexive strategies of the metafictionist. Characteristically, *The Satanic Verses* blends straightforward narrative with authorial commentary. Gibreel's visions are presented as parables or allegories and have the feel of dreams, while the frame story of the Indian star and Saladin is presented with a mixture of fantasy and realism. Readers who are familiar with the style of Rushdie's earlier novels will not be surprised to find in *The Satanic Verses* the same kind of slapstick, comic excess, and satiric energy that he has previously used. But they may be unprepared for the simple realism of this novel's ending and the pathos of the deathbed scene. Linguistically, Rushdie once again shows himself to be endlessly inventive. The novel is filled with puns, metaphors, and exact mimicry of different voices and dialects. Rushdie manages to move between Gibreel's visions and the present-day world with consummate skill. Nevertheless, there are stretches of the novel, especially near the middle when Gibreel and Saladin are trying to situate themselves in London, which are less than satisfying.

Literary Precedents

Rushdie alludes throughout the novel to numerous fictional works, leaving no doubt about the genealogy of *The Satanic Verses*. *The Thousand and One Nights* continues to be a major influence, especially in the way Gibreel's dreams are presented. The self-consciousness of Sterne and the "magical" realism of Márquez continue to be in evidence. But a few writers are acknowledged as influences implicitly or explicitly for the first time. The most prominent of them is Dickens, and English critics have been quick to point out the deliberateness with which Rushdie invokes *Our Mutual Friend* (1865). In his *Newsweek* essay, Rushdie also mentions Blake's "The Marriage of Heaven and Hell" (1790) as one of the formative influences on his effort to fictionalize "the inter-penetration of good and evil." In this same article, Rushdie credits the Russian novelist Mikhail Bulgakov's *The Master and Margarita* (1967) as the work which inspired him to write about devilish visitations. *The Satanic Verses* also has affiliations with the tales of Argentina's Jorge Louis Borges. And as has been pointed out above, Rushdie intentionally mimics the outlandish style of popular Indian cinema. Finally, the multiple endings given to the Rosa Diamond episode affiliate that part of the novel with the experimental fiction of John Fowles, especially his celebrated novel, *The French Lieutenant's Woman* (1969).

Other Works

Grimus, 1974 (novel); *The Jaguar Style: A Nicaraguan Journey*, 1987 (travel narrative-political memoir); "Prophet's Hair," *Atlantic*, June 1981 (short fiction); "Outside the Whale," *Granta*, 11/1983 (essay); "After Midnight," *Vanity Fair*, September 1987 (essay); "In Good Faith," *Newsweek*, February 12, 1990 (essay); "Is Nothing Sacred?" *Granta*, 31/1990 (essay). *Haroun and the Sea of Stories* (1990).

Additional Sources

Aramavudan, Srinvas. "Is No Fun, Yaar; Salman Rushdie's *The Satanic Verses*," *Diacritics*, 19, 2 (Summer 1989): 1-20. Focuses on the novel's satiric moments and religious and historical contexts.

Appignanesi, Lisa, and Sara Maitland, eds. *The Rushdie File*. Syracuse: Syracuse University Press, 1990. A comprehensive documentation of *The Satanic Verses* controversy.

Brigg, Peter. "Salman Rushdie's Novels: The Disorder in Fantastic Order," *World Literature Written in English*," 27, 1 (1987): 119-130. Treatment of the element of fantasy in the novels.

Brennan, Timothy. *Salman Rushdie and the Third World*. New York: St. Martin's, 1989. The only book-length work to analyze Rushdie's novels and a good account of his status as a "third world" writer.

Durix, Jean-Pierre. "The Artistic Journey in Salman Rushdie's *Shame*," *World Literature Written in English*," 23, 2 (1984): 451-463. Examines Rushdie's technique in the novel.

Kanaganayakam, C. "Myth and Fabulosity in *Midnight's Children*," *Dalhousie Review*, 67, 1 (1987): 86-98. Discussion of the book as *the* modern Indian novel in English.

Mukher Jee, Bharati. "Prophet and Loss." *Voice Literary Supplement,* March 1989, Number 2: 9-12. Sympathetic account of Rushdie's work by the Asian-American writer.

Pipes, Daniel. *The Rushdie Affair: The Novel, the Ayatollah and the West*. New York: Birch Dune Press, 1990. Attempts to describe and analyze the controversy around *The Satanic Verses*.

Suleri, Sara. "Contraband Histories: Salman Rushdie and the Embodiment of Blasphemy," *The Yale Review*, 78, 4 (1990): 604-624. Sophisticated defense of *The Satanic Verses*.

Weatherby, W. J. *Salman Rushdie: Sentenced to Death.* New York: Carrol & Graf, 1990. A biography and an account of *The Satanic Verses* affair; interesting and informative.

Wilson, Keith. *"Midnight's Children* and Reader Responsibility," *Critical Quarterly,* 26 (Autumn 1984): 23-27. Examines the role of the reader in uncovering the meaning of the novel.

Fakrul Alam
Clemson University

RAFAEL SABATINI
1875-1950

Publishing History

Born of an Italian father and English mother, in Jesi, Italy, April 29, 1875, Rafael Sabatini was raised in England and educated in Portugal and Switzerland. With all the travelling he did as a youngster, he quickly learned to master languages; by the time he was eighteen, he was fluent in six. Settling in Liverpool, he turned to writing fiction at about the age of twenty. It was more fun to write romances, he often said, than to read them. An avid reader throughout his childhood, he was steeped in the romanticism of Alexandre Dumas *père* and Jules Verne, as well as the histories of William Prescott. At first he wrote, he said, with no thought of publication in mind. He showed some of his stories to a journalist friend who not only liked them, but encouraged Sabatini to submit them to an editor. What was even more remarkable—to Sabatini at least—was that the stories were accepted for publication.

Balancing a full time job in commerce with his determination to write fiction, Sabatini labored on short stories at night. By 1899 he had moved up to the better paying, more prestigious markets. On the strength of Sabatini's short stories, Peter Keary, an editor with the Pearson organization, offered Sabatini a contract to write a novel. "I am disposed to regard that as the most singular event in my career," Sabatini later observed, "one of the most singular, indeed, that could befall an author: for I have certainly yet to meet another who could boast of having been commissioned to write his first book." The result of that commission, published in 1902, was the novel *The Lovers of Yvonne*. It was a juvenile effort, to be sure, which Sabatini would one day try to suppress. Still, it started him on a novelistic career that would span nearly half a century.

Like many "overnight" celebrities, Rafael Sabatini labored long and hard to achieve his success. He served a lengthy apprenticeship, producing a steady stream of novels, short stories, plays, and non-fiction, gradually refining his skills and techniques. His progress as a writer was not dramatic, but steady. After a decade, he was producing fine work such as two controversial biographies, the novels *Mistress Wilding*, *The Sea Hawk*, and *The Snare*, and the brilliant short novel collection *The Banner of the Bull*. Although now accomplished as a writer, his work remained largely unrecognized.

Sabatini struggled for roughly twenty years before he attained best-seller status. His income from his writing was so modest that he was forced to perform editorial work for the publisher Martin Secker, though he clearly found such work uncongenial. He made a comfortable living, and he had a loyal, if not huge, following in England. It wasn't until 1921 with the publication of *Scaramouche* that he achieved celebrity status.

In Sabatini's own words, "Publishers and editors had been slamming their doors in my face with the assertion that the American public was interested only in the present and the future, and not at all in the past with which I persisted in dealing." However, "By chance a publisher—a member of the firm of Houghton Mifflin Co., of Boston—happened to see the MS. of 'Scaramouche' and because he personally liked it, he decided to undertake the publication in spite of the general feelings against work of that type."

It turned out to be a happy decision for Houghton Mifflin, for not only did they become Sabatini's American publisher for the remainder of his life, but they made a fortune from the writer's works.

The response to *Scaramouche* was immediate. In two months the novel was into its sixth printing. Esther Forbes, then a publicist with Houghton Mifflin, recounted the frenzy that followed: "The publishers then found it difficult to reprint earlier Sabatini novels fast enough for the demand. At Riverside [Houghton Mifflin's publishing arm] eleven of his books, old and new, were on the press at the same time. Among the big moving picture producers there was a rush for movie rights. The bidding for 'Scaramouche' became furious . . . . Nor did 'Scaramouche' stop with the movies. It has been ably produced . . . on the legitimate stage . . . . Even the opera rights have been sold." Sabatini had arrived.

The following year, 1922, the writer achieved even greater success with the novel *Captain Blood*. The 1920s saw the high-water mark of Sabatini's popularity. Besides screenplays, scripts for the stage, and revisions of old works, Sabatini also wrote the little-known, but brilliant romance *Bellarion the Fortunate* in 1926.

The Depression struck a severe blow to the book industry. Sabatini was by no means exempt, and his popularity slipped. He tried a lecture tour in the U.S. to stimulate interest in his books but to no avail. Despite personal problems—the death of a beloved son, the breakup of his first marriage—Sabatini continued to produce at an astonishing rate. And if his sales figures did not reach the heady numbers of earlier years, his work still had plenty of loyal followers. The master story-teller could always be counted upon for an exciting read.

In 1931 Sabatini purchased a small country home in the bucolic English countryside near the Welsh border. There, with annual visits to Switzerland, he would spend the remaining twenty years of his life with his second wife.

Although Sabatini was as prolific as ever, producing at least one book a year, to a certain extent he was not as concerned with the issues that marked the finest of his fiction: a passion for justice and the delineation of the heroic, ideal man.

During the 1930s he wrote a great deal of short fiction, as well as sequels to *Scaramouche* and *Captain Blood*. That he was still capable of fine story-telling is shown by the taut spy thriller *Venetian Masque* (1934).

Illness plagued the writer in the 1940s, and for the first time in four decades of writing, he slowed down. He was, after all, sixty-five years old. Furthermore, being a cosmopolitan, at home in all the countries of Europe, he was depressed with the advent of World War II. His stepson died in a tragic airplane accident before his very eyes.

However, he managed to produce two brilliant books during the 1940s. The first was the excellent short story collection, *Turbulent Tales* (1946). The sixteen stories are the distillation of Sabatini's thirty years of short story writing. *Turbulent Tales* found an unlikely supporter in Ellery Queen who selected no less than five of the stories for publication in the *Ellery Queen Mystery Magazine*. In 1949 Sabatini produced the fine novel *The Gamester,* the story of a financial wizard and a study in economics and government policy. The unlikely villain is inflation—unusual subject matter for a swashbuckling novelist. It is also unusual for Sabatini in that the story analyzes an unhappy marriage, where a couple must seek understanding and communication if they are to save their marriage and their love.

When the writer died in his beloved Adelboden, Switzerland, February 13, 1950, the *New York Times* and London *Times*, among other newspapers, published lengthy obituaries. Sabatini was probably the last figure of a school of writing that had begun in the nineteenth century. He had carried its mantle with pride and honor for half a century.

He is buried in Adelboden in sight of the Swiss mountains that he loved. His wife created a beautiful grave site sculpture, on which is carved, "He was born with a gift of laughter and a sense that the world was mad."

Critical Reception, Honors, Popularity

Despite popular success and acclaim Sabatini has rarely been accorded critical attention. Except for a few articles, mostly at the height of his fame, little has been written about him or his fiction. There are several reasons for this.

First, after the appearance of *Scaramouche*, a flood of Sabatini novels of uneven quality appeared in the book stalls. Many critics erroneously thought Sabatini was in reality a fiction factory. Sabatini himself tried to suppress those least worthy of him, but without success.

More significantly, though—and Sabatini realized this himself—he was not of his time. Nurtured on the romanticism of the nineteenth century, he began writing when historical fiction was still the vogue. The early twentieth century was the time of F. Marion Crawford, Robert Louis Stevenson, Stanley Weyman, and Mary Johnston, of books like *The Prisoner of Zenda* and *The Scarlet Pimpernel*. But even as Sabatini wrote his first novels, historical fiction was on the decline. By the time Sabatini penned his masterpiece, *Scaramouche*, historical fiction had long since gone out of vogue. The new school of Hemingway, Fitzgerald, and Steinbeck was far removed from Sabatini's world of thrilling adventure and idealistic heroes. That he achieved popular success is quite remarkable—due, no doubt, to Sabatini's narrative skill. Regardless of the charges that have been leveled against Sabatini's fiction, no one can deny his matchless skill at sheer storytelling. "Sabatini is our most cunning weaver of fact into fiction," wrote the London *Sunday Times*, and it is a typical comment.

Sabatini was a literary loner and never part of the literary establishment. He disdained many of the contemporary literary values. For instance, he objected to "the insistence that every novelist should be no better than an elegant reporter, confining himself to subjects within his personal experience." Instead, Sabatini asserted, "The supreme and essential gift of the story-teller is a logically inventive mind functioning in a well-ordered and well-informed imagination, and that this may sit confidently and authoritatively in the place of personal experience." From Sabatini's perspective the "modern realistic school" of fiction frequently meant "a synthetic author, an uninspired university product, a chronicler of unimportant and mainly sordid trifles, whose unimaginative and uninventive art lies somewhere between the arts of photography and journalism."

Sabatini's defiance of the literary establishment is evident in an introduction he wrote to an anthology: "This is not a book for those exalted intellectuals to whom plot in a story is the sign of auctorial puerility, who deprecate invention in fiction, look askance on the romantic, and for whom no piece of writing can be distinguished if it has the temerity to be dramatic."

An outsider, Sabatini garnered little critical praise during his lifetime. In an age when plot was considered artistically fraudulent, emotionally cheap, and psychologically suspect Sabatini stood proudly in defense of the well-made story. He held the literary establishment in contempt, and they repaid him with silence. While most reviews were favorable, they tend to be of a minor nature, principally praising his storytelling ability.

What would give Sabatini greater satisfaction than critical praise is the knowledge that his work continues to be reprinted and read. *Scaramouche* has seen more than fifty editions. *Captain Blood* has sold more than a million copies. Open up nearly any of the reprinted volumes and you will see reprint figures in the hundred thousand range. Hearing that, Sabatini might be forgiven the sardonic smile for which his characters are well-known.

Analysis of Selected Titles

SCARAMOUCHE

Scaramouche, 1921, novel.

Social Concerns/Themes

Rafael Sabatini was skillful at combining political issues of high drama with the intense personal quests of the characters. This is as true in *Scaramouche* as it is in *Captain Blood, Bellarion the Fortunate,* or *The Banner of the Bull,* to name but a few of his novels. *Scaramouche* focuses upon the French Revolution as *The Carolinian* deals with the American Revolution. While the Monmouth Rebellion sets in motion the plot for *Captain Blood*, it is the conclusion of *Mistress Wilding*. Bellarion rises to eminence in the turbulent time of Cesare Borgia, and *The Banner of the Bull* is set during the same time. Within these dramatic times the characters strive for their own personal goals.

The French Revolution is more than merely a backdrop to the story of *Scaramouche*. Rather, it is at the core of the story—almost a character itself. Without the French Revolution, there would be no story.

André-Louis Moreau is the novel's pivotal character. A young man without patrimony, he seeks to avenge the wanton murder of his dearest friend by a cruel and ruthless aristocrat, the Marquis de La Tour d'Azyr. Unable to find justice in the courts of pre-revolutionary France, Moreau incites the populace of Brittany to rebel against the privileged class. The irony is that he has not "the illusion of liberty" that the revolutionists have. "It was no part of his concern to set about the regeneration of mankind, or even the regeneration of the social structure of France." His desire is simply personal revenge. This desire for revenge is further heightened when he discovers that the contemptible Marquis de La Tour d'Azyr seeks to wed the woman Moreau loves, the independent Aline de Kercadiou. After fanning the flames of rebellion, Moreau flees. Like Scaramouche, a stock figure in Italian Commedia Dell-Arte, he is forever stirring up trouble then dashing to safety.

Throughout *Scaramouche* Sabatini argues for an aristocracy not of birth but ability. "Man is the child of his own work. Let there be no inheriting of rights but from such a parent. Thus a nation's best will always predominate, and such a nation will achieve greatly," Moreau proclaims. At another time he states, "I desire a society which selects its rulers from the best elements of every class and denies the right of any class or corporation to usurp the government to itself—whether it be the nobles, the clergy, the bourgeoisie, or the proletariat. For government by any one class is fatal to the welfare of the whole." This vision of the self-made, self-governing man—efficacious and confident—accounts for at least some of the popularity of *Scaramouche* in America and even in England, where after World War I there was a rising consciousness of the inequities in a class-structured society.

Scaramouche is in many ways a study of the French Revolution. Moreau realizes that the well-spring of the revolution is not the down-trodden. "The suffers were ever the proletariat," he observes. "The men who sought to make this revolution, the electors—here in Paris as elsewhere—were men of substance, notable bourgeois, wealthy traders." They envied "the privileged, talked largely of equality—by which they meant an ascending equality that should confuse themselves with the gentry." Meanwhile, "The proletariat perished of want in its kennels." As the Revolution plunges towards chaos, repression and slaughter, Moreau recognizes that the future of the Revolution is futile. "The reins of government will be tossed to the populace, or else the populace, drunk with the conceit with which the Dantons and the Marats have filled it, will seize the reins by force. Chaos must follow, and a despotism of brutes and apes, a government of the whole by its lowest parts. It cannot endure, because unless a nation is ruled by its best elements it must wither and decay."

However, *Scaramouche* is more than a textbook of the French Revolution. It is a thrilling story, tightly-knit and elegantly told. The climax of the novel is contained in the very first paragraph of the book.

Characters

Scaramouche is as much a psychological study as it is an adventure novel. The dimensions of André-Louis Moreau and Marquis de La Tour d'Azyr rank them as two of Sabatini's finest creations. Indeed, *Scaramouche* should be viewed as a psychological journey of self-discovery.

The distinguishing attribute of a Sabatini hero is "the vision" that "pierces husks and shams to claim the core of reality for its own." Time and again, Sabatini used this as a benchmark of the heroic. Captain Blood is like Moreau. Cesare Borgia, a character in many of Sabatini's fictions, has profound insight into the motives of men.

Throughout, Moreau is viewed as a cynic; he himself claims as much. But in reality he cares too deeply—so deeply that he is compelled to hide his emotions, to hide the things that mean the most to him. Hence, he is always donning masks. *Scaramouche* is an apt mask, and when Moreau dons the trickster's apparel, he exclaims, "It is the first time in my life that I look what I am."

Moreau begins the novel by cynically using revolutionary rhetoric to further his personal goal—the destruction of Marquis de La Tour d'Azyr. Gradually "he came fully to believe in those things in which he had not believed when earlier he had preached them."

Sabatini was no less careful in his depiction of evil. He infused Marquis de La Tour d'Azyr with a stature few villains have attained. Ironically, while Moreau uses the revolution for a personal vendetta, the Marquis maintains nobly that what he did was not for personal gain, but rather to defend his class, the aristocracy. He faces death, as he faced life, "without fear and without deception." And Moreau himself defends the Marquis by deciding that he was, after all, "nurtured upon a code of shams," and not completely at fault.

That Sabatini wrote more than an adventure novel is evident in the climax of *Scaramouche*. With all of Paris crumbling around them, Sabatini could have dwelt on the characters' flight from the French capital. Recognizing, however, that the true climax of the novel pivoted on the revelation of the relationship of Moreau and the Marquis, Sabatini wisely brought the book to a swift conclusion, ignoring the obvious peril Revolutionary Paris could have for them. By doing so, Sabatini shifted the novel from the realm of adventure and focused on the psychological aspects of the story.

Techniques/Literary Precedents

Sabatini considered verisimilitude to be a central feature of good historical fiction and went to great lengths to develop his skill in this area. He was fond of trying to convince the reader that what was being presented was history, not fiction. He frequently cites fictitious references. For instance, in *Scaramouche*, Sabatini quotes letters that André-Louis wrote and he mentions a book the character wrote called his *Confessions*. *The Sea Hawk*, supposedly, is taken from "eighteen enormous folio volumes" of history written by Lord Henry Goade.

Another of Sabatini's favorite techniques—one he freely admits he learned from Dumas *père*—was to mingle real characters with fictional ones, actual events with created ones, in order to blur the distinction between fiction and history. So Mirabeau, Robespierre, and Danton—all architects of the Revolution—appear on Sabatini's stage.

Related Titles

Sabatini used the French Revolution in no less than seven novels, as well as many short stories. However, as a blend of passion, psychological insight, technique, and bravado storytelling, he never surpassed *Scaramouche*. At one time, Sabatini thought of turning *Scaramouche* into a trilogy. It never materialized, but he did publish a sequel in 1931, *Scaramouche the Kingmaker*. While technically adequate, most of the fire and passion of the first novel is missing, and André-Louis's concern for his future wife's fidelity becomes somewhat tedious. *The Lost King* (1937) focuses on the search for a successor to Louis XVI. *The Marquis of Carabas*, published in 1940, is a fine, but little-known Sabatini novel. During the desperate days of 1940 it was generally overlooked.

Adaptations

Sabatini has been at once lucky and unlucky in the adaptation of his novels to film. There can be little doubt that the film versions of *Scaramouche*, *Captain Blood*, and *The Sea Hawk* have kept Sabatini's titles familiar to the public. On the other hand, these very films often have little to do with his books.

In 1923 Rex Ingram directed the first screen version of *Scaramouche*, starring Ramon Novarro as Moreau, Alice Terry as Aline de Kercadiou, and Lewis Stone as the Marquis de la Tour d'Azyr. A 1952 version, directed by George Sidney, starred Stewart Granger, Eleanor Parker, and Mel Ferrer.

CAPTAIN BLOOD: HIS ODYSSEY

Captain Blood: His Odyssey, 1922, novel.

Social Concerns/Themes

For Peter Blood, scholar and doctor, the quest for justice is not an idle or abstract discussion. He is confronted with injustice of the most terrible kind: slavery. The terrible irony is that he is sentenced for performing an act of compassion, healing the wounded after a battle. "My business, my lord, was with his wounds, not his politics," he tells the judges. But bloody Lord Jeffreys, the King's judicial representative, will have none of it. He sentences Peter Blood to work in the plantations of the New World. Utilizing his medical skills, Blood escapes the worst of the sentence, and eventually, he organizes an escape and takes to the open sea as a pirate.

America and England have long had a love-affair with the outlaw, the individual who defines himself beyond the institutions of society. In England, Robin Hood is a prime example, as are the highwayman legends of Tom Evans and Dick Turpin. In the United States our outlaws have taken a decidedly western turn: Jesse James, the Lone Ranger, and Zorro. More modern examples are Bonnie and Clyde, and Jimmy Valentine. With *Captain Blood* and *The Sea Hawk* Sabatini added immeasurably to the history of the outlaw ideal in literature.

In retribution for his suffering, Captain Blood, as he comes to be called, becomes the scourge of the Caribbean. "For what he had suffered at the hands of Man he had chosen to make Spain the scapegoat," Sabatini says. Thus, he who began as a peaceful doctor becomes a feared outlaw. His experiences as a slave have left him a bitter man. "It came to Mr. Blood . . . that man—as he had long suspected—was the vilest work of God, and that only a fool would set himself up as a healer of a species that was best exterminated." Fool or not, however, he continues to exhibit compassion. " 'It is not human to be wise,' said Blood. 'It is much more human to err, though perhaps exceptional to err on the side of mercy. We'll be exceptional.' " One of the complex paradoxes of Sabatini's fiction is this desire at once to hold up a shining vision of the ideal man and at the same time to reflect the contempt in which he generally seemed to hold the human race. Captain Blood is at once sardonic and remorseless and chivalrous to the point of being foolhardy.

The justice Blood exacts on the Spanish Main is tempered by the love he has for his former master's daughter, Arabella Bishop. "The love that is never to be realized will often remain a man's guiding ideal," Sabatini observes. While his love serves to bring out the best in him, it also causes Blood anguish, for while he would have her admiration he attains only her contempt. The journey she takes to finally recognize Blood's essential nobility is long and arduous, but ultimately successful.

Characters

Like Moreau in *Scaramouche*, Peter Blood is a man of intellect who is torn from his contemplative life and thrust into a life of bold action. Also like Moreau, Blood seeks only to be left alone to pursue his quiet life, to detach himself from the insanity of war. Against his will he must confront injustice. Blood has the characteristic of being "an exceptional judge of men." He is self-sufficient, noble, and ruthless. For all his self-sufficiency, though, Captain Blood is a tormented man, and he gains our sympathy in a way that Moreau does not.

While Sabatini paints his chief characters in broad and bold swaths of white and black, he peoples the novel with fine minor characters. Lord Jeffreys, the Lord Chief Justice who sentences Blood to a life-time of misery, has "an oval face that was delicately beautiful." The "fine sensitiveness of those nostrils, the tenderness of those dark liquid eyes and the noble calm of that pale brow" belie the bloodthirsty nature of the judge. That mingling of nobility and baseness, that fevered beauty and excruciating pain makes Lord Jeffreys one of Sabatini's most intriguing personalities.

Lord Julian Wade is another character in which Sabatini has poured considerable ingenuity in mingling good and bad. "He is ingenious, tolerably accomplished, mildly dissolute, entirely elegant," Sabatini tells us. A creature of the court, he is "very sophisticated" and has "carefully educated tastes." He is melancholy and dreamy, but at the same time he is always observant and astute. While he opposes Captain Blood, Lord Julian is motivated by jealousy, and is not an active agent of evil to the degree Colonel Bishop is.

Literary Precedents

The direct influence for *Captain Blood* was Mary Johnston's *Prisoners of Hope*. Johnston was an American novelist (undeservedly forgotten) who wrote historical novels of her native Virginia. Sabatini was not reticent in declaring his admiration for Mary Johnston. When he achieved fame, he often spoke of his debt to her and how he learned valuable literary lessons from the American novelist. He said, "Her writings read as the chronicling not of things studied, but of things remembered, of things personally witnessed." This eye-witness quality he thought a major attribute of good fiction: "That, I think . . . is the highest quality you may look for in the historical novel."

Sabatini owed a more specific debt to Johnston, as well. *Prisoners of Hope* (1898), one of Johnston's finest efforts, is the story of a nobleman who is enslaved for treason and sent to the colony of Virginia. There he falls in love with the plantation owner's daughter, helps plan a slave revolt, and eventually escapes into the wilderness. Although the lives of Henry Pitman, Henry Morgan, and others were the basis of *Captain Blood*, still, the resemblance between *Captain Blood* and *Prisoners of Hope* is remarkable. He read and re-read the book, he said, studying her literary skills, so it is not at all surprising that he might use aspects of her plot.

As with his earlier novels, Sabatini was adroit at mingling facts and fiction, and *Captain Blood* is no exception. For instance, the life of Henry Morgan bears resemblance to part of *Captain Blood*; Blood becomes the governor of Jamaica, while Morgan served lieutenant-general of Jamaica.

Related Titles

Sabatini created two succeeding volumes of Captain Blood stories: *Captain Blood Returns* (also called *The Chronicles of Captain Blood*) in 1931 and *The*

Fortunes of Captain Blood in 1936. On the one hand it can be argued that they represent a failure of creative power. But several of the stories were actually written at about the same time as *Captain Blood*. For instance, "Blood Money," collected in *Captain Blood Returns* (1931), was originally published in 1921. The reason Sabatini wrote more adventures for his pirate friend was that Sabatini loved Peter Blood, and he thoroughly enjoyed his company.

In one of the convoluted twists and turns of the plot of *Captain Blood*, Sabatini has the gentleman-pirate say, "I am considering it—the profit that a man may find in the ignorance of others." In many respects that is the central point of the Captain Blood short stories. The plots often turn on the ignorance of a character, or the reader.

In the sequels Sabatini does not address the issue of justice as he did in the first novel. These stories, however, have another purpose. They are clever and difficult exercises in plot. Contemporary readers may not be moved by the climaxes, but they will delight in Sabatini's ingenuity in creating dangerous situations and exciting escapes for Blood.

Even in the smaller forms, Sabatini created some gems. For instance, in "The Expiation of Madame de Coulevain" and in "The Gratitude of Monsieur de Coulevain," both of which appear in *Captain Blood Returns*, Sabatini wrote genuinely moving stories of infidelity, unhappiness, despair, and marital discord that transcend mere storytelling. The conclusion of these two stories illustrates that Sabatini could weave a complex tale that need not end happily.

In 1932 Sabatini published *The Black Swan* in an attempt to recapture his waning popularity. The hero of *The Black Swan*, Charles de Bernis, is an obvious copy of Captain Blood—elegant, suave, and brave.

Adaptations

The first adaptation of *Captain Blood* was the 1924 silent film directed by David Smith and starring J. Warren Kerrigan as Captain Blood and Jean Paige as Arabella Bishop. In 1935 Michael Curtiz directed the classic film version of the novel, starring Errol Flynn and Olivia de Haviland. This is a splendid production that remains fairly close to Sabatini's novel. There is some condensation of characters and incident, but the film captures the spirit of the novel. Erich Wolfgang Korngold provided the stirring score for the film, as he did he for another Sabatini/Flynn collaboration: *The Sea Hawk*.

In 1950 Columbia produced *Fortunes of Captain Blood*, directed by Gordon Douglas, and starring Louis Hayward and Patricia Medina. It was based on Sabatini's short story collection, *The Fortunes of Captain Blood* (1936). In 1952

Colombia produced *Captain Pirate* with the same stars, based on another *Captain Blood* sequel called *Captain Blood Returns* (1931). A television film, *Captain Without a Country*, was produced in 1956 by Warner Brothers-TV.

THE SEA HAWK

The Sea Hawk, 1915, novel.

Social Concerns/Themes

Sabatini, who studied the histories of many countries, was fond of saying that no religion is exempt from the charge of bigotry. In *The Sea Hawk* Sabatini put forth the argument that perhaps the Muslim faith is as worthy, and perhaps more worthy, of respect as any Christian faith. Today, this may not seem an earth-shaking announcement, but in 1915, when the Muslim faith was still relatively strange to the English and American audiences, any defense of an exotic creed was unusual. Throughout his career, Sabatini spoke out for moderation, understanding, and compassion.

In *The Sea Hawk* Sir Oliver Tressilian suffers at the hands of Christians, and when he has the opportunity to join the Muslim ranks and make war on the Christians, he gladly does so. "Hell was surely made for Christians," exclaims Sir Oliver, "which may be why they seek to make earth like it." The Sea Hawk scorns a Christian faith built on hypocrisy, and he admires the Muslim for practicing what he preaches. He is not a convert, however. He recognizes that the Islamic nation is as bloodthirsty as the Christians, practicing the same infamous actions in the name of Allah. In his heart, he believes in neither.

Sabatini espoused a creed of tolerance, but in looking over history and in surveying his times—in which two world wars would devastate Europe—he was profoundly pessimistic. "The hypocrisy of man! There is no plumbing the endless depths of it!" exclaims Sir Oliver Tressilian. He was too often a witness of man's inhumanity to man.

Where Peter Blood is the victim of institutional injustice, Sir Oliver Tressilian is the victim of a personal injustice. He is betrayed into slavery by a cowardly and ungrateful brother. Worse, his own fiancée believes Sir Oliver guilty of murder and cowardice. In that respect *The Sea Hawk* is a darker vision of *Captain Blood*. While Peter Blood is ennobled by his love for Arabella Bishop, Oliver Tressilian is driven by his malevolent fate to violence and by his powerful love to bitterness.

Once again, Sabatini presents us with a war between justice and vengeance in the soul of one man. Sir Oliver, in his "season of truth," faces death heroically. One of his arch nemeses, Sir John, is his judge.

"Your task, Sir John," replies one of the characters, "is one of justice, not vengeance."

"A quibble, when all is said," Sir John replies.

Tressilian realizes that it is much more than a quibble. The recognition of that distinction is what makes him a hero.

Characters

Besides being fearless, Sir Oliver Tressilian is a thoughtful, brilliant leader. Tressilian's men realize that "his was the brain that had guided them to this swift sweet victory," and he continues to do so time and again. He and Captain Blood are brothers in this respect. Tressilian is quick-witted and insightful. An efficacious man, Tressilian declares, "In all my life I never found good in a fool and never trusted one—" Peter Blood believed the same thing. However, Tressilian lacks the cool detachment of Moreau or Blood. He is hot tempered, which proves to be his downfall.

Sabatini has often been criticized for creating women who are weak and simpering creatures. It is hard to see from where this criticism comes. Arabella Bishop gives as good as she gets in *Captain Blood*. Rosamund Godolphin, the heroine of *The Sea Hawk*, defends Sir Oliver at his trial with resourcefulness and skill. She exhibits, Sabatini tells us, the finest attributes of any of the male members of the Godolphin family. Certainly, she is a more admirable character than her weak and malicious brother.

Related Titles

Sabatini used the Islamic motif again in the 1939 novel, *The Sword of Islam*. As in *The Sea Hawk*, he presents the Muslims objectively, and they are no worse—nor better—than their Italian foes. *Captain Blood* and *The Sea Hawk* are, of course, closely linked in theme and subject matter. *The Hounds of God*, which takes place about the same time as *The Sea Hawk*, has as one of its settings the same Cornish seacoast, and deals partially with the Spanish Inquisition.

Adaptations

The first adaptation of *The Sea Hawk* was the 1924 silent film, directed by Frank Lloyd and starring Milton Sills as Sir Oliver Tressilian and Enid Bennett as Rosamund Godolphin. It was a successful, big budget production, which the *New*

York Times termed "far and away the best sea story that has ever been brought to the screen."

In 1940 Warner Brothers released *The Sea Hawk*, directed by Michael Curtiz and starring Errol Flynn and Brenda Marshall. As marvelous as this swashbuckling Flynn vehicle is, it really has nothing whatsoever to do with Sabatini's novel. It is taken from the screenplay "Beggars of the Sea." When Sabatini discovered how little the film had to do with his book, he tried to have his name removed from it. Sabatini's lawyers had already told him that Warner Brothers owned the rights to the title, *The Sea Hawk*, so there was really nothing he could do about that. Warner Brothers, believing that Sabatini's name had marquee value, paid the author to keep his name attached to the piece. Reluctantly, Sabatini agreed.

Other Titles

The Lovers of Yvonne (also published as *The Suitors of Yvonne*), 1902 (novel); *The Tavern Knight*, 1904 (novel); *Bardelys the Magnificent*, 1906 (novel); *The Trampling of the Lilies*, 1906 (novel); *Love-At-Arms*, 1907 (novel); *The Shame of Motley*, 1908 (novel); *St. Martin's Summer*, 1909 (novel); *Mistress Wilding* (also published as *Arms and the Maid* and *Anthony Wilding*), 1910 (novel); *The Lion's Skin*, 1911 (novel); *The Life of Cesare Borgia*, 1912 (biography); *The Justice of the Duke*, 1912 (short stories); *The Strolling Saint*, 1913 (novel); *Torquemada and the Spanish Inquisition*, 1913 (biography); *The Gates of Doom*, 1914 (novel); *The Banner of the Bull*, 1915 (novellas); *The Snare*, 1917 (novel); *The Historical Nights' Entertainment, First Series*, 1917 (fictionalized history); *The Historical Nights' Entertainment, Second Series*, 1919 (fictionalized history); *Fortune's Fool*, 1923 (novel); *The Carolinian*, 1924 (novel); *The Tyrant*, 1925 (play); *Bellarion the Fortunate*, 1926 (novel); *The Nuptials of Corbal*, 1927 (novella); *The Hounds of God*, 1928 (novel); *The Romantic Prince*, 1929 (novel); *The Reaping*, 1929 (novella); *The King's Minion* (also published as *The Minion*), 1930 (novel); *Captain Blood Returns* (also published as *The Chronicles of Captain Blood*), 1931 (short stories); *Scaramouche the Kingmaker*, 1931 (novel); *The Black Swan*, 1932 (novel); *The Stalking Horse*, 1933 (novel); *Heroic Lives*, 1934 (biographies); *Venetian Masque*, 1934 (novel); *Chivalry*, 1935 (short stories); *The Fortunes of Captain Blood*, 1936 (short stories); *The Lost King*, 1937 (novel); *The Historical Nights' Entertainment, Third Series*, 1938 (fictionalized history); *The Sword of Islam*, 1939 (novel); *The Marquis of Carabas* (also published as *Master-At-Arms*), 1940 (novel); *Columbus*, 1941 (novel); *King In Prussia* (also published as *The Birth of Mischief*), 1944 (novel); *Turbulent Tales*, 1946 (short stories); *The Gamester*, 1949 (novel); *A Fair Head of Angling Stories*, 1950 (short stories).

Additional Sources

Darrach, Brad. "Rapier Envy, Anyone?" *Time* (August 9, 1976). A brief look at a handful of Sabatini's reprinted novels. The most interesting aspect of this mixture of literary review and Freudian psychology, is Darrach's contention that Sabatini was an "existential" writer, "dancing on the abyss of nothingness."

Forbes, Esther. "Rafael Sabatini and His Conquest of Fiction." *Boston Evening Transcript* (June 28, 1924). Containing much biographical background as well as analysis, this article was written from information provided by Sabatini. However, it contains at least one blatant error: Sabatini had only one child, not two as stated in the article.

Knight, Jesse F. *The Business of Romance: The Literary Philosophy of Rafael Sabatini.* London: Libertarian Alliance, 1991. A discussion of Sabatini's literary philosophy.

―――――. *The Great Swashbuckler.* New York: Amereon, 1991. A succinct biography and the most thorough bibliography of Sabatini's works to date.

―――――. "The Swashbuckler as Serious Artist." *The Romantist* Nos. 9-10 (1991). A thorough examination of Sabatini's life and art.

Overton, Grant. "Salute to Sabatini." *The Bookman* (February 1925): 728-735.

Sabatini, Rafael. "Rafael Sabatini—Reviews His Own Career." *The Liverpolitan* (May 1935). Sabatini reviews his climb to fame.

―――――. "My New Adventures of Captain Blood," *Pearson's Magazine* (December 1929). Sabatini discusses his childhood and the roots of Captain Blood.

―――――, et al. "Adapted From the Novel . . ." (Symposium), *Strand Magazine* (November 1925). Sabatini talks about the relationship between films and novels.

Voorhees, Richard J. "The Return of Sabatini." *The South Atlantic Quarterly* 78 (1979): 195-204. Looks at the same reprinted novels as Darrash.

Jesse F. Knight

MARY LEE SETTLE
1918

Update

Mary Lee Settle's decidedly unsettled life—involving shifts between privilege and poverty, moves back and forth across the Atlantic, three husbands, and an up-and-down critical reputation—has finally become tranquil. She now lives happily in Virginia with her third husband, has a circle of literary friends in the Charlottesville area, and continues to be productive. She has published two novels since 1985, *Celebration* (1986) and *Charley Bland* (1989), and a number of her earlier works have been reissued in paperback by Scribner's Signature Editions. Critical articles on her work continue to appear, and her friend and fellow writer George Garrett has published a short book-length introduction, *Understanding Mary Lee Settle* (1988).

Additional biographical information has also become available. Settle is credited with establishing the now prestigious PEN/Faulkner Award for Fiction. She also overcame uterine cancer soon after her 1978 National Book Award for *Blood Tie* (1977). In 1987 she became a member of the Roman Catholic Church—a move that one could hardly anticipate from her writing, unless one read *Celebration* carefully.

Yet it increasingly appears that her work is much more autobiographical than previously recognized. Like *Blood Tie*, *Celebration* features the expatriate life that Settle once knew, and *Charley Bland* closely follows the outlines of a hometown love affair that Settle described in an essay for *Contemporary Authors: Autobiography Series*, Vol. 1 (1984). Both expatriate and hometown settings in Settle's work seem, to some extent, to reflect her complex reactions to her origins—the provincial elite circles of Appalachia, particularly in Charleston, West Virginia.

Analysis of Selected Titles

CELEBRATION

Celebration, 1986, novel.

Social Concerns/Themes

Although international in scope, the social concerns in *Celebration* are more or less incidental to the novel's main theme. These social concerns center on the encroachment of the modern world on traditional ways of life in Turkey and Africa, as when the isolated village of the Yezidi, a Kurdish tribe in eastern Turkey, is razed to make room for a highway. Similar depredations occur or can be observed as a group of gun-running mercenaries travel through eastern Africa on their way to deliver a load of goods to Sudanese rebels. To an alarming degree, the favored means of introducing traditional peoples to "civilization" seems to be modern warfare.

The novel's main characters are sophisticated refugees of these cultural clashes, people who have lived through awful events, who have experienced the death of loved ones or other terrible losses. They themselves have had close brushes with death; although scarred by their experiences, they are far from lost souls, and one theme of the novel is that such people have developed a heightened awareness and sensitivity to life. They have, as the novel's epigraph states it, crossed over the river Styx and their eyes have been opened. Hence they celebrate life even amid its shambles.

Characters
By chance, a group of such scarred, sensitive people come together in London, where they party and commiserate with each other. The main characters are Teresa Cerrutti, a thirty-year-old American anthropologist recovering from the death of her husband (an archaeologist bitten by poisonous snakes) and a successful operation for uterine cancer; Ewen McLeod, a Scots Highlander recovering from malaria and a bloody romp through eastern Africa with his gun-running Uncle Gordie; Noel Atherton, an English homosexual recovering from a disastrous affair with a Chinese lover in Hong Kong; and Father Pius Deng, a six-foot-nine Jesuit priest whose Dinka family and village in Africa were wiped out by warfare. There are also numerous minor characters, including a younger Frank Proctor (a prominent CIA agent in *Blood Tie*), who earns his CIA credentials here by listening through the wall for Teresa and Ewen to make love.

Unhappily there is not much to hear; Teresa and Ewen are too physically debilitated to consummate their love until months after they move in together. This dispiriting note seems, no doubt unintentionally, to set the tone for the entire novel. Although the disparate cast of characters sounds exotic and exciting, the characters do not live up to their billing. They are something of a bore: their stories are too broken up, their passions too enfeebled, and their personalities too unconvincing. The most sympathetic character is Father Pius Deng, who is gratuitously killed off at the end by a group of London punks. Apparently his death is meant to enforce the novel's theme, to provide a kind of tough final exam for the celebratory spirit.

Techniques/Literary Precedents

One reason this ambitious novel does not quite succeed could be Settle's choice of the point of view. In order to bring together all the loose strands and provide a unifying focus, Settle centers the novel on Teresa, whose point of view predominates. The other characters have to tell their stories to and through her, usually bit by bit as they get to know her or overcome their initial reluctance. Their stories are thus distanced, and the effect of the novel is an overabundance of talk. Worse, the stories are filtered through the sensibility of Teresa, who seems to possess no special talent for being a confidante except good hearing and confusion about her own life (she has been seeing an ineffectual therapist, Dr. Dangle). Presumably Teresa clarifies things for herself in the novel, but nevertheless, instead of offering wisdom, her point of view seems self-indulgent, overly dramatic, and banal. In the novel's own terms, if she has crossed the river Styx, where are the results? The same might be said for the novel's whole collection of confused misfits, except for Father Pius Deng, who spreads some soothing balm and seems the only real candidate for the novel's center.

Settle's use of a distancing point of view and central intelligence recalls the work of Joseph Conrad, particularly Conrad's character/narrator Marlow. Marlow plays a prominent role in Conrad's *Heart of Darkness* (from which Father Deng learns his English) and narrates numerous other works, sometimes tediously. In addition, some of Conrad's characters are known to cross the Styx, though doing so does not necessarily qualify them to become members of an exclusive London social club. Settle's idea about those who have crossed the Styx recalls F. Scott Fitzgerald's idea about the rich, and Ernest Hemingway's idea about bullfighters: they are different people from the rest.

Relation to Previous Work

Celebration bears some likeness to Settle's *Blood Tie*: both novels have a foreign setting, involve a diverse set of characters, and feature experimentation with point of view. But in *Celebration* the experimentation does not work as well, and a comparison with the earlier novel provides some evidence of how far and perhaps why Settle fell short. Yet in both cases (as in the case of her monumental Beulah Quintet) Settle's ambitions were undeniably grand.

CHARLEY BLAND

Charley Bland, 1989, novel.

Social Concerns/Themes

The theme of *Charley Bland*, as the author tells us again in an epigraph, is "profane love," which describes the doomed six-year love affair in the novel. This theme is bound up with the novel's social concerns, since the society in which the love affair occurs helps doom it. Set in the fictional town of Canona, West Virginia, modeled after the author's hometown of Charleston, the novel offers an uncanny study of family and class, focusing on the ingrown Appalachian coal town elite.

The society portrayed is one in which infantile patterns seem to prevail. The role and nickname of one's childhood hang on into adulthood and old age, and the games down at the Canona Country Club are only slightly more advanced versions of earlier ones: "He [Charley Bland] and Plain George Potter, his best friend, and some of the others, all in their golf shoes and Argyle sweaters like the Prince of Wales, drank bootleg whiskey and held a contest peeing up at the chandelier in the ballroom at Canona Country Club for bets. The rumor was that Kitty Puss Wilson was the judge."

A person's bonding to the social group is forever, and anything that happens outside the group is of no consequence. The mother of the thirty-five-year-old female narrator "wanted me home, meaning, of course, her home." The narrator's father also wishes she would stop writing those books in Paris, settle down back home, and make something of herself. When the narrator shows up at the Canona Country Club after "fifteen years of self-imposed exile," the same people she left behind are still there, and they accept her back as though she had never been gone.

Characters

Although outsiders would no doubt view the society depicted as unbelievably oppressive, its roles, rituals, and patterns represent a kind of safety to those on the inside. In effect, these people never have to leave the nest.

This sense of safety has a seductive allure to the unnamed narrator and helps explain why she, supposedly a smart woman, would fall for such a lout as Charley Bland. He reminds her of a tobacco-smelling fatherly figure, Bobby Low, whom she adored as a child. Her idea that she can transfer this childhood crush to Charley Bland, a forty-five-year-old bourbon-sipping bachelor and philanderer, is of course total folly, but then he is a handsome lout, a perpetual Peck's bad boy idolized by the community. Perhaps too, like all the other women, she thinks she can save him from himself.

Charley Bland does, indeed, need saving. Although idolized on the outside, he is a tragic figure inside, someone who has become imprisoned by his role and the society around him. The narrator appeals to him because she, worldly and traveled, has experienced the escape that he could never manage. So in a sense she is as much a romantic figure to him as he is to her.

The extent of Charley's imprisonment is clear. He still lives at "home" with his parents, where his smothering seventy-nine-year-old mother rules. Charley is hers. After Charley has had his fling with the narrator, his mother succeeds in breaking up the affair—just as the narrator's mother set it up in the first place.

Techniques/Literary Precedents

Charley Bland is, above all, a love story, but it also fits into the literary tradition that focuses on manners and mores, showing that Settle could have been an Appalachian Dorothy Parker or Jane Austen. However, *Charley Bland* lacks the satiric bite typical of most novels of manners. Instead, using a first-person point of view and a rather sympathetic tone, Settle has chosen to tell a straightforward story that reflects some ambivalence towards her own origins.

Relation to Previous Works

Charley Bland returns to the fictional city of Canona, the setting of most of Settle's novels, including the major part of the Beulah Quintet. In fact, *Charley Bland* might be seen as a spinoff of the Quintet's last volume, *The Killing Ground* (1982), where poor Charley's eventual suicide was first related. *Charley Bland* is also reminiscent of other Settle novels that concern themselves with manners, such as her first two works, *The Love Eaters* (1954) and *The Kiss of Kin* (1955), and particularly the autobiographical novel *The Clam Shell* (1971), in which Charley Bland also appears.

In comparison to much of Settle's previous work, *Charley Bland* stands out for the simplicity of its technique. In particular, Settle's supple and lucid style here might distinguish the novel as much as its depiction of manners.

Additional Sources

Bach, Peggy. "The Searching Voice and Vision of Mary Lee Settle." *The Southern Review* 20 (Autumn 1984): 842-850. Offers a general view.

Garrett, George. *Understanding Mary Lee Settle*. Columbia: University of South Carolina Press, 1988. A good full-length introduction, including a useful bibliography and index.

Joyner, Nancy Carol. "Mary Lee Settle's Connections: Class and Clothes in the Beulah Quintet." *The Southern Quarterly* 22 (Fall 1983): 33-45. Shows how Settle's concern with manners and social class extends into the Beulah Quintet.

Settle, Mary Lee. "Mary Lee Settle." In *Contemporary Authors: Autobiography Series*, Vol. 1, edited by Dedria Bryfonski. Detroit: Gale Research, 1984. Provides the fullest information on Settle's life.

Harold Branam
Temple University

SIDNEY SHELDON
1917

Update

Sidney Sheldon continues to be the number one best-selling novelist in the world. As of November 1988, the author had 150 books in print in 39 countries. *The Sands of Time* topped the best-seller list in January 1989. Sheldon now devotes much of his time and money to charitable causes and has emerged as a fierce opponent of censorship in the United States and abroad. When accused by fundamentalist evangelists of writing immoral books, he did not accept their judgment meekly. When a prominent evangelist, the Reverend Tom Williams, attempted not only to have Sheldon's books banned from public libraries but also tried to compile a list of prominent people who read his books, the author went on ABC's "Good Morning America" and confronted Williams directly. While researching the diamond industry for *Masters of the Game* in South Africa where his novels were banned, Sheldon went on a national television program to defend his works, and subsequently the South African government lifted the ban.

Sheldon contributes generously to the campaign to end illiteracy in this country. After the Los Angeles Public Library was seriously damaged by fire a few years ago, he supplied funds to help rebuild it. He is a supporter of the University of California Press and of the UCLA Friends of English. He sets up scholarships and newspapers in high schools with high dropout rates. He is a leading supporter of the Freedom to Read Foundation, an anti-censorship organization.

In his early seventies now, he still manages the same rigorous writing schedule that has worked so well for him. Sheldon visits the places he plans to use as settings for his books, whether in the American heartland or in the Basque country of northern Spain. He insists that his settings be as authentic as possible. After dictating a new novel from beginning to end to a secretary, he works over the resultant manuscript, often over two thousand pages, at least twelve times until he feels that his readers have been given what they have come to expect from a novel by Sidney Sheldon—a mixture of romance and intrigue they will find impossible to resist.

Sheldon has written a sequel to his 1974 blockbuster *The Other Side of Midnight*. Published by William Morrow, as were his other bestsellers, *Memories of Midnight* treats in great detail the machinations of the immensely powerful and wealthy shipping magnate Constantin Demeris, a character originally based on Aristotle Onassis. Demeris' prime motive is revenge, and his intended victim is poor, innocent Catherine Douglass. Catherine, at the end of *The Other Side of Midnight,* had taken refuge in a convent to escape the fate of her husband Larry and his mistress Noelle Page, both of whom were executed by Demeris. Much of the research Sheldon had done for the first novel is used again in the sequel.

Catherine Douglass, emotionally shattered before entering the convent, emerges into the outer world almost as naïve as she had been in the earlier book. Demeris has decided that she is a danger to him because she knows what he did to Larry and Noelle. At first he poses as her benefactor because he wants to first seduce and then destroy her. Her destruction will probably afford him more pleasure than the seduction since it better suits his cold, calculating nature. Catherine, suffering from amnesia, is not difficult to entrap. Vengeance is also the motive of the subplot as Demeris schemes the ruin of his chief rival and brother-in-law Spyros Lambrosa, a man nearly as villainous as he.

This novel invites comparison to Victorian melodramas and to the Elizabethan revenge tragedy, and in its plotting and characterizations is as awkward as Sheldon's previous performances. In its own fashion, however, it gives readers exactly what they want—a few hours' escape into a fascinating if grotesquely unreal world of adventure. *Memories of Midnight* climbed to the top of the best-seller lists the week of September 24, 1990 and remained number two on the list through October.

Analysis of Selected Titles

WINDMILLS OF THE GODS
Windmills of the Gods, 1987, novel.

Social Concerns Themes

One third of this novel is set in Romania, a country under the rule of Stalinist dictator Nicolae Ceausecu. Since Sheldon had visited Romania and had the cooperation of its government while doing his research, readers are told that Ceausecu has been succeeded by a man called Alexandros Ionescu who is even worse than Ceausecu. The dictator and his followers live in affluence, the people in extreme poverty. As a person who grew up during the Great Depression, Sheldon feels deep compassion for Romania's poor. In *Windmills of the Gods,* Mike Slade, who knows the country thoroughly, takes the new ambassador, Mary Ashley, to places where she can see how ordinary Romanians live—"the real Romania," as he says.

In 1989 the Iron Curtain crumbled, but as late as 1987 it was still firmly in place, and countries like Romania made excellent backgrounds for adventure novels. Sheldon introduces a secret organization of terrorists, the Patriots of Freedom, made up of political extremists of all persuasions who do not want the cold war to end.

The novel combines intrigue, romance, and international terrorism. As usual, the action takes place in a number of exotic foreign locales—Paris, Buenos Aires, and Bucharest. But many of Sheldon's foreign readers would consider Junction City, Kansas, almost as exotic. Accordingly, he researched this small city as thoroughly as the others.

Characters

The character types in *Windmills of the Gods* resemble those in his previous novels. His heroine is Mary Ashley, a housewife and mother who is also a teacher of political science at a Kansas university. She is as dedicated to her family as she is to her profession. Her articles on political science have been read with admiration by Paul Ellison, the recently elected president of the United States. She specializes in Eastern European studies and her classes are popular. Female students envy her beauty, and male students love her for it. She, typical of the innocence of Sheldon's heroines, is unaware of how her beauty affects them. Her husband, Edward Ashley, is a skilled surgeon who is equally dedicated to his profession. He will come to the assistance of anyone needing his services whether the patient can pay for them or not. This stereotyped couple has two beautiful children, and live a quiet life in Junction City, Kansas, a city chosen by Sheldon because it is as close to the center of the country as any place he could find on the map.

The president offers Mary the ambassadorship to Romania because of her expertise and because she is part Romanian. She at first refuses because it would mean a separation from her family since Edward cannot leave his patients. However, she is pressured by others who feel that she would be an excellent choice for this ambassadorship, including President Ellison, who believes that Mary could help ease East-West tensions. But the Patriots of Freedom want to set up a situation that would make any kind of détente impossible for generations. This supersecret organization consists of fanatical far-righters, Communists, and others, who want the cold war to continue indefinitely. Unknown to President Ellison, its controller is Stanton Rogers, his chief foreign affairs adviser whom he also considers a good friend. But Rogers, up to a few years before, had been as strong a candidate for the presidency as Ellison until a messy divorce ruined his political hopes. Now in his resentment he wants his friend's foreign policy utterly to fail. His scheme is to set Mary Ashley up in Bucharest and then to arrange for the murder of Mary and her children. He first gets rid of Edward Ashley through what seems to be an auto accident, and then goes to see Mary after a decent interval to convince her to accept the president's offer. Mary accepts, and goes to Washington for a briefing.

In Washington, Mary prepares for her life abroad by taking a number of crash courses, including one on the Romanian language. In her naiveté she commits several social gaffes, such as leaving an official party before the guest of honor, the vice-president, arrives and by calling on the Romanian Embassy unannounced. How a specialist in political science could be so unaware is never explained. Her closest associate in Romania, Mike Slade, a highly confident and handsome young man, considers her a bungling amateur, and she dislikes him because of his patronizing attitude. As Sheldon readers have come to expect, after Mary and Mike work together in Romania, they come to admire one another's abilities, and it is hinted that their relationship will develop into a stock romantic relationship.

The Patriots of Freedom see to it that Mary's blunders do not get the publicity that might be expected. This arouses the suspicions of an investigative reporter, Ben Cohn, who is trying to learn more about the organization. The Patriots frequently hire an international assassin known as the Angel, who lives in a Buenos Aires slum. He can be contacted only through a semi-literate peasant woman, Neusa Munez. Cohn goes to Buenos Aires trying to learn more about the Patriots from their agent and is murdered by Munez. It is later revealed that this grotesque woman is the Angel. She also kills the Romanian revolutionary leader Marin Groza who lives in Neuilly, a Paris suburb. The hopes of many of his countrymen depend on Groza, but he is a guilt-ridden creature who tries to atone for letting his wife and daughter be raped and murdered because he would not give the secret police the information they demanded of him. He hires prostitutes to beat him. The Angel hits upon a unique method to murder Groza, and she is hired to murder Mary and her children. In her own grisly fashion she is one of the more original characters in the book.

In Romania Mary suddenly ceases to be a naive blunderer and can take credit for several feats of diplomacy that even veteran professionals might envy. She is more than a match for Alexandros Ionescu, the president/dictator of the country. She manages the release of an American student arrested on drug charges. She persuades Ionescu to let a number of Jews leave the country after she has obtained the medicine needed to cure his son who is dying from botulism. She and Slade find they can work effectively together, but it is Mary who saves herself and her guests from the Angel's murderous plan to blow up the embassy.

The Angel has put explosives in some balloons that are decorating the embassy for a big party. Slade guesses what has happened, but does not know how to get the balloons out before their contents are detonated. Mary remembers that the roof of the ballroom will slide back, a feature introduced by an earlier ambassador, and the explosives float away; for once the Angel fails. Her last victim is Stanton Rogers whom she feels has betrayed her.

Apart from Ionescu and Rumanian officials, the people of Bucharest are not represented in the book. An exception is one of the chauffeurs at the embassy with whom Mary occasionally talks.

Techniques/Literary Precedents

Sheldon has said that he loves to write about women, and they continue to be his principal characters. In *Windmills of the Gods* he makes a woman, Neuse Munez, one of the novel's leading evil characters. As in past books several scenes form the background of the action. Sheldon also continues his practice of trying to make each chapter end in such a way that the reader is compelled to read on.

Through careful research Sheldon's fictional characters are assured of being placed in settings which are accurate in every possible detail. He loves visiting the places he intends to use. His books almost become guidebooks for those whose curiosity has been aroused. He describes Junction City, Kansas, as carefully as Bucharest, Romania.

Sheldon prefers calling himself a storyteller rather than a novelist, and despite his habitual use of clichés and stereotypical characters and situations, his plots hold the readers' attention. Most of his readers do not want subtlety and are content with suspense, violence, and explicit sex, normal or abnormal, which they can count on in his books.

Sheldon has found a formula that works for him and he continues to use it. *Windmills of the Gods* shows no particular improvement in style over previous works, but neither does he display any slackening of zest. Sheldon enjoys his writing, and his readers share his pleasures along with him.

THE SANDS OF TIME

The Sands of Time, 1988, novel.

Social Concerns/Themes

The Spanish Civil War, officially over in 1939 with the victory of General Franco's Nationalist forces, or fascists, still goes on through the efforts of separatist groups such as the Basque underground and the army which, while now serving a monarchy, still has in its ranks many officers and men who are unrepentant fascists. The Basques, lacking the men and the finances to fight open warfare, resort to the standard tactics of most twentieth-century terrorists—bombings, riots, and assassinations. Spain remains a divided and violent country with ancient enmities preventing any real settlement of its difficulties.

The Roman Catholic Church, having sided with the Republic during the later stages of the war met with reprisals at the end and is still facing hostility from the army and police. An order of nuns, the Cistercians of the Strict Observance, or Trappists, has a convent in Avila. Like their male counterparts, they observe strict silence, are constantly in prayer, and mortify their flesh—they still practice self-flagellation. After their convent is raided by soldiers, four members of the order flee north with a golden cross, the only object of value their order possesses. They are armed only with their piety and the discipline of their training, but three of them are very beautiful women.

These issues form the background of an adventure story involving flight and pursuit, romance and danger, and struggles against overwhelming dangers and temptations. The standard themes of adventure fiction clearly predominate in Sheldon's latest best seller.

Characters

The characters in *The Sands of Time* are similar to the heroes, heroines, and their antagonists who make up the cast in all of Sheldon's books. Ramon Acoca, the fascist colonel is a sadistic, but efficient army officer who takes his orders first of all from the Opus Mundo, a secret organization devoted to keeping the old scheme of things alive, and only secondarily from the monarchy he supposedly serves. He pursues Jaime Miro and the nuns relentlessly because the Opus Mundo has ordered him to destroy them and because he wants revenge against an enemy who has always outwitted him.

Jaime Miro is as ruthless as Acoca in his determination to give his people—the Basques—political independence. His family was destroyed during the war, an episode made famous by Picasso's painting, "Guernica." He is dedicated to fighting fascists to avenge his family. Sheldon's psychological and sociological explanations for his characters are facile to say the least.

While not a thorough-going cynic, Sheldon obviously believes that the attraction between a man and a woman is capable of overcoming any idealistic commitment. The principal characters of the book are four nuns—three actually, since one of them, Lucia Carmine, is a murderer who has disguised herself. While escaping from Colonel Acoca they join Miro's Basque terrorists, and two of the nuns, Sisters Megan and Graciela, after vain attempts to fight temptation, become lovers of Miro and Rubio Arzano respectively. Sister Teresa, an older woman and the most pious of the group renounces God during a gang rape, seizes a gun and kills several of her captors before the soldiers shoot her.

Lucia, the daughter of a Sicilian mafioso leader, has carried out a vendetta against her father's murderers by killing two of them. Wanted as an international fugitive, she is working her way to Switzerland where some of her father's money will be available. She falls in love with another of Miro's followers, Rubio Arzano, marries him later and becomes a farmer's wife in Southern France where they buy property. This is quite a change for a sophisticated and unscrupulous young woman.

Megan, it develops, is not an orphan Spanish girl at all, but Priscilla Scott, the heir to an international conglomerate. She falls in love with Jaime Miro and finally becomes his mistress. She will later assume control of the Scott enterprises after her aunt has confessed to abandoning her with a peasant family in Spain so that she and her weak husband could take over the conglomerate. Megan is as resourceful as most of Sheldon's heroines, learns everything she needs to become head of the business empire, and returns to Spain to rescue her lover from the death sentence imposed after his capture.

Of the three true nuns only Sister Graciela returns to the solitude and silence of the convent. After falling deeply in love with Ricardo Mellado and planning a life with him, as they are standing before a priest about to be married, the words of the service cause her to change her mind. "I am already married," she says. It will be some time and much penance before she will feel that her recent sins have been forgiven.

At best Sheldon provides some variations on stereotyped characters. Neither these people nor the plot in which they perform is particularly convincing. Sheldon seldom gives any indication that he has understood the personalities of his characters.

Techniques/Literary Precedents

That Sidney Sheldon is well acquainted with the tastes of his readers is obvious. He calls himself a perfectionist, and in his own way lives up to the claim. His books have all the necessary ingredients to assure their sales. He times erotic scenes and exciting events so that readers will not become bored with these long books. In *the Sands of Time* chapters end with cliff-hangers: "Rubio turned and watched in horror as Lucia disappeared downstream in the raging waters," and "The next instant an enormous gray wolf was flying at her throat." In the following chapters the scene shifts to feature other fugitives, and the fate of Lucia and

Garaciela, the nun attacked by the wolf, is not learned until the following chapters. This method of keeping up suspense is reminiscent of the old-time movie serials.

Sheldon researched this story by reading Bernard of Claivaux on the discipline he felt appropriate for his order. In an interview for *Publishers Weekly* Sheldon says that his secretary corresponded with Cistercian Convents of the Strict Observance. He himself toured Spain, including the Basque country. His basque terrorists speak Spanish however, and it is true that most Basques are, of necessity, bilingual. It was probably wise not to try to introduce their notoriously difficult language.

The Sands of Time is a typical Sheldon novel with stereotypical characters and a rather clumsy plot. As usual, Sheldon maintains suspense well and his readers will not be too critical of his poor literary standards.

Additional Sources

Interview with Sidney Sheldon. *Publishers Weekly* (November 25, 1988): 53-54. Sheldon's methods as an author, and his charities are covered in this interview.

Review of *The Sands of Time*. *Publishers Weekly* (September 23, 1988): 58. The book with its lively subplots moves along at a spirited pace.

Wells, Susan Spano. Review of *Windmills of the Gods*. New York Times Book Review (February 8, 1987): 25. Finds this book less entertaining than some of Sheldon's earlier work.

Karl Avery

ROBERT SILVERBERG
1935

Update

Since the publication of the enigmatic novel *Tom O'Bedlam* in 1985, Robert Silverberg's career has taken new directions. A major change in his personal life occurred when, following his divorce from Barbara Brown in 1986, he married Karen Haber, a talented young editor and writer, in 1987. By the end of the decade, they were collaborating on short fiction and had produced an ambitious novel, *The Mutant Season* (1989), the first volume of a projected series.

During this time, Silverberg's short fiction began to move beyond the limitations of sophisticated irony displayed in his stories for *Playboy* and other magazines, collected in *The Conglomeroid Cocktail Party* (1984). An amusing novelette for *Isaac Asimov's Science Fiction Magazine*, "Gilgamesh in the Outback" (1986), featuring the epic hero of *Gilgamesh the King*, won an unexpected Hugo Award; and "Sailing to Byzantium" (1985), a more literary effort for the same magazine, garnered Silverberg another Nebula award. Numerous other stories of considerable merit appeared also, and it was noticeable that some of them showed Silverberg extrapolating possible scenarios of ecological disaster in the near future, as in "Hot Sky," for *Playboy* (February 1990).

Silverberg continues to devote his energies to lengthy novels, as well. *Star of Gypsies* (1986) is an epic of a political struggle between a wily but essentially humane gypsy king and the irresponsible son who seeks to overthrow him. The novel was also distinguished by Silverberg's research into traditional gypsy culture, which is portrayed as surviving as an ethnic identity in a distant future.

Project Pendulum (1987) is a time travel tale for adolescents. *At Winter's End* (1988), the saga of a tribe of humans who emerge from life in caves several centuries after a nuclear holocaust, is one of Silverberg's best efforts. This work is the first in a projected trilogy; the second, *The New Springtime* was published in 1990, and the third is tentatively entitled *The Summer of Homecoming*, according to Silverberg's comments on his plans. Another recent novel, *Nightfall* (1990), written in collaboration with Isaac Asimov, is a dramatic expansion of the world of conflict of Asimov's celebrated classic short story "Nightfall," which first appeared in John W. Campbell's *Astounding Science Fiction* in 1941.

Silverberg opened the new decade with a second novel about Gilgamesh, *To the Land of the Living* (1990), and with the publication of his first major collaborative effort with Karen Haber, *The Mutant Season*. The Gilgamesh novel was a loose and episodic work growing out of Silverberg's novelettes about the hero's adventures in a purposeless world after death. But *The Mutant Season*, developed from a Silverberg short story, returned to a favorite theme—the maturation of humans possessing extraordinary talents as a result of mutation. In pursuing this theme, the authors describe a world in the near future much like ours, a setting that allows ample opportunity for political satire.

With the Winter's End trilogy and the series inaugurated by *The Mutant Season*, Silverberg appears to have set ambitious goals for himself, but he has expressed dissatisfaction with two facets of contemporary conditions that confront science fiction authors. In an address at the International Conference for the Fantastic in the Arts at Ft. Lauderdale in 1989, he criticized a perceived lack of discrimination in today's science fiction audience, and pointed out the constraints of current distribution methods, which channel most books through two major chains.

As a result of these factors, Silverberg considers his excursions into historical fiction with *Lord of Darkness* and *Gilgamesh the King* in the early 1980s to have been a mistake. Nevertheless, his invented realm of Majipoor has proved to be popular enough to prompt a paperback publisher (Tor Books) to issue a game-playing novel in that setting for Dungeons and Dragons enthusiasts. *Revolt in Majipoor* by Matt Costello (1987) allows its readers to make crucial choices at important turning points in the action. The existence of such a book suggests that Silverberg's work is more popular with younger readers than generally realized.

Some critics have expressed reservations about Silverberg's recent work. There is, however, a substantial body of opinion that continues to manifest confidence in the importance of his work. The recognition of Silverberg as a Guest of Honor by the IAFA Conference, his lengthening list of awards, and a forthcoming volume of critical essays from Greenwood Press, all attest to a growing awareness of his stature in the genre he has served so well.

Analysis of Selected Titles

STAR OF GYPSIES

Star of Gypsies, 1986, novel.

Social Concerns

At first glance, this novel seems remote from the major social issues of recent science fiction; however, it provides a lesson in Machiavellian politics used for humanitarian and liberal purposes. The main conflict of the novel concerns a power struggle between Yakoub, the King of the gypsies, and his son, Shandor, an ambitious and murderous egotist, who makes an ill-advised attempt to seize power over the gypsy realm.

Yakoub, the wily gypsy leader, is a master of devious political scheming, and his triumph in the novel comes from his ability to turn his captivity to his own purposes. In essence, the novel is a sophisticated hostage drama. Yakoub's knowledge of pragmatic politics also provides an intriguing contrast to the saintly idealism of Silverberg's liberal hero, Lord Valentine, especially as he is portrayed in *Valentine Pontifex*.

Another interesting social implication of the novel is its description of the culture of the gypsy nation or people, who are called the Rom (because of their use of the Romany language) in the novel. The gypsy nation is portrayed as a world of wily outsiders, who define themselves by their relationship with "the Gaje" or non-gypsies. In fact, the gypsy culture is depicted as the last group to maintain ethnic identity in the future of the novel, and Silverberg's identification with it may be traced to the dislike he has voiced in more than one story of a future where all cities and all cultures display a bland sameness.

Themes and Characters

A major theme is the importance of political pragmatism, as demonstrated not only by Yakoub's conflict with Shandor but by his skillful manipulation of relations with the empire. This theme is developed also in Yakoub's memories of his earlier life as a gypsy trickster. Yakoub's life has been a testimony to his survivor abilities and to his lusty enjoyment of the sensual pleasures of food and sexual gratification, as well as his delight in the trickery employed in his exercise of power.

Yakoub is the dominating character of the novel, and one of the supreme tricksters of science fiction and fantasy. Yakoub is cast in the tradition of the trickster heroes of E. R. Burroughs and their descendants, as created by such masters of adventure science fiction as Philip José Farmer (Kickaha in the *World of Tiers* Series) and Poul Anderson (Nicolas van Riijn in various novels). Though credible as a gypsy monarch, Yakoub is a larger-than-life Falstaff, whose craftiness and humor provide much of the novel's drama.

The rest of the characters are sketchily delineated, which may be the novel's main weakness. Shandor, Yakoub's antagonist, is seen almost entirely through Yakoub's comments about him, and, despite Shandor's acknowledged capacity for brutality, he never gains much respect for his villainy. Compared to Yakoub, Shandor seems to lack subtlety and cunning.

Yakoub's cousin Damiano has promising moments, and his surrogate son Chorian is adequately characterized; but neither character is memorable. Syluise, Yakoub's favorite lover, is an intriguing woman, but she is described chiefly through Yakoub's memories. Despite the possibilities of these characters, Yakoub remains in the forefront of the novel.

Techniques

Silverberg chose to tell *Star of Gypsies* as a first-person narrative, a technique used effectively in his historical novels. This viewpoint gives the reader insight into Yakoub's mind and allows the reader to experience Yakoub's richly textured memories. But the point of view also limits the author's depiction of other characters and prevents the reader from being present at some of the important moments of action, particularly during Yakoub's imprisonment.

Aside from the strengths and shortcomings of his choice of point of view, Silverberg's literary skills are displayed most clearly in his use of names and words with Romany origins. Because of the richness and amplitude of its language, the novel seems more like a romantic tale than a bare recital of its plot would suggest. Moreover, Yakoub's narrative is enriched by anecdotes and imagery derived from gypsy tradition—an accomplishment that heightens its credibility and testifies to a knowledge and narrative skill possessed by few other science fiction writers.

The future setting of *Star of Gypsies* is similar to the world of numerous science fiction epics in distant times, such as Isaac Asimov's Foundation series, the *Star Trek* adventures, and the world of Frank Herbert's Dune series. Precedents for political dramas also appear in mainstream novels, such as the works of Joseph Conrad, which are an acknowledged influence on Silverberg. The character of Yakoub offers a parallel, whether conscious or not, with the enigmatic duke in Shakespeare's *Measure for Measure*, who takes a leave of absence from power to observe how a more severe ruler fares in curbing his country's vices.

Other works that feature gypsies as central figures, either in science fiction, films, or mainstream literature, are rare. Gypsies appear in some German and Central European tales, and in Jewish folklore, though generally as secondary characters. In terms of fiction, only George Borrow, the nineteenth-century author of *Romany Rye*, has focused prominently on gypsy culture.

Relation to Previous Works

Silverberg's band of traveling entertainers in *Lord Valentine's Castle* suggests a gypsy troupe, and some of Valentine's adventures in the early parts of that novel are described in a tone anticipating Yakoub's reminiscences of his early life. Silverberg's extensive use of history and archeology in his non-fiction books of the 1960s no doubt provided some information about gypsy lore, as well as some of his understanding of practical politics.

THE MUTANT SEASON
The Mutant Season, 1989, novel, written with Karen Haber.

Social Concerns

Heralded as the first of a series by Silverberg and Haber, *The Mutant Season* explores the political and social tensions between American society and a well-organized minority of mutants with "wild talents" or such genetically superior traits as telepathy and telekinesis (the ability to levitate objects by mental action). The mutants of *The Mutant Season*, the gypsies of *Star of Gypsies*, the androids of *Tower of Glass*, and the shape-shifters of the Majipoor trilogy—all are representative of the outsider or the alienated rebel, as Silverberg himself points out in an introduction to the novel.

The novel sets out to explore society's fear of groups which appear to be different, and its resentment of superior talents when manifested by minorities. In its approach to this subject, the novel touches on many issues: hostility toward marriage between races and ethnic groups; political assassination; the rebellion of the younger generation; and short-sighted genetic experiments. Although the full implications of these themes are not developed in this book, succeeding volumes are certain to clarify the authors' positions on such matters.

The setting of the novel is essentially the contemporary world extrapolated thirty years into the future. Characters travel by "skimmer" above the surface of the planet. There were apparently a series of riots in 1995 when the existence of the mutants became public knowledge. But the world of *The Mutant Season* is clearly the metropolitan "global village," to use the phrase of the late Marshall McLuhan. Sex, credit, and media attention are all fairly easy to obtain for the characters; clear moral judgments and people of assured integrity are harder to find.

Themes/Characters

Silverberg and Haber focus the novel on two younger mutants, Michael and Melanie Ryton, who are coming into adulthood, and on two young women who are "normals," Andrea Greenberg and Kelly McLeod, both of whom become involved with the fates of the mutants. The presence of so many feminine protagonists is unusual for Silverberg, and probably indicates the influence of Haber in the collaboration. Obviously, too, the concentration on youthful leads almost makes the novel a study of various personal rites of passage from adolescence to adulthood.

Contrasting with the maturation and searches for identity of the protagonists, is the struggle of the mutant culture for recognition and equality. The fortunes of this cause shifts from a cautiously liberal advance under the guidance of their senator, Eleanor Jacobsen, to a different and more devious direction after Jacobsen's assassination. Her successor, the smooth and dishonest Stephen Jeffers, intends to co-opt the mutant cause in his own drive for power, which is connected with secret genetic research in Brazil.

The best drawn characters in the novel are Andrea (Andie) Greenberg, aide to senators Jacobsen and Jeffers, and Melanie Ryton, the rebellious daughter of a mutant leader. Michael Ryton, Melanie's brother, also has possibilities for character development because of his defiance of tradition and love for a "normal," Kelly McLeod; but his estrangement from McLeod and entrapment in a marriage with a scheming mutant girl are not credibly developed. More believable are Andrea's seduction by the clever Jeffers and Melanie's willful but foolish rebellion, wherein she becomes first an exotic dancer and then the mistress of a dangerous agent. At any rate, all the younger characters seem more strongly influenced by their emotions and sexual desires than by discretion—a feature of the novel that takes it nearer to conventional realism.

Techniques

Silverberg and Haber employ multiple narrative lines and a variety of points of view, but the novel follows rather conventional fiction techniques for the most part. The same narrative methods might be found in a work by James Michener or John Steinbeck, for example. The major exception to this pattern is found in some uses of telepathy in the second half of the novel, especially in the sections devoted to Michael Ryton's problems and in his relationship with the mysterious telepath Skerry, who seems to be lurking in the background, primed to emerge as a hero in the next novel.

By using materials that contradict conventional realism to describe the talents of the mutants and the future setting, Silverberg and Haber seem to rely on the illusion of narrative realism practiced in the contemporary thriller, especially a "techno-thriller" like *The Hunt for Red October*, to provide a sense of verisimilitude and suspense. By the end of the novel, several of the protagonists are in the kind of difficulties associated more with melodrama than science fiction; but the authors have withheld important revelations about the genetic research in Brazil and the long-range plans of their villain, Stephen Jeffers. In short, the grand design of the series has not been fully displayed in *The Mutant Season*.

Literary Precedents

Numerous popular novels of political conflict involving minority groups have established a tradition for *The Mutant Season*. Aside from Silverberg's own work, the models for this book would appear to include Robert Ludlum's and Tom Clancy's novels of international intrigue, and such political novels as Allen Drury's *Advise and Consent* (1959) and its numerous progeny. Science fiction, too, offers a lengthy list of tales and novels that describe a fear of mutants with extraordinary powers. Olaf Stapledon's *Odd John* (1934) describes the growth and tragic death of a boy with talents sufficient to make him seem superhuman, and, like Silverberg's and Haber's mutants, he and his counterparts organize themselves for protection against the normals.

In his introduction to the novel, Silverberg himself cites several other science fiction treatments of the mutant theme as possible influences: a pair of novels by John Taine (Eric Russell Bell) published in 1929 and 1931; stories by Edmond Hamilton ("He That Hath Wings," 1938) and Henry Kuttner (the "Baldy" series, 1945-1953); Wilmar Shiras's *Children of the Atom* (1948-50); Walter Miller's *A Canticle for Leibowitz*; Isaac Asimov's Foundation novels; John Wyndharn's novels; and Robert Heinlein's stories.

Two precedents that Silverberg fails to mention deserve comment. A. E. Van Vogt's *Slan* (1941) and Alfred Bester's *The Demolished Man* (1953), are both significant novels about telepaths with which Silverberg is familiar. The former deals with a telepathic genius who suffers from xenophobic persecution throughout his life; the latter presents mutants as honored members of a society, who use their talents to pursue and capture criminals. Silverberg and Haber's mutants are cast neither as the outcasts of *Slan* nor as the heroic role models of *The Demolished Man*; instead, they exist in a tenuous world where they are neither openly persecuted, nor fully accepted.

Relation to Previous Works

According to Silverberg's introduction to the novel, he and Haber developed the world of *The Mutant Season* out of a 1973 short story of the same name, a work only a few pages long. As a matter of fact, the story is different from the novel in many respects: it is a first-person narrative told from the point of view of an ordinary human rather than a mutant, and describes his reservations about accepting the mutants as equals. Silverberg also credits Byron Preiss with suggesting that he expand the world of the story into the setting for a series of novels.

Finally, Silverberg addresses the mutant theme in various early works, most notably the brilliantly written *Dying Inside* (1972). This ironic masterpiece describes the anguished alienation of David Selig, a telepath who can receive but not project messages, and who inadvertently witnesses the sufferings of numerous victims of society in the New York of the late 1960s.

Earlier Silverberg novels from his first major period (1968-1976) also show his mastery of the drama of political conflict, particularly *The Stochastic Man* (1975) and *Shadrach in the Furnace* (1976).

Other Titles
Beyond the Safe Zone, 1986 (short stories); *Project Pendulum*, 1987 (novel); *At Winter's End*, 1988 (novel); *To the Land of the Living*, 1990 (novel); *Nightfall*, 1990 (novel, with Isaac Asimov); *The New Springtime*, 1990 (novel).

Additional Sources
Elkins, Charles, ed. *Robert Silverberg's Many Trapdoors*. New York: Greenwood Press, 1991. A collection of critical essays by various academic scholars, this is a major addition to Silverberg studies, and includes Edgar L. Chapman's essay "Dying Inside."

Edgar L. Chapman
Bradley University

ISAAC BASHEVIS SINGER
1904

Update

Singer's literary career continues to be productive. In recent years he has published the short story collections, *Short Friday and Other Stories* (1983), *The Image and Other Stories* (1985), and *The Death of Methuselah and Other Stories* (1988), as well as the short novel *The King of the Fields*.

Singer's latest novel, *Scum* (1991), follows Max Barabander, a Polish exile to Buenos Aires, who as a boy in Poland was a criminal but who has parlayed his shrewdness into a successful business. After his son dies suddenly, Max returns to Warsaw hoping to regenerate his old sexual prowess. In Warsaw he is thrust into the heart of Jewish life and must reexamine beliefs he never really embraced. Between the rabbis' probing and the string of women who present themselves to him, Max embodies Singer's favorite theme, flesh and corruption. Devoid of faith, Max pursues any sensation with no thought of the cost to the innocent. Ultimately, Max cannot conquer the lust that drives him and is defeated. The bleakest of all Singer's works, *Scum* contains none of the innocence and joy of his stories of the Old World, where characters set into another era and culture speak of the universal ignorance of humankind.

Available biographical studies include Paul Kresh's *Isaac Bashevis Singer, The Magician of 86th Street* (1979) and *Love and Exile* (1984). Additional perspectives moderated by an interviewer/coauthor come in *Conversations with Isaac Bashevis Singer* (1985).

Analysis of Selected Titles

THE KING OF THE FIELDS
The King of the Fields, 1988, novel.

Social Concerns/Themes

A devout Jew wandering among Gentile cultures in an unclean world; superstitious, unsophisticated village folk who fear demons and spirits; characters struggling to survive clashes in political, religious and economic systems—none of these situations is new in the fictional world of Isaac Bashevis Singer. Nor is Singer's preference for the role of storyteller rather than that of a thinker with a clearly fixed world view. In *The King of the Fields* Singer recounts a parable of a devout Jew at the mercy of a tumultuous and often vicious Gentile world. While some might view the novel as a confirmation that Singer's work is basically pessimistic about human life and society, others see in it a fundamentally optimistic tale because the isolated Jew, Ben Dosa, eventually settles in a community of devout Jews, while the Gentile characters perpetuate a cycle of wanton, destructive domination.

Characters

The short, twelve-chapter novel follows the fortunes of a small tribal group in rural Poland, the Lesniks. At the outset, Krol Rudy (the Red King), a Pole, controls the Lesnik camp. The Lesnik leader, Cybula, has fled with others into the mountains. Krol Rudy takes Laska, Cybula's surviving daughter, as his wife, and he sets the Lesniks to clearing fields for the planting of grain. Krol Rudy also sends Nosek, a trusted associate, to persuade Cybula and other Lesniks to return to the lowland camp and live in peace under his rule.

Krol Rudy brings about several forms of cultural conflict. The Lesniks had been nomadic, forest-dwelling hunters and food gatherers. They have lost many men in battle with the Poles; many of their women have been raped and some are carrying children of the raiders; and they are unlikely to survive a hard winter in the mountains. Thus, they grudgingly and suspiciously accept Krol Rudy's plan to make the camp a farming site. From grain they can make bread enough for all to eat. From grain, they can also brew beer and vodka, and Krol Rudy himself succombs to alcoholism. His motions of peace, reconciliation and a more stable agricultural life only partially succeed.

Cybula, subordinate to Krol Rudy, remains responsible for the Lesniks in the camp—their housing needs, their legal disputes, and other soical needs. As father-in-law to the krol, he retains some political security, yet he is despised by Krol Rudy's Polish *kniezes* or knights. He serves as a focal character for the socio-political clashes in the Gentile society since he moves from krol to fugitive to a subordinate noble in a primitive ruling class, and then back to the position of krol when Krol Rudy grows incompetent. He returns to the role of fugitive when another Polish raider, Yodla, moves into the camp with more horsemen than the Cybula's warriors can resist.

Cybula acts to focus the religious conflicts in the novel. While his paramour, Kora, believes in spirits and demons, Cybula discounts the traditional animism of the Lesniks, nor does he embrace any of the parallel gods or spirits of the Poles.

The only supreme power Cybula acknowledges is Shmiercz, the god of death. All else he dismisses as superstition.

From the distant town of Miasto, Cybula and Nosek, a trusted Polish noble, bring Krol Rudy various tools and goods, as well as the Tatar concubine, Kosoka, and the Jewish shoemaker, Ben Dosa. With the late introduction of Ben Dosa into the narrative, Singer expands the cultural and religious conflicts of the novel. The Lesniks benefit from well-made shoes and clothing, yet Ben Dosa also speaks constantly of his God and the laws of his God. Befriending and trying to understand Ben Dosa, Cybula hears of a single, loving God who is in everything from stones and leaves to the human heart.

The strict mores and customs Ben Dosa observes contrast starkly with Cybula's willingness to rape on impulse, or to cohabit with both his young wife and her mother. Cybula supports Ben Dosa's instruction of children and adults in the Hebrew alphabet and Torah, the Five Books of Moses, even studying himself. He sees the devout Jew as a highly committed person, doing much good for the camp, but still as a stranger with a restrictive God. When Polish missionary bishop Mieczyslaw arrives, Cybula recognizes the similar views the Abrahamic faiths advance concerning the nature of God, but is dismayed by the conflicts over the role of Jesus Christ, and the bishop's emphasis on the view of the Jews as "Christ killers"—long an excuse for prejudice and violence against Jews in European history.

The religious issues, Cybula eventually decides, are "all lies." He publicly breaks up Kora's planned sacrifice of Kosoka to the goddess Baba Yaga, but succeeds only after he appeals to the camp's fear of chaos if he gives up leadership. His appeals to the religious principles of Ben Dosa and Bishop Mieczyslaw do not carry as much influence with the pagan Lesniks and Poles. When Cybula yields to Krol Yodla and his raiders, his own belief in the god of death draws him to apparent suicide.

While the reader ponders the benefits and liabilities of Judaism and Christianity through Cybula's perspective, Cybula remains a skeptical, almost agnostic pagan. It is Kora, Cybula's mother-in-law and lover who epitomizes pagan beliefs. Kora was the wife of Kostek, Cybula's best friend before Krol Rudy's attack. During the span of the novel, the widowed Kora shows insuppressible lust for Cybula, even though her daughter, Yagoda, is Cybula's wife. In her passion for Cybula, she even names him her god. When a Polish knight attacks Cybula one night, she not only kills the Pole in revenge, but also organizes a women's revolt that returns Cybula to power since Krol Rudy has lost effective control of the camp.

Cybula's release of the captive Kosoka and public shaming of Kora destroys their relationship for some time. Yet, after Cybula yields control of the camp to Yodla and flees with Yagoda, Kora cannot live without him. She catches up with them in the mountains and asks him to kill her. She admits to having lain with practically every available male in the camp—Lesnik or Pole. Her words and deeds exemplify no constructive hope in this life or the next, only unprincipled and sometimes murderous lust. Cybula accepts the satisfactions of sex and power that Kora can give, but he disdains her gods and spirits as meaningless figments of the imagination.

Ben Dosa, the shoemaker, tailor and furrier, carries the burden of representing his God and Torah to illiterate, savage Gentiles who live in a warring mixture of pagan cultures. He does not aim to convert them all to Judaism, but in teaching them to read and write he conveys what he can of God's laws. The ridicule of Ben Dosa by the pagan members of the camp and his opposition from the Christian bishop parallel the experiences of Jews in the Gentile world for centuries.

Ben Dosa teaches Kosoka his traditions of godliness, yet resists her wish for conversion. Thus he demonstrates the attraction Jewish traditions may hold for others, along with the reluctance of the more orthodox believers to accept outsiders. Ben Dosa's fate—settling in a supportive community and marrying a converted Kosoka—shows that even the very devout cannot avoid some influences of the wider world. It also gives the devout wanderer a home, even though the home is not Ben Dosa's first home, Babylon, nor is it a Zionist's ideal home, Jerusalem.

Techniques/Literary Precedents/Relation to Previous Works

In *The King of the Fields*, Singer composes a vague blend of references to time, melding the cultural traits of hunters, farmers, and city-dwellers into an almost timeless antiquity. His pagan male characters tend to seize what they want whenever they want. The female pagan characters generally serve the impulses or interests of the male. Nosek, the intellectual, worldly-wise Pole, displays political opportunism, but prefers a relationship with a young man to the exploitation of the available women.

In the sole Jewish character, Singer cannot fully develop the full range of viewpoints he knew in his early life among Hasidic Jews in Poland, but the characteristic impulse to separateness from Gentile society, paralleling an absolute devotion to God and Torah, is evident.

While the fate of the Jewish character is Singer's typical interest, the time and description given to the Gentiles in *The King of the Fields* is greater than that given to Ben Dosa. Viewing the novel as a parable of the fate of the Jew in Western society allows it to work effectively as a parallel both to life in earlier centuries and to conditions in Eastern Europe during the Nazi era.

The rapacity of the novel's Lesnik and Polish societies parallels the visciousness of Nazism, which attempted to revive ancient Teutonic paganism in Germany, encouraged free love for Aryan soldiers of the Third Reich, and institutionalized anti-Semitism. Assuredly, Germany itself is not the literal focus of Singer's novel; Poland is. But in most of Europe during the World War II era, anti-Semitic attitudes and policies grew fatally strong, despite the ideals of conventional Judaism and Christianity.

Additional Sources

Miller, David Neal. *Fear of Fiction: Narrative Strategies in the Works of Isaac Bashevis Singer*. Albany: State University of New York Press, 1985. Miller studies Singer's work within the context of Yiddish literature, focusing on Yiddish originals rather than stories translated into English. Still, he makes observations useful to the student of English translations as well.

Singer, Isaac Bashevis. *Love and Exile*. Garden City, NJ: Doubleday, 1985. This volume brings together Singer's three previous biographical works, *A Little Boy in Search of God*, *A Young Man in Search of Love*, and *Lost in America* along with a new introductory section, "The Beginning."

Singer, Isaac Bashevis, and Richard Burgin. *Conversations with Isaac Bashevis Singer*. Garden City, NY: Doubleday, 1985. Burgin has edited this material from interviews tape recorded intermittently over a span of two years.

Ralph S. Carlson
Azusa Pacific Unviersity

MARTIN CRUZ SMITH
1942

Update

Martin Cruz Smith has not been a prolific writer since his early work in pulp fiction. His major success, *Gorky Park* (1981), has been followed by only two others in the past decade: *Stallion Gate* (1986) and *Polar Star* (1989), the sequel to *Gorky Park*. His 1977 novel, *Nightwing*, was reprinted in 1987. In 1990, Smith was reported to be working on a third adventure of the Soviet detective, Arkady Renko, to be set among the Russian emigrés in Munich.

Analysis of Selected Titles

STALLION GATE

Stallion Gate, 1986, novel.

Social Concerns/Themes

Although the narrative of *Stallion Gate* can be admired for its technique—for the clarity with which Smith develops a number of intersecting plot lines and the ingenuity with which he blends the actions of his fictional and his historical characters—the novel's high ambitions are most evident in its treatment of its principal theme: the conflict between two visions of man's place in the world, that of the European scientific mind and that of the native American mind, a conflict set at a crucial time and place—Los Alamos and Trinity, New Mexico, 1943-1945 ("Stallion Gate" was Trinity's local name prior to atomic scientist Robert J. Oppenheimer's redesignation of it as the first nuclear test site). The first vision is that of such well-known scientists as Oppenheimer, Edward Teller, Enrico Fermi, and others; the second is that of the Pueblo Indians. Both visions are creative, but the scientists use their speculations and their technology to split the atom and produce a fission bomb; the Indians, possessing a radically different worldview, use quite different technology—dreams, dances, magic wands, pottery—for quite different ends. A secondary conflict emerges within the European-American community, as the visionary scientists find themselves increasingly at odds with the security-minded military authorities who sponsor the project.

The novel's protagonist, Sgt. Joe Peña, finds himself at the center of these conflicts. He is a Pueblo Indian who has been partially, but not entirely alienated from his family and his people by his cosmopolitan experiences as a professional boxer and jazz musician and by his service as a soldier. Joe finds himself sympathizing with both the scientists and the Indians. As Oppenheimer's driver/bodyguard (selected partly because he knew Oppenheimer as a boy), he develops a relationship with the scientist, and in a subplot he falls in love with a refugee mathematician, Anna Weiss. Joe becomes involved in the process of inventing the bomb—selecting the Trinity site, transporting radioactive materials, even climbing the tower at Trinity to free the prototype as it is raised to its final position.

But Joe Peña also rediscovers his inalienable links to his native American heritage—to the home of his dead mother, to the ceremonial dancing and clowning of his people. He responds to the New Mexican landscape itself—the deserts and mesas, the villages and ruins.

Joe's ambivalent position is epitomized in his relations with his uncle Ben and Ben's blind companion, Roberto. At one point the blind Roberto holds the scientist and traitor Klaus Fuchs captive at gunpoint; as a security officer, Joe's duty requires him to apprehend the pair; as an Indian and a man, he must prevent their apprehension. Inspired by images of the destructiveness that will be unleashed at Trinity, Ben and Roberto wander through the novel, warning Joe that the project must be stopped. They use "lightning wands" to invoke conflagrations that will disrupt the experimentation. Though he will not betray Oppenheimer and the project, Joe also refuses to betray Ben and Roberto, finally arranging for them to escape to Mexico.

The second challenge to Joe's loyalty to Oppenheimer comes from Captain Augustino, the head of security (a character based on the actual Captain Peer de Silva). Augustino assumes that the Europeans, who work under his protection at Los Alamos, are Communist subversives, and his suspicions focus upon Anna Weiss and Oppenheimer. Joe becomes caught between the political paranoia of military security and the apolitical innocence of the scientists.

Characters

Sgt. Joe Peña is the central character; he connects episodes of science and romance, jazz and boxing, mysticism and technology, humor and melodrama; he links the fiction and the history. As such, he is, as reviewers noted, overburdened. He is too excellent: he was an eighth-ranked heavyweight boxer; he played piano with the jazz greats; and he was in the Philippines with MacArthur. On July 15, 1945 he outboxes an opponent, uses $50,000 to buy a jazz club, ensures that Ben and Roberto escape to Mexico, and then, as the scientists count down the first atomic explosion at 5:30 a.m. on July 16, Joe wrestles with and kills his nemesis, Capt. Augustino, atop the tower at Trinity. And yet, despite the serendipity of his encounters, Joe emerges as a credible character, capable of carrying the thematic burden which Smith has placed on him.

The remaining characters are defined in vignettes. Though they too are burdened with thematic significance—Scientists, Indians, and Soldiers—all emerge as engaging persons. Characters such as Oppenheimer, General Groves, and Klaus Fuchs conform to their historical counterparts. The native American characters seem authentic in their beliefs and behaviors.

Techniques/Literary Precedents

Mixing historical and fictional characters and events has enjoyed a recent vogue in American fiction. It is a technique well-suited to Smith's style: his novels have always displayed a thorough knowledge of esoteric matters—Gypsy lore, bat behavior, Indian culture, and the minutiae of life in Moscow. In *Stallion Gate*, Smith applies this research method to recreating a historical context. Selecting a crucial moment in history, Smith has crafted an intelligent novel, which becomes neither a sophomoric melodrama, nor a thinly fictionalized lecture on bombmakers and bomb-making, nor a simplistic sermon on evil scientists and good Indians. There is, instead, enough drama (enough character, setting, and plot) to offset the lecture. The thematic conflicts, while not subtle, emerge concretely and organically within the drama.

The narrative follows a simple chronology. The action begins in November 1943, when Capt. Augustino recruits Joe, and ends the morning of July 16, 1945, when the bomb explodes. But within this linear development, Smith plays his themes artfully. The novel pauses several times to describe the techniques of different arts: jazz, boxing, pottery, dance, and construction of atomic bombs. The art of *Stallion Gate* is most like jazz, with Smith skillfully introducing and recalling his themes. Though flawed by the overdone excellence of the hero and the neatness of the timing, *Stallion Gate* is on the whole a fine and thoughtful novel.

Relation to Previous Works

Stallion Gate occupies an interesting position in Smith's development, as it comes between two major novels featuring the Russian detective, Arkady Renko. Smith began as a pulp writer and moved into what might be called increasingly ambitious pulps in the Gypsy novels and in *Nightwing*. Then, in *Gorky Park*, he used the subgenre of the detective story as the basis for a serious novel which presented and criticized a complex social reality.

Stallion Gate takes a further step away from popular conventions. The operative formula—that of espionage fiction—provides only an intermittent, minor plot line.

In the end, neither Capt. Augustino nor the reader cares much when Joe exposes Klaus Fuchs as the hidden threat to the project's security; the interest of the novel lies elsewhere. The central issue is that of subversion, but the real subversives prove to be Oppenheimer and his team, Ben and Roberto, and even Capt. Augustino. The jazz variations on the conventional formula are what really matter.

Stallion Gate returns at a higher level to some of the thematic concerns in *Nightwing*, with a Pueblo army sergeant replacing the Hopi deputy sheriff. Smith's next novel, *Polar Star* (1989) also looks backward. Smith brings back Arkady Renko from *Gorky Park*, thus transforming him from the protagonist of a novel to a series hero. In *Polar Star* Smith returns to a more straightforward, formulaic development of plot, that of the detective story. A body turns up in the first chapter; the investigator engages in the process of detection; there are complications—clues and red herrings; and the killer is revealed and disposed of in the penultimate chapter. Although less innovative than *Stallion Gate*, *Polar Star* presents a more plausible and clearly coherent narrative. Like *Gorky Park*, *Polar Star* sold half a million copies in hard-cover, whereas *Stallion Gate* only sold 40,000 copies.

Polar Star displays Smith's characteristic virtues. The context of the action—a Russian factory ship in the Bering Sea—has been carefully researched and is concretely imagined. Smith writes convincingly about the technology involved in sea fishing. The characters are diverse and plausible. Arkady Renko is the central figure. Following his successful but unorthodox resolution of the problem in *Gorky Park*, he has been expelled from the Party, subjected to "psychiatric rehabilitation," exiled to Siberia, and now serves as a seaman on a trawler sailing from Vladivostock. The appearance of the girl's body in the ship's fishing nets leads to Renko's peculiar resurrection as an investigator. In the process of solving the murder, Renko also uncovers smuggling and espionage.

Additional Sources

Beidler, Peter G. "The Indians in Martin Cruz Smith's *Nightwing*." *American Indian Quarterly* 5 (1979): 155-159.

Weber, Bruce. "Arkady Renko Goes to Munich." *New York Times Magazine* 7 (January 1990): 26-27+. A profile of Smith as he researches his third Arkady Renko novel.

J. K. Van Dover
Lincoln University

WALLACE STEGNER
1909

Publishing History

Wallace Stegner received his doctorate from the University of Iowa in 1935, and his revised dissertation *Clarence Edward Dutton: An Appraisal* was published the following year. His first novel, *Remembering Laughter,* was published in 1937; the book's success encouraged him to continue writing fiction. In 1937, Stegner became a teacher at the University of Utah, eventually moving to the University of Wisconsin. In 1940, he took a job as a part-time writing instructor at Harvard University. His fifth novel and seventh book, *The Big Rock Candy Mountain,* published in 1943, was his first major popular success.

In 1945, Stegner accepted a professorship at Stanford University, where he taught fiction writing until his retirement from teaching in 1971. During his years at Stanford he became recognized as one of America's best novelists and a foremost environmental activist. He recalls that in 1946, after years of being preoccupied with his dual careers as teacher and author, he became concerned with conserving those natural resources that figured so strongly in his fiction. Such was his prominence in efforts to protect the natural environment that he was named a Special Assistant to the Secretary of the Interior for 1961, and in 1962 he served on the National Parks Advisory Board. In 1971 he left Stanford to give full attention to his fiction.

Critical Reception, Honors, and Popularity

From the beginning of his career, Stegner has been taken seriously by literary critics. His early writings were praised for their realistic portrayals of the West. Of these works, *The Big Rock Candy Mountain* was held in especially high esteem, with critics ranking it as one of the best novels about western life. Until the publication of *Angle of Repose* in 1971, *The Big Rock Candy Mountain* was considered Stegner's best novel. Although some still maintain that it is Stegner's preeminent achievement, most critics now consider *Angle of Repose* to be superior. Some critics praise it as the best novel about the American West ever published. The novel blends a modern view of the West with that of the late nineteenth-century, revealing how the West has changed and showing what frontier values have survived. *Angle of Repose* received the 1972 Pulitzer Prize for fiction. Another novel, *The Spectator Bird*, published in 1976, won the 1977 National

Book Award for fiction. Through the years, Stegner has acquired a large and devoted audience; in 1990 his *Collected Stories* was a best seller.

Analysis of Selected Titles

ANGLE OF REPOSE

Angle of Repose, 1971, novel.

Social Concerns

In *Angle of Repose*, Stegner tries to show the value of history through the character Lyman Ward, who narrates the novel. Slowly dying from a crippling disease, Ward has retired to his grandparents' old home in the country. There, he tries to reconstruct their lives, partly because he wants to distract his mind from his disease and partly because he wants to understand himself better. It is his belief that by studying the past he will come to understand the present. He is somewhat nostalgic for the customs of the past. For instance, he complains about his assistant Shelly being *"ohne busthalter"*—meaning that she seldom wears a bra. The sexual titillation of Shelly's breasts makes him yearn for the more demure ways of his grandmother.

Lyman is a professional historian, and his research into the past is more than just a nostalgic yearning for more comfortable customs. In examining his grandparents' marriage he hopes to find clues to the reason why his own marriage has failed and clues to why life in the West has lost its dynamism and become aimless and drifting. He concludes that certain unique western values have been lost. For instance, he notes that marriage in his grandparents' day meant staying together through bad times as well as good, but modern marriage lacks this sense of commitment. When his disease began, Lyman was deserted by his wife. Shelly is in a loose relationship which she terms a marriage mostly to keep her parents happy. Her husband is a drug user who has threatened to kill her. Lyman does not fully understand why Shelly has a relationship that seems governed more by whim and convenience than commitment or love.

Themes

Lyman Ward is on a quest to understand why his life has taken the shape it has. He has trouble at first focusing on a theme for his fictionalized biography of his grandmother, Susan Burling Ward. In a conversation with his son, Rodman, he says, "I'm not writing a book of Western history .... I've written enough history books to know this isn't one. I'm writing about something else. A marriage, I guess." He decides that marriage is the main theme of his book. "What really interests me," he says, "is how two such unlike particles clung together, and under what strains, rolling downhill into their future until they reached the angle of repose where I knew them." When a rock rolls downhill, it eventually stops. Whatever the angle of the hill is where the rock has stopped is the "angle of repose." Lyman wants to know how the sixty-year marriage of his grandparents reached its angle of repose, the time at which it became fixed and permanent.

Lyman's biography is a wide-ranging study of his grandparents' marriage, which he follows from their courtship to the death of their daughter, Agnes. He notes that his grandfather, Oliver Ward, and his grandmother, Susan, had different temperaments and different values. Susan was from a genteel family; she associated with artists, writers, editors, and others attracted to the arts. Oliver was a tall, adventurous man who had dropped out of engineering school after two years. To him, the western frontier was a land of opportunity; it was a place where he could hone his engineering skills and make a name for himself. When he first saw Susan, he fell in love with her; her passion was more controlled, but she unhesitatingly accepted his marriage proposal. She had to wait several years for her husband to build a career in the West before she joined him. Later, she was separated from him for months at a time; she stayed in the East while he weathered winters trying to make homes for her. In spite of the separations, they remained committed to each other. *Angle of Repose* covers their lives until they were in their late thirties. By then, hardship and disappointment had distanced them from each other. Oliver took to drinking heavily, and Susan may have had an affair with Frank Sargeant, a man ten years younger than she and a colleague of her husband. In a mysterious way, Frank was involved in the accidental drowning of Agnes and committed suicide after her funeral. This event was the moment of the angle of repose. Oliver never quite forgave Susan for her involvement in the death of their daughter. In response Susan always showed him deference, as though their relationship was always shadowed by her guilt.

The theme of marriage also incorporates another theme common to much of Stegner's fiction: the relationship between the values of the East and those of the West. In a pattern found in such novels as *The Big Rock Candy Mountain*, the wife represents the genteel Victorian values of eastern society, while the husband represents the restless, questing values of the West. Some critics have suggested that the marriages of civilizing women and untamed, "natural" men represent a conflict between two different sets of American values: one cultured, settled, and refined, and the other crude and dynamic. Of these critics, most think Stegner advocates the values of the nineteenth-century western frontier. Others, however, suggest that he actually prefers the eastern values because the modern West has lost what once made it special. In *Angle of Repose*, both of these views are contradicted. According to Lyman, the idea of a West existing apart from the East is nonsense; without the East there would have been no West. To him, his grandmother Susan represents the multitude of family, business, and cultural ties that bound westerners to the East. In this view, the marriage of his grandparents represents the many compromises and adjustments Americans made to the frontier; they brought their values with them, and those values were then shaped to the requirements of a risky frontier life that demanded flexibility in people if they hoped to survive. This flexibility was not easy to come by, and the disappointments of Oliver and Susan's marriage suggest that the hardships of the frontier life sometimes overwhelmed people.

Characters

Angle of Repose has two main characters, Lyman Ward and his grandmother, Susan Burling Ward. Lyman narrates the novel, telling his own story while he tells Susan's story. The novel is full of his interjections, comments, and autobiography. A one-time college professor, he has lost half of one leg and his ability to turn his neck because of a bone disease. In great pain, he constantly gobbles down aspirin. His wife abandoned him and their marriage of more than twenty years when she learned of his illness. He has moved into his grandparents' old home, where he can sift through their letters and other papers. His son, Rodman, thinks he would be better off in a rest home; only fifty-eight, Lyman appears elderly and enfeebled. But he determinedly resists his son's desire to move him out of his grandparents' house. He believes his work there will help him keep meaning in his life.

Lyman admits that his values may be old-fashioned and that he has trouble with modern society. He sees his grandparents as examples of sound virtues that he finds lacking in the modern world. He admired his grandfather; when a child, Lyman felt especially safe in his strong presence. He also admired his grandmother as someone who, though bred to gentility, adjusted to the hardships involved in following her husband from job to job across the West and into Mexico. As he studies their marriage, Lyman gains new understanding of his friends, of Shelly, and at the end of the novel, even of his wife. Lyman's growth stems from what he uncovers about his grandparents. They were not paragons of the hardy virtues of a mythical old West. Instead, along with their good qualities, they had failings, disagreements, and petty disputes.

In Lyman's account, Susan had a hard time understanding Oliver, who sometimes withdrew and sulked when he was unhappy with her. She was used to bright, witty conversation; Oliver was quiet, soft-spoken, and usually kept his thoughts to himself. She loved the arts and throughout their marriage published her drawings and writings in eastern magazines; he was devoted to machines, to the movement of water and dirt for farms and mines. She thought that all they had to do was endure the West for a little while, and that after Oliver made their fortune, they would move back East, but this was never to be. Susan grew increasingly bitter about how her husband was often cheated by employers and claim jumpers, and about how he just shrugged off setbacks and started on a new project, rather than fighting for his rights. For instance, he invented "hydraulic cement," which is the type of cement used to make the foundations and walls of buildings. At the time such cement had to be imported from Europe. Oliver found a way to make cement using local resources. Unable to find a backer willing to build a cement factory, he dropped interest in the process without patenting it. That process became the standard one for making hydraulic cement throughout the country, but Oliver never profited from it. Such casualness about money angered Susan. After one disappointment too many, after years of hardship, she yielded to her unhappiness. Lyman, who narrates the story, refuses to explain what happened in detail, and sexually liberated Shelly thinks he is silly to be uneasy about discussing Oliver's and Susan's sexual problems. But Lyman shies away from it whenever his narrative comes upon sexual moments. Near the end of the novel, he sticks to dry historical evidence that suggests that Susan and Frank finally yielded to their attraction for each other, and that possibly, while in a sexual interlude, they forgot about Agnes, allowing her to drown.

Both Lyman and Susan are exceptional fictional creations. Lyman describes himself in vivid terms, and his comments about the world around him and the world of his grandparents reveal a full personality. He is a partisan of his grandmother, yet he is too honest to fail to reveal her as exactly what she was. He has a great personal stake in her because he hopes to learn through her why his own father was so bitter and taciturn, and why he became the person he is. He emerges as a complex, flawed man, not the stereotypical hero. Yet, he is heroic; he overcomes the loss of his wife, his illness, and his anger in order to pursue the truth. By the novel's end he is honest with himself in admitting his grandfather's failure to forgive and thereby admitting his own failure.

Susan is symbolic of the East trying to come to terms with the West. It is one of Stegner's outstanding achievements that he makes this symbolic figure fully human. He does this in part by allowing Susan to speak for herself in her letters to friends in the East—primarily Augusta, who married into high society. Although

Susan tells of her travels and feelings, she skirts discussion of her marriage. She is Victorian enough to want to keep her marital affairs private, although Lyman suggests that she is also ashamed of her rough-and-tumble husband who lacks the refinement she was brought up to admire. Since he is writing a fictionalized biography of Susan, Lyman invents dialogue and scenes that he thinks represent what Susan and others probably said and did. He is careful to separate his inventions from the historical facts. The fictionalized aspects of his account of Susan's life derive from what he knows of her through the historical record and from his own memories. She does not shed her youthful dreams easily; her anguish over her separation from the cultural centers of the East sometimes makes her cruel to her husband, and she blames him for her unhappiness. But her courage and determination to share her husband's life make her admirable.

Techniques

The form of *Angle of Repose* is that of a novel within a novel. The inner novel is Lyman's story of Susan; the outer one is the story of Lyman himself. This simultaneous telling of two stories is a clever device, and Stegner maintains a brilliant balance between them. This narrative approach allows Stegner to compare modern western society with that of the late nineteenth century. The weaving together of the two stories creates a set of contrasts: Lyman's failed marriage and Shelly's nonmarriage contrast with Oliver and Susan's long and successful marriage; the invasive soul-searching of Shelly's conversation contrasts with the witty yet reserved conversation of Susan's day; the efforts to incarcerate Lyman contrast with the relative privacy in the old West. There are also similarities. In Lyman's time it is still possible to maintain a degree of isolation from society; he retreats to the same lonely house that his grandparents had lived in. The problem of self-understanding and acceptance is still a problem; Oliver and Susan eventually came to a compromise and learned to accept each other, whereas Lyman is still learning how to accept his own faults.

The dual narrative structure of *Angle of Repose* also creates a spiritual history of the West. Lyman exposes his inner self to scrutiny, even while he pries into the heart of Susan. In fighting the hardships of the frontier and in persevering through great sorrow, Oliver and Susan reach deep into themselves, finding those elements in their personalities that make them westerners. They exhibit great moral courage, which may be at the root of the culture of the West. Lyman forces himself to search for such courage in himself; at the end when he says, "I lie wondering if I am man enough to be a bigger man than my grandfather," he acknowledges that coming to terms with western traditions and values means facing his inner, spiritual life, just as his grandparents had to confront theirs.

Another aspect of Stegner's fictional world is its realism. Several critics have noted that Stegner avoids the clichés of the legendary West. His characters are resolutely human; they are neither great heroes nor great villains, although they often exhibit heroism and villainy. This realism adds to the novel's power, making the characters seem like real people leading complex, difficult lives. Stegner has done extensive research into the history of the West and the everyday lives of its people. The projects in which Oliver becomes involved existed historically as Stegner relates them. Details as to clothing, housing, manners of speech, and other incidentals are authentic. This carefully constructed background contributes to the credibility of the characters and suggests that the novel is about real people.

In fact, the characters of Oliver and Susan are based on real people. Their marriage is patterned on that of Arthur De Wint Foote and Mary Hallock Foote. Arthur was an itinerant engineer and Mary was a writer and artist. Thus, when Lyman says that he is writing about why a marriage lasts, he is probably speaking for Stegner, whose novel is about marriage. This introduces one of the central problems in analyzing Stegner's works: How much is autobiographical? His intimate knowledge of the people and places of the West suffuses his writings, and his keen eye for detail is always at work. Lyman is a retired college history professor; at the time the novel was written, Stegner was a college writing professor. Lyman is deeply interested in how mixing fiction and fact can reveal truths about history that neither alone could uncover; this is a central aspect of Stegner's own creative work. The parallels between Lyman and Stegner are enough to encourage the unwary critic to assign Lyman's cynical personality to Stegner. Although Lyman sometimes acts as spokesman for Stegner, he is not Stegner. The two men do not share diseases, marriages, or personalities. On the other hand, as *The Big Rock Candy Mountain* shows, Stegner does use his own experiences to add to the authenticity of his fiction.

Literary Precedents

Angle of Repose is at once part of and outside the traditions of western literature. The novel's self-conscious realism separates it from most western fiction, which romanticizes the setting and peoples it with outsized heroes and villains. *Angle of Repose* is part of the historical record in which western society was built by miners from Cornwall, ladies from Vermont, and restless men who just wanted a place where they could live free. Some critics suggest that Stegner writes in a literary tradition called "realism" or "American Realism." This was the predecessor of the literary movement called "modernism" that dominated American literature for most of the twentieth century. Like realism, modernism emphasizes realistic action and dialogue, and both have a tendency to pessimism. However, modernism is also marked by a rejection of the validity of history and traditional values. Stegner's *Angle of Repose* exhibits a profound respect for history and traditional values, similar to writings of the Realists. Thus *Angle of Repose* is at least partly in the tradition of Twain's *The Adventures of Huckleberry Finn* (1884).

Like *Angle of Repose*, Twain's novel exhibits a passion for historical authenticity. As Huck and the escaped slave Jim drift down the Mississippi River, the dialects of the people on the shore change, varying from region to region. The geography, customs, and details of manners, clothing, and housing are all historically accurate. Like Stegner, Twain wrote about what he knew; before the Civil War, as a river boat pilot, he had visited the places he depicts in his novel.

Although *Angle of Repose* has much in common with American Realism, one should be aware of important differences. For instance, the influence of modern psychology would not be felt in Realist novels, but it is essential to the psychological realism of *Angle of Repose*. Further, the discussions of sexuality, especially lesbianism, are products of the frankness of modernism. *Angle of Repose* reflects the liberating spirit of modernism, which encouraged the incorporation of previously forbidden topics and language—such as obscenities—in fiction.

Although Twain's stern portrayal of the stupidity and cruelty of slavery in *The Adventures of Huckleberry Finn* creates a background of realism that is echoed in Stegner's *Angle of Repose*, the techniques of the novels differ in significant ways. For instance, in Twain's novel the view of frontiersmen is different. Huck's father, who represents the frontier figure, is illiterate, spiteful, ignorant, and a racist. For Stegner frontiersmen were not ignorant and without culture; they were educated, well read, and cared about their nation's culture. They were bound to civilization by thousands of invisible threads. In this sense, *Angle of Repose* is a unique statement, existing apart from the writings before it. Its literary precedent is the passionate search for truth that has motivated writers for thousands of years.

THE BIG ROCK CANDY MOUNTAIN
The Big Rock Candy Mountain, 1943, novel. Sequel: *Recapitulation,* 1979, novel.

Social Concerns
The Big Rock Candy Mountain focuses on the ending of the western frontier. Through the character of Bo Mason, the novel shows what happened to a society

of people whose temperaments were suited to a wide open frontier, but who had to adapt to the constraints of a settled society. In an interview Stegner said, "People like Bo Mason . . . grow up without history, and they live without history, without any sense of history. They're trapped in the present." This reflects Stegner's view of the American and Canadian Wests; each is without history—their people have to make their own history in the present. Bo Mason wanders about trying to escape from the need to create his own life, to make his own history. His wife Elsa yearns to settle in one place, but she is tied to a wandering frontiersman. The story of Bo, Elsa, and their children is the story of the people of the West who were born into a society with frontier traditions, but who had to live in the settled society of the twentieth-century West. The novel suggests that these people were displaced, without a time or locale to call their own.

The theme of abuse and familial violence is important to the relationships of the characters. Bo Mason is carefully developed; Stegner shows how he and his brothers were relentlessly brutalized by their father, Fred Mason. One after another, the brothers run away from their horrible home, making new lives for themselves wherever they can. Bo, the brightest of the children, acquires the most education, making it to the eighth grade. Properly educated, he might have become a poet. Instead, he must use his cleverness to make his way in the world. By running away from home, he gains some peace; it is a lesson he never forgets—when life is bad, run away. He wanders with his wife and children from one difficult situation to another. When Elsa falls terminally ill, he disappears for a time. In addition, as much as he detests his father, he cannot help reflecting him in his own abuse of his son Bruce. Stegner handles this material with sensitivity, showing how family life teaches children how to behave toward their own children, a fact that often produces frustrated, confused, and angry adults.

Themes

The Big Rock Candy Mountain is the story of a spiritual quest. Each of the three principal characters is searching for his or her own Eden. Bo seeks the freedom of wide open spaces with few social constraints. He pulls his family around with him as he searches for the big opportunity that will make him financially independent. He seems unaware that he is as much running away as he is searching. His brutal childhood chases him wherever he goes; his father's beatings have made him an angry man who is seldom sure of what he is angry about. His Eden would allow him to dissipate his angry energies in hunting and competing against nature for survival. Attracted by a frontier that no longer exists, pushed by a past he cannot escape, Bo is a tragic figure.

Elsa's Eden would be a nice house in a quiet town where she could set down roots. She wants to be respected in a community and to share her time with friends. Her dream is one that American families have long cherished: healthy children, a house of their own, community service, long-lasting friendships, and good educations for the children. Life with a frontiersman does not fulfill such dreams. She ends up focusing on her children, trying to give them a good family life. Perhaps she smothers Bruce's personality, who as a weak child seems to need extra care. Although Elsa's failure to achieve her dream makes her a melancholy figure, she at least knows what she wants. Neither Bo nor Bruce is sure of what his goal is; Elsa's certainty makes her the emotional core of the novel. It is always clear how far her actual life is from the life she hoped for.

By the end of *The Big Rock Candy Mountain*, Bruce is still unsure of what he wants. His Eden seems to be one in which he is the center of attention and where his dynamic and overbearing father is absent. Bruce is overshadowed by his father's powerful physical presence and strong personality. He wants to escape his father's influence and stand on his own.

Characters

The main figures in *The Big Rock Candy Mountain* are Bo, Elsa, and their younger son, Bruce. Bo is big, strong, and athletic. He played professional baseball for a time and was a candidate for the major leagues before a knee injury ended his career. He is bright and gregarious, with an easy manner that wins friends. He also has a quick mind; he uncovers cheats easily and can swiftly adjust to a dangerous situation. A man of the world, he is wise in the ways of earning money in the underworld—by gambling and by selling illegal liquor. He is also insecure and obsessed with a fear of failure. Elsa is at first taken with his charm, but she becomes alarmed when she sees him punch a vagrant. Bo is coldly merciless when protecting his interests, and the vagrant had been putting slugs into his hotel's slot machine.

Bo's charm eventually wins Elsa over. She has escaped an oppressive family situation and wants to make a life of her own. Dashing, handsome, and generous, Bo seems to be the husband who could help her build a new life. When she learns that her family wants her to stay away from him, Elsa becomes defiant. Her relationship with Bo resembles the marriage of Oliver and Susan in *Angle of Repose* in an important way. Like Susan, Elsa represents civilization; like Oliver, Bo represents the natural or untamed man. Elsa does not like moving about. She wishes to stay in one place, settle in, and make her roots in a community. She wants this stability for her children as well as for herself. Yet Bo cannot settle in one place. He is forever getting in trouble with the law, and he unconsciously seeks a frontier where he needs to answer only to nature, not to society. His quest is futile; wherever the frontier goes, society follows and settles in. By the time he has a family, the old West is gone; the new West is more Elsa's world than his. Elsa's desire for a peaceful, quiet, settled life, and Bo's hunger for a frontier life are in conflict. Unlike Oliver and Susan, Bo and Elsa do not reach a compromise.

Elsa is the focus of the conflict between Bo and Bruce. Bo wants to please her and, like a schoolboy, shows off for her. He initially wins her love through his courtesy and generosity. When she is outraged at his treatment of the vagrant, he leaves her gifts of wildfowl that he shot while hunting. His ability to hunt and his other frontier skills make him seem a fine, strong man. But he is also rigid and unable to adjust to a changing world. His generosity of the moment is offset by the pain he causes by moving Elsa frequently around the West.

Bruce, the weak son—a crybaby and mamma's boy—loves Elsa. Feeling rejected by a father he believes is insensitive and cruel, he emphasizes the kindnesses of his mother, devoting himself to her. When she falls terminally ill and his father disappears, he is triumphant. He has her all to himself. The return of his father is difficult for him to accept. Although *The Big Rock Candy Mountain* can be seen as a *bildungsroman*, Bruce does not really grow up. Sensitive, and intelligent, he fails to realize how his obsession with his mother leaves him spiritually stunted. At the novel's end, Bruce is still immature.

Techniques

Some critics object to the shifting point of view in *The Big Rock Candy Mountain*. The story is told from the perspectives of the different characters, shifting from one to another. To these critics, this technique is confusing. They would prefer the steadier view that the character Lyman Ward gives *Angle of Repose*. On the other hand, this shifting viewpoint allows the characters to reveal how they see their own lives. Without the scenes revealing Bruce's complex emotional life, he could seem only an annoying crybaby. Like his father, he is partly a product of his family life. His anger at his father seems natural, even sympathetic when seen from his point of view. After all, his father is sometimes brutal and cruel. Yet, Bo can be a sympathetic character. His horrible childhood is worse than what he inflicts on his children, and from his perspective he is being easier on them than his father was on him. He sees Bruce as a stubborn, disobedient child. When seen from Bo's perspective, Bruce seems provoking and selfish. Thus the shifting views help to build the psychological realism of the novel and help create a tone of fairness.

Stegner is open about the autobiographical elements of *The Big Rock Candy Mountain*, and a tone favoring one character over another might make all his observations in the novel seem untrustworthy. Stegner based the character Bruce on himself, admitting that he was something of a crybaby when he was young. Bo and Elsa represent Stegner's parents. Like the Mason family, the Stegner family moved often. The father was tough and cold; the mother was clinging. In *The Big Rock Candy Mountain*, Stegner works out some of his own anguish over his difficult childhood, and he develops an understanding of his parents. Yet one should take care not to overemphasize the autobiographical elements of the novel. Stegner uses his own family's life to provide a realistic background for the novel's events and to create psychologically believable characters, but ultimately the novel is a work of fiction. The events in the novel are not a literal transcription of Stegner's life. Further, the characters are not exactly like Stegner's family. For instance, Bruce does not quite grow up; in the sequel *Recapitulation*, he has remained unmarried through a long life. In real life, Stegner matured and made a place for himself in his career as college professor, author, and conservationist; his marriage has lasted over fifty years, and he raised a family of successful children.

Literary Precedents

The great, wandering epic structure of *The Big Rock Candy Mountain* resembles that of *The Adventures of Huckleberry Finn*. Each novel tries to capture the essence of its society while the main characters travel from place to place. Stegner himself compares his novel to Leo Tolstoy's *War and Peace* (1865-1869), suggesting that each novel has a loose structure that allows for the coverage of large social issues.

Related Titles

In *Recapitulation*, Bruce Mason returns to Salt Lake City and tries to sort out his childhood and youth. He is well off, successful in his line of work, and yet insecure. His having remained unmarried suggests that he never quite let go of his obsession with his mother—that he never quite grew up. In this novel, he tries to understand his parents and reconcile their world with the one in which he lives forty years later.

GENESIS

Gensis, 1962, novella.

Social Concerns

Genesis focuses on the hard lives of Canadian cowboys at the turn of the century. The ranch on which they work is owned by an absentee landlord who leaves the care of his cattle to hired hands. They must ride herd on a huge ranch that is as big as some European countries. During *Gensis,* they risk their lives to bring the cattle off the range for the winter. They endure backbreaking work, long hours, sunburn and frostbite for twenty dollars a month.

Themes

In this rite-of-passage story, nineteen-year-old Englishman Lionel Cullen—called "Rusty" for his red hair—passes into adulthood. The rite-of-passage theme differs from the coming-of-age theme by focusing on one key event that marks the transition into adulthood. In *Gensis,* the rite of passage is a two-week cattle drive through three terrible blizzards. At the beginning of the story, Rusty is a somewhat spoiled young man, looking for fun and adventure as a Canadian cowboy. After only a day of work, he realizes that riding herd is not an adventure; it is just plain hard work. Later, he contemplates what he might be doing instead of exhausting himself in painful labors. He could be going to Oxford University or sailing in a harbor while jeering at working sailors. He traveled to Canada over the objections of his family; like a spoiled child, he became more stubborn the more his family decried his whim to be a cowboy. He discovers that the life of a cowboy is not romantic, and he yearns to be free of his obligations to the men with whom he works. He imagines himself abandoning them and heading home. Yet, by the story's end, he has learned how to act like a man. He learns that saving another man's life is not heroism. On the range, that is merely doing what is expected; anything less would be cowardice. This realization on his part marks his transition into manhood.

Characters

Rusty is the main character of *Genesis.* He is only nineteen years old and eager for adventure. Almost everything about riding herd is new to him; as he learns the rules and nuances of his job, the reader gets a view of the life of Canadian cowboys in 1906. They have two kinds of horses: big ones that can endure terrible cold and smaller ponies that can maneuver around cattle easily but are not as sturdy as the large horses. There are different breeds of cattle on the range, and each kind must be kept separate from the others. Calves and yearlings are not as capable of enduring winter's hardships as older cattle, and they must be herded to the main ranch for care during the winter. As he gradually picks up on the details of cowboy life, Rusty finds a place for himself among the nine other cowboys he must work with.

At first Rusty yearns for an opportunity to do something heroic, so that the other men will accept him as a full-fledged cowboy. He is self-centered, easily annoyed, and eager for a respect that he does not realize cannot be easily earned. As he matures, he realizes that heroic acts are everyday experiences for cowboys. If they fail to look out for each other, they will not be able to do their jobs. When Rusty falls from his pony and is charged by a longhorn steer, he is saved by another rider. He feels humiliated by this, because he thinks he has looked unmanly in front of the others. Eventually, he learns that danger is always present and that helping or needing help is not a matter of concern to cowboys. Helping each other is just part of the routine; for Rusty to be accepted by the others, he must fit into the routine. He must prove himself rugged and trustworthy through many hardships. Through three freezing blizzards—with the last one nearly fatal—he endures, does his job, saves a life, and learns humility and self-confidence.

Techniques

The conflicts in *Genesis* are of three types: man against nature, man against man, and man against himself. The first conflict is readily apparent; nature is a formidable opponent. The Canadian winter is merciless and unrelenting. The range in November is bitterly cold; the sun is harsh and blinding; the wind burns the skin. At first the struggle against nature involves the cowboys trying to keep their herd together and driving it to safe places before the winter makes the task impossible. Their effort to do their jobs in such an unforgiving environment tests the men to the limits of their physical endurance. Yet, nature has even more demanding hardships in store. A blizzard forces them to retreat to their tent; afterwards they must reassemble the herd. Another blizzard forces the men to ride through snow on nearly dead ponies to again gather their cattle. A third blizzard overwhelms them, blowing over their tent and forcing them to leave the cattle to survive on their own. Through freezing temperatures and a violent wind, they hike to safety.

The man-against-man conflict is made to look petty and trivial in the story. Rusty's grievances against Spurlock are minor. Rusty is spoiling for a fight; he wants the men to respect him and believes that fighting and beating one of them would earn that respect. He sizes Spurlock up, measuring him against his own physical strengths. Spurlock is sixteen years older and had spent several years at a desk job. Spurlock does not like him, but the older man is not cruel. He merely makes cutting remarks and indicates that he thinks Rusty is spoiled and soft. The battle against natural hazards and Rusty's conflict within himself are more important than the man-to-man conflicts, which pale beside the life threatening dangers of the range.

Inner conflict is central to the development of Rusty's character. During one of the blizzards Rusty realizes, "The fact that he was here in a tent on the freezing Saskatchewan plains, that one decision rashly made and stubbornly stuck to had taken him not only out of the university, out of home, out of England, but out of a whole life and culture that had been assumed for him, left him dazed." During the hardships of the cattle drive he wrestles first with his desire to be accepted as a real cowboy and then with his desire to run away and return to a comfortable life. The privations caused by the winter storms force him to grow up; escape is not possible until the men reach the ranch house. He learns during the third blizzard that only by sticking together can the men survive. The conflict within himself is whether he will remain a spoiled, privileged person, or whether he will grow up and learn to respect other people. This conflict is only resolved at the story's end, when he comes to terms with his selfish desire to be the hero, to be the center of attention.

Other Titles (selected)

Clarence Edward Dutton: An Appraisal, 1936 (criticism); *Remembering Laughter*, 1937 (novel); *The Potter's House*, 1938 (novel); *On the Darkling Plain*, 1940 (novel); *Fire and Ice*, 1941 (novel); *Mormon Country*, 1942 (history); *Second Growth*, 1947 (novel); *The Preacher and the Slave*, 1950 (novel; also published as *Joe Hill: A Biographical Novel*); *The Women on the Wall*, 1950 (short stories); *The Writer in America*, 1951 (essays); *Beyond the Hundredth Meridian: John Wesley Powell and the Second Opening of the West*, 1954 (biography); *The City of the Living and Other Stories*, 1956; *A Shooting Star*, 1961 (novel); *Wolf Willow: A History, a Story, and a Memory of the Last Plains Frontier*, 1962 (history and fiction); *The Gathering of Zion: The Story of the Mormon Trail*, 1964 (history); *All the Little Live Things*, 1967 (novel); *The Sound of Mountain Water*, 1969 (essays); *The Uneasy Chair: A Biography of Bernard DeVoto*, 1974; *The Spectator Bird*, 1976 (novel); *One Way to Spell Man*, 1982 (nonfiction); *Crossing to Safety*, 1987 (novel); *The American West as Living Space*, 1987 (essays); *Collected Stories*, 1990.

Additional Sources

Ahearn, Kerry. "*The Big Rock Candy Mountain* and *Angle of Repose*: Trial and Culmination." In *Western American Literature* 10 (Spring 1975): 11-27. Ahearn compares the two novels, arguing that *Angle of Repose* is the better one.

Beetz, Kirk H. "Wallace Stegner." In *Research Guide to Biography and Criticism*, Vol. 5, edited by Walton Beacham. Washington, DC: Beacham Publishing, 1991. Surveys biographical, autobiographical, and critical sources for researching Stegner.

Canzoneri, Robert. "Wallace Stegner: Trial by Existence." *The Southern Review* 9 (October 1973): 796-827. Discusses the importance of realism in Stegner's fiction.

Dillman, Richard H. "Wallace Stegner." In *Critical Survey of Long Fiction: English Language Series*. Englewood Cliffs, NJ: Salem Press, 1983. This is a general introduction to Stegner's life and work, with special attention paid to *The Big Rock Candy Mountain*, *Angle of Repose*, and *Recapitulation*.

Hudson, Lois Phillips. "*The Big Rock Candy Mountain*: No Roots—and No Frontier." *South Dakota Review* 9 (Spring 1971): 3-13. Hudson discusses the "literal accuracy" of Stegner's novel.

Milton, John, et al., eds. "Wallace Stegner Number." *South Dakota Review* 23 (Winter 1985). This edition contains eight articles covering much of Stegner's work, plus a reprint of a 1971 interview.

Peterson, Audrey C. "Narrative Voice in Wallace Stegner's *Angle of Repose*." *Western American Literature* 10 (Summer 1975): 125-133. Peterson discusses the unconventional aspects of the narrative of the novel.

Robinson, Forrest G. "Wallace Stegner's Family Saga: From *The Big Rock Candy Mountain* to *Recapitulation*." *Western American Literature* 17 (Summer 1982): 101-116. Robinson examines how Stegner's views of the characters of the novels have changed over forty years.

Ronda, Bruce A. "Themes of Past and Present in *Angle of Repose*." *Studies in American Fiction* 10 (Autumn 1982): 217-226. Ronda examines the conflicting values in the novel.

Stegner, Wallace, and Richard W. Etulain. *Conversations with Wallace Stegner on Western History and Literature.* Salt Lake City: University of Utah Press, 1983. The conversations cover a wide range of Stegner's interests. This book includes chapters devoted to *The Big Rock Candy Mountain* and *Angle of Repose.*

Kirk H. Beetz
National University, Sacramento

AMY TAN
1952

Publishing History

Amy Tan began her writing career as a free-lance writer, publishing a business newsletter with a co-worker, after pursuing a doctorate in linguistics at the University of California, Berkeley. In 1985 she entered a Squaw Valley writers' workshop in California, intending to write a short story. This first story, "Endgame," was published in *FM* magazine, then reprinted by *Seventeen*. Encouraged by literary agent Sandra Dijkstra, Tan developed a formal proposal for a collection called "Wind and Water," which included her first stories. This collection, knit together to form a novel, became *The Joy Luck Club*, published by Putnam's in 1989. Besides "Endgame," some of the stories appeared in slightly different form in *The Atlantic, Grazia, Ladies Home Journal, The Francisco Focus*, and *The Short Story Review*.

Tan had another reason for beginning to write. When her mother became ill suddenly, Tan recalled something her mother had once asked her: "If I die, what would you remember?" Tan realized that in spite of hearing bits and pieces of stories from childhood on, she really didn't know much about her Chinese roots. She then resolved to visit China with her mother and to remember everything possible. Her first book, dedicated "To my mother and the memory of her mother," echoes this promise. Its epigraph reads: "You asked me once what I would remember. This, and much more." Tan is working on a new novel entitled *The Kitchen God's Wife*, which is scheduled for publication in June 1991.

Critical Reception, Honors, Popularity

From the beginning, Putnam's thought that *The Joy Luck Club* would receive serious literary attention, and thus promoted it intensively, using video, direct mailings, and prepublication quotations from notable authors, such as Alice Walker and Louise Erdrich. This instinct paid off; an associate publisher remarked that he had never before seen the kind of unanimous positive response to a first novel that Tan's work generated. *The Joy Luck Club* moved onto the *New York Times* bestseller list in April 1989. A few days later, the bidding for the paperback rights was frantic, with Vintage Books/Random House offering an unprecedented $1,238,000.

A *New York Times* book reviewer praised Tan's wonderful eye, fine ear, deep empathy, and "guilelessly straight-forward way of writing." Another New York reviewer called the book "not terribly deep" and "often burdened with symbols."

The *Los Angeles Times* said the effect of the book was to make the reader realize the power of every person's own amazing stories, a power to which "magicians of language" such as Tan hold the key.

Analysis of Selected Titles

THE JOY LUCK CLUB
The Joy Luck Club, 1989, novel.

Social Concerns/Themes

The Joy Luck Club achieves much of its power by tapping into aspects of myth. It deals with things lost and things found, with masks and unmasking, with reuniting, climbing, deceit, and discovery. It does this, not by retelling ancient myths, but by gradually revealing the real life stories of Chinese women and their Chinese-American daughters. The book is structured around the meetings of a long-standing mah-jong club in San Francisco. Jing-Mei Woo has been invited to replace her mother, Suyuan Woo, who died two months earlier. The club is the American version of a similar club, also named the Joy Luck Club, formed by Suyuan Woo in Kweilin, China, during the difficult time shortly before that city's fall to the Japanese.

Each of the sixteen chapters is a story told by one of the eight main characters: four mothers, four daughters; two stories each. The mother-daughter relationships, complicated by the great differences in the worlds in which the mothers and daughters grew up, create the dynamic tension. Which tensions are based upon these differences, which grow out of universal mother-daughter conflicts, neither the reader nor the characters involved can determine. But as these women tell their stories, a gradual awareness develops for how much of the past cannot be retrieved, and yet how pervasive it is in the present, and how it gives emotional shape and color to the present. That which is inherited from the past is shown in these stories to be the key to the survival, meaning, and value of these lives.

The mothers' values are a part of this past. As the daughters attempt to separate themselves, and search for their own way, they find in their identity with their mothers' pasts much to hold onto. For their own part, the mothers worry about not being able to communicate the past to their daughters, which may result in losing contact with them. Even language, which is very much a concern of this book, proves to be a barrier between mothers and daughters. One mother says, "And because I remained quiet for so long now my daughter does not hear me." Another, says the epigraph, waited in vain, "year after year, for the day she could tell her daughter this in perfect English."

Characters

The main characters in this novel are four women: China-born Suyuan Woo, An-Mei Hsu, Lindo Jong, and Ying-ying St. Clair; and their four daughters, American-born Jing-mei "June" Woo, Rose Hsu Jordan, Waverly Jong, and Lena St. Clair. Some readers have expressed difficulty in sensing a distinctness among the four mothers and the four daughters. The voices seem, at least on a first reading, too similar.

But if there is similarity in their voices and a sameness to the daughters' complaints about growing up Chinese-American, there is a brilliance of detail and individuality in the lives of the four women from China, who met and formed the San Francisco version of the Joy Luck Club in 1949. One cannot forget the picture of Suyuan Woo, fleeing Kweilin before the approaching Japanese army, leaving behind first her suitcases, then her food, and at last the twin daughters she could no longer carry. Or Linda Jong, getting out of a matchmaker marriage by her wits, getting to Peking, and getting out of the country. Or Ying-ying St. Clair and her stories of falling into Tai Lake at the celebration of the Moon Festival. Or An Mei Woo, with her memories of her sad and bitter mother, the unhappy fourth wife of a wealthy man.

The daughters show varying degrees of success, American-style. Waverly, learning to play with a cast-off chess set donated by Baptist ladies, becomes a chess prodigy; June is accused by her mother of being a "college drop-off"; Rose is being divorced by her dermatologist husband; Lena has a "balanced" marriage with a successful architect, balanced down to every dollar. One thing that unites all eight voices is their expression of things they wish they could communicate to one another.

Techniques

Like the four sides of the mah-jong table, the book is structured with an almost classical balance: four mothers' stories, four daughters' stories; then four more daughters' stories, four more mothers' stories, climaxing with a visit to China and the discovery of things long-lost.

Tan speaks with authentic voices, both American voices as heard in the next apartment ("You break your legs sliding down that bannister, I'm gonna break your neck"), and voices of Chinese mothers, such as comments about a handmade table: "What use for? You put something else on top, everything fall down. *Chunwana chihan.*"

Literary Precedents

Tan credits Louise Erdrich's *Love Medicine* (1984), a set of interwoven tales about Indian life, as a formative influence on her writing. *The Joy Luck Club* also is inevitably and frequently compared with its predecessors, Maxine Hong Kingston's three varied books: *The Woman Warrior, China Men,* and *Tripmaster Monkey.* Tan's book is less determinedly historical than *China Men,* less political than *Tripmaster Monkey*; it can be most productively compared with *The Woman Warrior* in its transformed amalgam of family history and myth, and it holds its own well in such a comparison.

Tan also credits a literary heritage of sermons by her Baptist minister father, family stories, Chinese fairy tales, and parables for influence on her work.

Adaptations

Tan reads from her book on audio tape by Dove. Movie rights are under negotiation.

Additional Sources

Feldman, Gayle. "*The Joy Luck Club*: Chinese Magic." *Publishers Weekly* (July 7, 1989): 24-26. A favorable review of Tan's first novel.

"Amy Tan, Author of *The Joy Luck Club.*" *Bestsellers 89* 3: 69-71. Brief biographical description.

Linda Yoder
Salem-Teikyo University

PETER TAYLOR
1917

Publishing History

Peter Matthew Hillsman Taylor was born on January 8, 1917, in the small west Tennessee town of Trenton. In 1924 his family moved to Nashville and in 1932 to Memphis. Each of these areas is important in Taylor's writing. In 1936 Taylor attended Southwestern University in Memphis, but was soon persuaded by his composition teacher, Allen Tate, to transfer to Vanderbilt University. Taylor's first stories were published in 1937 while he was still a student at Vanderbilt. At the departure of John Crowe Ransom, Taylor's mentor, Taylor left Vanderbilt and Nashville to return to Memphis. He soon resumed his studies and his writing, first at Kenyon College, then in graduate school at Louisiana State University where he studied with Robert Penn Warren and Cleanth Brooks before being drafted into the army in 1941. In 1948 Taylor's first collection of short stories, *A Long Fourth and Other Stories* was published, many others appearing in *The New Yorker*.

Since 1948 Taylor has published regularly and to acclaim. *A Woman of Means*, published in 1950, was followed by *The Widows of Thornton* (1954), *Tennessee Day in St. Louis* (1957), *In the Miro District* (1957), and *Happy Families Are All Alike*, which received the Ohioana Book Award in 1960. These were only the beginning of a distinguished literary career. Most recently, Taylor has published *The Old Forest and Other Stories* (1985) and *A Summons to Memphis* (1986). His *Collected Stories* were reissued in paperback in 1986.

Critical Reception, Honors, and Popularity

In addition to receiving the Ohioana Book Award for *Happy Families Are All Alike*, Taylor has received other recognition including the American Academy and Institute's Gold Medal for the Short Story in 1978 and a nomination for the American Book Award for *A Summons to Memphis* in 1986. He withdrew himself from consideration for the latter award.

Taylor has held teaching positions at numerous institutions: Indiana University, Kenyon College, the University of Chicago, Ohio State University, the University of North Carolina at Greensboro, the University of Virginia, and as a visiting professor at Harvard.

He has also been awarded a Guggenheim grant in 1950, a Fulbright grant in 1955, a National Institute of Arts and Letters grant in 1966, and a Rockefeller

Foundation grant in 1966. In May 1983 Taylor was inducted into the American Academy of Arts and Letters.

Analysis of Selected Titles

IN MIRO DISTRICT AND OTHER STORIES
In Miro District and Other Stories, 1974, short stories.

Social Concerns/Themes
In most of Taylor's work, his major concern is with change and the contrast that it produces between parents or grandparents and their children or grandchildren. In the title story, "In Miro District," the contrast is between a grandfather, who remembers Nashville by its ancient Spanish name, the Miro District, and his sometimes-wild grandson. In "The Captain's Son" the contrast is that of attitudes and lifestyles. Often the contrast and differing views results in conflict. The conflict in families and between friends provides a poignant comment on life in an ever-changing South.

Characters
All of the narrators of these stories are males representative of the younger generation. In "The Captain's Son," the narrator tells the story of his sister's marriage to a man reared in Memphis, a city of the modern world. Lila, the sister, is soon corrupted by her aimless husband. "Brother," as the narrator is called, recognizes this fact first, commenting that alcohol is the culprit. Lila and her husband soon retreat to Memphis and to silence, while the narrator goes on with his life facing a less-than-bright future.

"In Miro District" is about a young man's exploits, mostly sexual, and his grandfather's tyranny. The grandfather actually is not a tyrant but an understanding old man who is less stern than most adults would be given the circumstances. However, the gap between the grandfather and the grandson only widens as the young man grows older. The story ends with the young man's feelings of alienation and separation, revealing his lack of understanding of the character of his grandfather, the relative whom he probably most resembles.

Techniques
Taylor uses various approaches to the subject of family relationships and change. Of the eight narratives in this volume, four—"The Instruction of a Mistress,"

"The Hand of Emmagene," "Her Need," and "Three Heroines"—are in verse. The other four are more traditional short stories, filled with irony, the common problems of normal families, and situational humor. That the narrator of "The Captain's Son" suffers even though he is stable and astute is ironic, as is the narrator's alienation from his understanding grandfather in "In Miro District." Humorous vignettes are presented throughout the book, but the humor is quiet and subtle.

THE OLD FOREST AND OTHER STORIES
The Old Forest and Other Stories, 1985, short stories.

Social Concerns/Themes

Like *In Miro District*, this collection concentrates on family relationships and conflicts. "The Old Forest" is the story of social perceptions and the strong will that one must have not to allow those perceptions to shape events. The conflict between parents and children is explored in "The Gift of the Prodigal," a conflict that provides an old man with a purpose—to be a confidante to a son whose problems give the old man a sense of being needed. "Two Ladies in Retirement" shows the contrast between the way of living in an older town and a new way of life in a modern city.

Characters

Since the characters in the stories are so numerous and yet so similar, the characters in "Two Ladies in Retirement" can be seen as representative.

In this story three generations engage in a genteel battle of wills. The oldest group is represented by two aging women, Miss Betty Pettigru and her companion and cousin, Mrs. Florence Blalock. Because they are alone, they must move from Nashville to St. Louis, where they live with Miss Betty's relatives, the James Tollivers, representing the next younger group. The youngest group consists of the Tolliver children: Jimmy, Vance, and Landon. The old ladies worship the children and try to maintain their Nashville lifestyle in this extended family.

Conflict soon arises though. The servants' lives are disrupted when the old ladies move in; the order of the house changes; the boys change; and a showdown finally happens. The resolution is the realization that life cannot remain the same. All must change.

Techniques

Taylor again concentrates on familial conflict and psychological drama. The reader feels great empathy with the domestic situation and a better understanding of the way a geographical location can have a cultural hold on people years after they have left.

A SUMMONS TO MEMPHIS

A Summons to Memphis, 1986, novel.

Social Concerns/Themes

This novel, Taylor's most recent, is an extended study of his principle theme, well represented in his other work: the familial strife that arises in the face of change.

The change in this family is caused by a move that the family makes early in the narrator's life from the old southern town of Nashville to the modern southern city of Memphis. This changes the lives of the narrator's sisters, severely limiting their chances of making good marriages, eventually leaving them unmarried and dissatisfied. The stress that ensues after the move drives the eldest son to enlist, fight in the war, and die. And it compels the narrator to partially alienate himself from the family and move to New York and adopt a non-southern lifestyle.

Characters

In *A Summons to Memphis* the characters represent a family and the friends of that family. The father is forced to leave his home in Nashville because of a business disagreement that haunts the family even decades after the incident.

The family is brought together again when the children are middle-aged. Their widower father has decided to marry again and the two middle-aged but liberal-minded sisters have summoned their brother to return to Memphis to try and prevent the marriage. What ensues is a lengthy reminiscence about the family's move, the father's attempts to manipulate the lives of his children, and finally the children's attempts to tell an aged father how to live the few remaining years of his life.

Techniques

Taylor's major technique is the non-chronological revelation of the complexity of family relations. There is much irony and much humor in the situations, but the narrator recognizes the humor and irony only in hindsight and conveys it ambiguously. Throughout his literary career, Taylor's technique has remained basically the same, as have his themes, giving the reader the feeling that he is seeing pieces of a life collected in random order and put together much like a large, complicated jigsaw puzzle.

Literary Precedents
Taylor combines several traditions in his stories. His place in the southern tradition is obvious with his introversion, concentration on tradition, and scrutiny of private behavior. His preoccupation with psychology places him in the tradition of Henry James and others, although Taylor's style is quite dissimilar.

His short stories and novels are private rather than public, quiet rather than boisterous, contemplative rather than active. Readers more than likely will perceive the works as autobiographical in nature. However, this quality may be as much the effect Taylor's stories have upon the reader's identifying with events as it is the writer's personal story.

Other Titles
A Long Fourth and Other Stories, 1948; *A Woman of Means,* 1950 (novel); *The Widows of Thornton,* 1954 (short stories); *Tennessee Day in St. Louis: A Comedy,* 1957 (play); *Happy Families Are All Alike: A Collection of Stories,* 1959; *Miss Leonora When Last Seen and Fifteen Other Stories,* 1963; *Presences: Seven Dramatic Pieces,* 1973 (plays); *A Stand in the Mountains,* 1985 (play).

Additional Sources
Griffith, Albert J. *Peter Taylor.* New York: Twayne, 1970. An analysis of Taylor's works through 1969.

McAlexander, Hubert H. *Conversations with Peter Taylor.* Jackson: University Press of Mississippi, 1987. A collection of interviews and discussions with Taylor.

Lesa Dill
Western Kentucky University

PAUL THEROUX
1941

Update

Since the publication of the best-selling *The Mosquito Coast* in 1982, Paul Theroux's literary career has met with great success. He received American Book Award nominations for *The Old Patagonian Express* and *The Mosquito Coast*, and in 1986 *The Mosquito Coast* was made into a highly successful film; his novella, *Doctor Slaughter*, was adapted for the screen in 1986 as *Half Moon Street*. Theroux has also written two more bestsellers, *My Secret History* (1989), a novel, and *Riding the Iron Rooster* (1988), a travel book. Although Theroux owes some of the success of these books to the popularity of the film version of *The Mosquito Coast*, they are clearly the work of an evolving artist who continues to enthrall readers with his adventures while exploring the complexities of human nature.

Riding the Iron Rooster, which recounts Theroux's thirteen-month train trip through China, continues his use of travel experiences as a way of revealing the author's own character. For Theroux, travel writing gives a view into the writer's psyche. In addition, *Riding the Iron Rooster* examines how people are shaped by social traditions and pressures, especially their attitudes about sexuality, intellect, and freedom. This is a central theme that remains prominent in *My Secret History*.

My Secret History, although a strong novel, reveals that Theroux still struggles with his fiction. Without the framework of a journey around which to organize his material, Theroux occasionally falters in the presentation and thematic development. Nevertheless, *My Secret History* tackles major social and personal issues while entertaining readers with foreign locales and unforgettably offbeat characters.

Theroux's latest novel, *Chicago Loop* (1991), is less successful than *My Secret History*. The main character, a Chicago real estate developer, engages in kinky sex with women he meets through personal ads. During one of his trysts he murders the woman but blocks the horrible event from his memory. After other close calls he remembers, becomes remorseful, and turns transvestite, assuming the murdered woman's identity. In spite of strong writing, the unlikely plot in a serious novel sinks this latest effort.

Analysis of Selected Titles

MY SECRET HISTORY

My Secret History, 1989, novel.

Social Concerns/Themes

A common theme in the modern novel is the sense of alienation among people in contemporary society. *My Secret History* takes up this theme. The novel focuses on the life of Andre Parent, a Catholic who grows up in Boston during the 1950s and who copes with the repressive environment of his early life by living two lives—one open and conforming, the other secret and reckless. Through this novel, Theroux makes dual comments on modern society: that repressive and judgmental forces are driving everyone to hypocrisy and that such secrecy can go unchecked because of extreme isolation. Theroux suggests that people compartmentalize their lives to accommodate the conflicting demands of society and self. Because people are judgmental and dictatorial regarding the behaviors of others, they turn to secrecy in order to fulfill themselves without jeopardizing their status in the community. As Andre notes, "as soon as someone else's eyes are on us we are diminished—made into ugly miniatures of ourselves."

In the novel, Andre avoids social censure by ostensibly behaving in a respectable manner as a Peace Corps volunteer and headmaster of an African school. Simultaneously, he lives out his fantasy life of uninhibited sex with a variety of African girls whom he picks up each weekend at a local bar. Other characters have secrets as well. When Andre is a young man, he and several women from the Catholic church accompany one of the parish priests, Father Furty, on his boat where the women flirt with the priest and drink "bug juice" (alcoholic punch). On one trip, when Father Furty jokes that he hopes that "the Boss" (the Pastor) does not find out about their drinking, Andre notes that these "secret words seemed scandalous to [the women] and they laughed hard." With the seed planted in his mind as to how to live his life of hypocrisy, Andre eventually pushes this basic precept of secrecy to the limit, actually setting up two households (and two lives): one in England with his wife and son, and one in America with his mistress. As Andre notes while he sits in a hospital waiting room in Africa:

> In this waiting room no one is what he or she seems. The man with the little girl is not her father—he is a child molester. The married couple are actually saying good-bye—she is going to meet her lover, he's off to visit his mistress. The cowboy is a homo.

The prevalence of these secret histories underscores human isolation. Because Andre and these other characters live during a time when people are increasingly less connected with others, their secrets escape notice. At one point, for example, Andre states:

I had two lives but I had intimations today that because there were two they were both incomplete, I lived in the cracks between them—had only ever lived in that space. Outside it, among others, I was not Myself, and so no one knew me. Was that everyone's condition—that we were each of us unknown?

My Secret History answers "yes" to this question. The novel depicts contemporary society, worldwide, as failing to care for the individual, causing many to live fragmented and alienated existences.

The novel also addresses, although only cursorily, censorship (during a discussion about the ban of Henry Miller's work, a character responds "Imagine preventing people from reading something—as if reading is going to make us into monsters!") and abortion rights (two different characters describe the horrors of their illegal abortions). American elitism is also explored as Andre experiences prejudice from the wealthy who frequent the swimming pool where he lifeguards; Andre comments, "I had no money, and it seemed as if, having none, I did not exist."

Characters

My Secret History follows the tradition of a *bildungsroman* (a novel concerned with a youth's education and maturation), in which the protagonist, Andre Parent, changes from "innocent" to "experienced" in reaction to his environment. This transformation begins when his friend and confessor, Father Furty, dies. At a time when Andre's involvement with the Catholic Church is motivated by greed (as altar boy, if Andre serves for three funerals, he is "given" a wedding and money from the groom) or by guilt ("I had so often felt punished—ashamed and afraid—in the glare of God's sight.") Father Furty restores the humanity of the church for Andre. For example, Andre says that Father Furty "made happiness look natural and right," a much-needed balance to the extreme repression Andre had always associated with Catholicism. But when Father Furty dies and is considered a failure by the parishioners because of his alcoholism, in Andre's eyes the church has devalued a man whom he has loved. Ultimately Andre breaks from the church and remarks of the freedom he experienced "then I walked away and was aware in those seconds that my life had just begun—like a wheel slipping off an axle and rolling alone, and already it was spinning faster."

Andre eventually takes decisive steps to change his life and escape the drudgery and stupidity that he sees around him. As he says in the opening statement of the book "I was born poor in Rich America, yet my instincts were better than money and were for me a source of power." Rather than depending upon the church for guidance now, Andre begins to establish his own rules. After reading a poem by Baudelaire about a lover ("naked except for her jewels, wearing make up. Gleaming buttocks. Moorish slave. Like a captive tiger . . . she was black, and she yearned for him"), he is encouraged to escape America and its repressive atmosphere and go to Africa. There his desire to live a dual life becomes a dominant force in his plans.

For the remainder of the novel Andre is a divided character. Although he returns to a type of unity when he first meets his wife, he ultimately returns to the dual lifestyle, keeping a mistress in America and a wife in Britain. In the end it is only as a writer that Andre seems able to find contentment without deception. The creation of a third self, the self of the writer, frees Andre. He now keeps his literary ideas to himself, as "secrets" that he finds so vitally important. It is a transformation that Andre revels in. Speaking of a novel that he was working on, Andre explains that his wife "had not seen a word of it; no one had. That secrecy made me strong." Likewise, merely acting as an observer in his own life seems to him a viable continuation of his secret history. In the final scene of the novel, when Andre is faced with choosing his wife (who represents security and rationality) or his mistress (who represents eroticism and irrationality), he declares: "I know exactly what to do." Although his choice remains ambiguous to the reader, it seems likely that Andre will settle into a monogamous relationship since his writing can now fulfill his need for mystery.

Literary Precedents

Theroux has written in the Author's Note to *My Secret History* the following disclaimer: "Although some of the events and places depicted in this novel bear a similarity to those in my own life, the characters all strolled out of my imagination." Despite this statement, Andre Parent has a surprisingly large number of parallels to Theroux: both were brought up as Catholics in Massachusetts, both went to Nyasland (Malawi) as Peace Corps volunteers, both married British women, became successful writers, and eventually set up dual households in the United States and in Britain.

Like Saul Bellow in *Humboldt's Gift,* and John Irving in *The World According to Garp,* Theroux is writing in the semi-autobiographical fictional tradition. Although this method is widely acknowledged, Theroux's disclaimer hints at his discomfort with personal revelations.

Another literary influence on *My Secret History* is Joseph Conrad's *Heart of Darkness* (1902) and his treatment of the theme of the foreign exploitation of undeveloped countries. The character of Rockwell, for example, illustrates the tendency of foreigners to reshape an existing culture, to "improve" it, without considering the effects on the people. Rockwell, a Peace Corps worker, demonstrates his social insensitivity by creating an elaborate latrine for the African school based upon the architecture of the Alamo, while Andre's desire for unlimited and guiltless sex leads him to exploit local women.

The character of Andre has literary precedents at various stages in his life. The young Andre is reminiscent of James Joyce's character Stephen Daedalus in *A Portrait of the Artist as Young Man* (1916). Both Andre and Stephen are constantly oppressed by the consciousness of guilt because of a Catholic upbringing. At fifteen, Andre is reminiscent of J. D. Salinger's Holden Caulfield in *Catcher in the Rye* (1951): full of anger, rebellion, and indignation. For instance, Andre enjoys shocking people by declaring that he is a Communist.

Finally, as a man with two lives, Andre resembles the anonymous author of the Victorian novel, *My Secret Life* (1890). In *My Secret Life* the author recounts his rebellion against Victorian sexual repression; ostensibly he acts normally, but secretly he indulges in sexual exploits that are excessive and perverse. Although Andre is living in America during the 1950s, his statement that "everything enjoyable made me feel guilty" strongly connects him with the repressive lifestyle of the Victorians. Ultimately Andre, like the author of *My Secret Life*, escapes, not by abandoning what he considers sinful, but by living a dual existence.

Interestingly, in *Riding the Iron Rooster* Theroux mentions reading a Chinese novel, *Jin Ping Mei* (*The Golden Lotus*), similar to *My Secret Life* in that it was banned due to its eroticism. Theroux explains that he marveled at its blend of "manners, delicacy and smut" and suggests that if the Chinese were allowed to read the book, "they would discover a great deal about themselves": that what a society chooses to hide can be very revealing.

Relation to Previous Works

My Secret History has many ties with Theroux's travel stories, as well as the novel, *The Mosquito Coast*. Like the travel books, *My Secret History* incorporates Theroux's experiences in other countries and his belief that human nature is essentially the same worldwide. As he did in *The Mosquito Coast,* Theroux lambastes missionaries and all forms of narrow-mindedness, from egoistic foreign attempts to transform native cultures to the censorship of books.

Additional Sources

Review of *My Secret History*. *Library Journal* 114 (April 1, 1989): 115. Generally negative review which faults the novel's thematic development as well as its preoccupation with sex.

Review of *My Secret History*. *New Republic Society* 201 (July 17-24, 1989): 40. Insightful review with a special emphasis on the literary achievement of the work. Links the novel with Philip Roth's *The Anatomy Lesson* and *The Counterlife*, as well as with Don DeLillo's *White Noise*, as a novel that depicts "the dilemma of post-modernism with the juice of the nineteenth-century novel."

Review of *My Secret History*. *New Statesman* 2 (June 30, 1989): 33. This positive review notes that "Theroux's skill at incorporating foreign locations into his narratives leaves a number of other modern novelists looking amateurish." Its one negative comment concerns the possibility for reader alienation because of the high level of sex in the novel.

Review of *My Secret History*. *Time* 133 (May 22, 1989): 112. Declares the novel to be "the most consistently entertaining of the author's more than two dozen books" and notes the intense inner conflict of the protagonist, Andre Parent, as the great strength of the novel.

Nancy Wilson
Southwest Texas State University

SCOTT TUROW
1949

Publishing History

Scott Turow's literary career has taken some surprising twists and turns. Born April 12, 1949, to Dr. David D. Turow, a gynecologist, and his wife, Rita, in Chicago, Illinois, Turow started out to be a writer, studying under author Tillie Olsen while an undergraduate at Amherst College. During that period, two of his short stories were accepted for publication in the prestigious *Transatlantic Review*. In the fall of 1970, he entered the graduate writing program at Stanford University; he became an E. H. Jones Lecturer in Creative Writing from 1972 to 1975 and received his master's degree in 1974. He continued to publish stories and reviews in *Ploughshares, New England, Place*, and various newspapers. However, his first novel, *The Way Things Are*, was rejected by twenty-five publishers.

While researching that novel, which involved a rent strike, Turow became interested in the law and, frustrated with his writing career, entered Harvard Law School in 1975. At that time, he convinced Putnam's that a journal of first year experiences in law school would make an interesting book and, in 1977, while still a third-year student at Harvard, published *One L*.

After receiving his law degree, Turow went to work in the U. S. attorney's office in Chicago, helping to prosecute an undercover investigation of corruption in the Illinois courts. During his daily commute into Chicago, he began to work on the novel which was to become *Presumed Innocent* (1987). Interest in the novel was high; Turow finally decided to sign with Farrar, Straus, & Giroux who offered their largest advance ever for a first novel. Warner Books acquired the paperback rights for a record-breaking $3 million.

Despite the overwhelming success of *Presumed Innocent*, Turow still continues to practice law although he is now in private practice in Chicago. His second novel, *The Burden of Proof*, also published by Farrar, Straus, & Giroux, appeared in 1990. Once again, Warner Books acquired the paperback rights for a new record of $3.2 million. Forthcoming from Turow is a novel set in California and the Midwest.

Critical Reception, Honors, Popularity

With the exception of his unpublished first novel, Turow's literary efforts have been extremely well received. He won awards for his fiction in 1970 garnering honors from the Book-of-the-Month Club and the College English Association. One of his early stories, "A Classic Case," was named to the Roll of Honor of Best American Short Stories of 1971.

One L, published in 1977, became an immediate classic for first year law students. Over 300,000 copies have been sold in the United States as well as 25,000 in Japan.

His first published novel, *Presumed Innocent*, was a blockbuster; it sold 712,000 hard-cover copies and 4.3 million paperback copies in the U.S. alone. (There were also eighteen foreign language editions.) The novel was on the best-seller list for forty-four weeks, was a dual main selection of the Literary Guild, and the movie rights were sold for $1 million. Furthermore, the book was a critical success. Anne Rice, writing in the *New York Times Book Review*, declared, "From page one, the book consciously transcends the murder-mystery genre, combining whodunit suspense with an elegant style and philosophical voice."

Turow's latest effort, *The Burden of Proof*, published in 1990, also generated record numbers. It had a hard-cover first printing of 800,000 and went to the top of the best-seller list. However, critical reception for this second novel was less rapturous. A number of reviewers found the story, while not lacking in plot twists and turns, less compelling than *Presumed Innocent*.

Analysis of Selected Titles

ONE L

One L, 1977, autobiography.

Social Concerns

One L, Turow's account of his first year at Harvard Law School, reveals his fundamental concern with the training given to aspiring lawyers. As 550 of the best and brightest arrive at Harvard Law School to become one L's (the designation given to first year law students), they are systematically demoralized and defeated by the demanding workload and the rigors of the Socratic method. The students also worry that their indoctrination into the law has begun to alter their fundamental values. Gina Spitz, a one L, complains, "They're turning me into someone else. They're making me different."

Turow also questions whether law school training actually prepares students to face the difficult issues they will confront as lawyers. He observes, "Too much of what goes on around the law school and in the legal classroom seeks to tutor students in strategies for avoiding, for ignoring, for somehow subverting the unquantifiable, the inexact, the emotionally charged, those things which still pass in my mind under the label 'human.'"

Finally, Turow discusses a number of important issues about the profession—the reasons for increasing law school enrollment, the role of women and minorities in the profession, and the job prospects beyond law school.

Themes

In all his books, Turow is "fascinated by the extent to which the law define[s] our everyday lives." In this book, he shows the methods by which lawyers are trained to argue and to view the truth, a concern also at the heart of his two subsequent novels, *Presumed Innocent* and *The Burden of Proof*. Turow is intrigued with the law's central paradox: while it endeavors to standardize its judgments and eradicate ambiguity, the law also realizes that ambiguity forms the basis of most court cases. In its "war with ambiguity, with uncertainty," the law must presume that the truth may be discerned and that adequate judgments may be rendered.

More than the problems inherent in the law itself, Turow is concerned with how the single-minded pursuit of the law affects those who study it so assiduously. Over the course of the year, he becomes dramatically aware of how the tensions in law school exacerbate everyone's weaknesses.

Characters

One L traces the important relationships in law school between professors and students and the students and their peers and families. At the center of the work is Turow himself. Early on, he declares, "this book is not a novel. Everything I describe in the following pages happened to me." Turow carefully charts the changes he undergoes in his first year of law school; he proceeds from initial euphoria and love of the law to eventual burn-out and disillusionment to a gradual adoption of a more balanced approach to his studies. Along the way, he is alarmed by the changes he sees in himself and in the people around him. The extreme pressure to succeed brings out the worst in himself and in others; it also forces him to spend most of his waking hours consumed with the law and ignoring his understanding wife, Annette.

As he documents the changes in himself, Turow also sees the alterations in his group of friends, primarily those in his study group. Although he calls the book autobiographical, the other characters "are not the same as the friends and professors with whom I spent the year." Turow says that he "combined and altered personalities in order to represent more adequately the general character of my experience." The friends he made at law school illustrate the diversity of the students present. Among his closer friends are Terry Nazzario, a street-wise young man from Elizabeth, New Jersey, who becomes increasingly alienated from the classroom and spends most of his time studying law on his own in the library; Aubrey Drake, an older student who had already graduated from Harvard's business school and had an unsuccessful business career; and Stephen Litowitz, a doctor in sociology who came to law school to better his chances in finding a job in academe, but who becomes increasingly competitive and obsessed with making the Law Review, an honor reserved for only the top students.

Several professors also play important roles in the book. The most dominating figure is Rudolph Perrini who teaches the Contracts course. Both widely admired and feared, Perrini is an astute practitioner of the Socratic method in the classroom, making his students live in fear that they will be put on the spot and ridiculed. The teacher of the Torts class, William Zechman, also causes frustration in the classroom but for different reasons. At first, Zechman's propensity for showing the ambiguities in legal cases irritates his class, but when the validity of his approach becomes apparent, his popularity and esteem increases. Another popular instructor is Nicky Morris, a younger professor with a less rigid classroom style and a more philosophical approach to the law. Turow comes to value the instruction of Zechman and Morris whose concern for the law and its dilemmas appears genuine; he is less impressed by Perrini who seems more interested in manipulating students than in educating them.

Techniques

As a journal of Turow's first year in law school, *One L* follows a straightforward chronology that allows him to document his changing moods and perceptions. Yet Turow does more than provide a personal narrative, he also presents liberal doses of the material he was learning in his classes. His explanations of some of the moral dilemmas and technical points of law are similar to those he presents in *Presumed Innocent* and *The Burden of Proof*.

This book also reveals Turow's penchant for telling his story through the eyes of a single character who, despite his personal and professional difficulties, remains the reader's only source of information in the story.

Literary Precedents

One L, in many of its scenes, is highly reminiscent of the 1973 movie, *The Paper Chase*, (based on John Jay Osborn, Jr.'s 1971 novel) also set at Harvard Law

School. Both reveal the perpetual drive to receive good grades and both feature a demanding, autocratic professor, in *The Paper Chase*, Charles Kingsfield, and in *One L*, Rudolph Perrini. Yet, in the larger sense, *One L* is a classic initiation story, a *bildungsroman*, in which the young man is educated into a new way of life. Turow writes, "In baseball it's the rookie year. In the navy it is boot camp. In many walks of life there is a similar time of trial and initiation, a period when newcomers are forced to be victims of their own ineptness and when they must somehow master the basic skills of the profession in order to survive." Like Charles Dickens' *David Copperfield*, Turow has to adapt to a new world that forces him to learn a lot about himself, personally and professionally.

Related Titles

As in *Presumed Innocent* and *The Burden of Proof*, Turow focuses on the law and its ambiguities. He also begins illustrating the toll that the law can take on those who adopt it as a profession. The long demanding hours of law school eventually translate to the equal demands of the workplace that bring such trouble to his later protagonists, Rusty Sabich and Sandy Stern.

Interestingly enough, a Sandy Stern does appear in this book. However, this engineering student from MIT who eventually makes the Law Review is not the Argentinean-born Stern who plays a major role in both *Presumed Innocent* and *The Burden of Proof*.

PRESUMED INNOCENT

Presumed Innocent, 1987, novel.

Social Concerns

Presumed Innocent, Turow's first published novel, picks up on some of the same concerns as the autobiographical *One L*. Rather than focusing on law school, however, *Presumed Innocent* looks at the legal profession in practice. Turow seems particularly interested in the role that lawyers play in society. The protagonist, Rusty Sabich, a prosecuting attorney, declares, "I am a functionary of our only universally recognized system of telling wrong from right, a bureaucrat of good and evil." Yet, as the novel unfolds, Turow demonstrates how hard it may be to tell the two apart. Sabich's trial for the murder of his colleague and ex-lover Carolyn Polhemus reveals that his guilt or innocence is never really the question, but whether the evidence is sufficient to convict him. Sabich himself comments that

"Hedged by the formalities of the rules of evidence, our truthfinding system cuts off the corners on half of what is commonly known." Furthermore, the investigation into the murder reveals corruption riddling a system that is supposed to discover the truth and determine right from wrong. Sabich's ultimate question is "If we cannot find the truth, what is our hope of justice?"

Themes

Presumed Innocent revolves around questions of interpretation. Sabich is tried for the murder of Carolyn Polhemus because his motives seem the easiest to interpret: he was obsessed with his beautiful colleague who eventually dumped him for his boss, Raymond Horgan; because of his jealousy, he killed Carolyn and, with the specialized knowledge acquired from his job, made the scene of the crime look like a break-in, rape, and murder.

However, as both Sabich and the reader discover, the task of interpretation is not so easy. Throughout the novel, nearly every character is revealed to have a hidden agenda; their motives and actions become increasingly difficult to assess. Sabich has to change his estimations of everyone involved, including himself. No one is as they first appear. The readers must also grapple with the constantly shifting evidence. This struggle to find a convincing interpretation of events points to the difficulties inherent in the legal system. Ultimate truths and motives may never be determined, only acceptable interpretations.

Characters

Presumed Innocent has a large and rich cast of characters who all play critical roles in the development of the plot. At the center of the story is Rožat "Rusty" Sabich, thirty-nine, the son of a Yugoslavian immigrant who fled the Nazis. Sabich believes he has escaped the cruel and brutal world of wartime Europe to become a regular citizen of an unnamed midwestern city. Now the chief deputy in the prosecuting attorney's office, he is married to Barbara, a doctoral candidate in mathematics, and they have a nine-year-old son, Nat. Yet, as he gradually comes to realize, the dark forces that were part of his heritage, though tightly repressed, remain part of him.

Sabich was originally attracted to his wife, Barbara, because of her apparent normalcy. However, even though their marriage had been largely successful, Sabich gradually learns that she is a woman of "private and largely uncommunicated passions" whose fierce devotion to their son, Nat, and to himself, makes her a mystery to him. The depth of her emotions is dramatically revealed at the end.

Sabich also discovers that his boss, Raymond Horgan, has a number of surprises in his character as well. A consummate politician, he commanded Sabich's respect and loyalty for the past twelve years, even to the detriment of his own political ambitions. Horgan proves to have a number of potentially damaging secrets including a compromising affair with Carolyn and a mysterious file that reveals corruption within his administration.

Even the judge presiding over Sabich's trial, Larren Lyttle, is shown to be intimately connected with the case. Now a distinguished jurist, in the past Lyttle was involved both in taking bribes and with Carolyn Polhemus. These devastating secrets are in danger of being revealed during the trial.

The clever defense lawyer who subtly hints that he may reveal these secrets is Alejandro "Sandy" Stern, an Argentinean Jew, whose carefully theatrical performance in the courtroom ends up getting Sabich's case dismissed because of insufficient evidence. Stern remains an essentially mysterious character who knows more than he says and plays the legal game with skill regardless of the guilt or innocence of his client.

The only character who is as he appears is Dan "Lip" Lipranzer, a policeman who steadfastly helps Sabich untangle the threads of the convoluted mystery and remains loyal to his friend despite the evidence against him. Yet even Lip has his surprises; Sabich eventually learns that his friend concealed a crucial piece of evidence whose disappearance helped scuttle the prosecution's case against him. Although Sabich considers Lip his best friend, he also remains puzzled by this character whom he calls a "scholar of the underlife." Sabich is half-frightened by Lip and the world in which he travels, but his friendship with the policeman reveals his affinity for the darker side of life that he tries to deny.

Sabich's attraction to people with dark and threatening aspects is also exemplified in his relationship with Carolyn Polhemus. Her blind ambition leads her to use a series of men—Larren, Sabich, and Raymond—to achieve her aims, making her a rather unattractive character. Yet, as Sabich comes to realize, there was a painful life behind Carolyn's hard-bitten drive to success: her abused childhood, her never-talked about first marriage, her teenage son, and the corruption she was involved in. He also admires her efforts, futile though they may be, to deny or overcome those obstacles. Through Carolyn, Sabich begins to come to terms with his own past and his own pain.

Techniques

Turow presents his novel in a typical murder mystery format. Beginning slowly at Carolyn Polhemus's funeral, the story's pace quickens as it reveals the complicated relationships among its characters and then races to its surprising and disturbing conclusion.

Turow's choice of Sabich to narrate this story in the first person produces a number of interesting results. Sabich brings a lawyer's knowledge to his narration and is able to provide intriguing insight into the machinations of the legal process. Further, Sabich's narration involves the readers in the mystery and leads them to share in his confusion as more aspects of his case are revealed. However, Sabich also presents a disturbing challenge to the reader. Because of his emotionalism and extreme obsession with Carolyn, Sabich often makes the reader wonder if indeed he is a reliable narrator. Even at the end of the novel when the true murderer is revealed, a lingering doubt remains.

Literary Precedents

In many respects, *Presumed Innocent* falls squarely within the ranks of many murder mysteries. Turow is frequently compared to a number of writers in this genre, particularly Agatha Christie whose *Murder of Roger Ackroyd* (1926) set the standard for unreliable narrators in murder mysteries. It has also been compared to other trial books such as Robert Traver's *Anatomy of A Murder* (1958).

Turow, however, seeks to move beyond the constraints of the genre, and to look at the fate of a man trapped firmly in the coils of a system that may fail to deliver justice. The labyrinthine legal system in *Presumed Innocent* is reminiscent of the complexities of the case presented in *Jarndyce v. Jarndyce* in Charles Dickens' *Bleak House* (1852). Caught in a situation that he cannot control, Sabich even describes his situation as Kafkaesque. In particular, he shares affinities with Joseph K., the protagonist of Kafka's *The Trial* (1925) who finds himself accused of a mysterious crime. He also has much in common with Sherman McCoy, the protagonist of Tom Wolfe's *The Bonfire of the Vanities* (1987) who also discovers how the legal system can disrupt a man's life. Finally, as in Dostoyevsky's *The Brothers Karamazov* (1879-80), the troubled relationships in a family are explored in the context of a murder.

Related Titles

As in his other works, *One L* and *The Burden of Proof*, Turow explores the powers and limitations of the legal system. In all of these books, Turow probes to what extent we are capable of assessing the truth. To show how difficult a task this is, Turow always chooses to present his story from a single viewpoint, realizing the limitations inherent in that choice.

Turow's writing shows an increasing concern with the role of families. In *One L*, he chronicled some of the strains that law school put on his own marriage. In *Presumed Innocent*, he explores Sabich's complicated relationships with his father and his wife; and in *The Burden of Proof*, he turns once again to the character of Sandy Stern and the complex dynamic of his family. In each case, the protagonist must struggle to balance his obligations to his family and his profession.

Adaptations
Presumed Innocent was brought to the screen in 1990 in a film directed by Alan J. Pakula and with the screenplay by Pakula and Frank Pierson. The movie starred Harrison Ford as Sabich, Bonnie Bedelia as his wife, Brian Dennehy as Raymond Horgan, Paul Winfield as Judge Lyttle, Raul Julia as Sandy Stern, John Spencer as Lip Lipranzer, and Greta Scacchi as Carolyn Polhemus. Although many found the film's pace rather ponderous, critics generally praised *Presumed Innocent* for its adult concerns.

THE BURDEN OF PROOF
The Burden of Proof, 1990, novel.

Social Concerns
While *The Burden of Proof* maintains the interest in law demonstrated in Turow's two earlier works, the novel's main emphasis is on the troubled relationships within the Stern family and the quest of Sandy Stern for self-definition following the mysterious suicide of his wife Clara after thirty-one years of marriage. During the course of the novel, Stern must come to grips with the "imponderable duties darkly rooted in the hard soil of [his] own sense of filial and professional obligation." Stern must also learn to venture out of the neatly ordered world he has created for himself to explore the reason for his wife's suicide; he must rethink the assumptions of his own life.

The novel also explores, as *Presumed Innocent* did to a lesser extent, the assimilation of political refugees into the American landscape. Like Rožat Sabich who Americanizes his name to Rusty, Alejandro "Sandy" Stern comes to realize the legacy of his past; his feelings of being an outsider led to his career as a defense attorney and colored his dealings with his family and associates.

Themes

Like *Presumed Innocent*, *The Burden of Proof* is a mystery with the death of an enigmatic woman at its center. Each book forces the protagonist on a journey of outward and inward exploration to probe his life and his relationship with the dead woman. Each character is so intent on creating a semblance of "normal" life that he refuses to acknowledge the darker influences in his life until he is compelled to confront them. With Clara's suicide, Sandy must examine his own failings in his relationships with his wife and children. At the same time, he comes to realize that the interpretations he has made of other people or events are flawed.

Characters

The central characters of *The Burden of Proof* are nearly all members of the Stern family. At the center of the novel is Alejandro "Sandy" Stern, Sabich's defense lawyer from *Presumed Innocent*. As this novel indicates, Sabich's trial increased Stern's practice, and he seems the model of the successful professional. However, when he comes home to discover his wife dead in the garage with only the note, "Can you forgive me?", the fifty-six-year-old Stern is forced to face the deficiencies and failures in his life.

He comes to realize that he had avoided looking at the darker aspects of his wife, including the fact that she had always been an unhappy, secretive woman. As flashbacks in the book reveal, he found Clara's past a mystery; he never really understood how he, a poor immigrant, had been able to marry Clara Mittler, the daughter of a prominent and wealthy attorney. Clara's death forces him to reexamine and analyze their relationship as he had never before done.

Stern also confronts the mysteries embedded in his three children—Peter, a doctor, whose troubled relationship with his father continues to deteriorate after his mother's death; Marta, a legal-aid lawyer in New York who comes to her father's assistance when he becomes involved in legal proceedings; and Kate, his youngest daughter, whose beauty seems to have shielded her from many of life's harsh realities. Each of these children hides secrets whose revelation forces Stern to reevaluate his original views of them.

Also important in the story is Dixon Hartnell, husband of Stern's beloved sister, Silvia. Dixon, head of a commodities futures trading empire and owner of Maison Dixon, a brokerage house, is Stern's chief client and often the bane of his existence. Stern half admires this powerful, womanizing, and self-confident businessman as the prototypical American and half despises the pain that this self-involved man is capable of inflicting on those around him.

Dixon's shady dealings bring Stern into contact with Sonia Klonsky, an assistant U.S. attorney. Klonsky, after spending a decade in various graduate programs, had now embarked on a demanding law career while in her early forties. Stern finds this woman, in the midst of her first pregnancy after a bout with breast cancer and in a shaky marriage, a compelling figure; she seems to offer the enticing prospect of starting over again. He gradually overcomes his infatuation with her and eventually marries Helen Dudak, an old family friend now divorced from her husband. Like Stern, Helen has learned to adapt to the single life after the security of a long-term relationship. They both have learned by their failures and are ready for the demands of a new marriage.

Techniques

Turow's plotting technique in *Burden of Proof* is basically the same as in *Presumed Innocent*. Although the novel seems to be written in retrospect (Stern's eventual marriage to Helen Dudak is revealed in the book's first sentence), most of the action takes place in the present tense. While the book is written from the third, not the first, person point of view, the story is told exclusively from Stern's perspective. Thus the reader, once again, must work side-by-side with the protagonist to decipher the book's mysteries. As in *Presumed Innocent*, Turow uses extensive flashback sequences to show the protagonist's relationship with the dead woman.

One intriguing symbol Turow employs in the novel is Stern's glass desk. This desk, chosen by an interior decorator hired by Clara, had never been a favorite with him. Even after many years, he "was still not accustomed to looking down and seeing the soft expanse of his lap." This desk, so reminiscent of Clara and so emblematic of Stern's aversion to clear-sightedness, is shattered during the final scene between Dixon and him when many of the novel's secrets are revealed. From that meeting, Stern emerges feeling like a different person.

Literary Precedents

At one point, late in the novel, Stern sees that "The walls were closing in on Dixon, as on some Poe character." In its revelation of the dark secrets embedded in families, *The Burden of Proof* may be an echo of a work like "The Fall of the House of Usher" (1839). The tortured family conflicts in the novel have their literary roots as far back as Sophocles' Oedipus plays. The image of the family disintegrating around the figure of the mother is also seen in Eugene O'Neill's autobiographical play *Long Day's Journey into Night* (1956). The quest for a more mature understanding of life also forms the basis of novels by two of Turow's favorite authors—Leo Tolstoy's *War and Peace* (1864-69) and Saul Bellow's *Herzog* (1964).

Related Titles

The Burden of Proof is intimately connected to *Presumed Innocent*. Not only are Stern and his wife Clara characters in the earlier novel, but the reader also learns in the second novel that Sabich is now a judge. Yet these books are linked by more than the characters. Their structures and concerns are also similar. Both novels feature protagonists who must cope with their parents' pasts as political refugees. Both of these men are married to complex and mysterious women whose tightly reined-in emotions yield explosive results when released. Both become infatuated with troubled women who offer something they feel is lacking in their lives. Finally, both must interpret the mystery behind the death of a woman that forces them to explore regions of themselves previously ignored.

Other Titles

"The Carp Fish," 1970 (short story); "A Classic Case," 1971 (short story); "The Tenure Trap," 1987 (book review); "Law School Vs. Reality," 1988 (essay).

Additional Sources

Eden, Kathy. *Poetic and Legal Fiction in the Aristotelian Tradition*. Princeton, NJ: Princeton University Press, 1986. An interesting exploration of the Aristotelian correspondence between legal and poetic procedure.

Ferguson, Robert A. *Law and Letters in American Culture*. Cambridge: Harvard University Press, 1984. Gives a historical overview of a number of American literary figures who have also been lawyers and discusses the influence of the law on their writings.

Goldstein, Paul. "Scott Turow." *Publishers Weekly* (July 10, 1987): 52-53. Interview with Turow at the publication of *Presumed Innocent*.

Gray, Paul. "Burden of Success." *Time* (June 11, 1990): 69-72. Cover story on Turow that provides a good background on his career at the publication of *The Burden of Proof*.

Meier, Robert H. "Getting Away with Murder." *Armchair Detective* 21, 2 (Spring 1988): 150-152. Argument from a lawyer offers a reappraisal on who really killed Carolyn Polhemus.

Shear, Jeff. "A Lawyer Courts Best-Sellerdom." *New York Times Magazine* (June 7, 1987): 54+. A useful combination of personal history and interview published just before the publication of *Presumed Innocent*.

Smith, Carl S., ed. *Law and American Literature: A Collection of Essays*. New York: Knopf, 1983. Provides several good essays on the law in American literature and a useful bibliography.

Weisburg, Richard H. *The Failure of the Word: The Protagonist as Lawyer in Modern Fiction*. New Haven: Yale University Press, 1984. Discussion of Dostoyevsky's legal novels, the French legal novels, especially those of Camus, and Melville's *Billy Budd*.

Yeazell, Stephen C. "Corruption, Fiction, and Law." *New Literary History* 13, 11 (Autumn 1981): 89-102. An intriguing exploration of some of the problems of interpretation confronted by both the law and by literature.

Sharon L. Gravett
Valdosta State College

ANNE TYLER
1941

Update

The Accidental Tourist, published in 1985, was made into a movie in 1989. Geena Davis won an Academy Award for best supporting actress for her portrayal of Muriel, and the movie won the New York Film Critics Best Picture of the Year Award. Since *The Accidental Tourist*, Anne Tyler has published *Breathing Lessons*. Critically acclaimed, this best-selling novel won a second Pulitzer Prize for Tyler and was a Book-of-the Month Club main selection.

Analysis of Selected Titles

BREATHING LESSONS
Breathing Lessons, 1988, novel.

Social Concerns/Themes

Breathing Lessons relates one day in the life of Ira and Maggie Moran—the day they travel to Deer Lick, Pennsylvania, to attend the funeral of Maggie's best friend's husband and detour to visit their estranged daughter-in-law and their granddaughter, Leroy. But in essence the novel covers their whole life together as each remembers the years they have known each other. Once again, Tyler makes family a major theme, this time focusing on marriage. In earlier novels she exposed the idea of the perfect family as a myth; here she reveals that the perfect marriage is also an illusion. In an era of increasing divorce rates, serial marriages or relationships, and disillusionment with the institution of marriage, such a focus reflects a sensitivity to current social realities.

In *Breathing Lessons*, Tyler gives readers a picture of a good marriage versus a perfect marriage. Maggie and Ira Moran have been married for twenty-eight years. The marriage has lasted because they have somehow both tolerated and loved each other. Though they have disagreed about their children, bickered, and at times gotten on each other's nerves, they have also lifted each other up and learned to accommodate their respective eccentricities and weaknesses. Theirs is a study in acceptance and willingness to bend. They have a rock-solid core of affection that allows them to get past the times when their differences put them at odds. At one point, angry at Ira, Maggie gets out of the car and walks down the road as he drives off. Shortly afterward, he comes up behind her at a convenience store, and they simply pick up a conversation and come together again. In contrast is the dissolved marriage of their son, Jesse, and his wife, Fiona, a marriage Maggie wants desperately to repair. These two have never learned to bend. Maggie is probably right when she notes that they care for each other, but each is so concerned about losing face and being vulnerable that they can never connect.

A secondary theme, certainly from Maggie's perspective, is the empty nest syndrome. Her son has his own apartment and is involved with his band; her daughter-in-law moved out years ago with Maggie's only grandchild, Leroy; and her daughter is ready to go to college. Maggie's efforts to bring Fiona and Leroy back "home" are more than a romantic desire to reunite the spatting lovers; she wants to fill her own life. Maggie is by nature a nurturer and eager to be an integral part of people's lives. Now there is no one to watch grow, and she wants her granddaughter to fill the void.

Characters

Maggie is a romantic who wants to rearrange reality to suit her notions of how things should be. She reasons that since Jesse and Fiona once loved each other, they should be reunited as a loving family. Because Maggie so desperately wants this, she exaggerates and manipulates. For instance, she leads Fiona to think that Jesse is pining for her and has saved her tortoiseshell soapbox for years as a memento of her. In fact, Jesse has forgotten all about it and has a new girlfriend. Maggie's intentions are good, but she ends up interfering.

Ira represents the steadying influence of the realist. Whereas Maggie wants to rearrange relationships, Ira accepts things as they are. His granddaughter moved out years ago; and he accepts that he no longer has anything to do with her, even though it is clear, when Maggie forces him to visit, that he is missing a relationship that he would enjoy. Thus, what at first may seem a strength of character can be a detriment. Without Maggie to encourage or sometimes even nag him, he would spend his whole life working in the frame shop or playing solitaire.

Techniques/Literary Precedents

Limiting the action of a novel to one day in the life of ordinary people was an experiment for James Joyce in *Ulysses,* and it is a new technique for Tyler. Like Joyce, she uses flashbacks to circumvent the temporal constraint, and she takes the reader on detours and side trips to reveal character and add action. The tension between the Morans' seemingly ordinary day trip and the odd twists and turns on the journey is the perfect illustration of the novel's central idea. Each day of life or marriage is both the same old routine and a unique experience; people can live life without thinking about it—like breathing—or be open to each day's vagaries, accepting them when necessary and enjoying them when possible. Like Molly at the end of *Ulysses*, Maggie affirms at the end of *Breathing Lessons* her willingness to live and love, despite the disappointments of the day, and of the years past. Kissing Ira's cheekbone and settling in for a good night's sleep, she prepares for the next day's journey with Ira.

Relation to Previous Works

Once again Tyler creates characters that are at once quirky and ordinary, and she continues to employ humor skillfully. In *Breathing Lessons*, she has maintained the light humorous touch that was the hallmark of *The Accidental Tourist*. Examples are the opening accident with the newly repaired car and Maggie's madcap ride in a laundry cart during a fire drill at the nursing home. But she also uses the darker humor typical of novels like *Dinner at the Homesick Restaurant* and *Celestial Navigation*. The trip to the horse races, where Ira's sister lines up marshmallows while Jesse and Fiona fight the battle that ends their shaky marriage, and the macabre funeral for Max, where his widow Serena dresses in red and the funeral guests sing the songs of the fifties that they sang at Max and Serena's wedding are both funny and sad.

As in *Dinner at the Homesick Restaurant*, Tyler employs the technique of reviewing the same events through different characters' eyes. Telling and retelling events from first Maggie's and then Ira's perspective allows Tyler to develop the two characters' different outlooks and to show how they play off each other in the marriage. For instance, Maggie remembers the time of having babies and young children as an expansion of her world; for Ira the children were an intrusion.

While each character is an individual, some characters resemble those in earlier novels. Maggie, like Ezra in *Dinner at the Homesick Restaurant*, is foiled in her attempts to reunite the family. She is, however, feistier and less easily trampled than Ezra. Like Muriel in *The Accidental Tourist*, she has a knack for being at ease with anyone in a matter of minutes, but Muriel has a streak of steely realism and practicality that Maggie lacks. Ira, like Macon Leary in *The Accidental Tourist*, revels in order and control but has an underlying sensitivity that takes someone like a Maggie (or a Muriel) to bring out.

Additional Sources

Elkins, Mary J. "*Dinner at the Homesick Restaurant*: Anne Tyler and the Faulkner Connection." *Atlantis* 10, 2 (Spring 1985): 93-105. Compares *Dinner at the Homesick Restaurant* and William Faulkner's *As I Lay Dying*, finding similar concerns with "family dynamics and destinies" and the "mysterious bonds" that unite families. Tyler differs notably in being ultimately less pessimistic.

Gullette, Margaret Morganroth. "The Tears (and Joys) Are in the Things: Adulthood in Anne Tyler's Novels." *New England Review and Breadloaf Quarterly* 7, 3 (Spring 1985): 93-105. Discusses the tension "between family obligation and personal expansion" that is central to Tyler's characters.

Jones, Anne G. "Home at Last and Homesick Again: The Ten Novels of Anne Tyler." *The Hollins Critic* 23, 2 (April 1986): 1-14. Discusses Tyler's use of home and family as metaphors of "personal psychic growth" and as a means of exploring people in close relationships.

Robertson, Mary F. "Anne Tyler: Medusa Points and Contact Points." In *Contemporary American Women Writers: Narrative Strategies*, edited by Catherine Rainwater and William Scheick. Lexington: University Press of Kentucky, 1985. Discusses Tyler's narrative strategies, in particular her disruption of readers' expectations of a conventional family novel, and her depiction of family as a reflection of order and disorder both in society and the individual.

Rebecca Kelly
Southern College of Technology

JOHN UPDIKE
1932

Update

Updike has maintained his reputation as one of America's most prolific and successful writers. His recent publications include a collection of short stories, *Trust Me* (1987), a novel, *S.* (1988), a volume of selected memoirs, *Self-Consciousness* (1989), and another novel in the series about Harry Angstrom, *Rabbit at Rest* (1990), which received the National Book Critics Circle Award for fiction in 1991. The critics' citation said that the book "brings to a close a work which will stand as one of the major achievements of American fiction in the 20th century." Updike's reviews and critical essays continue to appear in *The New Yorker*. Four decades of public acceptance have neither compromised his talent for social comedy nor lessened his desire to explore new forms of romance and satire. While one recent novel takes the form of letters and tapes from a contemporary Hester Prynne who commits adultery with a spurious religious leader, another is focused upon the thoughts of an aging basketball player in the twilight zone of Reagan and Bush.

Analysis of Updike's fiction and poetry continues to be a growth industry for scholars and critics. Not only does his work occupy a regular section in the annual volume *American Literary Scholarship,* but a growing number of critics in France, Italy, Germany, Japan, and the Soviet Union are contributing analysis and commentary. Although the chorus of praise remains mixed with a few negative voices, Updike's reputation at home and abroad appears more than ever to be firmly established.

Analysis of Selected Titles

S.

S., 1988, novel.

Social Concerns/Themes

S. is a novel about a woman's search for sensual and spiritual fulfillment. In typical Updike fashion her attempt to find Nirvana involves a series of comic turns and remains inconclusive. The heroine leaves her husband and respectable life in Massachusetts in order to join a religious commune in Arizona headed by a man who pretends to be a holy master from India. Life at the commune turns out to be a charade of spiritual enlightenment, a comic rite of sexual initiation, and a wild mixture of jealousy, fraud, embezzlement, and self-deception. The leader of the commune is an imposter who actually comes from a poor suburb of the heroine's native Boston. She is more disappointed by the revelation of his class status than by the exposure of his pseudoreligious credentials. The comedy of adultery is complete when the narrator learns that her husband is about to marry her best friend and confidante.

Updike's contemporary romance is a mixture of social and religious satire. He explores the delusions of trying to escape from an empty marriage, the pratfalls of a religious commune, and the infinite capacity of the heart and soul to experience desire and betrayal. The road to Nirvana in *S.* is a sad and comic journey into a contemporary maze of self-deception.

Characters

The entire novel is told in the voice of Sarah Worth as represented by letters and tapes mailed to relatives and friends from a motel near the Arizona commune. Other voices only enter when Sarah reports conversations in her letters or happens to catch the guru's voice on her tape recorder. The main character is thus a narrator whose point of view dominates the novel, but her limited understanding is apparent, and the reader must look between the lines for the truth of what is happening.

Sarah Worth is modeled after Hester Prynne, the heroine of Nathaniel Hawthorne's *The Scarlet Letter* (1850). She has a daughter named Pearl, a husband who is a physician, and a mother descended from the Prynne family. As a modern character, however, she also has a dentist, lawyer, and hairdresser. What she needs, of course, is the fulfillment of heart and soul that also fascinated and eluded Hester Prynne. Adultery with a pious hypocrite, as Hester discovered, only compounds the feeling of loss and despair. Sarah also wanders "in the dark labyrinth of mind," and like Hawthorne's character finds "a home and comfort nowhere."

At the religious commune Sarah is given the name "Kundalini" which Updike defines as "coiled up" or "the serpent of female energy." Sarah has left her husband at the beginning of the novel in part to assert her independence and feminine power, but in Arizona she finds several women competing for the attention of their supposed religious master. She learns more about jealousy and seduction than any promised form of enlightenment, but she does have an affair with the guru before discovering that he really comes from Boston. After liberating herself from him at the end of the novel, Sarah is still unable to sort out the needs of flesh and spirit. At least she is not without material resources. Several pieces of inherited silverware are thought about with comic regularity, and she does manage to embezzle hundreds of thousands of dollars from the Treasury of Enlightenment.

The other important character in the novel is the cult leader, Updike's contemporary version of Arthur Dimmesdale. Sarah commits adultery with Art Steinmetz for two reasons: she thinks he radiates divine power, and on a deeper level she may feel that he is a replacement for the Jewish boy her parents would not allow her to marry in the first place. Art is a chameleon who presents himself as the Arhat, or "deserving one," who claims to have reached a high level of enlightenment. His particular deserts include women, limousines, and the power of religious language. Sarah and Hester, no doubt, are attracted to their men of God because sex and religion are twin expressions of their desire for satisfaction and fulfillment. Both find a mixture of faith and hypocrisy because the false saviors are designed by male authors to attract and disappoint their frustrated heroines.

Techniques/Literary Precedents

S. is a contemporary example of an eighteenth-century narrative tradition, a novel in the form of letters. Updike updates the epistolary form by introducing tape-recorded messages. He also limits and controls the narrative by having all of the letters come from a single character. In this way Sarah's mind is the stage for all that happens in the novel. Her feelings and thoughts, however compromised and mistaken, are the comedy and drama of Updike's narrative.

Another of Updike's techniques is the frequent repetition of the Hindu vocabulary in vogue at the religious commune. Not only is Sarah given a new name, she also learns a whole new language for dealing with her thoughts and feelings. One source of the guru's power, of course, is his apparent ownership of a foreign and exotic language. Updike clearly has fun by writing his novel in both English and Sanskrit. He even provides a glossary of words for the unenlightened.

The most important precedent for S.'s character is Hawthorne's *The Scarlet Letter*. Updike makes this quite clear by quoting two descriptions of Hester Prynne to serve as an epigraph for his novel. The many echoes of Hawthorne not only challenge the reader to make connections, but they also lend historical depth to Updike's contemporary story.

Relation to Previous Works

The subject of adultery is seldom missing from Updike's twelve earlier novels. The success of *Couples* in 1968 was the occasion for Updike's first appearance on the cover of *Time* magazine. Adultery and its consequences remain central in the series of novels from *Rabbit, Run* (1960) to *Rabbit at Rest* (1990), and the subject even receives a supernatural treatment in *The Witches of Eastwick* (1984). Updike has explored numerous points of view for adultery in his fiction, but lately, in *The Witches of Eastwick* and now more thoroughly in *S.*, he has presented the subject from a female perspective, or, some contend, a caricature of such a perspective.

Updike's fascination with Hawthorne's fiction is apparent in much of his recent work. Hawthorne was the topic of his 1979 lecture at the American Academy of Arts and Letters. That author was again on Updike's mind when he wrote about witchcraft and adultery in *The Witches of Eastwick*. His recent novels *Roger's Version* (1986) and *S.* are both modern derivatives of *The Scarlet Letter*. Indeed, the two can be read as different versions of Hawthorne's famous romantic triangle. Perhaps the only point of view that Updike has yet to explore is that belonging to Pearl, although her marriage to wealth and nobility in the Old World is foretold in *S.*

RABBIT AT REST

Rabbit at Rest, 1990, novel.

Social Concerns/Themes

Rabbit at Rest is the fourth and final novel in Updike's series on the adventures and fate of Harry Angstrom. By focusing on the life of an average American character, Updike has assembled a portrait of American culture and its disintegration that now spans more than three decades. The latest episode includes the issues of drug addiction, business corruption, the AIDS epidemic, the selling of America to foreign investors, and the fate of women in a declining job market. The novel is a detailed reflection of the news stories so prevalent in the year George Bush inherits a debt-ridden America.

Rabbit at Rest is also the portrait of a family, three generations of Angstroms, who show how difficult it is to live in a contemporary America filled with debt, drugs, and sterile retirement communities. The first scene of the novel, a family visit to the Florida condominium where Harry and Janice now hope to spend half the year, establishes Updike's concern with the tension and pathos of trying to be grandparents, parents, and especially children. The family is severely tested by Harry's worsening heart condition, his son's cocaine habit, and the frequent demands of the next generation. The revelation of Harry's adultery with his daughter-in-law, however, proves to be the catalyst that destroys the family unity. Only his final heart attack prompts a family reunion in his hospital room at the end of the novel. The theme of adultery and its consequences is familiar territory in Updike's fiction, but the familial nature of the two people's relationship is a new way for Updike to represent America's decadence.

The subject explored most frequently in the novel is human mortality. After his initial heart attack, thoughts of dying are often in the shadows of Harry's mind. The news on television is full of disaster, with another plane crash or a hurricane ready to attack the coast. The novel has its share of worried doctors, intensive care units, and technical descriptions of how the heart does or does not work. Amid his thoughts of death, Harry often wonders whether there is any point to his earthly existence. "Nothing matters very much," he thinks, "we'll all soon be dead." The morbid thoughts of the title character form a long chronicle of dying, but he cannot be "at rest" with himself or the world before his heart stops. At the end of the novel his damaged heart is beyond repair, but Updike leaves Harry Angstrom typically wondering how much he should say to his anxious son.

Characters/Relation to Previous Works

Updike introduced the character of Harry Angstrom as a young man in *Rabbit Run* in 1960. His nickname comes from his fame as a high school basketball player, and his inclination to run away from responsibility is clearly indicated in this first novel of the series. After his wife accidentally drowns their infant daughter, thoughts of death begin to invade and challenge his youthful sense of wellbeing. The fortunes of Harry Angstrom rise and fall in three more novels, but he remains a character who never regains the pleasure of success that he enjoyed as a young basketball player. Through more than a thousand pages of nostalgia and melancholy Rabbit fails to come to terms with the various stages of his life or to satisfy the repeated demands of his heart.

Harry learns more about drugs and death in the second novel of the series, *Rabbit Redux*, when his life in the late 1960s is challenged by a runaway girl and a black veteran. Angstrom is beset with one disaster after another while the television reports the futile news of war from Vietnam: his mother is dying, he loses his job, his wife has an affair, their house burns down, and the runaway girl dies in the flames. Despite a rather passive response to this sea of troubles, Rabbit remains a sympathetic character as he feels his way through the void left by his broken marriage and the failure of his dreams.

Harry and Janice are more or less reconciled in the third novel of the series, *Rabbit is Rich*, and some inherited money adds a few opportunities for pleasure in their middle age. Troubles with their son, however, continue to illustrate Updike's theme of family tension and frustration. The shadows of death also continue to loom as the senior generation passes away and Harry and Janice become grandparents themselves.

The final novel of the series, *Rabbit at Rest*, follows Harry through a year of heart trouble and family crisis. He cannot help but think of himself as "fifty-five and fading." Images of death appear from all directions: his golf partners in Florida discuss their heart operations, his mistress in Pennsylvania dies after a long painful disease, and Harry almost loses his own life early in the novel when he takes his granddaughter sailing off the Florida coast. To readers long familiar with Rabbit's self-indulgence and rather morbid soul-searching, it comes as no surprise that he is unable to cope with his own heart condition or with his son's addiction to cocaine. Still his long and futile quest for happiness remains a drama with considerable feeling, dark comedy, and pathos. The quest returns him in his mind to the lost glory of his youth, and thus it is appropriate for his final heart attack to occur when he attempts to play basketball with a nameless teenager.

Techniques/Literary Precedents

Updike's fiction is well-known for its realistic style that renders every nuance and texture of daily life. The use of this technique in *Rabbit at Rest* almost affords too much of a good thing, however. Details of contemporary America accumulate for more than five hundred pages. The reader may weary of hearing about every physical sensation, pain, desire, regret, and heart murmur that worry Harry Angstrom, but Updike pays such loving attention to detail. The resulting style forms the semblance of a life fully resonant with the experiences of decades. The more Rabbit suffers in his fifties, the more he relives the various stages of his life, and Updike's realistic style is appropriate for characterizing the complex layers of memory.

The tradition of literary realism offers several precedents for Updike, but he probably learned most about the use of interior monologue in fiction from the examples of James Joyce and Marcel Proust. By creating a series of novels to follow the thoughts and feelings of his title character, Updike demonstrates that the mind is truly an echo chamber of experience and memory.

The realistic style of *Rabbit at Rest* also includes intimate descriptions of many sights and sounds that form a sharp and comic satire of contemporary America. Whether he describes a retirement community in Florida or suburban life in Pennsylvania, Updike is unsparing in his perception of significant and often comic detail. His ability to create fictional characters against a backdrop of contemporary news events places him in the American tradition of literary realism which owes much to writers like John Steinbeck and John Dos Passos. When it comes, however, to reflecting the shadows of mortality in the mind of an average American character, John Updike is unsurpassed. By creating a series of novels about Harry Angstrom that now spans more than three decades, Updike has to some extent become his own literary precedent.

Additional Sources

Berryman, Charles. *Decade of Novels, Fiction of the 1970s: Form and Challenge*. Troy, NY: Whitston, 1990. Includes a chapter on Updike's fiction with special attention to *Rabbit Redux*.

Greiner, Donald J. "Updike on Hawthorne," *Nathaniel Hawthorne Review 13*, 1: 1-4. In this interview, Updike talks about *The Scarlet Letter* and the character of Chillingworth.

Mellard, James M. *Doing Tropology: Analysis of Narrative Discourse*. Urbana: University of Illinois Press, 1987. Includes an analysis of Updike's *The Centaur* in terms of Hayden White's theory of tropes.

Miyake, Takuo. *Reading American Literature: From Hawthorne to Pynchon*. Kyoto: Apollon-sha, 1987. Includes a study of the narrative style in Updike's Rabbit trilogy.

Charles Berryman
University of Southern California

LEON URIS
1924

Update

Commenting on his craft in a 1985 interview, Leon Uris said, "A writer must be driven, have determination, and willpower. He must have a sense of inspiration. He must be willing to face rejection and to overcome the fear of writer's block if he intends to succeed in this business. And he had better be ready to stand alone. He had also better be ready to work twenty years before he becomes an 'overnight sensation.' " Of his characters in *Exodus,* Uris commented in 1988 that "Those characters were chessmen placed to carry along a historical story." Of his more recent novel, *Mitla Pass,* Uris said, "it's the story of one man fighting his demons. . . . It deals more with inner themes than anything I've ever written. It's the first book of mine, I would say, in which the character is more important than the history." When asked about Israel, Uris replied, "I think they are handling the situation correctly over there at the present time" (1988). "Unfortunately," he remarked, "for most of our history, Jews have had to use words because we had no armies. Now we've got an army and everybody's on our case."

The immense popularity of *Exodus* continues, with sales by the late 1980s topping seven million copies in paperback. At that time the hardcover edition had never been out of print.

Uris was awarded an honorary doctorate degree by Lincoln College (Springfield, Illinois) in 1985 and was honored by the B'nai B'rith in 1988.

Analysis of Selected Titles

MITLA PASS

Mitla Pass, 1988, novel.

Social Concerns/Themes

The title of *Mitla Pass* refers to the location of a 1956 military objective in the Middle East, and Uris' inclusion of maps indicates the increasing symbolic importance of Mitla Pass in the novel. (The maps locate the pass in the northwest of the Sinai Peninsula; the maps themselves respectively bear the headings "The Sinai Campaign, October 1956" and "The Sinai Campaign, October 29—November 5, 1956.") In strategic terms, as the novel opens, while Anglo-French forces are to be deployed to regain the use of the Suez Canal, the Israelis are preparing to launch Operation Kadesh, "to free the blockaded passage to the Red Sea." Historically, by international agreement, the Suez Canal had been open to all nations since 1888; however, Egypt denied canal access to Israeli shipping in 1950, a situation that, despite U.N. efforts, persisted even after the Sinai Campaign. In the novel Uris explains that "Israel wasn't going to initiate a war unless she was forced. She was undermanned and underarmed against Egypt alone." In Uris' recreation, crisis arises when Egypt's President Gamal Abdel Nasser

> seized the Suez Canal and evicted the British and the French. He had closed the Strait of Tiran, at the tip of the Sinai Peninsula, to Israeli shipping. He had turned the Gaza Strip into one enormous terrorist base which violated the Israeli border hourly. He had massed a huge army in the Sinai armed with a larder filled with Russian weapons. The bottom line was that Israel had no choice other than military action...

"Every assessment was frightfully the same: *Israel must win the war in the first four days. A prolonged conflict in which every Arab nation would join would be disastrous.*" There is a chance that Jordan, Syria, and Iraq might join in the conflict. Israel's defense of the Mitla Pass is described in the novel as "the linchpin of the entire operation" for Israeli strategy.

The protagonist of the novel, Gideon Zadok, is an American writer and ex-marine who accompanies the Israeli troops at Mitla Pass. Major themes of the novel emerge from war having implications both for the individual and the nation. Mitla Pass, itself, helps bring into focus the contrast between the peacetime environment and wartime conditions. Peace is associated with fields where "wheat was young and still green and the fields were speckled with thousands of blood-red poppies." In war the "blood-red poppies" of such fields are replaced by a field hospital where floors of operating rooms "always had a half inch of blood" on which medical workers "slipped and fell and were drenched in blood a half-dozen times a day."

Other themes are developed through the personal wars that wound Zadok, the battles that he was born into. Family politics result in his growing up between a single parent situation and a larger extended family. Sexual politics lead him into messy entanglements. His stint in Hollywood writing for a studio brings problems as well as success, and fragments the continuity of what had been his way of life. Loyalty to his dream of becoming a writer requires the courage to face what almost shatters him—in terms of both his personal wars and wartime experiences.

The themes related to Zadok's struggle to survive are also interconnected. From his participation in war—either experienced, witnessed, or related to him—Zadok distills personal loyalty as an ideal. Family politics encourage him to value personal devotion, and sexual politics place Zadok in a position where conflicting claims are made in the name of loyalty. Variations on the theme of loyalty are at the core of *Mitla Pass*, and Zadok, in trying to express his allegiance to what is true, demonstrates a loyalty that is central to the theme of the novel.

Characters

Gideon Zadok, an American writer visiting Israel to research a novel, finds himself a witness to battle at the time of the Sinai Campaign. In the lulls created by the disruption of routine that times of crisis create, Zadok has ample time to contemplate his past, as well as his present predicament. He meditates on a range of subjects: his youth, a time of emotional and material deprivation; his becoming a marine; his early marriage; his struggle to become a writer; the success and cynicism he finds in Hollywood; and his ongoing extra-marital affair that currently catches him between his mistress and his wife. In both the past and the present, Zadok experiences crossfire in more ways than one.

As Zadok delineates his life story, certain attachments emerge as the ground of his loyalties—personal and professional—as well as the conflicts he encounters. The male characters who emerge from his family past tend to be desolate in their isolation, and their female counterparts tend to be maternal and/or matriarchal figures. In the present, Zadok is in the process of choosing between his mistress, Natasha, and his wife, Val, and their two daughters. His array of attachments becomes clear when he faces the prospect of the outbreak of war: "You can't divide fear up into halves and quarters, but I knew I was more afraid for Israel than for myself . . . or Val . . . or the girls. I was very afraid for Natasha."

Gideon Zadok and his future wife meet when he "was in Marine uniform and she was a student." A whirlwind courtship is followed by marriage at an early age, the birth of two daughters, and Gideon's becoming a successful scriptwriter. But Gideon and Val begin to squabble, and both seek extra-marital comfort. Val's support for Gideon's chosen path evaporates. She pushes him away from novel writing and toward more lucrative scriptwriting; she also demands that he make choices that he regards as morally ambiguous. During this prelude to his affair with Natasha, Gideon increasingly feels himself imprisoned as his world becomes maddeningly reduced to "Golden handcuffs. Mink-lined cells." Even his body revolts against Val's neglect of ethical considerations and her relentless greed: "My asthma was returning. I hadn't had an attack in fifteen years."

Zadok subsequently leaves for Israel, where his wife and daughters later join him as he works on his novel. In Israel he meets Natasha Solomon, a woman so stunningly beautiful that Prime Minister David Ben-Gurion, exhausted and about to sign a document as his nation is on the brink of war, pauses to admire her. Natasha is from Hungary; she is a "survivor of Auschwitz," although the rest of her family were killed in the gas chambers. The affair between Gideon and Natasha is fiery: according to a friend of Gideon's, their first meeting looked like the inflaming of "a couple of dormant volcanos." The fire subsides somewhat for Gideon, and as the novel ends, he and Val reunite in Rome, where she and the girls were taken when the fighting broke out. For Gideon, Val and Natasha respectively represent reason and passion. He maintains that they "come from two different planets" and that he experiences a need for both. The novel includes one winning description of a wife, Gideon's aunt.

In delineating Gideon's family history, Uris speaks of Russia, Poland, and "the establishment of a huge reservation in which the Jews had to live and beyond which the Jews were forbidden to go." Uris mentions that the "Pale of Settlement" constituted "one monstrous ghetto," where people "were trapped ... and reduced to basic survival." This aspect of the novel, while part of Gideon's family history, has vital connections to themes explored in *Mitla Pass*. One theme related to characterization is the profound relation of history to the individual. Natasha outlives the Holocaust, but not its harms. Shlomo Bar Adon, Gideon's friend and his guide to Israel, has "a theory that Moses and the tribes came through Mitla Pass during the Exodus from Egypt. I wrote my master's thesis on the realities behind the biblical fantasies." Thematically, among other things, *Mitla Pass* presents the impulse of loyalty toward historical truth and moral vision.

An aspect of characterization that applies to Zadok and other characters has to do with sexual conventions, roles, and stereotyping. Gideon states that there have been two women he could "trust": his teacher, Miss Abigail Winters, who thought that Gideon "would become a writer one day," and his sister, Molly. Both women depart from convention. His sister played a semi-maternal role, and "Miss Abigail Winters was no ordinary sixth-grade teacher" but "a very rare person, a woman flier, an aviatrix." She encourages Gideon to write, and gives him the most exhilarating experience of his childhood—a plane ride. It is to her that Gideon expresses his distaste for the racist belittlement conventionally accepted at school. The novel closes with an italicized passage set off from the rest of the text; this concluding passage is a reminder of Gideon's childhood introduction to the possibility of flight. In *Mitla Pass* Uris attacks any form of bigotry that would block the ability of anyone to soar, and he explicitly treats the subject of sexual stereotyping. Gideon explains to Val that "Little boys have to be little men the minute they're born. The pressure is on for them to be tough—don't cry—look how strong he is.'' He also remarks that the family dog ''is probably the best in the world at fake macho.''

Techniques

Mitla Pass interleaves passages describing Gideon Zadok's present, his past, the past of some of his relatives, and both past and present as seen by various people close to Gideon. This diversity of views, concerns, and times enables Uris to unite otherwise disparate themes and motifs. The novel's continuity emerges from character and theme, rather than from a strictly followed chronology or plot. Uris divides his text into numerous short sections within five larger divisions. These conspicuous subdivisions give the text the texture of a journal or diary. The labelled subdivisions, which occur frequently, reflect the novel's concern with history as a theme. The scope of the novel, the combined presence of realism and romanticism, and the heroic central character all relate the novel to the world of the epic.

Relation to Previous Works

Mitla Press, compared to *Exodus* and *The Haj*, is addressed more to the individual (as potential hero), although all three novels treat the subjects of heroism, nationhood, and identity. *Exodus* and *The Haj* present individual dramas in the context of the quest for identity, especially as related to nationhood, but *Mitla Pass* conveys the protagonist's struggle to survive on his own terms, outside any national drama. In *Mitla Pass*, loyalty to a moral vision is of paramount importance. The novel is a cluster of stories that finally reveal a portrait of loyalty, a theme that links the worlds and ideals of *Exodus*, *The Haj*, and *Mitla Pass*.

Joy Kuropatwa
Brescia College

GUY VANDERHAEGHE
1951

Update
Critics remain strongly divided on the merits of Guy Vanderhaeghe's fiction. Vanderhaeghe features social outcasts, misfits, and losers in his work, and the critics who complain about this argue that the characters are shallow and repulsive. In defense of Vanderhaeghe, other critics point out that his fiction gives voice to those people who are too often ignored by society.

Whatever the critics' opinions, Vanderhaeghe continues to receive his share of awards. His latest novel, *Homesick* (1989), received the 1990 City of Toronto Book Award, while his earlier acclaimed collection of short stories, *Man Descending* (1982), earned him the Faber Prize in England in 1985. Vanderhaeghe also received a Canadian Council Senior Grant Award in 1989.

In April 1991 Vanderhaeghe's play, *I Had a Job I Liked. Once.*, opened at Persephone Theater in Saskatoon. He is currently writing a collection of short stories, and continues to work on a historical novel that reflects his interest (and bachelor's degree) in British imperial history. Like his previous works, *Homesick* has been translated into Dutch.

Analysis of Selected Titles

HOMESICK
Homesick, 1989, novel.

Social Concerns
The seemingly unavoidable, self-imposed isolation present among family members permeates *Homesick;* the characters' self-involvement and stubborn pride thwart almost all direct communication, empathy, and understanding. Set in the remote reaches of Saskatchewan, the fictional town of Connaught is as physically removed from the cities to the east as the family members—Alec Monkman, his daughter Vera Miller, and her son Daniel—are psychologically isolated from one another. Life, however, is not static and by the novel's end there is evidence of growth. The year is 1959, decades before sociologists coined the terms "dysfunctional family" and "toxic parents," but Guy Vanderhaeghe's characters would fit nicely into contemporary group therapy—that is, if they could ever arrive at the self-awareness necessary to propel them to seek help. But this is 1959, and the

characters are not self-examining. Instead, they spend their lives fruitlessly hoping for others to change.

Repressed hostility between father and daughter keeps the family's past ever present and serves to lock relationships in animosity. Change is possible through the new generation, represented here by Daniel, and through the intervention of outsiders. Daniel forges a relationship with Alec which Vera resents. Her own growth was fostered, years earlier, by her brief marriage to Daniel's father. Alec's survival since the death of his wife twenty years earlier has been due largely to his association with Stutz, a man with no family of his own. Stutz has come through as a spokesman for Alec when communication with Vera has ceased, and he serves as a parent figure to Daniel as Alec nears death. Stutz also is the one who saved the mysterious brother Earl from a fire and he helps Vera by supplying the start-up money for her restaurant venture. But Stutz is not the only element making this business enterprise a possibility. The invasion of Connaught by an American mining company is preceded by a Portuguese street-paving crew that gives a spark to Vera's business. For Vanderhaeghe growth is dependent on the connections of the individual, the family, and the community.

Themes/Characters

Homesick portrays the binding force of family ties, even in the face of enormous emotional pain. Vanderhaeghe's unsophisticated characters drag their emotional baggage with them throughout the novel, allowing repression and projection to prevent any kind of resolution. Three generations are each represented by a single living family member; although Vera's brother, Earl, whose whereabouts we do not know until near the novel's end, is conspicuously present by his absence.

None of these characters is especially likeable. All are lonely. Alec Monkman turned to alcoholism when he was unable to cope with his wife's death twenty years before the novel opens. Instead of parenting his two children, Alec depended on them—Vera to become the homemaker and substitute mother to Earl, and Earl to accompany him on late-night drunken drives through the countryside. After Vera leaves home, Monkman finds another caretaker in Stutz, who continues to do much of Alec's emotional work throughout the novel.

Alec is connected to the memory of his dead wife until, at the end, after Vera and Daniel have left him, he finally hears the sound of his own voice. Left on his own, with only sporadic, forbidden visits from his grandson Daniel, Alec suffers a stroke but stubbornly refuses to call for help. Scars on the floor of his house show that he shuffled around for at least three days using a kitchen chair as a walker. As the novel opens, he has a recurring dream of being trapped beneath the ice on a lake. Following his stroke, his single word to Daniel is "fro'en," and his only word to Vera at his deathbed is "Cold." Alec is a frozen man; he dies without fully connecting with anyone in life. Vera finally gives him all the warmth she has to give, but it is too late.

True reconciliation between Alec and Vera is impossible, as Vera shares her father's pride and self-righteousness. Some critics have found Vera shrill and unsympathetic, and indeed she is prone to self-pity that alternates with self-congratulation. Her coping strategy is to flee unpleasant situations, and this often brings her opportunities. Vera leaves home at age seventeen and gains a sense of self-importance in the army. She rebuffs the sexual advances of soldiers, vowing that they will never "take" her. Later, fleeing the advances of a coworker, Thomas, she is rescued by the man who becomes her husband and father of her child. The marriage is said to have been an idyllic two years, but the reader has no sense of the intimacy of the union. Fearing the delinquency of her son, Vera returns to her father's home after a seventeen-year absence. But when one of her father's drinking buddies makes sexual advances, Vera again leaves her father's house, only to be rescued by Stutz. Vera has a history of inability to synthesize the episodes of her life. She marries a man who knows nothing of her roots, then returns to a family who never knew her husband. Her saving strength is perseverance. But her stoicism goes for naught. It is only at her father's deathbed that Vera refuses to quit on him. She endures, but while estranged from her father, Vera clings to the expectation that he will admit his wrongs.

Daniel brings some objectivity and insight into the family. He is its hope for the future, acting to bridge the gap between his mother and grandfather even though he cannot reunite them. Daniel has the most self-awareness in the family, along with the clearest view of the others. Yet, finding no peers, he too remains a lone, isolated figure. He comes to realize that he loves his grandfather, but he never gets the chance to tell him.

The characters who are most sympathetic, and perhaps most interesting, are already dead. Martha, Alec's wife, and Stanley, Vera's husband, are only sketchily presented—a disappointment, as a developed sense of these two marriages would add depth to the surviving characters. And Earl, a timid boy, unleashes his anger toward his life and his father in a nearly fatal fire after which he lapses into madness. He lives on in an inscription on a downtown Connaught wall: "Forever and Beyond alone." Vera's abandonment of Earl is not fully brought to consciousness within her, and her self-absorption obscures a full-blown sense of guilt.

Techniques/Literary Precedents

The bleakness of this family's life is reflected in the bleak countryside Vanderhaeghe describes. Movement in the characters' lives is the result of external control or natural consequences—a death, an influence exerted by another. This fits the description of Canadians having a tradition of being managed by others.

The juxtaposition of past and present, and the shifting points of view distance readers from the characters; this is an effective and appropriate device because the characters themselves are not comfortable with intimacy.

Despite this overriding bleakness, *Homesick* is not without its comic moments. There are some fine episodes portraying Vera's experience as a theater employee, complete with an ostentatious uniform and colorful coworkers. Vanderhaeghe gives us a collection of "oddballs and misfits," reminiscent of characters from his *Man Descending* and *My Present Age*. His first novel offered a lighter treatment of failing relationships. *Homesick* has been criticized for having two-dimensional characters, yet that is the appearance of repressed individuals. The plot element which brings the novel closest to a soap-opera formula is the well-kept secret of the whereabouts of Earl. It seems unlikely that Vera, with her drive to make her father look bad, would shy away from a confrontation on that point. But to compare the novel to a hackneyed television-movie plot, as one critic has, seems unfair; there is subtle complexity here, which largely remains unspoken. There is no easy resolution at the end, no real feeling of satisfaction. The surviving characters of *Homesick* still have their own work cut out for them. Perhaps they will benefit in the age of self-help, after all.

Additional Sources

Andrew, Ruby. Review of *Homesick*. *Macleans's* (October 23, 1989): 69. Sees the novel's "basic elements as hackneyed as a TV movie," "with two-dimensional characters," "tone-deaf dialogue," and "precious little story to tell."

Bauer, Douglas. Review of *Homesick*. *New York Times Book Review* (June 17, 1990): 15. Sees Vera as whining and Earl's whereabouts as a problem with plot.

Garrod, Andrew, ed. Interview with Vanderhaeghe. *In Speaking for Myself*. St. John's, Newfoundland: Breakwater Books, 1986.

Steinberg, Sybil. Review of *Homesick*. *Publishers Weekly* (March 16, 1990). "The novel ultimately succeeds as a quiet, moving story of family forgiveness."

Twigg, Alan, ed. Interview with Vanderhaeghe. In *Strong Voices*. Madeira Park, BC: Harbour Publishing, 1988.

Lynn LaPorte

MARIO VARGAS LLOSA
1936

Update

From 1989 to 1990 Mario Vargas Llosa's literary reputation and activity were subordinate to his political ambitions. He ran for the presidency of his native Peru, representing the views of a centrist, conservative coalition that advocated a free-market economy and the elimination of government involvement and interference in the economy. Interventionist policies, associated with the previous administration of Alán García, were held responsible for the country's serious economic stagnation and its inability to finance its foreign debt. In spite of his international literary reputation, his access to the international media, and support from the Peruvian middle class, Vargas Llosa lost the election to a university professor and agricultural engineer of Japanese ancestry whose political platform was more palatable to the majority of the Peruvian people.

Analysis of Selected Titles

IN PRAISE OF THE STEPMOTHER

In Praise of the Stepmother, 1990, novel. *Elogio de la madrastra*, 1988.

Social Concerns

The upper middle class Peruvian family of *In Praise of the Stepmother* is an affluent and congenial group. While the novel takes place exclusively within the confines of the family home in Lima, it is clear that they enjoy a seemingly normal relationship with the outside world: business associates, friends, and school. Don Rigoberto, the head of the household, is the manager of an insurance company. A widower, he marries Lucrecia, a forty-year-old divorcee. Doña Lucrecia enjoys the fruits of her privileged lifestyle; during the day she directs the household staff, goes shopping, plays bridge, and attends to the care of Don Rigoberto's son, the angelic looking Alfonso, a prepubescent boy of indeterminate age. At night, she partakes of her husband's rich sexual rituals and fantasies and is a passive yet willing partner to his imaginative sensual flights of fancy and constant experimentation.

Doña Lucrecia, a warm, sensual, and "still beautiful" woman is happily married and loves Don Rigoberto. Her new life is clouded by only one worry, her concern over gaining young Alfonso's love and trust. Her friends caution her about this all too common challenge of stepmotherhood. And while for much of the novel the reader is led to believe that Lucrecia has been able to escape the stereotypical forebodings of her friends, Vargas Llosa delivers a potent surprise at the end: a stepmother, if not inherently evil as in *Cinderella* and *Snow White*, can be made evil, and the seemingly innocent stepchild is the vehicle through which this unlikely goal is achieved. Traditional expectations of the roles of child and stepparent are completely reversed when the potential victim becomes the victimizer; the frail motherless child turns into the avenger and the helpless stepmother becomes an unsuspecting casualty. Here Vargas Llosa gives a new twist to the age-old family dynamic.

Themes

Conceived as a novel of eroticism, this short work is centered on the quest for worldly happiness and the individual's prospects of attaining it. The medium of the quest is sensory and sexual fulfillment, and Vargas Llosa's characters conduct their lives assuming that this fulfillment is both the cause and the effect of their happiness. As in other erotic texts, the characters' responses and relationships are fueled exclusively by sensual and sexual stimulation, and the mutual satisfaction gained from sexual encounters is in turn a reaffirmation of their sense of contentment and well being, of success and happiness. Sexual stimulation for Rigoberto, however, is not spontaneously generated but rather slowly achieved through an elaborate nightly toilette and the inspirational power of the artistic erotica he keeps locked up in the living room. By appealing to so much external stimulation, the character's predicament revolves around a number of questions: Is worldly happiness really possible? Are reality and happiness essentially incompatible? How long can happiness last? Is happiness only possible, as in the story, when one resorts to fantasy?

Although at times risible and esoteric, Don Rigoberto's habits and sexual poses are essentially harmless. In spite of the ritualistic even fetishistic way in which he pursues his pleasures, he is neither prurient nor abusive; his obsessions are diverting rather than threatening and his goals lofty rather than demeaning and malevolent. He is reasonably certain that in Lucrecia he has found an ideal mate, and that the happiness they enjoy at the beginning of the novel is sure to last forever.

He, of course, is wrong, and the threat to their eternal contentment comes from none other than his son Alfonso, the seemingly pure and angelic child who has never given his father any trouble, whose innocent appearance and habits belie a shrewd and manipulative mind and a malevolence that is truly formidable. In fact, innocence, its role and meaning, is the second important theme of the book. It is clear that the father, for all his eccentricities, is a good, kind, innocent and honest individual. His son, on the other hand, for all his cherubic appearance, his youth, size, age, and fragility, is a monster.

A third, and less explicit, theme that emerges from the novel is the historically recurrent predicament of women, portrayed as the embodiment of the virgin, the whore, or the fallen Eve. Vargas Llosa makes productive use of this traditional topology. Chapter 14 of the novel, for example, revolves around a description of Fra Angelico's painting *The Annunciation* in which the presence of a rosy youth with wings informs Mary of her impending maternity and the virgin birth of a son. And while the angelic youth helps Mary prepare for her unexpected fate of "queen of all men," the youth of the novel, unlike Jesus, brings betrayal rather than exaltation to Lucrecia. At the same time, Lucrecia represents sexual fulfillment for Don Rigoberto, and this carnal aspect of a woman's role is reinforced through painted images in which the female is portrayed as the object of a specific sexual fantasy. Lucrecia, in the end, fails both as (step)mother and mistress. The rosy youth of the story, Alfonso, rejects her as his stepmother, in this case his virgin mother, and he conspires to end her relationship with Don Rigoberto by manipulating and seducing her. Lucrecia, like Eve after the Fall, becomes an outcast.

Characters

The four characters of the novel are sketchily described, and their present circumstances are limited to the details that permit the development of the action of the novel. Since the story takes place in a few day's time, the characters remain largely devoid of a past.

Don Rigoberto is, by far, the novel's most interesting character, not because he is especially complex but because Vargas Llosa relishes in his quirks and describes them in titillating detail, creating what Anthony Burgess calls "the pornography of hygiene." Don Rigoberto is compulsive about his personal cleanliness and his bodily functions. He appreciates them as marvelous and necessary, to be worshipped both for their sake as well as for the sake and welfare of the whole body. He devotes a day a week to the care of a different member or organ: Monday, hands; Tuesday, feet; Wednesday, ears; Thursday, nose; Friday, hair; Saturday, eyes, and Sunday, skin. He cleans, soaps, oils, dries, buffs, and trims, and then contemplates his handiwork with the satisfaction of having reached—or at least approximated—however momentarily, perfection. After such nightly ablutions, he goes into the bedroom, where Lucrecia awaits him in readiness. In their lovemaking, he pretends to be a different lover each time, finding inspiration in art; he pretends, for example, to be Candaules, King of Lydia, after the 17th century painting by Jacob Jordaenes by the same name; he owns a copy of Kenneth Clark's book *The Nude*, which he views with relish in the privacy of his living room.

Lucrecia, the wife, is loving, warm, and well meaning. Wishing to be accepted and loved by her stepson, she allows herself to be seduced by him, a circumstance that in her own mind, foments family unity. She also comes to believe that it enhances her own enjoyment of sex with her husband. In fact, she asserts that through the experience she has finally learned the meaning of emancipation. Of course this sense of elation is temporary and ends when little Alfonso exposes her. The reader never learns how she reacts to this betrayal and to Rigoberto's decision to banish her from their home.

Throughout, Lucrecia seems somewhat naive, even after her supposed "emancipation." She does evolve somewhat as a character, a development indicated when Rigoberto, coming to bed without having assumed a sexual identity for the night, asks her to choose one for him, to which she responds that she would rather choose one for herself.

Alfonso is the real perverse character of the novel. Though sweet in both appearance and speech, he possesses a precocious intelligence and a masterful ability to deceive. He seduces his stepmother by threatening suicide if she does not respond physically to his affectionate advances. Although he does not appear to be old enough for adult sexual relations, he is able to perform. Lucrecia comes to believe that their sexual encounters are perfectly innocent and harmless because the child is devoid of malice. She is, of course, completely wrong. Alfonso has deliberately entrapped her; he seduces her in order to get rid of her. He exposes his stepmother to his father (asking him what "orgasm" means, a word he says Lucrecia uses after lovemaking) and by writing about it in a free composition assignment for school.

The fourth and last character of the novel is Justiniana, the maid, who serves as messenger, witness, and interlocutor for Lucrecia, Alfonso, and the author. At the end of the book, aware of Alfonso's role in the stepmother's downfall, she confronts the child only to hear that he did it for her, not for his own dead mother. A startled Justiniana (called Justita, an endearing diminutive used only by Alfonso) rushes out of his bedroom as he begins to shower her with passionate kisses, just as he had done with his more naive and unsuspecting stepmother at the start of the novel.

Techniques

In Praise of the Stepmother consists of fourteen chapters and an Epilogue. As he did in *Aunt Julia and the Scriptwriter* (1982), Vargas Llosa interpolates related materials into the main plot of the story. Chapters 2, 5, 7, 9, 12, and 14 contain a color print of a famous painting accompanied by a narration, each from a separate voice, associating the narrator's reading of the picture to the authoritative version of the plot provided by an omniscient and detached third person narrator who controls the more realistic aspects of the novel. Rigoberto, Lucrecia, Alfonso, and perhaps even Justiniana, all become the protagonist/narrator of one of the paintings by Jordaenes, Boucher, Titian, Francis Bacon, Fernando de Szyszlo, and Fra Angelico. This rather heterogenous collection of prints share the fact that they could be viewed as depicting various aspects of sensuality, from the voyeuristic to the immaculate. The remainder of the chapters relate the domestic life of Don Rigoberto and his family and his diligent bathroom rituals and techniques. Vargas Llosa excels at describing the details of Don Rigoberto's grooming, especially in the chapter devoted to the ear.

Aside from the technique of interpolating chapters about art, enhanced by the inclusion of color reproductions, Vargas Llosa avoids the use of more complex structures. The novel is easy to read and brief, under 150 pages long.

WHO KILLED PALOMINO MOLERO?

Who Killed Palomino Molero?, 1987, novel. *¿Quién mató a Palomino Molero?*, 1986.

Social Concerns

In this short novel, as in *The Time of the Hero*, Vargas Llosa portrays the deep chasm that separates Peru's ruling elite, the white descendants of European settlers, and the *cholos* or part-Indian, part-European Peruvians who make up the majority of the country's population. The story opens with the discovery of the corpse of an air force enlisted man, Palomino Molero, a *cholo*, the victim of a brutal murder. The local police, or *Guardia Civil*, consisting of *cholo* officers, Lieutenant Silva and his assistant Sergeant Lituma, are called upon to investigate. Lituma is a member of the "Inconquistables" a group of comrades, now adult, first introduced member of the "Inconquistables" a group of comrades, now adult, first introduced by Vargas Llosa as the youthful and somewhat aimless gang of the same name in his novel *The Green House* (1968).

Silva and Lituma's investigation quickly takes them to the air force base in Piura (a town which Vargas Llosa also wrote about in *The Green House*) where they try to piece together the victim's last days. They are belittled and dismissed by the commanding officer of the base, Colonel Mindreau.

Mindreau makes no secret of his lack of respect for these local policemen. He treats them with scorn and bans them from the base, insisting that they are not only outside their jurisdiction but that a military investigation has already been carried out, clearing all military personnel. In spite of Mindreau's intimidating tactics—these are so obvious that the reader cannot help but suspect that Mindreau is either directly implicated or part of a cover up—Lieutenant Silva slowly unravels the details of the murder. Molero's death seems inevitable because he commits the cardinal sin of falling in love with Mindreau's daughter Alicia. The doomed romance between the pampered only child of an air force commanding officer and Palomino Molero, a *cholo*, serves to encapsulate the novel's principal social concern—the vast and unbridgeable differences that separate Peruvians of different social classes. Even Alicia, whose love for Palomino leads her to defy her father's authority, justifies her attraction by praising Palomino's musical talents, his unexpectedly refined manners, and a physical appearance that belies his true ethnicity. His name, however, reveals his *cholo* ancestry, and remains a source of embarrassment for Alicia.

The way in which the establishment, in this case an elite air force officer corps, carries out and covers up Molero's murder makes clear the extent to which the Peruvian upper class is willing to go to protect itself from interlopers.

Themes

Vargas Llosa demonstrates that psychologically uncomplicated and socially unpretentious characters—such as Molero, his mother, the local saloon keepers, the town whores, and the *Guardia Civil*—can never receive fair and just treatment from the Peruvian establishment. Silva's great detective skills, which consist of a mixture of patience, reason, deep intuition, and a knowledge of human nature, result in his and his assistant's effective punishment rather than reward. He and Lituma are transferred from the warm coastal region where the novel takes place to their own gulags in remote outposts in the cold and inhospitable Peruvian highlands. This serves as a permanent reminder of the risks of defying the implicit rules of a rigorously hierarchical society.

The hopelessness of the *cholo*'s predicament, echoed in other Vargas Llosa novels, is neither revealing nor interesting here. It serves to weaken an already weak and predictable plot, loosely structured as a detective story.

Characters

The reader is seldom surprised by the reactions of the characters in *Who Killed Palomino Molero?* Even Lituma's naive and matter-of-fact acceptance of the obvious as truth, in contrast to Silva's more reticent and cerebral approach, does not lull the reader into sharing his world view. Vargas Llosa's characters seem static and one-dimensional. For example, Lieutenant Silva's relentless infatuation with Doña Adriana, the plump and vivacious restaurant keeper, could be a potentially amusing counterpoint to the detective's cool and unflappable demeanor. This tension, however, is awkwardly resolved. Silva, all talk, is unable to perform sexually when Adriana entices him into her bed. Doña Adriana pretends to relent to Silva's sexual advances only to expose him. And while Silva's sexual impotence serves to mirror his social impotence, his predicament is not presented in a way that enhances the reader's understanding of his character or sheds any light on the complexities of the machismo it pretends to expose.

Vargas Llosa attempts to add an element of depth to the characters, and the story, by introducing a psychological twist to the plot. The death of Molero was precipitated by his affair with Alicia, and Mindreau's central role in the murder was not merely an example of a father who disapproves of the uneven love match. More elaborate explanations emerge. Alicia, who confirmed to the police her father's guilt, also claimed that she had to submit routinely to her father's sexual abuse. After each sexual encounter, she reported, Mindreau, in tears would beg her forgiveness. Mindreau's version to Silva, however, differs substantially from his daughter's. He tells the lieutenant that Alicia was mentally unstable, suffering from delusions that world-renown specialists had been unable to cure. According to Mindreau, his daughter hated him and blamed him, totally without cause, for the death of her mother. He, in turn, devoted his entire life and fortune to the child's well-being. These revelations make the outcome of the story predictable. Mindreau, who prided himself in being a strict follower of the rules, could not tolerate failure and exposure. He kills both his daughter and himself. The locals, however, find the details of the story entirely too bizarre. They prefer to think that it was invented by the authorities to protect the base personnel and cover up the murder of a *cholo;* or that smugglers from neighboring Ecuador were responsible; or that Mindreau had been the head of a spy ring selling military secrets.

Techniques

Vargas Llosa uses an omniscient narrator who moves frequently through time and space and juxtaposes his voice with present time dialogue, adding both detail and perspective to his characters' rather straightforward discourse. He also enriches the narrative with a few, telling details about the major and minor characters and the physical setting of the story. He thus creates an evocative visual landscape in spite of the absence of careful and elaborate descriptions or familiar references. Molero's guitar, a dinner menu at a local tavern, dilapidated pick-up trucks, and Dona Adriana's clothes are a few examples.

Literary Precedents

Vargas Llosa is self-referential in *Who Killed Palomino Molero?*, exploring characters and locales he introduced twenty years earlier in *The Green House*. The elements of a detective novel should not detract from the fact that this is not essentially about who killed Molero, but about Peru's social conditions and the hopelessness of those marginalized by the system. Vargas Llosa has been their pre-eminent voice.

Additional Sources

Castro-Klarén, Sara. *Understanding Mario Vargas Llosa*. Columbia: University of South Carolina Press, 1990. A helpful and serious analysis of the most important of Vargas Llosa's works and literary techniques.

Geisdorfer Feal, Rosemary. *Novel Lives: The Fictional Autobiographies of Guillermo Cabrera Infante and Mario Vargas Llosa*. Chapel Hill: University of North Carolina Press, 1986. A study of the interplay between fiction and biography in the novels of Vargas Llosa and Cabrera Infante, an important contemporary Cuban writer.

Vargas Llosa, Mario. *A Writer's Reality*. Ed. with an introduction by Myron I. Lichtblau. Syracuse, NY: Syracuse University Press, 1991. This work is made up of a series of lectures delivered by Vargas Llosa at Syracuse in 1988 covering a variety of themes such as the autobiographical elements of six of his novels, and the influences of Borges and Sartre, among others, in his writing.

Urquidi Illanes, Julia. *My Life with Mario Vargas Llosa.* Trans. by C. R. Perricone. New York: Peter Lang, 1988. A first person account of her life with the author written by his aunt and first wife, the older woman who was the inspiration for Vargas Llosa's novel *Aunt Julia and the Scriptwriter.* While the work contains some interesting insights, it is of limited value in understanding Vargas Llosa's literary accomplishments.

Clara Estow
University of Massachusetts, Harbor Campus

JOHN VARLEY
1947

Update

Recently, most of John Varley's time has been devoted to producing the motion-picture version of his novel, *Millennium*. He is currently under contract to write two new novels for Berkley Publishing Group, and is reported at work on the first of them.

Analysis of Selected Titles

TANGO CHARLIE AND FOXTROT ROMEO

Tango Charlie and Foxtrot Romeo, 1986, novella.

Social Concerns

In *Tango Charlie and Foxtrot Romeo* civil servants and politicians cynically debate the fate of a child discovered living in a quarantined space station. They are driven more by fear of popular opinion than by any desire to do what is morally right. This common portrait of public servants can be found in numerous works of fiction. Of more topical interest is the disease Neuro-X, which resembles AIDS in the fear that it generates in people. One character, Doctor Blume, even suggests that "Neuro-X destroyed her immune system," a characteristic of AIDS. In the novel, Neuro-X is a virulent disease that is transmitted in mysterious ways. No safeguard seems effective. Even physicians dressed in airtight suits catch the disease and die within days. The disease is confined to a space station and a space ship, both of which have been quarantined, and the space station left to orbit the moon. Thirty years later observers learn that a living girl who appears about seven years old is on board. Her presence on the station opens a vigorous debate among people on Luna (the Moon) about whether the child's life or the safety of the public is more important. Should the child be saved, even though she may be a carrier of the deadliest disease known to humanity? Should the station be destroyed and the girl killed in order to safeguard against the possibility of Neuro-X being transmitted to the general population? These matters echo some of the debate about AIDS, particularly when there was doubt about how the disease was transmitted. Just how much risk should the general public be expected to accept?

When does discrimination against those with the disease exceed justification and become cruel prejudice?

Themes

Tango Charlie and Foxtrot Romeo is a moving story of the struggle to save a stranded child. The mere fact that a child is in danger moves some characters to want to save her. When the "child" turns out actually to be over thirty years old, the decision to save her or not becomes more complicated, as if an adult's life were less valuable than that of a child. Still, the girl looks very young, and in many ways she is mentally a child. Her confusion about what is happening endears her to Corporal Anna-Louise Bach and Megan Galloway, who decides to help her regardless of her real age. This theme of mortality is emphasized by the initial reaction to the discovery of the girl's real age: could she hold the secret of immortality, freedom from death? Then the harsh reality of the girl's situation dashes the observers' hopes, and debate focuses on whether the girl can be saved. The theme of mortality is enriched by the question of whether anyone would be eager to save the child if she were a mature woman; Varley offers no answers, and the question remains unresolved and troubling.

Characters

Corporal Anna-Louise Bach is the point-of-view character for most of *Tango Charlie and Foxtrot Romeo*. She is too acid-tongued for her own good and has been placed in a dead-end job because she failed to show respect to incompetent superiors. She supervises the crew of the New Dresden Police Department's monitoring room. When the presence of a living person on the space station Tango Charlie is suspected, this crew activates the station's few functioning cameras and observes the girl. Bach is a sad, lonely figure. She is attracted to vacuous, muscular men and drifts from one unfulfilling love affair to another. She empathizes with the isolation of the girl and acts out of morality and emotion, rather than regard for public opinion.

The little girl calls herself Charlie. Why she has remained a child for more than thirty years is a mystery, although the disease Neuro-X might be a factor. She is Tango Charlie's only human survivor, kept company by the descendants of Shetland Sheepdogs that survived the Neuro-X plague, as well as by Tik-Tok, the space station's computer. Her time is spent maintaining the space station and raising Shetland Sheepdogs to exacting dog-show competition standards. Tik-Tok makes sure that Charlie follows a busy daily schedule of chores, sees to it that she eats nutritious meals, and encourages her to bathe and groom herself. She is lonely but does not know it. When first seen on camera, she presents a startling picture; with makeup smeared on her face like war paint, she seems surrounded by a sea of flowing dogs wherever she goes. Her courage in the face of isolation and her childlike innocence help make *Tango Charlie and Foxtrot Romeo* one of Varley's most passionate and moving works.

The news reporter Megan Galloway is an unusual character. Once paralyzed from the neck down, she became famous as a mechanized being who moved with the aid of a golden exoskeleton. She became famous because of her ability to exploit the glamorous and erotic possibilities her extraordinarily beautiful exoskeleton offered. Medical science eventually advanced enough to restore most of her natural mobility, although she walks with a cane. Now a glamorous reporter, she wears ornaments that resemble parts of her discarded exoskeleton. When she learns through informants of Charlie's plight, she takes an immediate interest in the child's welfare. Beneath her cynical shell, there is a responsible and caring person who tempers her desire for a good story with compassion. Like Charlie, she is something of a freak; she empathizes strongly with the little girl's loneliness and creates a plan to save the child. She is a bizarre, otherworldly figure, yet with a core of humanity that makes her a believable, sympathetic character.

Techniques

Tango Charlie and Foxtrot Romeo resembles a tragic drama in which the plot leads inevitably to catastrophe (usually death) for the main character. Although Bach does not die, her efforts end in disaster. Like a tragedy, Varley's novel is plotted in movements in which certain elements dominate. *Tango Charlie and Foxtrot Romeo* is first a mystery story in which Bach and others try to learn the truth about who is on the space station; then a moral story in which characters are ethically tested by the plight of the girl; and finally a suspense story in which the protagonists struggle to save Charlie from certain death. Each movement reveals different aspects of the characters. For instance, in the mystery movement, Bach demonstrates her quick mind; in the moral movement, she reveals a depth of emotions that have not been expressed through her shallow love life; and in the suspense movement, she shows the courage of her convictions.

By shifting scenes back and forth from Bach to Charlie, Varley gives the reader a rounded view of the little girl. At first, she greets the mystery of her discovery with irritation—she is a busy person with no time to waste talking with outsiders.

As she warms to Bach, Charlie feels the loneliness of her isolation and expresses despair at losing her loved ones. First she cries for a dead puppy; later she faces up to the pain caused by her mother's death. Her courage in these situations seems natural. Varley includes character touches, such as her literal-mindedness when asked questions, that make her seem believable. When she finally puts her trust in Bach, she reaches a level of maturity that exceeds that of the adults who are trying to help her. She confronts the universal human problem of mortality and overcomes her fear of death.

A tragedy touches on matters of universal human importance, and as the plot unfolds it humanizes and explores these themes. *Tango Charlie and Foxtrot Romeo* does this, making it a remarkable literary work. If there is a false note, it is Bach's seeming failure to grow. Her grief yields to the passage of time and yet another brawny man. On the other hand, this woman, who was resigned to her fate as the oldest recruit in the police force, has discovered in herself the capacity to do what is right in spite of powerful opposition, and the courage to risk her future for someone who cannot defend herself.

Literary Precedents

Perhaps the most famous science fiction book to deal with an attempt to control a virulent disease is *The Andromeda Strain* by Michael Crichton (1969). Although that novel features people sealed in a research laboratory for somewhat the same reasons Charlie is sealed in her space station, its themes are very different. The motion picture *Silent Running* (1971) features a man isolated on a space station that contains some of the last examples of earth's natural world. He kills others and eventually kills himself to protect the wildlife on the station, leaving one lonely little robot to care for the living things. Like *Tango Charlie and Foxtrot Romeo*, the movie evokes strong emotions, although it lacks the thoughtfulness of Varley's novella. The conflict between incompetent civil servants and compassionate ones is an old idea, featured in many works of fiction. *Tango Charlie and Foxtrot Romeo* is exceptional for its presentation of the problems of mortality through a character who is at once a little girl and a woman, as well as for its well-paced plot and genuine emotional content.

Related Titles

The imaginary future of *Tango Charlie and Foxtrot Romeo* appears in at least one other of Varley's works, the novella *Blue Champagne*. There, the character

Megan Galloway also appears. She is paralyzed from the neck down but moves with the aid of an elaborate golden exoskeleton. In *Tango Charlie and Foxtrot Romeo*, recent medical advances have given her back much of her natural mobility, although she uses a cane to help her walk.

Additional Sources
"Varley, John." In *Reader's Guide to Twentieth-Century Science Fiction*. Edited by Marilyn P. Fletcher. Chicago: American Library Association, 1989. Offers mostly plot summaries of Varley's fiction, with a brief discussion of his themes and style.

Kirk H. Beetz
National University, Sacramento

KURT VONNEGUT
1922

Update

Since 1985, Kurt Vonnegut has published two novels—*Bluebeard* (1987) and *Hocus Pocus* (1990)—both of which have attracted a mixture of praise and censure from critics. Much of the critical disagreement centers on Vonnegut's conscious use of "anti-novelistic" techniques and devices, such as an intrusive author, a non-linear plot structure, and the inclusion of seemingly irrelevant passages that interrupt the story line. Vonnegut uses these techniques because he believes that the traditional novel is dead; he sets out to write "anti-novels" in which conventional expectations about the novel are thwarted.

As early as *The Sirens of Titan* (1959), Vonnegut established the anti-novel form and techniques which he has used ever since: a main character or first person narrator who ranges back and forth in time, nightmarish and bloody events which overwhelm the characters, interruptions that break up the action and narration, and a whimsical or pseudo-scientific view of the purpose of existence (in *Deadeye Dick*, when one is born a peephole opens; when one dies, it closes). How one responds to Vonnegut's later novels depends on whether one accepts and enjoys this form. Vonnegut is currently working on a new novel, *Fates Worse Than Death*, scheduled for publication in August of 1991.

Analysis of Selected Titles

DEADEYE DICK

Deadeye Dick, 1982, novel.

Social Concerns

In *Deadeye Dick* Vonnegut continues to voice his now familiar concern that modern technology has gone out of control. For example, a mantelpiece which no-one knows is radioactive kills one of the characters, and, worse, a neutron bomb explodes over the center of the action, Midland City (another of Vonnegut's narrative substitutes for Indianapolis, his childhood home). Vonnegut also continues to investigate the role of the artist in society by making his main character a failed playwright who is more noted for accidentally shooting someone than for his literary efforts.

Themes

The role of chance in human life continues to fascinate Vonnegut. Society tells its young that if they behave in a certain manner, certain things will happen; therefore, one should behave in the socially approved way so that good things will happen. In nineteenth-century America, the genteel tradition assumed that literature should show its readers proper ideals and values. In Europe, critics assumed that art was designed to instruct and improve. Thomas Hardy was condemned for allowing happenstance to rule at crucial points in such novels (*Tess of the D'Urbervilles,* 1891). Hardy responded that accident is a determinant of human existence more often than is acknowledged. Vonnegut seems to believe that accident is the *major* determinant of human existence.

There is simply no way to know, believes Vonnegut, whether any action will have a good or bad outcome. The central event of *Deadeye Dick* occurs when Rudy Waltz, the main character, at the age of twelve, fires one of his father's guns at random and the stray bullet fatally wounds a pregnant housewife. Young Rudy thus becomes a double or "mass" murderer and acquires the taunting nickname "Deadeye Dick" which follows him throughout his life. When Rudy's father, Otto, was studying art in Vienna, he befriended his fellow art student, the young Adolf Hitler, loaned Hitler his coat when Hitler sold his own for food, and bought one of his paintings so that he wouldn't starve. These humane gestures saved the life of the greatest mass murderer of all time.

When Otto Waltz comes to the police station to rescue his son, the police savagely beat both of them. This action brings up another of Vonnegut's favorite themes, the brutality of institutional response to human misfortune. It is not just that the police enjoy violence and, because they are police, get to use it in an official fashion; institutions are set up according to logical patterns, and people who support those institutions must act as their logic tells them to act, even if that action is itself not reasonable. The logic of the law says that every unsocial act has a perpetrator who must be punished; reason easily shows that Rudy was not responsible for his act, but it is more frightening to accept that the event was an accident, because that admission would undercut the logical ground on which human institutions rest. So Rudy and Otto must be beaten without reason.

Even more disturbing than accepting chance as a primary cause is the corollary that guilt would also disappear. Rudy became a mass murderer by accident and thus should not be condemned, but Adolf Hitler became a mass murderer by the same process, and therefore, neither should he be condemned. Vonnegut implies that emotion saves people from this moral nightmare. Because human life is too much for all people, the appropriate response to it is not blame or credit but compassion.

Characters

As often happens in Vonnegut's novels, there is really only one character (in this case, Rudy Waltz), a narrative voice who ranges back and forth over a given period (those of his life and of his parents), describing the other characters, whom the reader rarely confronts directly. Rudy has failed as a playwright, but he is a good cook, and he spices his narrative with recipes. Rudy settles down to a career as a pharmacist, but he is interrupted at his duties almost nightly by callers asking if he is Deadeye Dick. He is living in Haiti when he begins to tell his story.

The rest of Rudy's family is as strange as Vonnegut's characters usually are. His father supports his friend Hitler before World War II and is condemned for this once hostilities occur; his mother is done in by her own mantelpiece, and brother Felix eventually becomes head of the National Broadcasting Company but forsakes it all to return to Midland City. Other characters include Fred T. Barry, owner of Barrytron, the largest employer in Midland City, but not a happy man, and Celia Hoover, whom Rudy loves but with whom he can never establish a relationship. She commits suicide by swallowing Drano.

Police Chief Francis X. Morissey is someone whose life Vonnegut compares and contrasts with that of Rudy. When Rudy fires his fatal shot, Morissey at first wants to hush up the fact of the child's involvement, an odd reaction from a law enforcement officer. Later the reader discovers why. The most famous unsolved murder in the area is that of August Gunther, whose headless body was found in a creek after he left his house to go hunting. Many years later Rudy finds out that Gunther was accidentally shot by Morissey, who never revealed his role in the affair. This episode underlines another of Vonnegut's ideas, the failure of easy moralistic answers. Honesty is the best policy, and confession is good for the soul; Rudy owns up to his accident and is pilloried for life, while Morissey keeps quiet about a similar incident and becomes a community leader.

Techniques

The literary techniques of *Deadeye Dick* are similar to those in most of Vonnegut's other novels. There is a sentimental, resigned, and eccentric first person narrator who relates his tale in short chapters with many divisions within the chapters. There are also various "interrupters," that is, material that some critics have deemed irrelevant. In *Deadeye Dick*, Rudy's interpolated recipes break up the story. Sometimes he presents the story in the form of a play, since he wanted to be a playwright.

In *Deadeye Dick*, there is no real plot, but instead a collection of anecdotes. Vonnegut brings himself into the book by writing an introduction in which he explains its meaning and lists its symbols before the book has even begun. The purpose of these elements is not just to disarm and slyly poke fun at literary critics but to encourage his audience just to enjoy reading his writing rather than to try to puzzle out some hidden meaning. Vonnegut wants to put it all on the surface.

Literary Precedents

Vonnegut's most obvious literary precedents are his own works, but critics have compared his approach to writing to that of an improvising jazzman. For Vonnegut plot and character are not as interesting as the sentence he is writing, just as the jazz musician cares about the song only as a means to the end of self-expression. Vonnegut is often compared to Jack Kerouac, but the two free form writers improvise in different ways. Another literary ancestor is Laurence Sterne, whose novel *Tristram Shandy* (1759-1767) is more important for how it is written than what is said.

Relation to Previous Works

Most critics regard Vonnegut's early work, specifically *Mother Night* (1961), *Cat's Cradle* (1963), and *Slaughterhouse-Five* (1969) as his best, and subsequent works are always compared to those benchmark novels. From the beginning of his career, Vonnegut has enjoyed plugging the same characters in and out of his books. Rabo Karabekian, who appears briefly in *Deadeye Dick*, will become the main character of Vonnegut's next novel, *Bluebeard* (1987). The novelist himself speaks directly in *Deadeye Dick*, as he did in *Slaughterhouse-Five* and *Breakfast of Champions* (1973).

GALAPAGOS

Galapagos, 1985, novel.

Social Concerns

Vonnegut's view of human society is grimmest in this novel. Human life has led to utter failure and the devastation of the planet. The story is told from the temporal perspective of one million years in the future, by which time the human race has devolved into amphibian creatures that resemble seals or walruses, with a small brain and flippers instead of hands. Big brains and hands were the human body parts that caused trouble in the past, as people used their big brains to hatch schemes and their hands to hurt other people.

Themes

Galapagos is one of Vonnegut's strongest statements—in philosophical as well as literary terms—of his basic assumption that life is simply too much for people. In this novel he suggests that life of any sort may have been a cosmic mistake, and he further proposes that the only solution for the human race may be to reverse the process by which we arrived at such a position of dominance over other life forms and return to the kind of simple aquatic creatures that we once were. The only trouble with this solution is that it will take worldwide catastrophe, good luck, and a million years to accomplish.

Early in his career, Vonnegut was mistakenly labelled as a science fiction writer because his novels were sometimes set in the future and involved space travel. A pure science fiction writer is concerned with the logical application of a scientific idea to a narrative setting; Vonnegut is really interested in morality, and he uses fantastic settings and scientific gimmicks to titillate and involve the reader in his world view. Vonnegut's explanation of time travel, the Tralfamadorean chronosynclastic infundibulum, is a satire, rather than a genuine use of a scientific idea. But in *Galapagos*, Vonnegut bases his novel on scientific discoveries more than in any work since *Cat's Cradle*, which is really about the atomic bomb.

This novel is set in the Galapagos Islands where Charles Darwin found the keys to his theory of evolution. Darwin recognized that a number of highly unusual life forms had developed there because the animals were isolated from the mainland and developed specific adaptations. From this observation Darwin concluded that all life had developed, or evolved, in a similar fashion. The Galapagos Islands were a happy accident, a living laboratory of evolution. Vonnegut suggests that human beings need a similar lucky break, but a reversal of the process that Darwin described. Fortunately (from Vonnegut's viewpoint), a group of travellers are stranded on one of these islands while disasters, including worldwide economic collapse, food riots, political upheavals, and a plague which renders women sterile, destroy the rest of the human population. The survivors lose those pesky brains and hands and can be peaceful again.

Another of Vonnegut's themes, the dominance of technology and our inability to control it, appears in *Galapagos* in the form of Mandarax, an electronic gadget no bigger than a hand calculator which is a combination encyclopedia and problem solver that renders human brain activity pointless. Enraged, one of the characters finally throws the instrument in the sea. Like ice-nine in *Cat's Cradle*, Mandarax is a symbol both of humanity's intellectual ability and of its inability to control it.

Characters

Vonnegut can take his readers a million years into the future because his narrator is a ghost who experiences all history simultaneously. The ghost is none other than Leon Trotsky Trout, son of the famous science fiction writer, Kilgore Trout, who appears so often in Vonnegut's works. Leon was decapitated while building a ship in a Scandinavian shipyard, so his spirit haunts the ship, *Bahia de Darwin*. The ghost begins the story in 1986. Since 1986 is one year after the book's actual date of publication, by this time setting alone Vonnegut suggests an imminent world catastrophe. The *Bahia de Darwin* is in the harbor of Quayaquil, Ecuador as the passengers prepare for the "nature cruise of the century" to the nearby Galapagos. Unfortunately—or fortunately, since in Vonnegut's novels either choice is correct—the "cruise" never really takes place, because rebellion and riot break out in the city and several of the passengers are killed before the ship leaves the harbor, not on a cruise but in an attempt to escape. The ship wrecks on one of the Galapagos, and once again the islands serve the function of saving an endangered species—humankind.

Leon tells little about life a million years in the future, since his aim is to explain where that life came from. He repeatedly states that things are much better a million years from now without those big brains and hands and implies that people are mostly concerned with food-gathering. Among the other characters are James Wait, a con man who plans to victimize the passengers; Adolf von Kleist, captain of the *Bahia de Darwin*, who becomes the father of the new human race; Mary Hepburn, a high school teacher from upstate New York who becomes its midwife; Zenji Hiroguchi, a Japanese computer expert; his pregnant wife Hisako; and Andrew MacIntosh, an American financial wizard.

One of Vonnegut's narrative jokes involves Zenji and Andrew. When the novel begins, it appears that a major plot element will concern the efforts of these two to control the world's computer markets. Instead, both are shot to death before the "cruise" begins. Zenji's unborn baby, Akiko, turns out to be of vital importance, though. Luckily, her grandmother was exposed to radiation at Hiroshima, and Akiko is born a furry mutant, just the right kind of creature to serve (along with some other survivors) as mother of the new human race.

Techniques

Vonnegut's interrupters in *Galapagos* are quotations from literature which he uses to comment on the action and which Leon says are summoned up from Mandarax. Leon also places an asterisk before the name of anyone who dies before the book ends. This device is an example of Vonnegut's familiar anti-novelistic technique of destroying suspense while maintaining curiosity. There is no question of how the book will end, as Leon tells the reader early that Von Kleist will be the father of the new human race, but since one cannot imagine how this can be, one keeps reading. Another interrupter is a transcript of the *Tonight Show* which brings Johnny Carson into the novel.

Literary Precedents

Galapagos has been compared to another bitter futurist satire, Samuel Butler's *Erewhon* (1872), which is also heavily indebted to Darwinian theory. Also, in this book Vonnegut comes closest in outlook to that of his American humorist ancestor, Mark Twain.

Relation to Previous Works

With its backdrop of world catastrophe and emphasis on science run wild and humankind powerless to stop it, *Galapagos* most closely resembles *Cat's Cradle*. In that novel ice-nine destroys the world; in *Galapagos* humankind puts an end to "the world as we know it." Ever since a Tralfamadorean cadet destroyed the universe in *Slaughterhouse-Five*, apocalypse has been one of Vonnegut's favorite motifs.

HOCUS POCUS

Hocus Pocus, 1990, novel.

Social Concerns

In *Hocus Pocus* Vonnegut again invokes his familiar themes of technology out of control and humankind's puny efforts to control it. But in this novel a much more specific and contemporary failure of the big brain creatures is noted: racism. Blacks and Hispanics, the traditional targets of this psychological and social disease, are now joined by the Japanese, whom Americans resent because of their growing economic dominance.

Themes

Once again Vonnegut tells his readers that everything is going to pieces and nothing can be done about it. As an example of the futility of man's efforts to forestall at least some of the trouble, the main character, Eugene Debs Hartke, teaches at Tarkington, a college at the end of one of the Finger Lakes in western New York. The college and its location are another of Vonnegut's private jokes; Vonnegut's *alma mater* is Cornell, also located in the Finger Lake district. Tarkington is a college for dyslexics, but the main activity there is sexual adventuring and spying on one another. The college has a museum of perpetual motion machines, all failures of course, another of Vonnegut's bitter comments on humankind's abilities to keep pace with its dreams.

Racism appears in the story when Hartke is sent to a prison primarily populated by blacks and operated by the Japanese. The prisoners revolt and attack the town across the lake, butchering most of the previously introduced characters in garish methods which Hartke describes blandly. This is nothing shocking to him; he served in Viet Nam. After the uprising is suppressed, Hartke, who had nothing to do with it, is accused of being the leader, since everyone assumes that the black inmates were not intelligent enough to start a revolt on their own.

Characters

Eugene Debs Hartke is the main character of *Hocus Pocus*, or more accurately, his observations are. An "editorial note" at the beginning of the book announces that the reader is about to read Hartke's diary. The character's name is another joke; Eugene Debs was a socialist crusader, and Vance Hartke was a liberal senator from Vonnegut's home state, Indiana, one of the most conservative areas in the country. Thus Hartke's name is a reflection of national confusion. Most of the action occurs in 2001, another joke, since that year is not only the beginning of a bright new century but the title of a film which suggests a new beginning for the human race. Such a future is hardly likely, says Vonnegut.

Hartke's life, as revealed in his diary, is an excuse for Vonnegut to comment indirectly on many contemporary events and our reactions to them. One of the buildings at Tarkington is named Samoza Hall after the fallen Nicaraguan dictator, a detail suggesting that society really values only money and power, in whatever form they may appear.

Other characters include the president of the college, Tex Johnson, and his wife Zuzu, to whom Hartke makes love at every spare moment. Hartke cannot understand why Kimberley Wilder, a student, spends so much time around him and finally learns that she is recording everything he says as evidence of his traitorous behavior. Hartke is sent to prison as a result of Kimberley's attentions. With this episode Vonnegut suggests that in spite of people's intellectual capacity, their primary activities are sex for the bored and gossip and spying for the sexless.

Techniques

Critics frequently complain that Vonnegut's anti-novelistic short chapters, non sequiturs, and digressions either draw attention to themselves and thus defeat their purpose (to make the reader forget that he or she is reading a novel) or simply are not interesting or funny. The "editorial note" at the beginning of the book states that Hartke's diary was written in prison and therefore on scraps and bits of paper, so some of the entries are quite short. The diary was not put in order by its author, so the fragments appear at random. This "explanation" is Vonnegut's way of telling his critics that he is going to write as he pleases, although it does provide some justification for the novel's form.

Vonnegut's repeated catch phrase in *Hocus Pocus* (similar to "So it goes" in *Slaughterhouse-Five*) is a favorite expression of one of the characters, Jack Patton: "I had to laugh like hell." With this phrase, Vonnegut may be agreeing with Mark Twain that laughter is the best response to the madness of human life.

Literary Precedents

The diary form of *Hocus Pocus* is similar to that of early novels such as Daniel Defoe's *Robinson Crusoe* (1719) and Victorian thrillers such as Bram Stoker's *Dracula* (1897) which maintain the reader's interest in a fantastic story by means of an ordinary and believable epistolary or journalistic narrative technique.

Relation to Previous Works

The nearly contemporary setting and autobiographical backward glance from late in life suggest Vonnegut's earlier works *Jailbird* (1979) and *Bluebeard*. Another detail is reminiscent of *Sirens of Titan*, in which the reader learns that the purpose of the earth and the life on it is to aid a Tralfamadorean space ship get across the universe with its vital message, "greetings." In *Hocus Pocus*, Hartke finds a science fiction story in the magazine *Black Garterbelt* (a reminder that truth often turns up in the most unusual places) in which life on earth may be a breeding ground for germs as they evolve into forms able to withstand the rigors of space travel.

Additional Sources

Brodrick, Jeffrey. "On and Off." *National Review* 34 (December 10, 1982): 1558-1559. Brodrick admires Vonnegut's improvisational approach and regards *Deadeye Dick* as evidence of the novelist's growing maturity.

de Mott, Benjamin. "A Riot of Randomness." *New York Times Book Review* (October 17, 1982): 1. Sees Vonnegut as a soft-hearted moralist and judges *Deadeye Dick* to be better than *Jailbird* but not as good as *Slaughterhouse-Five*.

McInerney, Jay. Review of *Galapagos*. *New York Times Book Review* (September 9, 1990): 12. Admires Vonnegut for continuing to ask the kinds of big questions that a child asks and regards *Hocus Pocus* as Vonnegut's most contemporary and realistic novel in years.

Moore, Lorrie. Review of *Galapagos*. *New York Times Book Review* (October 6, 1985): 7. Regards Vonnegut as a better narrator than plotter. Notes that for Vonnegut survival is not a matter of being fit but being lucky.

Skow, John. "And So It Went." *Time* 136 (September 9, 1990): 73. Admires Vonnegut's prophetic vision as revealed in *Hocus Pocus* but thinks that Hartke is too slight a character to convey it.

Towers, Robert. Review of *Galapagos*. *New York Review of Books* 32 (December 19, 1985): 23-25. Regards *Galapagos* as Vonnegut's strongest work since *Slaughterhouse-Five*.

Jim Baird
University of North Texas

ALICE WALKER
1944

Update

After *The Color Purple* established Alice Walker as America's foremost black female novelist, the reading public waited seven years for her next novel, *The Temple of My Familiar*. During that time Walker worked in active support of numerous causes: abortion rights, the anti-apartheid movement, nuclear disarmament, animal rights, and protection of old-growth forests in California and rain forests in Brazil. Her 1987 nonfiction collection, *Living by the Word*, includes essays, lectures, letters, and journal entries on a wide range of topics that relate to the health of the individual, society, race, nation, and planet.

While not a critical success, *The Temple of My Familiar* was commercially successful, remaining on *The New York Times* best-seller list for over four months. Walker made her first national promotional tour for the book and the paperback rights sold for reportedly $2 million. She currently resides in California, where she has a townhouse in San Francisco and a cabin in the mountains.

Since becoming the first black woman to win the Pulitizer Prize, Walker has attracted increased critical attention. Book-length critical studies of her work have yet to appear, but, in 1988, *Alice Malsenior Walker: An Annotated Bibliography* was published, containing over four hundred annotated entries.

Analysis of Selected Titles

THE TEMPLE OF MY FAMILIAR
The Temple of My Familiar, 1989, novel.

Social Concerns/Themes

An old saying goes: "There are two kinds of people in the world—the kind who divide the world into two kinds of people, and the kind who don't." Walker—who has been accused of seeing the world in terms of black and white, female and male, right and wrong—celebrates in *The Temple of My Familiar* the connectedness of all things. This theme had not previously been central to her fiction. Walker is still concerned with race and sexual relationships and still views the world from the perspective of a black womanist. But with her focus on cosmic consciousness, the label "black womanist" seems too narrow to define her new approach. Although some critics have expanded the label to "new age black womanist," Walker has supplied her own description: "My full title that I've given myself at this juncture is pagan agnostic ecstatic." Whatever the label, she has undeniably broadened her social concerns. Since Walker has always expressed a strong concern for the rights of the excluded and exploited, it is not surprising that she would extend that concern to animal rights and the protection of the environment.

The "familiar" of the title, in fact, (in a more egalitarian way) refers to pets, which have long suffered in their relationship with humanity. According to one of Walker's characters, Lissie, familiars were once treated by women as companions and equals, but that relationship threatened male hegemony and they were driven away. In other stories in the book, Walker describes with equal indignation the wanton destruction of South American rain forests, African complicity with Western powers who dump radioactive wastes in Africa, and the destruction of the ozone layer. In the face of these assaults on the defenseless, Walker contends "it is fatal to see yourself as separate." For her, healthy change will come only when society learns to see itself from a holistic perspective, and with the understanding that all are one.

Walker takes great pains to remythologize the past from a new perspective, presenting a counter discourse to the white male version of the last 500,000 years of human history. Walker's method is to speak through Lissie, a continually reincarnated character, who now tells "dream memories" of former lives. In one of her memories she recalls a time when women had a non-exploitative relationship with animals. In a revision of the biblical story of humanity's separation from Eden, it is a man who brings evil into creation by killing the woman's snake-like familiar. To avert charges of reverse sexism, Walker has Lissie confess that she herself was this man in one of her previous incarnations, and that he was the first white (albino) man. Walker, thus, achieves one of her goals with this story: "to reconnect us to our ancestors. All of us." The white race can be traced back to an African mother.

Walker's view of "connectedness" includes the sexes as well as the races. In another incarnation, Lissie confesses that she was a white woman who passively watched while people of color suffered. Despite her intentions, the danger of Walker's homogenized view of the sexes and races is that it tends to dilute moral responsibility for racism and sexism since, in Walker's view, women and men, and blacks and whites have merely traded places throughout the cycles of human history.

Characters

The Temple of My Familiar contains more characters than all of Walker's other novels combined, including several that reappear from *The Color Purple*. Drawn from various continents, the number and diversity of these characters are appropriate to the theme of the connectedness of each and all. The concept of the unity of all people is further reinforced by having the central characters, who live continents apart physically and mentally, cross paths and develop intimate relationships during the course of the novel.

Lissie and Zede are the two characters who most clearly carry the novel's message of the need for a new vision. Zede, like Lissie, has "dream memories" of her ancestors who trace their lineage from Latin America back to Africa. In her many incarnations Lissie has been both animal and human, male and female, white and black. Although she has more often been exploited than the exploiter, she has been and done all. Both characters (especially Lissie), function primarily as symbols rather than realistic characters.

The other female characters, Fanny and Carlotta, struggle to achieve the self-realization Lissie and Zede have already won. They chafe within the narrow roles defined by the dominant culture. Fanny is unhappy with her subordinate role in both her marriage and a racist society. She has a hatred of oppressors that she fears she cannot control. To develop her sense of selfhood she travels to Africa to observe and learn from female relatives. Carlotta, a much different type of woman, faces essentially the same problem. Abandoned by her husband, she becomes the submissive woman for Fanny's husband that Fanny refused to be. She acts and dresses the part but ultimately, like Fanny, remains unsatisfied. Her search for identity also takes her through new age approaches such as massage and yoga. However, she only discovers her identity through community with other womanists, in particular, through her relationship with Fanny.

If female characters in Walker's novel have to learn to reject the marginalized roles assigned them, Walker's male characters have to learn to accept the side of themselves that they have marginalized—the feminine side. Two of the three male characters have a developed feminine side. Hal, Lissie's husband, is so sensitive to the birth of his wife's first child that he gives up sex to avoid causing such pain, yet he loves delivering his wife's babies (who are fathered by other men). He is effective as a symbol, but as a character he borders on the absurd. Arveyda, the other sensitive black male character, is a new age music star, but with a domestic side. He bakes whole wheat bread and after reading some womanist tracts his wife brings home, he recognizes their author, Shug, as his spiritual mother. Suwelo is the male character most intent on learning to develop his feminine side. Through Lissie's tutelage, he learns to give up his love of pornography, a fetish that symbolizes his desire to continue the oppression of women, and is brought to see women as equals.

By the novel's conclusion, Walker's main characters have all reached the same philosophical viewpoint: nothing is to be excluded from the circle of life. In *The Color Purple*, Celie says that if God listened to black women, life would sure be different. *The Temple of My Familiar* illustrates the efforts of black womanists to transform the world by reviewing the past and countering divisive forces in the present.

Techniques/Literary Precedents

Walker's principal technique in *The Temple of My Familiar* is to revise the Western representation of reality, which depicts itself as separate from and superior to other cultures, by telling stories that stress connection and equality. In her own words, Walker has said: "What I'm doing is literally trying to reconnect us to our ancestors. All of us. I'm really trying to do that because I see that ancient past as the future, that the connection that was original is a connection; if we can affirm it in the present, it will make a different future." From her characters, then, come stories that challenge the established view. Fanny unearths stories of black contributions to American history that have been neglected or suppressed. Lissie presents reinterpretations of ancient myths. Zede recounts horrors and heroism that would have been left in the jungle and out of recorded history. This deconstructive technique might well have been acquired from the feminist movement or from modern critical theory; however, Walker was most probably influenced by the Black Aesthetic of the 1960s. As Elliott Butler-Evans explained the goals of that movement: "The major thrust of Black Aesthetic narratives as oppositional or alternative texts was the production of alternative representations of black life, positing significant self-reconstruction and definition, and the deconstruction of the ideological assumptions underpinning Western constructions of reality."

Walker employs the same deconstructive technique not only on broad cultural topics but also on the characters' personal relationships. In *The Temple of My Familiar* the traditional institution of marriage is a failure. Exclusive pairs fail because one of the partners is always privileged. To achieve sexual egalitarianism, paired relationships must open into triangular ones. Triangles are, after all, woman's sign of peace throughout the novel. Hal and Lissie's relationship is troubled until it opens to include Rafe. Fanny and Suwelo's relationship is exploitative until Arveyda enters in. Arveyda and Carlotta's relationship is marred by jealousy until she is able to accept her mother as having been Arveyda's lover. Paired relationships are broken and eventually characters are healed by the love triangle, which in traditional Western literature invariably spelled disaster. In Walker's novels, however, the destructive triangle is transformed into a circle of cooperation and equality.

The Temple of My Familiar is a unique novel, with few literary precedents. Much like Lissie's dream familiar, it isn't recognizably bird, fish, or reptile. Nevertheless, Walker would claim to owe a debt to Zora Neale Hurston to whom she has often referred as her literary foremother. Hurston's novel, *Their Eyes Were Watching God*, is also concerned with the search for identity in an oppressive and exploitative world. While both novels are concerned with the same struggle, however, the solutions are different. Hurston's character achieves her identity by adhering to her individual artistic vision, while Walker's characters achieve whole, healthy identities through participation in a community of people with a holistic vision of life.

The Temple of My Familiar has perhaps been most influenced by Virginia Woolf's *Orlando* (1928). Walker quotes from the opening of Woolf's novel in an epigraph. Woolf's central character, Orlando, experiences life as a male and later as a female over a period of three centuries. Most importantly, Woolf uses this fantastic technique to expose cultural biases and illustrate the essential equality of the sexes. Walker quotes a passage in *Orlando* in which the young man is batting at the shrunken and suspended head of a Moor. It could be that Walker, while acknowledging her predecessor, is also calling attention to Woolf's selective view of equality.

Relation to Previous Works

In *The Temple of My Familiar* Walker's revolutionary anger of previous works has been displaced by a conciliatory tone, or what she calls a form of "prayer." No antagonists obstruct the development towards pagan ecstasy; consequently, the novel lacks the dramatic intensity that characterized Walker's earlier fiction.

Her projected audience is different as well. Walker was willing to sell the movie rights to *The Color Purple* because she wanted to reach that audience who would not read the novel. *The Temple of My Familiar*, a far more consciously literary work, concerns comfortable middle class professionals, who lounge in kitchens, living rooms, hot tubs, and engage in consciousness-raising discussions. Certainly there will be no movie made of *The Temple of My Familiar;* Walker is addressing a different audience altogether.

The themes that endeared Walker to feminists remain: men are humanized by adopting womanist perspectives, and women are empowered through the community of other women. However, the emphasis on unity rather than the struggle to attain unity has sublimated potential conflict in the novel and, to some critics, resulted in a preachy novel that neither offends nor inspires.

Additional Sources

Bush, Trudy Bloser. "Transforming Vision: Alice Walker and Zora Neale Hurston." *The Christian Century* (November 16, 1988): 1035-1039. Compares Hurston's and Walker's approaches to female empowerment.

Butler-Evans, Elliott. *Race, Gender, and Desire: Narrative Strategies in the Fiction of Toni Cade Bambara, Toni Morrison, and Alice Walker*. Philadelphia: Temple University Press, 1989. Discusses the influence of the Black Aesthetic and the feminist movement on Walker's narrative strategy.

Coetzee, J. M. "The Beginnings of (Wo)man in Africa." *New York Times Book Review* (April 30, 1989): 7. Maintains there are "certain brute realities that cannot be willfully ignored" and so dismisses Walker's revisionary historical approach.

Dreifus, Claudia. "Alice Walker: 'Writing To Save My Life.'" *The Progressive* (August 1989): 29-31. Interview with Walker about *The Temple of My Familiar*.

Hite, Molly. *The Other Side of the Story: Structures and Strategies of Contemporary Feminist Narrative*. Ithaca: Cornell University Press, 1989. Regards *The Color Purple* as a romance.

Pratt, Louis H., and Darnell D. Pratt. *Alice Malsenior Walker: An Annotated Bibliography: 1968-1986*. Westport, CT: Meckler, 1988.

Walker, Alice. "Coral and Turquoise." *New Statesman & Society* (September 15, 1989). Describes composition of *The Temple of My Familiar*.

Wolcott, James. "Party of Animals." *The New Republic* (May 29, 1989): 28-29. Calls Walker's book "the nuttiest novel I've ever read."

Dennis Baeyen
Cuesta College

JOSEPH WAMBAUGH
1937

Update

In 1987 Joseph Wambaugh published *Echoes in the Darkness,* a true crime account that attempts to explain how a group of people who are aware that one of their acquaintances has been threatened with murder, do nothing to protect her or her young children. Wambaugh describes the events leading up to the triple murder, the ensuing investigation, the arrest and trial of the suspects, and the effect of these events on those involved. He also begins a discussion of sociopathy, which he defines as an incurable indifference to the needs and rights of others.

In 1989 Wambaugh published *The Blooding*, which was praised for the excellence of its writing and the clarity with which it explained the new technique of genetic fingerprinting. A nonfiction account of the investigation of two brutal rape-murders which occurred in England, it continues Wambaugh's exploration of sociopathy. The recently developed technique of genetic fingerprinting was used to clear a suspect who had confessed to the crimes. The real murderer was caught when it came to light that he had convinced someone else to take blood and saliva tests in his place. Both *Echoes in the Darkness* and *The Blooding* were best sellers.

Analysis of Selected Titles

THE GOLDEN ORANGE

The Golden Orange, 1990, novel.

Social Concerns/Themes

The Golden Orange refers to Orange County, California, home of the very rich and the very weird. This area of California, including Newport Harbor, the Pacific coast, and Catalina Island, is magnificent, and many of its inhabitants are beautiful; but this paradise is fast being ruined by the greed of its multi-millionaire businessmen and the women who set out to trap them for financial gain. Towns like Newport Beach are also polluted by drug addicts and other petty criminals.

Wambaugh is appalled by the gross materialism that has come to be identified with Orange County. Some of the funnier passages in the novel mock the Southern California yuppie lifestyle: grocery stores that sell white truffles at $1,600 dollars a kilo, individually wrapped white eggplants, and elephant garlic in little white nets; the diesel Mercedes Benz as a despised automobile fit only for employees running errands; women over forty who maintain perfect bodies by means of plastic surgery and constant exercise; huge yachts that never leave Newport Harbor.

He also notes the difficulty of police work in an area where the rich cheat their insurance companies and criminals seem to have more rights than policemen. In such a society only the quixotic would insist on total honesty.

Characters

The major characters are Winnie Farlowe, an alcoholic policeman who retired early because of an injury sustained in chasing a burglar; Buster Wiles, a policeman who does not want to be killed; and Tess Binder, a rich woman who desires to be much richer. Tess seduces Winnie and leads him to fall in love with her. She discourages him from giving up alcohol, the better to control him. Winnie tries to keep his wits about him, but until he hits bottom, he is totally in her control. Only when he sobers up can he realize what has been done to him.

Tess has no goals but a perfect body and the vast sums of money needed to clothe it perfectly. She needs to be the envy of her friends, whose vocation is the acquisition of wealth, usually through marriage and generous divorce settlements. She comes close to falling in love with Winnie, but the intensity of her greed prevents her from entering fully into any other emotion.

Wambaugh's minor characters are well-drawn and entertaining. Chip Simon is the perfect yuppie lawyer who imitates the actor Michael Douglas' hair style and his devotion to greed, as portrayed in the film *Wall Street*. Corky Peebles is an expert on assessing the net worth of everyone around her. The barflies who are Winnie's drinking companions provide more comic touches. They include Guppy Stover, who has never gotten over the fact that she was jilted in 1945; Bilge O'Toole, who races his turtle, Irma, against Regis, a turtle owned by Carlos Tuna; and Spoon, who owns the bar, Spoon's Landing, and plays the spoons as a musical instrument.

Winnie is the sympathetic character whom the reader wants to warn against the manipulations of Tess and his own self-destructive drinking. It is clear that he is in danger from both. Tess appears too compliant and eager to ply him with liquor. Clearly she is up to something. As it turns out, she means Winnie no real harm, but her need for money is much greater than her need for him.

Techniques/Literary Precedents

The Golden Orange seems to be an old-fashioned whodunit. Called upon to protect Tess from a dangerous killer, Winnie begins to suspect that her father's death was a homicide. Later on, another suspicious death occurs, and he holds himself responsible until he begins to suspect his closest friend.

Wambaugh withholds information about the relationship between Winnie's friend Buster and Tess in order to keep the reader, as well as Winnie, in suspense. We know that Winnie is really a good person, despite his unfortunate addiction to drink, and that Tess is not a good person, because of the many hints Wambaugh provides. Tess is a temptress and a dangerous woman; she does all she can to corrupt the naive hero. In this sense, she is a direct descendant of the seductresses created by late romantic British poets of the nineteenth century, such as Algernon Swinburne and Oscar Wilde.

Winnie would like to be the conventional hard-boiled detective in the tradition of Dashiel Hammet's tough and incorruptible operatives. He is also the heir of the wounded hero such as Jake Barnes in Ernest Hemingway's *The Sun Also Rises*, and his character can be traced to the Byronic hero of the early nineteenth century. Unlike earlier heroes, however, Winnie cannot drink with impunity, nor can he solve the mystery until he comes to terms with his alcoholism. American novels of the 1920s, particularly those by Ernest Hemingway, F. Scott Fitzgerald and John Dos Passos often portrayed binges and hangovers, usually idealizing excessive drinking as the height of sophisticated behavior. Wambaugh, on the contrary, shows the destructive aspect of alcohol with devastating realism.

The social satire in the novel is reminiscent of that of nineteenth-century British novelists Charles Dickens and William Thackeray, and the British eighteenth-century poets Jonathan Swift and Alexander Pope. Swift and Pope were particularly incensed by women who attempted to improve their appearance through artificial means.

Relation to Previous Works

The Golden Orange, Wambaugh's first novel in five years, shares with his nonfiction works on crime, the conviction that criminals have sociopathic personalities that are incurable. He reminds us of the viciousness of these criminals in a scene in which a tape of a tortured child's screams is played. The murderer made the tape for his own enjoyment.

The California setting is familiar from Wambaugh's previous works; *The Golden Orange* is not set in a slum or a ghetto, however, but in one of the wealthiest communities in America. Life here is very different from English middle-class life portrayed in the nonfiction *The Blooding*, but it seems just as authentic.

Unlike Wambaugh's earlier books, *The Golden Orange* deals with the difficulties inherent in every person's life, not just those of police officers. In Wambaugh's late twentieth-century America, it is difficult just to get by, and almost impossible to survive honorably. Yet Wambaugh believes that a spark of decency still exists in even the most unlikely people.

Additional Sources

Friedman, Kinky. "Life in a Spiritual Towaway Zone." *New York Times Book Review* (May 6, 1990): 7, 9. Review of *The Golden Orange*.

Barbara J. Horwitz
Long Island University
C. W. Post Campus

EUDORA WELTY
1909

Update

Since *The Optimist's Daughter* (published first in 1969 in *The New Yorker* and issued in book form by Random House in 1972), Eudora Welty has concentrated upon collections of her photographs, stories, and essays. In 1971 Random House published *One Time, One Place: Mississippi in the Depression; A Snapshot Album*, a widely praised collection of photographs taken during her employment by the Works Project Administration (WPA). *The Eye of the Story: Selected Essays and Reviews* followed in 1978. The 1980 volume, *The Collected Short Stories of Eudora Welty*, is a testament to Welty's stature as a short story writer. In April 1983, she was invited to give the first series of the William E. Massey Lectures in American Civilization at Harvard University. Her lectures ("Listening," "Learning to See," and "Finding a Voice") were published in 1984 as *One Writer's Beginnings* and became a bestseller.

Analysis of Selected Titles

THE OPTIMIST'S DAUGHTER
The Optimist's Daughter, 1972, novel.

Social Concerns

Like her fellow Mississippian William Faulkner, Eudora Welty deals with the conflicting behavioral codes of the waning southern gentry and the emerging lower class. Because the events are seen from Laurel's patrician perspective, the treatment of Fay and her family is almost entirely unsympathetic.

Considering her stepmother a gold-digger, Laurel McKelva Hand has neither accepted the "unsuitable" woman her father married nor understood the reasons for his choice. She avoided any association with Fay until Judge McKelva's surgery forces them to spend hours together in the hospital. Angered by Fay's failure to conform to the code of wifely solicitude which Becky McKelva undoubtedly would have upheld, Laurel makes only token gestures toward communication with Fay, and these Fay rebuffs.

Fay's lack of concern also irks Dr. Courtland, Judge McKelva's surgeon and longtime friend. She minimizes the severity of her husband's damaged retina, attempting to dissuade him from the surgery. The hospital nurse too is annoyed by Fay's selfishness, as she scolds the Judge for spoiling her visit to New Orleans, insists that he look at the shoes she has bought, and finally shakes him. Likewise, all the women of Mount Salus, Mississippi, are especially offended by Fay's excessive and inappropriate show of grief at her husband's funeral, and Laurel is embarrassed, considering such behavior an affront to the memory of her mother.

On the other hand, Fay belongs to a subculture which does not accept the code of reserve and propriety so important to Laurel and her friends. In the hospital waiting room, the Dalzell family echo Fay's complaints about the condescending attitudes of the doctor and nurse, and accepting her as one of their own, they comfort her when the Judge dies, while glaring at Laurel as an outsider. At the Judge's funeral, Mrs. Chisom, Fay's mother, considers Fay's wailing and flinging herself on the casket a demonstration of love and grief second only to her own. Even Laurel is drawn to Fay's silent, but observant, nephew Wendell. Also appealing is the simple dignity of Grandpa Chisom, who brings Laurel a sack of pecans which he has shelled as he traveled by bus to the funeral.

Themes

In *One Writer's Beginnings*, Eudora Welty discusses her lifelong awareness of time. In *The Optimist's Daughter*, an example of the highly introspective fiction that Welty has called "inside stories," Laurel must become aware of time and learn to deal with the changes it brings. Unlike the rose everyone refers to as "Becky's climber," the human characters cannot continue to thrive indefinitely. When the novel opens, Becky McKelva has already been dead for more than ten years, and within a few pages the Judge too dies. The remainder of the novel chronicles Laurel's thoughts and feelings as she attempts to regain her emotional security by cleaning and rearranging the furniture until her family home looks as it did when her mother was alive. Only when Laurel has spent several days alone in the house and has reviewed all her family history, pleasant and unpleasant, can she destroy the most intimate artifacts of her mother's life. Relinquishing ownership of the house to Fay frees Laurel, just as being driven out of the house allows the trapped chimney swift to survive and to return to its own environment.

Although Laurel is a middle-aged widow, her experience is in essence a belated coming of age. Her brief, childless marriage has actually changed her life very little; she recalls the marriage as "perfect," but her husband—who seems to exist primarily in her dreams—is almost a chivalric abstraction to her. Likewise, despite the unhappy experiences of the intervening years, her parents remain for her the dashing, heroic figures and the romantic lovers of the family stories she heard in childhood. Certain of her father's literary taste, she dutifully reads *Nicholas Nickleby* to him for hours, and only after his death does she realize that Dickens was her mother's favorite author. When she returns to Mount Salus, time seems frozen at a point just before her wedding; her bridesmaids gather to welcome her, and they engage in the same conversations and exchange the same "secret" signals that they used when they were young girls. Only when Laurel achieves the maturity to accept change can she accurately evaluate herself and her future.

A third theme is the complex nature of reality. Initially everything seems simple to Laurel, but she soon learns otherwise. Her father's eye operation is not precisely routine, but neither is it considered life-threatening; nevertheless, even though the surgery is successful and the recuperation is proceeding according to Dr. Courtland's expectations, the Judge dies. Similarly, Laurel has always considered her parents' marriage the perfect union of two virtually identical personalities; however, as she sorts through her mother's letters, she is forced to comprehend that her parents were not always completely compatible or idyllically happy. Further, Laurel sees Fay as a totally insensitive interloper who has taken advantage of the Judge and desecrated Becky's shrine—her home. Eventually, though, Laurel must accept her father's relationship with Fay as his way of satisfying his need to continue living after his wife's death and his daughter's departure. Likewise, once Laurel understands that tangible reminders—such as the soapstone boat her father carved and the breadboard her husband made—are less significant than memories, she can endure Fay's determined efforts to place the stamp of her personality upon the McKelva house. Finally, as Laurel hears her father's longtime friends and associates idealize the Judge beyond her recognition, she realizes that the townspeople have begun to create their own mythical Judge Clinton McKelva, a collection of images that resemble the actual man perhaps even less than her own memories. In short, once again Welty demonstrates that reality is a series of layers, some pleasant and some unpleasant, and that one's perception is subtly modified by each new realization.

Characters

The central character in *The Optimist's Daughter* is Laurel McKelva Hand, but since she is also the narrative voice, her personality must be deduced largely from her actions and her reactions to other characters. Somewhat condescending toward Fay and others whose status she considers inferior, Laurel has always taken for granted her relationships with her family and with the people of Mount Salus. She has reacted to the challenge of her mother's powerful personality by making a life for herself in the North, but she considers herself a dutiful daughter, remaining by her father's bedside and reading to him for hours, even though this seems less spectacular than her mother's heroism in a similar situation. Before her period of self-imposed isolation in the family home, Laurel repressed all negative memories of her mother, and she remains bound by the past. To free herself, she must complete an inward journey through time, examining her parents' history as well as her own and recognize her tendency to romanticize her family as myth. Until she understands the complexity of truth, Laurel is helpless to deal with the unpleasant elements in her life, but once she sees confluence as the essence of human existence, she gains a strength of her own—parallel to, but different from, her mother's.

Fay McKelva (née Wanda Fay Chisom), Judge McKelva's second wife, is the antithesis of Laurel and her mother. A typist employed by the Judge during a legal convention, she is as loud, crude, and overblown as Becky was quiet, reserved, and understated. To the chagrin of most of the Mount Salus women, Fay does not even attempt to conform to their code of appropriate behavior, and her display of grief for the Judge is so excessive that all of them consider it fakery designed to enlist the sympathy of the town's sentimental men. Secretive about herself and her background, Fay also rebuffs Laurel's attempt to get to know her. When Laurel asks about her family, Fay says they are all dead and—perhaps echoing Becky's stories of caring for her dying father—that she nursed Grandpa Chisom through his final illness and he died in her arms. She seems unembarrassed by the contradictions when Grandpa shows up at the funeral, having come by bus from Bigbee, Mississippi. The rest of the reportedly dead family—Mrs. Chisom, Sis, Bubba, and Wendell—then arrive from their home in Madrid, Texas. In fact, emphasizing the reversal in which she is surrounded by family and Laurel is alone, Fay vehemently declares the importance of close family ties and impulsively decides to return to Texas with her loving family.

The "optimist" is Clinton McKelva, retired judge and leading citizen of Mount Salus, Mississippi. Laurel regards him as isolated by his illness, but he has evidently long been aware of the breakdown in communication between himself and his daughter. Hospitalized following eye surgery, he must lie absolutely still, and he gradually retreats within himself, becoming increasingly reluctant to make the effort to speak or follow Laurel's movements with his good eye. Until his marriage to Fay, Laurel has never distinguished between his personality and her mother's; and she is amazed at the changes she sees in him. She observes that he has never before described himself as an optimist, and she regards this remark—like his marriage to Fay and his subsequent indulgence of her—as further evidence of a weakness and folly probably resulting from his age. Laurel does not understand the attraction between Fay and her father because she cannot comprehend his need for a relationship with a woman who is not as strong as, or perhaps stronger, than he.

A background presence in the novel is Becky Thurston McKelva, the Judge's first wife. As Laurel and the townspeople remember her, Becky represents an unmatchable ideal. Not only was she the perfect mother, homemaker, and hostess, but she was unbelievably brave, having run back into her burning home to retrieve her set of Dickens's novels and, alone, having transported her dying father by raft to Baltimore for medical treatment. Only gradually do Laurel's memories of her mother's later blindness, bitterness, and paranoia emerge, suggesting that Becky was not completely perfect after all.

Techniques

As in her earlier work, Welty displays an outstanding eye for detail and ear for dialect, which contributes to the believability of her characters. As the reader moves with Laurel through the house and relives with her the family history, the abundance of physical detail reinforces the reflective, almost brooding, tone and creates the sense of awe with which she must approach the past. Likewise, Welty's accurate recording of metaphor, vocabulary, syntax, and idiom brings individuality to stock characters such as the sentimental Major Bullock, the genteel Miss Adele, the whining Dalzell family, and the comically pretentious Chisoms. Moreover, as in her other fiction, Welty distinguishes between the characters who are talkers and those who avoid talk or, like Fay, use it as a means to conceal their feelings.

Welty makes limited, but effective use of symbols. For example, there are parallels between Laurel and the chimney swift trapped in the McKelva house. Neither the bird nor Laurel can find a way out of this captivity, but for both of them the alternatives are being forced out or destroyed. Once driven out, both are able to soar.

The theme of nature's continuity—as opposed to human mortality—is introduced by the Judge's reference to cutting back Becky's climber, a hardy rose loved by his first wife. The Judge's attitude towards the past is seen in his spur-of-the-moment decision to prune the rose: unlike his daughter, he is not obsessed with objects and their associations with the past. He tends the rose, not according to the traditional schedule, but during an idle moment when he happens to notice it. Also in cutting back Becky's climber, the Judge prepares for new growth in the next season, for another stage in the rose's development.

In contrast, Laurel is caught up in physical objects. She carefully removes the nail polish from her father's antique desk, eliminating all trace of Fay's destructive presence. Coming upon the little soapstone boat in which her father carved his initials, C C M McK, she offers it as a memento to Adele Courtland, the woman she would have chosen as her father's second wife. Only later does she understand the reason Adele refuses it. When she finds the breadboard her husband made for her mother, now badly scarred by Fay's cracking of walnuts, Laurel intends that this will be her only memento of her past. In forcing Fay to relinquish it, she sees that to Fay it is meaningless except as a symbol of power, and suddenly she knows that for her too its value is symbolic. Laurel recognizes a more powerful symbol in her recurring dream of seeing the confluence of the Ohio and Mississippi Rivers, and she realizes that the greatest confluence is human memory.

Relation to Previous Works

Perhaps the clearest parallel to *The Optimist's Daughter* is Welty's first full-length novel, *Delta Wedding* (1946). Both works portray a family involved in a significant ritual: a marriage in *Delta Wedding* and a funeral in *The Optimist's Daughter*. In each case the family also must deal with an outsider of a different social class; Troy Flavin of *Delta Wedding* is only sightly more acceptable to the clannish Fairchild family than Fay is to Laurel and the women of Mount Salus. In fact, both novels capture the dual nature of the close-knit southern family which nurtures those people born into it, but isolates in-laws as outsiders. Similar themes are developed in *The Ponder Heart*, whose narrator is a less introspective and more comic version of Laurel.

ONE WRITER'S BEGINNINGS

One Writer's Beginnings, 1984, memoirs.

Themes

More memoir than actual autobiography, *One Writer's Beginnings* is divided into three sections corresponding to Eudora Welty's three lectures in April 1983 for the William E. Massey Lecture Series in American Civilization at Harvard University. Each section develops a separate theme.

"Listening," a discussion of sounds and their effect upon the writer-to-be, begins with a description of the many clocks in the Welty household and the subsequent influence of time upon the eldest child, Eudora. Until she had younger brothers for playmates, Welty spent most of her time listening to adults as they talked and read aloud. She also describes learning to read silently and yet "hearing" the words in the books she borrowed from Jackson's Carnegie Library. As a result, she developed the ability to sense when words and sentences sound right, and she has remained conscious of the way her writing sounds. In this section too she credits her brothers with helping her develop the good sense of humor essential for a writer.

"Learning to See" focuses upon the backgrounds of the Welty and Andrews families, beginning with Welty's recollections of the family's summer travels, by automobile, to visit the Weltys in Ohio and the Andrewses in West Virginia. Christian Welty's cheerful attitude toward the journey led his wife to refer to him frequently as an optimist. From the pleasures and difficulties of the journey itself, Welty soon turns to an exploration of her parents' relationship with the Andrews family. Clearly Chestina Andrews Welty served as the model for the most admirable traits of Becky Thurston McKelva.

"Finding a Voice" chronicles Welty's individual development, including an account of her railroad journey with her father, a possible inspiration for a similar account in *Delta Wedding*. She describes the types of writing she did at Mississippi State College for Women and at the University of Wisconsin, where she transferred in her junior year. However, she ascribes much of her literary development to her days as a junior publicity agent for the Works Project Administration, when she traveled through the state of Mississippi, using camera and pen to record everyday life during the Great Depression. In particular she mentions the origins of the bottle tree ("Livvie") and "gone to borry some fire" ("The Death of a Traveling Salesman").

External influences alone do not make a writer, however, and Welty also explains how she searched for connection and sequence in experience, especially after her father's relatively sudden death at age fifty-two. Although she insists that no single character is her spokesman, Welty apparently embarked upon an inward journey of discovery parallel to that of Laurel McKelva Hand, arriving at a similar theory of confluence through human memory, the belief that all which is remembered joins and continues to live.

Characters

The central character is, of course, Eudora Welty herself. Although she mentions people associated in various ways with the Welty family, the only other significant characters are her parents, Christian and Chestina Andrews Welty.

Techniques

As in all of Eudora Welty's writing, the meticulous attention to physical detail makes experiences come alive for the reader.

Relation to Previous Works

While *One Writer's Beginnings* probably is the most closely related to *The Optimist's Daughter*, reading these memoirs leads to a more complete understanding of all of Welty's fiction.

Additional Sources

"Eudora (Alice) Welty." In *Contemporary Literary Criticism*. Vol. 33. Detroit: Gale, 1985. Collected excerpts from a number of scholarly articles analyzing various Welty novels and stories.

VandeKieff, Ruth M. "Eudora Welty." In *Dictionary of Literary Biography Yearbook*. Detroit: Gale, 1987. Discussion of Welty's literary theories and practices with special emphasis upon *Eye of the Story* and *One Writer's Beginnings*.

"Welty, Eudora." In *Contemporary Authors*. Vol. 12. Detroit: Gale, 1974. List of works and biographical information with a few critical comments and a brief bibliography.

Charmaine Allmon Mosby
Western Kentucky University

MORRIS WEST
1916

Update

Morris West continues to enjoy tremendous popularity worldwide. His novels have been translated into twenty-seven languages and attract a wide readership. Having returned to residence in Australia after years of living away from his native land, he maintains his interest in contemporary world events and world crises, using them as the springboard for his creative works. A deeply religious man who spent twelve years of his life in a monastery, West remains concerned about issues affecting the Roman Catholic faith and its place in the modern world. He seems especially interested in the role the concept of evil plays in modern philosophy and theology. He says that evil "is the absence of everything human, a black hole in a collapsed cosmos in which even the face of God is eternally invisible." This idea is featured prominently in *Lazarus*, the concluding novel of a trilogy that includes *The Shoes of the Fisherman* (1963), and *The Clowns of God* (1981).

West's latest novel, *Masterclass* (1991), is a thriller that takes readers into the world, and underworld, of international art collecting. The protagonist is art historian Max Mather, who is repaying favors to his millionairess lover by researching her family archives. She bequeaths him a memento of his choice from the family holdings, and he selects a package containing what he believes are Raphael drawings, although the other family members have no idea of the value of his choice. In a scam to have his Raphaels "discovered" in order to avoid legal recourse by the family, he joins forces with gallery owner Anne-Maire Loredon, his ex-lover who has become entangled in the murder of one of her artists. As the story unfurls, Morris weaves a morality tale whose moral center is the function of deception in making choices.

Analysis of Selected Titles

CASSIDY

Cassidy, 1986, novel.

Social Concerns/Themes

Morris West's *Cassidy* is a novel with global as well as personal dimensions. The title character is an influential Australian politician who has become rich and politically powerful by establishing contacts with various underworld figures in his own country and abroad. Upon his death, he leaves the settlement of his estate to his son-in-law Martin Gregory, the real protagonist of the novel. Gregory was once Cassidy's protégé but became estranged from his father-in-law. As Gregory tries to unravel the complicated skein of associations through which Cassidy amassed his considerable fortune, the reader is shown the pervasive influence of criminal elements on contemporary politics and international business. The novel suggests that honest men have little hope of ridding society of this corruption.

Concurrent with this global concern is a more individual one: Gregory's personal quest for knowledge. Once Cassidy's apparent business heir, and partially responsible for Cassidy's estrangement from his only daughter, Gregory seeks to understand the man who has poisoned his own life and that of his family. Underlying this search is the archetypal quest of a son to kill or replace the father, for although Cassidy himself may be dead, his memory haunts Gregory and his wife. West is as interested in dramatizing the expurgation of this powerful father-figure from Martin Gregory's life as he is in exposing the seamy underside of politics and international business.

Characters

As the title suggests, the figure of Charles Parnell Cassidy, head of one of Australia's major provinces, dominates the action of the novel. Yet Cassidy appears only briefly in the novel. Martin Gregory, his son-in-law, is a successful lawyer with substantial connections to the London banking industry. Estranged from his father-in-law because of Cassidy's high-handed treatment of everyone with whom he comes in contact, Gregory has established himself on another continent. When he finds himself made executor of Cassidy's estate, he is forced to re-enter the world of Australian politics—a world riddled with criminal elements. The novel is built around Gregory's transformation as he adapts himself to the ruthless ways of Cassidy's associates.

Carrying out the terms of the will, Gregory learns to deal with corrupt politicians, drug dealers who have infiltrated legitimate business interests in Australia (and throughout the world), as well as gangsters and military men who find murder a simple method of removing obstacles to their financial and political comfort. In the course of the novel Gregory is constantly tempted to compromise his own ethics in an attempt to extricate himself and his family from this web of underworld intrigue. Additionally, there is a strong subplot involving the love-hate relationship Gregory and his wife have for Cassidy, whom they revered and admired but whose ruthlessness and disregard for law they could not understand or accept.

Techniques
Cassidy is first and foremost an adventure novel. Heavily dependent on plotting and suspense devices, the novel moves quickly from incident to incident. The narrative is told from the point of view of Martin Gregory, and it achieves its impact from the sense of discovery and the impending doom that he feels as he learns the details of Cassidy's political empire. West devotes little attention to character development (minor characters are especially superficial) or to an examination of motives. Setting is suggested rather than detailed; West's interest lies primarily in exploring the events in which his protagonist is involved. Like many popular novels, *Cassidy* relies on the reader's acceptance of conventional morality regarding such issues as drugs and prostitution, and of the reader's often strong, if unexpressed, interest in power politics and sexual relationships.

Relation to Previous Works
Cassidy is another in West's series of novels that use the contemporary scene as a backdrop for his exploration of men and women in conflict. The protagonist of this novel is strongly reminiscent of John Spada in *Proteus* (1979) and of Gunnar Thorkild in *The Navigator* (1976); all three find themselves in conflict with global forces that threaten the stability of world order, and all three must find ways to extricate themselves and their loved ones from situations that pose serious personal danger.

LAZARUS
Lazarus, 1990, novel.

Social Concerns/Themes
Lazarus is West's third novel about the modern Roman Catholic papacy. In it, conservative Pope Leo XIV undergoes major heart by-pass surgery. He emerges from the operation a new man in several respects, most notably in his view of the future of his Church. Through his protagonist, West explores the inner workings of the Vatican bureaucracy and how Church politics influence the doctrines that Catholics throughout the world are expected to follow. At the heart of the novel

are two central questions. Should the Church continue as it has for centuries, recognizing the pronouncements of past popes as inviolable dictates, binding for all time? Or is it time for Rome to admit that dogmas imposed by former pontiffs need to be be modified to fit changing societies and advances in technology?

West is on the side of those who would like to see the Church initiate reforms and promulgate more relaxed rules regarding subjects such as birth control. West's views are expressed obliquely yet clearly in his careful delineation of characters who represent differing viewpoints within the Church. Those who opt for a revision of the Church's position on many social issues and who question the current methods by which the Church is run, receive more sympathetic treatment. Indeed, the protagonist himself moves gradually from a hard-line position on issues of doctrine toward a view that decentralization in decision-making and toleration of differences are in the best interests of the Church.

As in several of his earlier novels, notably *The Clowns of God* (1981) and *Cassidy* (1987), West gives substantial attention to the problem of international terrorism. When his protagonist chooses to have his heart by-pass operation at a private clinic in Rome, he becomes a target of opportunity for Middle East radicals who wish to assassinate him as a means of demonstrating their ability to kill anyone, anywhere. The Mossad, the Israeli intelligence agency, steps in to protect the pontiff, foiling the terrorists' scheme. The terrorists come to consider the success of their mission a point of honor, and much of the last quarter of the novel builds to the climax of the terrorist assassination attempt.

The combination of these themes suggests West's deep philosophical interest in questions he considers of vital importance. How can people live the good life in an increasingly complex and dangerous world? Can one good person make a difference? Can religion offer a plausible antidote to the chaos and evil that seem to dominate everyday living, not only for those in positions of importance in society, but for the common man and woman as well? The events he depicts in *Lazarus* offer glimmers of hope that the answer to all these questions is a qualified "yes." But the novel is hardly a resounding affirmation that man has much hope for changing the world for good at any time in the near future.

Characters/Techniques

A host of characters populates *Lazarus,* and West constantly shifts the point of view among them to give readers a varied perspective on the action. As one might expect, the author's primary focus is on Pope Leo XIV, formerly Cardinal Ludovico Gadda, an Italian who has succeeded the mystic Gregory XVII upon the latter's abdication. Gregory had thrown the Church into turmoil by claiming to have had a private revelation of the end of the world, and by proposing radical alterations in the way the Church should conduct its affairs. Leo XIV, a hard-line traditionalist, who has worked to reaffirm the traditional teachings and practices of the Church, undergoes a spiritual experience as a result of his heart surgery. One of the central concerns in *Lazarus* is Leo's attempt to reverse the policies he established before his surgery; he finds considerable opposition both from within and without the Vatican. Simultaneously, he becomes an assassination target for Arab terrorists who want to make a political statement about their power in Europe. Hence, Leo, his advisors, and friends must cope with a looming threat to his personal safety while trying to deal with the monumental change in philosophy the pontiff wishes to bring about in the Church.

As he does in most of his novels, West introduces a number of characters of various nationalities whose lives are intertwined with his protagonist's. Anton Drexel, an elderly German who is the senior Cardinal at the Vatican, helps Leo overcome his doubts about reforming the Church. He also takes Leo to his farm near Rome to recuperate, and there introduces him to the group of handicapped children he supports. Among them is Britte Lundberg, a brilliant child whose mother is a nurse at the clinic where Leo's heart surgery is performed. Tove Lundberg, a Swede, is a sensitive woman who nevertheless cannot believe in religion; she presents a gentle foil to Leo's insistence on the religious dimensions of human activity. Sergio Salviati, Leo's surgeon, is an Italian Jew; through him the pope comes under the protection of Israel's secret intelligence agency, the Mossad. Two Irish priests also play key roles in the book: Malachy O'Rahilly is the pope's personal secretary—and an alcoholic; Matt Neylen, a junior Vatican diplomat, suffers a crisis of faith and leaves the priesthood. These characters provide ample opportunities for West to introduce the conflicts that Leo must confront and, through the pope's reactions, to make shrewd observations about the possibilities—and limitations—that men of goodwill have to shape the world for good.

Related Titles

Though it can be read independently of its predecessors in West's trilogy, *Lazarus* contains many references to the two other novels that deal with the issue of the Roman Catholic papacy: *The Shoes of the Fisherman* (1963) and *The Clowns of God* (1981). In each, West traces the career of an extraordinary pope who is forced to confront a world where technology offers new challenges to traditional Roman Catholic teaching. The three major characters are strikingly different, yet their responses to the crises they face share certain important similarities. When pressed to act, they do so with a firm faith that God will guide their actions and that anything done from motives of love for their fellow humans will somehow come to good. All three novels suggest—with subtle irony—both the efficacy of the religious approach to solving world problems, and the inadequacy of such methods in circumstances where other men act without respect for individual or collective human dignity.

Additional Sources

West, Morris L. "A Perception of Evil." *America* 166 (December 23-30, 1989): 466-469. The novelist explores the nature of evil as it is manifested in the modern world, offering possible theological explanations for the phenomenon. Valuable companion piece for students of West's novels, most of which deal with this subject as a prominent theme.

―――――. "The Seven Deadly Sins." *America* 167 (April 28, 1990): 422-426. Autobiographical account of West's days as a monk, providing an explanation of some of his reasons for leaving the monastery. Useful to explain West's continuing interest in religious matters, especially those dealing with Roman Catholicism.

Laurence W. Mazzeno
Mesa State College

T. H. WHITE
1906-1964

Publishing History

Terence Hanbury White had an extensive and unusually varied literary career. Famous for mainly one work, the very popular *The Once and Future King* (1958), he published several other novels, diaries, journals, poems, and considerable nonfiction. His first book was *Loved Helen and Other Poems,* published in both England and the United States in 1929, the year of his graduation from Cambridge. He then began work on five novels at the same time, including two mysteries, *Dead Mr. Nixon* (1931) and *Darkness at Pemberley* (1932). White published two other novels, *They Winter Abroad* (1932) and *First Lesson* (1932), under the pseudonym of James Aston. Although most of his novels were unsuccessful, his journals *England Have My Bones* (1936) and *The Goshawk* (1951), and his translation, *The Bestiary: A Book of Beasts* (1954), were well-received by critics. His only successful novel apart from his Arthurian works was *Mistress Masham's Repose* (1954). Two of his works were published posthumously, *America at Last* (1965) and *The Book of Merlyn* (1977). White's masterpiece, *The Once and Future King,* was published as a single work in 1958, but the first three books of the tetralogy had previously been published separately: *The Sword in the Stone* (1938), *The Witch in the Wood* (later to be called *The Queen of Air and Darkness,* 1939), and *The Ill-Made Knight* (1940).

Critical Reception, Honors, Popularity

Although widely acknowledged as a major writer, T. H. White has had an extraordinarily uneven career in terms of both popular and critical acclaim. Best known for his Arthurian tetralogy, he began his career writing poetry but was never recognized as a poet. He then turned to fiction, producing five novels which failed to attract a readership. Always experimental, he wrote mysteries, adventures, and romances. His fictional masterpiece *The Once and Future King,* however, was an instant and overwhelming success. Its first book, *The Sword in the Stone,* was popular with readers of all ages and inspired the Walt Disney film of the same name. The entire work was received enthusiastically by readers and reviewers alike in England and the United States. Its adaptation to a Broadway musical and later to a film attests to its success, as does its impact on the popular modern image of medieval life.

White's sequel to Jonathan Swift's *Gulliver's Travels* (1726), *Mistress Masham's Repose*, is a minor satirical masterpiece. It has not achieved the popularity it deserves because it has been mistakenly regarded as a children's book. Ironically, Swift's satire suffered the same fate.

Analysis of Selected Titles

THE ONCE AND FUTURE KING
The Once and Future King, 1958, novel.

Social Concerns/Themes

The central theme of this ambitious retelling of the Arthurian legend is the conflict of Might and Right. White remarked that he had the Matter of Britain on his mind for twenty years, wanting "to deal with every side of it—with the clash between Might and Right, man's place in nature, and the problem of war" along with the personal tragedy of King Arthur. In the first book, *The Sword in the Stone*, which takes place during the childhood of Wart (young Arthur's nickname), the future king is taught by Merlyn to abhor the unnaturalness of war. The boy learns through observing the geese fly overhead that boundaries are imaginary lines, not worth fighting for. As a king facing battle at the end of the final book (*Candle in the Wind*), he reiterates his lifelong belief that war is "fought about nothing—literally nothing." Although belligerence and violence exist in nature, only humans fight to prove who is right about imaginary matters like boundaries. It is Arthur's goal to defend and preserve Right rather than to impose control through the use of force.

Closely related to the theme of conflict is that of man's role in nature. White's intense interest in the natural world gave him a perspective of distance on humanity, which he found sadly wanting in many ways. Many of his views are represented through Merlyn, whose tutoring of Wart establishes the idealism of the future King Arthur. In the opening book of the tetralogy, several episodes satirize human nature in comparison with other creatures. White points out, for example, that only six species kill their own members, five of which are ants; the sixth is human. In the episode in which Wart talks with an embryo, the point is made that whereas other species requested God at their creation to give them specific distinguishing traits, the humans did not ask for any one in particular but simply thanked God for giving them a multitude of natural gifts. The badger, however, asserts that the human race has misused those gifts in order to become the dominant race.

Also important in the opening work is the theme of education. White believed in the value and joy of learning but was highly critical of institutional education. Several passages satirize private schools, probably reflecting the author's own unhappy experiences. Merlyn's inspiring soliloquy on learning praises it as a source of lifelong pleasure and fulfillment. As he demonstrates with his pupil Wart, however, experience is a better teacher than textbooks. Merlyn's oneness with nature enables him to provide the future king with direct experience of its many wonders.

Nature is also a major theme in the book. Not only does Wart learn about various animal species through his transformations but he also lives close to the rhythms of nature. In White's idealized depiction of rural life in medieval England, the seasonal cycle is the basis for most activities. The distinctive joys of spring, summer, fall, and winter delight all who live in this setting.

Partly because of its closeness to nature, the medieval way of life becomes a theme in the book. White found much to object to in modern industrialized society, and in his revisioning of the Arthurian age he focuses on the advantages of rural life, of handicrafts, of outdoor sports and activities. The line between work and play is slight, so that, for example, haying is both at once. The communal festivities at holidays are depicted as appealing to all, young and old, rich and poor.

Finally, the timelessness of the ideal Camelot is a pervasive theme. White deliberately incorporates many anachronisms, particularly in regard to Merlyn, who lives backwards in time. Often for comic effect, these violations of realistic time nonetheless make a point about the eternal image of the ideal life.

Characters

It is one of the paradoxes of the traditional Arthurian legend that King Arthur is one of the least individualized of the many characters. In a sense this is inevitable since he is the hero-king, a mythic entity rather than an individual. White's characterization transcends this limitation by showing Arthur's development from youth to maturity. The young Wart is realistically portrayed, effectively contrasted with his step-brother Kay. Wart's zest for experience, his tenderness and sensitivity to nature and its creatures, his strong ethical convictions—all help to distinguish him as a promising prince. As Arthur the King he comes to recognize himself as fated for tragic failure, but at the end, when he calmly awaits what he knows will be his last battle, he feels "clear-headed" and "ready to begin again."

The most original and memorable character is Merlyn, who undertakes the tutelage of Wart. Living backwards in time gives him insights unavailable to others, and frequently his moral examples are drawn from recent history. In a long discussion with Arthur about whether Might should enforce Right he cites his memory of a certain Austrian who felt that way. Often his confusion of memory and prophecy is comic, as he is uncertain whether an event is past or about to occur. Another source of comedy is his occasional absent-minded spells that go wrong.

Merlyn's appearance is striking but also somewhat comic. He wears a tall, pointed hat; his long, flowing gown is imprinted with the signs of the zodiac and other cabalistic symbols; he has a long white beard and carries a wand of lignum. Perched on his shoulder most of the time is his owl, Archimedes, who nests in his hair and leaves droppings over his gown. The wizard is in part a self-image of the author, who also had an owl named Archimedes.

Merlyn is also a serious character. An ideal tutor for Wart, partly because of his oneness with nature, he is able to transform Wart into many different animals through his magic. He also offers the mature King Arthur sage advice on ruling the kingdom. It is ultimately the memory of the wizard's instruction that cheers Arthur on the eve of his doom. White's Merlyn is a masterful characterization.

Another highly original character is Lancelot, hero of the third book, *The Ill-Made Knight*. White interprets the tradition of the knight "mal fait" as suggesting physical ugliness as well as sinfulness. Lancelot has an extremely ugly face, which he views frequently in a shiny kettle surface. Partly because of this defect, he is determined to become the best knight in the entire world. This dichotomy between the terrible physical reality and the noble spiritual ideal becomes the clue to Lancelot's inner conflict. White's character is therefore much more complex than in the medieval sources. Ever torn between his sexual desires and his spiritual aspirations, manifested in love for both Guenevere and Arthur, Lancelot struggles to become godlike. Eventually the ill-made knight, in spite of his guilt, is permitted to perform a minor miracle, healing a wounded comrade, achieving a moral victory even though he is not destined to attain the Grail that he seeks.

White's villains are less complex than his heroes. Both Morgause, the title role in *The Queen of Air and Darkness,* and Mordred are as much symbols of evil as characters. Morgause (supposedly based on White's mother) is cruel, selfish, and unable to love without dominating. A destructive force, she becomes almost a personification of a malign fate. Both her seduction of Arthur, resulting in the incestuous birth of Mordred, and her influence on her four sons contribute to Arthur's downfall.

Mordred is the other major villain. On one level he is the revengeful child of an adulterous and incestuous relationship, determined to destroy the guilty father. On another, however, he is a symbol of evil, always dressed in black and devoted to destruction. His life purpose is to destroy the man who gave him life and the ideals of Camelot which he represents. Relentlessly wicked, he gleefully contemplates the enmity between Arthur and Lancelot and brazenly tries to marry Guenevere in the king's absence.

Guenevere, the major female role, is neither hero nor villain. Not a strong character, she does not share the idealism of either her husband or her lover, but rather vacillates between loyalty and treachery. A self-centered woman, she is also pathetic in her continual loneliness, as both men are often away on quests or in battles. The only other significant female character is Elaine, who seduces Lancelot and produces Galahad, the son destined to achieve the Grail. A lesser Guenevere, she is also somewhat pathetic and wilfully selfish.

White is extremely skilled in his creation of minor comic figures, especially in *The Sword in the Stone*. Madame Mim, a fairy tale witch, rivals Merlyn in wizardly skills. At one point the two engage in a dazzling battle of spells, a delightfully comic vignette. Morgan le Fay, also an enchantress, is, like Merlyn, an anachronistic figure. Her household boasts items like chocolates and cigarettes. Wart's adoptive father, Ector, is a satiric portrayal of an English country squire. King Pellinore is a satirical image of the medieval knight. The object of his quest, the Questing Beast, is a loving creature who dotes on her pursuer and languishes when he momentarily forgets to chase her. Even Merlyn's owl, Archimedes, has a true personality—wise and sardonic in his comments to his master.

Many of the other characters from the Arthurian legend find a place in the pages of White's vast retelling, but most have relatively minor roles. Morgause's four sons, for example, are active briefly, but only Gawain is developed as an individual. Sensitive to the ambiguities of right and wrong, he is nonetheless committed to killing his friend Lancelot, who unwittingly brought about the death of his two younger brothers.

Literary Techniques

White's most distinctive technique in *The Once and Future King* is his modulation of comic and tragic tone. The work as a whole moves from comedy through tragedy to an ending that suggests rebirth and renewal. The first book, dealing with Wart's joyful childhood, is primarily comic and satiric. Under the light tone of the surface narrative, however, there is a persistent dark message. Even one of the most famous scenes, the hilarious fight between King Pellinore and Sir Grummore, not only satirizes the medieval mode of fighting but also reveals the disturbing fact that both men feel the need to fight. Wart's various animal transformations also suggest a serious challenge to human belief and behavior within their amusing narratives. The Might vs. Right conflict becomes the subject of a sombre debate in the second book. Intimations of the ultimate tragedy are indicated throughout the middle books. In the final book, White transcends the tragic conclusion even as the tragic mode replaces the comic. Although Arthur's ideal Camelot has failed and he is about to be killed by Mordred, he feels hope for the future, and the book ends with the words, "The Beginning."

Another of White's techniques is his skillful use of anachronism, both for comic and thematic purposes. Merlyn and Morgan le Fay demonstrate the comic uses, particularly in their homes. The wizard's cottage is a remarkable collection of items, including mythic animals and the *Encyclopedia Britannica*. Morgan's house boasts a variety of twentieth-century treats and devices. More subtly, however, White incorporates anachronism as thematic commentary on the material. Throughout the story, the contrasts and similarities of medieval and modern life interpenetrate. Finally, White uses anachronistic language for the sake of realistic character portrayal. The Arthurian figures do not speak in epic fashion or high style but instead converse in a colloquial contemporary manner; Lancelot and Guenevere call each other Lance and Jenny.

Relation to Previous Works

Although *The Once and Future King* is unique in White's literary works, it is related to several other books in its concern with the Matter of Britain taken in its broadest sense. His journal *England Have My Bones* deals with Britain, as does his novel *Farewell Victoria*. Furthermore, the love of nature and all its creatures, which is so evident in the tetralogy, appears in many of his other works.

Literary Precedents

In a large sense, White's only predecessor is Sir Thomas Malory, who in the fifteenth century pulled together for the first time the entire body of Arthurian material in his *Le Morte Darthur* (1485). Although there have been several major retellings of the legend in the twentieth century, none precedes White's work. His only predecessor in the comic-ironic vision of Arthurian romance was Mark Twain, whose negative attitude toward the Middle Ages was the opposite of White's profound admiration for the medieval world.

Adaptations

The first book in the tetralogy, *The Sword in the Stone*, was adapted to film by Walt Disney (1963). In 1960, *The Once and Future King* was adapted to the stage in the Broadway musical, *Camelot,* by Alan Jay Lerner and Frederick Lowe. The musical was enormously successful, and White himself saw seventy performances of it. The cast included Richard Burton, Julie Andrews, Roddy McDowell, Robert Goulet, and Robert Coote.

Additional Sources
Crane, John K. *T. H. White.* New York: Twayne, 1974. A general study of the writings of White, with a long chapter on *The Once and Future King.* The author deals with the work as a whole and with the four separate volumes.

Kellman, Martin. *T. H. White and the Matter of Britain.* Lewiston, NY: Edwin Mellen, 1988. A critical overview of White's writings as they deal with the large subject of the Matter of Britain. Detailed chapters are devoted to *The Sword in the Stone* and *The Ill-Made Knight,* which the author regards as White's masterpieces.

Nellis, Marilyn. "Anachronistic Humor in Two Arthurian Romances of Education: *To The Chapel Perilous* and *The Sword in the Stone.*" *Studies in Medievalism* (Fall 1983): 57-77. A careful and perceptive study of the comic anachronisms in both novels and their relevance to the theme of education. About half of the article is devoted to White.

Charlotte Spivack
University of Massachusetts at Amherst

P. G. WODEHOUSE
1881-1975

Publishing History

From relatively modest beginnings with "school stories," P. G. Wodehouse was always successful as a writer. When he graduated from school he had already sold an essay, "Some Aspects of Game Captaincy," to *The Public School Magazine*. For the next two years, while working in London for the Hong Kong and Shanghai Bank (1900-1902), he sold about eighty stories and essays to various magazines. His first novel, *The Pothunters*, was originally designed to be a serial but, when the magazine failed, its publishers brought out the work in book form. In 1903, the same company published a sequel, *The Prefect's Uncle*, and a collection of previously serialized stories, *St. Austin's*. For another publisher, *The Gold Bat* was serialized and then published in book form, followed by *The Head of Kays* (1905), and *The White Feather* (1907, previously serialized). Both *The Pothunters* and *The Gold Bat* have recently been issued in paperback, and many of the early stories appear in volumes collected and edited by David Jasen.

The second phase of Wodehouse's publishing career lasted from 1904, when he first visited the United States while on vacation from the *Globe*, to the outbreak of World War II. At the beginning of this period he was doing hack work for various magazines and writing lyrics for stage musicals. Success in selling short stories to *The Saturday Evening Post*, *Cosmopolitan*, and *Colliers* induced him to travel frequently to New York, starting in 1909; throughout the war years, having been turned down for the army because of weak eyes, he continued to produce short stories and novels. He also collaborated on a number of plays, contributing both song lyrics and dialogue. His partnership with Guy Bolton and Jerome Kern led to a series of musical hits in the 1920s and 1930s; the best known of his lyrics is probably "Bill" from *Showboat* (a show in which, ironically, he did not otherwise collaborate at all). Wodehouse wrote about his theatrical work in his autobiographical works. In 1906 he brought out his first "adult" novel, *Love Among the Chickens*, in which the immortal Stanley Featherstonehaugh Ukridge first appears. This was soon followed by perhaps his best school story, *Mike*, in 1909. (*Mike*, his longest novel, was reissued in 1953 as two separate books: *Mike at Wrykyn* and *Mike and Psmith*. The second half had already been reissued in 1935, in slightly different form, as *Enter Psmith*.)

In 1914, Wodehouse married Ethel Rowley; the happy marriage was to last more than sixty years. In 1915, both Jeeves and Blandings Castle entered publishing history, and the next decade saw the beginnings of the Mulliner stories and the golf stories. Wodehouse spent several unproductive stints in Hollywood—unproductive in terms of Hollywood's rejection of his scripts, but productive for him in terms of fictional material. Stories, novels, and plays continued to roll from Wodehouse's typewriter at rate of more than eight typed pages a day. At perhaps the high point of Wodehouse's reputation, in 1939, Oxford conferred an honorary degree upon him: a late consolation, though a magnificent one, for his family's inability to send him to the university many years earlier.

Then came the turning point in Wodehouse's literary (and personal) reputation: World War II, which decisively ended the long and peaceful second phase of Wodehouse's publishing career. Interned by the Germans while he was staying at Le Touquet, Wodehouse was released two months before his sixtieth birthday. He made five broadcasts, and public opinion has split into several camps ever since. Some, perhaps the majority, see Wodehouse as an innocent, unaware of the propaganda value of his remarks. At one extreme are those, including some American experts on propaganda, who see the broadcasts as clever disinformation. At the other extreme are the hard-liners, originally led by Duff Cooper and by "Cassandra" of the *Daily Mirror* (William Connor), presenting Wodehouse as an actual traitor. Connor made a vitriolic attack on Wodehouse in July 1941, the effects of which were to last for many years. Despite the storm over the broadcasts, Wodehouse continued writing through both his German internment and a short postwar French internment, and his books continued to sell—well over 400,000 copies in Britain alone, during the war years.

After the war, from 1947 to the end of his life, Wodehouse lived in the United States, still turning out from eight to as many as twenty-five pages a day, still selling briskly. Although he would not for many years regain his personal popularity, neither the quality of his work nor its sales appeal diminished. Several of Wodehouse's best-loved books appeared during this third and last phase of his long publishing career. A relative downturn in sales during the 1950s was balanced by the beginnings of a strong paperback selling trend when Penguin reprinted five Wodehouse volumes in 1948, followed by further reprints which continue to the present. In 1956, Wodehouse's regular British publisher began bringing out a uniform edition which included both new books and reissues of older titles. This is known as the "autograph" edition and is considered the standard text of the nondramatic works.

On Wodehouse's eightieth birthday in 1961 publishers brought out several books by and about him to mark the occasion. Recordings and television adaptations began to appear. Ten years later, on Wodehouse's ninetieth birthday, a new Jeeves book was published simultaneously on both sides of the Atlantic (though, characteristically, with two different titles). A week before his death, Wodehouse appeared in an introductory talk for *Wodehouse Playhouse*. The day of his death, he was at work on *Sunset at Blandings* and took part of the manuscript with him to the hospital. (Richard Usborne later completed *Sunset at Blandings* from the author's notes and plot outlines.) Such is the continuing demand for Wodehouse's comedy that various reprints, new anthologies of previously uncollected stories, repackagings of stories on particular themes, and biographies continue to be published.

Critical Reception, Honors, Popularity

Wodehouse's stylized comedy appeals to highbrow and middlebrow alike and has seldom received a really negative review. Although a good deal of academic criticism has appeared, especially since his death, Wodehouse has attracted more appreciations and tributes than searching analysis. There is a much larger number of reminiscences of Wodehouse, bibliographies, collectors' manuals, and the like, than there is literary criticism.

Admirers of Wodehouse fall mainly into two groups: fanatic readers, and practicing writers. Members of the former group tend to know all the details of every Wodehouse venue, and can remember which girl was engaged to Bertie Wooster in which novel; the closest analogy would probably be to readers of the Sherlock Holmes stories. The second group, practicing writers, tends not only to enjoy Wodehouse's comedy but also to consider him very much underrated.

Only one serious question has ever affected Wodehouse's reputation: the German broadcasts. For many years after the war, the BBC (even though its board had not originally supported Connor's attack in 1941) banned the broadcast of works by or about Wodehouse, or even of songs with lyrics by him. Some British libraries stopped buying his books, and at least one is said to have disposed of its Wodehouse collection. Oxford was urged to withdraw the honorary degree (and did not), while his beloved school, Dulwich College, considered expunging his name (and did). As late as 1961, Evelyn Waugh had difficulty getting permission to air a tribute to Wodehouse on his eightieth birthday.

By simply surviving, continuing to write, and showing his unvarying good humor, Wodehouse outlasted the controversy. Malcolm Muggeridge, who had taken up his cause at the end of the war, went on defending him; so did George Orwell. Dulwich College quietly reinstated him at the end of the war and, soon after his death, dedicated a "Wodehouse Corner" in its library to his memorabilia (including his last typewriter). Evelyn Waugh did succeed in getting the BBC to air the eightieth birthday tribute in October 1961 and called it, significantly, "An Act of Homage and Reparation." Meanwhile, believing Wodehouse's eightieth birthday to be a year earlier than in fact it was, his American publisher had taken out a large advertisement in the *New York Times* in which some eighty well known writers, including W. H. Auden, Graham Greene, Ogden Nash, and Lionel Trilling, saluted his art. Finally, in 1975, Wodehouse was named Knight Commander of the Order of the British Empire (along with another controversial exile, Charlie Chaplin), in the New Year's Honors List.

Various selections from Wodehouse's works have been translated into French, Italian, Spanish, German, Dutch, the Scandinavian languages, Polish, Ukrainian, and many non-Indo-European languages, including Finnish, Hungarian, and Turkish. There are also translations into Latin and Esperanto. Richard Usborne gives a good account of the problems of translating Wodehouse, and the Pierpont Morgan/Oxford centenary volume has a useful bibliography.

Analysis of Selected Titles

SUMMER LIGHTNING

Summer Lightning, 1929, novel. British title *Fish Preferred*.

Social Concerns/Themes

Though Jeeves must certainly be Wodehouse's best known and best loved character, Blandings Castle is the ultimate Wodehouse locale. In his tribute for Wodehouse's eightieth birthday, Evelyn Waugh called the Blandings gardens "the original gardens from which we are all exiled." An idealized country setting, Blandings is the place where people come to be made whole and have their problems solved. It is a utopia where the sun always shines and where, though social distinctions are carefully observed, social class never controls destiny. Freddie Threepwood, Lord Emsworth's second son, marries an American girl who turns out to be not only a relative of the Castle gardener, McAllister ("The Custody of the Pumpkin") but also the daughter of an American millionaire. In America, the languidly aristocratic Freddie becomes a surprisingly successful salesman of dog biscuits—so successful that he intimidates his visiting father, who feels compelled to compete by selling Encyclopedias of Sport ("Birth of a Salesman"). One of Lord Emsworth's many wards wants to marry a chorus girl, Sue Brown, who is in fact the daughter of a chorus girl once loved by the earl's brother Galahad (*Summer Lightning* and *Heavy Weather*); the only person against this arrangement is the earl's unpleasant sister, who disapproves of chorus girls and has planned a dynastic marriage for each of her younger relatives.

Characters

Clarence, ninth Earl of Emsworth, is an unprepossessing figure, lean and limp, a bit past sixty, who clearly prefers pigs to people. This preference is scarcely surprising, given the charm and bulk of his beloved prize sow, Empress of Blandings. Beneath Lord Emsworth's placid exterior, though, he shares the Wodehouse desire to thwart the inconveniences of the system and to resist tyranny, especially when represented by his sister, Lady Constance Keeble (who bears a close resemblance to Bertie Wooster's Aunt Agatha). Nine other sisters threaten the peace of Blandings from time to time, all tall and queenly except Hermione, who resembles a cook. The only brother, Galahad Threepwood, is an aging boulevardier whose exploits at the racetrack and elsewhere alarm his family. Lord Emsworth benevolently shelters a series of beautiful young females (usually nieces or other relatives) and tries to smooth the path of romance for them. In this he is assisted by his imperturbable butler, Beach, who somewhat resembles a countrified Jeeves. Less reliably on his side are his irascible Scottish gardener, McAllister, and his pig man, George Cyril Wellbeloved. Wellbeloved, who is first lured away by a rival landowner and later buys a thriving pub with an inheritance, is one of a long line of Blandings pigkeepers, each of whom brings various complications to Lord Emsworth's life.

Techniques/Literary Precedents

As usual, Wodehouse juggles several parallel plots in *Summer Lightning*. The main story concerns the romance between Lord Emsworth's ward Ronnie Fish and the chorus girl Sue Brown. Their main goal is to get Lord Emsworth's blessing (and a check) while fending off the rival suitors who threaten both of them. In the Blandings tradition, at least one character (this time, Sue Brown) arrives impersonating someone else (her rival, the wealthy Myra Schoonmaker). Meanwhile, Lord Emsworth faces the prospect of an unwelcome secretary, Baxter, and seeks his missing pig, the beloved Empress of Blandings, abducted by an unknown pignapper. The farcelike plot devices of the impersonator (who constantly risks detection) and the stolen pig (which constantly moves from one hiding place to another) were to become staple elements in the Blandings books. The dramatic origins of the stolen-pig farce are obvious. The lover who can only be near the loved one if in a disguise owes much to stage comedy—including Shakespeare's as well as the Broadway musical.

Relation to Previous Works

Blandings Castle first beguiled the public in *Something New* (1915, British title *Something Fresh*), then in *Leave It to Psmith* (1923). These were followed by *Summer Lightning* (1929), marking the first appearance of Galahad Threepwood, *Heavy Weather* (1933), which occurs ten days later, and *Uncle Fred in the Springtime* (1939), in which Lord Ickenham assumes the role usually played by Galahad. Following these were *Full Moon* (1947), *Pigs Have Wings* (1952), *The Brinkmanship of Galahad Threepwood* (1965, British title *Galahad at Blandings*), *No Nudes Is Good Nudes* (1970, British title *A Pelican at Blandings*, 1969), and the novel Wodehouse was working on the day he died, *Sunset at Blandings* (completed by Richard Usborne, published 1977 in Britain and 1978 in the United States). Short stories were collected in *Blandings Castle* (1935), which also contains non-Blandings stories, and in *Crime Wave at Blandings* (1937, British title *Lord Emsworth and Others*).

Adaptations

Building on the success of *The World of Wooster* (see below), the BBC launched a Blandings series, "Blandings Castle," in 1967. Although it starred Sir Ralph Richardson as Lord Emsworth and, in an unforgettable role, Stanley Holloway as the pigman, this series never reached the level of popularity of *The World of Wooster*.

UNCLE FRED FLITS BY

"Uncle Fred Flits By," 1936, short story.

Social Concerns/Themes

Uncle Fred's main purpose in life is to spread sweetness and light, and he usually does this on visits to his nephew Pongo Twistleton-Twistleton of the Drones Club. Though himself the fifth Earl of Ickenham, Uncle Fred is practically anarchistic in his desire to stir up society. Aside from an ingrained dislike of constables and magistrates, Uncle Fred distrusts most social distinctions. Presented with a suburban girl whose family disapproves of her marrying a young man who jellies eels, he makes it his job to bring off the match, on principle. Later, he encourages his old friend Peasemarch, a butler, to marry his employer's sister (*Cocktail Time*).

Characters

Uncle Fred (Lord Ickenham) is one of Wodehouse's immortals. Uncle of Pongo Twistleton-Twistleton of the Drones Club, he comes to London very seldom because his domineering wife keeps him at home. He combines the most amusing features of the Earl of Emsworth and the young rowdies of the Drones Club, while also quoting nearly as much as Jeeves. Pongo's role in this story is that of a straight man, a witness who can later relate the story to his friends at the club.

Techniques/Literary Precedents

Once again, the dominant influence is probably stage farce. The fast-moving comedy of mistaken identities and pretended speechlessness includes a good deal of gesturing and devices such as hiding behind sofas, and owes much to Wodehouse's dramatic training. So does the tight structure; even in this short piece, Wodehouse's narrative is divided into scenes. The first scene deals with Uncle Fred's securing shelter from the rain by pretending to be a veterinarian; the second with his arranging the match between two perfect strangers, this time while impersonating a relative; the third with his alerting the real homeowner to the presence of "intruders" in his house, this time claiming to be a neighbor. A very brief prelude and epilogue allow Uncle Fred and Pongo to converse, since during the three main scenes Pongo is alleged to be deaf and dumb.

Relation to Previous Works

Like the other stories in *Young Men in Spats*, "Uncle Fred Flits By" has to do with the misadventures of a member of the Drones Club, Pongo Twistleton-Twistleton. One Drones story appears in *The Crime Wave at Blandings* (1937) and many in *Eggs, Beans, and Crumpets* (1940). Bertie Wooster, of course, is also a Drone, so many of the Bertie-and-Jeeves short stories, and several of the novels, involve other Drones. This is the first of the Uncle Fred stories; later, Uncle Fred was to star in *Uncle Fred in the Springtime* (1939), set at Blandings, and in *Uncle Dynamite* (1948), *Cocktail Time* (1958), and *Service with a Smile* (1962).

THE TRUTH ABOUT GEORGE

"The Truth About George," 1927, short story.

Social Concerns/Themes

As so often happens in the golden world of Wodehouse, the goodhearted hero—or nonhero—gets his wish by dint of his basic worth and, mostly, by sheer chance. Though determined and resourceful, George really does not conquer his shyness and stammer by his own efforts but by a series of incredible coincidences. In this he resembles many of Wodehouse's other nonheroes, from Pongo and Lord Emsworth right up to Bertie Wooster.

Literary Techniques

Like many Mulliner stories, "The Truth about George" has a linear plot involving several well-defined episodes. The initial problem is George's stammer; the complication, his love for an attractive fellow crossword puzzle addict. The main action of the story takes place on the day George goes to London to consult a specialist and is advised to talk to three strangers a day and, when unable to speak, to resort to singing. On the train home, he meets first a fellow stammerer, then an escaped lunatic, and finally a woman who thinks *he* is the escaped lunatic—an impression which George only strengthens by offering her his thermos and singing "Tea for Two." The ensuing chase over the fields to his cottage ends with George able to declare his love. Because it is constructed in scenes, and because of the dramatic possibilities of his speechless gesturing and his sudden bursts of song, this story has adapted exceptionally well to television.

Characters

George Mulliner resembles most of Mr. Mulliner's other nephews in being decent, rather obtuse, and lacking in assertion. The London doctor and the lady on the train fall into the category of middle class stereotypes, and the girl, as so often in Wodehouse, will obviously manage George's life for him to the slightest detail.

Relation to Previous Works

This story occurs in the first Mulliner collection, *Meet Mr. Mulliner* (1928, British edition 1927). The format, in which Mr. Mulliner tells his audience at the Angler's Rest stories about the mishaps of his many nephews and other young relatives, was repeated in *Mr. Mulliner Speaking* (1930, British edition 1929), *Mulliner Nights* (1933), and some stories included in *Blandings Castle* (1935) and *Young Men in Spats* (1936). It is similar to the format of the many golf stories told by the Oldest Member, and to some of the Drones Club stories.

Adaptations

Most successful of all the adaptations has probably been the *Wodehouse Playhouse* of the mid-1970s. These episodes are based chiefly on the Mulliner stories (with some from the world of golf), and star Pauline Collins and John Alderton. The programs include short introductory segments by Wodehouse himself, who was filming one only a week before his death. "The Truth About George" is generally agreed to be one of the best.

JOY IN THE MORNING

Joy in the Morning, 1946, novel. British edition 1947.

Social Concerns/Themes

Bertie and Jeeves nearly always strive to preserve the status quo—sometimes against considerable odds. Many readers have noticed that Bertie seldom acts; he reacts. Here, as usual, he responds to a call for help (strengthened by Jeeves's desire to be near a river where there is good fishing), and finds himself embroiled with two romances, a missing brooch, a sailor costume, a visiting financier, and a Boy Scout who burns his cottage, Wee Nooke, to the ground. The solutions to these various problems involve minor violence, disguises, blackmail, locking people up, and just plain lying. At the end, everything is just as it was—except that the romance of Boko and Nobby will now succeed, thanks to an infusion of money from Lord Worplesdon.

Some critics have surmised that Boko's stupidity in this postwar novel may reflect Wodehouse's own sense of having made a fool of himself through the German broadcasts. This seems quite possible; Bertie constantly speaks of Boko as a writer, and therefore an idiot, while this explicit connection is not made in previous books (though Wodehouse does have other silly writers).

Characters

Like so many other readers' favorites, this novel revolves around the immortal duo of Bertie Wooster and Jeeves. Bertie belongs to the class of likeable young men represented elsewhere by the members of the Drones Club (*Young Men in Spats*) to which he himself belongs, by Archibald Moffam (*Indiscretions of Archie*), and by so many of the younger relatives of Mr. Mulliner (*Mr. Mulliner Speaking*). All of these young men may descend from Psmith, who had his origin in the later school stories (*Mike*, 1909), but who grew to relative adulthood and starred in many later novels. Bertie, an independently wealthy young man in his mid-twenties, spends most of his time getting out of scrapes he has landed in through a series of unlikely coincidences; these usually involve romance, money, and domineering relatives.

Jeeves, on the other hand, has no real counterpart elsewhere in Wodehouse's works. A large and impressive figure, he seems not to move like ordinary people but rather to materialize suddenly, often where he is least expected. "Shimmer" is a word Bertie often uses to describe the way Jeeves suddenly appears at his side. His noble head bulges at the back and he eats a great deal of fish—both signs of his immense brain power. He speaks largely in quotations, is never perturbed, and can find a solution to any problem. He even foresees Bertie's bunglings and allows for them in his plans.

Techniques/Literary Precedents

Tight plotting and constant wordplay hold this novel together. Two parallel plots concern Bertie's efforts to keep his nemesis and former fiancée, Florence Craye, engaged to D'Arcy ("Stilton") Cheesewright, who has become a policeman, and Boko Fittleworth's efforts to get permission to marry Zenobia ("Nobby") Hopwood. The connection between the two romance plots is Lord Worplesdon, who is the second husband of Bertie's dreaded Aunt Agatha and is also Florence's father and Nobby's guardian. Leverage over Lord Worplesdon comes about through his need for a secret meeting with Chichester Clam, an American millionaire with whom he has business dealings.

The novel is leavened with an unusually fine series of quotations by Jeeves, linguistic felicities by Bertie, and examples of total idiocy by Boko Fittleworth. The whole experience, complete with fiendish Boy Scout, burning house, sailor costumes, and much more, is justly summed up afterward, by Bertie, as "the Steeple Bumpleigh Horror."

Relation to Previous Works

Though by no means the first of the Bertie-and-Jeeves books, many readers consider this the best. Jeeves arrived on the scene in the story "Extricating Young Gussie," which appeared in the *Saturday Evening Post* in 1915. He developed through a series of stories—*My Man Jeeves*, 1919, revised with additional stories as *Carry On, Jeeves*, 1925 (British edition 1927); *Jeeves*, (British title *The Inimitable Jeeves*), 1923; *Very Good, Jeeves*, 1930. His first appearance in a full-length novel was *Thank You, Jeeves* (1934), followed by *The Code of the Woosters*

(1938), a novel particularly admired by Wodehouse fans. After *Joy in the Morning* (1946) came *The Return of Jeeves* (1954; British title *Ring for Jeeves*, 1953); *Bertie Wooster Sees It Through* (1955; British title *Jeeves and the Feudal Spirit*, 1954); *Jeeves In the Offing* (1960; British title *How Right You Are, Jeeves*); *Stiff Upper Lip, Jeeves* (1963); *Jeeves and the Tie That Binds* (1971; British title *Much Obliged, Jeeves*); and *Aunts Aren't Gentlemen* (1974; British title *The Cat-Nappers*).

Adaptations

Many have attempted, with varying degrees of success, to reduce Wodehouse's verbal comedy to fit the screen. The BBC adapted a number of Jeeves and Bertie stories in 1965, with Ian Carmichael as Bertie and Dennis Price as Jeeves; Wodehouse had a rather mixed opinion of this casting. More recently, the immortal duo have appeared in a series, "Jeeves and Wooster," produced for Granada television and broadcast in the United States on Public Broadcasting's Masterpiece Theatre. These episodes feature reminiscent introductions by Alistair Cooke and postludes by the two lead actors, Stephen Fry and Hugh Laurie. There have also been several audio issues, including *The Code of the Woosters* (1989).

Other Titles (Selected)

Bring On the Girls, 1953 (autobiography); *America, I Like You*, 1956 (autobiography); *Author! Author!*, 1962 (autobiography); *Wodehouse on Crime: A Dozen Tales of Fiendish Cunning*, 1981 (short stories); *The Uncollected Wodehouse*, 1976 (short stories); *The Swoop! and Other Stories*, 1979 (short stories); *The Eighteen-Karat Kid*, 1980 (short stories); *Fore! The Best of Wodehouse on Golf*, 1983 (short stories); *A Wodehouse Bestiary*, 1985 (short stories); *Yours, Plum*, 1990 (letters, edited by Lady Frances Lonsdale Donaldson).

Additional Sources

Cazalet-Keir, Thelma. *Homage to P. G. Wodehouse*. London: Barrie & Jenkins, 1973. A collection of essays in appreciation, including tributes from Lord David Cecil, Sir John Betjeman, Malcolm Muggeridge, and Auberon Waugh. The editor was the sister-in-law of Wodehouse's beloved stepdaughter, Leonora.

Connolly, Joseph. *P. G. Wodehouse: An Illustrated Biography, With Complete Bibliography and Collector's Guide*. London: Orbis, 1979. A knowledgeable and humorous account of Wodehouse's life and works, with numerous photographs and an excellent bibliography of first editions (including descriptions of dust jackets and estimates of value).

Donaldson, Lady Frances Lonsdale. *P. G. Wodehouse: A Biography*. New York: Alfred A. Knopf, 1982. The authorized biography, by a family friend.

Fogle, Richard Harter. "Saki and Wodehouse." In *The English Short Story, 1880-1945*, edited by Joseph M. Flora. Boston: Twayne, 1985. Places Wodehouse in historical context.

Green, Benny. *P. G. Wodehouse: A Literary Biography*. New York: Rutledge Press, 1981.

Hall, Robert A., Jr. *The Comic Style of P. G. Wodehouse*. Hamden, CT: Archon, 1974. A well informed analysis of plot types, character types, and stylistic devices by a linguistics expert who is also a Wodehouse admirer.

Heineman, James H., and D. R. Bensen. *P. G. Wodehouse: A Centenary Celebration, 1881-1981*. New York: Pierpont Morgan Library and Oxford University Press, 1981. A collection of essays in appreciation, opening with a reprint of Wodehouse's own "How I Write My Books" and continuing with pieces on, among other things, Hollywood, illustrations, crime, Wodehouse, and scripture. Nearly half (eighteen) of the essays deal with bibliographical subjects.

Jasen, David A. *P. G. Wodehouse: A Portrait of a Master*. Rev. ed. New York: Continuum, 1981. A thorough biography, with particular emphasis on publishing history, by a Wodehouse scholar who was responsible for the reissue of much previously uncollected Wodehouse.

Morris, J. H. C. *Thank You, Wodehouse*. New York: St. Martin's, 1981. With contributions by A. D. Macintyre and an introduction by Frances Donaldson. A series of amusing pieces on the minutiae of the Wodehouse world: who, really, was Aunt Dahlia's husband Tom Travers? Could Ronnie Fish have been illegitimate? Where exactly is Market Blandings?

Sproat, Iain. *Wodehouse at War*. New Haven and New York: Ticknor and Fields, 1981. A thorough account of the broadcast controversy, with numerous excerpts from the actual broadcasts, from letters to newspapers, and from interviews with witnesses.

Usborne, Richard. *The Penguin Wodehouse Companion*. London: Penguin, 1988. Combines and updates parts of *Wodehouse at Work to the End* (1961, revised 1976) with parts of *A Wodehouse Companion* (1981), by the world's foremost expert on Wodehouse. Includes plot summaries of the novels and an excellent annotated bibliography of books and articles about Wodehouse.

―――――. *After Hours with P. G. Wodehouse*. London: Heineman, 1991. Usborne collects fifteen of his essays, articles, and talks that address such matters as Wodehouse's creation of Jeeves, his depiction of dogs and cats, and scholarship on Wodehouse

Voorhees, Richard J. *P. G. Wodehouse*. Twayne, 1966. A straightforward biography, with critical analysis.

―――――. *P. G. Wodehouse*. In *Dictionary of Literary Biography*, 34 (British Novelists, 1880-1929: Traditionalists), edited by Thomas F. Staley. Detroit: Gale, 1985. An excellent brief introduction to Wodehouse's career, with photographs and a useful primary bibliography.

Caroline C. Hunt
College of Charleston

TOM WOLFE
1931

Update

The Bonfire of the Vanities proved to be Wolfe's greatest commercial success. After months on the best seller list, the paperback edition of the novel likewise enjoyed best seller status. The popular appeal of the novel was heightened by striking parallels to at least two celebrated legal cases in New York City: those of Bernhard Goetz and of Tawana Brawley. Commentators were quick to compare Brawley's advisor, Reverend Al Sharpton, and the fictional Reverend Bacon.

Analysis of Selected Titles

THE BONFIRE OF THE VANITIES
The Bonfire of the Vanities, 1987, novel.

Social Concerns

The Bonfire of the Vanities deals with what Wolfe calls the "big, rich slices of contemporary life" that he believes modern authors have too long neglected or completely ignored. These are the details of life in a metropolis—race relations, the mass media, the law, and the class structure—handled in a highly realistic manner.

Sherman McCoy, a prodigiously successful bond trader at a prestigious Wall Street firm, is involved in a car accident in which his mistress, Maria Ruskin, fatally injures a young man, Henry Lamb, in the South Bronx. Seen by some as "the Great White Defendant," Sherman is arrested and arraigned, humiliated by and paraded before the press in a spectacle motivated by the political ambitions of various powerful individuals. Disgraced and ostracized, Sherman quickly loses his wealth, wife, job, home, mistress, friends, all sense of privilege and security, and possibly even his family.

Essential to the telling of these events is the fact that Sherman is a member of the wealthy elite and that Henry Lamb is a poor, black man. Both live in the most powerful, fascinating city of the late twentieth century, but whereas Henry Lamb lives in a public housing project in one of the worst neighborhoods, Sherman has a charmed existence in the most glamorous, expensive, and insulated quarter of the city.

The social worlds within New York are as highly stratified as they are diverse. Wolfe's meticulous attention to details underscores the status of characters ranging from crack dealers to business tycoons. Rarely does Wolfe fail to mention the ceiling height or decor of a room through which his characters move. How much characters earn, their ethnicity, speech, affectations, background, and clothing are all details emblematic of their culture, values, and nature. For example, the district attorney, seeking to establish credibility for "the crack king of Evergreen Avenue," is careful to costume him for an appearance before a jury in a button-down oxford shirt and loafers rather than his habitual windbreaker and sneakers. Even among the very wealthy, status and class remain virtual obsessions. Sherman, for instance, often travels in social circles of the *nouveaux riche* that he, educated at the finest preparatory schools and universities, occasionally finds contemptible.

Wolfe sets most of the legal action of his novel in the Bronx, which has one of the highest crime rates in the world. He graphically depicts the process by which criminal cases in the Bronx are handled by an overworked and underpaid staff of assistant district attorneys, judges, and police. The entire judicial system is so entrenched in bureaucracy, legalism, and politics that only the Irish cops and lawyers, who tenaciously adhere to a rigid code governing not only their demeanor but the exchange of favors and "contracts," emerge as less than despicable.

The racial tensions depicted in the novel are, like everything else, orchestrated and controlled by various forces that place greater emphasis on what an individual represents than on the individual himself. While virtually all of the lawyers, judges, and court personnel in the Bronx Country Building are white, the majority of those involved in the crimes—perpetrators and victims alike—are not. The aggressive prosecution of a white male, especially a rich, well-educated one from Park Avenue, for a crime against a poor black from the Bronx with no criminal record, is a rare opportunity for the Bronx district attorney to show his electorate that he is not a racist, but a servant of the people. In the media circus that follows his accident, Sherman becomes the representative of a society that community activists, led by the sensationalistic Reverend Bacon, blame for the ills of the poor, the minorities, and the oppressed.

Like the district attorney and his assistants, the journalists and television reporters allow themselves to be manipulated in their presentation of "news." Peter Fallow, a reporter for *The City Light* newspaper, for example, is fed stories by a lawyer, Al Vogel, who is anything but disinterested in the case of Henry Lamb. Television reporters usually follow the stories that first appear in newspapers with little regard for truth or accuracy. In accepting exclusives on stories in exchange for featured coverage, television reporters simply broadcast events staged for broadcast and are often more willingly and shamelessly manipulated than Fallow.

Characters

The Bonfire of the Vanities traces the descent of Sherman McCoy from the heights of financial success on Wall Street and Park Avenue through his arrest and arraignment in the bowels of the Bronx County Building to his contemplation of suicide. At the beginning of the novel, Sherman fancies himself "A Master of the Universe," a titan, a mover and shaker of world finance. He is so wrapped up in himself that he sees his wealth and status as license for his various indulgences: expensive clothing, his affair with Maria Ruskin, his solipsism, and his credo "insulate, insulate."

When his seven-year-old daughter asks him what he does for a living, Sherman is unable to simplify the world of leveraged buy-outs, and his wife Judy explains that he lives off the "crumbs" of other people's transactions. Sherman takes offense at Judy's deprecation of his work, but this is only one of the first of Sherman's many humiliations. So mortifying is his arrest and arraignment, described in a brilliant chapter entitled "Styrofoam Peanuts," that Sherman convincingly describes it as a death for himself. Although Sherman may never gain self-knowledge, he does overcome much of his arrogance. He does realize that in insulating himself from crime, poverty, and misery, he has also insulated himself from reality.

The epilogue, which purports to be a newspaper article from the *New York Times* that appears a year after the novel's end, summarizes the entire novel in describing Sherman's arraignment for the death of Henry Lamb wearing not a two thousand dollar suit but "an open-necked sport shirt, khaki pants, and hiking shoes." The epilogue also reveals the widely diverse effects of Sherman's case on the likes of Larry Kramer, Peter Fallow, and Maria Ruskin, in what might have otherwise occupied several thousand additional pages of fiction.

Despite his vanity, Sherman is hardly the villain of the piece. In fact, most of the other major characters are equally if not more selfish, greedy, and unprincipled. The flamboyant Reverend Bacon not only orchestrates the attacks on the mayor of New York City described in the Prologue and those on Sherman, but has also misappropriated and probably stolen $350,000 in seed money for the Little Shepherd Day Care Center. Peter Fallow, who is as lazy as his name suggests, is perhaps the most dislikeable character in Wolfe's entire novel. A parasite, opportunist, and cynic, Fallow's professional career is as reprehensible as his personal life. Larry Kramer, who struggles to support his family on the pitiful "$25,000-after-taxes" a year he earns as the assistant district attorney handling Sherman's case, views Sherman with a mixture of envy and contempt. Kramer, too, believes that he is entitled to indulge his own appetites in an affair that ends, like Sherman's, on the bonfire of vanities.

Techniques/Literary Precedents

Wolfe tells his story in the same style that characterizes his new journalism. Just as he appropriated fictional techniques for non-fiction, he freely uses non-fictional techniques in fiction. The latter, however, is nothing new. Wolfe laments the disappearance of novels, such as those by Dickens, Thackerey, Balzac, and Zola, alive with convincing precision that revealed how people in great cities lived during a particular age. Infused with immensely realistic detail, *The Bonfire of the Vanities* is as credible in describing the holding pens in the Bronx as it is in chronicling a glamorous dinner party on the Upper East Side. In addition, Wolfe effectively uses language to express not only a character's status but personality as well.

Unlike most of his non-fictional work, Wolfe employs omniscient narration that allows him to develop a variety of characters and freely comment on their motivations, inner thoughts, and backgrounds.

Relation to Previous Work

The Bonfire of the Vanities was originally serialized in *Rolling Stone* magazine in 1984-1985, but the final novel varies dramatically from the serialization. In the earlier version, Sherman, a largely sympathetic character often referred to as "the Great Observer," was a writer rather than an ego-maniacal bond trader. That transformation of Sherman's character is the crucial difference between the serialization and the published novel: many of the details of the serialized Sherman presented him as a victim, but most of his good intentions are subdued if not altogether lost in the published novel. Written to meet deadlines, the serialization lacks the balance, fluidity, and polish of the published novel.

The Bonfire of the Vanities is perhaps most closely related to *Radical Chic and Mau-Mauing the Flak Catchers* (1970) as both are concerned with social status and racial tensions. Freed from the constraints of factual accounts, Wolfe's novel relentlessly pursues the hypocrisy, irony, and self-absorption that exists in every strata of society.

Adaptations

The Bonfire of the Vanities was adapted for a film, released in the winter of 1990, directed by Brian DePalma, best known for his Hitchcock homages (such as *Obsession*) and violent crime epics like *Scarface* and *The Untouchables*. Tom Hanks plays Sherman McCoy, with a supporting cast that includes Bruce Willis as

Larry Kramer, Melanie Griffith as Maria Ruskin, Morgan Freeman, F. Murray Abraham, Kim Cattrall, and Saul Rubinek. The playwright Michael Cristofer wrote the screenplay from Wolfe's novel.

The filming itself aroused considerable controversy. Under pressure from community groups that vehemently objected to the negative way in which the Bronx is depicted in Wolfe's novel, filmmakers agreed to photograph footage showing more positive features of the Bronx: its zoo and botanical gardens, for example.

Yet another controversy arose when Wolfe appeared with Spike Lee, the author and director of *Do the Right Thing*, on a panel sponsored by the CORO Foundation in New York City in May 1990. Lee charged that the screenplay of *The Bonfire of the Vanities* drastically altered the end of Wolfe's novel so that Henry Lamb did not die, but instead simply walked out of the hospital one day. Wolfe responded by emphasizing that since he had not authored the screenplay, he had no knowledge of or control over such a change. There are also considerable differences between Wolfe's story and the film, such as Sherman's acquittal, the judge's moralistic speech, and Maria's character. The film also loses the important ambiguity of whether Sherman's car actually hurt Henry Lamb.

Additional Sources

Andrew, James. Review of *The Bonfire of the Vanities*. *Christian Science Monitor* (November 3, 1987): 20. A complimentary review, commenting that the novel "invites comparison with Dickens."

Conroy, Frank. Review of *The Bonfire of the Vanities*. *New York Times Book Review* (November 1, 1987): 1. A good review, despite its observation that Wolfe's social commentary may be "too much of a good thing."

Edwards, Thomas R. Review of *The Bonfire of the Vanities*. *New York Review of Books* No. 1 (February 4, 1988): 8-9. Edwards comments that "the world pictured is mainly a theater of malice, and it seems tempting to ask why the book has sold so many copies."

Lehmann-Haupt, Christopher. Review of *The Bonfire of the Vanities*. *The New York Times* (October 22, 1987): C-25. Calls the novel "an impressive performance," but observes that finding comedy in detailing ethnic conflict is playing with fire.

Levine, A. "Tom Wolfe: the Years of Living Prosperously." *U.S. News and World Report* 107 (December 25, 1989): 117. In this interview, Wolfe describes his life after the publication of *The Bonfire of the Vanities*.

Rich, Frank. Review of *The Bonfire of the Vanities*. *The New Republic* 197 (November 23, 1987): 42. Accuses Wolfe of lacking the desire or the ability to chronicle all of the levels of New York society; instead, Rich claims, he merely focuses his efforts on the Bronx and Park Avenue.

Wolfe, Tom. "Stalking the Billion-Footed Beast: A Literary Manifesto for the New Social Novel." *Harper's* (November 1989): 45-56. This article was a rationale for his writing *The Bonfire of the Vanities* as an effort to reclaim a great American tradition of the realistic social novel from the hands of absurdists, "K'mart realists," and antiseptic novelists. Wolfe's manifesto triggered a wide and sometimes vicious response. *Harper's,* for which Wolfe serves as a contributing editor, solicited and ran letters [*Harper's* (February 1990): 4-14] from Philip Roth, Walker Percy, Scott Spencer, Alison Lurie, Madison Smartt Bell, Jim Harrison, Mary Gordon, T. Coraghessan Boyle, and John Hawkes, all of whom objected to at least part of Wolfe's analysis of the state of contemporary fiction.

Yardley, Jonathan. Review of *The Bonfire of the Vanities*. *The Washington Post* (October 25, 1987): 3. Judges that *"The Bonfire of the Vanities* is a superb human comedy and the first novel ever to get contemporary New York, in all its arrogance and shame and heterogeneity and insularity, exactly right," but warns that nearly everyone will take offense at it.

Joan F. Dean
University of Missouri-Kansas City

CHELSEA QUINN YARBRO
1942

Update

Over three years Yarbro produced a new trilogy featuring Atta Olivia Clemens (Olivia), a character introduced in *Blood Games* (1980), the third novel in the Saint-Germain series. The new series, *A Flame in Byzantium* (1987), *Crusader's Torch* (1988), and *A Candle for D'Artagnan* (1989), carries on the story of Olivia's life as a vampire. The vampire-hero of the original series, Saint-Germain, appears in these novels only in the letters he sends to Olivia. After these three books, which mark the sixth, seventh, and eighth of the Saint-Germain group, the hero himself may be expected to reappear.

Yarbro also published another novel in the genre of apocalyptic or holocaust fiction, *Firecode* (1987). Similar to *The Time of the Fourth Horseman* (1976) and *False Dawn* (1978), Yarbro confronts the reader with a frightening vision of overwhelming destruction, and creates heroines who must survive the ravages of disease, fire, and disaster.

In 1989 Yarbro's *Beastnights* appeared in a paperback edition. It is the story of a Vietnam veteran who developed mental problems while a prisoner of war, and has turned into a serial killer who strikes only when it's raining.

Analysis of Selected Titles

FLAME IN BYZANTIUM

A Flame in Byzantium, 1987, novel. Prequel: *Blood Games: A Novel of Historical Horror*, 1980, novel. Sequels: *Crusader's Torch*, 1988, novel; *A Candle for D'Artagnan*, 1989, novel.

Social Concerns/Themes

In the last book of the Saint-Germain trilogy, *Blood Games*, Olivia appears as the oppressed wife of an important man, who repeatedly brutalizes her and allows her to be raped by gladiators. Saint-Germain saves Olivia from this brutality, and they fall in love, demonstrating Yarbro's persistent theme that no vampire has ever wreaked as much havoc as mortal men. At Olivia's insistence, Saint-Germain makes her a vampire (not immortal, but with a very long life span). Olivia then flees Rome with her vampire bondsman, Niklos, when the Ostrogoths invade.

Now five-hundred-years-old, they settle in Constantinople during the reign of Justinian and Theodora. There, they discover that the city has been newly converted to Christianity. Conditions have become severely restrictive of women's rights. The city is infested with spies. Olivia's pagan Roman customs are seen as threatening, and her self-confident femininity causes her to become the victim of persecution. As the Saint-Germain novels have made clear, water is particularly dreaded by vampires, though not nearly so much as fire. Sentenced to be drowned, she nearly dies, but is saved by Niklos. A brief love affair with a mortal, Captain Drosos, ends sadly.

Characters

In keeping with her feminist leanings, Yarbro presents a heroine who asserts her rights against social oppression, at a time when the new state religion of Christianity is driving out and repressing the old pagan ways.

In the Saint-Germain trilogy, Atta Olivia Clemens was saved from her tomb by her lover, Saint-Germain, and vindicated by the Emperor Titus Flavius Vespasianus after he orders the public beheading of her vicious husband Justus as punishment for his brutality. Once free of the sexual dominance and violence of her husband (whom she tolerated only because he held her entire family's fate in his hands), Olivia was free to develop her true personality. In the trilogy she loves only liberated men, although Yarbro seems to prefer that they be males who are of a martial bent, perhaps the more to underscore their gentility and considerate treatment of women. The male romantic characters in each book are much like one another, whether they be knight or army officer or musketeer. These are women's fantasy books, and those heroes, who are not princes or counts, need uniforms.

Techniques/Literary Precedents

Yarbro's Saint-Germain series falls easily into the category of historical romance, with the added interest of a vampire hero, or in the case of this sub-trilogy, heroine. These books are unique among vampire novels in that the author uses the longevity of the central characters to take advantage of every historical setting that appeals to her. Her intent is to recreate the period and its particular brand of oppression in order that her protagonists may war against the establishment of that day and either help illustrate the brutality of men or to combat it. The vampirism becomes less important with each novel, and the ironic contrast between the view of vampires as terrifying and dangerous and the reality of how humans can massacre enormous numbers in short periods of time, becomes less significant.

A reviewer commented that *A Flame in Byzantium* is not a horror novel because "any horror stems not from vampirism but from human acts in an age of religious persecution." The reviewer felt that Olivia's vampirism was "a subplot in an excellent historical novel." Another critic, however, complained that fans of the occult would feel cheated, while lovers of historical fiction would consider Yarbro's work inadequate. "As history," said the *Kirkus Review*, "her novels are like tales heard over a car radio, vaguely entertaining but quickly forgotten."

CRUSADER'S TORCH

Crusader's Torch, 1988, novel. Prequels: *Blood Games: A Novel of Historical Horror*, 1980, novel; *A Flame in Byzantium*, 1987, novel. Sequel: *A Candle for D'Artagnan*, 1989, novel.

Social Concerns/Themes

The second novel in the trilogy leaps ahead to the twelfth century, where Olivia is now eleven hundred years old. Living in Tyre, she wishes to return to Rome, but the city is suffering at the hands of the Crusaders, most notably Richard the Lion-hearted. The walls are falling, and there is fever in the aqueducts. Olivia is forced to flee an invading army led by Saladin. Attacked at sea, she nearly dies swimming to Cyprus.

Characters

In this novel Olivia's inevitably ill-fated love for a mortal man centers upon a Hospitaller knight who gives her his "body and blood." Unfortunately, he has a rare disease. At the end of the novel, Olivia decides to take her chances in Rome.

Techniques/Literary Precedents

While most critics ignored *Crusader's Torch*, a critic for *Science Fiction Chronicle* declared it a success. "This series," he wrote, "would have been successful even without the supernatural protagonists" that made it valuable to fans of the occult, because Yarbro excels at depicting history. He pronounced *Crusader's Torch* "a first rank novel by any standard."

A CANDLE FOR D'ARTAGNAN

A Candle for D'Artagnan, 1989, novel.

Social Concerns/Themes

The final novel of the trilogy finds Olivia a wealthy Roman widow living in the seventeenth century and now sixteen hundred years old. The plot revolves around papal intrigue, the deaths of the French Cardinal Richelieu and Louis XIII, and the regency of Louis XIV.

Yarbro has always used the theme of vampirism partly as a topic of interest in itself and partly as a means to carry her readers on an erratic course through history in which she dwells heavily upon the inhumanity of men, most particularly the cruelty of adult males to women. A sub-theme is always sex/romance with Olivia, as it was with Saint-Germain. As a genuine, and not a "second-hand" vampire, Saint-Germain will live forever. In this new trilogy Yarbro has focused upon the life of a liberated woman, rather than upon the vampire who liberated her. Thus the theme of feminism is given more explicit attention through the personality of the protagonist. As long as there are vampire fans, people will buy these books. The Olivia trilogy will also attract those who look for books with strong female protagonists. What it will not attract is fans who prefer literature that is not heavily propagandistic.

Characters

Olivia has been befriended by the pope and his cardinals, who send her on a special mission to Paris. There, she is to aid and observe Abbe Guilio Mazarini, a spy for the Holy See, and to provide him with a place to hold meetings. Mazarini is in Paris at the invitation of Cardinal Richelieu, head churchman in France and a cohort of King Louis XIII. Olivia again falls in love with a mortal man, this time with d'Artagnan, musketeer and comrade of the musketeers from Dumas's novel *The Three Musketeers* (1844)—Isaac de Portau (Porthos), Armand de Sillegue d'Athos (Athos), and Herni d'Aramitz (Aramis). He becomes a vampire at her hands in order to spend more time with her, even though she warns him that they will never be immortal.

Relation to Previous Works

These three novels, as noted above, are a sub-trilogy within the open-ended series dominated by the male vampire, Saint-Germain. They are of a piece with them in terms of technique and authorial intent, and are linked by the fact that Atta Olivia Clemens is the creature of Saint-Germain, although he does not figure in the plots of these books. Olivia was created in *Blood Games* (1980), which was set in ancient Rome, and is now presumably gone as of the third novel in this trilogy. Given, However, Yarbro's penchant for jumping about in history, there is always the possibility that she will return to some interesting date in Olivia's fifteen-hundred-year life span and add yet another episode.

FIRECODE
Firecode, 1987, novel, written as Quinn Yarbro.

Social Concerns/Themes
Firecode belongs to Yarbro's second most typical form of fiction, the apocalyptic or holocaust novel. As with *False Dawn* and *The Time of the Fourth Horseman*, she appeals to the reader's paranoia to create a sense of helplessness in the face of mass death and destruction. Here, the fear is that of the innumerate who fear the dominance of computers and their incomprehensible "number-crunching" in the late twentieth century. Needless to say, the computers bring ruin to humankind.

Characters
The central character is a statistician named Carter Milne. When a series of incredibly destructive fires of unknown origin break out all over North America, she correlates all the data using computers, which is ironic because the fault lies with computers to begin with. Carter is opposed by those who disagree with her theories and by the FBI, which hopes to isolate the cause of the fires and to use it as a weapon against enemies of the United States. By using a female detective/mathematician, Yarbro makes the point that stereotypes of women as less rational or mathematically talented are to be rejected. Carter Milne is presented as a role model for female readers.

Techniques/Literary Precedents
Firecode is a science fiction novel in which a holocaust is threatened. As in all of Yarbro's novels, there is a supernatural or mystical component to the plot. In this case, Carter Milne solves the mystery of the fires when she happens upon ancient mystical books in her new house, which she buys after her husband, a victim of mysterious forces, burns up the old house with himself inside. To modernize the novel and to take credit away from religious mystics, Yarbro

demonstrates that the mystics are only half right—there is something out there that is inadvertently summoned by the computers, but it is an actual physical "something." One reviewer termed this something a "whatsit, a natural phenomenon, a resonance with reality." What occurs is simply that when the thousands of computers clicking away happen to hit upon a specific sequence of numbers, fire is called down from this "whatsit," destroying the typist and everything around.

The reviewer was scornful of this premise because the sequence of death numbers is only fifteen digits long. He reasons that society as a whole probably hits upon this number thousands of times every day. As he points out, such a weak basis for our fear is merely "the night terror of someone who belongs to a different millennium and does not really comprehend that new-fangled thing called arithmetic and how it helps one control the world." It is ironic that Yarbro's attempt to create a non-stereotypical woman mathematician/statistician is crippled by her own ignorance of mathematical probability.

Relation to Previous Works

Although *Firecode* is clearly related to Yarbro's other apocalyptic science fiction novels, it is also related to her detective novels that feature a male American Indian lawyer/detective, Charlie Spotted Moon. Whereas Charlie uses some sort of Indian sixth sense to solve crimes, Milne does not rely on "feminine intuition" but on a liberated woman's analytical powers. Further, as in Yarbro's two other apocalyptic novels, the blame falls upon a corrupt, short-sighted, or insensitive humanity that has allowed technology to get out of control.

In *False Dawn*, pollution runs rampant, destroying many present forms of life and most of humanity. In *Fourth Horseman*, there was a deliberate decision of Malthusian-minded scientists to destroy the least desirable one third of the world's population by substituting placebos for vaccinations. In *Firecode*, our data-processing equipment mindlessly turns upon and destroys humanity. This final novel is easily the least convincing of the three.

Additional Sources

Amantia, A. M. B. Review of *A Flame in Byzantium*. *Library Journal* (September 1, 1987): 202.

D'Ammassa, Don. Review of *Crusader's Torch*. *Science Fiction Chronicles* (February 1989): 10.

———. Review of *Beastnights*. *Science Fiction Chronicles* (June 1989): 41.

Easton, Tom. Review of *Firecode*. *Analog* (October 1987): 179.

Steinberg, Sybil. Review of *A Candle for D'Artagnan*. *Publishers Weekly*. (October 6, 1989): 80.

Kay Kinsella Rout
Michigan State University

ROGER ZELAZNY
1937

Update

Roger Zelazny continues as one of science fiction and fantasy's most prolific and popular authors. The last five years have seen the publication of two Hugo-winning shorter pieces—"Twenty-four Views of Mount Fuji by Hokusai" (1985) and "Permafrost" (1986)—the children's novel *A Dark Travelling* (1989), and the story collection *Frost and Fire* (1989). But his major effort has been the completion of a second series of novels set in the fantasy universe of Amber. Four Amber novels have been published since 1985, and at least one more is in preparation.

While Zelazny is well-regarded within science fiction circles, as attested by the two recent Hugos, recent reviews suggest a degree of critical coolness. Detractors argue that he has failed to live up to his initial promise, that his work often shows signs of haste and carelessness, or that he merely rehashes earlier themes and devices. There is a measure of truth to these criticisms; some of the novels show signs of hasty construction or repeat earlier successes. His admitted practice of starting a story without knowing where it is going gives his work considerable spontaneity, but it can also lead to sloppiness, padding, and dead ends. Each of the Amber sequences has really been one long novel published as several shorter novels over a period of years. This has resulted in a great deal of expositional repetition and aggravated the problem of loose ends and false starts. It seems likely that both sets of Amber books would have been significantly improved by extensive editing once Zelazny actually knew the final shape of the plot.

Zelazny's novels will always be compared with his brilliant early work, which had a remarkable impact upon science fiction. Still, he remains a gifted storyteller and one of the genre's distinctive voices. His exploration of the themes of maturity, death, and immortality, the power of his imagination, and the quality of his best writing set him apart from writers who are only entertainers. The weaknesses of some of his recent work perhaps typify the dilemma of the writer who strives for both artistic and commercial success.

Analysis of Selected Titles

THE SECOND CHRONICLES OF AMBER

The Second Chronicles of Amber, novel series (including *Trumps of Doom*, 1985; *Blood of Amber*, 1986; *Sign of Chaos*, 1987; *Knight of Shadows*, 1989).

Social Concerns/Themes

The first Chronicle of Amber ends at the Courts of Chaos, where Corwin, Prince of Amber, meets for the first time his son Merlin. Indeed the reader learns that the whole five-novel sequence has been a story told by Corwin to Merlin—a kind of autobiography and apologia. The second chronicle is Merlin's story.

Merlin is the son of Corwin and Dara, Princess of Chaos, Corwin's one-time lover and more recently his bitter enemy. Thus he is a son both of Amber and Chaos and a pivotal figure in the ongoing struggle between those two opposed realms. While the plot defies easy summary, it turns on Merlin's attempt to discover who is trying to kill him, a quest that involves him in a dizzying array of political machinations, family feuds, and lovers' vendettas. The struggle culminates in what appears to be an ultimate conflict between the powers of the Logrus and the Unicorn, the rival metaphysical entities underlying Chaos and Amber. If this sounds confusing, it is, and Zelazny further complicates the plot by adding characters and plot twists at virtually every turn.

The reader has the strong sense of a writer delighting in making up his story as he goes along, but at least one reviewer has unflatteringly compared the novels to a television soap opera, with the frequent cliffhanger endings, the discovery of new relatives every few episodes, and the general sense of an author writing himself in and out of corners.

The principal theme of the first Amber sequence is the need for a dynamic balance between freedom (or chaos, energy) and pattern (or law, order, form), which are represented by Chaos and Amber. Chaos is the primordial condition of existence; Amber, long thought by its inhabitants to be the original world, is an offshoot of Chaos, the product of the genius of a rebel Lord of Chaos who created a Pattern. Zelazny is here playing a variation on numerous creation accounts which portray the beginning of the universe not as a creation from nothing, but as the triumph of order over chaos. What makes Zelazny's version different is his celebration of balance. There is no suggestion that he regards order as morally or metaphysically superior to Chaos; it is a mistake to regard Chaos as evil and Amber as good. More precisely, his pairs are freedom and law, energy and pattern. None of the Amber books offers the opposition between good and evil seen in Christian-based fantasies like J. R. R. Tolkien's *The Lord of the Rings*. On the contrary, the ideal requires a continuous balance between opposites, not the triumph of one over the other.

While it is impossible to make a definitive pronouncement on the themes of a novel sequence still in progress, Merlin's parentage is perhaps suggestive of the main thematic line. As a child of both Chaos and Amber, one whose sole allegiance has been demanded by each side, Merlin plays a critical thematic role.

Through the fourth novel he has resisted efforts of the Logrus and the Unicorn to recruit him, insisting upon his dual allegiance to Amber and Chaos. It is likely that the ultimate resolution of the plot will revolve around Merlin's choices and that the precarious balance of Chaos and Amber will depend upon his ability and willingness to be true to both sides of his heritage, to both poles of his being.

Characters

The growth of the protagonist—or his failure to grow—is at the heart of virtually all of Zelazny's fiction. In most genre fiction the protagonist solves a problem or defeats an enemy. If there is any hint of moral, emotional, or psychological growth, it may seem merely formulaic or simply incidental to the plot. In Zelazny's best work, however, the development of the protagonist is both central and problematic. His heroes are always attractive, but they are usually morally flawed or psychologically stunted. Their problem is not only to complete a quest or defeat an enemy, but to deepen their own humanity.

Merlin, despite the fact that he is a sorcerer, a warrior, and a prince of two magical realms, faces some rather prosaic problems. He is a young man trying to come to terms with his family: a famous (and absent) father who is a stranger yet intimately familiar; a protective mother who hates his father; and a jealous and resentful step-brother. In addition, Merlin's former lover now bitterly resents him because (as he is beginning to understand) he was unable to trust her or confide in her. Merlin is also trying to discover himself, to learn who he is and what he believes. Zelazny has transposed these common human problems to the level of high fantasy.

Merlin's step-brother Jurt and former lover Julia are both actively engaged in trying to kill him, using assassins, supernatural creatures, and a variety of magical spells. His mother saddles him with a guardian spirit which can temporarily possess any handy body to save Merlin from harm. And his father, though never actually present, still seems hauntingly near at hand. His family difficulties, moreover, involve concerns over the succession to the two major thrones of the universe. His own choices are apt to affect countless lives and the political and ontological balance of that universe. Nonetheless, the problems with which Merlin has to deal are recognizably human ones: can he be true to others and remain true to himself? Will his level of moral maturity match his power? Will he grow to meet the challenges he faces?

Techniques/Literary Precedents

The second Amber sequence, like the first, is structured in part as a mystery story. Merlin attempts to discover who is trying to kill him and learns that there may be more enemies and more plots than he first imagined and that there are threats to more than just Merlin himself. Again, as in the first series, the hero spends a good deal of time listening to the stories of other characters—friends, enemies, and those who switch sides—as he tries to piece together a coherent account from their partial and contradictory tales. There is less reliance on the epic techniques of the first sequence and a greater concentration on magic and court intrigue.

Zelazny's wide reading is reflected in his highly allusive style. Echoes of dozens of other works permeate the novel's texture. For example the name Merlin for a young sorcerer is at the very least suggestive, though it is not yet clear how much Zelazny will exploit the Arthurian parallel. There is a sustained allusion to Lewis Carroll's *Alice in Wonderland* (1865), especially in a lengthy dream passage, and perhaps the invocation of Carroll suggests something of the novel's playful and often satiric tone.

Relation to Previous Work

Zelazny's principal precedent is his own first sequence of Amber novels. Although he introduces new elements, Zelazny mainly elaborates on his previously created universe. Amber/Chaos/Shadow are not as fully realized as Tolkien's Middle Earth or Stephen R. Donaldson's The Land, for example. One has the sense that while there may be a good deal of vivid action going on in the foreground, the rest of the stage is decked with rather flimsy and ill-assorted props dredged from a theatrical company's archives. And yet there are hints, especially in the recent *Knight of Shadows*, that Zelazny intends to explore the underlying significance of Amber and Chaos in much greater depth. Zelazny's fans may well hope so, for Amber has lost much of its original freshness and excitement.

Another problem with the second series is the fact that thus far Merlin is a less interesting character than Corwin. He lacks Corwin's maturity and painful experiences; as yet his emotional and psychological growth is more anticipated than real. Thus far, Zelazny seems to be capitalizing, admittedly in a generally entertaining way, on a previous success. Up to this point, the new Amber novels share the fate of most sequels: to be compared to the original and found wanting.

Additional Sources

Lindskold, Jane M. "All Roads *Do* Lead to Amber." *Extrapolation* 31, 4 (Winter 1990): 326-332. Explores the sources of names and characters, with primary attention given to the first series.

Slater, Niall W. "Of Memory and Desire: Zelazny's Platonism." *Classical and Modern Literature: A Quarterly* 9, 2 (Fall 1988): 65-71. One of very few scholarly articles yet to appear on the Amber novels. Slater points out the Platonic sources of Amber, but misses the importance of balance between Chaos and Amber.

Zelazny, Roger. "Fantasy and Science Fiction: A Writer's View." In *Intersections: Fantasy and Science Fiction*, edited by George E. Slusser and Eric S. Rabkin. Carbondale: Southern Illinois University Press, 1987. A brief essay comparing science fiction and fantasy.

Kevin P. Mulcahy
Rutgers University

APPENDIX I
TITLES GROUPED BY SOCIAL ISSUES AND THEMES

Academia/Education
Because It Is Bitter, and Because It Is My Heart (Joyce Carol Oates)
Coyote Waits (Tony Hillerman)
Cyteen (C. J. Cherryh)
Folk of the Air, The (Peter S. Beagle)
Free-Lance Pallbearers, The (Ishmael Reed)
Giles Goat-Boy or, The Revised New Syllabus (John Barth)
God's Grace (Bernard Malamud)
Hocus Pocus (Kurt Vonnegut)
House for Mr Biswas, A (V. S. Naipaul)
In Country (Bobbie Ann Mason)
J R (William Gaddis)
Last Notes From Home (Frederick Exley)
Man Made of Words, The (N. Scott Momaday)
Marya: A Life (Joyce Carol Oates)
More Die of Heartbreak (Saul Bellow)
Mumbo Jumbo (Ishmael Reed)
Mystic Masseur, The (V. S. Naipaul)
No More Saturday Nights (Norma Klein)
Once and Future King, The (T. H. White)
One L (Scott Turow)
Prayer for Owen Meany, A (John Irving)
Stones of Nomuru, The (L. Sprague de Camp)

Adolescence
Always Coming Home (Ursula K. Le Guin)
Angel with the Sword (C. J. Cherryh)
Because It Is Bitter, and Because It Is My Heart (Joyce Carol Oates)
Beet Queen, The (Louise Erdrich)
Blood of Requited Love (Manuel Puig)
Brown Girl, Brownstones (Paule Marshall)
Captain and the Enemy, The (Graham Greene)
Cat's Eye (Margaret Atwood)
Cyteen (C. J. Cherryh)
Dead Father, The (Donald Barthelme)
Deadeye Dick (Kurt Vonnegut)
Eyes of the Dragon, The (Stephen King)
Fade (Robert Cormier)
Fast Lanes (Jayne Anne Phillips)
Floating Opera, The (John Barth)
Gallowglass (Ruth Rendell as Barbara Vine)
Game of Empire, The (Poul Anderson)
Garden-Party, The (Katherine Mansfield)

Giles Goat-Boy or, The Revised New Syllabus (John Barth)
House of Stairs, The (Ruth Rendell as Barbara Vine)
How I Grew (Mary McCarthy)
In My Father's House (Ernest J. Gaines)
In Miro District and Other Stories (Peter Taylor)
J R (William Gaddis)
K. (Mary Roberts Rinehart)
Lover, The (Marguerite Duras)
Marya: A Life (Joyce Carol Oates)
Midnight's Children (Salman Rushdie)
Moon and the Face, The (Patricia A. McKillip)
Mutant Season, The (Robert Silverberg)
My Secret History (Paul Theroux)
No More Saturday Nights (Norma Klein)
Old Forest and Other Stories, The (Peter Taylor)
Once and Future King, The (T. H. White)
Picturing Will (Ann Beattie)
Prayer for Owen Meany, A (John Irving)
Quinn's Book (William Kennedy)
Rusalka (C. J. Cherryh)
Sea Wall, The (Marguerite Duras)
Shame (Salman Rushdie)
Summons to Memphis, A (Peter Taylor)
Tales of the South Pacific (James A. Michener)
Taming the Star Runner (S. E. Hinton)
Tehanu (Ursula K. Le Guin)
Till We Meet Again (Judith Krantz)
Tracks (Louise Erdrich)
Vineland (Thomas Pynchon)
You Must Remember This (Joyce Carol Oates)

Alienation/Loneliness
Acres and Pains (S. J. Perelman)
Always Coming Home (Ursula K. Le Guin)
Angle of Repose (Wallace Stegner)
At the Bay (Katherine Mansfield)
Because It Is Bitter, and Because It Is My Heart (Joyce Carol Oates)
Beet Queen, The (Louise Erdrich)
Being Invisible (Thomas Berger)
Beloved (Toni Morrison)
Big Rock Candy Mountain, The (Wallace Stegner)
Bourne Ultimatum, The (Robert Ludlum)
Bridesmaid, The (Ruth Rendell)
Captain and the Enemy, The (Graham Greene)
Cardinal of the Kremlin, The (Tom Clancy)
Carpenter's Gothic (William Gaddis)
Cat's Eye (Margaret Atwood)
Close Quarters (William Golding)
The Counterlife (Philip Roth)
Country Place (Ann Petry)
Crying of Lot 49, The (Thomas Pynchon)
Cyteen (C. J. Cherryh)
Dark Laughter (Sherwood Anderson)

Appendix I

Dark Tower Series, The (Stephen King)
Deadeye Dick (Kurt Vonnegut)
Death of Artemio Cruz (Carlos Fuentes)
Devices and Desires (P. D. James)
Difficulties with Girls (Kingsley Amis)
Exile, The (William Kotzwinkle)
Eyes of the Dragon, The (Stephen King)
Fade (Robert Cormier)
Fast Lanes (Jayne Anne Phillips)
Feast of Snakes, A (Harry Crews)
Fencepost Chronicles, The (W. P. Kinsella)
Fire Down Below (William Golding)
Folks That Live on the Hill, The (Kingsley Amis)
Fool's Run (Patricia A. McKillip)
Freaky Deaky (Elmore Leonard)
Galapagos (Kurt Vonnegut)
Gallowglass (Ruth Rendell as Barbara Vine)
Game of Empire, The (Poul Anderson)
Garden of Eden, The (Ernest Hemingway)
Gathering of Old Men, A (Ernest J. Gaines)
Gerald's Party (Robert Coover)
God Knows (Joseph Heller)
God's Grace (Bernard Malamud)
Golden Orange, The (Joseph Wambaugh)
Gravity's Rainbow (Thomas Pynchon)
Guerrillas (V. S. Naipaul)
Handmaid's Tale, The (Margaret Atwood)
Harmful Intent (Robin Cook)
Her Mother's Daughter (Marilyn French)
Hermit of 69th Street, The (Jerzy Kosinski)
His Little Women (Judith Rossner)
Hocus Pocus (Kurt Vonnegut)
Homesick (Guy Vanderhaeghe)
Hook, Line, Sinker (Len Deighton)
Hot Jazz Trio (Wm. Kotzwinkle)
House for Mr Biswas, A (V. S. Naipaul)
House of Stairs, The (Ruth Rendell as Barbara Vine)
House Made of Dawn (N. Scott Momaday)
In My Father's House (Ernest J. Gaines)
In Miro District and Other Stories (Peter Taylor)
Joy Luck Club, The (Amy Tan)
J R (William Gaddis)
Keep the Change (Thomas McGuane)
Killshot (Elmore Leonard)
Knockout Artist, The (Harry Crews)
Last Notes From Home (Frederick Exley)
Love in the Time of Cholera (Gabriel García Márquez)
Lover, The (Marguerite Duras)
Marya: A Life (Joyce Carol Oates)
Midnight's Children (Salman Rushdie)

Moderato Cantabile (Marguerite Duras)
Moon and the Face, The (Patricia A. McKillip)
More Die of Heartbreak (Saul Bellow)
Most of S. J. Perelman, The (S. J. Perelman)
Moviegoer, The (Walker Percy)
Mutant Season, The (Robert Silverberg)
My Àntonia (Willa Cather)
My Secret History (Paul Theroux)
Novelty (John Crowley)
Old Gringo, The (Carlos Fuentes)
Old Devils, The (Kingsley Amis)
Old Forest and Other Stories, The (Peter Taylor)
Origin of the Brunists, The (Robert Coover)
Other Side, The (Mary Gordon)
Paladin of the Lost Hour (Harlan Ellison)
Paradise (Donald Barthelme)
Praisesong for the Widow (Paule Marshall)
Prelude (Katherine Mansfield)
Princess Bride, The (William Goldman)
Pubis Angelical (Manuel Puig)
Quinn's Book (William Kennedy)
Rat, The (Günter Grass)
Recognitions, The (William Gaddis)
Roma Mater (Poul Anderson)
Rusalka (C. J. Cherryh)
Russia House, The (John le Carré)
Satanic Verses, The (Salman Rushdie)
Sea Wall, The (Marguerite Duras)

Second Coming, The (Walker Percy)
Secret Pilgrim, The (John le Carré)
Shadows (John Gardner)
Shame (Salman Rushdie)
Silent Gondoliers, The (William Goldman)
Silver Pillow, The (Thomas M. Disch)
Snow White (Donald Barthelme)
Soft Monkey (Harlan Ellison)
Sphere (Michael Crichton)
Square, The (Marguerite Duras)
Star of Gypsies (Robert Silverberg)
Stillness (John Gardner)
Stones of Nomuru, The (L. Sprague de Camp)
Story of My Life (Jay McInerney)
Summons to Memphis, A (Peter Taylor)
Taming the Star Runner (S. E. Hinton)
Tango Charlie and Foxtrot Romeo (John Varley)
Tracks (Louise Erdrich)
Tripmaster Monkey: His Fake Book (Maxine Hong Kingston)
Universal Baseball Association, The (Robert Coover)
V. (Thomas Pynchon)
Veiled One, The (Ruth Rendell)
Vineland (Thomas Pynchon)
War (Marguerite Duras)
Weaveworld (Clive Barker)
Westward Ha! (S. J. Perelman)
When Harry Met Sally (Nora Ephron)
Where I'm Calling From (Raymond Carver)

Winesburg, Ohio (Sherwood Anderson)
You Must Remember This (Joyce Carol Oates)

American Dream, The
Acres and Pains (S. J. Perelman)
Angle of Repose (Wallace Stegner)
Autobiography of Miss Jane Pittman, The (Ernest J. Gaines)
Because It Is Bitter, and Because It Is My Heart (Joyce Carol Oates)
Beet Queen, The (Louise Erdrich)
Being Invisible (Thomas Berger)
Big Town, The (Ring Lardner)
Big Rock Candy Mountain, The (Wallace Stegner)
Billy Bathgate (E. L. Doctorow)
Bonfire of the Vanities, The (Tom Wolfe)
Brown Girl, Brownstones (Paule Marshall)
Burden of Proof, The (Scott Turow)
Carpenter's Gothic (William Gaddis)
Country Place (Ann Petry)
Dark Laughter (Sherwood Anderson)
Deadeye Dick (Kurt Vonnegut)
Emperor of America (Richard Condon)
Exile, The (William Kotzwinkle)
Golden Orange, The (Joseph Wambaugh)
Guerrillas (V. S. Naipaul)
Her Mother's Daughter (Marilyn French)
House for Mr Biswas, A (V. S. Naipaul)
Houseguest, The (Thomas Berger)
Icarus Agenda, The (Robert Ludlum)
In My Father's House (Ernest J. Gaines)
J R (William Gaddis)
Keep the Change (Thomas McGuane)
Killing Mister Watson (Peter Matthiessen)
Last Notes From Home (Frederick Exley)
Mary and the Giant (Philip K. Dick)
Midnight Examiner, The (William Kotzwinkle)
Most of S. J. Perelman, The (S. J. Perelman)
Mutant Season, The (Robert Silverberg)
My Àntonia (Willa Cather)
Other Side, The (Mary Gordon)
Paradise (Donald Barthelme)
Picturing Will (Ann Beattie)
Public Burning, The (Robert Coover)
Quinn's Book (William Kennedy)
Shiloh and Other Stories (Bobbie Ann Mason)
Stillness (John Gardner)
Toynbee Convector, The (Ray Bradbury)
Tracks (Louise Erdrich)
Trust (George V. Higgins)
Universal Baseball Association, The (Robert Coover)
Victories (George V. Higgins)

Vineland (Thomas Pynchon)
Westward Ha! (S. J. Perelman)
Where I'm Calling From (Raymond Carver)
You Must Remember This (Joyce Carol Oates)

Animals
Acres and Pains (S. J. Perelman)
Alaska (James A. Michener)
Alnilam (James Dickey)
Always Coming Home (Ursula K. Le Guin)
Bingo (Rita Mae Brown)
Feast of Snakes, A (Harry Crews)
Galapagos (Kurt Vonnegut)
Genesis (Wallace Stegner)
God's Grace (Bernard Malamud)
Most of S. J. Perelman, The (S. J. Perelman)
Picture This (Joseph Heller)
Prayer for Owen Meany, A (John Irving)
Rat, The (Günter Grass)
Sphere (Michael Crichton)
Taming the Star Runner (S. E. Hinton)
Tango Charlie and Foxtrot Romeo (John Varley)
Temple of My Familiar, The (Alice Walker)
We Are Still Married (Garrison Keillor)
Westward Ha! (S. J. Perelman)
Whistlejacket (John Hawkes)

Art/Artists
Acres and Pains (S. J. Perelman)
Autobiography of Miss Jane Pittman, The (Ernest J. Gaines)
Because It Is Bitter, and Because It Is My Heart (Joyce Carol Oates)
Being Invisible (Thomas Berger)
Big Room, The (Michael Herr)
Carpenter's Gothic (William Gaddis)
Cat's Eye (Margaret Atwood)
Complete Short Stories of Ernest Hemingway, The (Ernest Hemingway)
Crying of Lot 49, The (Thomas Pynchon)
Dead Father, The (Donald Barthelme)
Exile, The (William Kotzwinkle)
Fade (Robert Cormier)
Folk of the Air (Peter Beagle)
Foucault's Pendulum (Umberto Eco)
Free-Lance Pallbearers, The (Ishmael Reed)
Garden of Eden, The (Ernest Hemingway)
Gift of Asher Lev, The (Chaim Potok)
Graveyard for Lunatics, A (Ray Bradbury)
Gravity's Rainbow (Thomas Pynchon)
Hermit of 69th Street, The (Jerzy Kosinski)
His Little Women (Judith Rossner)
Hot Jazz Trio, The (William Kotzwinkle)

Appendix I   1315

House for Mr Biswas, A (V. S. Naipaul)
Je ne parle pas français (Katherine Mansfield)
J R (William Gaddis)
Keep the Change (Thomas McGuane)
Man-Eater of Malgudi, The (R. K. Narayan)
Midnight Examiner, The (William Kotzwinkle)
Midnight's Children (Salman Rushdie)
Misery (Stephen King)
Mitla Pass (Leon Uris)
Most of S. J. Perelman, The (S. J. Perelman)
My Secret History (Paul Theroux)
Novelty (John Crowley)
Paradise (Donald Barthelme)
Picturing Will (Ann Beattie)
Pillars of the Earth (Ken Follett)
Reckless Eyeballing (Ishmael Reed)
Recognitions, The (William Gaddis)
Satanic Verses, The (Salman Rushdie)
Shame (Salman Rushdie)
Silent Gondoliers, The (William Goldman)
Skinny Legs and All (Tom Robbins)
Snow White (Donald Barthelme)
Stillness (John Gardner)
Tripmaster Monkey: His Fake Book (Maxine Hong Kingston)
Truth about Lorin Jones, The (Alison Lurie)
Vineland (Thomas Pynchon)
Whistlejacket (John Hawkes)

Betrayal
Cardinal of the Kremlin, The (Tom Clancy)
Clear and Present Danger (Tom Clancy)
Game of Empire, The (Poul Anderson)
Russia House, The (John le Carré)

Black Identity
All God's Children Need Traveling Shoes (Maya Angelou)
Autobiography of Miss Jane Pittman, The (Ernest J. Gaines)
Because It Is Bitter, and Because It Is My Heart (Joyce Carol Oates)
Beloved (Toni Morrison)
Brown Girl, Brownstones (Paule Marshall)
Chosen Place, The Timeless People, The (Paule Marshall)
Different Kind of Christmas, A (Alex Haley)
Free-Lance Pallbearers, The (Ishmael Reed)
Gathering of Old Men, A (Ernest J. Gaines)
Guerrillas (V. S. Naipaul)
Hocus Pocus (Kurt Vonnegut)
In My Father's House (Ernest J. Gaines)
Mumbo Jumbo (Ishmael Reed)
Narrows, The (Ann Petry)

Praisesong for the Widow (Paule Marshall)
Q Clearance (Peter Benchley)
Quinn's Book (William Kennedy)
Sphere (Michael Crichton)
Street, The (Ann Petry)
Temple of My Familiar, The (Alice Walker)

Business/Corporate World
Acres and Pains (S. J. Perelman)
Being Invisible (Thomas Berger)
Bonfire of the Vanities, The (Tom Wolfe)
Burden of Proof, The (Scott Turow)
Carpenter's Gothic (William Gaddis)
Cassidy (Morris West)
Crying of Lot 49, The (Thomas Pynchon)
Deadeye Dick (Kurt Vonnegut)
Exile, The (William Kotzwinkle)
Financial Expert, The (R. K. Narayan)
Galapagos (Kurt Vonnegut)
Gravity's Rainbow (Thomas Pynchon)
Guerrillas (V. S. Naipaul)
Hocus Pocus (Kurt Vonnegut)
J R (William Gaddis)
Mortal Fear (Robin Cook)
Most of S. J. Perelman, The (S. J. Perelman)
Picture This (Joseph Heller)
Rabbit at Rest (John Updike)
Rat, The (Günter Grass)
Something In the Air (Emma Lathen)
Straight (Dick Francis)
Strong Medicine (Arthur Hailey)
Theft, A (Saul Bellow)
Vineland (Thomas Pynchon)
Westward Ha! (S. J. Perelman)

Children in Distress
Autobiography of Miss Jane Pittman, The (Ernest J. Gaines)
Because It Is Bitter, and Because It Is My Heart (Joyce Carol Oates)
Beet Queen, The (Louise Erdrich)
Big Rock Candy Mountain, The (Wallace Stegner)
Cat's Eye (Margaret Atwood)
Charlie and the Chocolate Factory (Roald Dahl)
Cyteen (C. J. Cherryh)
Devices and Desires (P. D. James)
Exile, The (William Kotzwinkle)
Fade (Robert Cormier)
Four Million, The (O. Henry)
Gallowglass (Ruth Rendell as Barbara Vine)
Game of Empire, The (Poul Anderson)
Gravity's Rainbow (Thomas Pynchon)
House for Mr Biswas, A (V. S. Naipaul)
In My Father's House (Ernest J. Gaines)
J R (William Gaddis)
Just As Long As We're Together (Judy Blume)
Marya: A Life (Joyce Carol Oates)
Picturing Will (Ann Beattie)
Rat, The (Günter Grass)
Sea Wall, The (Marguerite Duras)

Some Can Whistle (Larry McMurtry)
Taming the Star Runner (S. E. Hinton)
Tango Charlie and Foxtrot Romeo (John Varley)
Taste for Death, A (P. D. James)
Tehanu (Ursula K. Le Guin)
Tracks (Louise Erdrich)
Trimmed Lamp, The (O. Henry)
Vineland (Thomas Pynchon)
War (Marguerite Duras)
You Must Remember This (Joyce Carol Oates)

Class Conflict
Acres and Pains (S. J. Perelman)
Alaska (James A. Michener)
All God's Children Need Traveling Shoes (Maya Angelou)
Autobiography of Miss Jane Pittman, The (Ernest J. Gaines)
Bearkeeper's Daughter, The (Gillian Bradshaw)
Because It Is Bitter, and Because It Is My Heart (Joyce Carol Oates)
Beloved (Toni Morrison)
Big Town, The (Ring Lardner)
Big Rock Candy Mountain, The (Wallace Stegner)
Bonfire of the Vanities, The (Tom Wolfe)
Bridesmaid, The (Ruth Rendell)
Bridge of Lost Desire, The (Samuel R. Delany)
Chosen Place, The Timeless People, The (Paule Marshall)
Close Quarters (William Golding)
Country Place (Ann Petry)

Different Kind of Christmas, A (Alex Haley)
Fade (Robert Cormier)
Fencepost Chronicles, The (W. P. Kinsella)
Fire Down Below (William Golding)
First Man in Rome, The (Colleen McCullough)
Four Million, The (O. Henry)
Galapagos (Kurt Vonnegut)
Garden-Party, The (Katherine Mansfield)
Gathering of Old Men, A (Ernest J. Gaines)
Golden Orange, The (Joseph Wambaugh)
Guerrillas (V. S. Naipaul)
Handmaid's Tale, The (Margaret Atwood)
Hawaii (James A. Michener)
Hocus Pocus (Kurt Vonnegut)
House for Mr Biswas, A (V. S. Naipaul)
Houseguest, The (Thomas Berger)
Imperial Purple (Gillian Bradshaw)
J R (William Gaddis)
Killing Mister Watson (Peter Matthiessen)
Knockout Artist, The (Harry Crews)
Love in the Time of Cholera (Gabriel García Márquez)
Lover, The (Marguerite Duras)
Moderato Cantabile (Marguerite Duras)
Most of S. J. Perelman, The (S. J. Perelman)
My Secret History (Paul Theroux)

Narrows, The (Ann Petry)
Old Gringo, The (Carlos Fuentes)
Optimist's Daughter, The (Eudora Welty)
Origin of the Brunists, The (Robert Coover)
Paradise (Donald Barthelme)
Picture This (Joseph Heller)
Praisesong for the Widow (Paule Marshall)
Quinn's Book (William Kennedy)
Recognitions, The (William Gaddis)
Renegades of Pern (Anne McCaffrey)
Rummies (Peter Benchley)
Rusalka (C. J. Cherryh)
Scaramouche (Rafael Sabatini)
Sea Wall, The (Marguerite Duras)
Southern Family, A (Gail Godwin)
Tales of the South Pacific (James A. Michener)
Taming the Star Runner (S. E. Hinton)
Trimmed Lamp, The (O. Henry)
Uncle Fred Flits By (P. G. Wodehouse)
Veiled One, The (Ruth Rendell)
Vineland (Thomas Pynchon)
War (Marguerite Duras)
Westward Ha! (S. J. Perelman)
Who Killed Palomino Molero? (Mario Vargas Llosa)

Classical Greece/Rome
Beacon at Alexandria, The (Gillian Bradshaw)
Candle for D'Artagnan, A (Chelsea Quinn Yarbro)
Crusader's Torch (Chelsea Quinn Yarbro)
Firebrand, The (Marion Zimmer Bradley)
First Man in Rome, The (Colleen McCullough)
Flame in Byzantium (Chelsea Quinn Yarbro)
Picture This (Joseph Heller)
Roma Mater (Poul Anderson)
Skinny Legs and All (Tom Robbins)
Warrior Queens, The (Lady Antonia Fraser)

Colonialism/National Aggression
Alaska (James A. Michener)
Angel with the Sword (C. J. Cherryh)
Captain and the Enemy, The (Graham Greene)
Chosen Place, The Timeless People, The (Paule Marshall)
Dragonsdawn (Anne McCaffrey)
Emperor of America (Richard Condon)
Game of Empire, The (Poul Anderson)
Gravity's Rainbow (Thomas Pynchon)
Guerrillas (V. S. Naipaul)
Hawaii (James A. Michener)
House for Mr Biswas, A (V. S. Naipaul)
Lover, The (Marguerite Duras)
Magicians of Gor (John Norman)
Man-Eater of Malgudi, The (R. K. Narayan)

Appendix I

Midnight's Children (Salman Rushdie)
Mongoose R.I.P. (William F. Buckley, Jr.)
Mumbo Jumbo (Ishmael Reed)
Mystic Masseur, The (V. S. Naipaul)
Novelty (John Crowley)
Picture This (Joseph Heller)
Roma Mater (Poul Anderson)
Satanic Verses, The (Salman Rushdie)
Sea Wall, The (Marguerite Duras)
Shame (Salman Rushdie)
Stones of Nomuru, The (L. Sprague de Camp)
Tales of the South Pacific (James A. Michener)
Whirlwind (James Clavell)

Coming-of-Age
Autobiography of Miss Jane Pittman, The (Ernest J. Gaines)
Because It Is Bitter, and Because It Is My Heart (Joyce Carol Oates)
Beet Queen, The (Louise Erdrich)
Big Rock Candy Mountain, The (Wallace Stegner)
Billy Bathgate (E. L. Doctorow)
Blood of Requited Love (Manuel Puig)
Brown Girl, Brownstones (Paule Marshall)
Captain and the Enemy, The (Graham Greene)
Cat's Eye (Margaret Atwood)
Close Quarters (William Golding)
Cyteen (C. J. Cherryh)
Dead Father, The (Donald Barthelme)
Eyes of the Dragon, The (Stephen King)
Fade (Robert Cormier)
Fast Lanes (Jayne Anne Phillips)
Fencepost Chronicles, The (W. P. Kinsella)
Fire Down Below (William Golding)
Garden-Party, The (Katherine Mansfield)
Gathering of Old Men, A (Ernest J. Gaines)
Genesis (Wallace Stegner)
Giles Goat-Boy or, The Revised New Syllabus (John Barth)
God Knows (Joseph Heller)
Happy Turnip, The (Thomas M. Disch)
Harrowing of Gwynedd, The (Katherine Kurtz)
Honorable Barbarian, The (L. Sprague de Camp)
House for Mr Biswas, A (V. S. Naipaul)
How I Grew (Mary McCarthy)
In Praise of the Stepmother (Mario Vargas Llosa)
In My Father's House (Ernest J. Gaines)
In Country (Bobbie Ann Mason)
In Miro District and Other Stories (Peter Taylor)
J R (William Gaddis)
Just As Long As We're Together (Judy Blume)
K. (Mary Roberts Rinehart)
Little Governess, The (Katherine Mansfield)

Love in the Time of Cholera (Gabriel García Márquez)
Lover, The (Marguerite Duras)
Marya: A Life (Joyce Carol Oates)
Midnight's Children (Salman Rushdie)
Moon and the Face, The (Patricia A. McKillip)
Mutant Season, The (Robert Silverberg)
My Secret History (Paul Theroux)
My Àntonia (Willa Cather)
No More Saturday Nights (Norma Klein)
Old Forest and Other Stories, The (Peter Taylor)
Once and Future King, The (T. H. White)
One L (Scott Turow)
Optimist's Daughter, The (Eudora Welty)
Picturing Will (Ann Beattie)
Prayer for Owen Meany, A (John Irving)
Princess Bride, The (William Goldman)
Quinn's Book (William Kennedy)
Recognitions, The (William Gaddis)
Second Chronicles of Amber, The (Roger Zelazny)
Secret Pilgrim, The (John le Carré)
Shame (Salman Rushdie)
Silent Gondoliers, The (William Goldman)
Silver Pillow, The (Thomas M. Disch)
Sot-Weed Factor, The (John Barth)
Story of My Life (Jay McInerney)
Summons to Memphis, A (Peter Taylor)
Tales of the South Pacific (James A. Michener)
Taming the Star Runner (S. E. Hinton)
Tehanu (Ursula K. Le Guin)
Tracks (Louise Erdrich)
When Harry Met Sally (Nora Ephron)
Whistlejacket (John Hawkes)
Winesburg, Ohio (Sherwood Anderson)
You Must Remember This (Joyce Carol Oates)

Corruption
Angel with the Sword (C. J. Cherryh)
Big Room, The (Michael Herr)
Billy Bathgate (E. L. Doctorow)
Bridesmaid, The (Ruth Rendell)
Burden of Proof, The (Scott Turow)
Cardinal of the Kremlin, The (Tom Clancy)
Carpenter's Gothic (William Gaddis)
Cassidy (Morris West)
Clear and Present Danger (Tom Clancy)
Coyote Waits (Tony Hillerman)
Cyteen (C. J. Cherryh)
Dark Tower Series, The (Stephen King)
Emperor of America (Richard Condon)
Exile, The (William Kotzwinkle)

Appendix I

Fade (Robert Cormier)
Fire Down Below (William Golding)
First Man in Rome, The (Colleen McCullough)
Galapagos (Kurt Vonnegut)
Gallowglass (Ruth Rendell as Barbara Vine)
Game of Empire, The (Poul Anderson)
Gerald's Party (Robert Coover)
Golden Orange, The (Joseph Wambaugh)
Gravity's Rainbow (Thomas Pynchon)
Guerrillas (V. S. Naipaul)
Harmful Intent (Robin Cook)
Harrowing of Gwynedd, The (Katherine Kurtz)
House for Mr Biswas, A (V. S. Naipaul)
In Praise of the Stepmother (Mario Vargas Llosa)
Je ne parle pas français (Katherine Mansfield)
J R (William Gaddis)
Killing Time in St. Cloud (Judith Guest and Rebecca Hill)
Killing Mister Watson (Peter Matthiessen)
Little Governess, The (Katherine Mansfield)
Love Killers, The (Jackie Collins)
Midnight's Children (Salman Rushdie)
Mortal Fear (Robin Cook)
Old Gringo, The (Carlos Fuentes)
Out on the Cutting Edge (Lawrence Block)
Picturing Will (Ann Beattie)
Pillars of the Earth (Ken Follett)
Presumed Innocent (Scott Turow)
Public Burning, The (Robert Coover)
Rabbit at Rest (John Updike)
Rat, The (Günter Grass)
Recognitions, The (William Gaddis)
Roma Mater (Poul Anderson)
Sands of Time, The (Sidney Sheldon)
Satanic Verses, The (Salman Rushdie)
Sea Wall, The (Marguerite Duras)
Secret Pilgrim, The (John le Carré)
Shadows (John Gardner)
Shame (Salman Rushdie)
Straight (Dick Francis)
Trust (George V. Higgins)
V. (Thomas Pynchon)
Victories (George V. Higgins)
Vineland (Thomas Pynchon)
Who Killed Palomino Molero? (Mario Vargas Llosa)
Windmills of the Gods (Sidney Sheldon)
Wonderful Years, Wonderful Years (George V. Higgins)

Counterculture
Always Coming Home (Ursula K. Le Guin)
Angel with the Sword (C. J. Cherryh)
Crying of Lot 49, The (Thomas Pynchon)
Fast Lanes (Jayne Anne Phillips)
Folk of the Air, The (Peter S. Beagle)

Freaky Deaky (Elmore Leonard)
Gallowglass (Ruth Rendell as Barbara Vine)
Gathering of Old Men, A (Ernest J. Gaines)
Giles Goat-Boy or, The Revised New Syllabus (John Barth)
Guerrillas (V. S. Naipaul)
Hot Jazz Trio, The (William Kotzwinkle)
House of Stairs, The (Ruth Rendell as Barbara Vine)
J R (William Gaddis)
Midnight Examiner, The (William Kotzwinkle)
Origin of the Brunists, The (Robert Coover)
Public Burning, The (Robert Coover)
Radio Free Albemuth (Philip K. Dick)
Rat, The (Günter Grass)
Recognitions, The (William Gaddis)
Skinny Legs and All (Tom Robbins)
Sphere (Michael Crichton)
Story of My Life (Jay McInerney)
Vineland (Thomas Pynchon)

Crime
Because It Is Bitter, and Because It Is My Heart (Joyce Carol Oates)
Beloved (Toni Morrison)
Big Rock Candy Mountain, The (Wallace Stegner)
Billy Bathgate (E. L. Doctorow)
Bonfire of the Vanities, The (Tom Wolfe)

Bridesmaid, The (Ruth Rendell)
Burden of Proof, The (Scott Turow)
Carpenter's Gothic (William Gaddis)
Cassidy (Morris West)
Circular Staircase, The (Mary Roberts Rinehart)
Clear and Present Danger (Tom Clancy)
Cyteen (C. J. Cherryh)
Devices and Desires (P. D. James)
Fade (Robert Cormier)
Feast of Snakes, A (Harry Crews)
Financial Expert, The (R. K. Narayan)
Foucault's Pendulum (Umberto Eco)
Freaky Deaky (Elmore Leonard)
Gallowglass (Ruth Rendell as Barbara Vine)
Gathering of Old Men, A (Ernest J. Gaines)
Gerald's Party (Robert Coover)
Golden Orange, The (Joseph Wambaugh)
Graveyard for Lunatics, A (Ray Bradbury)
Gravity's Rainbow (Thomas Pynchon)
Guerrillas (V. S. Naipaul)
House for Mr Biswas, A (V. S. Naipaul)
Joey's Case (K. C. Constantine)
J R (William Gaddis)
Killing Time in St. Cloud (Judith Guest and Rebecca Hill)
Killing Mister Watson (Peter Matthiessen)

Appendix I

Killshot (Elmore Leonard)
Lamb to the Slaughter (Roald Dahl)
Last Notes From Home (Frederick Exley)
Love Killers, The (Jackie Collins)
Midnight Examiner, The (William Kotzwinkle)
Moderato Cantabile (Marguerite Duras)
Out on the Cutting Edge (Lawrence Block)
Patriot Games (Tom Clancy)
Presumed Innocent (Scott Turow)
Recognitions, The (William Gaddis)
Rummies (Peter Benchley)
Sands of Time, The (Sidney Sheldon)
Shadows (John Gardner)
Shame (Salman Rushdie)
Skinwalkers (Tony Hillerman)
Soft Monkey (Harlan Ellison)
Something In the Air (Emma Lathen)
Straight (Dick Francis)
Taste for Death, A (P. D. James)
Tehanu (Ursula K. Le Guin)
Theft, A (Saul Bellow)
Ticket to the Boneyard, A (Lawrence Block)
Tough Guys Don't Dance (Norman Mailer)
Tracks (Louise Erdrich)
Trust (George V. Higgins)
Veiled One, The (Ruth Rendell)
Victories (George V. Higgins)
Vineland (Thomas Pynchon)
Who Killed Palomino Molero? (Mario Vargas Llosa)

Death
Alnilam (James Dickey)
Angle of Repose (Wallace Stegner)
Autobiography of Miss Jane Pittman, The (Ernest J. Gaines)
Beloved (Toni Morrison)
Bridesmaid, The (Ruth Rendell)
Burden of Proof, The (Scott Turow)
Carpenter's Gothic (William Gaddis)
Celebration (Mary Lee Settle)
Clear and Present Danger (Tom Clancy)
The Counterlife (Philip Roth)
Dark Tower Series, The (Stephen King)
Deadeye Dick (Kurt Vonnegut)
Death of Artemio Cruz (Carlos Fuentes)
Devices and Desires (P. D. James)
Exile, The (William Kotzwinkle)
Fade (Robert Cormier)
Fast Lanes (Jayne Anne Phillips)
Feast of Snakes, A (Harry Crews)
Floating Opera, The (John Barth)
Galapagos (Kurt Vonnegut)
Garden-Party, The (Katherine Mansfield)
Gerald's Party (Robert Coover)
God Knows (Joseph Heller)
Golden Orange, The (Joseph Wambaugh)
Graveyard for Lunatics, A (Ray Bradbury)
Gravity's Rainbow (Thomas Pynchon)
Great Sky River (Gregory Benford)

Guerrillas (V. S. Naipaul)
Happy Turnip, The (Thomas M. Disch)
Hermit of 69th Street, The (Jerzy Kosinski)
Hocus Pocus (Kurt Vonnegut)
Homesick (Guy Vanderhaeghe)
House of Stairs, The (Ruth Rendell as Barbara Vine)
House for Mr Biswas, A (V. S. Naipaul)
J R (William Gaddis)
Killing Time in St. Cloud (Judith Guest and Rebecca Hill)
Lamb to the Slaughter (Roald Dahl)
Last Notes From Home (Frederick Exley)
LETTERS (John Barth)
Love in the Time of Cholera (Gabriel García Márquez)
Misery (Stephen King)
Mongoose R.I.P. (William F. Buckley, Jr.)
Mystic Masseur, The (V. S. Naipaul)
Novelty (John Crowley)
Old Gringo, The (Carlos Fuentes)
Optimist's Daughter, The (Eudora Welty)
Patriot Games (Tom Clancy)
Pillars of the Earth (Ken Follett)
Presumed Innocent (Scott Turow)
Pubis Angelical (Manuel Puig)
Public Burning, The (Robert Coover)
Quinn's Book (William Kennedy)
Rabbit at Rest (John Updike)
Rat, The (Günter Grass)
Recognitions, The (William Gaddis)

Roma Mater (Poul Anderson)
Sands of Time, The (Sidney Sheldon)
Satanic Verses, The (Salman Rushdie)
Secret Pilgrim, The (John le Carré)
Shadows (John Gardner)
Shame (Salman Rushdie)
Soft Monkey (Harlan Ellison)
Sphere (Michael Crichton)
Tango Charlie and Foxtrot Romeo (John Varley)
Taste for Death, A (P. D. James)
Tracks (Louise Erdrich)
Truth about Lorin Jones, The (Alison Lurie)
Universal Baseball Association, The (Robert Coover)
Veiled One, The (Ruth Rendell)
Vineland (Thomas Pynchon)
War (Marguerite Duras)
Weaveworld (Clive Barker)
Whirlwind (James Clavell)
Windmills of the Gods (Sidney Sheldon)

Drug/Alcohol Abuse

Because It Is Bitter, and Because It Is My Heart (Joyce Carol Oates)
Cardinal of the Kremlin, The (Tom Clancy)
Carpenter's Gothic (William Gaddis)
Clear and Present Danger (Tom Clancy)
Coyote Waits (Tony Hillerman)
Dark Tower Series, The (Stephen King)
Devices and Desires (P. D. James)

Appendix I

Emperor of America (Richard Condon)
Folks That Live on the Hill, The (Kingsley Amis)
Gerald's Party (Robert Coover)
Golden Orange, The (Joseph Wambaugh)
J R (William Gaddis)
Killing Time in St. Cloud (Judith Guest and Rebecca Hill)
King of the Fields, The (Isaac Bashevis Singer)
Knockout Artist, The (Harry Crews)
Last Notes From Home (Frederick Exley)
Marya: A Life (Joyce Carol Oates)
Misery (Stephen King)
Out on the Cutting Edge (Lawrence Block)
Picturing Will (Ann Beattie)
Rabbit at Rest (John Updike)
Recognitions, The (William Gaddis)
Rock Star (Jackie Collins)
Rummies (Peter Benchley)
Russia House, The (John le Carré)
Sea Wall, The (Marguerite Duras)
Shadows (John Gardner)
Stillness (John Gardner)
Story of My Life (Jay McInerney)
Strong Medicine (Arthur Hailey)
Taming the Star Runner (Hinton)
Taste for Death, A (P. D. James)
Vineland (Thomas Pynchon)

Elderly/Aging
Alnilam (James Dickey)
Angle of Repose (Wallace Stegner)
Autobiography of Miss Jane Pittman, The (Ernest J. Gaines)
Bingo (Rita Mae Brown)
Charlie and the Chocolate Factory (Roald Dahl)
Circular Staircase, The (Mary Roberts Rinehart)
Dead Father, The (Barthelme)
Deadeye Dick (Kurt Vonnegut)
Death of Artemio Cruz (Carlos Fuentes)
Devices and Desires (P. D. James)
Fade (Robert Cormier)
Friend of My Youth (Alice Munro)
Gathering of Old Men, A (Ernest J. Gaines)
God Knows (Joseph Heller)
House of Stairs, The (Ruth Rendell as Barbara Vine)
House for Mr Biswas, A (V. S. Naipaul)
Lazarus (Morris West)
LETTERS (John Barth)
Love in the Time of Cholera (Gabriel García Márquez)
Mortal Fear (Robin Cook)
Old Forest and Other Stories, The (Peter Taylor)
Old Devils, The (Kingsley Amis)
Other Side, The (Mary Gordon)
Paradise (Donald Barthelme)
Rabbit at Rest (John Updike)
Rat, The (Günter Grass)
Sea Wall, The (Marguerite Duras)
Second Coming, The (Walker Percy)
Some Can Whistle (Larry McMurtry)
Spence + Lila (Bobbie Ann Mason)

Square, The (Marguerite Duras)
Star of Gypsies (Robert Silverberg)
Summons to Memphis, A (Peter Taylor)
Tehanu (Ursula K. Le Guin)
2061: Odyssey Three (Arthur C. Clarke)
Veiled One, The (Ruth Rendell)

Environment/Ecology
Acres and Pains (S. J. Perelman)
Alaska (James A. Michener)
Always Coming Home (Ursula K. Le Guin)
Angle of Repose (Wallace Stegner)
Cat's Eye (Margaret Atwood)
Cyteen (C. J. Cherryh)
Desert Solitaire (Edward Abbey)
Dragonsdawn (Anne McCaffrey)
Galapagos (Kurt Vonnegut)
Gravity's Rainbow (Thomas Pynchon)
Great Sky River (Gregory Benford)
Guerrillas (V. S. Naipaul)
Handmaid's Tale, The (Margaret Atwood)
Hawaii (James A. Michener)
House Made of Dawn (N. Scott Momaday)
House for Mr Biswas, A (V. S. Naipaul)
J R (William Gaddis)
Keep the Change (Thomas McGuane)
Killing Mister Watson (Peter Matthiessen)
Most of S. J. Perelman, The (S. J. Perelman)

Origin of the Brunists, The (Robert Coover)
Rat, The (Günter Grass)
Sphere (Michael Crichton)
Tales of the South Pacific (James A. Michener)
Temple of My Familiar, The (Alice Walker)
Toynbee Convector, The (Ray Bradbury)
Tracks (Louise Erdrich)
Veiled One, The (Ruth Rendell)
Vineland (Thomas Pynchon)
Way to Rainy Mountain, The (N. Scott Momaday)
Westward Ha! (S. J. Perelman)

Espionage/Terrorism
Bourne Identity, The (Robert Ludlum)
Candle for D'artagnan, A (Chelsea Quinn Yarbro)
Cardinal of the Kremlin, The (Tom Clancy)
Cyteen (C. J. Cherryh)
Devices and Desires (P. D. James)
Hook, Line, Sinker (Len Deighton)
Gallowglass (Ruth Rendell as Barbara Vine)
Icarus Agenda, The (Robert Ludlum)
Mongoose R.I.P. (William F. Buckley, Jr.)
Patriot Games (Tom Clancy)
Red Storm Rising (Tom Clancy)
Russia House, The (John le Carré)
Secret Pilgrim, The (John le Carré)
Shining Through (Susan Isaacs)

Appendix I

Evil
Autobiography of Miss Jane Pittman, The (Ernest J. Gaines)
Boomerang (Barry Hannah)
Bourne Ultimatum, The (Robert Ludlum)
Candle for D'Artagnan, A (Chelsea Quinn Yarbro)
Captain and the Enemy, The (Graham Greene)
Clear and Present Danger (Tom Clancy)
Crusader's Torch (Chelsea Quinn Yarbro)
Crying of Lot 49, The (Thomas Pynchon)
Dark Tower Series, The (Stephen King)
Devices and Desires (P. D. James)
Exile, The (William Kotzwinkle)
Eyes of the Dragon, The (Stephen King)
Fade (Robert Cormier)
Feast of Snakes, A (Harry Crews)
Flame in Byzantium (Chelsea Quinn Yarbro)
Foucault's Pendulum (Umberto Eco)
Gallowglass (Ruth Rendell as Barbara Vine)
Gerald's Party (Robert Coover)
God's Grace (Bernard Malamud)
Golden Orange, The (Joseph Wambaugh)
Gravity's Rainbow (Thomas Pynchon)
Great Sky River (Gregory Benford)
House of Stairs, The (Ruth Rendell as Barbara Vine)
In Praise of the Stepmother (Mario Vargas Llosa)
J R (William Gaddis)
Killing Mister Watson (Peter Matthiessen)
Lazarus (Morris West)
Midnight Examiner, The (William Kotzwinkle)
Misery (Stephen King)
Mutation (Robin Cook)
Patriot Games (Tom Clancy)
Picturing Will (Ann Beattie)
Queen of the Damned, The (Anne Rice)
Rat, The (Günter Grass)
Recognitions, The (William Gaddis)
Roma Mater (Poul Anderson)
Satanic Verses, The (Salman Rushdie)
Shadows (John Gardner)
Shame (Salman Rushdie)
Silver Pillow, The (Thomas M. Disch)
Some Can Whistle (Larry McMurtry)
Sphere (Michael Crichton)
Star of Gypsies (Robert Silverberg)
Taste for Death, A (P. D. James)
V. (Thomas Pynchon)
War (Marguerite Duras)
Weaveworld (Clive Barker)

Existentialism
Carpenter's Gothic (William Gaddis)
Djinn (Alain Robbe-Grillet)
Exile, The (William Kotzwinkle)
Floating Opera, The (John Barth)
Gerald's Party (Robert Coover)

Giles Goat-Boy or, The Revised New Syllabus (John Barth)
Guerrillas (V. S. Naipaul)
Handmaid's Tale, The (Margaret Atwood)
House for Mr Biswas, A (V. S. Naipaul)
Moviegoer, The (Walker Percy)
Recognitions, The (William Gaddis)
Second Coming, The (Walker Percy)
Shadows (John Gardner)
Sot-Weed Factor, The (John Barth)
Sphere (Michael Crichton)

Family Relationships
Acres and Pains (S. J. Perelman)
Alaska (James A. Michener)
All God's Children Need Traveling Shoes (Maya Angelou)
Alnilam (James Dickey)
Angle of Repose (Wallace Stegner)
At the Bay (Katherine Mansfield)
Autobiography of Miss Jane Pittman, The (Ernest J. Gaines)
Beacon at Alexandria, The (Gillian Bradshaw)
Because It Is Bitter, and Because It Is My Heart (Joyce Carol Oates)
Beet Queen, The (Louise Erdrich)
Beloved (Toni Morrison)
Big Rock Candy Mountain, The (Wallace Stegner)
Bingo (Rita Mae Brown)
Blood of Requited Love (Manuel Puig)
Bourne Ultimatum, The (Robert Ludlum)
Breathing Lessons (Anne Tyler)
Bridesmaid, The (Ruth Rendell)
Brown Girl, Brownstones (Paule Marshall)
Burden of Proof, The (Scott Turow)
Captain and the Enemy, The (Graham Greene)
Cat's Eye (Margaret Atwood)
Charley Bland (Mary Lee Settle)
Charlie and the Chocolate Factory (Roald Dahl)
Circular Staircase, The (Mary Roberts Rinehart)
Complete Short Stories of Ernest Hemingway, The (Ernest Hemingway)
The Counterlife (Philip Roth)
Country Place (Ann Petry)
Cyteen (C. J. Cherryh)
Dead Father, The (Donald Barthelme)
Death of Artemio Cruz (Carlos Fuentes)
Devices and Desires (P. D. James)
Different Kind of Christmas, A (Alex Haley)
Dragonsdawn (Anne McCaffrey)
Emperor of America (Richard Condon)
Exile, The (William Kotzwinkle)
Eyes of the Dragon, The (Stephen King)
Fade (Robert Cormier)
Fast Lanes (Jayne Anne Phillips)
Feast of Snakes, A (Harry Crews)
Fencepost Chronicles, The (W. P. Kinsella)
Financial Expert, The (R. K. Narayan)

Appendix I

Firebrand, The (Marion Zimmer Bradley)
Folks That Live on the Hill, The (Kingsley Amis)
Free-Lance Pallbearers, The (Ishmael Reed)
Garden-Party, The (Katherine Mansfield)
Gathering of Old Men, A (Ernest J. Gaines)
Gift of Asher Lev, The (Chaim Potok)
God Knows (Joseph Heller)
God's Grace (Bernard Malamud)
Golden Orange, The (Joseph Wambaugh)
Great Sky River (Gregory Benford)
Handmaid's Tale, The (Margaret Atwood)
Hawaii (James A. Michener)
Heirs of Hammerfell, The (Marion Zimmer Bradley)
Her Mother's Daughter (Marilyn French)
His Little Women (Judith Rossner)
Homesick (Guy Vanderhaeghe)
House for Mr Biswas, A (V. S. Naipaul)
Houseguest, The (Thomas Berger)
How I Grew (Mary McCarthy)
Imperial Purple (Gillian Bradshaw)
In Praise of the Stepmother (Mario Vargas Llosa)
In My Father's House (Ernest J. Gaines)
In Miro District and Other Stories (Peter Taylor)
In Country (Bobbie Ann Mason)
Joey's Case (K. C. Constantine)

Joy Luck Club, The (Amy Tan)
Joy in the Morning (P. G. Wodehouse)
J R (William Gaddis)
Just As Long As We're Together (Judy Blume)
K. (Mary Roberts Rinehart)
Keep the Change (Thomas McGuane)
Killing Time in St. Cloud (Judith Guest and Rebecca Hill)
Killshot (Elmore Leonard)
Last Notes From Home (Frederick Exley)
Light Can Be Both Wave and Particle (Ellen Gilchrist)
Lover, The (Marguerite Duras)
Marya: A Life (Joyce Carol Oates)
Midnight's Children (Salman Rushdie)
Moon and the Face, The (Patricia A. McKillip)
More Die of Heartbreak (Saul Bellow)
Most of S. J. Perelman, The (S. J. Perelman)
Moviegoer, The (Walker Percy)
Mutant Season, The (Robert Silverberg)
Mystic Masseur, The (V. S. Naipaul)
Narrows, The (Ann Petry)
No More Saturday Nights (Norma Klein)
Old Forest and Other Stories, The (Peter Taylor)
Old Devils, The (Kingsley Amis)
One Writer's Beginnings (Eudora Welty)

One L (Scott Turow)
Optimist's Daughter, The (Eudora Welty)
Origin of the Brunists, The (Robert Coover)
Other Side, The (Mary Gordon)
Paradise (Donald Barthelme)
Picture This (Joseph Heller)
Picturing Will (Ann Beattie)
Praisesong for the Widow (Paule Marshall)
Prayer for Owen Meany, A (John Irving)
Prelude (Katherine Mansfield)
Presumed Innocent (Scott Turow)
Pubis Angelical (Manuel Puig)
Public Burning, The (Robert Coover)
Quinn's Book (William Kennedy)
Rabbit at Rest (John Updike)
Rat, The (Günter Grass)
Recognitions, The (William Gaddis)
Renegades of Pern (McCaffrey)
Rummies (Peter Benchley)
Rusalka (C. J. Cherryh)
Satanic Verses, The (Salman Rushdie)
Sea Wall, The (Marguerite Duras)
Second Chronicles of Amber, The (Roger Zelazny)
Secret Pilgrim, The (John le Carré)
Shame (Salman Rushdie)
Shiloh and Other Stories (Bobbie Ann Mason)
Shining Through (Susan Isaacs)
Silver Pillow, The (Thomas M. Disch)
Southern Family, A (Gail Godwin)
Spence + Lila (Bobbie Ann Mason)

Square, The (Marguerite Duras)
Star of Gypsies (Robert Silverberg)
Stillness (John Gardner)
Story of My Life (Jay McInerney)
Straight (Dick Francis)
Street, The (Ann Petry)
Summer Lightning (Wodehouse)
Summons to Memphis, A (Peter Taylor)
Taming the Star Runner (S. E. Hinton)
Taste for Death, A (P. D. James)
Tehanu (Ursula K. Le Guin)
Temple of My Familiar, The (Alice Walker)
Theft, A (Saul Bellow)
Till We Meet Again (Judith Krantz)
To Sail Beyond the Sunset (Robert A. Heinlein)
Tracks (Louise Erdrich)
Truth about Lorin Jones, The (Alison Lurie)
Veiled One, The (Ruth Rendell)
Vineland (Thomas Pynchon)
War (Marguerite Duras)
Way to Rainy Mountain, The (N. Scott Momaday)
We Are Still Married (Garrison Keillor)
Westward Ha! (S. J. Perelman)
Where I'm Calling From (Raymond Carver)
Whistlejacket (John Hawkes)
Who Killed Palomino Molero? (Mario Vargas Llosa)
Winesburg, Ohio (Sherwood Anderson)
You Must Remember This (Joyce Carol Oates)

Feminism/Women's Issues

Alaska (James A. Michener)
All God's Children Need Traveling Shoes (Maya Angelou)
Always Coming Home (Ursula K. Le Guin)
Angel with the Sword (Cherryh)
Angle of Repose (Wallace Stegner)
Autobiography of Miss Jane Pittman, The (Ernest J. Gaines)
Beacon at Alexandria, The (Gillian Bradshaw)
Because It Is Bitter, and Because It Is My Heart (Joyce Carol Oates)
Beet Queen, The (Louise Erdrich)
Being Invisible (Thomas Berger)
Beloved (Toni Morrison)
Big Rock Candy Mountain, The (Wallace Stegner)
Bingo (Rita Mae Brown)
Brown Girl, Brownstones (Paule Marshall)
Candle for D'Artagnan, A (Chelsea Quinn Yarbro)
Cat's Eye (Margaret Atwood)
Circular Staircase, The (Mary Roberts Rinehart)
City of Sorcery, The (Marion Zimmer Bradley)
Crusader's Torch (Chelsea Quinn Yarbro)
Cyteen (C. J. Cherryh)
Dead Father, The (Donald Barthelme)
Devices and Desires (P. D. James)
Fencepost Chronicles, The (W. P. Kinsella)
Firecode (Chelsea Quinn Yarbro)
Flame in Byzantium (Chelsea Quinn Yarbro)
Friend of My Youth (Alice Munro)
Galapagos (Kurt Vonnegut)
Gerald's Party (Robert Coover)
Guerrillas (V. S. Naipaul)
Guide, The (R. K. Narayan)
Handmaid's Tale, The (Atwood)
Her Mother's Daughter (Marilyn French)
His Little Women (Judith Rossner)
In Country (Bobbie Ann Mason)
J R (William Gaddis)
K. (Mary Roberts Rinehart)
Killashandra (Anne McCaffrey)
Light Can Be Both Wave and Particle (Ellen Gilchrist)
Love Killers, The (Jackie Collins)
Lover, The (Marguerite Duras)
Magicians of Gor (John Norman)
Mammoth Hunters (Jean Auel)
Marya: A Life (Joyce Carol Oates)
Moderato Cantabile (Marguerite Duras)
Moon and the Face, The (Patricia A. McKillip)
My Secret History (Paul Theroux)
Narrows, The (Ann Petry)
Other Side, The (Mary Gordon)
Paradise (Donald Barthelme)
Picturing Will (Ann Beattie)
Plains of Passage, The (Jean M. Auel)
Prayer for Owen Meany, A (John Irving)
Pubis Angelical (Manuel Puig)
Queen of the Damned, The (Anne Rice)

Quinn's Book (William Kennedy)
Rat, The (Günter Grass)
Reckless Eyeballing (Ishmael Reed)
Recognitions, The (William Gaddis)
Roma Mater (Poul Anderson)
S. (John Updike)
Sea Wall, The (Marguerite Duras)
Serenissima: A Novel of Venice (Erica Jong)
Shame (Salman Rushdie)
Shiloh and Other Stories (Bobbie Ann Mason)
Snow White (Donald Barthelme)
Sphere (Michael Crichton)
Square, The (Marguerite Duras)
Stillness (John Gardner)
Story of My Life (Jay McInerney)
Street, The (Ann Petry)
Taste for Death, A (P. D. James)
Tehanu (Ursula K. Le Guin)
Temple of My Familiar, The (Alice Walker)
Theft, A (Saul Bellow)
Till We Meet Again (Judith Krantz)
To Sail Beyond the Sunset (Robert A. Heinlein)
Tracks (Louise Erdrich)
Truth about Lorin Jones, The (Alison Lurie)
Vineland (Thomas Pynchon)
War (Marguerite Duras)
Warrior Queens, The (Lady Antonia Fraser)
We Are Still Married (Garrison Keillor)
Whirlwind (James Clavell)
Whistlejacket (John Hawkes)
Windmills of the Gods (Sidney Sheldon)
You Must Remember This (Joyce Carol Oates)

Freedom (The Nature of)
Angel with the Sword (C. J. Cherryh)
Autobiography of Miss Jane Pittman, The (Ernest J. Gaines)
Being Invisible (Thomas Berger)
Big Rock Candy Mountain, The (Wallace Stegner)
Bingo (Rita Mae Brown)
Blood of Requited Love (Manuel Puig)
Captain Blood (Rafael Sabatini)
Desert Solitaire (Edward Abbey)
Different Kind of Christmas, A (Alex Haley)
Exile, The (William Kotzwinkle)
Gathering of Old Men, A (Ernest J. Gaines)
Guerrillas (V. S. Naipaul)
Handmaid's Tale, A (Margaret Atwood)
House for Mr Biswas, A (V. S. Naipaul)
In My Father's House (Ernest J. Gaines)
Integral Trees, The (Larry Niven)
J R (William Gaddis)
K. (Mary Roberts Rinehart)
Keep the Change (Thomas McGuane)
Lazarus (Morris West)
Love in the Time of Cholera (Gabriel García Márquez)
Lover, The (Marguerite Duras)
Magicians of Gor (John Norman)
Midnight's Children (Rushdie)

Appendix I

Misery (Stephen King)
Mitla Pass (Leon Uris)
Moderato Cantabile (Marguerite Duras)
Mutant Season, The (Robert Silverberg)
Narrows, The (Ann Petry)
Novelty (John Crowley)
Paradise (Donald Barthelme)
Praisesong for the Widow (Paule Marshall)
Recognitions, The (William Gaddis)
Scaramouche (Rafael Sabatini)
Sea Wall, The (Marguerite Duras)
Sea Hawk, The (Rafael Sabatini)
Shadows (John Gardner)
Skinny Legs and All (Tom Robbins)
Street, The (Ann Petry)
Taming the Star Runner (S. E. Hinton)
War (Marguerite Duras)
Whirlwind (James Clavell)

Friendship

Acres and Pains (S. J. Perelman)
All God's Children Need Traveling Shoes (Maya Angelou)
Beet Queen, The (Louise Erdrich)
Bliss (Katherine Mansfield)
Boomerang (Barry Hannah)
Carpenter's Gothic (William Gaddis)
Cat's Eye (Margaret Atwood)
Celebration (Mary Lee Settle)
City of Sorcery, The (Marion Zimmer Bradley)
Close Quarters (William Golding)
Dark Tower Series, The (Stephen King)
Dark Laughter (Sherwood Anderson)
Different Kind of Christmas, A (Alex Haley)
Eyes of the Dragon, The (Stephen King)
Fencepost Chronicles, The (W. P. Kinsella)
Fire Down Below (Wm. Golding)
Folks That Live on the Hill, The (Kingsley Amis)
Gallowglass (Ruth Rendell as Barbara Vine)
Game of Empire, The (Poul Anderson)
Gathering of Old Men, A (Ernest J. Gaines)
Genesis (Wallace Stegner)
Gerald's Party (Robert Coover)
Gift of Asher Lev, The (Chaim Potok)
God Knows (Joseph Heller)
Golden Orange, The (Joseph Wambaugh)
Graveyard for Lunatics, A (Ray Bradbury)
Guerrillas (V. S. Naipaul)
Handmaid's Tale, The (Margaret Atwood)
Houseguest, The (Thomas Berger)
How I Grew (Mary McCarthy)
In Miro District and Other Stories (Peter Taylor)
Je ne parle pas français (Katherine Mansfield)
Joy in the Morning (P. G. Wodehouse)

J R (William Gaddis)
Just As Long As We're Together (Judy Blume)
Last Notes From Home (Frederick Exley)
Midnight Examiner, The (William Kotzwinkle)
Most of S. J. Perelman, The (S. J. Perelman)
My Àntonia (Willa Cather)
Old Devils, The (Kingsley Amis)
Paladin of the Lost Hour (Harlan Ellison)
Paradise (Donald Barthelme)
Picturing Will (Ann Beattie)
Prayer for Owen Meany, A (John Irving)
Pubis Angelical (Manuel Puig)
Quinn's Book (William Kennedy)
Recognitions, The (William Gaddis)
Rummies (Peter Benchley)
Some Can Whistle (Larry McMurtry)
Stillness (John Gardner)
Story of My Life (Jay McInerney)
Summons to Memphis, A (Peter Taylor)
Truth about Lorin Jones, The (Alison Lurie)
Universal Baseball Association, The (Robert Coover)
Veiled One, The (Ruth Rendell)
Westward Ha! (S. J. Perelman)
When Harry Met Sally (Nora Ephron)
Whirlwind (James Clavell)
Winesburg, Ohio (Sherwood Anderson)
Wonderful Years, Wonderful Years (George V. Higgins)
You Know Me Al (Ring Lardner)

Generational Differences
All God's Children Need Traveling Shoes (Maya Angelou)
Alnilam (James Dickey)
Angle of Repose (Wallace Stegner)
Autobiography of Miss Jane Pittman, The (Ernest J. Gaines)
Beet Queen, The (Louise Erdrich)
Big Rock Candy Mountain, The (Wallace Stegner)
Breathing Lessons (Anne Tyler)
Cat's Eye (Margaret Atwood)
Dead Father, The (Donald Barthelme)
Fade (Robert Cormier)
Fast Lanes (Jayne Anne Phillips)
Friend of My Youth (Alice Munro)
Gathering of Old Men, A (Ernest J. Gaines)
Gift of Asher Lev, The (Chaim Potok)
God Knows (Joseph Heller)
Golden Orange, The (Joseph Wambaugh)
Handmaid's Tale, The (Margaret Atwood)
Her Mother's Daughter (Marilyn French)
House for Mr Biswas, A (V. S. Naipaul)
In My Father's House (Ernest J. Gaines)
In Miro District and Other Stories (Peter Taylor)

Appendix I

Joy Luck Club, The (Amy Tan)
J R (William Gaddis)
LETTERS (John Barth)
Light Can Be Both Wave and Particle (Ellen Gilchrist)
Midnight's Children (Salman Rushdie)
No More Saturday Nights (Norma Klein)
Old Devils, The (Kingsley Amis)
Other Side, The (Mary Gordon)
Paradise (Donald Barthelme)
Secret Pilgrim, The (John le Carré)
Shiloh and Other Stories (Bobbie Ann Mason)
Some Can Whistle (Larry McMurtry)
Spence + Lila (Bobbie Ann Mason)
Summer Lightning (P. G. Wodehouse)
Summons to Memphis, A (Peter Taylor)
Taming the Star Runner (S. E. Hinton)
Till We Meet Again (Judith Krantz)
Veiled One, The (Ruth Rendell)
Vineland (Thomas Pynchon)

Government/Politics
Alaska (James A. Michener)
All God's Children Need Traveling Shoes (Maya Angelou)
Autobiography of Miss Jane Pittman, The (Ernest J. Gaines)
Bonfire of the Vanities, The (Tom Wolfe)
Captain and the Enemy, The (Graham Greene)
Cardinal of the Kremlin, The (Tom Clancy)
Carpenter's Gothic (William Gaddis)
Clear and Present Danger (Tom Clancy)
Desert Solitaire (Edward Abbey)
Dragonsdawn (Anne McCaffrey)
Emperor of America (Richard Condon)
Eyes of the Dragon, The (Stephen King)
First Man in Rome, The (Colleen McCullough)
Game of Empire, The (Poul Anderson)
Gathering of Old Men, A (Ernest J. Gaines)
Gravity's Rainbow (Thomas Pynchon)
Guerrillas (V. S. Naipaul)
Handmaid's Tale, The (Margaret Atwood)
Harrowing of Gwynedd, the (Katherine Kurtz)
Hawaii (James A. Michener)
Hook, Line, Sinker (Len Deighton)
House for Mr Biswas, A (V. S. Naipaul)
Icarus Agenda, The (Robert Ludlum)
Imperial Purple (Gillian Bradshaw)
In My Father's House (Ernest J. Gaines)
J R (William Gaddis)
Midnight's Children (Salman Rushdie)
Mongoose R.I.P. (William F. Buckley, Jr.)

Mutant Season, The (Robert Silverberg)
Mystic Masseur, The (V. S. Naipaul)
Novelty (John Crowley)
Patriot Games (Tom Clancy)
Picture This (Joseph Heller)
Pubis Angelical (Manuel Puig)
Public Burning, The (Robert Coover)
Q Clearance (Peter Benchley)
Radio Free Albemuth (Philip K. Dick)
Rat, The (Günter Grass)
Red Storm Rising (Tom Clancy)
Renegades of Pern (Anne McCaffrey)
Scaramouche (Rafael Sabatini)
Shame (Salman Rushdie)
Skinny Legs and All (Tom Robbins)
Sot-Weed Factor, The (John Barth)
Star of Gypsies (Robert Silverberg)
Tango Charlie and Foxtrot Romeo (John Varley)
Till We Meet Again (Judith Krantz)
Trust (George V. Higgins)
V. (Thomas Pynchon)
Victories (George V. Higgins)
War (Marguerite Duras)
Warrior Queens, The (Lady Antonia Fraser)
We Are Still Married (Garrison Keillor)
Whirlwind (James Clavell)

Greed/Materialism
Alaska (James A. Michener)

Angel with the Sword (C. J. Cherryh)
Big Town, The (Ring Lardner)
Big Room, The (Michael Herr)
Billy Bathgate (E. L. Doctorow)
Bonfire of the Vanities, The (Tom Wolfe)
Bridesmaid, The (Ruth Rendell)
Brown Girl, Brownstones (Paule Marshall)
Carpenter's Gothic (William Gaddis)
Country Place (Ann Petry)
Crying of Lot 49, The (Thomas Pynchon)
Cyteen (C. J. Cherryh)
Desert Solitaire (Edward Abbey)
Dragonsdawn (Anne McCaffrey)
Emperor of America (Richard Condon)
Fade (Robert Cormier)
Feast of Snakes, A (Harry Crews)
Financial Expert, The (R. K. Narayan)
First Man in Rome, The (Colleen McCullough)
Four Million, The (O. Henry)
Galapagos (Kurt Vonnegut)
Gallowglass (Ruth Rendell as Barbara Vine)
Golden Orange, The (Joseph Wambaugh)
Graveyard for Lunatics, A (Ray Bradbury)
Gravity's Rainbow (Thomas Pynchon)
Guerrillas (V. S. Naipaul)
Guide, The (R. K. Narayan)

Handmaid's Tale, The (Margaret Atwood)
Hawaii (James A. Michener)
Hocus Pocus (Kurt Vonnegut)
House of Stairs, The (Ruth Rendell as Barbara Vine)
House for Mr Biswas, A (V. S. Naipaul)
Houseguest, The (Thomas Berger)
Icarus Agenda, The (Robert Ludlum)
Imperial Purple (Gillian Bradshaw)
J R (William Gaddis)
Keep the Change (Thomas McGuane)
Knockout Artist, The (Harry Crews)
Love in the Time of Cholera (Gabriel García Márquez)
Lover, The (Marguerite Duras)
Moderato Cantabile (Marguerite Duras)
My Uncle Oswald (Roald Dahl)
Naked in Garden Hills (Harry Crews)
Narrows, The (Ann Petry)
Picture This (Joseph Heller)
Rat, The (Günter Grass)
Recognitions, The (William Gaddis)
Renegades of Pern (Anne McCaffrey)
Rock Star (Jackie Collins)
Roma Mater (Poul Anderson)
S. (John Updike)
Satanic Verses, The (Salman Rushdie)
Sea Wall, The (Marguerite Duras)
Shame (Salman Rushdie)
Something In the Air (Emma Lathen)
Stones of Nomuru, The (L. Sprague de Camp)
Straight (Dick Francis)
Taste for Death, A (P. D. James)
Theft, A (Saul Bellow)
Trimmed Lamp, The (O. Henry)
2061: Odyssey Three (Arthur C. Clarke)
V. (Thomas Pynchon)
Veiled One, The (Ruth Rendell)
Vineland (Thomas Pynchon)
War (Marguerite Duras)

Heroism (The Nature of)
Alnilam (James Dickey)
Autobiography of Miss Jane Pittman, The (Ernest J. Gaines)
Bourne Ultimatum, The (Robert Ludlum)
Captain Blood (Rafael Sabatini)
Cardinal of the Kremlin, The (Tom Clancy)
Clear and Present Danger (Tom Clancy)
Close Quarters (William Golding)
Dark Tower Series, The (Stephen King)
Dragonsdawn (Anne McCaffrey)
Emperor of America (Richard Condon)
Exile, The (William Kotzwinkle)
Fire Down Below (William Golding)
Gathering of Old Men, A (Ernest J. Gaines)
Genesis (Wallace Stegner)

God Knows (Joseph Heller)
Golden Orange, The (Joseph Wambaugh)
Great Sky River (Gregory Benford)
Guerrillas (V. S. Naipaul)
Guide, The (R. K. Narayan)
Icarus Agenda, The (Robert Ludlum)
In My Father's House (Ernest J. Gaines)
Killing Mister Watson (Peter Matthiessen)
Last Notes From Home (Frederick Exley)
Marya: A Life (Joyce Carol Oates)
Mongoose R.I.P. (William F. Buckley, Jr.)
Mutant Season, The (Robert Silverberg)
My Àntonia (Willa Cather)
O Pioneers! (Willa Cather)
Once and Future King, The (T. H. White)
Patriot Games (Tom Clancy)
Picturing Will (Ann Beattie)
Prayer for Owen Meany, A (John Irving)
Quinn's Book (William Kennedy)
Red Storm Rising (Tom Clancy)
Rusalka (C. J. Cherryh)
Russia House, The (John le Carré)
Scaramouche (Rafael Sabatini)
Sea Hawk, The (Rafael Sabatini)
Shadows (John Gardner)
Shining Through (Susan Isaacs)
Sphere (Michael Crichton)
Star of Gypsies (Robert Silverberg)
Tales of the South Pacific (James A. Michener)
Tough Guys Don't Dance (Norman Mailer)
Toynbee Convector, The (Ray Bradbury)
2061: Odyssey Three (Arthur C. Clarke)
Universal Baseball Association, The (Robert Coover)
War (Marguerite Duras)
Whirlwind (James Clavell)

Hollywood
Crying of Lot 49, The (Thomas Pynchon)
Exile, The (William Kotzwinkle)
Golden Orange, The (Joseph Wambaugh)
Graveyard for Lunatics, A (Ray Bradbury)
Most of S. J. Perelman, The (S. J. Perelman)
Pubis Angelical (Manuel Puig)
Rock Star (Jackie Collins)
Rummies (Peter Benchley)
Till We Meet Again (Judith Krantz)

Homosexuality/Lesbianism
Bingo (Rita Mae Brown)
Bridge of Lost Desire, The (Samuel R. Delany)
Cardinal of the Kremlin, The (Tom Clancy)
Celebration (Mary Lee Settle)
Devices and Desires (P. D. James)
Difficulties with Girls (Kingsley Kingsley Amis)
Folks That Live on the Hill, The (Kingsley Amis)

Garden of Eden, The (Ernest
  Hemingway)
Guerrillas (V. S. Naipaul)
Handmaid's Tale, The (Margaret
  Atwood)
House of Stairs, The (Ruth Rendell
  as Barbara Vine)
Je ne parle pas français (Katherine
  Mansfield)
Joey's Case (K. C. Constantine)
Picturing Will (Ann Beattie)
Recognitions, The (William Gaddis)
Roma Mater (Poul Anderson)
Sands of Time, The (Sidney
  Sheldon)
Truth about Lorin Jones, The
  (Alison Lurie)

Imagination
Acres and Pains (S. J. Perelman)
Autobiography of Miss Jane
  Pittman, The (Ernest J. Gaines)
Beet Queen, The (Louise Erdrich)
Carpenter's Gothic (William
  Gaddis)
Cat's Eye (Margaret Atwood)
Dead Father, The (Donald
  Barthelme)
Exile, The (William Kotzwinkle)
Fade (Robert Cormier)
Folk of the Air, The (Peter S.
  Beagle)
Fool's Run (Patricia A. McKillip)
Gathering of Old Men, A (Ernest J.
  Gaines)
Gerald's Party (Robert Coover)
Graveyard for Lunatics, A (Ray
  Bradbury)

Great Sky River (Gregory Benford)
Guerrillas (V. S. Naipaul)
Handmaid's Tale, The (Margaret
  Atwood)
Hot Jazz Trio, The (William
  Kotzwinkle)
House for Mr Biswas, A (V. S.
  Naipaul)
J R (William Gaddis)
K. (Mary Roberts Rinehart)
Man Made of Words, The (N. Scott
  Momaday)
Midnight's Children (Salman
  Rushdie)
Mitla Pass (Leon Uris)
Moon and the Face, The (Patricia
  A. McKillip)
Most of S. J. Perelman, The (S. J.
  Perelman)
Once and Future King, The (T. H.
  White)
One Writer's Beginnings (Eudora
  Welty)
Origin of the Brunists, The (Robert
  Coover)
Paradise (Donald Barthelme)
Picture This (Joseph Heller)
Picturing Will (Ann Beattie)
Princess Bride, The (William
  Goldman)
Recognitions, The (William Gaddis)
Satanic Verses, The (Salman
  Rushdie)
Shame (Salman Rushdie)
Skinny Legs and All (Tom
  Robbins)
Snow White (Donald Barthelme)
Sphere (Michael Crichton)
Stillness (John Gardner)

Universal Baseball Association, The (Robert Coover)
Way to Rainy Mountain, The (N. Scott Momaday)
Weaveworld (Clive Barker)
Westward Ha! (S. J. Perelman)
Whistlejacket (John Hawkes)

Individualism
Acres and Pains (S. J. Perelman)
Angle of Repose (Wallace Stegner)
Autobiography of Miss Jane Pittman, The (Ernest J. Gaines)
Beet Queen, The (Louise Erdrich)
Being Invisible (Thomas Berger)
Big Rock Candy Mountain, The (Wallace Stegner)
Breathing Lessons (Anne Tyler)
Close Quarters (William Golding)
Dark Tower Series, The (Stephen King)
Dark Laughter (Sherwood Anderson)
Desert Solitaire (Edward Abbey)
Dragonsdawn (Anne McCaffrey)
Exile, The (William Kotzwinkle)
Fire Down Below (William Golding)
Floating Opera, The (John Barth)
Game of Empire, The (Poul Anderson)
Guerrillas (V. S. Naipaul)
Handmaid's Tale, The (Margaret Atwood)
Happy Turnip, The (Thomas M. Disch)
House for Mr Biswas, A (V. S. Naipaul)
Houseguest, The (Thomas Berger)

Icarus Agenda, The (Robert Ludlum)
Joy in the Morning (P. G. Wodehouse)
J R (William Gaddis)
Keep the Change (Thomas McGuane)
Killashandra (Anne McCaffrey)
Midnight's Children (Salman Rushdie)
Mongoose R.I.P. (William F. Buckley, Jr.)
Most of S. J. Perelman, The (S. J. Perelman)
Mutant Season, The (Robert Silverberg)
Old Gringo, The (Carlos Fuentes)
Picture This (Joseph Heller)
Picturing Will (Ann Beattie)
Public Burning, The (Robert Coover)
Recognitions, The (William Gaddis)
S. (John Updike)
Serenissima: A Novel of Venice (Erica Jong)
Shadows (John Gardner)
Skinny Legs and All (Tom Robbins)
Skinwalkers (Tony Hillerman)
Some Can Whistle (Larry McMurtry)
Sphere (Michael Crichton)
Till We Meet Again (Judith Krantz)
To Sail Beyond the Sunset (Robert A. Heinlein)
Tracks (Louise Erdrich)
Westward Ha! (S. J. Perelman)
Winesburg, Ohio (Sherwood Anderson)

Individuals versus Societal Institutions

Acres and Pains (S. J. Perelman)
Alnilam (James Dickey)
Autobiography of Miss Jane Pittman, The (Ernest J. Gaines)
Beet Queen, The (Louise Erdrich)
Blood of Requited Love (Manuel Puig)
Bridesmaid, The (Ruth Rendell)
Bridge of Lost Desire, The (Samuel R. Delany)
Brown Girl, Brownstones (Paule Marshall)
Captain Blood (Rafael Sabatini)
Cardinal of the Kremlin, The (Tom Clancy)
Carpenter's Gothic (William Gaddis)
Cassidy (Morris West)
Circular Staircase, The (Mary Roberts Rinehart)
Close Quarters (William Golding)
Country Place (Ann Petry)
Crying of Lot 49, The (Thomas Pynchon)
Cyteen (C. J. Cherryh)
Desert Solitaire (Edward Abbey)
Fade (Robert Cormier)
Fast Lanes (Jayne Anne Phillips)
Fencepost Chronicles, The (W. P. Kinsella)
Fire Down Below (William Golding)
Four Million, The (O. Henry)
Gallowglass (Ruth Rendell as Barbara Vine)
Gathering of Old Men, A (Ernest J. Gaines)
Gift of Asher Lev, The (Chaim Potok)
Giles Goat-Boy or, The Revised New Syllabus (John Barth)
Golden Orange, The (Joseph Wambaugh)
Gravity's Rainbow (Thomas Pynchon)
Great Sky River (Gregory Benford)
Guerrillas (V. S. Naipaul)
Guide, The (R. K. Narayan)
Handmaid's Tale, The (Margaret Atwood)
Hermit of 69th Street, The (Jerzy Kosinski)
Hocus Pocus (Kurt Vonnegut)
House of Stairs, The (Ruth Rendell as Barbara Vine)
House for Mr Biswas, A (V. S. Naipaul)
In My Father's House (Ernest J. Gaines)
J R (William Gaddis)
K. (Mary Roberts Rinehart)
Keep the Change (Thomas McGuane)
Killing Mister Watson (Peter Matthiessen)
LETTERS (John Barth)
Lover, The (Marguerite Duras)
Man-Eater of Malgudi, The (R. K. Narayan)
Mary and the Giant (Philip K. Dick)
Midnight's Children (Salman Rushdie)
Moderato Cantabile (Marguerite Duras)
More Die of Heartbreak (Saul Bellow)

Most of S. J. Perelman, The (S. J. Perelman)
Mutant Season, The (Robert Silverberg)
My Secret History (Paul Theroux)
Mystic Masseur, The (V. S. Naipaul)
Novelty (John Crowley)
Picture This (Joseph Heller)
Picturing Will (Ann Beattie)
Presumed Innocent (Scott Turow)
Public Burning, The (Robert Coover)
Q Clearance (Peter Benchley)
Radio Free Albemuth (Philip K. Dick)
Rat, The (Günter Grass)
Recognitions, The (William Gaddis)
Satanic Verses, The (Salman Rushdie)
Scaramouche (Rafael Sabatini)
Sea Hawk, The (Rafael Sabatini)
Sea Wall, The (Marguerite Duras)
Secret Pilgrim, The (John le Carré)
Shame (Salman Rushdie)
Silent Gondoliers, The (William Goldman)
Sphere (Michael Crichton)
Square, The (Marguerite Duras)
Stallion Gate (Martin Cruz Smith)
Taming the Star Runner (S. E. Hinton)
Tracks (Louise Erdrich)
Trimmed Lamp, The (O. Henry)
Tripmaster Monkey: His Fake Book (Maxine Hong Kingston)
Trust (George V. Higgins)
Uncle Fred Flits By (P. G. Wodehouse)
V. (Thomas Pynchon)
Veiled One, The (Ruth Rendell)
Victories (George V. Higgins)
Vineland (Thomas Pynchon)
Westward Ha! (S. J. Perelman)
Whirlwind (James Clavell)
Wonderful Years, Wonderful Years (George V. Higgins)

Intercultural Conflicts
Acres and Pains (S. J. Perelman)
Alaska (James A. Michener)
Always Coming Home (Ursula K. Le Guin)
Autobiography of Miss Jane Pittman, The (Ernest J. Gaines)
Beacon at Alexandria, The (Gillian Bradshaw)
Bearkeeper's Daughter, The (Gillian Bradshaw)
Because It Is Bitter, and Because It Is My Heart (Joyce Carol Oates)
Beet Queen, The (Louise Erdrich)
Beloved (Toni Morrison)
Brown Girl, Brownstones (Paule Marshall)
Carpenter's Gothic (William Gaddis)
Celebration (Mary Lee Settle)
Chosen Place, The Timeless People, The (Paule Marshall)
Fade (Robert Cormier)
Fencepost Chronicles, The (W. P. Kinsella)
Fool's Run (Patricia A. McKillip)
Free-Lance Pallbearers, The (Ishmael Reed)
Gathering of Old Men, A (Ernest J. Gaines)

Appendix I

Genesis (Wallace Stegner)
God Knows (Joseph Heller)
God's Grace (Bernard Malamud)
Guerrillas (V. S. Naipaul)
Hawaii (James A. Michener)
Heirs of Hammerfell, The (Marion Zimmer Bradley)
Hocus Pocus (Kurt Vonnegut)
Honorable Barbarian, The (L. Sprague de Camp)
House Made of Dawn (N. Scott Momaday)
House for Mr Biswas, A (V. S. Naipaul)
Icarus Agenda, The (Robert Ludlum)
Imperial Purple (Gillian Bradshaw)
Joy Luck Club, The (Amy Tan)
J R (William Gaddis)
King of the Fields, The (Isaac Bashevis Singer)
Lover, The (Marguerite Duras)
Midnight's Children (Salman Rushdie)
Moon and the Face, The (Patricia A. McKillip)
Mutant Season, The (Robert Silverberg)
My Secret History (Paul Theroux)
Mystic Masseur, The (V. S. Naipaul)
Narrows, The (Ann Petry)
Old Gringo, The (Carlos Fuentes)
Origin of the Brunists, The (Robert Coover)
Patriot Games (Tom Clancy)
Plains of Passage, The (Jean M. Auel)
Quinn's Book (William Kennedy)

Recognitions, The (William Gaddis)
Roma Mater (Poul Anderson)
Satanic Verses, The (Salman Rushdie)
Shame (Salman Rushdie)
Skinny Legs and All (Tom Robbins)
Skinwalkers (Tony Hillerman)
Sphere (Michael Crichton)
Stallion Gate (Martin Cruz Smith)
Star of Gypsies (Robert Silverberg)
Stones of Nomuru, The (L. Sprague de Camp)
Street, The (Ann Petry)
Tales of the South Pacific (James A. Michener)
Talking God (Tony Hillerman)
Tracks (Louise Erdrich)
V. (Thomas Pynchon)
Westward Ha! (S. J. Perelman)
Whirlwind (James Clavell)

International Politics
Bourne Ultimatum, The (Robert Ludlum)
Captain and the Enemy, The (Graham Greene)
Carpenter's Gothic (William Gaddis)
Clear and Present Danger (Tom Clancy)
Complete Short Stories of Ernest Hemingway, The (Ernest Hemingway)
The Counterlife (Philip Roth)
Cyteen (C. J. Cherryh)
Deadeye Dick (Kurt Vonnegut)
Exile, The (William Kotzwinkle)
Galapagos (Kurt Vonnegut)

Gravity's Rainbow (Thomas Pynchon)
Guerrillas (V. S. Naipaul)
Hook, Line, Sinker (Len Deighton)
House for Mr Biswas, A (V. S. Naipaul)
J R (William Gaddis)
Lazarus (Morris West)
Marya: A Life (Joyce Carol Oates)
Midnight's Children (Salman Rushdie)
Mongoose R.I.P. (William F. Buckley, Jr.)
Most of S. J. Perelman, The (S. J. Perelman)
Mutant Season, The (Robert Silverberg)
Mystic Masseur, The (V. S. Naipaul)
Patriot Games (Tom Clancy)
Red Storm Rising (Tom Clancy)
Russia House, The (John le Carré)
Secret Pilgrim, The (John le Carré)
Shame (Salman Rushdie)
Skinny Legs and All (Tom Robbins)
V. (Thomas Pynchon)
Vineland (Thomas Pynchon)
War (Marguerite Duras)
Westward Ha! (S. J. Perelman)
Whirlwind (James Clavell)
Windmills of the Gods (Sidney Sheldon)

Jewish Concerns
Acres and Pains (S. J. Perelman)
Beacon at Alexandria, The (Gillian Bradshaw)
Carpenter's Gothic (William Gaddis)
The Counterlife (Philip Roth)
Gift of Asher Lev, The (Chaim Potok)
God Knows (Joseph Heller)
God's Grace (Bernard Malamud)
How I Grew (Mary McCarthy)
Icarus Agenda, The (Robert Ludlum)
King of the Fields, The (Isaac Bashevis Singer)
Lazarus (Morris West)
Mitla Pass (Leon Uris)
More Die of Heartbreak (Saul Bellow)
Most of S. J. Perelman, The (S. J. Perelman)
Public Burning, The (Robert Coover)
Reckless Eyeballing (Ishmael Reed)
Recognitions, The (William Gaddis)
Shining Through (Susan Isaacs)
Skinny Legs and All (Tom Robbins)
Till We Meet Again (Judith Krantz)
War (Marguerite Duras)
Westward Ha! (S. J. Perelman)

Justice
Autobiography of Miss Jane Pittman, The (Ernest J. Gaines)
Because It Is Bitter, and Because It Is My Heart (Joyce Carol Oates)
Bonfire of the Vanities, The (Tom Wolfe)
Bourne Ultimatum, The (Robert Ludlum)
Burden of Proof, The (Scott Turow)

Appendix I

Captain Blood (Rafael Sabatini)
Clear and Present Danger (Tom Clancy)
Different Kind of Christmas, A (Alex Haley)
Exile, The (William Kotzwinkle)
Fool's Run (Patricia A. McKillip)
Gathering of Old Men, A (Ernest J. Gaines)
God Knows (Joseph Heller)
God's Grace (Bernard Malamud)
Golden Orange, The (Joseph Wambaugh)
Guerrillas (V. S. Naipaul)
House for Mr Biswas, A (V. S. Naipaul)
Icarus Agenda, The (Robert Ludlum)
In My Father's House (Ernest J. Gaines)
Joey's Case (K. C. Constantine)
Killing Mister Watson (Peter Matthiessen)
Lazarus (Morris West)
Mutant Season, The (Robert Silverberg)
Mystic Masseur, The (V. S. Naipaul)
One L (Scott Turow)
Patriot Games (Tom Clancy)
Picture This (Joseph Heller)
Presumed Innocent (Scott Turow)
Public Burning, The (Robert Coover)
Recognitions, The (William Gaddis)
Scaramouche (Rafael Sabatini)
Sea Hawk, The (Rafael Sabatini)
Shadows (John Gardner)
Tehanu (Ursula K. Le Guin)

Tracks (Louise Erdrich)
Trust (George V. Higgins)
Victories (George V. Higgins)
War (Marguerite Duras)
Wonderful Years, Wonderful Years (George V. Higgins)

Law Enforcement/Legal Systems
Autobiography of Miss Jane Pittman, The (Ernest J. Gaines)
Bonfire of the Vanities, The (Tom Wolfe)
Carpenter's Gothic (William Gaddis)
Clear and Present Danger (Tom Clancy)
Coyote Waits (Tony Hillerman)
Devices and Desires (P. D. James)
Gathering of Old Men, A (Ernest J. Gaines)
Gerald's Party (Robert Coover)
Golden Orange, The (Joseph Wambaugh)
Guerrillas (V. S. Naipaul)
Handmaid's Tale, The (Margaret Atwood)
Harmful Intent (Robin Cook)
Hocus Pocus (Kurt Vonnegut)
In My Father's House (Ernest J. Gaines)
Joey's Case (K. C. Constantine)
J R (William Gaddis)
Killshot (Elmore Leonard)
Lamb to the Slaughter (Roald Dahl)
One L (Scott Turow)
Out on the Cutting Edge (Lawrence Block)
Picture This (Joseph Heller)
Presumed Innocent (Scott Turow)

Shadows (John Gardner)
Skinwalkers (Tony Hillerman)
Talking God (Tony Hillerman)
Taste for Death, A (P. D. James)
Trust (George V. Higgins)
Victories (George V. Higgins)
Vineland (Thomas Pynchon)
Wonderful Years, Wonderful Years (George V. Higgins)

Man and Nature
Acres and Pains (S. J. Perelman)
Alaska (James A. Michener)
Always Coming Home (Ursula K. Le Guin)
Angle of Repose (Wallace Stegner)
Big Rock Candy Mountain, The (Wallace Stegner)
Carpenter's Gothic (William Gaddis)
Cat's Eye (Margaret Atwood)
Chosen Place, The Timeless People, The (Paule Marshall)
Close Quarters (William Golding)
Desert Solitaire (Edward Abbey)
Dragonsdawn (Anne McCaffrey)
Fire Down Below (Wm. Golding)
Galapagos (Kurt Vonnegut)
Genesis (Wallace Stegner)
God's Grace (Bernard Malamud)
Handmaid's Tale, The (Margaret Atwood)
Hawaii (James A. Michener)
Killing Mister Watson (Peter Matthiessen)
Light Can Be Both Wave and Particle (Ellen Gilchrist)
Man-Eater of Malgudi, The (R. K. Narayan)

Midnight's Children (Salman Rushdie)
More Die of Heartbreak (Saul Bellow)
Most of S. J. Perelman, The (S. J. Perelman)
My Àntonia (Willa Cather)
Novelty (John Crowley)
O Pioneers! (Willa Cather)
Once and Future King, The (T. H. White)
Origin of the Brunists, The (Robert Coover)
Rat, The (Günter Grass)
Recognitions, The (William Gaddis)
Shadows (John Gardner)
Sphere (Michael Crichton)
Tales of the South Pacific (James A. Michener)
Vineland (Thomas Pynchon)
Westward Ha! (S. J. Perelman)

Marriage
Acres and Pains (S. J. Perelman)
Angle of Repose (Wallace Stegner)
At the Bay (Katherine Mansfield)
Autobiography of Miss Jane Pittman, The (Ernest J. Gaines)
Because It Is Bitter, and Because It Is My Heart (Joyce Carol Oates)
Being Invisible (Thomas Berger)
Big Rock Candy Mountain, The (Wallace Stegner)
Bingo (Rita Mae Brown)
Bliss (Katherine Mansfield)
Bourne Ultimatum, The (Robert Ludlum)
Breathing Lessons (Anne Tyler)

Appendix I

Burden of Proof, The (Scott Turow)
Carpenter's Gothic (William Gaddis)
Cat's Eye (Margaret Atwood)
Circular Staircase, The (Mary Roberts Rinehart)
The Counterlife (Philip Roth)
Dark Laughter (Sherwood Anderson)
Dead Father, The (Donald Barthelme)
Devices and Desires (P. D. James)
Difficulties with Girls (Kingsley Amis)
Exile, The (William Kotzwinkle)
Fast Lanes (Jayne Anne Phillips)
Feast of Snakes, A (Harry Crews)
Friend of My Youth (Alice Munro)
Garden of Eden, The (Ernest Hemingway)
Gerald's Party (Robert Coover)
Gift of Asher Lev, The (Chaim Potok)
God Knows (Joseph Heller)
Handmaid's Tale, The (Margaret Atwood)
Her Mother's Daughter (Marilyn French)
Homesick (Guy Vanderhaeghe)
Honorable Barbarian, The (L. Sprague de Camp)
Hook, Line, Sinker (Len Deighton)
House for Mr Biswas, A (V. S. Naipaul)
House of Stairs, The (Ruth Rendell as Barbara Vine)
Houseguest, The (Thomas Berger)
In Praise of the Stepmother (Mario Vargas Llosa)
In Miro District and Other Stories (Peter Taylor)
In My Father's House (Ernest J. Gaines)
J R (William Gaddis)
K. (Mary Roberts Rinehart)
Lamb to the Slaughter (Roald Dahl)
Last Notes From Home (Frederick Exley)
Love in the Time of Cholera (Gabriel García Márquez)
Midnight's Children (Salman Rushdie)
Moderato Cantabile (Marguerite Duras)
More Die of Heartbreak (Saul Bellow)
Most of S. J. Perelman, The (S. J. Perelman)
Moviegoer, The (Walker Percy)
Old Forest and Other Stories, The (Peter Taylor)
Old Devils, The (Kingsley Amis)
Other Side, The (Mary Gordon)
Paradise (Donald Barthelme)
Picture This (Joseph Heller)
Picturing Will (Ann Beattie)
Prelude (Katherine Mansfield)
Pubis Angelical (Manuel Puig)
Public Burning, The (Robert Coover)
Q Clearance (Peter Benchley)
Quinn's Book (William Kennedy)
Recognitions, The (William Gaddis)
Roma Mater (Poul Anderson)
S. (John Updike)
Second Coming, The (Walker Percy)

Shame (Salman Rushdie)
Shiloh and Other Stories (Bobbie Ann Mason)
Shining Through (Susan Isaacs)
Skinny Legs and All (Tom Robbins)
Snow White (Donald Barthelme)
Southern Family, A (Gail Godwin)
Square, The (Marguerite Duras)
Stillness (John Gardner)
Summons to Memphis, A (Peter Taylor)
Taste for Death, A (P. D. James)
Temple of My Familiar, The (Alice Walker)
Theft, A (Saul Bellow)
Till We Meet Again (Judith Krantz)
To Sail Beyond the Sunset (Robert A. Heinlein)
Tough Guys Don't Dance (Norman Mailer)
Truth about Lorin Jones, The (Alison Lurie)
Veiled One, The (Ruth Rendell)
Vineland (Thomas Pynchon)
War (Marguerite Duras)
We Are Still Married (Garrison Keillor)
Westward Ha! (S. J. Perelman)
Whirlwind (James Clavell)
Whistlejacket (John Hawkes)
Wonderful Years, Wonderful Years (George V. Higgins)

Mental Illness/Psychiatry
Bourne Ultimatum, The (Robert Ludlum)
Bridesmaid, The (Ruth Rendell)
Carpenter's Gothic (William Gaddis)
Cat's Eye (Margaret Atwood)
Cyteen (C. J. Cherryh)
Dark Tower Series, The (Stephen King)
Exile, The (William Kotzwinkle)
Fast Lanes (Jayne Anne Phillips)
Fool's Run (Patricia A. McKillip)
Gallowglass (Ruth Rendell as Barbara Vine)
Garden of Eden, The (Ernest Hemingway)
Golden Orange, The (Joseph Wambaugh)
Gravity's Rainbow (Thomas Pynchon)
House of Stairs, The (Ruth Rendell as Barbara Vine)
In My Father's House (Ernest J. Gaines)
J R (William Gaddis)
Last Notes From Home (Frederick Exley)
Lover, The (Marguerite Duras)
Midnight's Children (Salman Rushdie)
Misery (Stephen King)
Origin of the Brunists, The (Robert Coover)
Picturing Will (Ann Beattie)
Recognitions, The (William Gaddis)
Satanic Verses, The (Salman Rushdie)
Sea Wall, The (Marguerite Duras)
Second Coming, The (Walker Percy)
Shadows (John Gardner)
Shame (Salman Rushdie)

Appendix I

Silver Pillow, The (Thomas M. Disch)
Soft Monkey (Harlan Ellison)
Stillness (John Gardner)
Universal Baseball Association, The (Robert Coover)
Veiled One, The (Ruth Rendell)
Vineland (Thomas Pynchon)
Who Killed Palomino Molero? (Mario Vargas Llosa)
Wonderful Years, Wonderful Years (George V. Higgins)

Mentors
Autobiography of Miss Jane Pittman, The (Ernest J. Gaines)
Beet Queen, The (Louise Erdrich)
Bourne Ultimatum, The (Robert Ludlum)
Captain and the Enemy, The (Graham Greene)
Charlie and the Chocolate Factory (Roald Dahl)
Cyteen (C. J. Cherryh)
Dead Father, The (Donald Barthelme)
Fade (Robert Cormier)
Fire Down Below (William Golding)
Gathering of Old Men, A (Ernest J. Gaines)
Genesis (Wallace Stegner)
Icarus Agenda, The (Robert Ludlum)
In My Father's House (Ernest J. Gaines)
J R (William Gaddis)
Last Notes From Home (Frederick Exley)

Marya: A Life (Joyce Carol Oates)
More Die of Heartbreak (Saul Bellow)
Narrows, The (Ann Petry)
Paradise (Donald Barthelme)
Picture This (Joseph Heller)
Picturing Will (Ann Beattie)
Snow White (Donald Barthelme)

Native American
Beet Queen, The (Louise Erdrich)
Coyote Waits (Tony Hillerman)
Fencepost Chronicles, The (W. P. Kinsella)
House Made of Dawn (N. Scott Momaday)
Skinwalkers (Tony Hillerman)
Talking God (Tony Hillerman)
Tracks (Louise Erdrich)
Way to Rainy Mountain, The (N. Scott Momaday)

Nature
Acres and Pains (S. J. Perelman)
Always Coming Home (Ursula K. Le Guin)
Carpenter's Gothic (William Gaddis)
Desert Solitaire (Edward Abbey)
Galapagos (Kurt Vonnegut)
Genesis (Wallace Stegner)
House Made of Dawn (N. Scott Momaday)
Light Can Be Both Wave and Particle (Ellen Gilchrist)
Lover, The (Marguerite Duras)
Moderato Cantabile (Marguerite Duras)

More Die of Heartbreak (Saul
　Bellow)
Most of S. J. Perelman, The (S. J.
　Perelman)
My Àntonia (Willa Cather)
O Pioneers! (Willa Cather)
Rusalka (C. J. Cherryh)
Taming the Star Runner (S. E.
　Hinton)
Tehanu (Ursula K. Le Guin)
Way to Rainy Mountain, The (N.
　Scott Momaday)
Westward Ha! (S. J. Perelman)

Nonconformity
Acres and Pains (S. J. Perelman)
Beet Queen, The (Louise Erdrich)
Being Invisible (Thomas Berger)
Cat's Eye (Margaret Atwood)
Charlie and the Chocolate Factory
　(Roald Dahl)
Circular Staircase, The (Mary
　Roberts Rinehart)
Cyteen (C. J. Cherryh)
Desert Solitaire (Edward Abbey)
Difficulties with Girls (Kingsley
　Amis)
Exile, The (William Kotzwinkle)
Fire Down Below (William
　Golding)
Firebrand, The (Marion Zimmer
　Bradley)
First Man in Rome, The (Colleen
　McCullough)
Folks That Live on the Hill, The
　(Kingsley Amis)
Golden Orange, The (Joseph
　Wambaugh)
Graveyard for Lunatics, A (Ray
　Bradbury)
Guerrillas (V. S. Naipaul)
Handmaid's Tale, The (Margaret
　Atwood)
Hermit of 69th Street, The (Jerzy
　Kosinski)
Hot Jazz Trio, The (William
　Kotzwinkle)
House of Stairs, The (Ruth Rendell
　as Barbara Vine)
House for Mr Biswas, A (V. S.
　Naipaul)
Houseguest, The (Thomas Berger)
Je ne parle pas français (Katherine
　Mansfield)
K. (Mary Roberts Rinehart)
Keep the Change (Thomas
　McGuane)
Lover, The (Marguerite Duras)
Man-Eater of Malgudi, The (R. K.
　Narayan)
Midnight Examiner, The (William
　Kotzwinkle)
Moderato Cantabile (Marguerite
　Duras)
Most of S. J. Perelman, The (S. J.
　Perelman)
Mutant Season, The (Robert
　Silverberg)
My Uncle Oswald (Roald Dahl)
My Secret History (Paul Theroux)
Picture This (Joseph Heller)
Q Clearance (Peter Benchley)
Recognitions, The (William Gaddis)
Sea Wall, The (Marguerite Duras)
Skinny Legs and All (Tom
　Robbins)
Summons to Memphis, A (Peter
　Taylor)

Taming the Star Runner (S. E. Hinton)
Tango Charlie and Foxtrot Romeo (John Varley)
Till We Meet Again (Judith Krantz)
Tracks (Louise Erdrich)
Tripmaster Monkey: His Fake Book (Maxine Hong Kingston)
Uncle Fred Flits By (P. G. Wodehouse)
Vineland (Thomas Pynchon)
War (Marguerite Duras)
Westward Ha! (S. J. Perelman)

Past (Significance of)
Alaska (James A. Michener)
Angle of Repose (Wallace Stegner)
Autobiography of Miss Jane Pittman, The (Ernest J. Gaines)
Beacon at Alexandria, The (Gillian Bradshaw)
Beloved (Toni Morrison)
Bourne Ultimatum, The (Robert Ludlum)
Burden of Proof, The (Scott Turow)
Candle for D'Artagnan, A (Chelsea Quinn Yarbro)
Cat's Eye (Margaret Atwood)
Chosen Place, The Timeless People, The (Paule Marshall)
Crusader's Torch (Chelsea Quinn Yarbro)
Crying of Lot 49, The (Thomas Pynchon)
Cyteen (C. J. Cherryh)
Dark Tower Series, The (Stephen King)
Dead Father, The (Donald Barthelme)
Deadeye Dick (Kurt Vonnegut)
Exile, The (William Kotzwinkle)
Fast Lanes (Jayne Anne Phillips)
Flame in Byzantium (Chelsea Quinn Yarbro)
Folk of the Air, The (Peter S. Beagle)
Foucault's Pendulum (Umberto Eco)
Freaky Deaky (Elmore Leonard)
Friend of My Youth (Alice Munro)
Galapagos (Kurt Vonnegut)
Gathering of Old Men, A (Ernest J. Gaines)
Gift of Asher Lev, The (Chaim Potok)
God Knows (Joseph Heller)
Graveyard for Lunatics, A (Ray Bradbury)
Gravity's Rainbow (Thomas Pynchon)
Handmaid's Tale, The (Margaret Atwood)
Hawaii (James A. Michener)
House of Stairs, The (Ruth Rendell as Barbara Vine)
In My Father's House (Ernest J. Gaines)
Joy Luck Club, The (Amy Tan)
Keep the Change (Thomas McGuane)
Killing Mister Watson (Peter Matthiessen)
Light Can Be Both Wave and Particle (Ellen Gilchrist)
Love in the Time of Cholera (Gabriel García Márquez)

Lover, The (Marguerite Duras)
Midnight's Children (Salman Rushdie)
Mitla Pass (Leon Uris)
Mongoose R.I.P. (William F. Buckley, Jr.)
Most of S. J. Perelman, The (S. J. Perelman)
My Àntonia (Willa Cather)
Novelty (John Crowley)
O Pioneers! (Willa Cather)
Old Devils, The (Kingsley Amis)
Once and Future King, The (T. H. White)
One Writer's Beginnings (Eudora Welty)
Optimist's Daughter, The (Eudora Welty)
Other Side, The (Mary Gordon)
Paradise (Donald Barthelme)
Picture This (Joseph Heller)
Praisesong for the Widow (Paule Marshall)
Presumed Innocent (Scott Turow)
Public Burning, The (Robert Coover)
Quinn's Book (William Kennedy)
Rat, The (Günter Grass)
Recognitions, The (William Gaddis)
Renegades of Pern (Anne McCaffrey)
Sands of Time, The (Sidney Sheldon)
Satanic Verses, The (Salman Rushdie)
Secret Pilgrim, The (John le Carré)
Shame (Salman Rushdie)
Snow White (Donald Barthelme)
Some Can Whistle (Larry McMurtry)
Sphere (Michael Crichton)
Square, The (Marguerite Duras)
Stones of Nomuru, The (L. Sprague de Camp)
Theft, A (Saul Bellow)
V. (Thomas Pynchon)
Vineland (Thomas Pynchon)
Way to Rainy Mountain, The (N. Scott Momaday)
Westward Ha! (S. J. Perelman)
Whistlejacket (John Hawkes)
You Must Remember This (Joyce Carol Oates)

Physical Disability
Alnilam (James Dickey)
Angle of Repose (Wallace Stegner)
Beet Queen, The (Louise Erdrich)
Dark Tower Series, The (Stephen King)
Galapagos (Kurt Vonnegut)
God Knows (Joseph Heller)
Graveyard for Lunatics, A (Ray Bradbury)
Hocus Pocus (Kurt Vonnegut)
House of Stairs, The (Ruth Rendell as Barbara Vine)
Midnight's Children (Salman Rushdie)
Misery (Stephen King)
Prayer for Owen Meany, A (John Irving)
Shadows (John Gardner)
Truth About George, The (P. G. Wodehouse)
War (Marguerite Duras)

Appendix I 1353

Political/Social Protest
Alaska (James A. Michener)
All God's Children Need Traveling Shoes (Maya Angelou)
Angel with the Sword (C. J. Cherryh)
Autobiography of Miss Jane Pittman, The (Ernest J. Gaines)
Beloved (Toni Morrison)
Captain and the Enemy, The (Graham Greene)
Carpenter's Gothic (William Gaddis)
The Counterlife (Philip Roth)
Cyteen (C. J. Cherryh)
Desert Solitaire (Edward Abbey)
Devices and Desires (P. D. James)
Different Kind of Christmas, A (Alex Haley)
Exile, The (William Kotzwinkle)
Fencepost Chronicles, The (W. P. Kinsella)
Folk of the Air, The (Peter S. Beagle)
Foucault's Pendulum (Umberto Eco)
Gathering of Old Men, A (Ernest J. Gaines)
Gravity's Rainbow (Thomas Pynchon)
Guerrillas (V. S. Naipaul)
Handmaid's Tale, The (Margaret Atwood)
Hawaii (James A. Michener)
House Made of Dawn (N. Scott Momaday)
Icarus Agenda, The (Robert Ludlum)
In Country (Bobbie Ann Mason)
In My Father's House (Ernest J. Gaines)
Integral Trees, The (Larry Niven)
J R (William Gaddis)
LETTERS (John Barth)
Midnight's Children (Salman Rushdie)
Mongoose R.I.P. (William F. Buckley, Jr.)
Mystic Masseur, The (V. S. Naipaul)
Naked in Garden Hills (Harry Crews)
Patriot Games (Tom Clancy)
Picture This (Joseph Heller)
Prayer for Owen Meany, A (John Irving)
Pubis Angelical (Manuel Puig)
Public Burning, The (Robert Coover)
Q Clearance (Peter Benchley)
Radio Free Albemuth (Philip K. Dick)
Rat, The (Günter Grass)
Recognitions, The (William Gaddis)
Satanic Verses, The (Salman Rushdie)
Sea Wall, The (Marguerite Duras)
Shame (Salman Rushdie)
Skinny Legs and All (Tom Robbins)
Stallion Gate (Martin Cruz Smith)
Star of Gypsies (Robert Silverberg)
Tales of the South Pacific (James A. Michener)
Tripmaster Monkey: His Fake Book (Maxine Hong Kingston)
V. (Thomas Pynchon)
Veiled One, The (Ruth Rendell)

Vineland (Thomas Pynchon)
War (Marguerite Duras)
Whirlwind (James Clavell)

Poverty
Angel with the Sword (C. J. Cherryh)
Billy Bathgate (E. L. Doctorow)
Blood of Requited Love (Manuel Puig)
Charlie and the Chocolate Factory (Roald Dahl)
Crying of Lot 49, The (Thomas Pynchon)
Devices and Desires (P. D. James)
Four Million, The (O. Henry)
Garden-Party, The (Katherine Mansfield)
Guerrillas (V. S. Naipaul)
House for Mr Biswas, A (V. S. Naipaul)
K. (Mary Roberts Rinehart)
Knockout Artist, The (Harry Crews)
Lover, The (Marguerite Duras)
Mystic Masseur, The (V. S. Naipaul)
Picturing Will (Ann Beattie)
Quinn's Book (William Kennedy)
Sea Wall, The (Marguerite Duras)
Shiloh and Other Stories (Bobbie Ann Mason)
Southern Family, A (Gail Godwin)
Square, The (Marguerite Duras)
Street, The (Ann Petry)
Taste for Death, A (P. D. James)
Trimmed Lamp, The (O. Henry)
Winesburg, Ohio (Sherwood Anderson)

Quest/Journey
Alaska (James A. Michener)
Alnilam (James Dickey)
Angle of Repose (Wallace Stegner)
Autobiography of Miss Jane Pittman, The (Ernest J. Gaines)
Being Invisible (Thomas Berger)
Beloved (Toni Morrison)
Blood of Requited Love (Manuel Puig)
Charlie and the Chocolate Factory (Roald Dahl)
City of Sorcery, The (Marion Zimmer Bradley)
Close Quarters (William Golding)
Crying of Lot 49, The (Thomas Pynchon)
Cyteen (C. J. Cherryh)
Dark Tower Series, The (Stephen King)
Dark Laughter (Sherwood Anderson)
Dead Father, The (Donald Barthelme)
Djinn (Alain Robbe-Grillet)
Fade (Robert Cormier)
Fast Lanes (Jayne Anne Phillips)
Fire Down Below (Wm. Golding)
Folk of the Air, The (Peter S. Beagle)
Fool's Run (Patricia A. McKillip)
Galapagos (Kurt Vonnegut)
Gallowglass (Ruth Rendell as Barbara Vine)
Game of Empire, The (Poul Anderson)
Genesis (Wallace Stegner)
Giles Goat-Boy or, The Revised New Syllabus (John Barth)

Appendix I

Gravity's Rainbow (Thomas Pynchon)
Great Sky River (Gregory Benford)
Guerrillas (V. S. Naipaul)
Guide, The (R. K. Narayan)
Handmaid's Tale, The (Margaret Atwood)
Harrowing of Gwynedd, the (Katherine Kurtz)
Hawaii (James A. Michener)
Honorable Barbarian, The (L. Sprague de Camp)
Hook, Line, Sinker (Len Deighton)
Hot Jazz Trio, The (William Kotzwinkle)
House of Stairs, The (Ruth Rendell as Barbara Vine)
House for Mr Biswas, A (V. S. Naipaul)
House Made of Dawn (N. Scott Momaday)
Icarus Agenda, The (Robert Ludlum)
In My Father's House (Ernest J. Gaines)
Keep the Change (Thomas McGuane)
Knockout Artist, The (Harry Crews)
Love in the Time of Cholera (Gabriel García Márquez)
Midnight's Children (Salman Rushdie)
Mitla Pass (Leon Uris)
Moon and the Face, The (Patricia A. McKillip)
More Die of Heartbreak (Saul Bellow)
My Uncle Oswald (Roald Dahl)
Mystic Masseur, The (V. S. Naipaul)
Once and Future King, The (T. H. White)
Picturing Will (Ann Beattie)
Plains of Passage, The (Jean M. Auel)
Prayer for Owen Meany, A (John Irving)
Princess Bride, The (William Goldman)
Quinn's Book (William Kennedy)
Random Walk: A Novel for a New Age (Lawrence Block)
Recognitions, The (William Gaddis)
S. (John Updike)
Sands of Time, The (Sidney Sheldon)
Satanic Verses, The (Salman Rushdie)
Second Chronicles of Amber, The (Roger Zelazny)
Secret Pilgrim, The (John le Carré)
Shadows (John Gardner)
Shame (Salman Rushdie)
Skinny Legs and All (Tom Robbins)
Some Can Whistle (Larry McMurtry)
Sot-Weed Factor, The (John Barth)
Square, The (Marguerite Duras)
Temple of My Familiar, The (Alice Walker)
Theft, A (Saul Bellow)
Tough Guys Don't Dance (Norman Mailer)
Tracks (Louise Erdrich)
Tripmaster Monkey: His Fake Book (Maxine Hong Kingston)

2061: Odyssey Three (Arthur C.
    Clarke)
V. (Thomas Pynchon)
Vineland (Thomas Pynchon)
Way to Rainy Mountain, The (N.
    Scott Momaday)
Weaveworld (Clive Barker)
Westward Ha! (S. J. Perelman)
Whirlwind (James Clavell)
Winesburg, Ohio (Sherwood
    Anderson)

Racism
Alaska (James A. Michener)
All God's Children Need Traveling
    Shoes (Maya Angelou)
Autobiography of Miss Jane
    Pittman, The (Ernest J. Gaines)
Because It Is Bitter, and Because It
    Is My Heart (Joyce Carol Oates)
Beet Queen, The (Louise Erdrich)
Beloved (Toni Morrison)
Blood of Requited Love (Manuel
    Puig)
Bonfire of the Vanities, The (Tom
    Wolfe)
Brown Girl, Brownstones (Paule
    Marshall)
Carpenter's Gothic (William
    Gaddis)
Different Kind of Christmas, A
    (Alex Haley)
Fade (Robert Cormier)
Free-Lance Pallbearers, The
    (Ishmael Reed)
Game of Empire, The (Poul
    Anderson)
Gathering of Old Men, A (Ernest J.
    Gaines)

Guerrillas (V. S. Naipaul)
Handmaid's Tale, The (Margaret
    Atwood)
Hawaii (James A. Michener)
Hocus Pocus (Kurt Vonnegut)
In My Father's House (Ernest J.
    Gaines)
Killing Mister Watson (Peter
    Matthiessen)
Lover, The (Marguerite Duras)
Mammoth Hunters, The (Jean M.
    Auel)
Mumbo Jumbo (Ishmael Reed)
Mutant Season, The (Robert
    Silverberg)
Mystic Masseur, The (V. S.
    Naipaul)
Narrows, The (Ann Petry)
Plains of Passage, The (Jean M.
    Auel)
Quinn's Book (William Kennedy)
Reckless Eyeballing (Ishmael Reed)
Rummies (Peter Benchley)
Satanic Verses, The (Salman
    Rushdie)
Sea Wall, The (Marguerite Duras)
Sphere (Michael Crichton)
Street, The (Ann Petry)
Tales of the South Pacific (James
    A. Michener)
Tracks (Louise Erdrich)
V. (Thomas Pynchon)
Who Killed Palomino Molero?
    (Mario Vargas Llosa)

Redemption
Alaska (James A. Michener)
Autobiography of Miss Jane
    Pittman, The (Ernest J. Gaines)

Celebration (Mary Lee Settle)
Dark Tower Series, The (Stephen King)
Dead Father, The (Donald Barthelme)
Eyes of the Dragon, The (Stephen King)
Foucault's Pendulum (Umberto Eco)
Gathering of Old Men, A (Ernest J. Gaines)
Golden Orange, The (Joseph Wambaugh)
Hawaii (James A. Michener)
House Made of Dawn (N. Scott Momaday)
In My Father's House (Ernest J. Gaines)
Last Notes From Home (Frederick Exley)
Moviegoer, The (Walker Percy)
Old Devils, The (Kingsley Amis)
Origin of the Brunists, The (Robert Coover)
Picturing Will (Ann Beattie)
Quinn's Book (William Kennedy)
Random Walk: A Novel for a New Age (Lawrence Block)
Second Coming, The (Walker Percy)
Story of My Life (Jay McInerney)
Theft, A (Saul Bellow)
Weaveworld (Clive Barker)

Regional Identity
Acres and Pains (S. J. Perelman)
Alaska (James A. Michener)
All God's Children Need Traveling Shoes (Maya Angelou)
Autobiography of Miss Jane Pittman, The (Ernest J. Gaines)
Beet Queen, The (Louise Erdrich)
Boomerang (Barry Hannah)
Cat's Eye (Margaret Atwood)
Country Place (Ann Petry)
Desert Solitaire (Edward Abbey)
Fade (Robert Cormier)
First Man in Rome, The (Colleen McCullough)
Friend of My Youth (Alice Munro)
Gathering of Old Men, A (Ernest J. Gaines)
Genesis (Wallace Stegner)
Guerrillas (V. S. Naipaul)
Hawaii (James A. Michener)
House for Mr Biswas, A (V. S. Naipaul)
House Made of Dawn (N. Scott Momaday)
Houseguest, The (Thomas Berger)
In My Father's House (Ernest J. Gaines)
In Country (Bobbie Ann Mason)
Love in the Time of Cholera (Gabriel García Márquez)
Most of S. J. Perelman, The (S. J. Perelman)
Moviegoer, The (Walker Percy)
Mystic Masseur, The (V. S. Naipaul)
Old Devils, The (Kingsley Amis)
Origin of the Brunists, The (Robert Coover)
Prayer for Owen Meany, A (John Irving)
Rusalka (C. J. Cherryh)
Second Coming, The (Walker Percy)

Shiloh and Other Stories (Bobbie Ann Mason)
Sot-Weed Factor, The (John Barth)
Spence + Lila (Bobbie Ann Mason)
Tracks (Louise Erdrich)
Way to Rainy Mountain, The (N. Scott Momaday)
We Are Still Married (Garrison Keillor)
Westward Ha! (S. J. Perelman)
Whirlwind (James Clavell)
Windmills of the Gods (Sidney Sheldon)

Religion
Alaska (James A. Michener)
Angel with the Sword (C. J. Cherryh)
Autobiography of Miss Jane Pittman, The (Ernest J. Gaines)
Beacon at Alexandria, The (Gillian Bradshaw)
Boomerang (Barry Hannah)
Carpenter's Gothic (William Gaddis)
City of Sorcery, The (Marion Zimmer Bradley)
The Counterlife (Philip Roth)
Devices and Desires (P. D. James)
Feast of Snakes, A (Harry Crews)
Firebrand, The (Marion Zimmer Bradley)
Foucault's Pendulum (Umberto Eco)
Friend of My Youth (Alice Munro)
Gift of Asher Lev, The (Chaim Potok)
God Knows (Joseph Heller)
God's Grace (Bernard Malamud)
Guide, The (R. K. Narayan)
Handmaid's Tale, The (Margaret Atwood)
Happy Turnip, The (Thomas M. Disch)
Harrowing of Gwynedd, the (Katherine Kurtz)
Hawaii (James A. Michener)
Hermit of 69th Street, The (Jerzy Kosinski)
House for Mr Biswas, A (V. S. Naipaul)
Icarus Agenda, The (Robert Ludlum)
In My Father's House (Ernest J. Gaines)
King of the Fields, The (Isaac Bashevis Singer)
Last Notes From Home (Frederick Exley)
Lazarus (Morris West)
Marya: A Life (Joyce Carol Oates)
Moviegoer, The (Walker Percy)
Mumbo Jumbo (Ishmael Reed)
Mystic Masseur, The (V. S. Naipaul)
Origin of the Brunists, The (Robert Coover)
Other Side, The (Mary Gordon)
Pillars of the Earth (Ken Follett)
Queen of the Damned, The (Anne Rice)
Radio Free Albemuth (Philip K. Dick)
Rat, The (Günter Grass)
Reckless Eyeballing (Ishmael Reed)
Recognitions, The (William Gaddis)
Roma Mater (Poul Anderson)
S. (John Updike)

Appendix I

Sands of Time, The (Sidney Sheldon)
Satanic Verses, The (Salman Rushdie)
Sea Hawk, The (Rafael Sabatini)
Second Coming, The (Walker Percy)
Shame (Salman Rushdie)
Skinny Legs and All (Tom Robbins)
Stones of Nomuru, The (L. Sprague de Camp)
Taste for Death, A (P. D. James)
Way to Rainy Mountain, The (N. Scott Momaday)
Whirlwind (James Clavell)

Revenge
Autobiography of Miss Jane Pittman, The (Ernest J. Gaines)
Being Invisible (Thomas Berger)
Bourne Ultimatum, The (Robert Ludlum)
Captain Blood (Rafael Sabatini)
Clear and Present Danger (Tom Clancy)
Crying of Lot 49, The (Thomas Pynchon)
Eyes of the Dragon, The (Stephen King)
Fade (Robert Cormier)
Fencepost Chronicles, The (W. P. Kinsella)
First Man in Rome, The (Colleen McCullough)
Fool's Run (Patricia A. McKillip)
Gathering of Old Men, A (Ernest J. Gaines)
God Knows (Joseph Heller)
God's Grace (Bernard Malamud)
Graveyard for Lunatics, A (Ray Bradbury)
Guerrillas (V. S. Naipaul)
House for Mr Biswas, A (V. S. Naipaul)
Houseguest, The (Thomas Berger)
Icarus Agenda, The (Robert Ludlum)
In My Father's House (Ernest J. Gaines)
King of the Fields, The (Isaac Bashevis Singer)
Lamb to the Slaughter (Roald Dahl)
Love Killers, The (Jackie Collins)
Misery (Stephen King)
Mongoose R.I.P. (William F. Buckley, Jr.)
Naked in Garden Hills (Harry Crews)
Patriot Games (Tom Clancy)
Princess Bride, The (William Goldman)
Renegades of Pern (Anne McCaffrey)
Rusalka (C. J. Cherryh)
Sands of Time, The (Sidney Sheldon)
Satanic Verses, The (Salman Rushdie)
Scaramouche (Rafael Sabatini)
Sea Hawk, The (Rafael Sabatini)
Ticket to the Boneyard, A (Lawrence Block)
V. (Thomas Pynchon)
Weaveworld (Clive Barker)
Whirlwind (James Clavell)

Whistlejacket (John Hawkes)
Windmills of the Gods (Sidney Sheldon)

Romantic Love
All God's Children Need Traveling Shoes (Maya Angelou)
Angel with the Sword (C. J. Cherryh)
Angle of Repose (Wallace Stegner)
Autobiography of Miss Jane Pittman, The (Ernest J. Gaines)
Being Invisible (Thomas Berger)
Breathing Lessons (Anne Tyler)
Captain Blood (Rafael Sabatini)
Captain and the Enemy, The (Graham Greene)
Carpenter's Gothic (William Gaddis)
Charley Bland (Mary Lee Settle)
Circular Staircase, The (Mary Roberts Rinehart)
Complete Short Stories of Ernest Hemingway, The (Ernest Hemingway)
Exile, The (William Kotzwinkle)
Fade (Robert Cormier)
Firebrand, The (Marion Zimmer Bradley)
First Man in Rome, The (Colleen McCullough)
Folks That Live on the Hill, The (Kingsley Amis)
Four Million, The (O. Henry)
Game of Empire, The (Poul Anderson)
Garden of Eden, The (Ernest Hemingway)
God Knows (Joseph Heller)
Golden Orange, The (Joseph Wambaugh)
Gravity's Rainbow (Thomas Pynchon)
Guerrillas (V. S. Naipaul)
Guide, The (R. K. Narayan)
Handmaid's Tale, The (Margaret Atwood)
Heirs of Hammerfell, The (Marion Zimmer Bradley)
Honorable Barbarian, The (L. Sprague de Camp)
Houseguest, The (Thomas Berger)
Icarus Agenda, The (Robert Ludlum)
In Miro District and Other Stories (Peter Taylor)
K. (Mary Roberts Rinehart)
Killashandra (Anne McCaffrey)
Love in the Time of Cholera (Gabriel García Márquez)
Magicians of Gor (John Norman)
Mammoth Hunters, The (Jean M. Auel)
Midnight Examiner, The (William Kotzwinkle)
Midnight's Children (Salman Rushdie)
Mongoose R.I.P. (William F. Buckley, Jr.)
Most of S. J. Perelman, The (S. J. Perelman)
Moviegoer, The (Walker Percy)
Mutant Season, The (Robert Silverberg)
My Uncle Oswald (Roald Dahl)
Narrows, The (Ann Petry)
Old Forest and Other Stories, The (Peter Taylor)

Old Devils, The (Kingsley Amis)
Picturing Will (Ann Beattie)
Plains of Passage, The (Jean M. Auel)
Princess Bride, The (William Goldman)
Q Clearance (Peter Benchley)
Quinn's Book (William Kennedy)
Renegades of Pern (Anne McCaffrey)
Roma Mater (Poul Anderson)
Rummies (Peter Benchley)
Russia House, The (John le Carré)
S. (John Updike)
Sands of Time, The (Sidney Sheldon)
Scaramouche (Rafael Sabatini)
Sea Hawk, The (Rafael Sabatini)
Second Coming, The (Walker Percy)
Serenissima: A Novel of Venice (Erica Jong)
Shame (Salman Rushdie)
Snow White (Donald Barthelme)
Stillness (John Gardner)
Stones of Nomuru, The (L. Sprague de Camp)
Story of My Life (Jay McInerney)
Theft, A (Saul Bellow)
Till We Meet Again (Judith Krantz)
Tracks (Louise Erdrich)
Truth About George, The (P. G. Wodehouse)
War (Marguerite Duras)
When Harry Met Sally (Nora Ephron)
Whirlwind (James Clavell)
Whistlejacket (John Hawkes)
Who Killed Palomino Molero? (Mario Vargas Llosa)
Windmills of the Gods (Sidney Sheldon)
Winesburg, Ohio (Sherwood Anderson)

Rural Life

Acres and Pains (S. J. Perelman)
Always Coming Home (Ursula K. Le Guin)
Angle of Repose (Wallace Stegner)
Autobiography of Miss Jane Pittman, The (Ernest J. Gaines)
Because It Is Bitter, and Because It Is My Heart (Joyce Carol Oates)
Beet Queen, The (Louise Erdrich)
Big Rock Candy Mountain, The (Wallace Stegner)
Financial Expert, The (R. K. Narayan)
Gathering of Old Men, A (Ernest J. Gaines)
Genesis (Wallace Stegner)
Happy Turnip, The (Thomas M. Disch)
Homesick (Guy Vanderhaeghe)
In My Father's House (Ernest J. Gaines)
Marya: A Life (Joyce Carol Oates)
Most of S. J. Perelman, The (S. J. Perelman)
My Àntonia (Willa Cather)
O Pioneers! (Willa Cather)
Rusalka (C. J. Cherryh)
Shiloh and Other Stories (Bobbie Ann Mason)
Spence + Lila (Bobbie Ann Mason)
Stillness (John Gardner)

Summer Lightning (P. G. Wodehouse)
Tehanu (Ursula K. Le Guin)
Trust (George V. Higgins)
Victories (George V. Higgins)
Winesburg, Ohio (Sherwood Anderson)

Sexual Politics
Bearkeeper's Daughter, The (Gillian Bradshaw)
Beet Queen, The (Louise Erdrich)
Big Town, The (Ring Lardner)
Blood of Requited Love (Manuel Puig)
Boomerang (Barry Hannah)
Bridge of Lost Desire, The (Samuel R. Delany)
Brown Girl, Brownstones (Paule Marshall)
Carpenter's Gothic (Wm. Gaddis)
Cat's Eye (Margaret Atwood)
Circular Staircase, The (Mary Roberts Rinehart)
Cyteen (C. J. Cherryh)
Dead Father, The (Donald Barthelme)
Difficulties with Girls (Kingsley Amis)
Folks That Live on the Hill, The (Kingsley Amis)
Gerald's Party (Robert Coover)
God Knows (Joseph Heller)
God's Grace (Bernard Malamud)
Golden Orange, The (Joseph Wambaugh)
Guerrillas (V. S. Naipaul)
Handmaid's Tale, The (Margaret Atwood)

J R (William Gaddis)
K. (Mary Roberts Rinehart)
Keep the Change (Thomas McGuane)
King of the Fields, The (Isaac Bashevis Singer)
Lamb to the Slaughter (Roald Dahl)
LETTERS (John Barth)
Magicians of Gor (John Norman)
Midnight Examiner, The (William Kotzwinkle)
Mitla Pass (Leon Uris)
More Die of Heartbreak (Saul Bellow)
Mutant Season, The (Robert Silverberg)
My Uncle Oswald (Roald Dahl)
Narrows, The (Ann Petry)
Old Devils, The (Kingsley Amis)
Paradise (Donald Barthelme)
Picture This (Joseph Heller)
Plains of Passage, The (Jean M. Auel)
Pubis Angelical (Manuel Puig)
Queen of the Damned, The (Anne Rice)
Rat, The (Günter Grass)
Recognitions, The (William Gaddis)
Roma Mater (Poul Anderson)
Second Coming, The (Walker Percy)
Serenissima: A Novel of Venice (Erica Jong)
Snow White (Donald Barthelme)
Sphere (Michael Crichton)
Stillness (John Gardner)
Stones of Nomuru, The (L. Sprague de Camp)
Story of My Life (Jay McInerney)

Appendix I 1363

Street, The (Ann Petry)
Theft, A (Saul Bellow)
Till We Meet Again (Judith Krantz)
Tracks (Louise Erdrich)
Warrior Queens, The (Lady Antonia Fraser)
When Harry Met Sally (Nora Ephron)
Whirlwind (James Clavell)
Whistlejacket (John Hawkes)
Windmills of the Gods (Sidney Sheldon)

Sexuality

Angle of Repose (Wallace Stegner)
Autobiography of Miss Jane Pittman, The (Ernest J. Gaines)
Being Invisible (Thomas Berger)
Bingo (Rita Mae Brown)
Bliss (Katherine Mansfield)
Blood of Requited Love (Manuel Puig)
Boomerang (Barry Hannah)
Bridesmaid, The (Ruth Rendell)
Carpenter's Gothic (William Gaddis)
Cat's Eye (Margaret Atwood)
The Counterlife (Philip Roth)
Cyteen (C. J. Cherryh)
Dead Father, The (Donald Barthelme)
Devices and Desires (P. D. James)
Difficulties with Girls (Kingsley Amis)
Exile, The (William Kotzwinkle)
Fade (Robert Cormier)
Feast of Snakes, A (Harry Crews)
Friend of My Youth (Alice Munro)
Gallowglass (Ruth Rendell as Barbara Vine)
Garden of Eden, The (Ernest Hemingway)
Gerald's Party (Robert Coover)
God Knows (Joseph Heller)
Gravity's Rainbow (Thomas Pynchon)
Guerrillas (V. S. Naipaul)
Handmaid's Tale, The (Margaret Atwood)
Hermit of 69th Street, The (Jerzy Kosinski)
His Little Women (Judith Rossner)
Hocus Pocus (Kurt Vonnegut)
Homesick (Guy Vanderhaeghe)
Hot Jazz Trio, The (William Kotzwinkle)
House of Stairs, The (Ruth Rendell as Barbara Vine)
How I Grew (Mary McCarthy)
In Praise of the Stepmother (Mario Vargas Llosa)
In My Father's House (Ernest J. Gaines)
Je ne parle pas français (Katherine Mansfield)
Joey's Case (K. C. Constantine)
J R (William Gaddis)
Lover, The (Marguerite Duras)
Magicians of Gor (John Norman)
Midnight Examiner, The (William Kotzwinkle)
Moderato Cantabile (Marguerite Duras)
More Die of Heartbreak (Saul Bellow)
Mutant Season, The (Robert Silverberg)

My Uncle Oswald (Roald Dahl)
My Secret History (Paul Theroux)
Naked in Garden Hills (Harry Crews)
Old Gringo, The (Carlos Fuentes)
Paradise (Donald Barthelme)
Picturing Will (Ann Beattie)
Prayer for Owen Meany, A (John Irving)
Recognitions, The (William Gaddis)
Rock Star (Jackie Collins)
Roma Mater (Poul Anderson)
Rusalka (C. J. Cherryh)
S. (John Updike)
Sea Wall, The (Marguerite Duras)
Second Coming, The (Walker Percy)
Serenissima: A Novel of Venice (Erica Jong)
Silver Pillow, The (Thomas M. Disch)
Skinny Legs and All (Tom Robbins)
Snow White (Donald Barthelme)
Sot-Weed Factor, The (John Barth)
Square, The (Marguerite Duras)
Story of My Life (Jay McInerney)
Temple of My Familiar, The (Alice Walker)
Theft, A (Saul Bellow)
To Sail Beyond the Sunset (Robert A. Heinlein)
Tracks (Louise Erdrich)
War (Marguerite Duras)
Whistlejacket (John Hawkes)
You Must Remember This (Joyce Carol Oates)

Slavery
All God's Children Need Traveling Shoes (Maya Angelou)
Autobiography of Miss Jane Pittman, The (Ernest J. Gaines)
Bearkeeper's Daughter, The (Gillian Bradshaw)
Beloved (Toni Morrison)
Bridge of Lost Desire, The (Samuel R. Delany)
Different Kind of Christmas, A (Alex Haley)
Imperial Purple (Gillian Bradshaw)
Magicians of Gor (John Norman)

Supernatural Phenomena/Powers
Alnilam (James Dickey)
Autobiography of Miss Jane Pittman, The (Ernest J. Gaines)
Beloved (Toni Morrison)
Candle for D'Artagnan, A (Chelsea Quinn Yarbro)
City of Sorcery, The (Marion Zimmer Bradley)
Crusader's Torch (Chelsea Quinn Yarbro)
Cyteen (C. J. Cherryh)
Dark Tower Series, The (Stephen King)
Exile, The (William Kotzwinkle)
Fade (Robert Cormier)
Financial Expert, The (R. K. Narayan)
Firecode (Chelsea Quinn Yarbro)
First Man in Rome, The (Colleen McCullough)
Flame in Byzantium (Chelsea Quinn Yarbro)

Appendix I

Folk of the Air, The (Peter S. Beagle)
Foucault's Pendulum (Umberto Eco)
Gift of Asher Lev, The (Chaim Potok)
Gravity's Rainbow (Pynchon)
Guide, The (R. K. Narayan)
Harrowing of Gwynedd, the (Katherine Kurtz)
Honorable Barbarian, The (L. Sprague de Camp)
Hot Jazz Trio, The (William Kotzwinkle)
House for Mr Biswas, A (V. S. Naipaul)
Man-Eater of Malgudi, The (R. K. Narayan)
Midnight's Children (Salman Rushdie)
Most of S. J. Perelman, The (S. J. Perelman)
Mutant Season, The (Robert Silverberg)
Mystic Masseur, The (V. S. Naipaul)
Paladin of the Lost Hour (Harlan Ellison)
Prayer for Owen Meany, A (John Irving)
Princess Bride, The (William Goldman)
Queen of the Damned, The (Anne Rice)
Quinn's Book (William Kennedy)
Radio Free Albemuth (Philip K. Dick)
Random Walk: A Novel for a New Age (Lawrence Block)

Roma Mater (Poul Anderson)
Rusalka (C. J. Cherryh)
Second Chronicles of Amber, The (Roger Zelazny)
Shame (Salman Rushdie)
Silver Pillow, The (Thomas M. Disch)
Skinwalkers (Tony Hillerman)
Sphere (Michael Crichton)
Taste for Death, A (P. D. James)
2061: Odyssey Three (Clarke)
Weaveworld (Clive Barker)

Technology/Industrialization/Science

Acres and Pains (S. J. Perelman)
Angel with the Sword (C. J. Cherryh)
Angle of Repose (Wallace Stegner)
Cardinal of the Kremlin, The (Tom Clancy)
Carpenter's Gothic (William Gaddis)
Crying of Lot 49, The (Thomas Pynchon)
Cyteen (C. J. Cherryh)
Desert Solitaire (Edward Abbey)
Devices and Desires (P. D. James)
Firecode (Chelsea Quinn Yarbro)
Fool's Run (Patricia A. McKillip)
Galapagos (Kurt Vonnegut)
Gravity's Rainbow (Thomas Pynchon)
Great Sky River (Gregory Benford)
Handmaid's Tale, The (Margaret Atwood)
Hocus Pocus (Kurt Vonnegut)
Integral Trees, The (Larry Niven)
J R (William Gaddis)

Light Can Be Both Wave and Particle (Ellen Gilchrist)
Moon and the Face, The (Patricia A. McKillip)
Most of S. J. Perelman, The (S. J. Perelman)
Rat, The (Günter Grass)
Robots of Dawn, The (Isaac Asimov)
Sphere (Michael Crichton)
Stallion Gate (Martin Cruz Smith)
Stones of Nomuru, The (L. Sprague de Camp)
Tango Charlie and Foxtrot Romeo (John Varley)
Toynbee Convector, The (Ray Bradbury)
2061: Odyssey Three (Arthur C. Clarke)
V. (Thomas Pynchon)
Veiled One, The (Ruth Rendell)
Vineland (Thomas Pynchon)
Westward Ha! (S. J. Perelman)

Urban Life
Acres and Pains (S. J. Perelman)
Bearkeeper's Daughter, The (Gillian Bradshaw)
Being Invisible (Thomas Berger)
Big Town, The (Ring Lardner)
Bonfire of the Vanities, The (Tom Wolfe)
Bridesmaid, The (Ruth Rendell)
Brown Girl, Brownstones (Paule Marshall)
Charlie and the Chocolate Factory (Roald Dahl)
Crying of Lot 49, The (Thomas Pynchon)

Dark Laughter (Sherwood Anderson)
Four Million, The (O. Henry)
Golden Orange, The (Joseph Wambaugh)
House for Mr Biswas, A (V. S. Naipaul)
Houseguest, The (Thomas Berger)
Imperial Purple (Gillian Bradshaw)
J R (William Gaddis)
Knockout Artist, The (Harry Crews)
Midnight Examiner, The (William Kotzwinkle)
Most of S. J. Perelman, The (S. J. Perelman)
Mystic Masseur, The (V. S. Naipaul)
Paradise (Donald Barthelme)
Picture This (Joseph Heller)
Quinn's Book (William Kennedy)
Rat, The (Günter Grass)
Recognitions, The (William Gaddis)
Satanic Verses, The (Salman Rushdie)
Snow White (Donald Barthelme)
Soft Monkey (Harlan Ellison)
Story of My Life (Jay McInerney)
Street, The (Ann Petry)
Theft, A (Saul Bellow)
Ticket to the Boneyard, A (Lawrence Block)
Toynbee Convector, The (Ray Bradbury)
Trimmed Lamp, The (O. Henry)
Veiled One, The (Ruth Rendell)
Westward Ha! (S. J. Perelman)
When Harry Met Sally (Nora Ephron)

Appendix I

Violence

Alaska (James A. Michener)
Alnilam (James Dickey)
Autobiography of Miss Jane Pittman, The (Ernest J. Gaines)
Because It Is Bitter, and Because It Is My Heart (Joyce Carol Oates)
Big Rock Candy Mountain, The (Wallace Stegner)
Billy Bathgate (E. L. Doctorow)
Boomerang (Barry Hannah)
Bourne Ultimatum, The (Robert Ludlum)
Bridesmaid, The (Ruth Rendell)
Candle for D'Artagnan, A (Chelsea Quinn Yarbro)
Carpenter's Gothic (William Gaddis)
Cassidy (Morris West)
Clear and Present Danger (Tom Clancy)
Complete Short Stories of Ernest Hemingway, The (Ernest Hemingway)
The Counterlife (Philip Roth)
Coyote Waits (Tony Hillerman)
Crusader's Torch (Chelsea Quinn Yarbro)
Cyteen (C. J. Cherryh)
Deadeye Dick (Kurt Vonnegut)
Devices and Desires (P. D. James)
Exile, The (William Kotzwinkle)
Fade (Robert Cormier)
Feast of Snakes, A (Harry Crews)
Firebrand, The (Marion Zimmer Bradley)
Flame in Byzantium (Chelsea Quinn Yarbro)
Freaky Deaky (Elmore Leonard)
Galapagos (Kurt Vonnegut)
Gallowglass (Ruth Rendell as Barbara Vine)
Gathering of Old Men, A (Ernest J. Gaines)
God Knows (Joseph Heller)
God's Grace (Bernard Malamud)
Golden Orange, The (Joseph Wambaugh)
Graveyard for Lunatics, A (Ray Bradbury)
Gravity's Rainbow (Thomas Pynchon)
Great Sky River (Gregory Benford)
Guerrillas (V. S. Naipaul)
Handmaid's Tale, The (Margaret Atwood)
Hawaii (James A. Michener)
Heirs of Hammerfell, The (Marion Zimmer Bradley)
Icarus Agenda, The (Robert Ludlum)
In Country (Bobbie Ann Mason)
Joey's Case (K. C. Constantine)
Killing Mister Watson (Peter Matthiessen)
Killshot (Elmore Leonard)
King of the Fields, The (Isaac Bashevis Singer)
Knockout Artist, The (Harry Crews)
Lamb to the Slaughter (Roald Dahl)
Lazarus (Morris West)
Lover, The (Marguerite Duras)
Man-Eater of Malgudi, The (R. K. Narayan)
Marya: A Life (Joyce Carol Oates)
Midnight Examiner, The (William Kotzwinkle)

Midnight's Children (Salman Rushdie)
Misery (Stephen King)
Moderato Cantabile (Marguerite Duras)
Old Gringo, The (Carlos Fuentes)
Patriot Games (Tom Clancy)
Quinn's Book (William Kennedy)
Rat, The (Günter Grass)
Recognitions, The (William Gaddis)
Renegades of Pern (Anne McCaffrey)
Rummies (Peter Benchley)
Sea Wall, The (Marguerite Duras)
Secret Pilgrim, The (John le Carré)
Shadows (John Gardner)
Shame (Salman Rushdie)
Skinny Legs and All (Tom Robbins)
Skinwalkers (Tony Hillerman)
Soft Monkey (Harlan Ellison)
Some Can Whistle (Larry McMurtry)
Sphere (Michael Crichton)
Tales of the South Pacific (James A. Michener)
Taming the Star Runner (S. E. Hinton)
Taste for Death, A (P. D. James)
Ticket to the Boneyard, A (Lawrence Block)
Tough Guys Don't Dance (Norman Mailer)
V. (Thomas Pynchon)
Veiled One, The (Ruth Rendell)
Vineland (Thomas Pynchon)
War (Marguerite Duras)
Whirlwind (James Clavell)
Whistlejacket (John Hawkes)
Windmills of the Gods (Sidney Sheldon)
You Must Remember This (Joyce Carol Oates)

War/Military
Alnilam (James Dickey)
Beacon at Alexandria, The (Gillian Bradshaw)
Beet Queen, The (Louise Erdrich)
Cardinal of the Kremlin, The (Tom Clancy)
Clear and Present Danger (Tom Clancy)
Complete Short Stories of Ernest Hemingway, The (Ernest Hemingway)
Emperor of America (Richard Condon)
Exile, The (William Kotzwinkle)
Firebrand, The (Marion Zimmer Bradley)
First Man in Rome, The (Colleen McCullough)
Galapagos (Kurt Vonnegut)
Game of Empire, The (Poul Anderson)
God Knows (Joseph Heller)
Gravity's Rainbow (Thomas Pynchon)
Great Sky River (Gregory Benford)
Guerrillas (V. S. Naipaul)
Handmaid's Tale, The (Margaret Atwood)
Heirs of Hammerfell, The (Marion Zimmer Bradley)
Hocus Pocus (Kurt Vonnegut)
In Country (Bobbie Ann Mason)
Lover, The (Marguerite Duras)

Appendix I

Magicians of Gor (John Norman)
Midnight's Children (Salman Rushdie)
Mongoose R.I.P. (William F. Buckley, Jr.)
Old Gringo, The (Carlos Fuentes)
Picture This (Joseph Heller)
Prayer for Owen Meany, A (John Irving)
Quinn's Book (William Kennedy)
Rat, The (Günter Grass)
Red Storm Rising (Tom Clancy)
Roma Mater (Poul Anderson)
Shame (Salman Rushdie)

Sphere (Michael Crichton)
Stallion Gate (Martin Cruz Smith)
Stones of Nomuru, The (L. Sprague de Camp)
Tales of the South Pacific (James A. Michener)
V. (Thomas Pynchon)
War (Marguerite Duras)
Warrior Queens, The (Lady Antonia Fraser)
Whirlwind (James Clavell)
Who Killed Palomino Molero? (Mario Vargas Llosa)

APPENDIX II
SOCIAL ISSUES AND THEMES GROUPED BY TITLES

Acres and Pains (S. J. Perelman)
familial relationships
male/female relationships
personal values
social relationships
social and individual foibles

Alaska (James A. Michener)
exploitation of primitive races
exploitation of nature
man's intolerance and inhumanity toward his fellow man
racial bigotry
religious prejudice and persecution

All God's Children Need Traveling Shoes (Maya Angelou)
African-American expatriates
belonging
nostalgia
realization of American bonds
search for an identity
slavery

Always Coming Home (Ursula K. Le Guin)
absurdity of war
ecological consciousness
economic justice
matriarchal versus patriarchal society
socialism versus capitalism

Alnilam (James Dickey)
aviation
blindness and enlightenment
individual versus society
reason and mysticism
search for lost son
violence
World War II

Angel with the Sword (C. J. Cherryh)
aristocracy
caste system
female domination
outsider
poverty as a chief motivation for success

Angle of Repose (Wallace Stegner)
changing marital views
frontier America
present clarified by the past
ties between eastern and western America
value of history
values of the American West

At the Bay (Katherine Mansfield)
ages of mankind
male/female roles
time

Autobiography of Miss Jane Pittman, The (Ernest J. Gaines)
conflict between age and youth
interracial relationships

passive versus active resistance
persistence of racism/lack of
  civil rights
spiritual authenticity gained
  through suffering
survival/endurance of hardship

**Beacon at Alexandria, The
(Gillian Bradshaw)**
coexistence of Jewish and Christian
  communities
discrimination against women
ethnic diversity
Helenistic world
medical ethics
religious factionalism

**Bearkeeper's Daughter, The
(Gillian Bradshaw)**
importance of the silk trade
military prowess
role of religion in politics
slavery

**Because It Is Bitter, and
Because It Is My Heart
(Joyce Carol Oates)**
civil rights
emotional barriers
photography
popular culture
social mobility
Vietnam

Beet Queen, The (Louise Erdrich)
independent women
cultural identity and heritage
survival in alien cultures

Being Invisible (Thomas Berger)
amoral world of commerical art
coming of age
discovery of talent and control of it
power of money and social success
re-discovery of romantic love
satire on modern manners and
  values
urbanization and urban values

Beloved (Toni Morrison)
American "amnesia"
coexistence of past and present
intercultural understanding
live full or die
maternal abuse
mother-daughter bonding
physical/psychological torture

**Big Rock Candy Mountain, The
(Wallace Stegner)**
child abuse across generations
frontier America and its
  disappearance
making history where there is
  no history
running away from problems
search for a personal Eden

Big Room, The (Michael Herr)
celebrity image versus sincere self
emptiness of Las Vegas
American popular culture

Big Town, The (Ring Lardner)
the era of the 1920s
Search for identity
Lost illusions

Billy Bathgate (E. L. Doctorow)
lost innocence
gangsters
morality
rags to riches
survival through resourcefulness
  and independence

Bingo (Rita Mae Brown)
adultery
influence of commercial interests
  on editorial freedom
optimism
rivalry
tolerance and respect for
  individuals

Bliss (Katherine Mansfield)
middle-class manners
self delusion

**Blood of Requited Love
(Manuel Puig)**
contemporary Brazil
Third World economics

**Bonfire of the Vanities, The
(Tom Wolfe)**
media/journalism
status in society
legal system
the American dream

Boomerang (Barry Hannah)
autobiography
memory and the past
male bonding
southern authors

**Bourne Ultimatum, The
(Robert Ludlum)**
agnosticism and atheism
identity crisis
morality in a godless universe
searching for meaning in life
searching for self-knowledge

Breathing Lessons (Anne Tyler)
breaking up of the traditional
  family
empty-nest syndrome
husband/wife relationship
middle age
myth of the perfect marriage
parent/child relationship
romantic versus realist

Bridesmaid, The (Ruth Rendell)
bad choices
bad luck
obsessive behavior
revelation of character by dwellings
sexual bondage

**Bridge of Lost Desire, The
(Samuel R. Delany)**
fetishism
language/narrative theory
prehistory
slavery
sword-and-sorcery

**Brown Girl, Brownstones
(Paule Marshall)**
cultural alienation
immigrant assimilation
role of individual in a community

Appendix II

rural and urban conflict
sexism and racism
experience of black female

**Burden of Proof, The
(Scott Turow)**
adjustment to the death of a spouse
business corruption
difficulties of marriage
family conflict
immigrant assimilation

**Candle for D'Artagnan, A
(Chelsea Quinn Yarbro)**
espionage
man's cruelty to woman
papal intrigue
vampirism

**Captain and the Enemy, The
(Graham Greene)**
alternative family relationships
good and evil
nature of love
personal loyalty
political involvement
U.S./Central American relations

Captain Blood (Rafael Sabatini)
fate/chance
heroism
image of the outlaw
individualism
intellectual leadership
love as purifying force
man's inhumanity to man
unjust social institutions

**Cardinal of the Kremlin, The
(Tom Clancy)**
Afghan guerrillas
cold war
false impressions
modern war technology
Strategic Defense Initiative
treason
war in Afghanistan

**Carpenter's Gothic
(William Gaddis)**
contemporary apocalypse/cold war
military ideology
evangilism
government corruption
media
nihilism

Cassidy (Morris West)
Australian politics
drug dealers infiltrating legitimate
  business
love-hate relationship among
  family members
pervasive influence of crime on
  politics and business

Cat's Eye (Margaret Atwood)
artist's evolution
commercialism/consumerism
entropy in modern world
memory

Celebration (Mary Lee Settle)
celebration of life
comfort of friends
destruction of traditional societies
experience of personal loss

gun-running
informal support group
sensitivity to life

Charlie and the Chocolate Factory (Roald Dahl)
addiction to television
gluttony
selfishness
spoiled children

Charley Bland (Mary Lee Settle)
Appalachian coal town elite
infantile patterns
ingrown society
manners and mores
oppressive society
safety of social roles
smothering mothers
social rituals

Chosen Place, The Timeless People, The (Paule Marshall)
African diaspora
American and western colonialism
cultural and national identity and independence
economics and industrialization
industrialization and the Third World
interdependence of nature and humans
Western and European customs imposed at expense of natives

Circular Staircase, The (Mary Roberts Rinehart)
innovative ideas
modernism

City of Sorcery, The (Marion Zimmer Bradley)
democratic egalitarian system versus authoritarian hierarchy
resistance to partriarchal structures
search for individual identity and community
vision ideal of utopian sisterhood

Clear and Present Danger (Tom Clancy)
Columbian drug cartel
cruelty
effects of illegal drugs on American society
Hispanic Americans
international drug smuggling
limitations of presidential power

Close Quarters (William Golding)
acquiring sense of self
experience of facing grave danger
leadership, qualities/kinds of
military (naval) discipline
responsibility for actions
risk taking

Complete Short Stories of Ernest Hemingway, The
Christian sacrifice and communion
Communism and Fascism
illusory nature of victory in war
moral responsibility
Spanish Civil War

The Counterlife (Philip Roth)
alter egos
alternative versions of living
modernist theme

Country Place (Ann Petry)
impact of materialism
lost ideas and aspirations
provincialism
spiritual poverty

Coyote Waits (Tony Hillerman)
academic politics
academic research versus restrictions/taboos of ethnic cultures
anthropology
Butch Cassidy

**Crusader's Torch
(Chelsea Quinn Yarbro)**
ill-fated love between a mortal and a vampire
individual surviving against impossible odds

**Crying of Lot 49, The
(Thomas Pynchon)**
conspiracy
communication theory
disguise
music and song
revenue theory
West coast life

Cyteen (C. J. Cherryh)
bureaucracy
man's relation to non-human species
military-industrial complex
sadism
terrorism

**Dark Laughter
(Sherwood Anderson)**
frustrated ambitions
human relationships
industrialization
rejection
small-town life

**Dark Tower Series, The
(Stephen King)**
change/entropy
moral integrity and responsibility
post-apocalyptic future
sacrifice
the importance of myth on history

**Dead Father, The
(Donald Barthelme)**
factitiousness of all framing devices
necessity of living in a permanent state of uncertainty
Oedipal conflict
undermining of all forms of authority

Deadeye Dick (Kurt Vonnegut)
chance/accident
conventional morality
guilt
institutional violence
irony
nuclear radiation

**Death of Artemio Cruz
(Carlos Fuentes)**
aging and memory
love and hate in the family
personal and political history
personal success and failure
social and class change
trust and the loss of trust

Desert Solitaire (Edward Abbey)
conservation versus development
dangers of big government/big business
importance of the individual
individual versus society
living in step with the natural world

Devices and Desires (P. D. James)
abortion
deterioration of family life and society
English middle class
nuclear energy
sexually abused children
terrorism

Different Kind of Christmas, A (Alex Haley)
dictates of conscience
human dignity
man's interdependence
moral conflict
rightness versus popularity
rigidity of position
slavery
ultimate rights

Difficulties with Girls (Kingsley Amis)
middle-class values
office politics
psychology
publishing business
sexual infidelity

Djinn (Alain Robbe-Grillet)
Oedipus myth
reality versus illusion
uncertainty/vagueness about time, space and identity

Dragonsdawn (Anne McCaffrey)
exploration
genetic manipulation
intercultural cooperation
sacrifice
utopia

Emperor of America (Richard Condon)
administration of Ronald Reagan
American military command policies
Nicaragua's Sandinista government
television's influence on Americans

Exile, The (William Kotzwinkle)
alienation of artist from society
corrupting influences of contemporary culture
manifestations of subconscious desires
nature of evil
struggle for the artist to maintain integrity in his work

Eyes of the Dragon, The (Stephen King)
manipulation and power
sibling rivalry
spying
storytelling

Fade (Robert Cormier)
discrimination
illusion and reality

Appendix II

importance of family
mortality
secret sin
sexual and moral maturation
social isolation

Fast Lanes (Jayne Anne Phillips)
divorce
dysfunctional families
impermanence of human relationships
sanity as a precarious balance
  between reality and illusion
self-delusion

Feast of Snakes, A (Harry Crews)
cruelty
decadence of contemporary society
failure of social structures
infidelity
rape/sexual abuse
religious fanaticism
snakes

**Fencepost Chronicles, The
(W. P. Kinsella)**
alienation and courses of action
rites of passage

**Financial Expert, The
(R. K. Narayan)**
dubious paths to wealth
tradition and modernity
transience of human actions
true and false riches
wealth versus knowledge

**Firebrand, The
(Marion Zimmer Bradley)**
fall of Troy
Great Goddess/Earth Mother
mythology

Firecode (Chelsea Quinn Yarbro)
apocalypse/holocaust
danger of computers and advanced
  technology

**Fire Down Below
(William Golding)**
accepting self
acquiring sense of self
facing grave danger
friendship
leadership
responsibility for actions
risk taking

**First Man in Rome, The
(Colleen McCullough)**
ambition and drive to succeed
interpersonal relationships
love, obsessive and unrequited
loyalty
mythology
political power and corruption
Roman cultural, political and
  military history
women's roles

**Flame in Byzantium (Chelsea
Quinn Yarbro)**
destructive capacity of humans
individual fighting the established
  order
threat of strong feminine
  characteristics
vampirism

Floating Opera, The (John Barth)
critique of the subject
filiation and authority
existentialism
personality
rationality
self-consciousness
suicide

Folk of the Air, The (Peter S. Beagle)
idealism of the flower generation
innocence rediscovered through music and magic
nostalgia for the 1960s

Folks That Live on the Hill, The (Kingsley Amis)
coping with a changing society
emotional needs
ethnic diversity
functioning of a community

Fool's Run (Patricia A. McKillip)
communication
madness
music
symbolism

Foucault's Pendulum (Umberto Eco)
creative process
paranoia
radical politics
secret societies

Four Million, The (O. Henry)
coincidence
hope/glamour
importance of the quality of life
money
power of love
urban environment

Freaky Deaky (Elmore Leonard)
criminality
escapism
search for identity

Free-Lance Pallbearers, The (Ishmael Reed)
American political system
class conflicts within the black community
debate over the nature and purpose of art
examination of "western/European/Christian tradition"
parody of black autobiography/narrative
warped nature of the academic community

Friend of My Youth (Alice Munro)
constraints of small-town life
contemporary women's relationship to women of an earlier generation
problems involved in bridging gender gaps

Galapagos (Kurt Vonnegut)
apocalypse
artificial intelligence
atomic power
computers
evolutionary theory
ghosts

Appendix II

Gallowglass (Ruth Rendell as Barbara Vine)
abnormal sexuality
sadism
torture

Game of Empire, The (Poul Anderson)
distrust of big government
quest for political power
search for meaning in life
self-pity is contemptible

Garden-Party, The (Katherine Mansfield)
bourgeois values
morality
social satire

Garden of Eden, The (Ernest Hemingway)
androgeny
craft of writing
high human cost of art
initiation into knowledge of
  betrayal and loss
sex role reversals/inversions
sexual liberation

Gathering of Old Men, A (Ernest J. Gaines)
cooperative rescue/community
rescuing individual and self
passive versus active resistance
positive versus negative aspects
  of change
race relations/awareness

Genesis (Wallace Stegner)
Canadian cattle ranching
living up to one's obligations
  to others
rite of passage
work ethic

Gerald's Party (Robert Coover)
art and pornography
epistemology
hedonism and its implications
illusion and reality
memory and its tyranny
narcissism
rationalism and randomness

Gift of Asher Lev, The (Chaim Potok)
artist's relation to family and
  community
conflict and reconciliation
cycles of life
exile and return
fathers and sons
relation of past, present, and future
religion versus secularism
role of Jews in the world

Giles Goat-Boy or, The Revised New Syllabus (John Barth)
American academia
cold war politics
myth
origins
psychological doubling
tragic view
twins

God Knows (Joseph Heller)
adultery
desire for reconciliation
difficulties of growing old
father/son relationships
patriarchal authority

God's Grace (Bernard Malamud)
instinct to aggression is supreme
mingling of realism and fantasy
nuclear war
rebuilding civilization based on
  mutual respect and love

**Golden Orange, The
(Joseph Wambaugh)**
alcoholism
alienation
class conflict
collapse of family
collapse of traditional values
greed
materialism
societal corruption

**Graveyard for Lunatics, A
(Ray Bradbury)**
distinction between life and death
living in the present versus living
  in the past
living well
past encroaching on the present
studio system of Hollywood

**Gravity's Rainbow
(Thomas Pynchon)**
conspiracy
missile technology
music and song

mythology
psychology
World War II

**Great Sky River
(Gregory Benford)**
collapse of society
enduring human spirit
family ties
future of humanity
nature of artificial intelligence
radical physical change versus
  unchanging human nature
technological innovation

Guerrillas (V. S. Naipaul)
cultural alienation

Guide, The (R. K. Narayan)
accepting one's fate
disease of worldliness
going beyond the self
Rogue's progress
seeking true self-realization
tradition and modernity
true path to sainthood

**Handmaid's Tale, The
(Margaret Atwood)**
class stratification
feminism/sexism
individual versus social institutions
nature of freedom
social violence

**Happy Turnip, The
(Thomas M. Disch)**
afterlife
closeness created by shared meals

Appendix II

fear
social prejudice
telepathy
unity of living things

Harmful Intent (Robin Cook)
corrupt attorneys
medical malpractice

**Harrowing of Gwynedd, The
(Katherine Kurtz)**
death and transfiguration
group identity
individual responsibility
oppression and survival

Hawaii (James A. Michener)
bigotry
exploitation of nature
exploitation of primitive races
journey
man's inhumanity to fellow men
melting pot of humanity
religious persecution

**Heirs of Hammerfell, The
(Marion Zimmer Bradley)**
encounter of culture with nature
feuding
mythology
nobility
telepathy

**Hermit of 69th Street, The
(Jerzy Kosinski)**
creativity
identity
revenge

sexual relations
victims

**Her Mother's Daughter
(Marilyn French)**
acculturation of immigrant families
  in America
autonomy and selfhood
economic mobility
motherhood and/or mother-daughter
  relationships
work and its impact on the
  individual

**His Little Women
(Judith Rossner)**
connection between fiction and real
  life
father-daughter relationships
importance of traditional values
role of the writer
sisterhood both within a family and
  among women generally
women's liberation/feminism

Hocus Pocus (Kurt Vonnegut)
dyslexia
Japanese, relations with
prisons
technological failures
Vietnam war

Homesick (Guy Vanderhaeghe)
alcohol as a panacea for emotional
  pain
Canadian small-town life
death of a spouse
dysfunctional families

**Honorable Barbarian, The
(L. Sprague de Camp)**
definition of civilization
magic

**Hook, Line, Sinker
(Len Deighton)**
alienation
bureaucracy
cold war/espionage
international intrigue

**Hot Jazz Trio, The
(William Kotzwinkle)**
allure of magic and metaphysics
appeal of the surreal
interchangeability of historic epochs
juxtaposition of varying cultural
  modes
psychic transformation
romance of the bohemian life

**House for Mr Biswas, A
(V. S. Naipaul)**
cultural alienation

**Houseguest, The
(Thomas Berger)**
breakdown of manners and civility
infidelity
initiation of feminine protagonist
satirical view of modern values
urban frustration

**House Made of Dawn
(N. Scott Momaday)**
cultural heritage/tradition
fragmentation and healing
identity

individual and community
oral traditions
silencing

**House of Stairs, The (Ruth
Rendell as Barbara Vine)**
process of writing

How I Grew (Mary McCarthy)
the aging process
contemporary manners and culture
tempering of emotional intensity by
  time and circumstance

**Icarus Agenda, The
(Robert Ludlum)**
Arab culture
Middle Eastern politics
Palestinian terrorism

**Imperial Purple
(Gillian Bradshaw)**
cultural diversity
nature of political intrigue
slavery
way of life in fifth-century
  Roman Empire

In Country (Bobbie Ann Mason)
American history
individual and the State
mourning
popular culture
veterans issues
Vietnam

**In Miro District and Other
Stories (Peter Taylor)**
complexity of love

Appendix II

family conflict
necessity of family
old and new South
social change

**In My Father's House
(Ernest J. Gaines)**
denial
family responsibility
father-son alienation
fight for social/political justice
irrevocable loss versus regeneration
public versus private self
redemption as ongoing process

**In Praise of the Stepmother
(Mario Vargas Llosa)**
art and eroticism
childhood and innocence
fetishism
eroticism
innocence
search for happiness
stepmotherhood

Integral Trees, The (Larry Niven)
dangers inherent in scientific
  progress
freedom bringing danger as well as
  excitement
need for exploration and discovery

**Je ne parle pas français
(Katherine Mansfield)**
androgyny
anti-feminism
masks
post World War II alienation
self-gratification

sexual ambiguity
sexual victimization

Joey's Case (K. C. Constantine)
corruption of justice
macho ethic and its role in
  competition and patriotism
pornography and censorship
sexual/psychological motivation
  for crime
use and misuse of power in the
  legal system

**Joy in the Morning
(P. G. Wodehouse)**
class distinctions
master/servant relationship

Joy Luck Club, The (Amy Tan)
aspects of myth
Chinese women and their Chinese-
  American daughters
deceit
importance of passing on traditions
  to future generations
mah-jong

J R (William Gaddis)
classical music
junk mail
poetry
stocks

**Just As Long As We're Together
(Judy Blume)**
childhood friendships
divorce and its impact on children
jealosy
puberty

school related issues
sibling relationships

K. (Mary Roberts Rinehart)
corruption
lost aspirations
medical ethics

**Keep the Change
(Thomas McGuane)**
disconnectedness of American life
infection of American life by the
 corporate ethic
infinite adaptability of interpretation
interweaving of fraud and honesty
persistence of illusion

Killashandra (Anne McCaffrey)
ambition/excellence
manipulation and power
masks and personas
mining
music

**Killing Mister Watson
(Peter Matthiessen)**
human propensity for myth making
inability to escape American
 concern for racial make-up
individual responsibility for
 collective act of violence
superiority of the primitive over
 the civilized

**Killing Time in St. Cloud
(Judith Guest and Rebecca Hill)**
Catholicism
parental pressures
respectability and hypocrisy

Killshot (Elmore Leonard)
criminality
cultural rootlessness

**King of the Fields, The
(Isaac Bashevis Singer)**
intertribal feuding
Judaism versus Christianity versus
 Paganism
primitive tribal life in rural Poland
superstition

**Knockout Artist, The
(Harry Crews)**
affluent sophisticates of New
 Orleans
integrity as saving value
mentors
perverse value structure of modern
 society
prostitution
self abuse
use of other people as objects

**Lamb to the Slaughter (Roald
Dahl)**
devotion to duty
devotion to marriage
devotion to one's children

**Last Notes From Home
(Frederick Exley)**
alcoholism and madness
brotherly love/bonds of home
demise of heroes in the twentieth
 century
imagined life
myth of the "American Dream"
shame of failure

Appendix II

Lazarus (Morris West)
modern Roman Catholic papacy
international terrorism
modification of dogmas to changing
  societies and technologies
Vatican bureaucracy and politics

LETTERS (John Barth)
history and historiography
language and writing
order and contingency
repetition
tragic view

**Light Can Be Both Wave and
Particle (Ellen Gilchrist)**
middle age/maturity
pregnancy/birth
search for roots/home

**Little Governess, The
(Katherine Mansfield)**
loss of innocence
temptation

**Love in the Time of Cholera
(Gabriel García Márquez)**
reality versus illusion

Love Killers, The (Jackie Collins)
women as "warriors"

Lover, The (Marguerite Duras)
child abuse
eroticism
escape
exploitation
father-daughter relationships
tenderness

Magicians of Gor (John Norman)
biological determinism
nature of reality
political propaganda
treatment of war veterans

**Mammoth Hunters, The
(Jean M. Auel)**
acceptance
genius
lying
man and society
prehistoric man

**Man-Eater of Malgudi, The
(R. K. Narayan)**
aggressive individual versus
  unchanging society
good versus evil
identification with another
progress versus tradition

**Man Made of Words, The
(N. Scott Momaday)**
language and identity
native American identity
personal and cultural memory
story telling/verbal tradition

**Mary and the Giant
(Philip K. Dick)**
capitalism
entertainment world
female "awakening"

**Marya: A Life
(Joyce Carol Oates)**
emotional barriers
family violence

female heroism
French feminism
search for the mother
torture

**Midnight Examiner, The
(William Kotzwinkle)**
appeal of language
bizarre excesses of contemporary
  culture
chaos of the modern city
nature of transformative fantasy
poignance of individual friendships
virtues and burdens of eccentricity

**Midnight's Children
(Salman Rushdie)**
breakup of traditional family
  structures
innocence and experience
modern Indian's predicament
national history and individual
  progress
post-colonial history
quest for identity

Misery (Stephen King)
reasonableness of the psychotic
survival and pain
writer's craft

Mitla Pass (Leon Uris)
diaspora
Sinai Campaign
writer's craft

**Moderato Cantabile
(Marguerite Duras)**

bourgeois society
hypocrisy
monotony
satire
passion

**Mongoose R.I.P.
(William F. Buckley, Jr.)**
Cuban-American relations
espionage
foreign policy
intelligence operations
international politics
Nikita Khrushchev
nuclear threat
politics
President John F. Kennedy
U.S. government policy

**Moon and the Face, The
(Patricia A. McKillip)**
communication
interplanetary travel

**More Die of Heartbreak
(Saul Bellow)**
Don Juanism
plants
political bossism
popular culture
Russian literature
search for love

Mortal Fear (Robin Cook)
good science gone wrong
health care
health insurance
health maintenance organizations

Appendix II

Most of S. J. Perelman, The (S. J. Perelman)
familial relationships
male/female relationships
personal values
social relationships
social and individual foibles
social intercourse
travel

Moviegoer, The (Walker Percy)
alienation
Catholicism
Christian Existentialism
Kierkegaard
love, marriage
the movies
the South

Mumbo Jumbo (Ishmael Reed)
black nationalism
historical revision
racial politics-manipulation of blacks by whites
struggle between Judeo-Christian ethic and Neo-HooDoo aesthetic

Mutant Season, The (Robert Silverberg)
hostility toward inter-racial marriage
political assassination
resentment of superior talent when manifested by minorities
society's fear of what appears different
telepathy and telekinesis

Mutation (Robin Cook)
bio-molecular research
exceptional children
genius
surrogate motherhood

My Ántonia (Willa Cather)
frontier life
immigration
love
memory
motherhood
myth
pastoralism
settlement
small-town life

My Secret History (Paul Theroux)
American elitism
censorship
human alienation
hypocrisy
lost innocence/gained experience
rationality versus irrationality
sexuality and identity

Mystic Masseur, The (V. S. Naipaul)
cultural alienation (Trinidad)

My Uncle Oswald (Roald Dahl)
breeding geniuses
fornication/sexual intercourse

Naked in Garden Hills (Harry Crews)
absurdist use of mythic parallels
allegory
contemporary industrialization

humans surviving on their own
  resources in a world of
  shifting values
phosphate mining
triumph of decadent humanism

Narrows, The (Ann Petry)
intersocioeconomic class conflicts
racial and sexual politics
role of black women in society
violence and materialism of
  American culture

**No More Satuday Nights
(Norma Klein)**
adjusting to college
alternative sex roles
single-parent families
teenage pregnancy

Novelty (John Crowley)
concepts and interactions of time,
  history, and creativity
self-alienation
time travel
writer's block

Old Devils, The (Kingsley Amis)
changing society
emotional fulfillment
functioning of a community

**Old Forest and Other Stories,
The (Peter Taylor)**
conflicting lifestyles
old and new South
roles of the young and old
stereotypes
romantic love and conflicts

Old Gringo, The (Carlos Fuentes)
complexity of love
disillusionment and pessimism
internal and external change
political upheaval
social change
youth and age

One L (Scott Turow)
law and its ambiguities
moral challenges of the law
philosophy of law
philosophy of legal instruction
stresses and strains of a legal
  education

**One Writer's Beginnings
(Eudora Welty)**
memory and its role in development of artist's imagination
role of individual experiences
  in an author's development
sound as a creative stimulus
time and resulting changes

**Once and Future King, The
(T. H. White)**
Arthurian legend
conflict of might and right
human's misuse of their natural
  gifts
modern industrial society versus
  the advantages of rural life
unnaturalness of war
value and joy of learning by
  experience

O Pioneers! (Willa Cather)
frontier life

immigration
love
myth
settlement

**Optimist's Daughter, The
(Eudora Welty)**
conflicting behavioral codes
continuity in nature and human
  relationships
myth versus reality
perception and perspective (point of
  view)
struggle to control (power,
  especially over others)

**Origin of the Brunists, The
(Robert Coover)**
charisma and the search for
  miracles
cults as responses to a world
  devoid of meaning
dominant personalities
nature of reality
philosophical systems
randomness versus design
religious movements

Other Side, The (Mary Gordon)
fragmentation of families
immigrant experience
love-hate relationships between
  family members
politics of the working class
value and destructive power of
  self-sacrifice

**Out on the Cutting Edge
(Lawrence Block)**
brutality of cities
homelessness
New York City real estate market

**Paladin of the Lost Hour
(Harlan Ellison)**
responsibility
time puzzle

Paradise (Donald Barthelme)
city life as a state of mind
mid-life crisis
quest for satisfaction ends in
  disillusionment
sexual and economic exploitation
social responsibility

Patriot Games (Tom Clancy)
Anglo-Irish politics
courage
cowardice
fear
hatred
Irish Republican Army

Picture This (Joseph Heller)
art and history as merely deceptive
  illusions of reality
capitalism
cynicism
evolution of money
failure of democracy to improve
  everyday life

Picturing Will (Ann Beattie)
art as escape from life
broken marriages, marital infidelity
career versus personal life
child nurturing

drug trade/trafficking
men as nurturers of children
psychological problems/denial of
  feelings
role of imagination

Pillars of the Earth (Ken Follett)
abiding nature of love
clash of ideas
cruelty and revenge
importance of a vision
poverty and creativity
unselfish and selfish dreams

**Plains of Passage, The
(Jean M. Auel)**
abuse fostering abuse
loyalty of animals
prehistoric man
respect for contributions of all
  individuals
scientific discovery

**Praisesong for the Widow
(Paule Marshall)**
double cultural identity
identity and roots in African
  heritage
lost culture/cultural alienation
materialism and spiritual poverty

**Prayer for Owen Meany, A
(John Irving)**
illegitimacy
nontraditional family
public/private education
social stratification
Vietnam

Prelude (Katherine Mansfield)
ages of mankind
male/female relationships
time

Presumed Innocent (Scott Turow)
ambiguities of the law
emotional duplicity
failure of truth-finding systems
problems of interpretation
quest for self understanding

**Princess Bride, The
(William Goldman)**
absurdity of modern world
contrast between romantic and
  real love
courage and beauty
modern imagination
modern world and imagination
trials and tribulation
violence

Pubis Angelical (Manuel Puig)
Argentine politics
fascism
mother/daughter relationships
reality versus illusion

**Public Burning, The
(Robert Coover)**
ambition
execution as public ritual
myth of the scapegoat
political paranoia
political power
radical politics and repression
treason

Q Clearance (Peter Benchley)
bureaucratic inefficiency
egomania in national leaders
family conflicts
intense competitive nature
role of chance/coincidence
satire as a check on the irrational
secrecy in national politics

Queen of the Damned, The (Anne Rice)
anticipated obsolescence of religion
family as foundation of eternal life
importance of family
morality

Quinn's Book (William Kennedy)
history of newspapers and reporting
background history of the theater
journey motif
rites of passage

Rabbit at Rest (John Updike)
adultery
AIDS
women in a declining job market
selling of America to foreigners

Radio Free Albemuth (Philip K. Dick)
extraterrestrial intelligence
governmental repression
music as subversion
perception and reality

Random Walk: A Novel for a New Age (Lawrence Block)
alchemy
astrology
Eastern religions
New Age healing

Rat, The (Günter Grass)
academic/scholarly integrity
children and posterity
cultural alienation
doomsday/nuclear holocaust
economics and industrialization
electronic technology and truth
facism
futurism
genetic manipulation
media/television
pollution/destruction of the environment
pornography
science and social responsibility
space satellite travel

Reckless Eyeballing (Ishmael Reed)
historical revision
North/South difference
race relations between blacks and Jews
"war" between black male writers and black female writers
(white) feminism

Recognitions, The (William Gaddis)
alchemy
mythology
witchcraft

Red Storm Rising (Tom Clancy)
cold war
fear

militarism
NATO versus the Warsaw Pact
politics of oil supplies
rationale for nuclear war
technology of modern warfare
wastefulness of war
World War III

Renegades of Pern
(Anne McCaffrey)
ambition
archeology
exploration and colonization
leadership

Robots of Dawn, The
(Isaac Asimov)
compromise between technophilia
 and respect for human individuals
state of robots in futuristic society
warning against easy solutions
 technology offers

Rock Star (Jackie Collins)
depravity of the rock music world
tribulations of fame

Roma Mater (Poul Anderson)
control over one's destiny
creating a prosperous society
good and bad leadership
history in the making
human love
nature of religious faith
public welfare
religious persecution
religious politics
state religions

Rummies (Peter Benchley)
delusions/self-deceptions of
 alcoholics
effects of racism in professional life
hypocrisy in spiritual leaders
leveling of class distinctions in
 extreme situations
marital problems of alcoholics
treatment of alcoholics by AA
 methods

Rusalka (C. J. Cherryh)
childhood and fatherhood
corruption of power
myth as elemental narrative
regeneration

Russia House, The
(John le Carré)
abuse of human rights by the USSR
 during glasnost
corruption of the human spirit by
 having to lie
flaws in international nuclear
 strategy
inherent value of individual lives
softening of the cold war

S. (John Updike)
adultery
fraudulent religious cults
search for Nirvana
self deception

Sands of Time, The
(Sidney Sheldon)
adaption of former nun to the
 conglomerate business world

basque terrorists in comtemporary
 Spain
fascist activities in post Franco
 Spain
lingering effects of the Spanish
 Civil War
mafia operations
nuns of the Cisterians of the Strict
 Observance

**Satanic Verses, The
(Salman Rushdie)**
Indian diaspora
interpenetration of good and
 evil love
metamorphosis
monomania/fanaticism
nature of religious faith
quest for identity

Scaramouche (Rafael Sabatini)
emotional alienation
fate
French Revolution
heroism versus greed and
 corruption
historical forces
individualism
intelligence as driving human force
unjust social institutions

Sea Hawk, The (Rafael Sabatini)
compassion
intellectual leadership
man's inhumanity to man
religious bigotry
the clash of civilizations
unjust social institutions

**Sea Wall, The
(Marguerite Duras)**
escape
expolitation
father-daughter relationships
money problems
monotony
sickness

**Second Chronicles of Amber, The
(Roger Zelazny)**
freedom and order
nature of reality
moral growth
power and responsibility

**Second Coming, The
(Walker Percy)**
alienation
Christian Existentialism
love, marriage, sex
the South
suicide

**Secret Pilgrim, The
(John le Carré)**
dehumanization of individual lives
 by warfare and international
 conflict
end of the cold war
evils wrought by communists
need for spying
value of defending western liberties

**Serenissima: A Novel of Venice
(Erica Jong)**
alternative history
sexual liberation

Shakespeare, William
Shylock
sixteenth-century English literature
Venice, Italy/Renaissance
woman's sexuality

Shadows (John Gardner)
artificial intelligence
crime
existentialism and freedom
nature and origins of fear
restoring order to the community
voluntary amnesia

Shame (Salman Rushdie)
idealism
oppression of women
power and corruption
psychic damage
revenge

**Shiloh and Other Stories
(Bobbie Ann Mason)**
American cultural history
commodification
disappointment
loss of the self
popular culture
post-industrial society

Shining Through (Susan Isaacs)
Nazi Germany
personal risk
social class and mobility
World War II era

Silent Gondoliers, The (William Goldman)
absurdity of life
courage and unselfishness
cultural alienation
determination and willpower
dreams and reality
individualism

**Silver Pillow, The
(Thomas M. Disch)**
caring for the mentally ill
morality

**Skinny Legs and All
(Tom Robbins)**
failure of Christianity in Western
  culture
sexuality
individual spiritual growth
love and freedom
radical politics
religious fundamentalism
twentieth-century art

Skinwalkers (Tony Hillerman)
Alzheimer's disease
collision of tribal beliefs and
  modern skepticism
delving into the occult
intrusion of modern world into traditional native American culture
Navajo society

Snow White (Donald Barthelme)
consumerism
democratization of politics, sex,
  economics, literature, and
  linguistics
omnipresent dissatisfaction

Appendix II

Soft Monkey (Harlan Ellison)
homelessness

**Some Can Whistle
(Larry McMurtry)**
aging and reclusiveness
insulating qualities of great wealth
living with loss of loved one
redemptive power of unselfish love
relationship between absentee father
 and adult child

**Something In the Air
(Emma Lathen)**
drug distribution
financial establishment
labor/management
women's awakening to power
work ethic

**Sot-Weed Factor, The
(John Barth)**
American colonial culture
existentialism
identity
psychological doubling
responsibility
self and authority
twins

**Southern Family, A
(Gail Godwin)**
altering memory to suit one's needs
conflicting obligations to family
 and self
negative effect a class society has
 on those trapped in it
southern culture and values
suicide

**Spence + Lila
(Bobbie Ann Mason)**
disease
post-industrial society
role/psychology of the mother
sibling relationships

Sphere (Michael Crichton)
consequences of sexual and racial
 discrimination
emotion versus intellect
group dynamics
nature of reality
power of the imagination
problem solving
the scientific method

Square, The (Marguerite Duras)
lack of ambition
lower social classes
monotony
rootlessness

**Stallion Gate
(Martin Cruz Smith)**
atomic bomb
jazz
native Americans
New Mexico
Oppenheimer, J. Robert

**Star of Gypsies
(Robert Silverberg)**
gypsy culture
importance of political pragmatism
maintaining ethnic identity

Stillness (John Gardner)
art as restorative enactment

domestic conflict
female submissiveness
left brain/right brain contrasts
writing as psychotherapy

**Stones of Nomuru, The
(L. Sprague de Camp)**
alternative evolution
blighted love
tradition versus change

**Story of My Life
(Jay McInerney)**
art and life
coming of age
honesty
love versus sex
order versus chaos

Straight (Dick Francis)
ambition
idealism

Street, The (Ann Petry)
black women's identity and role in culture
economic racism
impact of classism, racism, and sexism
link/separation between the individual and the community
materialism

Strong Medicine (Arthur Hailey)
animal experimentation
testing of drugs

Summer Lightning (P. G. Wodehouse)
aristocracy
impersonations
nostalgia
utopia

**Summons to Memphis, A
(Peter Taylor)**
aging parents
breaking with the family
change in lifestyles
family responsibility
family secrets
generational changes and conflict

**Tales of the South Pacific
(James A. Michener)**
anti-authoritarianism
bigotry
brotherhood of man
effects of war and violence on man
effects of war on the environment

Talking God (Tony Hillerman)
archeological plundering of ancient burial grounds
conflict between American culture, tribal customs and metaphysics
Navajo society
the search for knowledge that encroaches upon cultural traditions

**Taming the Star Runner
(S. E. Hinton)**
adolescents in gangs
inevitability of change
mystical power of animals (especially horses and cats)
need to belong
Oedipal conflicts

Tango Charlie and Foxtrot Romeo (John Varley)
image of a child versus the image of an adult
morality versus fear
mortality and immortality
plague

Taste for Death, A (P. D. James)
abortion
disintegration of society
English middle class/petty aristocracy
juvenile crime
revolution
sexual infidelity
suicide

Tehanu (Ursula K. Le Guin)
child abuse
gender roles
social justice

Temple of My Familiar, The (Alice Walker)
concern for the rights of the excluded and exploited
connectedness of all things
race and sexual relations
reincarnation

Theft, A (Saul Bellow)
ethnic difference
mother-daughter relationships
submissive husbands
women in corporate life

Ticket to the Boneyard, A (Lawrence Block)
fatalism
insecurity of urban life
misogyny
prostitution

Till We Meet Again (Judith Krantz)
anti-Semitism
increasing sexual openness of women
increasing importance of air travel
monotony, futility, and horror of war
tradition as a stabilizing force
World War I and II

To Sail Beyond the Sunset (Robert A. Heinlein)
decay of manners
failure of American educational system
incest
mentorship
nature of reality

Tough Guys Don't Dance (Norman Mailer)
adultery
amnesia
fragility of masculine ego
universal struggle between God and Devil
unsolved murders

Toynbee Convector, The (Ray Bradbury)
dangers of despair
problems of the present can be solved

remaking the future
value of believing in a better future

Tracks (Louise Erdrich)
encroaching of white civilization on native American life
relation of native Americans to dominant culture

Trimmed Lamp, The (O. Henry)
coincidence
hope/glamour
importance of the quality of life
money
power of love
urban environment

Tripmaster Monkey: His Fake Book (Maxine Hong Kingston)
Chinese Americans
need to belong
persuasive nature of popular culture
poets
prejudice
quest to reconcile self and society

Trust (George V. Higgins)
car dealers
consequences of deception
trust

Truth About George, The (P. G. Wodehouse)
antihero or nonhero
appearance versus reality
bougeois stereotypes
discrimination

Truth about Lorin Jones, The (Alison Lurie)
male/female conflicts
parenting
self-identity

2061: Odyssey Three (Arthur C. Clarke)
economics of racism
revolutionary progress of humankind
space exploration
telecommunications and society

Uncle Fred Flits By (P. G. Wodehouse)
impersonations
suburbs
trickster figure

Universal Baseball Association, The (Robert Coover)
God's relationship to creation
magic and beauty of excellence
real world versus created world
relation between imagination and reality
theological and philosophical systems

V. (Thomas Pynchon)
artificial intelligence
conspiracy
entropy
European avant-garde
journal style
repression

Appendix II

Veiled One, The (Ruth Rendell)
anti-nuclear lobbying
hypocrisy in communications media
societal pretention
welfare systems that fail their
　recipients
well-intentioned police efforts
　that misfire

Victories (George V. Higgins)
car dealers
1960s
trust

Vineland (Thomas Pynchon)
governmental conspiracies
hippies
marijuana, use of
1960s
supernatural beings
television

War (Marguerite Duras)
dictatorship
divorce
fear
French Resistance
suffering
traitors
World War II

**Warrior Queens, The
(Lady Antonia Fraser)**
persistence of stereotypes
sterotypes about women warriors
　formulated by men
uses made by women rulers of their
　femininity

women as rulers
women as military leaders
women as effective statespersons
(Elizabeth I, Catherine the Great)

**Way to Rainy Mountain, The
(N. Scott Momaday)**
anthropology
myth/legend
native American culture
oral traditions
personal and family history

**We Are Still Married
(Garrison Keillor)**
importance of place and back-
　ground in shaping of attitudes
roles of women
roles of the writer
satire of political, social, and
　cultural fads

Weaveworld (Clive Barker)
enduring nature of friendship
power of the imagination
power of evil
realism and surrealism
trust

Westward Ha! (S. J. Perelman)
exploration of the human condition
　through travel metaphor
familial relationships
male/female relationships
personal values
romantic fantasy
social relationships
social and individual foibles

**When Harry Met Sally
(Nora Ephron)**
food
male friendships and sports
opposite-sex friendships
urban upper middle-class
yuppie culture

**Where I'm Calling From
(Raymond Carver)**
futility
hope
seeking of happiness
struggle for survival

Whirlwind (James Clavell)
denial of individual rights
overthrow of the Shah of Iran and triumph of Ayatollah Khomeini
philosophical and moral differences between East and West

Whistlejacket (John Hawkes)
beauty of the physical form of women
castration of the male
cruelty and art
objectification of women
ritualized lives
sexual predation
sexual liberation of women
wasted lives of the leisure class

**Who Killed Palomino Molero?
(Mario Vargas Llosa)**
child abuse
class structure
crime detection
forbidden love
military life
Third World living conditions

**Windmills of the Gods
(Sidney Sheldon)**
academic life in a midwestern university
cold war in Eastern Europe
Communist Russia and its rulers
innocence of young women in the world of terrorism
international intrigue and terrorism

**Winesburg, Ohio
(Sherwood Anderson)**
cultural deprivation
dullness
folk-tale quality
isolation
sensitive people
small town lives

Wonderful Years, Wonderful Years (George V. Higgins)
ambition
integrity
justice
loyalty
paranoia
politics
social anatomy

You Know Me Al (Ring Lardner)
baseball
vernacular narrative

Appendix II

You Must Remember This
(Joyce Carol Oates)
abortion
atomic bomb
boxing
incest
McCarthyism
1950s
popular culture

APPENDIX III
CONTENTS BY GENRE

Adventure
Angelou, Maya
Barthelme, Donald
Cherryh, C. J.
Clancy, Tom
Clavell, James
Collins, Jackie
Crichton, Michael
De Camp, L. Sprague
Gaddis, William
Gaines, Ernest J.
Greene, Graham
Haley, Alex
Kennedy, William
King, Stephen
Kotzwinkle, William
McCaffrey, Anne
McKillip, Patricia A.
Pynchon, Thomas
Sabatini, Rafael
Sheldon, Sidney
Stegner, Wallace
Theroux, Paul
Wambaugh, Joseph
West, Morris
White, T. H.

African American Women
Marshall, Paule

Allegory
Narayan, R. K.
Grass, Günter

Autobiographical Fiction
Exley, Frederick
Kosinski, Jerzy
Turow, Scott

Bildungsroman
Cather, Willa
Hinton, S. E.
Marshall, Paule
McInerney, Jay
Oates, Joyce Carol

Detective/Mystery
Asimov, Isaac
Benchley, Peter
Block, Lawrence
Bradbury, Ray
Cherryh, C. J.
Constantine, K. C.
Cook, Robin
Coover, Robert
Cormier, Robert
Crichton, Michael
Dahl, Roald
Eco, Umberto
Ellison, Harlan
Francis, Dick
Gardner, John
Guest, Judith
Hill, Rebecca
Hillerman, Tony
James, P. D.
Lathen, Emma

Appendix III

Leonard, Elmore
Mailer, Norman
Pynchon, Thomas
Reed, Ishmael
Rendell, Ruth
Rinehart, Mary Roberts
Robbe-Grillet, Alain
Turow, Scott
Vargas Llosa, Mario
Wambaugh, Joseph
Yarbro, Chelsea Quinn

Epistolary Novel
Barth, John

Experimental/Avant-garde
Anderson, Sherwood
Barth, John
Barthelme, Donald
Coover, Robert
Dickey, James
Duras, Marguerite
Erdrich, Louise
Exley, Frederick
Gaddis, William
Grass, Günter
Hawkes, John
Kosinski, Jerzy
Kotzwinkle, William
Le Guin, Ursula K.
Mansfield, Katherine
Matthiessen, Peter
Morrison, Toni
Naipaul, V. S.
Puig, Manuel
Pynchon, Thomas
Reed, Ishmael
Robbe-Grillet, Alain
Robbins, Tom

Roth, Philip
Rushdie, Salman

Fable
Disch, Thomas M.
Malamud, Bernard
Narayan, R. K.
Rushdie, Salman

Fantasy
Anderson, Poul
Atwood, Margaret
Barker, Clive
Barth, John
Barthelme, Donald
Beagle, Peter S.
Berger, Thomas
Bradley, Marion Zimmer
Cherryh, C. J.
Coover, Robert
Cormier, Robert
Dahl, Roald
De Camp, L. Sprague
Delany, Samuel R.
Disch, Thomas M.
Goldman, William
Grass, Günter
Heinlein, Robert A.
Jong, Erica
King, Stephen
Kotzwinkle, William
Kurtz, Katherine
Le Guin, Ursula K.
Malamud, Bernard
Niven, Larry
Norman, John
Perelman, S. J.
Pynchon, Thomas
Robbins, Tom

Rushdie, Salman
Vonnegut, Kurt
White, T. H.
Zelazny, Roger

Folk Epic
Gaines, Ernest J.

Gothic
Gaddis, William
King, Stephen
Rushdie, Salman

Historical
Anderson, Poul
Angelou, Maya
Barth, John
Benchley, Peter
Bradley, Marion Zimmer
Bradshaw, Gillian
Buckley, William F.
Cather, Willa
Cherryh, C. J.
Clavell, James
Coover, Robert
Eco, Umberto
Follett, Ken
Fraser, Lady Antonia
Fuentes, Carlos
Gaines, Ernest J.
García Márquez, Gabriel
Grass, Günter
Haley, Alex
Herr, Michael
Isaacs, Susan
Jong, Erica

Kennedy, William
Kotzwinkle, William
Marshall, Paule
Mason, Bobbie Ann
McCullough, Colleen
Michener, James A.
Momaday, N. Scott
Morrison, Toni
Pynchon, Thomas
Rushdie, Salman
Sabatini, Rafael
Sheldon, Sidney
Stegner, Wallace
Uris, Leon
White, T. H.
Yarbro, Chelsea Quinn

Horror
Barker, Clive
Cook, Robin
Cormier, Robert
Crichton, Michael
Disch, Thomas M.
King, Stephen
Kotzwinkle, William
Pynchon, Thomas
Rendell, Ruth
Rice, Anne
Rushdie, Salman

Juvenile
Blume, Judy
Cormier, Robert
Dahl, Roald
Hinton, S. E.
King, Stephen
Klein, Norma
Le Guin, Ursula K.

Appendix III

Law
Higgins, George V.
Turow, Scott

Mainstream
Amis, Kingsley
Anderson, Sherwood
Atwood, Margaret
Beattie, Ann
Bellow, Saul
Berger, Thomas
Blume, Judy
Brown, Rita Mae
Carver, Raymond
Cather, Willa
Clavell, James
Collins, Jackie
Crews, Harry
Crichton, Michael
Crowley, John
Dick, Philip K.
Doctorow, E. L.
Erdrich, Louise
French, Marilyn
Gaines, Ernest J.
Gardner, John
Gilchrist, Ellen
Godwin, Gail
Gordon, Mary
Grass, Günter
Guest, Judith
Hannah, Barry
Heller, Joseph
Hemingway, Ernest
Herr, Michael
Higgins, George V.
Hill, Rebecca
Irving, John
Isaacs, Susan

Kennedy, William
Kinsella, W. P.
Klein, Norma
Lurie, Alison
Mason, Bobbie Ann
Matthiessen, Peter
McCarthy, Mary
McGuane, Thomas
McInerney, Jay
McMurtry, Larry
Munro, Alice
Naipaul, V. S.
Oates, Joyce Carol
Percy, Walker
Perelman, S. J.
Potok, Chaim
Pynchon, Thomas
Reed, Ishmael
Rossner, Judith
Settle, Mary Lee
Stegner, Wallace
Tan, Amy
Taylor, Peter
Turow, Scott
Tyler, Anne
Updike, John
Vanderhaeghe, Guy
Vargas Llosa, Mario
Walker, Alice
Welty, Eudora
Wolfe, Tom

Philosophical Ideas
Abbey, Edward
Anderson, Sherwood
Atwood, Margaret
Barth, John
Berger, Thomas
Coover, Robert

Cormier, Robert
Crichton, Michael
Crowley, John
Eco, Umberto
Gaddis, William
Gardner, John
Golding, William
Grass, Günter
Heller, Joseph
Kingston, Maxine Hong
Le Guin, Ursula K.
Marshall, Paule
Naipaul, V. S.
Narayan, R. K.
Oates, Joyce Carol
Percy, Walker
Petry, Ann
Potok, Chaim
Pynchon, Thomas
Robbe-Grillet, Alain
Theroux, Paul
Uris, Leon
Vonnegut, Kurt
West, Morris

Romance
Anderson, Sherwood
Auel, Jean M.
Barthelme, Donald
Benchley, Peter
Berger, Thomas
Bradley, Marion Zimmer
Cherryh, C. J.
Ephorn, Nora
García Márquez, Gabriel
Jong, Erica
Kennedy, William
King, Stephen
Kotzwinkle, William

McCaffrey, Anne
Naipaul, V. S.
O. Henry
Petry, Ann
Rinehart, Mary Roberts
Sabatini, Rafael
Settle, Mary Lee
Sheldon, Sidney
Updike, John
Yarbro, Chelsea Quinn

Satire/Humor
Abbey, Edward
Amis, Kingsley
Barth, John
Barthelme, Donald
Beattie, Ann
Bellow, Saul
Benchley, Peter
Berger, Thomas
Bradbury, Ray
Condon, Richard
Coover, Robert
Dahl, Roald
Ephron, Nora
Gaddis, William
Goldman, William
Grass, Günter
Heinlein, Robert A.
Irving, John
Keillor, Garrison
Kinsella, W. P.
Kosinski, Jerzy
Kotzwinkle, William
Lardner, Ring
Lurie, Alison
Malamud, Bernard
Mansfield, Katherine
Naipaul, V. S.

Appendix III

Narayan, R. K.
O. Henry
Percy, Walker
Perelman, S. J.
Pynchon, Thomas
Reed, Ishmael
Robbins, Tom
Rushdie, Salman
Tyler, Anne
Vonnegut, Kurt
Wambaugh, Joseph
White, T. H.
Wodehouse, P. G.
Wolfe, Tom

Science Fiction
Anderson, Poul
Asimov, Isaac
Barker, Clive
Benford, Gregory
Bradbury, Ray
Bradley, Marion Zimmer
Cherryh, C. J.
Clancy, Tom
Clarke, Arthur C.
Cook, Robin
Crichton, Michael
De Camp, L. Sprague
Dick, Philip K.
Ellison, Harlan
Grass, Günter
Heinlein, Robert A.
King, Stephen
McCaffrey, Anne
McKillip, Patricia A.
Niven, Larry
Norman, John
Varley, John

Vonnegut, Kurt
Yarbro, Chelsea Quinn
Zelazny, Roger

Spy/Thriller
Benchley, Peter
Buckley, William F.
Cherryh, C. J.
Clancy, Tom
Deighton, Len
Greene, Graham
Isaacs, Susan
Le Carré, John
Ludlum, Robert
Pynchon, Thomas
Rendell, Ruth
Sheldon, Sidney
Smith, Martin Cruz

Stream of Consciousness
Duras, Marguerite
Mansfield, Katherine

Theological/Spiritual
Block, Lawrence
Coover, Robert
Disch, Thomas M.
Eco, Umberto
Gaines, Ernest J.
Heller, Joseph
Irving, John
Kurtz, Katherine
Morrison, Toni
Naipaul, V. S.
Narayan, R. K.
Percy, Walker
Potok, Chaim

Rushdie, Salman
Sheldon, Sidney
Singer, Isaac Bashevis
West, Morris

INDEX OF TITLES
ANALYZED IN THE 1991 UPDATE

Acres and Pains (Perelman), 972
Alaska (Michener), 877
All God's Children Need Traveling Shoes (Angelou), 52
Alnilam (Dickey), 377
Always Coming Home (Le Guin), 745
Angel With the Sword (Cherryh), 229
Angle of Repose (Stegner), 1159
At the Bay (Mansfield), 788
Autobiography of Miss Jane Pittman, The (Gaines), 477
Beacon at Alexandria, The (Bradshaw), 184
Bearkeeper's Daughter, The (Bradshaw), 186
Because It Is Bitter, and Because It Is My Heart (Oates), 945
Beet Queen, The (Erdrich), 428
Being Invisible (Berger), 142
Beloved (Morrison), 897
Big Town, The (Lardner), 722
Big Room, The (Herr), 598
Big Rock Candy Mountain, The (Stegner), 1165
Billy Bathgate (Doctorow), 388
Bingo (Brown), 193
Bliss (Mansfield), 792
Blood of Requited Love (Puig), 1006
Bonfire of the Vanities, The (Wolfe), 1291
Boomerang (Hannah), 557

Bourne Ultimatum, The (Ludlum), 768
Breathing Lessons (Tyler), 1203
Bridesmaid, The (Rendell), 1048
Bridge of Lost Desire, The (Delany), 365
Brown Girl, Brownstones (Marshall), 802
Burden of Proof, The (Turow), 1198
Candle for D'Artagnan, A (Yarbro), 1299
Captain and the Enemy, The (Greene), 542
Captain Blood (Sabatini), 1119
Cardinal of the Kremlin, The (Clancy), 241
Carpenter's Gothic (Gaddis), 471
Cassidy (West), 1265
Cat's Eye (Atwood), 68
Celebration (Settle), 1127
Charley Bland (Settle), 1170
Charlie and the Chocolate Factory (Dahl), 342
Chosen Place, The Timeless People, The (Marshall), 803
Circular Staircase, The (Rinehart), 1063
City of Sorcery (Bradley), 176
Clear and Present Danger (Clancy), 244
Close Quarters (Golding), 522
Complete Short Stories of Ernest Hemingway, The, 593

Counterlife, The (Roth), 1090
Country Place (Petry), 985
Coyote Waits (Hillerman), 615
Cradle (Clarke), 253
Crusader's Torch (Yarbro), 1299
Crying of Lot 49, The (Pynchon), 1017
Cyteen (Cherryh), 226
Dark Laughter (Anderson), 47
Dark Tower Series, The (King), 666
Dead Father, The (Barthelme), 104
Deadeye Dick (Vonnegut), 1237
Death of Artemio Cruz, The (Fuentes), 459
Desert Solitaire (Abbey), 2
Devices and Desires (James), 638
Different Kind of Christmas, A (Haley), 554
Difficulties with Girls (Amis), 18
Djinn (Robbe-Grillet), 1071
Dragonsdawn (McCaffrey), 824
Emperor of America (Condon), 268
Exile, The (Kotzwinkle), 700
Eyes of the Dragon, The (King), 663
Fade (Cormier), 308
Fast Lanes (Phillips), 992
Feast of Snakes, A (Crews), 322
Fencepost Chronicles, The (Kinsella), 681
Financial Expert, The (Narayan), 919
Fire Down Below (Golding), 524
Firebrand, The (Bradley), 179
Firecode (Yarbro), 1301
First Man In Rome, The (McCullough), 839
Flame in Byzantium (Yarbro), 1297

Floating Opera, The (Barth), 89
Folk of the Air, The (Beagle), 111
Folks That Live on the Hill, The (Amis), 10
Fool's Run (McKillip), 858
Foucault's Pendulum (Eco), 411
Four Million, The (O. Henry), 952
Freaky Deaky (Leonard), 755
Free-Lance Pallbearers, The (Reed), 1032
Friend of My Youth (Munro), 901
Galapagos (Vonnegut), 1240
Gallowglass (Rendell), 1052
Game of Empire, The (Anderson), 37
Garden of Eden, The (Hemingway), 585
Garden-Party, The (Mansfield), 797
Gathering of Old Men, A (Gaines), 489
Genesis (Stegner), 1169
Gerald's Party (Coover), 302
Gift of Asher Lev, The (Potok), 998
Giles Goat-Boy or, The Revised New Syllabus (Barth), 94
God Knows (Heller), 574
God's Grace (Malamud), 781
Golden Orange, The (Wambaugh), 1253
Graveyard for Lunatics, A (Bradbury), 164
Gravity's Rainbow (Pynchon), 1020
Great Sky River (Benford), 138
Guerrillas (Naipaul), 913
Guide, The (Narayan), 921
Handmaid's Tale, The (Atwood), 62
Happy Turnip, The (Disch), 384
Harmful Intent (Cook), 284

Harrowing of Gwynedd, The (Kurtz), 711
Hawaii (Michener), 872
Heirs of Hammerfell, The (Bradley), 181
Her Mother's Daughter (French), 454
Hermit of 69th Street, The (Kosinski), 688
His Little Women (Rossner), 1079
Hocus Pocus (Vonnegut), 1243
Homesick (Vanderhaeghe), 1219
Honorable Barbarian, The (De Camp), 356
Hook, Line, Sinker (Deighton), 360
Hot Jazz Trio, The (Kotzwinkle), 697
House Made of Dawn (Momaday), 885
House for Mr Biswas, A (Naipaul), 910
House of Stairs, The (Rendell), 1050
Houseguest, The (Berger), 145
How I Grew (McCarthy), 835
Icarus Agenda, The (Ludlum), 763
Imperial Purple (Bradshaw), 189
In Country (Mason), 813
In My Father's House (Gaines), 485
In Praise of the Stepmother (Vargas Llosa), 1223
In Miro District and Other Stories (Taylor), 1180
Integral Trees, The (Niven), 929
Je ne parle pas français (Mansfield), 794
Joey's Case (Constantine), 274
Joy Luck Club, The (Tan), 1176

Joy in the Morning (Wodehouse), 1286
J R (Gaddis), 468
Just as Long as We're Together (Blume), 160
K. (Rinehart), 1067
Keep the Change (McGuane), 847
Killashandra (McCaffrey), 829
Killing Time in St. Cloud (Guest and Hill), 546
Killing Mister Watson (Matthiessen), 819
Killshot (Leonard), 757
King of the Fields, The (Singer), 1149
Knockout Artist, The (Crews), 325
Lamb to the Slaughter (Dahl), 340
Last Notes From Home (Exley), 436
Lazarus (West), 1267
LETTERS (Barth), 96
Light Can Be Both Wave and Particle (Gilchrist), 512
Little Governess, The (Mansfield), 786
Love in the Time of Cholera (García Márquez), 500
Love Killlers, The (Collins), 262
Lover, The (Duras), 399
Magicians of Gor (Norman), 933
Mammoth Hunters, The (Auel), 78
Man Made of Words, The (Momaday), 891
Man-Eater of Malgudi, The (Narayan), 924
Mary and the Giant (Dick), 372
Marya: A Life (Oates), 941
Midnight Examiner, The (Kotzwinkle), 693

Midnight's Children (Rushdie), 1097
Misery (King), 670
Mitla Pass (Uris), 1214
Moderato Cantabile (Duras), 396
Mongoose R.I.P. (Buckley), 197
Moon and the Face, The (McKillip), 856
More Die of Heartbreak (Bellow), 123
Mortal Fear (Cook), 280
Most of S. J. Perelman, The (Perelman), 976
Moviegoer, The (Percy), 961
Mumbo Jumbo (Reed), 1034
Mutant Season, The (Silverberg), 1145
Mutation (Cook), 282
My Uncle Oswald (Dahl), 346
My Secret History (Theroux), 1184
My Ántonia (Cather), 214
Mystic Masseur, The (Naipaul), 907
Naked in Garden Hills (Crews), 318
Narrows, The (Petry), 987
No More Saturday Nights (Klein), 685
Novelty (Crowley), 336
O Pioneers! (Cather), 210
Old Devils, The (Amis), 15
Old Forest and Other Stories, The (Taylor), 1181
Old Gringo, The (Fuentes), 461
Once and Future King, The (White), 1272
One Writer's Beginnings (Welty), 1262
One L (Turow), 1191
Optimist's Daughter, The (Welty), 1257
Origin of the Brunists, The (Coover), 288
Other Side, The (Gordon), 533
Out on the Cutting Edge (Block), 155
Paladin of the Lost Hour (Ellison), 418
Paradise (Barthelme), 107
Patriot Games (Clancy), 237
Picture This (Heller), 578
Picturing Will (Beattie), 115
Pillars of the Earth (Follett), 441
Plains of Passage, The (Auel), 81
Praisesong for the Widow (Marshall), 805
Prayer for Owen Meany, A (Irving), 625
Prelude (Mansfield), 788
Presumed Innocent (Turow), 1194
Princess Bride, The (Goldman), 528
Pubis Angelical (Puig), 1002
Public Burning, The (Coover), 298
Q Clearance (Benchley), 131
Queen of the Damned, The (Rice), 1056
Quinn's Book (Kennedy), 654
Rabbit at Rest (Updike), 1210
Radio Free Albemuth (Dick), 373
Random Walk: A Novel for a New Age (Block), 153
Rat, The (Grass), 537
Reckless Eyeballing (Reed), 1039
Recognitions, The (Gaddis), 466
Red Storm Rising (Clancy), 234
Renegades of Pern (McCaffrey), 827
Robots of Dawn, The (Asimov), 57

Index of Titles

Rock Star (Collins), 264
Roma Mater (Anderson), 23
Rummies (Benchley), 134
Rusalka (Cherryh), 231
Russia House, The (le Carré), 732
S. (Updike), 1207
Sands of Time, The (Sheldon), 1137
Satanic Verses, The (Rushdie), 1104
Scaramouche (Sabatini), 1116
Sea Hawk, The (Sabatini), 1123
Sea Wall, The (Duras), 399
Second Chronicles of Amber, The (Zelazny), 1304
Second Coming, The (Percy), 965
Secret Pilgrim, The (le Carré), 737
Serenissima: A Novel of Venice (Jong), 645
Shadows (Gardner), 508
Shame (Rushdie), 1101
Shiloh and Other Stories (Mason), 810
Shining Through (Isaacs), 630
Silent Gondoliers, The (Goldman), 530
Silver Pillow, The (Disch), 381
Skinny Legs and All (Robbins), 1075
Skinwalkers (Hillerman), 610
Snow White (Barthelme), 101
Soft Monkey (Ellison), 419
Some Can Whistle (McMurtry), 863
Something In the Air (Lathen), 727
Sot-Weed Factor, The (Barth), 92
Southern Family, A (Godwin), 516
Spence + Lila (Mason), 815
Sphere (Crichton), 332
Square, The (Duras), 393
Stallion Gate (Smith), 1154

Star of Gypies (Silverberg), 1142
Stillness (Gardner), 505
Stones of Nomuru, The (De Camp), 352
Story of My Life (McInerney), 852
Straight (Francis), 444
Street, The (Petry), 983
Strong Medicine (Hailey), 550
Summer Lightning (Wodehouse), 1281
Summons to Memphis, A (Taylor), 1182
Tales of the South Pacific (Michener), 868
Talking God (Hillerman), 612
Taming the Star Runner (Hinton), 620
Tango Charlie and Foxtrot Romeo (Varley), 1232
Taste for Death, A (James), 634
Tehanu: The Last Book of Earthsea (Le Guin), 749
Temple of My Familiar, The (Walker), 1247
Theft, A (Bellow), 127
Ticket to the Bone Yard, A (Block), 157
Till We Meet Again (Krantz), 705
To Sail Beyond the Sunset (Heinlein), 567
Tough Guys Don't Dance (Mailer), 777
Toynbee Convector, The (Bradbury), 168
Tracks (Erdrich), 432
Trimmed Lamp, The (Henry), 954
Tripmaster Monkey: His Fake Book (Kingston), 676
Trust (Higgins), 604

Truth about Lorin Jones, The
  (Lurie), 773
Truth About George, The
  (Wodehouse), 1284
2061: Odyssey Three (Clarke), 250
Uncle Fred Flits By (Wodehouse),
  1283
Universal Baseball Association, The
  (Coover), 293
V. (Pynchon), 1013
Victories (Higgins), 604
Veiled One, The (Rendell), 1046
Vineland (Pynchon), 1025
War (Duras), 404
Warrior Queens, The (Fraser), 449
Way to Rainy Mountain, The
  (Momaday), 889
We Are Still Married (Keillor), 648

Weaveworld (Barker), 85
Westward Ha! (Perelman), 974
When Harry Met Sally (Ephron),
  423
Where I'm Calling From (Carver),
  203
Whirlwind (Clavell), 257
Whistlejacket (Hawkes), 560
Who Killed Palomino Molero?
  (Vargas Llosa), 1227
Windmills of the Gods (Sheldon),
  1134
Winesburg, Ohio (Anderson), 45
Wonderful Years, Wonderful Years
  (Higgins), 601
You Must Remember This (Oates),
  943
You Know Me Al (Lardner), 719

CUMULATIVE INDEX

Bolded numbers are *1991 Update* entries; PF = Entries in *Beacham's Popular Fiction in America;* WF = Entries in *Popular World Fiction.*

Abbey, Edward, **1-9**
Adams, Alice, PF 1-4
Adams, Richard, PF 5-13
Agee, James, WF 1-6
Alexander, Lloyd, WF 7-13
Algren, Nelson, WF 14-24
Allen, Woody, PF 14-20
Alther, Lisa, PF 21-26
Amis, Kingsley, **10-22**, WF 25-29
Anderson, Poul, **23-42**, PF 27-35
Anderson, Sherwood, **43-51**
Andrews, V. C., WF 30-33
Angelou, Maya, **52-55**, PF 36-41
Archer, Jeffrey, WF 34-41
Arnow, Harriette Simpson, WF 42-49
Asimov, Isaac, **56-60**, PF 42-51
Atwood, Margaret, **61-76**, PF 52-67
Auchincloss, Louis, WF 50-60
Auel, Jean M., **77-84**, PF 68-72
Bach, Richard, PF 73-78
Baldwin, James, PF 79-88
Barker, Clive, **85-87**, WF 61-70
Barth, John, **88-99**
Barthelme, Donald, **100-110**
Basso, Hamilton, WF 71-79
Beagle, Peter S., **111-113**, WF 80-87
Beattie, Ann, **114-122**, PF 89-96
Beauvoir, Simone De, WF 88-100
Bellow, Saul, **123-130**, WF 101-111
Benchley, Peter, **131-137**, PF 97-101

Benford, Gregory, **138-141**, PF 102-107
Berger, Thomas, **142-150**, PF 108-121
Bester, Alfred, **151-152**, PF 122-135
Blasco Ibáñez, Vincente, WF 112-123
Blatty, William Peter, PF 136-139
Blish, James, WF 124-135
Block, Lawrence, **153-159**, PF 140-150
Blume, Judy, **160-163**, PF 151-157
Böll, Heinrich, WF 136-145
Borges, Jorge Luis, WF 146-154
Boucher, Anthony, WF 155-158
Bourgaily, Vance Nye, WF 159-168
Bradbury, Ray, **164-174**, PF 158-167
Bradley, Marion Zimmer, **175-183**, PF 168-178
Bradshaw, Gillian, **184-191**, WF 169-175
Brand, Max, WF 176-196
Brautigan, Richard, PF 179-186
Brown, Rita Mae, **192-196**, PF 187-193
Buck, Pearl S., WF 197-207
Buckley, William F., **197-200**, PF 194-200
Buechner, Frederick, WF 208-220
Buell, John, PF 201-206

Bulgakov, Mikhail Afanasievich,
  WF 221-228
Burroughs, Edgar Rice,
  WF 229-241
Cain, James M., PF 207-215
Caldwell, Erskine, **201-202**,
  WF 242-251
Caldwell, Taylor, PF 216-224
Camus, Albert,
  WF 252-261
Capote, Truman, WF 262-272
Carver, Raymond, **203-206**, PF
  225-231
Cather, Willa, **207-224**
Chandler, Raymond, PF 232-239
Charnas, Suzy McKee, PF 240-246
Cheever, John, PF 247-257
Cherryh, C. J., **225-232**,
  PF 258-266
Christie, Agatha, WF 273-280
Clancy, Thomas L., Jr., **233-249**,
  PF 267-272
Clark, Mary Higgins, WF 281-284
Clarke, Arthur C., **250-256**,
  WF 285-294
Clavell, James, **257-261**,
  PF 273-279
Colette, WF 295-311
Collins, Jackie, **262-267**,
  PF 280-283
Colwin, Laurie, WF 312-317
Conan Doyle, Arthur, WF 318-335
Condon, Richard, **268-273**,
  PF 284-290
   rad, Joseph, WF 336-352
   stantine, K. C., **274-279**,
  WF 353-361
Cook, Robin, **280-285**,
  WF 362-368

Coover, Robert, **286-306**
Cormier, Robert, **307-315**,
  WF 369-379
Cortázar, Julio, WF 380-390
Cozzens, James Gould, PF 291-298
Crews, Harry, **316-330**
Crichton, Michael, **331-335**,
  WF 391-399
Cronin, A. J., WF 400-407
Cross, Amanda, PF 299-306
Crowley, John, **336-338**,
  WF 408-414
Dahl, Roald, **339-351**
De Camp, L. Sprague, **352-359**,
  WF 415-427
Deighton, Len, **360-364**,
  WF 428-435
Delany, Samuel R., **365-370**,
  WF 436-444
Delillio, Don, PF 307-317
Derleth, August, PF 318-331
Dick, Philip K., **371-376**,
  PF 332-342
Dickey, James, **377-380**,
  PF 343-347
Didion, Joan, PF 348-356
Disch, Thomas M., **381-387**,
  PF 357-367
Doctorow, E. L., **388-391**,
  PF 368-375
Donaldson, Stephen R.,
  WF 445-454
Dos Passos, John, WF 455-473
Du Maurier, Daphne, WF 474-480
Duras, Marguerite, **392-410**
Durrell, Lawrence, WF 481-493
Eco, Umberto, **411-416**,
  WF 494-499
Ellis, Bret Easton, PF 376-379

Ellison, Harlan, **417-422**,
PF 380-393
Emerson, Ralph Waldo,
PF 394-400
Ephron, Nora, **423-427**,
WF 500-507
Erdrich, Louise, **428-435**,
PF 401-405
Exley, Frederick, **436-440**,
PF 406-410
Farmer, Philip José, PF 411-422
Farrell, James Thomas,
WF 508-519
Fast, Howard Melvin, PF 423-435
Faulkner, William, WF 520-532
Findley, Timothy, WF 533-543
Finney, Jack, PF 436-443
Fitzgerald, F. Scott, WF 544-557
Fleming, Ian, WF 558-568
Follett, Ken, **441-443**, PF 444-455
Fowles, John, PF 456-465
Francis, Dick, **444-448**, PF 466-473
Fraser, Lady Antonia, **449-453**,
PF 474-479
French, Marilyn, **454-458**,
PF 480-484
Fuentes, Carlos, **459-464**
Gaddis, William, **465-474**
Gaines, Ernest J., **475-498**
Gann, Ernest K., PF 485-495
García Márquez, Gabriel, **499-504**,
WF 569-577
Gardner, Erle Stanley, PF 496-503
Gardner, John, **505-511**,
PF 504-522
Garrett, Randall, WF 578-589
Gilchrist, Ellen, **512-515**,
PF 523-526
Godden, Rumer, WF 590-598

Godwin, Gail, **516-521**, PF 527-533
Golding, William, **522-527**,
WF 599-607
Goldman, William, **528-532**,
PF 534-541
Gordon, Mary, **533-536**,
PF 542-545
Grass, Günter, **537-541**,
WF 608-617
Grau, Shirley Ann, WF 618-622
Graves, Robert, WF 623-633
Greeley, Andrew, PF 546-552
Greene, Graham, **542-545**,
WF 634-645
Grey, Zane, WF 646-654
Grimes, Martha, PF 553-558
Guest, Judith, **546-549**, PF 559-563
Hailey, Arthur, **550-553**,
PF 564-567
Haley, Alex, **554-556**, PF 568-574
Halliday, Brett, PF 575-582
Hammett, Dashiell, WF 655-666
Hannah, Barry, **557-559**,
WF 667-673
Hansen, Joseph, PF 583-589
Hawkes, John, **560-566**,
WF 674-680
Haycox, Ernest, WF 681-687
Heinlein, Robert A., **567-573**,
PF 590-599
Heller, Joseph, **574-582**,
PF 600-612
Hemingway, Ernest, **583-597**,
WF 688-702
Herbert, Frank, PF 613-622
Herlihy, James Leo, PF 623-627
Herr, Michael, **598-600**,
PF 628-631
Herriot, James, PF 632-636

Hersey, John, WF 703-714
Hesse, Hermann, WF 715-724
Higgins, George V., **601-607**,
    PF 637-642
Hillerman, Tony, **608-619**
Himes, Chester, PF 643-653
Hinton, S. E., **620-624**,
    WF 725-735
Hoban, Russell, PF 654-660
Hobson, Laura, WF 736-742
Holt, Victoria, WF 743-750
Horgan, Paul, WF 751-758
Hunter, Evan, WF 759-768
Hutchinson, A. S. M., WF 769-774
Huxley, Aldous, WF 775-781
Irving, John, **625-629**, PF 661-671
Isaacs, Susan, **630-633**, PF 672-678
Jackson, Shirley, WF 782-788
Jaffe, Rona, PF 679-683
Jakes, John, WF 789-796
James, P. D., **634-644**, PF 684-693
Jenkins, Dan, WF 797-802
Johnson, Diane, PF 694-699
Jones, James, PF 700-705
Jong, Erica, **645-647**, PF 706-712
Kafka, Franz, WF 803-812
Kaufman, Bel, WF 813-818
Kazantzakis, Nikos, WF 819-826
Keillor, Garrison, **648-652**,
    PF 713-717
Kemelman, Harry, WF 827-833
Kennedy, William, **653-662**,
    PF 718-725
Kerouac, Jack, PF 726-731
Kesey, Ken, PF 732-746
King, Stephen, **663-675**,
    PF 747-758
Kingston, Maxine Hong, **676-680**,
    WF 834-841

Kinsella, W. P., **681-684**,
    PF 759-766
Kirkwood, James, WF 842-851
Klein, Norma, **685-687**,
    PF 767-774
Knowles, John, WF 852-857
Koen, Karleen, WF 858-863
Kosinski, Jerzy, **688-692**,
    PF 775-789
Kotzwinkle, William, **693-704**,
    PF 790-796
Krantz, Judith, **705-710**,
    PF 797-806
Kundera, Milan, WF 864-873
Kurtz, Katherine, **711-716**,
    PF 807-812
L'Amour, Louis, WF 874-886
L'Engle, Madeleine,
    PF 853-862
Lardner, Ring **717-726**
Lathern, Emma, **727-731**,
    PF 813-820
Lawrence, D. H., WF 887-896
Le Carré, John, **732-743**,
    PF 821-829
Le Guin, Ursula K., **744-753**,
    PF 838-844
Lee, Harper, PF 830-837
Leiber, Fritz, PF 845-852
Leonard, Elmore, **754-762**,
    PF 863-870
Lewis, C. S., WF 897-909
Lewis, Sinclair, WF 910-916
Lindbergh, Anne Morrow,
    WF 917-924
London, Jack, WF 925-936
Lord, Bette Bao, WF 937-942
Lovecraft, H. P., WF 943-954
Lowry, Malcolm, WF 955-969

Ludlum, Robert, **763-772**,
PF 871-877
Lurie, Alison, **773-776**, PF 878-881
MacDonald, John D., PF 882-891
MacDonald, Ross, PF 892-901
MacInnes, Helen, WF 970-976
Mailer, Norman, **777-780**,
WF 977-988
Malamud, Bernard, **781-784**,
PF 902-916
Malraux, André, WF 989-994
Mann, Thomas, WF 995-1007
Mansfield, Katherine, **785-800**
Marquand, John P., WF 1008-1015
Marshall, Catherine, WF 1016-1025
Marshall, Paule, **801-808**
Mason, Bobbie Ann, **809-818**
Matthiessen, Peter, **819-822**,
PF 917-924
Maugham, W. Somerset,
WF 1026-1035
McBain, Ed (See Hunter, Evan)
McCaffrey, Anne, **823-833**,
PF 925-931
McCarthy, Mary, **834-836**,
PF 932-941
McCarthy, Cormac, WF 1036-1043
McCullers, Carson, PF 942-949
McCullough, Colleen, **837-846**,
PF 950-955
McGuane, Thomas, **847-851**,
PF 956-963
McInerney, Jay, **852-855**,
PF 964-970
McKillip, Patricia, **856-861**,
PF 971-976
McMurtry, Larry, **862-865**,
PF 977-982
Metalious, Grace, PF 983-993

Michener, James, **866-883**
Miller, Henry, PF 1011-1017
Miller, Walter M., Jr.,
PF 1018-1023
Milne, A. A., WF 1044-1050
Mishima, Yukio, WF 1051-1059
Mitchell, Margaret, WF 1060-1071
Momaday, N. Scott, **884-896**
Monsarrat, Nicholas,
WF 1072-1078
Morrison, Toni, **897-900**,
PF 1024-1032
Morse, L. A., PF 1033-1042
Munro, Alice, **901-904**,
WF 1079-1087
Nabokov, Vladimir Vladimirovich,
WF 1088-1099
Naipaul, V. S., **905-916**
Narayan, R. K., **917-928**
Nin, Anaïs, PF 1043-1049
Niven, Larry, **929-932**,
PF 1050-1058
Norman, John, **933-939**,
WF 1100-1106
Norris, Frank, WF 1107-1122
Norton, Andre, WF 1123-1129
Oates, Joyce Carol, **940-949**,
PF 1059-1067
O'Connor, Flannery, PF 1068-1078
O'Dell, Scott, WF 1130-1138
O'Hara, John, WF 1139-1148
O. Henry, **950-959**
Olsen, Tillie, WF 1149-1154
Orwell, George, PF 1079-1089
Parker, Robert B., PF 1090-1097
Pasternak, Boris, WF 1155-1161
Paton, Alan, WF 1162-1178
Percy, Walker, **960-969**
Perelman, S. J., **970-981**

Petry, Ann, **982-991**
Phillips, Jayne Anne, **992-997**,
  WF 1179-1183
Piercy, Marge, PF 1098-1107
Plain, Belva, PF 1108-1110
Plath, Sylvia, WF 1184-1190
Porter, Gene Stratton,
  WF 1191-1203
Porter, Katherine Anne,
  WF 1204-1213
Porter, William Sydney (See O.
  Henry)
Portis, Charles, PF 1111-1117
Potok, Chaim, **998-1001**,
  PF 1118-1130
Proust, Marcel, WF 1214-1221
Puig, Manuel, **1002-1010**,
  WF 1222-1233
Puzo, Mario, PF 1131-1138
Pym, Barbara, WF 1234-1244
Pynchon, Thomas, **1011-1029**
Queen, Ellery, PF 1139-1153
Rand, Ayn, WF 1245-1252
Rawlings, Marjorie Kinnan,
  WF 1253-1261
Reed, Ishmael, **1030-1044**
Remarque, Erich Maria,
  WF 1262-1274
Renault, Mary, PF 1154-1161
Rendell, Ruth, **1045-1055**,
  WF 1275-1280
Rice, Anne, **1056-1060**,
  PF 1162-1165
Rinehart, Mary Roberts, **1061-1070**
Robbe-Grillet, Alain, **1071-1074**,
  WF 1281-1287
Robbins, Harold, PF 1166-1176
Robbins, Tom, **1075-1078**,
  PF 1177-1182

Rossner, Judith (Perelman),
  1079-1088, PF 1183-1196
Roth, Philip, **1089-1093**,
  PF 1197-1203
Ruark, Robert, WF 1288-1293
Rushdie, Salman, **1094-1111**
Russ, Joanna, PF 1204-1213
Sabatini, Rafael, **1112-1126**
Saint-Exupéry, Antoine de,
  WF 1294-1303
Salinger, J. D.,
  PF 1214-1220
Sanders, Lawrence, WF 1304-1309
Sarraute, Nathalie, WF 1310-1316
Sartre, Jean-Paul, WF 1317-1328
Sayers, Dorothy L., WF 1329-1342
Schaefer, Jack, PF 1221-1226
Schmitz, James H., PF 1227-1236
Schulberg, Budd, WF 1343-1352
Segal, Erich, PF 1237-1245
Settle, Mary Lee, **1127-1132**,
  PF 1246-1254
Shaara, Michael, WF 1353-1360
Shaw, Irwin, WF 1361-1372
Sheldon, Sidney, **1133-1140**,
  WF 1373-1382
Shellabarger, Samuel,
  WF 1383-1392
Silverberg, Robert, **1141-1148**,
  WF 1393-1406
Simenon, Georges, WF 1407-1413
Sinclair, Upton, WF 1414-1419
Singer, Isaac Bashevis, **1149-1153**,
  WF 1420-1428
Sjöwal, Maj, WF 1429-1438
Smith, Thorne, WF 1439-1445
Smith, Betty, PF 1255-1262
Smith, Martin Cruz, **1154-1157**,
  PF 1263-1269

Solzhenitsyn, Aleksandr,
  WF 1446-1457
Southern, Terry, PF 1270-1276
Spencer, Scott, PF 1277-1282
Spillane, Mickey, PF 1283-1287
Steel, Danielle, PF 1288-1296
Stegner, Wallace, **1158-1174**
Stein, Gertrude, WF 1458-1464
Steinbeck, John, WF 1465-1475
Stewart, Mary, PF 1297-1303
Stone, Irving, PF 1304-1314
Stone, Robert, PF 1315-1323
Stout, Rex, PF 1324-1337
Straub, Peter, WF 1476-1481
Sturgeon, Theodore, WF 1482-1494
Styron, William, PF 1338-1349
Susann, Jacqueline, PF 1350-1359
Tan, Amy, **1175-1178**
Tarkington, Booth, WF 1495-1511
Taylor, Peter, **1179-1183**
Terkel, Studs, WF 1512-1516
Theroux, Paul, **1184-1189**,
  PF 1360-1367
Thomas, D. M., WF 1517-1523
Thompson, Hunter S.,
  PF 1368-1372
Thurber, James, WF 1524-1538
Tolkien, J. R. R., WF 1539-1549
Toole, John Kennedy,
  WF 1550-1553
Tryon, Thomas, PF 1373-1380
Turow, Scott, **1190-1202**
Tyler, Anne, **1203-1206**,
  PF 1381-1386
Updike, John, **1207-1213**,
  PF 1387-1394
Uris, Leon, **1214-1218**,
  PF 1395-1402
Van Vogt, A. E., WF 1554-1567

Vanderhaeghe, Guy, **1219-1222**,
  PF 1403-1410
Vargas Llosa, Mario, **1223-1231**,
  WF 1568-1577
Varley, John, **1232-1236**,
  WF 1578-1588
Vidal, Gore, PF 1411-1422
Vine, Barbara (See Rendell, Ruth)
Vonnegut, Kurt, **1237-1246**,
  PF 1423-1432
Wahlöö, Per, WF 1429-1438
Walker, Alice, **1247-1252**,
  PF 1433-1443
Wallace, Irving, PF 1444-1453
Wambaugh, Joseph, **1253-1256**,
  PF 1454-1460
Warren, Robert Penn,
  WF 1589-1606
Waugh, Evelyn, WF 1607-1617
Wells, H. G., WF 1618-1636
Welty, Eudora, **1257-1264**,
  WF 1367-1647
Werfel, Franz, WF 1648-1657
West, Jessamyn, WF 1658-1666
West, Morris, **1265-1270**,
  PF 1461-1466
West, Nathaniel, WF 1667-1674
West, Rebecca, WF 1675-1684
Westlake, Donald, PF 1467-1475
Wharton, Edith, WF 1685-1693
White, E. B., WF 1694-1703
White, T. H., **1271-1277**
Wiesel, Elie, WF 1704-1709
Williams, Charles, WF 1710-1715
Wister, Owen, WF 1716-1724
Wodehouse, P. G., **1278-1290**
Wolfe, Tom, **1291-1296**,
  PF 1476-1482
Wolfe, Thomas, WF 1725-1734

Wouk, Herman, PF 1483-1489
Wright, Harold, Bell,
 WF 1735-1744
Wright, Richard, WF 1745-1757
Yarbro, Chelsea Quinn, **1297-1303**,
 PF 1490-1497
Yerby, Frank G., PF 1498-1509
Yourcenar, Marguerite,
 WF 1758-1764
Zelazny, Roger, **1304-1308**,
 PF 1510-1518